Lecture Notes in Artificial Intelligence   12331

Subseries of Lecture Notes in Computer Science

Series Editors

Randy Goebel
University of Alberta, Edmonton, Canada
Yuzuru Tanaka
Hokkaido University, Sapporo, Japan
Wolfgang Wahlster
DFKI and Saarland University, Saarbrücken, Germany

Founding Editor

Jörg Siekmann
DFKI and Saarland University, Saarbrücken, Germany

More information about this series at http://www.springer.com/series/1244

Maki Sakamoto · Naoaki Okazaki ·
Koji Mineshima · Ken Satoh (Eds.)

New Frontiers
in Artificial Intelligence

JSAI-isAI International Workshops, JURISIN,
AI-Biz, LENLS, Kansei-AI
Yokohama, Japan, November 10–12, 2019
Revised Selected Papers

Springer

Editors
Maki Sakamoto
The University of Electro-Communications
Tokyo, Japan

Naoaki Okazaki
Tokyo Institute of Technology
Tokyo, Japan

Koji Mineshima
Keio University
Tokyo, Japan

Ken Satoh
National Institute of Informatics
Tokyo, Japan

ISSN 0302-9743   ISSN 1611-3349 (electronic)
Lecture Notes in Artificial Intelligence
ISBN 978-3-030-58789-5   ISBN 978-3-030-58790-1   (eBook)
https://doi.org/10.1007/978-3-030-58790-1

LNCS Sublibrary: SL7 – Artificial Intelligence

© Springer Nature Switzerland AG 2020
This work is subject to copyright. All rights are reserved by the Publisher, whether the whole or part of the material is concerned, specifically the rights of translation, reprinting, reuse of illustrations, recitation, broadcasting, reproduction on microfilms or in any other physical way, and transmission or information storage and retrieval, electronic adaptation, computer software, or by similar or dissimilar methodology now known or hereafter developed.
The use of general descriptive names, registered names, trademarks, service marks, etc. in this publication does not imply, even in the absence of a specific statement, that such names are exempt from the relevant protective laws and regulations and therefore free for general use.
The publisher, the authors and the editors are safe to assume that the advice and information in this book are believed to be true and accurate at the date of publication. Neither the publisher nor the authors or the editors give a warranty, expressed or implied, with respect to the material contained herein or for any errors or omissions that may have been made. The publisher remains neutral with regard to jurisdictional claims in published maps and institutional affiliations.

This Springer imprint is published by the registered company Springer Nature Switzerland AG
The registered company address is: Gewerbestrasse 11, 6330 Cham, Switzerland

Preface

The Japanese Society for Artificial Intelligence (JSAI) is a premier academic society that focuses on artificial intelligence (AI) in Japan and was established in 1986. The JSAI International Symposium on Artificial Intelligence (JSAI-isAI 2019) was the 11th international symposium on AI supported by the JSAI. JSAI-isAI 2019 was successfully held during November 10–12 at Keio University in Yokohama, Japan. 113 people from 8 countries participated and 7 invited talks were presented. The JSAI-isAI 2019 included four workshops. 75 papers were submitted and 46 papers were selected for presentation at the workshops. This volume, *New Frontiers in Artificial Intelligence: JSAI-isAI 2019 Workshops*, is the post-proceedings of JSAI-isAI 2019. From the four workshops (JURISIN 2019, AI-Biz 2019, LENLS 16, and Kansei-AI 2019), 26 papers were carefully selected and revised according to the comments of the Workshop Program Committees. The acceptance rate was about 56%. This resulted in the excellent selection of papers that were representative of some of the topics of AI research both in Japan and in other parts of the world.

The 13th International Workshop on Juris-Informatics (JURISIN 2019) was held with the support of JSAI in association with JSAI International Symposia on AI (JSAI-isAI 2019). Juris-informatics was organized to discuss legal issues from the perspective of information science. Compared with the conventional AI and law, this workshop covered a wide range of topics, including any theories and technologies which are not directly related with juris-informatics but have a potential to contribute to this domain.

Artificial Intelligence of and for Business (AI-Biz 2019) was the 4th workshop hosted by the Business Informatics (SIG-BI) of JSAI and we believe the workshop was successful, because of very wide fields of business and AI technology, including for human capital, industry classifications, capturing mercurial customers, variable selection, organizational performance, traffic congestion, visualization of R&D project, credit risk, ecocars, stock price prediction, and so on.

Logic and Engineering of Natural Language Semantics (LENLS 16) was the 14th event in the series, and it focused on the formal and theoretical aspects of natural language. LENLS is an annual international workshop recognized internationally in the formal syntax-semantics-pragmatics community. It has been bringing together, for discussion and interdisciplinary communication, researchers working on formal theories of natural language syntax, semantics and pragmatics, (formal) philosophy, AI, and computational linguistics.

Kansei and Artificial Intelligence (Kansei-AI 2019) was the first international workshop on artificial affective (Kansei) intelligence. The scope of this workshop was research of science and engineering related to value judgements made through the five senses, such as image processing, tactile engineering, acoustics, machine learning, sensitivity engineering, and natural language processing.

It is our great pleasure to be able to share some highlights of these fascinating workshops in this volume. We hope this book will introduce readers to the state-of-the-art research outcomes of JSAI-isAI 2019, and motivate them to participate in future JSAI-isAI events.

July 2020

Maki Sakamoto
Naoaki Okazaki
Koji Mineshima
Ken Satoh

Organization

JURISIN 2019

Workshop Chairs

Makoto Nakamura   Niigata Institute of Technology, Japan
Satoshi Tojo   Japan Advanced Institute of Science and Technology, Japan

Program Committee

Thomas Ågotnes   University of Bergen, Norway
Michał Araszkiewicz   Jagiellonian University, Poland
Ryuta Arisaka   National Institute of Informatics, Japan
Marina De Vos   University of Bath, UK
Juergen Dix   Clausthal University of Technology, Germany
Víctor Rodríguez Doncel   Universidad Politecnica de Madrid, Spain
Randy Goebel   University of Alberta, Canada
Guido Governatori   NICTA, Australia
Tokuyasu Kakuta   Chuo University, Japan
Yoshinobu Kano   Shizuoka University, Japan
Takehiko Kasahara   Toin Yokohama University, Japan
Mi-Young Kim   University of Alberta, Canada
Sabrina Kirrane   Vienna University of Economics and Business, Austria
Le-Minh Nguyen   Japan Advanced Institute of Science and Technology, Japan
Katumi Nitta   Tokyo Institute of Technology, Japan
Ginevra Peruginelli   ITTIG-CNR, Italy
Seiichiro Sakurai   Meiji Gakuin University, Japan
Ken Satoh   National Institute of Informatics and Sokendai, Japan
Akira Shimazu   Japan Advanced Institute of Science and Technology, Japan
Kazuko Takahashi   Kwansei Gakuin University, Japan
Katsuhiko Toyama   Nagoya University, Japan
Masaharu Yoshioka   Hokkaido University, Japan
Yueh-Hsuan Weng   Tohoku University, Japan

Steering Committee

Takehiko Kasahara   Toin Yokohama University, Japan
Makoto Nakamura   Niigata Institute of Technology, Japan
Katsumi Nitta   Tokyo Institute of Technology, Japan
Seiichiro Sakurai   Meiji Gakuin University, Japan
Ken Satoh   National Institute of Informatics and Sokendai, Japan

| Satoshi Tojo | Japan Advanced Institute of Science and Technology, Japan |
| Katsuhiko Toyama | Nagoya University, Japan |

Advisory Committee

Trevor Bench-Capon	The University of Liverpool, UK
Tomas Gordon	Fraunfoher FOKUS, Germany
Henry Prakken	Utrecht University and University of Groningen, The Netherlands
John Zeleznikow	Victoria University, Australia
Robert Kowalski	Imperial College London, UK
Kevin Ashley	University of Pittsburgh, USA

AI-Biz 2019

Workshop Chair

| Takao Terano | Chiba University of Commerce, Japan |

Workshop Co-chairs

| Setsuya Kurahashi | University of Tsukuba, Japan |
| Hiroshi Takahashi | Keio University, Japan |

Program Committee

Reiko Hishiyama	Waseda University, Japan
Manabu Ichikawa	National Institute of Public Health, Japan
Yoko Ishino	Yamaguchi University, Japan
Hajime Kita	Kyoto University, Japan
Hajime Mizuyama	Aoyama Gakuin University, Japan
Chathura Rajapaksha	University of Kelaniya, Sri Lanka
Masakazu Takahashi	Yamaguchi University, Japan
Shingo Takahashi	Waseda University, Japan
Takashi Yamada	Yamaguchi University, Japan

LENLS 16

Workshop Chair

| Naoya Fujikawa | University of Tokyo, Japan |

Workshop Co-chairs

Elin McCready	Aoyama Gakuin University, Japan
Daisuke Bekki	Ochanomizu University, Japan
Koji Mineshima	Keio University, Japan

Program Committee

Naoya Fujikawa	University of Tokyo, Japan
Elin McCready	Aoyama Gakuin University, Japan
Daisuke Bekki	Ochanomizu University, Japan
Koji Mineshima	Keio University, Japan
Alastair Butler	Hirosaki University, Japan
Richard Dietz	University of Tokyo, Japan
Yurie Hara	Hokkaido University, Japan
Magdalena Kaufmann	University of Connecticut, USA
Yoshiki Mori	University of Tokyo, Japan
David Y. Oshima	Nagoya University, Japan
Katsuhiko Sano	Hokkaido University, Japan
Osamu Sawada	Kobe University, Japan
Wataru Uegaki	The University of Edinburgh, UK
Katsuhiko Yabushita	Naruto University of Education, Japan
Tomoyuki Yamada	Hokkaido University, Japan
Shunsuke Yatabe	Kyoto University, Japan
Kei Yoshimoto	Tohoku University, Japan

KANSEI-AI 2019

Workshop Chair

Koichi Yamagata	The University of Electro-Communications, Japan

Workshop Co-chair

Yuji Nozaki	The University of Electro-Communications, Japan

Program Committee

Koichi Yamagata	The University of Electro-Communications, Japan
Yuji Nozaki	The University of Electro-Communications, Japan

Sponsored By

The Japan Society for Artificial Intelligence (JSAI)

Contents

KANSEIAI 2019

JURISIN 2019

Juris-Informatics (JURISIN) 2019

Makoto Nakamura[1] and Satoshi Tojo[2]

[1] Niigata Institute of Technology, Japan
[2] Japan Advanced Institute of Science and Technology, Japan

The Thirteenth International Workshop on Juris-Informatics (JURISIN 2019) was held with a support of the Japanese Society for Artificial Intelligence (JSAI) in association with JSAI International Symposia on AI (JSAI-isAI 2019). JURISIN was organized to discuss legal issues from the perspective of information science. Compared with the conventional AI and law, JURISIN covers a wide range of topics, including any theories and technologies which is not directly related with juris-informatics but has a potential to contribute to this domain.

Thus, the members of Program Committee (PC) are leading researchers in various fields: Thomas Ågotnes (University of Bergen), Michał Araszkiewicz (Jagiellonian University), Ryuta Arisaka (National Institute of Informatics), Marina De Vos (University of Bath), Juergen Dix (Clausthal University of Technology), Victor Rodriguez Doncel (Universidad Politecnica de Madrid), Randy Goebel (University of Alberta), Guido Governatori (CSIRO), Tokuyasu Kakuta (Chuo University), Yoshinobu Kano (Shizuoka University), Takehiko Kasahara (Toin Yokohama University), Mi-Young Kim (University of Alberta), Sabrina Kirrane (Vienna University of Economics and Business), Makoto Nakamura (Niigata Institute of Technology), Le-Minh Nguyen (JAIST), Katumi Nitta (Tokyo Institute of Technology), Ginevra Peruginelli (ITTIG-CNR), Seiichiro Sakurai (Meiji Gakuin University), Ken Satoh (National Institute of Informatics and Sokendai), Akira Shimazu (JAIST), Kazuko Takahashi (Kwansei Gakuin University), Satoshi Tojo (JAIST), Katsuhiko Toyama (Nagoya University), Masaharu Yoshioka (Hokkaido University), Yueh-Hsuan Weng (Tohoku University). The collaborative work of computer scientists, lawyers and philosophers is expected to contribute to the advancement of juris-informatics and it is also expected to open novel research areas.

Despite the short announcement period, twenty-one papers were submitted. Each paper was reviewed by three members of PC. This year, we allow a double submission to JURIX 2019 and four papers were withdrawn because of acceptance to JURIX 2019 and eleven papers were accepted in total. The collection of papers covers various topics such as legal reasoning, argumentation theory, social simulation, application of AI and informatics to law, application of natural language processing and so on. As invited speakers, we have Professor Dan Jerker B. Svantesson from Bond University, Australia and Professor Floris Bex from Utrecht University and Tilburg University, the Netherlands.

After the workshop, six papers were submitted for the post proceedings. They were reviewed by PC members again and five papers were finally selected. Followings are their synopses.

Takahiro Komamizu, Kazuya Fujioka, Yasuhiro Ogawa and Katsuhiko Toyama explore relevant parts between legal documents using substructure matching. Legal documents are typically hierarchically structured. This paper focuses on ordinances and rules (OR documents for short) in the local governments, which are designed for social lives under the governments. Experimental evaluation on real OR documents in Japan demonstrates that the proposed algorithm successfully discovers relevant parts of OR documents.

Jieh-Sheng Lee and Jieh Hsiang propose to measure patent claim generation by span relevancy. Their long-term goal of patent claim generation is to realize "augmented inventing" for inventors by leveraging new Deep Learning techniques. In order to generate patent claims with reasonable quality, a fundamental question is how to measure the quality. They tackle the problem from the perspective of claim span relevancy as a proof of concept.

Juliano Rabelo, Mi-Young Kim, Randy Goebel, Masaharu Yoshioka, Yoshinobu Kano and Ken Satoh summarize the evaluation of the 6th Competition on Legal Information Extraction/Entailment (COLIEE 2019). The competition consists of four tasks. Participation was open to any group in the world, based on any approach. Eleven different teams participated in the case law competition tasks, some of them in more than one task. They summarize each team's approaches, their official evaluation, and analysis on their data and submission results.

Emilio Serrano and Ken Satoh present an agent-based model (ABM) for exploring pension law and social security policies. This paper contributes with an agent-based model for computer-aided law education in this field. This model is a simplified representation of the complex reality of pension systems, to the point that the reality is understandable and analytically manageable. Experimental results indicate that a constant or increasing population of uniformly distributed ages is not enough to ensure the sustainability of pension systems as backbone of the welfare state.

Gabriela Ferraro, Ho-Pun Lam, Silvano Colombo Tosatto, Francesco Olivieri, Mohammad Badiul Islam, Nick van Beest and Guido Governatori show automatic extraction of legal norms. This paper address two major questions related to this problem: (i) what are the challenges in formalising legal documents into a machine understandable formalism? (ii) to what extent can the data-driven state-of-the-art approaches developed in the Natural Language Processing (NLP) community be used to automate the normative mining process. The results of their experiments indicate that NLP technologies such as relation extraction and semantic parsing are promising research avenues to advance research in this area.

Finally, we wish to express our gratitude to all those who submitted papers, PC members, discussant and attentive audience.

Exploring Relevant Parts Between Legal Documents Using Substructure Matching

Takahiro Komamizu$^{(\boxtimes)}$, Kazuya Fujioka, Yasuhiro Ogawa,
and Katsuhiko Toyama

Nagoya University, Nagoya, Japan
`taka-coma@acm.org`, `{yasuhiro,toyama}@is.nagoya-u.ac.jp`

Abstract. Legal documents are typically hierarchically structured. This paper focuses on ordinances and rules (OR documents for short) in the local governments, which are designed for social lives under the governments. OR documents are composed of provisions for social lives in various aspects such as healthy development of youths and landscape preservation. OR documents in different local governments share common provisions but also include different provisions depending on their social situations. There is a large demand on helping governmental officers draft OR documents, especially searching "relevant parts" of OR documents. To help drafting OR documents, this paper designs the relevancy of OR documents with two basic measurements; matching ratio and provision commonality. Based on the relevancy, this paper develops a structured document search algorithm for OR documents. Experimental evaluation on real OR documents in Japan demonstrates that the proposed algorithm successfully discovers relevant parts of OR documents.

Keywords: Structured document search · Substructure matching · Legal document · Ordinance and rules

1 Introduction

Finding *relevant* ordinances and rules (OR documents for short) in different local governments is crucial for governmental officers, who draft OR documents. Based on social situations in a local government, its officers need to draft OR documents to protect social lives under the government. For instance, the Protection of Young Persons Ordinance is designed to protect young persons from various harmful activities such as drug abuses, violences and blackmails. To draft OR documents, governmental officers typically imitate existing OR documents in other local governments. To this end, the officers first search OR documents related to a drafting document, second determine provisions to reuse from the search results, and last modify the provisions so as to fit to their social situations.

In a broad vision for helping the officers draft OR documents, a system having the following functionalities is demanded. One functionality is searching OR documents from existing OR documents, which are gathered from other

© Springer Nature Switzerland AG 2020
M. Sakamoto et al. (Eds.): JSAI-isAI 2019, LNAI 12331, pp. 5–19, 2020.
https://doi.org/10.1007/978-3-030-58790-1_1

governments. The other functionality is finding relevant provisions between two OR documents, where one is a drafting document and another is a reference document. The former can be achieved by the information retrieval techniques (e.g., [5]). In a practical use case, eLen Regulation Database [11] is a search system for ordinances of Japanese local governments. In eLen, an edit distance-based approach is used for retrieving ordinances. While, the latter has not been studied well. In particular, to the best of our knowledge, this paper is the first work that develops the functionality in the legal domain.

The search task of finding relevant provisions between OR documents is formalized as follows. Given two OR documents, which share common (broad) provisions, the task is to find part pairs of the documents, which correspond to relevant (narrow) provisions, and to emphasise their commonalities and differences. For instance, assuming that the OR documents as the landscape ordinances in two towns (Ami, Ibaraki, Japan and Shichigashuku, Miyagi, Japan). They share the common broad provision, which is "landscape". The ordinance of Ami town contains narrow provisions such as the responsibility of the mayor and the subsidy. That of Shichigashuku town also contains provisions about the responsibility of the mayor and the subsidy. The subsidy provisions of these towns have different structures and contents in the corresponding articles. The search task is to find the common contents and different contents between the provisions. Note that, in this paper, a provision is defined as a part of the OR document; that is, the OR document itself can be a provision and a sentence of the document can also be a provision. This is because structural granularities of provisions are different in different OR documents. This flexibility of the search space makes the search task challenging.

To tackle the challenge, the basic idea in this paper is that provisions are organized in a hierarchical manner. Since OR documents are hierarchically structured, the documents are regarded as tree structured documents; thus, the provisions are the subtrees in the documents. Hence, the search task becomes another task for determining relevant subtree pairs of the OR documents. One may think that structural similarity [12] is important, while another may think that textual similarity is important [5] for OR document search. However, OR documents in different governments do not necessarily share common structures.

Preliminary observations on OR documents give an inspiration that textual similarity is suitable for finding relevant provisions, and structural information is helpful to explore units of provisions in a document. As mentioned above, OR document drafters tend to imitate the existing OR documents as many as possible to reduce their efforts. As a results of the imitation, there are lots of similar sentences. More interestingly, there are exactly same sentences, which occurs more than 10,000 OR documents. For the similar sentences, there are small differences on the numeric values (e.g., year, the number of people, etc.), the organization names, and so on. These indicates that the textual similarity between sentences is useful for finding relevant sentences (i.e., the narrowest level of provisions). In addition, the structural information of OR documents are useful for aggregating the similarities on the broader levels of provisions. Suppose that two articles from two OR documents respectively have two sentences. When there are a bijective relationship of equivalence between these sentences, the two articles are also the same provision. This indicates that when narrow provisions under a broad provision are similar to those under another broad provisions, the broad provisions are also similar. Therefore, the structural information is helpful to explore the provisions between OR documents.

Based on the inspiration, in this paper, a relevancy metric is defined, which is composed of two similarity measurements (*matching ratio* and *provision commonality*) between subtrees of OR documents. The matching ratio measures matching node ratio between two subtrees, while the provision commonality measures how evenly matched nodes appear in the leaf nodes. Intuitively, the matching ratio measures ordinary similarities of subtrees, while the provision commonality measures how many different nodes (or narrow provisions) are included. To make the relevancy metric flexible on application requirements, the relevancy metric is designed by a linear combination of these measurements, where the weight controls how many new provisions are expected in results. This paper develops an algorithm which explores subtree pairs for a given query document and an OR database. To avoid redundant results, the algorithm explores subtree pairs which are maximal.

Contributions of this paper is summarized as follows.

- **Dedicated structured legal document search**: This paper models a dedicated structured document search in the legal domain. The search requirement is different from conventional structured document search discussed in XML search and others (see Sect. 2).
- **Relevancy metric for structured document**: In order to realize the search model, this paper proposes a relevancy metric which is a linear combination of matching ratio and provision commonality measurements. In addition to the straightforward similarity measurement, the matching ratio, this paper integrates the provision commonality measurement which allows search results to contain extra parts of documents. Based on the measurement, this paper develops an algorithm for the search model.
- **Experimental evaluation on real-world data**: This paper evaluates the proposed metric using real-world data which is OR documents from Japanese local governments, and the evaluation demonstrates that the proposed metric successfully evaluates relevant parts of OR documents.

The rest of this paper is organized as follows: Sect. 2 explains distinctions of this paper from existing literatures. Section 3 introduces the OR documents and the search requirement on them. Section 4 discusses the proposed relevancy metric and the search algorithm, and Sect. 5 showcases the evaluation of the proposed method in the real-world data. Finally, Sect. 6 concludes this paper.

2   Related Work

This paper deals with OR document search, especially finding relevant parts of the documents. The parts here mean that contiguous sub-documents, in other words, suppose that an OR document as a tree-structured document, the parts are subtrees of the document. The OR document search in this paper is related to (1) legal document search and (2) structured document search. The subsequent subsections introduce related works in terms of these two aspects.

2.1   Legal Document Search

To the best of our knowledge, this paper is the first attempt dealing with finding pairs of relevant parts of legal documents. Most likely, two kinds of legal document search tasks are related to this paper: one is the document-level similarity search and the other is the keyword search. The document-level similarity search receives a query legal document and a set of legal documents as inputs, and outputs similar documents to the query document in the set. The keyword search task is to find related documents to input keywords.

Document-level similarity search task is mainly motivated to find similar legal documents to discover commonalities of documents [5], or to find citations between legal documents [14]. Fujioka et al. [5] have proposed a neural model-based OR document search mechanism which aims to capture the semantic relatedness between OR documents using a word embedding technique (i.e., Doc2Vec [9]). Panagis et al. [14] aims to discover (implicit) citations in the cases to laws by employing a text similarity approach. Their approach utilizes a bag of words model and discovers citations in the paragraph level using Tversky index as the similarity measurement. These works focus on finding only related documents or paragraphs, while this paper aims at finding related provisions represented as parts of documents. More importantly, this paper allows acceptable differences of the provisions, while the related works above do not.

Keyword search task is an adaptation of IR techniques for legal documents. The legal document search is a noticeable IR domain, because of increasing amount of digitalized legal documents. For instance, Locke and Zuccon have a published legal document search test collection [10]. In more technical point of views, Arora et al. [1] have motivated to use typical phrases in legal documents to improve the legal document search quality. Similarly, Landthaler et al. [8] aim to improve the search quality by taking a semantic similarity (i.e., word embedding-based similarity) into account. These works indicate that phrasing and semantics are helpful components on the legal document search if the input keywords are given by (non-expert) users. On the other hand, this paper aims at comparing legal documents which typically have few different words with semantically similar meanings because of ambiguity avoidance.

2.2   Structured Document Search

Legal documents are typically large structured documents which is sectioned into several parts in a hierarchical manner. This fact suggests to use structured document search techniques which have been persistently studied on XML data. XML data can be roughly classified into two groups [16]: one is data-centric and the other is document-centric XML data (a.k.a. content-oriented). Schemas of data-centric XML data are designs of objects where XML tags can be regarded as hierarchical attributes, while those of document-centric XML data preserve document structures where the data are still understandable without XML tags. OR documents are classified into the document-centric group.

Since structured documents have tree-structure, the tree edit distance (TED) [3] is one of major approaches to measure similarities between trees [2,12]. TED works well on data-centric XML data, however, does not work well on document-centric XML data because structural information in document-centric XML data are not consistent among different data. Takenaka et al. [18] have tried to measure similarities between legal XML documents by using TED, and they have shown that TED and a text-based similarity [17] have similar tendency. This is because TED is not suitable for measuring similarities between document-centric XML data. In another perspective, fragmentation of XML data [7,15] is to discover meaningful subtrees in the data. This can be applied to document-centric XML data. However, the fragmentation determines units of search results *in advance*, therefore, it misses flexibility which is crucial in the search setting of this paper. XML document comparison also has been proposed (for instance, ID-based matching approach [4] which utilizes ID attributes in XML tags, and structural similarity approach [13]). However, these are suitable for data-centric XML data but not for document-centric.

3   OR Documents: Ordinances and Rules

Ordinances and Rules are the fundamental declarations of social designs, especially under local governments in Japan. OR documents are composed of various provisions which aim at protecting social lives. The Protection of Young Persons Ordinance is a typical ordinance. However, importantly, ordinances in different local governments differ each other in terms of both composed provisions and document structures. Since different regions have different issues, composed provisions may differ. On the other hand, OR documents do not have standardized structural formats like granularities of sections and itemization rules. Due to these differences, finding reference OR documents has required human labours. The rest of this section defines OR documents as tree-structured document in Sect. 3.1 and relevant OR document search task in Sect. 3.2.

3.1   OR Document as a Tree-Structured Document

An OR document is a hierarchically structured document, therefore it can be regarded as a tree structure. Note that this paper ignores reference relationships in an OR document, in other words, no loop exists, therefore, OR document has tree structure. Also, this paper assumes texts only exist in leaf nodes. An OR document is a ordered tree $T = \langle V, S, E, r \rangle$, where V is a set of nodes, $E \subseteq V \times V$ is a set of edges, $r \in V$ is a root node of T, S is a set of text nodes and a text node $s \in S$ is associated with a text $X \in \Sigma^+$ which is mapped by a function $text : S \rightarrow \Sigma^+$ where Σ^+ is the Kleene plus of an alphabet Σ^1. As basic operations of tree T, the following functions are defined: (1) $children : V \rightarrow 2^{V \cup S}$ returns a set of child nodes, (2) $parent : V \cup S \rightarrow V$ returns a parent node, (3) $ancestor : V \cup S \rightarrow 2^{V \cup S}$ returns a set of ancestor nodes or self, and (4) $descendant : V \cup S \rightarrow 2^{V \cup S}$ returns a set of descendant nodes or self.

Chapter I General Rules
  Article 1 Purpose
    (1) The purpose of this Ordinance is to protect young persons by preventing activities which tends to hinder sound upbringing and to contribute to sound upbringing of young persons.
  Article 2 Standard for Operation
    (1) This Ordinance shall apply to the minimum extent necessary to achieve the purpose in the preceding article and shall operate in a manner that does not unduly restrict the rights and freedoms of the citizens.
  Article 3 Responsibilities of Protection
    (1) All prefectural residents are required to protect young persons from the environment that hinders the sound upbringing of young persons and to make positive efforts to ensure the sound upbringing of young persons.
  Article 4 Definitions
    (1) "young person" means a person under 18 years of age.
    (2) "vending machine" means an equipment for the sale of goods, which is capable of selling the goods contained in the equipment without face-to-face contact (Excluding images transmitted using telecommunications equipment that are transmitted through a monitor screen.) between a person engaged in the sale of goods and a customer.

$$\vdots$$

Chapter II Prohibition of acts tends to impede the sound upbringing of young persons

$$\vdots$$

Fig. 1. OR document example: Protection of Young Persons Ordinance

Figure 1 shows a part of an OR document, the Protection of Young Persons Ordinance in Aichi prefecture, Japan[2]. The OR document has virtual top-level node which contains several chapters as its children, chapters have articles as their children, articles have paragraphs (each starts from Arabic numerals with round brackets), and so on. For example, node v corresponding with **Chapter I** has children $children(v) = \{v_1, v_2, \ldots, v_{n_v}, s\}$ where each v_i corresponds with an article (like v_1 corresponds with **Article 1**), n_v is the number of children

---

[1] This paper assumes a space symbol is also included in Σ.
[2] https://www.pref.aichi.jp/uploaded/attachment/200892.pdf (in Japanese). Note that texts in the figure are translated by authors of this paper, so they are not official translations.

of v and $s \in S$ corresponds with a text node. Typically, nodes in higher levels contain title texts in their text nodes for explaining children, and nodes in lowest levels contain text sentences describing parts of provisions. Continue the aforementioned example, v has text $text(s)$ (where $s \in children(v) \cap S$) which is "General Rules". Similarly, node u corresponding with paragraph `(1)` of `Article 1` in `Chapter I` has text $text(s)$ where $s \in children(u) \cap S$ which is "The purpose of this ... young persons".

Table 1. Use case: matched paragraphs about "council" in landscape ordinances in two towns (Ami town, Ibaraki, Japan and Shichigashuku, Miyagi, Japan). #A and #P columns show the numbers of articles and paragraphs, respectively. Article Title column shows titles of articles and, if two or more paragraphs are in an article, the content description of a paragraph is shown in a bracket.

Ami town			Shichigashuku town		
#A	#P	Article Title (Content desc.)	#A	#P	Article Title (Content desc.)
23	1	Establishment	11	1	Council (Establishment)
24	1	Deliberation matters	11	2	Council (Deliberation matters)
25	1	Counsel	11	3	Council (Counsel)
26	1	Organization (#Committee)	12	1	Organization (#Committee)
26	2	Organization (Conditions)	12	3	Organization (Conditions)
26	3	Organization (Temporary com.)			
27	1	Term of service (Basic)	12	2	Organization (Term of service)
27	2	Term of service (Substitute)			
27	3	Term of service (Temporary com.)			
28	1	Chairperson (Election)			
28	2	Chairperson (Chairperson)			
28	3	Chairperson (Vice chairperson)			
29	1	Convention (Summons)			
29	2	Convention (Resolution)			
30	1	Section			

3.2 OR Document Search

As mentioned above, OR documents of different governments may differ in terms of composed provisions and document structures. For instance, the Protection of Young Persons Ordinance in Aichi prefecture, Japan mainly declares to protect young persons from indecent contents like advertisements and books. On the other hand, a related ordinance in Ishikawa prefecture, Japan[3] declares to protect young persons from not only indecent contents but also alcohols, drugs, etc.

Such differences are important for whom drafting OR documents, since drafters tend to imitate multiple reference OR documents. The differences are

---

[3] https://www.pref.ishikawa.lg.jp/kodomoseisaku/plan-jyourei/documents/jyoureizenbunh3002-2.pdf (in Japanese).

not only important for the drafters but also social analysts who research on differences of OR documents among governments. In summary, requirements for the differences of relevant OR documents are as follows: (1) users want parts (subtrees) of OR documents in an OR database *topically related* to a query document, (2) users want *slightly different* subtrees rather than exact matching for the purpose of observing the differences, and (3) users thus want to know *commonalities and differences* between subtrees from OR database and the query document.

Table 1 showcases an example of OR document comparisons, which is a paragraph comparison of articles about councils in landscape ordinances. The OR documents come from two towns in Japan, namely, Ami town and Shichigashuku town. Each row in the table represents corresponding paragraphs between the OR documents, where the combination of article number #A and paragraph number #P identifies paragraphs on each document. The table indicates three facts; (1) The number of paragraphs about the council is different, that is, there are potential provisions for the Shichigashuku ordinance; (2) There is a matching between two (Paras. 1 and 2 in Art. 27 on the left hand ordinance) with one (Para. 2 in Art. 13 on the right hand ordinance) paragraphs; and (3) The orders of paragraphs can differ (paragraphs in Art. 12 in the right hand ordinance do not appear in the same order in the left hand ordinance).

4   Structured Document Search for OR Documents

This paper proposes an OR document search method which deals with the requirements in Sect. 3. The proposed method is composed of two parts: (1) a relevancy metric between subtrees of OR documents and (2) a search algorithm which highlights common parts and different parts in a result subtree pairs.

4.1   Relevancy Metric

The proposed relevancy metric is the composition of two similarity measurements, namely, *matching ratio* and *provision commonality*. The former quantifies the topical similarity between two subtrees of OR documents, and the latter quantifies the commonality (or the inverse of differences) between subtrees.

The proposed metric assumes a set M of text node matching is given. The matching can be calculated by any means, but it must be deterministic. In other words, given two trees T_1 and T_2, the text node matching is a function $f : S_1 \times S_2 \to \{0, 1\}$, where S_1 and S_2 are text nodes of T_1 and T_2, respectively, and 1 means 'matched' and 0 otherwise. Since recent literatures typically use probabilistic approaches, they are required to convert their results from probabilistic to deterministic. For instance, the decision boundary by a threshold is a promising conversion. However, to decide suitable conversion criteria is troublesome. Therefore, the proposed metric depends on the deterministic approaches.

The matching ratio measurement calculates the mean ratio of matching text nodes in both trees, which is formally defined as Definition 1.

Definition 1 (Matching Ratio). *Given two trees $T_1 = \langle V_1, E_1, S_1, r_1 \rangle$, $T_2 = \langle V_2, E_2, S_2, r_2 \rangle$ whose textual matching is $M \subseteq S_1 \times S_2$, the matching ratio $R(T_1, T_2, M)$ is the geometric mean of ratios of matched text nodes over the total number of text nodes*

$$R(T_1, T_2, M) = \sqrt{\frac{|M_1|}{|S_1|} \cdot \frac{|M_2|}{|S_2|}} \,,$$

where M_1 and M_2 are sets of unique text nodes in M w.r.t. T_1 and T_2.

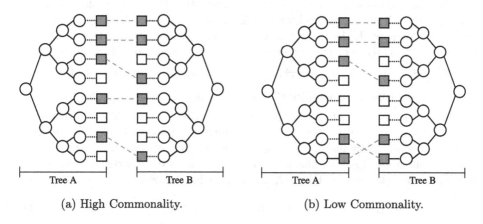

(a) High Commonality.   (b) Low Commonality.

Fig. 2. Tree comparisons, each of which have same matching ratios, with different provision commonalities. Two trees (A and B) are compared, where circles represent intermediate nodes and squares represent texts nodes. Orange texts indicate matched texts and orange dashed lines show textual matchings. (Color figure online)

The matching ratio can capture how largely two trees have matching text nodes, however, it cannot distinguish how the matching text nodes are distributed in sequences of text nodes. Figure 2 illustrates this situation, that is both comparisons (Fig. 2(a) and Fig. 2(b)) have the same matching ratio (i.e., 0.63). If the matching text nodes are distributed evenly in the sequences of text node, the subtrees share common provisions (Fig. 2(a)). On the other hand, meaning that if the matching nodes are biased, the subtrees include separate provisions (Fig. 2(b), the trees both contain a subtree with no matching text node). To capture this, the provision commonality measurement calculates the number of longest consecutive non-matched text nodes. This number estimates the size of different provisions in a subtree against the other, therefore, in order to measure commonality, the inverse of the number is calculated. As a similarity measurement, the provision commonality calculates the average of the inverses for given two trees. The provision commonality is formalized as Definition 2.

Definition 2 (Provision Commonality). *Given two trees* $T_1 = \langle V_1, E_1, S_1, r_1 \rangle$, $T_2 = \langle V_2, E_2, S_2, r_2 \rangle$ *whose textual matching is* $M \subseteq S_1 \times S_2$, *the provision commonality* $C(T_1, T_2, M)$ *of the trees is the geometric mean of the inverse numbers of longest consecutive non-matched text nodes*

$$C(T_1, T_2, M) = \sqrt{\frac{1}{L(T_1, M) + 1} \cdot \frac{1}{L(T_2, M) + 1}} \, ,$$

where $L : (T, M) \to \mathbb{N}$ *returns the length of the longest consecutive non-matched text nodes in tree* T.

The two comparisons in Fig. 2 demonstrates the difference of the provision commonalities between trees whose matching ratios are same. The comparison in Fig. 2(a) represents higher provision commonality since matching text nodes are distributed broadly over the sequences of text nodes, where its provision commonality is $C(A, B) = \sqrt{\frac{1}{1+1} \cdot \frac{1}{2+1}} = 0.41$. While, the comparison in Fig. 2(b) has lower provision commonality (i.e., $C(A, B) = \sqrt{\frac{1}{3+1} \cdot \frac{1}{2+1}} = 0.29$).

As mentioned in Sect. 3, the preference on the commonality of provisions is different on application scenarios. Therefore, the proposed relevancy metric includes a controllable parameter $w \in [0, 1]$ which indicates allowable differences between subtrees. That is, the lower w is, the more differences are expected. Formally, the relevancy metric, rel, is calculated as follows:

$$rel(T_1, T_2, M) = (1 - w) \cdot R(T_1, T_2, M) + w \cdot C(T_1, T_2, M) \tag{1}$$

4.2   Search Algorithm

The objective of the search algorithm is, given two OR document trees, to find pairs of subtrees of the documents, where the subtrees in each pair is relevant in terms of rel function (Eq. 1) and relevancy threshold θ. In a naïve approach, it firstly enumerates all subtree pairs from given two trees and then it evaluates rel function with θ. Obviously, this is computationally inefficient. Also, the naïve approach generates *redundant* results, meaning that the results include two pairs where trees of one pair are both subtrees of respective trees in the other pair. For the clarity of results, the redundancy should be avoided.

The search algorithm introduces a text matching-oriented bottom-up enumeration for computation cost reduction and a maximality check for redundancy avoidance. In order to discuss maximality of pairs of subtrees, the partial order $\preceq$ between the pairs of subtrees rooted by v_1 and v_2 are defined as follows:

$$(v_1, v_2) \preceq (v_1', v_2') \iff v_1' \in ancestor(v_1) \wedge v_2' \in ancestor(v_2) \, ,$$

where $(v_1, v_2) = (v_1', v_2')$ if and only if $v_1 = v_1'$ and $v_2 = v_2'$. Based on the partial order of pairs, the set $P \subseteq V_1 \times V_2$ of maximal pairs is defined as follows:

$$P = \{p \in V_1 \times V_2 \mid \nexists p' \in P, p \preceq p'\}$$

Algorithm 1. Search Algorithm

Input: $T_1 = \langle V_1, E_1, S_1, r_1 \rangle$, $T_2 = \langle V_2, E_2, S_2, r_2 \rangle$, $M \subseteq S_1 \times S_2$, θ
Output: P
1:   $P \leftarrow \{\}$
2:   **for** $(s_1, s_2) \in M$ **do**   ▷ Start from only matched text nodes.
3:      $C = \{(v_1, v_2) \mid v_1 = ancestor(s_1), v_2 \in ancestor(s_2)\}$
4:      **for** $(v_1, v_2) \in C$ **do**
5:         **if** $\nexists (v_1', v_2') \in P, (v_1, v_2) \preceq (v_1', v_2')$ **then**
6:            **if** $rel(v_1, v_2) \geq \theta$ **then**   ▷ Find relevant pair.
7:                $P \leftarrow P \backslash \{(v_1', v_2') \in P \mid (v_1', v_2') \preceq (v_1, v_2)\}$
8:                $P \leftarrow P \cup \{(v_1, v_2)\}$
9:            **end if**
10:        **end if**
11:     **end for**
12: **end for**

The proposed search algorithm traverses all nodes which are ancestors of matched text nodes and eliminates pairs from the set P whenever it discovers pairs which cannot be in P. The algorithm is summarized in Algorithm 1. The inputs of the algorithm are two OR documents T_1, T_2, a set M of precomputed matching text node pairs, and a threshold θ. The traverse starts from each of matching pair (s_1, s_2) in M (line 2). This avoids all combinations of nodes in T_1 and T_2. Then, for each ancestor node pair (line 3), the algorithm checks whether the pair is relevant (line 8). During the traverse, the current candidate pair is checked whether it can be in P (line 5), and, when relevant pair is discovered, pairs in P are examined whether they can be in P (line 9).

5 Experimental Evaluation

This section shows evaluation of the proposed method by measuring correct matching of articles of ordinances. Since OR document search is an immature research area, there is no suitable data for the evaluation. In order to evaluate the proposed method, this paper utilizes a survey on landscape ordinances [6], which classifies articles into 18 classes. The classified articles are used for the evaluation in a way that pairs of articles sharing same classes are those which the proposed method should discover. Based on this strategy, precisions, recall, and F1-measure are calculated for evaluation. The rest of this section introduces the experimental setting and the evaluation results.

5.1 Settings

Dataset. Ito [6] has surveyed inclusions of specific classes of provisions (e.g., screening, council and prohibitions) in articles of the landscape ordinances. Based on the survey, articles are classified into 17 specific classes and one miscellaneous class. The landscape ordinances described in the survey are obtained from eLen

Regulation Database[4] which contains ordinances of local governments from all over Japan. There are six ordinances which have not been amended after the survey are obtained. Therefore, the six ordinances are used in the evaluation. The precomputed matching text node set M is calculated using term frequency-based cosine similarity with threshold. Firstly, each text node is represented as a bag-of-words representation. Using the representations, cosine similarities among all combinations of text nodes between ordinances are computed. Given similarity threshold (0.4 in this experiment), the matching text node set M is obtained.

Methodology. The evaluation is realized as a class estimation problem. One of the six ordinances is selected as a query ordinance whose articles are assigned to classes. For the query ordinance, the proposed method with threshold $\theta = 0.35$ is applied to determine relevant parts (not necessarily articles) of the other ordinances. Then, classes of articles in the query ordinance is propagated to the relevant parts of the other ordinances. There are three exceptional processes: (1) If matched parts of a pair are both below the article level, the pair is discarded; (2) If the matched part in the query ordinance is above the article level, the descendant articles of the part in the other ordinance are classified into all classes of the descendant articles of the part in the query ordinance; and (3) If the matched part in the other ordinance is above the article level, the descendant articles of the part are classified into the class of the part in the query ordinance.

Baseline. A competitor for the proposed method is a heuristic approach. The heuristic approach only compares articles in a query ordinance and the other ordinances by the same relevancy metrics as the proposed method (Eq. 1). This approach is expected to be good performance if there is a one-to-one relationship for each class. In other words, this approach can be poor performance if consecutive articles belong to same classes, since they are estimated separately while the proposed method estimates them at once.

Metrics. The classification results are evaluated by precision, recall and F1-measure. The precision is the ratio of correctly estimated classes over the estimated classes, the recall is the ratio of correctly estimated classes over the true classes, and F1-measure is the harmonic mean of the precision and the recall. The classification include the miscellaneous class which is not always meaningful, therefore, in the evaluation, the metrics are calculated in both cases, one (called *optimistic*) includes the miscellaneous class and the other (called *skeptical*) excludes the miscellaneous class.

5.2   Results

Table 2 showcases the evaluation results where (a) is the optimistic case and (b) is the skeptical case. In the optimistic case, the proposed method significantly outperforms the baseline method, while comparable in the skeptical case. This result indicates that the proposed method performs well even without a priori

---

[4] https://elensv.e-legislation.jp/.

knowledge, which expected parts are articles. These methods have lower precision scores but higher recall scores. In the real application scenario, higher recall is preferable because users do not want to miss relevant parts of ordinances.

Table 2. Evaluation results. The best scores are boldfaced.

(a) Optimistic.

Method	Precision	Recall	F1-measure
Baseline	0.34	**0.81**	0.48
Proposed	**0.51**	0.79	**0.62**

(b) Skeptical.

Method	Precision	Recall	F1-measure
Baseline	**0.39**	0.83	**0.53**
Proposed	0.37	**0.83**	0.51

Table 3. Matched provision related about "council" in landscape ordinances in two towns (Ami town, Ibaraki, Japan and Shichigashuku town, Miyagi, Japan)

Ami town	Shichigashuku town
Article 23, Chap. 3	Article 11
Article 24, Chap. 3	
Article 25, Chap. 3	
Chap. 3 (Article 23 - 30)	Article 12

Use Case. Table 1 demonstrates an example result obtained by the proposed method. The table shows paragraph comparison of "council"-class articles of the landscape ordinances from two towns, namely, Ami town and Shichigashuku town. It is noteworthy that the proposed method discovers the correspondences with regardless of the order of the paragraphs and the granularity of parts (i.e., Para. 1 and 2 of Art. 27 in the query ordinance are corresponding with Para. 2 of Art. 12 in the other ordinance). This result suggests that governmental officers in Shichigashuku town may need to consider the inclusion of "temporary committee" of the organization into their ordinance, since paragraphs (Para. 3 in Art. 26 and Para. 3 in Art. 27) about it are missing.

Table 3 shows a part of matching by the proposed method. The table shows three matched provisions in different levels. The first three rows show a many-to-one matching between articles, and the last row shows a one-to-one matching between a chapter and an article. The first three rows are also observable in Table 1. Each of Arts. 23–25 in the ordinance of Ami town consists of one paragraph, while Art. 11 in that of Shichigashuku town consists of three paragraphs. Each of the paragraphs in Art. 11 in the Shichigashuku town corresponds with Arts. 23–25 in the ordinance of Ami town. On the other hand, the Chap. 3 of the ordinance of Ami town matches with Art. 12 in that of Shichigashuku town. As shown in Table 1, there are two matchings that Para. 2 of the Art. 12 in

Shichigashuku town matches with two paragraphs in Art. 27, Chap. 3 in Ami town, and the other paragraphs in the Art. 12 match with paragraphs in Art. 26, Chap. 3. In this case, the matching ratio is still high, thus the Art. 12 and one-level higher level the Chap. 3 are matched.

6   Conclusion

This paper models the OR document search as a task finding relevant subtree pairs of OR documents by regarding as tree-structured documents. This paper deals with the OR search task by the relevancy metric composed of two similarity measurements, namely, the matching ratio and the provision coverage. To find relevant pairs of subtrees, this paper proposes a text matching-oriented algorithm. Experimental evaluation demonstrates practical effectiveness of relevant OR document discovery.

For the future direction, the proposed algorithm will be expanded for other datasets like contracts, privacy policies and so on. Privacy policies are regarded more and more important for both users and service providers, therefore, service providers should prepare privacy policies with sufficient contents. However, it is not easy to provide enough privacy policies from scratch. The proposed algorithm can help find provisions in privacy policies which is not yet included in the drafting privacy policies. Furthermore, other legal documents including contracts are also expected applications of the proposed algorithm.

Acknowledgements. This work was supported by JSPS KAKENHI Grant Number JP18H03492 and the Artificial Intelligence Research Promotion Foundation.

References

1. Arora, P., Hossari, M., Maldonado, A., Conran, C., Jones, G.J.F.: Challenges in the development of effective systems for professional legal search. In: Proceedings of ProfS/KG4IR/DATA:SEARCH@SIGIR 2018, pp. 29–34 (2018)
2. Augsten, N., Barbosa, D., Böhlen, M.H., Palpanas, T.: Efficient top-k approximate subtree matching in small memory. IEEE Trans. Knowl. Data Eng. **23**(8), 1123–1137 (2011)
3. Bille, P.: A survey on tree edit distance and related problems. Theoret. Comput. Sci. **337**(1–3), 217–239 (2005)
4. Cobena, G., Abiteboul, S., Marian, A.: Detecting changes in XML documents. In: Proceedings of ICDE 2002, pp. 41–52 (2002)
5. Fujioka, K., Nakamura, M., Ogawa, Y., Ohno, T., Toyama, K.: Search method for ordinances and rules in Japanese local governments based on distributed representation. In: Proceedings of KSE 2017, pp. 185–190 (2017)
6. Ito, S.: Jichitai hatsu no seisaku kakushin: Keikan jorei kara keikanho e (Local Government Policy Innovation: From the Landscape Ordinance to the Landscape Act). Bokutakusha (2006). (in Japanese)
7. Komamizu, T., Amagasa, T., Kitagawa, H.: A framework of faceted navigation for XML data. In: Proceedings of iiWAS **2011**, pp. 28–35 (2011)

8. Landthaler, J., Waltl, B., Holl, P., Matthes, F.: Extending full text search for legal document collections using word embeddings. In: Proceedings of JURIX 2016, pp. 73–82 (2016)
9. Le, Q.V., Mikolov, T.: Distributed representations of sentences and documents. In: Proceedings of ICML 2014, pp. 1188–1196 (2014)
10. Locke, D., Zuccon, G.: A test collection for evaluating legal case law search. In: Proceedings of SIGIR 2018, pp. 1261–1264 (2018)
11. Nakamura, M., Kakuta, T.: Development of the eLen regulation database to support legislation of municipalities. In: JURIX 2014, pp. 185–186 (2014)
12. Nierman, A., Jagadish, H.V.: Evaluating structural similarity in XML documents. In: Proceedings of WebDB@PODS/SIGMOD 2002, pp. 61–66 (2002)
13. de Oliveira, A.M.: An efficient similarity-based approach for comparing XML documents. Inf. Syst. **78**, 40–57 (2018)
14. Panagis, Y., Sadl, U., Tarissan, F.: Giving every case its (legal) due - the contribution of citation networks and text similarity techniques to legal studies of European Union law. In: Proceedings of JURIX 2017, pp. 59–68 (2017)
15. Pradhan, S.: An algebraic query model for effective and efficient retrieval of XML fragments. In: Proceedings of VLDB 2006, pp. 295–306 (2006)
16. Sherkhonov, E.: Data exchange for document-centric XML. In: Proceedings of PhD Symposium@SIGMOD 2014, pp. 26–30 (2014)
17. Takenaka, Y., Wakao, T.: Automatic generation of article correspondence tables for the comparison of local government statutes. Nat. Lang. Process. **19**(3), 193–212 (2012)
18. Takenaka, Y., Wakao, T.: Similarity measure among structures of local government statute books based on tree edit distance. In: KSE 2015, pp. 49–54 (2015)

PatentTransformer-1.5: Measuring Patent Claim Generation by Span Relevancy

Jieh-Sheng Lee[✉] [iD] and Jieh Hsiang

Department of Computer Science and Information Engineering, National Taiwan University, Taipei, Taiwan
{d04922013,hsiang}@csie.ntu.edu.tw

Abstract. PatentTransformer is our codename for patent text generation based on Transformer-based models. Our long-term goal of patent claim generation is to realize "augmented inventing" for inventors by leveraging new Deep Learning techniques. We envision the possibility of building an "auto-complete" function for inventors to conceive better inventions in the era of artificial intelligence. In order to generate patent claims with reasonable quality, a fundamental question is how to measure the quality. In PatentTransformer-1.5, we tackle the problem from the perspective of claim span relevancy as a proof of concept. Patent claim language was rarely explored in the NLP field. In this work, we propose a span-based approach and a generic framework to measure patent claim generation quantitatively. In order to study the effectiveness of patent claim generation, we define a metric to measure whether two consecutive spans in a generated patent claims are relevant. We treat such relevancy measurement as a span-pair classification problem, following the concept of natural language inference. Technically, the span-pair classifier is implemented by fine-tuning a pre-trained language model. The patent claim generation is implemented by fine-tuning the other pre-trained model. Specifically, we fine-tune a pre-trained Google BERT model to measure the patent claim spans generated by a fine-tuned OpenAI GPT-2 model. In this way, we re-use two of the state-of-the-art pre-trained models in the NLP field. Our result shows the effectiveness of the span-pair classifier after fine-tuning the pre-trained model. It further validates the quantitative metric of span relevancy in patent claim generation. Particularly, we found that the span relevancy ratio measured by BERT becomes lower when the diversity in GPT-2 text generation becomes higher.

Keywords: Patent · Claims · Classification · Text generation · BERT · GPT-2 · NLI · NLG · NLP

J.-S. Lee—Admitted in New York and passed the USPTO patent bar exam. Currently a Ph.D. candidate focusing on Deep Learning for patents and an in-house patent counsel at Novatek Microelectronics Corp.

ⓒ Springer Nature Switzerland AG 2020
M. Sakamoto et al. (Eds.): JSAI-isAI 2019, LNAI 12331, pp. 20–33, 2020.
https://doi.org/10.1007/978-3-030-58790-1_2

1   Introduction

1.1   Patent Law and Deep Learning

Patents are granted to inventions that meet three basic legal requirements in general: utility, novelty, and nonobviousness. Utility is the requirement that an invention must have a useful function of some kind. Novelty is the requirement that an invention must be substantially different from everything that has been published or known before. Nonobviousness is the requirement that an invention cannot have been obvious to a person having ordinary skill in the art. From the perspective of NLP and Deep Learning, we hypothesize that the nonobviousness problem is a reinforcement learning problem between inventor/patent practitioner and patent examiner. The novelty problem is a search problem in essence. The utility problem is an NLI (Natural Language Inference) problem. In this paper, we focus on the utility perspective in the patent claim generation problem. Without a way to measure the likelihood of meeting the utility requirement, a patent claim generator may generate something novel and nonobvious but not useful at all.

1.2   Augmented Inventing

The ultimate goal of our research is an "augmented inventing" system. We envision an "auto-complete" use case in which, if an inventor is just contemplating and has no whole picture in mind yet, a function like patent claim generation may augment the inventor to conceive better inventions. For example, the interactive augmented- inventing system can suggest next words, phrases, claim spans or even new ideas based on user's input. Such active learning between human and machine may open a window for both qualitative and quantitative analysis on augmented inventing. By measuring how the inventor responds to the system, it is possible to collect human annotations for supervised learning. In order to facilitate supervised learning in the future, it is essential to generate patent claims with reasonable quality for inventors to appreciate. This paper is a step toward such a direction. We measure the quality by span relevancy and assume that a suitable range of span relevancy means a reasonable quality. It is noted that the relevancy measurement is implemented in an unsupervised fashion. By doing so, we have a chance to combine both unsupervised learning and supervised learning in the future.

1.3   A Span-Based Approach

In the NLP field, language modeling is the task of predicting what word comes next. Instead of working on word level, we propose a span-based modeling approach to predict what text span may come next. The text spans in this work are claim spans in patent claims. A patent claim defines the scope of the legal protection conferred by a patent. Most of the time a patent has several claims to define its scope. The reason why it might be possible to build a function to evaluate the utility requirement is that a granted claim is presumed to have met the utility requirement. It could be said that granted patents are human-annotated and possible for supervised learning. The problem lies in how to identify and make use of such annotations.

We identify two types of human annotation in patent claims: explicit and implicit. The explicit annotation is manifested by the dependency between an independent claim and a dependent claim. For example, a dependent claim such as "2. The method of claim 1, wherein...." defines a dependency between claim 2 and claim 1. The implicit annotation is based on the property of element combination. In patent claim language, an invention could be decomposed into inventive elements and conceptually, for a classification task, the order of the elements describing how they work collectively does not matter. The identification and boundary of an inventive element is, therefore, an implicit annotation. Such a property of being able to combine elements in different order is pretty unique, compared with other mainstream NLP research.

Leveraging both the explicit and implicit of annotations is the reason why supervised learning might be feasible for learning the utility requirement. Before building training datasets, a technical problem is how to identify the inventive elements in a patent claim. The format of patent claims provides an answer. A patent claim is required to be a single sentence. Since it defines a technical scope to be protected, a patent claim is usually much longer than an ordinary sentence. Such an unusual length is a challenge to most inventors and even to patent practitioners. Therefore, it is common to split a claim into text spans. A claim span is a segment of claim text. For example, the claim 1 of US9229634B2 is divided into spans as Fig. 1. A claim span for readability is a suitable approximation of an inventive element. We assume such approximation sufficient for proof of concept in this work and leave finer approximation to the future, such as training a neural network to split a longer span into shorter ones.

1.4   Span-Pair Classification

Based on the utility requirement, we treat two spans in a patent claim relevant to a useful function of some kind and relevant to each other. We further take such a relevance problem as a classification problem and the classification is binary: relevant or irrelevant. Our goal is to train a neural network to predict the relevancy between two claim spans. For example, in Fig. 1, the span 1-1, 1-2, 1-3 and 1-4 are relevant to each other. The span 2-1 and 2-2 are relevant to each other. In addition, since the claim 2 is dependent on the claim 1, the span 2-1 and 2-2 are relevant to all spans in the claim 1 too. We collect such intra-claim span pairs and inter-claim span pairs and build a dataset of relevant span pairs.

Training a binary classifier needs both positive records and negative records. The relevant span pairs are positive records. As for negative records, we leverage the current patent classification system, such as CPC (Cooperative Patent Classification) [1], and apply negative sampling to select claim spans from non-overlapped patent classes. For example, the subclass labels of the '634 patent

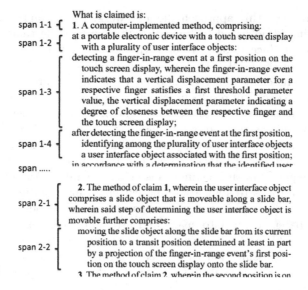

What is claimed is:

span 1-1 { 1. A computer-implemented method, comprising:

span 1-2 { at a portable electronic device with a touch screen display
with a plurality of user interface objects:

span 1-3 { detecting a finger-in-range event at a first position on the
touch screen display, wherein the finger-in-range event
indicates that a vertical displacement parameter for a
respective finger satisfies a first threshold parameter
value, the vertical displacement parameter indicating a
degree of closeness between the respective finger and
the touch screen display;

span 1-4 { after detecting the finger-in-range event at the first position,
identifying among the plurality of user interface objects
a user interface object associated with the first position;

span ..... in accordance with a determination that the identified user

span 2-1 { 2. The method of claim 1, wherein the user interface object
comprises a slide object that is moveable along a slide bar,
wherein said step of determining the user interface object is
movable further comprises:

span 2-2 { moving the slide object along the slide bar from its current
position to a transit position determined at least in part
by a projection of the finger-in-range event's first position on the touch screen display onto the slide bar.

3. The method of claim 2, wherein the second position is on

Fig. 1. Spans in the '634 patent

are G06F and H04M. The claim spans from patents without any of the same labels are sampled randomly. We assume that such claim spans would be negative records and suitable for building a dataset of irrelevant span pairs. After having both of the relevant or irrelevant span pairs, we formulate the span-pair relevancy problem as a sentence-pair classification problem.

It is noted that patents with different subject matters, such as process, machine, manufacture, and composition of matter, may have different average span lengths or different average numbers of spans per claim. We avoid any manual feature engineering and hypothesize that the neural network can learn different subject matters in one model well based on two assumptions: (1) The span boundaries are annotated by humans for easier comprehension. Therefore, it should be feasible for the neural network to learn such comprehensible spans. It might also be possible that the neural network can estimate what kind of subject matter a patent claim is. (2) As mentioned in Sect. 1.3, it should be possible to train a neural network to calculate more fine-grained span boundaries. By doing so, the relation between spans in different subject matters should be similar from a data perspective. In our previous works [2,3] and this work, we didn't encounter any issue requiring different treatments for different subject matters. We leave the validation of the aforementioned assumptions to the future.

1.5 Patent Claim Generation with GPT-2

Initially, we tried patent claim generation at span level by using an ad hoc span-pair classifier. We thought that, by ranking the relevancy concerning all existing spans, it might be possible to provide candidate spans based on user's input. Unfortunately, this approach did not work. As a binary classifier, its relevancy ranking is polarized to binary results most of the time. The neural network cannot produce ranking results with finer granularity. After knowing the effectiveness of the GPT-2 by Radford et al. [4], we switched gear to such a model for patent claim generation. Deep learning and pre-training models have demonstrated excellent results in several language tasks recently. Especially, GPT-2 has become state-of-the-art for text generation. For the details in patent claim generation, please refer to our previous work [2]. In that work, we add a special span separator "@@@" to the patent claims in training data. Our purpose was to measure how fast a GPT-2 model can learn from a patent corpus. We observed the frequency of such claim spans being generated. An auxiliary usage of the span separator is to split a long patent claim into multiple claim spans for readability. In this work, the span separator enables one more use case. By splitting a patent claim into spans and arranging them as span pairs, we found that the problem of measuring two consecutive spans can be formulated as a sentence-pair classification task. Measuring text relevancy is a proxy of measuring text generation quality. Details of building a span-pair classifier are explained in Sect. 3.

In terms of implementation, our patent claim generation is based on the default unconditional random sampling algorithm provided in GPT-2. The sampling is a *top_k* random sampling algorithm with a default k value 40. It means sorting by probability and zeroing out anything below the 40th token when sampling. The quality of generated text depends on the distribution of reasonable words in the top 40 tokens. If there are many words one could sample from reasonably, the quality would be higher. If there are only a few reasonable words to sample from, the quality would be lower. We experiment with different k values in this work. We also hypothesize that a higher k value will generate patent claims with higher diversity and the span-pair relevancy will, therefore, become lower. To our knowledge, our previous work [2] is the first to generate patent claims by transfer learning with a Transformer [5] model. It is also the first time that a machine can generate patent claims in a massive way. Therefore, there is no baseline model for us to benchmark with. As a quick reference, on the surface form, the following is one positive example generated in our previous work:

A deep learning method for drones, comprising the following steps:

a. creating an initial base grid and a final base grid by calculating a first total number of points and a first distance between the final base grid and the initial base grid;

b. setting up a first grid with a plurality of cells;

c. setting up a second grid with a plurality of cells;

d. setting up a third grid with a plurality of cells, wherein each cell of the second grid is connected to each cell of the third grid;

e. calculating a plurality of total distance durations for each cell in the second grid and the third grid;

f. calculating a plurality of total distance durations for each cell in the first grid and the second grid; and g. calculating a plurality of total distance durations for each cell in the final grid and the first grid.

...

The following is one negative example in our previous work. The generated text is too repetitive. Interested readers can check our project repository or try patent claim generation with our sample code.

...

wherein one or more of the control signal sets are used to generate a plurality of image display,
wherein one or more of the control signal sets are used to generate a plurality of new image display,
...

2   Framework

We propose a generic framework for text generation and quality measurement based on Transformer architecture. To our knowledge, at least in the patent domain, our work is the first to combine two Transformer models into one framework. The objective of the framework is to study the correlation between text generation by one Transformer model and the relevancy measurement by the other Transformer model. Since this approach is new, there is no baseline framework for us to benchmark with. In Fig. 2, on the right-hand side, the quality measurement is based on a fine-tuned Transformer Encoder. The Encoder is the BERT model by Devlin et al. [6]. BERT is a language representation model which stands for Bidirectional Encoder Representations from Transformers. We leverage the BERT model by fine-tuning the pre-trained BERT model released by Google [7]. In Sect. 3, we describe how to build a span-pair classifier based on BERT. On the left-hand side, the text generation is based on a fine-tuned Transformer Decoder. The Decoder is the GPT-2 model. We leverage the GPT-2 model by fine-tuning the pre-trained GPT-2 model released by OpenAI [8]. In the training data for the GPT-2 model, we add a special span separator to the patent claims so that generated text contains the span separator for post-processing. The *top_k* random sampling algorithm in GPT-2 source code is controlled by its parameter k. By using different k values, we can generate patent claims with different randomness and quality. In our framework, after text generation, the next step is to split the generated patent claims into span pairs. The span pairs are then fed to the fine-tuned BERT for measuring relevancy. Measuring the generated text completes an iteration of data flow in the framework. In Sect. 4, we describe how to fine-tune the GPT-2 model for text generation in more details.

In this framework, we treat the fine-tuned models as building blocks and they are replaceable. In fact, it is preferable but not necessary to use Transformer

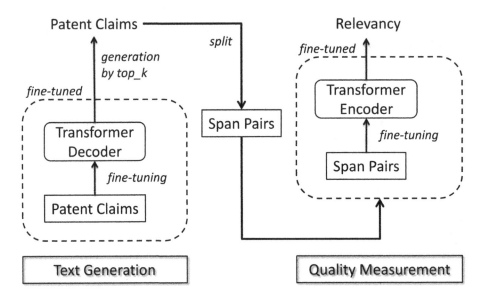

Fig. 2. Framework of text generation & measurement

Decoder for text generation and use Transformer Encoder for quality measurement. Conversely, a Transformer Encoder can be used for text generation. A Transformer Decoder can be used for quality measurement too. If the Encoder and the Decoder of the same Transformer are co-trained, it is also possible to use the same Transformer for both text generation and quality measurement. Whether this kind of replacement is better is another research topic. At the moment of this writing, BERT and GPT-2 are the best available Encoder and Decoder respectively. For example, using BERT for text generation is feasible by Wang and Cho [9] but it does not outperform GPT-2. There are several competing Transformer-based models emerging too, such as RoBERTa [10], MASS [11], XLNet [12] and ERNIE 2.0 [13]. This is the reason why we generalize our implementation from the perspective of a framework. Our current work is a baseline for benchmarking in the future.

It is noted that OpenAI proposes a similar idea in their recent lease of the 1.5B pre-trained model. According to their blog [14], the detection of GPT-2 generated content is still challenging. The way they detect it is to build a sequence classifier by fine-tuning a RoBERTa model to classify the outputs from the 1.5B GPT-2 model versus WebText, the dataset used to train the GPT-2 model. It means that OpenAI leverages a Transformer-based model to measure the content generated by another Transformer-based model. The idea fits well with the dual-Transformer framework in this paper.

3   Build a Span-Pair Classifier Based on BERT

Sentence pair classification has been a type of problem for a long time. Conventionally the goal of the sentence pair classification is to predict whether the second sentence is an entailment, contradiction, or neutral. In this work, we simplify the prediction as a binary classification to entail relevancy or irrelevancy in terms of the utility requirement for patents. One recent approach to text classification problems is fine-tuning a pre-trained BERT model. Such an approach produced the state-of-the-art models for several sentence pair classification tasks, e.g., MNLI, QQP, QNLI, SST-2, CoLA, STS-B, MRPC, and RTE. Therefore, we leverage this fine-tuning approach to build our span-pair classifier. Besides, such a fine-tuning approach applies to other text classification problems as well. For example, a new state-of-the-art result for patent classification based on BERT is produced in our previous work [3].

3.1   Data Pipeline

A data pipeline of preprocessing is required in order to split the raw text of patent claims into span pairs. There are three stages in our data pipeline: (1) raw data collection, (2) claim span identification, and (3) span combination. Although raw data is available on the USPTO Open Data Portal [15], we found it easier to leverage the Google Patents Public Datasets on BigQuery [16]. A dataset based on SQL lowers the entry barrier of data preparation. In our project repository, we share our SQL statement [17] as a better way than sharing conventional raw data for two reasons: (1) Separation of concerns. If the shared raw data contains pre-processing or post-processing specific to a problem or solution, it will be harder for other researchers to reuse for different data processing. (2) Clarity and flexibility. A SQL statement is more precise and easier to revise.

At the second stage, we split patent claim text into claim spans on a heuristic basis. Very often patent practitioners use semicolon or comma to separate a long patent claim into multiple lines. The character return between lines was omitted in our queried data. Therefore, a convenient trick is to make use of such omissions to identify claim spans. Such a heuristic span identification might be not perfect, but this kind of data approximation is sufficient for proof of concept in our work.

At the third stage, the span combination includes two types of data preparation: positive sampling and negative sampling. Generating relevant span pairs as positive records is more intuitive. If the claim is an independent claim having $n1$ spans, $n1 * (n1 - 1)$ span pairs will be generated. If the claim is a dependent claim having $n2$ spans and depending on a claim having $n3$ spans, $n2 * n3$ spans will be generated in addition to $n2 * (n2 - 1)$ spans. We skipped the scenario of multiple dependencies since it does not occur often.

Generating irrelevant span pairs (span1, span2) as negative records is trickier. The number of records based on negative sampling is twice the number of records of positive sampling because we define two types of negative sampling. Type (a) is to randomly pick a span2 which does not share any CPC Subclass label (e.g., "G06F") with the span1. Under the CPC hierarchy, a Section label is higher and more inclusive than a Subclass label. Based on this hierarchy, we design type (b) to pick another span2 which shares the same Section label (e.g.., "G") with the span1 but does not share any Subclass label. We hypothesize that the two spans in type (a) could be farther away in tensor space and easier for a neural network to learn. By adding the type (b), the two spans could be closer but still irrelevant. This may make the neural network generalize better. We leave the validation of this hypothesis to the future.

One more consideration at the span combination stage is to avoid data explosion. In fact, a patent may have many claims and a claim may have many spans. In this work, we cap both the number of claims per patent and the number of spans per claim to 20. In addition, due to resource constraint, our datasets cover the first month of year 2013 to 2016 only. The number of span pairs in our datasets are 3,826,027 (2013), 3,257,617 (2014), 3,316,532 (2015) and 3,728,207 (2016) respectively, as shown in Table 1. We found such datasets sufficient to show the stability of accuracy in our results. We leave broader coverages and different approaches of span combination to the future.

Table 1. Evaluation result (accuracy in percentage)

Test	2013		2014		2015		2016	
Fine-tuning	pos & neg	pos only	pos & neg	pos only	pos & neg	pos only	pos & neg	pos only
2013	97.09	96.08	93.07	87.19	92.79	86.37	92.74	86.24
2014			97.09	95.73	92.56	84.99	92.44	84.87
2015					96.99	95.90	92.70	85.94

pos = positive sampling (i.e., relevant span pairs),
neg = negative sampling (i.e., irrelevant span pairs)
Dataset is limited to January, due to cloud resource constraint.
Number of records:
2013: 3,826,027 (pos & neg), 1,412,983 (pos only)
2014: 3,257,617 (pos & neg), 1,128,790 (pos only)
2015: 3,316,532 (pos & neg), 1,158,265 (pos only)
2016: 3,728,207 (pos & neg), 1,364,092 (pos only)

4   Measuring Text Generation by Span Relevancy

Before measuring text generation, we have to build a fine-tuned GPT-2 model for text generation first. We leverage the same codebase in our previous work [2] and fine-tune the pre-trained 345M model released by OpenAI again. In the followings, we describe the dataset for fine-tuning, parameters to experiments and our measurement results.

4.1   Data

Our dataset to fine-tune the pre-trained GPT-2 model contains 180,000 patent claims. It is composed of three smaller datasets, and each dataset has 60,000 records. The first smaller dataset belongs to CPC Class A (Human Necessities) and its data period is from year 2011 to 2014. The second one belongs to CPC Class G (Physics) and has the same data period. The third one belongs to both CPC Class A and G. Due to fewer records being available, the data period for the third dataset is from 2000 to 2016 so that 60,000 records can be collected. These three datasets are prepared for our next paper in which we plan to observe the detail transition in GPT-2 fine-tuning. For possible integration of these two papers in the future, we decide to leverage the same datasets in this work.

4.2   Method and Experimental Setup

According to Radford et al. [4], GPT-2 is a successor to GPT (Generative Pre-Training) which uses a Transformer-based architecture as its language model. GPT-2 largely follows the details of the original GPT model with a few modifications, particularly a larger model size and more training data. When a large language model is trained on a sufficiently large and diverse dataset, it is able to perform well across many domains and datasets. In GPT-2, text generation is based on top_k random sampling. The random sampling can be either conditional or unconditional. The authors use k value as 40 in their experiments and show several state-of-the-art results. In our work, we tested the top_k unconditional sampling in GPT-2 with different k values: 3, 40, 100, 1000 and 10000. We chose 100, 1000 and 10000 as different orders of magnitude for observation. If k is 1, the generated text will be repetitive. To avoid the problem, we chose 3 for experiments. These numbers are ad hoc and can be adjusted if needed. When fine-tuning the pre-trained GPT-2 model, we keep most of the hyperparameters in our previous work [2] and we set warmup step as 1,000 and training step as 10,000 to reach a reasonable training loss empirically. After fine-tuned, for each experiment, we generate 512 patent claims. These patent claims contain span separators since the GPT-2 model has been fine-tuned with patent claims containing span separators. Based on the output, we split a generated patent claim into spans and combine two consecutive claim spans as a span pair. On average, each patent claim contains 4.34 span pairs.

4.3   Results

The purpose of this work is to propose a generic framework for text generation and quality measurement. Measuring the overall quality of text generation is a challenging problem. In this work, we treat span relevancy as a global quality metric and also a proof of concept of the framework. It is open for future researchers to devise more models and metrics to measure more qualities of text generation. Based on GPT-2 and BERT, Table 2 shows our experiment results. The relevancy ratio in the table is defined as the total number of relevant pairs divided by the total number of all generated pairs. As described in Sect. 1.5, the top_k random sampling algorithm decides how many tokens to sample according to the k value. For example, the default k value 40 will zero out anything below the 40th token. If the k value is too high, more lower-probability tokens will be sampled and the quality of text generation might be lower. If the k value is too low, the quality of text generation may be higher but the diversity of generated text might be reduced. We hypothesized that a higher k value will generate patent claims with higher diversity and the span-pair relevancy will be lower. Our experiment results validate the hypothesis. A higher k value (more randomness) actually produces a lower relevancy ratio between spans. An example of low relevancy in our test results is: "providing a first device that" and "has a first surface and a second surface." In contrast, an example of high relevancy is: "has a first surface and a second surface" and "said first surface and second surface defined by a cross-section and an axis on the first surface and extending from an outer edge of said first surface to a periphery of said first surface."

Table 2. TableRelevancy ratio of generated patent claims

top_k	3	40	100	1,000	10,000
Relevant pairs	2,592	2,117	1,992	1,671	1,401
Irrelevant pairs	205	202	210	323	419
Relevancy ratio	92.67%	91.28%	90.83%	83.80%	76.97%

In Table 2, the ratio is 92.67% (highest) when k is 3 (lowest), and the ratio is 76.97% (lowest) when k is 10,000 (highest). Between these two experiments, the relevancy ratio decreases when the randomness in GPT-2 increases. Such a correlation between randomness and relevancy is intuitive, and it is probably observable if mechanical Turk is involved for manual evaluations. To our knowledge, this work is the first to define a quality metric at span level for GPT-2 text generation. It is noted the *top_k* in our experiment is exemplary. The other parameters in GPT-2 sampling algorithm can also be tested for observing their effect on text generation quality, e.g. measuring different *temperature* values in the sampling algorithm.

4.4   Universal Sentence Encoder

In this section, we leverage the Universal Sentence Encoder (USE) [18,19] as a different way to measure text generation quality. The USE model encodes text into high-dimensional vectors that can be used for text classification, semantic similarity, clustering, and other natural language tasks. We use the model to calculate the semantic similarity within span pairs. The results in Table 3 are based on the same span pairs in Table 2. The TensorFlow Hub hosts two architectures of the USE model: DAN (Deep Averaging Network) and Transformer. We experimented with the latest versions of both architectures. To make it a simple baseline, we didn't fine-tune these two pre-trained models with our patent data.

Similar to the tendency span relevancy, our results show that a higher k value (more randomness) for text generation will make the semantic similarity of

Table 3. Average similarity of span pairs

top_k	3	40	100	1,000	10,000
USE (DAN v.4) [20]	43.83%	38.89%	36.71%	33.03%	29.03%
USE (Transformer v.5) [17]	45.69%	40.27%	38.16%	34.00%	29.92%

two consecutive spans lower. It is noted that measuring the semantic similarity is different from measuring the relevancy. Such a comparison is pertinent is because patent claim spans often contain the same or similar text from other claim spans. The objective of a patent claim is to describe a technical invention as precise as possible so that the described patent claims can meet the "written description" requirement in patent laws. A claimed subject matter lacking a proper antecedent basis in the patent specification can be invalidated. Such a requirement makes the semantic similarity between spans a feasible indicator to measure the overall quality of text generation. Also, using the USE model to measure text generation quality is another example of our framework.

4.5 GitHub

We made our PatentTransformer project available for researchers [17]. The "v1.5" directory is specific to this work, and it contains our sample code, test data, test results, and fine-tuned model for measuring span relevancy. The test data for both Table 2 and Table 3 are archived as "span_pairs.k.[n].txt" ([n] = 3, 40, 100, 1000 and 10000) in the "v1.5/test_data" directory. The test results are archived in the "v1.5/test_results" directory. At the moment of this writing, the "v1" directory covers our previous work [2] for generating patent claims by fine-tuning a GPT-2 model. We envision a next version that will also control patent text generation by structural metadata. Structural metadata includes patent title, abstract, and dependent claim, and independent claim. We make use of the relations between metadata and build a text-to-text generation flow, for example, from a few words to a patent title, from the title to an abstract, from the abstract to an independent claim, and from the independent claim to multiple dependent claims.

5 Conclusion

Patents might be an ideal data source for inventors to move toward human-machine co-inventing in the long run. The emergence of Transformer models such as BERT and GPT-2 is a paradigm shift and a tremendous opportunity for patent researchers. Our contributions in this work include: (1) proposing a framework of using one Transformer to measure the other Transformer, (2) fine-tuning a pre-trained BERT model as a classifier of span-pair relevancy, and (3) using the classifier to measure the patent claims generated by a pre-trained GPT-2 model. Our result validates the quantitative metric of relevancy in patent claim generation. Notably, the span relevancy ratio calculated by BERT becomes higher when the diversity in GPT-2 text generation becomes lower. By having a way to measure text generation quantitatively, we expect to push text generation quality further in the future.

References

1. Cooperative Patent Classification System. https://www.cooperativepatentclassi fication.org. Accessed 2 Mar 2020
2. Lee, J.-S., Hsiang, J.: Patent Claim Generation by Fine-Tuning OpenAI GPT-2 (2019)
3. Lee, J.-S., Hsiang, J.: PatentBERT: Patent Classification with Fine-Tuning a pretrained BERT Model (2019)
4. Radrof, A., Wu, J., Child, R., Luan, D., Amodei, D., Sutskever, I.: Language models are unsupervised multitask learners. Technical report, OpenAI (2018)
5. Vaswani, A., et al.: Attention is all you need. In: Advances in Neural Information Processing Systems, pp. 5998–6008 (2017)
6. Devlin, J., Chang, M.-W., Lee, K., Toutanova, K.: BERT: pre-training of deep bidirectional transformers for language understanding. In: Proceedings of NAACL-HLT, pp. 4171–4186 (2018)
7. (GitHub) google-research/bert. https://github.com/google-research/bert. Accessed 2 Mar 2020
8. (GitHub) openai/gpt-2. https://github.com/openai/gpt-2. Accessed 2 Mar 2020
9. Wang, A., Cho, K.: BERT has a mouth, and it must speak: BERT as a Markov random field language model. In: Proceedings of the Workshop on Methods for Optimizing and Evaluating Neural Language Generation (NeuralGen), pp. 30–36 (2019)
10. Liu, Y., et al.: RoBERTa: A Robustly Optimized BERT Pretraining Approach (2019)
11. Song, K., Tan, X., Qin, T., Lu, J., Liu, T.-Y.: MASS: masked sequence to sequence pre-training for language generation. In: Proceedings of the 36th International Conference on Machine Learning, Long Beach, California (2019)
12. Yang, Z., Dai, Z., Yang, Y., Carbonell, J., Salakhutdinov, R., Le, Q.V.: XLNet: generalized autoregressive pretraining for language understanding. In Advances in Neural Information Processing Systems 32 (NIPS 2019), Pre-proceedings, pp. 5754–5764 (2019)
13. Sun, Y., et al.: ERNIE 2.0: a continual pre-training framework for language understanding. In: Accepted by AAAI 2020 (2019)
14. GPT-2: 1.5B Release. https://openai.com/blog/gpt-2-1-5b-release. Accessed 2 Mar 2020
15. USPTO Open Data Portal. https://developer.uspto.gov/. Accessed 2 Mar 2020
16. Google Patents Public Datasets on BigQuery. https://console.cloud.google.com/ bigquery?p=patents-public-data. Accessed 2 Mar 2020
17. (GitHub) PatentTransformer. https://github.com/jiehsheng/PatentTransformer. Accessed 2 Mar 2020
18. Cer, D., et al.: Universal sentence encoder for English. In: EMNLP 2018 - Conference on Empirical Methods in Natural Language Processing, System Demonstrations, Proceedings, pp. 169–174 (2018)

19. Google Patents Public Datasets on BigQuery. https://console.cloud.google.com/bigquery?p=patents-public-data. Accessed 2 Mar 2020

20. Universal-sentence-encoder (V4). https://tfhub.dev/google/universal-sentence-encoder/4. Accessed 2 Mar 2020

21. Universal-sentence-encoder-large (V5). https://tfhub.dev/google/universal-sentence-encoder-large/5. Accessed 2 Mar 2020

A Summary of the COLIEE 2019 Competition

Juliano Rabelo[1,2(✉)], Mi-Young Kim[1,3], Randy Goebel[1,2],
Masaharu Yoshioka[4,5,6], Yoshinobu Kano[7], and Ken Satoh[8]

[1] Alberta Machine Intelligence Institute, Edmonton, AB, Canada
{rabelo,miyoung2,rgoebel}@ualberta.ca
[2] University of Alberta, Edmonton, AB, Canada
[3] Department of Science, Augustana Faculty, Camrose, AB, Canada
[4] Graduate School of Information Science and Technology, Kita-ku, Sapporo-shi,
Hokkaido, Japan
yoshioka@ist.hokudai.ac.jp
[5] Global Station for Big Date and Cybersecurity, Global Institution for Collaborative
Research and Education, Kita-ku, Sapporo-shi, Hokkaido, Japan
[6] Hokkaido University, Kita-ku, Sapporo-shi, Hokkaido, Japan
[7] Faculty of Informatics, Shizuoka University,
Naka-ku, Hamamatsu-shi, Shizuoka, Japan
kano@inf.shizuoka.ac.jp
[8] National Institute of Informatics, Hitotsubashi, Chiyoda-ku, Tokyo, Japan
ksatoh@nii.ac.jp

Abstract. We summarize the evaluation of the 6th Competition on
Legal Information Extraction/Entailment (COLIEE 2019). The competition consists of four tasks: two on case law and two on statute law. The
case law component includes an information retrieval task (Task 1), and
the confirmation of an entailment relation between an existing case and
an unseen case (Task 2). The statute law component also includes an
information retrieval task (Task 3) and an entailment/question answering task (Task 4), which attempts to confirm whether a particular statute
applies to a yes/no question. Participation was open to any group in the
world, based on any approach. Eleven different teams participated in the
case law competition tasks, some of them in more than one task. We
received results from 7 teams for Task 1 (15 runs) and 7 teams for Task
2 (18 runs). For the statute law tasks, 8 different teams participated,
some in more than one task. Seven teams submitted a total of 13 runs
for Task 3, and 7 teams submitted a total of 15 runs for Task 4. Here
we summarize each team's approaches, our official evaluation, and some
analysis of the variety of methods that produced the evaluation results.

Keywords: Legal documents processing · Textual entailment ·
Information retrieval · Classification · Question answering

© Springer Nature Switzerland AG 2020
M. Sakamoto et al. (Eds.): JSAI-isAI 2019, LNAI 12331, pp. 34–49, 2020.
https://doi.org/10.1007/978-3-030-58790-1_3

1   Introduction

The Competition on Legal Information Extraction/Entailment (COLIEE) is a series of evaluation competitions intended to build a research community, and to accelerate the development of the state of the art for information retrieval and entailment using legal texts. It is usually co-located with JURISIN, the Japanese Artificial Intelligence Society Juris-Informatics workshop series, which was created to promote community discussion on both fundamental and practical issues on legal information processing. The intention is to broadly embrace multiple disciplines, including law, social sciences, information processing, logic and philosophy, and the existing conventional "AI and law" area. In alternate years, COLIEE is organized as a workshop at the International Conference on AI and Law (ICAIL), which was the case in 2017 and 2019.

In COLIEE editions 2014 to 2017, there were two tasks (information retrieval (IR) and entailment) using Japanese Statute Law (civil law). Since COLIEE 2018, two new tasks (IR and entailment) were introduced, which use Canadian case law (Tasks 1 and 2).

Task 1 is a legal case retrieval task, and it involves reading a new case Q, and identifying supporting cases S1, S2, ..., Sn from the provided case law corpus, hypothesized to support the decision for Q. Task 2 is a legal case entailment task, which involves the identification of a paragraph or paragraphs from existing cases, which are alleged to entail a given fragment of a new case. For the information retrieval task (Task 3), based on the discussion about the analysis of previous COLIEE IR tasks, we modify the evaluation measure of the final results and also ask the participants to submit a ranked list of relevant article results to inform a detailed discussion on the difficulty of the questions. For the entailment task (Task 4), we analyze accuracy of case analysis to expose issues with characterization of case attributes, in addition to evaluation of accuracy as in previous COLIEE tasks.

The rest of the paper is organized as follows: Sects. 2, 3, 4, 5 decribe each task, presenting their definitions, datasets, list of approaches submitted by the participants, and results attained. Section 6 presents final some final remarks.

2   Task 1 - Case Law Information Retrieval

2.1   Task Definition

This task consists in finding which cases, in the set of candidate cases, should be "noticed" with respect to a given query case. "Notice" is a legal technical term that identifies a legal case description that is considered to be relevant to a query case. More formally, given a query case q and a set of candidate cases $C = \{c_1, c_2, ..., c_n\}$, the task is to find the supporting cases $S = \{s_1, s_2, ..., s_n \mid s_i \in C \wedge noticed(s_i, q)\}$ where $noticed(s_i, q)$ denotes a relationship which is true when $s_i \in S$ is a noticed case with respect to q.

2.2 Dataset

The training dataset consists of 285 base cases, each with 200 candidate cases from which the participants must identify those that should be noticed with respect to the base case. The official COLIEE test dataset has 61 cases has their golden labels, disclosed only after the competition results were published. Table 1 summarizes the properties of those datasets.

Table 1. Summary for the case law retrieval task datasets

Property	Training	Testing
Number of base cases	285	61
Total number of candidate cases	57,000	12,200
Total number of noticed cases	1486 (2.60%)	330 (2.70%)

2.3 Approaches

Seven teams submitted a total of 15 runs for this task. Deep learning techniques and machine learning based classifiers were commonly used. More details on these alternative approaches are described below:

- **CACJ (one run)** [3] applies a machine learning based classifier using features extracted from the cases header (i.e., it does not consider any of the case contents).
- **CLArg (one run)** [17] describes an approach based on vector representation of cases, in combination with two different classifiers: random forests and k-nearest neighbours.
- **HUKB (one run)** [26] improved their previous system, used on the 2018 COLIEE edition (which was based on the use of structural information which considers a case as composed of three sections: header, facts and footer), by incorporating the use of case metadata: date, to exclude candidates more recent than the base case, and topics.
- **IITP (three runs)** [4] uses a combination of Deep Learning techniques, such as Doc2Vec, and Information Retrieval techniques, such as BM25, to tackle the task 1 challenge.
- **ILPS (three runs)** [21] combines text summarizing and a generalized language model (BERT) in order to assess pairwise relevance. To overcome a limitation of the framework on handling text fragments longer than 512 tokens, the authors apply summarization techniques over the case contents. The generated embeddings are then used as input to an MLP classifier.
- **JNLP (three runs)** [23] applies a summarization model that encodes a document into a continuous vector space, which embeds the summary properties of the document. The authors combine such encoded representation with latent and lexical features extracted from different parts of a given query and its candidates.

– **UA (three runs)** [19] developed an approach based on the use of the Universal Sentence Encoder to generate a vector representation of both the base case and each candidate, followed by the calculation of a similarity score using a cosine measure (this approach was used as the baseline for this task).

2.4 Results

The F1-measure is used to assess performance in this task. We use a simple baseline model that uses the Universal Sentence Encoder to encode each candidate case and base case into a fixed size vector, and then applies the cosine distance between both vectors. The baseline result was 0.3560 (precision: 0.3333, recall: 0.3443, for a threshold of 0.57 minimum similarity). The actual results of the submitted runs by all participants are shown on Table 2, from which it can be seen that only 1 team could not reach the baseline.

Table 2. Results attained by all teams on the test dataset of task 1.

Team	Submission file	Precision	Recall	F1-score
JNLP	JNLP.task_1.pl.txt	0.6000	0.5545	0.5764
JNLP	JNLP.task_1.ple.txt	0.6000	0.5545	0.5764
JNLP	JNLP.task_1.p.txt	0.5934	0.5485	0.5701
ILPS	BERT_Score_0.946.txt	0.6810	0.4333	0.5296
HUKB	task1.HUKB	0.7021	0.4000	0.5097
ILPS	BM25_Rank_6.txt	0.4672	0.5182	0.4914
ILPS	BERT_Score_0.96.txt	0.8188	0.3424	0.4829
IITP	task1.IITPdocBM.txt	0.6368	0.3879	0.4821
IITP	task1.IITPBM25.txt	0.6256	0.3848	0.4765
CLArg	CLarg.txt	0.9266	0.3061	0.4601
IITP	task1.IITPd2v.txt	0.4653	0.3455	0.3965
UA	UA_0.57.txt	0.3560	0.3333	0.3443
UA	UA_0.52.txt	0.3513	0.3364	0.3437
UA	UA_0.54.txt	0.3639	0.3242	0.3429
CACJ	submit_task1_CACJ01.csv	0.2119	0.5848	0.3110

Table 2 shows JNLP attained the best result for the F1-score. CLArg had the best score when only precision is considered, whereas CACJ had the best recall score. The F1-score for CLArg and CACJ, however, were not among the best ones for this task, which shows the difficulty of finding the right balance in order to achieve good overall performance in this task.

3 Task 2 - Case Law Entailment

3.1 Task Definition

Given a base case and an extracted specific fragment together with a second case that is relevant in respect to the base case, this task consists in determining which paragraphs of the second case entail that fragment of the base case. More formally, given a base case b and its entailed fragment f, and another case r represented by its paragraphs $P = \{p_1, p_2, ..., p_n\}$ such that $noticed(b, r)$ as defined in Sect. 2 is true, the task consists in finding the set $E = \{p_1, p2, ..., p_m \mid p_i \in P\}$ where $entails(p_i, f)$ denotes a relationship which is true when $p_i \in P$ entails the fragment f.

3.2 Dataset

The training dataset has 181 base cases, each with its respective entailed fragment in a separate file. For each base case, a related case represented by a list of paragraphs is given, from which must be identified is the paragraph(s) that entail the base-case-entailed fragment. The test dataset has 44 cases and was initially released without the golden labels, which were only disclosed after the competition results were published. Table 3 summarizes the properties of those datasets.

Table 3. Summary for the case law entailment task datasets

Property	Training	Testing
Number of base cases	181	44
Total paragraphs in the related cases	5,814	1,448
Total true entailing paragraphs	202 (3.47%)	45 (3.10%)

3.3 Approaches

Seven teams submitted a total of 18 runs to this task. The most used techniques were those based on transformer methods, such as BERT [2] or ELMo [18]. More details on the approaches are show below.

- **IeLab**[1] (three runs)] used an IR-based technique which selects terms from the entailed fragments and the candidates using inverse document frequency and part of speech information.

---

[1] This is an interesting approach worth further investigation, however the paper describing the method lacked important information and thus was not accepted for publication on the COLIEE proceedings.

- **IITP (three runs)** [4] describes an approach which uses BM25, an Information Retrieval technique, and Doc2Vec, a Deep Learning based technique, for this task.
- **JNLP (three runs)** has not submitted a paper describing the details of their approach for task 2, but they devised deep learning based methods for other tasks of COLIEE 2019 (e.g., [16]).
- **TRCase (one run)** [13] applies a ranking algorithm which uses word embeddings and textual similarity features to determine entailment relationships between a candidate paragraph and an entailed fragment. The authors observe that the set of selected features provide better results when applied to a ranking approach, rather than a supervised classifier.
- **TTCL (three runs)** presents an approach based on a generalized language model using BERT for the case law entailment task, and compared that approach with an SVM baseline approach. To overcome the framework limitation of 512 tokens, the authors apply BERT at a sentence level, considering a paragraph to be an entailing example when one or more sentences are classified as entailing one or more sentences from the entailed fragment.
- **UA (three runs)** [19] proposes an approach which relies the extraction of similarity measures between the candidate paragraph and the entailed fragment; the application of BERT on those two pieces of text; use of a threshold-based classifier; and post-processing the results considering the a priori probability determined by the data distribution on the training samples.
- **UBLTM (two runs)** has not submitted a paper describing the details of their approach.

3.4 Results

The F1-measure is used to assess performance in this task. The score attained by a simple baseline model which uses the Universal Sentence Encoder to encode each candidate paragraph and the entailed fragment into a fixed size vector and applies the cosine distance between both vectors was 0.1760 (precision: 0.1375, recall: 0.2444, for a threshold of 0.75 minimum similarity). The actual results of the submitted runs by all participants are shown on Table 4, from which it can be seen that only 2 runs had a performance worse than the baseline score (however, the teams which sent those submissions also got better results on other runs).

From Table 4, one can see UA attained the best result for the F1-score, the official metric used in this task. However, IITP and TRCase achieved comparable results for the F1-score. It is also worth noting that IITP attained the best score considering only precision, and TTCL got the best recall score.

Table 4. Results attained by all teams on the test dataset of task 2.

Team	Submission file	Precision	Recall	F1-score
UA	UA_0.400000.txt	0.6538	0.7556	0.7010
UA	UA_0.250000.txt	0.6364	0.7778	0.7000
IITP	task2.iitpBM25.txt	0.7045	0.6889	0.6966
UA	UA_0.300000.txt	0.6296	0.7556	0.6869
TRCase	TRCase_colie_test_submission_task2	0.6818	0.6667	0.6742
IITP	task2.iitp2docBM.txt	0.6591	0.6444	0.6517
JNLP	JNLP.task_2.lex.txt	0.5909	0.5778	0.5843
TTCL	uncased758256.txt	0.4000	0.8000	0.5333
TTCL	uncased758voted.txt	0.3882	0.7333	0.5077
TTCL	uncased758512.txt	0.3780	0.6889	0.4882
ielab	ielabsen.txt	0.4545	0.4444	0.4494
ielab	ielabphrase.txt	0.3409	0.3333	0.3371
ielab	ielabterm.txt	0.2273	0.2222	0.2247
UBLTM	UBLTM_T2_2.txt	0.1273	0.6222	0.2113
UBLTM	UBLTM_T2_1.txt	0.1182	0.5778	0.1962
JNLP	JNLP.task_2.cls-elmo.txt	0.1364	0.1333	0.1348
JNLP	JNLP.task_2.cls-elmobert.txt	0.0682	0.0667	0.0674
IITP	task2.iitp2D2v.txt	0.0455	0.0444	0.0449

4   Task 3 - Statute Law Information Retrieval

4.1   Task Definition

This task involves reading a legal bar exam question Q, and identification of a subset of Japanese Civil Code Articles S_1, S_2,..., S_n from the entire Civil Code which are those appropriate for answering the question such that

$$Entails(S_1, S_2, ..., S_n, Q) \text{ or } Entails(S_1, S_2, ..., S_n, \text{ not } Q).$$

Given a question Q and the all Civil Code Articles, the participants are required to retrieve the set of "$S_1, S_2, ..., S_n$" as the answer of this track.

4.2   Dataset

For task 3, questions related to Japanese civil law were selected from the Japanese bar exam. The organizers provided a data set used for previous bar law exams, translated to English [8–10, 25] as training data (717 questions), with new questions selected from the 2018 bar exam as test data (98 questions). The number of questions classified by the number of relevant articles is listed in Table 5.

Table 5. Number of questions classified by number of relevant articles

Number of relevant article(s)	1	2	3	5	Total
Number of questions	80	15	2	1	98

4.3   Approaches

The following seven teams submitted 13 runs in total. Four teams (HUKB, JNLP, KIS and UA) had participated in previous editions, and three teams (DBSE, EVORA and IITP) were new competitors. Common techniques used in the system were well known IR engine mechanisms such as elasticsearch[2], Terrier [12], Indri [22], gensim[3], scikit-learn[4] with various scoring function such as TF-IDF, BM25. For the indexing, the most common method was ordinal word base indexing with stemming. Several teams use N-gram, word sequence, Word2Vec [15] and Doc2Vec [11].

- **DBSE (one run)** [24] used BM25 scoring of elasticsearch and Word2Vec [15] based similarity scoring. They finally select the one or more results from them.
- **EVORA (three runs)** [20] uses Terrier IR platform with different scoring function with two query sets (original and keyword selection) and two article database (original articles and keyword selected articles).
- **HUKB (one run)** [26] uses sentence structure analysis to extract condition part and argument part of the query and articles and compare the similarity using Indri IR system. Final results are calculated by SVMRank using those features.
- **KIS (two runs)** [5] uses Doc2Vec [11] for generating document embedding vector and calculate similarity among query and articles. They also use TF-IDF to select important keywords for generating document embedding. Final results are selected by considering the score difference between the top ranked and candidate documents.
- **IITP (two runs)** [4] uses BM25 module of gensim and tfidf module of scikit learn.
- **JNLP (two runs)** [1] proposed to use different indexing method for TF-IDF calculation (N-gram, verb-phrase, noun-phrase) and calculate similarity using cosine similarity. Final results are selected by considering the score difference between the i-th ranked document and $i + 1$-th ranked one.
- **UA (two runs)** [14] uses the TF-IDF model and language model as an IR module.

The teams which participated in the previous COLIEE proposed an extension or equivalent system for Task 3, and new teams proposed methods.

---

[2] https://www.elastic.co/.
[3] https://radimrehurek.com/gensim/.
[4] https://scikit-learn.org.

4.4   Results

Table 6 shows the evaluation results of submitted runs. The official evaluation measures used in this task were macro average of F2 measure, precision, and recall. We also calculate the mean average precision (MAP), recall at k (R_k: recall calculated by using the top k ranked documents as returned documents) by using the long ranking list (100 articles). Table 6 shows UA-TFIDF achieved the best F2 score among all submitted runs. KIS_2 had the highest recall score. For the longer ranked list, EVORA is better than others.

Table 6. Evaluation results of submitted runs (Task 3) and the corresponding organizers' run

runid	lang	ret.	rel.	F2	Prec.	Rec.	MAP	R_5	R_{10}	R_{30}
DBSE	E	172	54	0.466	0.454	0.493	0.512	0.512	0.620	0.669
EVORA1	E	98	56	0.533	0.571	0.529	**0.628**	**0.669**	0.744	**0.851**
EVORA2	E	98	56	0.533	0.571	0.529	0.617	0.653	0.744	0.835
EVORA3	E	98	56	0.529	0.571	0.524	0.624	0.653	**0.752**	0.835
iitpBM25	E	98	48	0.447	0.490	0.442	0.541	0.620	0.669	0.760
iitptfidf	E	98	43	0.401	0.439	0.396	0.506	0.570	0.628	0.752
JNLP-tf	E	165	64	0.534	0.459	0.582	0.598	0.653	0.686	0.769
JNLP-tfnv	E	171	61	0.505	0.403	0.562	0.575	0.595	0.653	0.769
UA-LM	E	98	48	0.452	0.490	0.447	0.541	0.554	0.636	0.727
UA-TFIDF	E	98	58	**0.549**	**0.592**	0.544	0.618	0.620	0.694	0.760
HUKB	J	98	44	0.414	0.449	0.410	0.494	0.488	0.612	0.727
KIS	J	404	69	0.503	0.423	0.613	0.562	0.628	0.711	0.835
IS_2	J	408	**72**	0.503	0.427	**0.637**	0.540	0.653	0.744	0.835

Figures 1, 2 and 3 show an average of evaluation measure for all submission runs. As we can see from Fig. 1, there are many easy questions for which almost all systems can retrieve relevant articles. Figures 2 and 3 show there are also many queries for which none of the systems can retrieve relevant articles.

One of the example of this issue is H30-1-A: "An unborn child may not be given a gift on the donor's death." and relevant article is Article 3 "The enjoyment of private rights shall commence at birth." There is no common words between the query and a relevant article and it requires knowledge about relationship between "commence at birth" and "unborn" for understanding the relationship. In order to analyze the improvement of the system for such difficult questions, it is necessary to compare the retrieval performance for such difficult queries.

5   Task 4 - Statute Law Entailment

5.1   Task Definition

Task 4 requires determination of entailment relationships between a given problem sentence and article sentences. Competitor systems should answer "yes" or "no" regarding the given problem sentences and given article sentences. Until COLIEE 2016, the competition had only pure entailment tasks, where t1 (relevant article sentences) and t2 (problem sentence) were given. Due to the limited number of available problems, COLIEE 2017 and 2018 did not retain this style of task. In the Task 4 of COLIEE 2019, we returned to the pure textual entailment task to attract more participants, allowing more focused analyses.

5.2   Dataset

Our training dataset and test dataset are the same as Task 3. Questions related to Japanese civil law were selected from the Japanese bar exam. The organizers provided a data set used for previous campaigns as training data (717 questions) and new questions selected from the 2018 bar exam as test data (98 questions).

5.3   Approaches

The following seven teams submitted their results (15 runs in total). Two teams (KIS and UA) had experience in submitting results in the previous campaign. We describe each system's overview below.

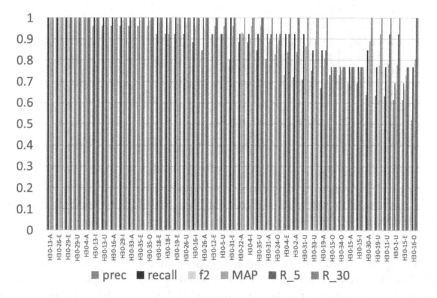

Fig. 1. Averages of precision, recall, F2, MAP, R_5, and R_30 for easy questions with a single relevant article

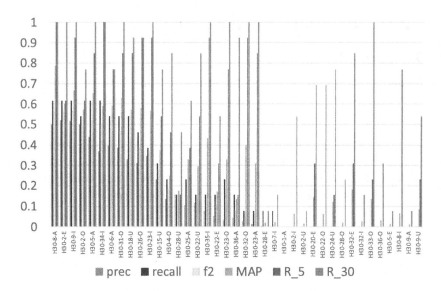

Fig. 2. Averages of precision, recall, F2, MAP, R_5, and R_30 for non-easy questions with a single relevant article

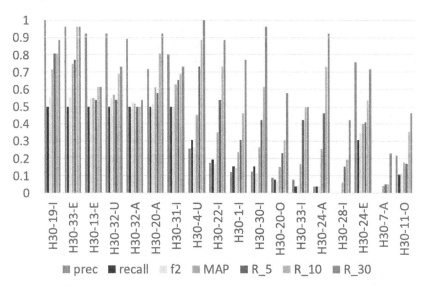

Fig. 3. Averages of precision, recall, F2, MAP, R_5, and R_30 for non-easy questions with multiple relevant articles

- **UA** [14] uses condition/conclusion/exception detection rules, and negation dictionaries created manually. They translated original Japanese texts into Korean by machine translation, employed their own Korean parser and

Korean resources. **UA_Ex** uses Excite machine translation service, **UA_Go** uses Google machine translation service.

- **KIS** [6] parses sentences into predicate-argument structures to compare t1/t2 pairs, detecting negations and conditions. They use an ensemble of different comparison criteria (**KIS_3module**), then adding their own synonym dictionary (**KIS_dic**) or using FrameNet (**KIS_frame**).
- **IITP** [4] uses BERT with a BERT-base model.
- **DBSE** [24] uses an ensemble of stacked LSTMs.
- **JNLP** [16] indirectly solves the original problem with a derived problem with more abundant data. They trained using a stacked GRU.
- **TR** [7] uses BERT large model with decomposable attention (**TRAttn**), and similarity features (**TRSimFeat**).
- **EVORA** [20] used deep neural networks based methods, such as embedding by FastText (**EVORA1**), LSTM (**EVORA2**) and CNN (**EVORA3**).

5.4 Results

Evaluation was based on accuracy. Table 7 shows evaluation results of Task 4 for each submitted run. Because an entailment task is essentially a complex composition of different subtasks, we manually categorized our test data into categories, depending on what sort of technical issues are required to be resolved. Table 8 shows our categorization results. As this is a composition task, overlap is

Table 7. Evaluation results of submitted runs (Task 4)

Team	Dataset language	# of correct answers (98 problems in total)	Accuracy
UA_Ex	Japanese	67	0.6837
KIS_3module	Japanese	61	0.6224
IITP	English	58	0.5918
KIS_dic	Japanese	58	0.5918
UA_Go	Japanese	58	0.5918
KIS_frame	Japanese	57	0.5816
DBSE	English	56	0.5714
JNLP.t = 98	English	56	0.5714
TRAttn	English	55	0.5612
TRSimFeat	English	52	0.5306
JNLP.t = 85	English	51	0.5204
EVORA1	English	50	0.5102
JNLP.t = 78	English	48	0.4898
EVORA3	English	47	0.4796
EVORA2	English	44	0.4490

Table 8. Technical category statistics of questions, and correct answers of submitted runs for each category in numbers of counts and percentages[a].

Category	#	a	%	b	%	c	%	d	%	e	%	f	%	g	%	h	%	i	%	j	%	k	%	l	%	m	%	n	%	o	%
Conditions	83	47	.57	44	.53	34	.41	38	.46	49	.59	40	.48	42	.51	46	.55	52	.63	50	.60	47	.57	48	.58	44	.53	57	.69	51	.61
Pers. role	66	36	.55	37	.56	24	.36	26	.39	40	.61	34	.52	35	.53	38	.58	43	.65	39	.59	41	.62	35	.53	34	.52	46	.70	37	.56
Pers. Reltnshp	66	36	.55	37	.56	24	.36	26	.39	40	.61	34	.52	35	.53	38	.58	43	.65	39	.59	41	.62	35	.53	34	.52	46	.70	37	.56
Negation	44	27	.61	24	.55	20	.45	20	.45	26	.59	22	.50	19	.43	26	.59	26	.59	29	.66	23	.52	23	.52	22	.50	26	.59	24	.55
Entailment	33	18	.55	14	.42	18	.55	15	.45	16	.48	15	.45	10	.30	16	.48	21	.64	19	.58	19	.58	18	.55	16	.48	20	.61	18	.55
Dependency	28	12	.43	14	.50	10	.36	11	.39	14	.50	10	.36	17	.61	16	.57	19	.68	17	.61	18	.64	19	.68	12	.43	21	.75	17	.61
Ambiguity	26	11	.42	14	.54	9	.35	14	.54	12	.46	10	.38	15	.58	17	.65	15	.58	15	.58	11	.42	12	.46	14	.54	17	.65	13	.50
Legal terms	24	12	.50	11	.46	11	.46	14	.58	12	.50	9	.38	14	.58	18	.75	13	.54	12	.50	15	.63	15	.63	13	.54	17	.71	15	.63
Anaphora	22	12	.55	13	.59	9	.41	12	.55	13	.59	13	.59	13	.59	13	.59	16	.73	12	.55	14	.64	9	.41	9	.41	18	.82	14	.64
Verb paraphrs	21	11	.52	12	.57	8	.38	8	.38	15	.71	10	.48	10	.48	11	.52	10	.48	13	.62	11	.52	12	.57	10	.48	13	.62	9	.43
Morpheme	18	13	.72	7	.39	6	.33	8	.44	13	.72	13	.72	11	.61	9	.50	12	.67	11	.61	13	.72	14	.78	12	.67	14	.78	14	.78
Case role	17	8	.47	10	.59	6	.35	8	.47	12	.71	7	.41	8	.47	10	.59	9	.53	7	.41	7	.41	11	.65	8	.47	9	.53	8	.47
Pred. argument	14	5	.36	7	.50	6	.43	7	.50	10	.71	7	.50	7	.50	8	.57	9	.64	7	.50	9	.64	9	.64	5	.36	11	.79	7	.50
Article search	11	5	.45	6	.55	4	.36	7	.64	8	.73	7	.64	6	.55	3	.27	8	.73	8	.73	5	.45	4	.36	4	.36	10	.91	7	.64
Paraphrase	11	4	.36	6	.55	5	.45	7	.64	3	.27	1	.09	7	.64	7	.64	9	.82	3	.27	10	.91	4	.36	7	.64	8	.73	5	.45
Itemized	8	6	.75	4	.50	5	.63	3	.38	5	.63	4	.50	3	.38	4	.50	4	.50	6	.75	4	.50	6	.75	5	.63	6	.75	5	.63
Normal terms	7	3	.43	3	.43	2	.29	5	.71	4	.57	2	.29	4	.57	4	.57	5	.71	5	.71	4	.57	3	.43	2	.29	5	.71	4	.57
Calculation	2	1	.50	1	.50	1	.50	1	.50	1	.50	1	.50	1	.50	1	.50	1	.50	1	.50	1	.50	1	.50	1	.50	2	1.00	2	1.00

[a] Alphabetical letters stand for team names; a: DBSE, b: EVORA1, c: EVORA2, d: EVORA3, e: IITP, f: JNLP: t = 78, g: JNLP: t = 85, h: JNLP(t = 98), i: KIS_3module, j: KIS_dic, l: TRAttn, m: TRSimFeat, n: UA.Ex, o: UA_Go, respectively. Team columns stand for their number of correct answers for corresponding category.

allowed between categories. Our categorization is based on the original Japanese version of the legal bar exam.

Although some cells show better results than others, none of the current systems could have solved problem types of more complex semantics, e.g., anaphora resolution. Overall we require a more precise survey of system differences, especially which components are more or less complete solutions that produce predictably correct results.

6   Final Remarks

We have summarized the results of the COLIEE 2019 competition. In case law, Task 1 deals with the retrieval of noticed cases, and Task 2 poses the problem of identifying which paragraphs of a relevant case entail a given fragment of a new case. In statute law, Task 3 is about retrieving articles to decide the appropriateness of the legal question, and Task 4 is a task to entail whether the legal question is correct or not. Eleven (11) different teams participated in the case law competition (some of them in both tasks). We received results from 7 teams for Task 1 (a total of 15 runs), and 7 teams for Task 2 (a total of 18 runs). Regarding the statute law tasks, there were 8 different teams participating, some in both tasks. 7 teams submitted 13 runs for Task 3, and 7 teams submitted 15 runs for Task 4.

A variety of methods were used for Task 1: classification using only features extracted from the case header, random forest and k-NN classifiers, exploitation of the case structure information, deep learning based techniques (such as transformer methods and tools such as the Universal Sentence Encoder), lexical and latent features, embedding summary properties, and information retrieval techniques were the main ones. For Task 2, transformer-based tools such as BERT and ELMo were prevalent, but IR techniques and textual similarity features have also been applied. The results attained were satisfactory, but there is much room for improvement, especially if one considers the related issue of explaining the predictions made; deep learning methods, which showed promising results this year, would not be so appropriate in a scenario where explainability is key. For future editions of COLIEE, we plan to continue to expand the data sets in order to improve the robustness of results, as well as introducing evaluation of explainability-aware tasks or requirements into the competition.

For Task 3, we found there are three types of questions in the test data (easy questions, difficult questions with vocabulary mismatch, and questions with multiple answers). Most of the submission systems are good at retrieving relevant answers for easy questions, but it is still difficult to retrieve relevant articles for other question types. It may be necessary to focus on such question types to improve the overall performance of the IR system. For Task 4, overall performance of the submissions is still not sufficient to use their systems in real applications, mainly due to lack of coverage for some classes of problems, such as anaphora resolution. We found this task is still a challenging one, and requires deeper analysis of semantic issues in the general application of natural language processing.

Acknowledgements. This research was supported by the National Institute of Informatics, Shizuoka University, Hokkaido University, and the University of Alberta's Alberta Machine Intelligence Institute (Amii). Special thanks to Colin Lachance from vLex for his unwavering support in the development of the case law data set, and to continued support from Ross Intelligence and Intellicon.

References

1. Dang, T.B., Nguyen, T., Nguyen, L.M.: An approach to statute law retrieval task in COLIEE-2019. In: Proceedings of the 6th Competition on Legal Information Extraction/Entailment. COLIEE 2019 (2019)
2. Devlin, J., Chang, M., Lee, K., Toutanova, K.: BERT: pre-training of deep bidirectional transformers for language understanding. CoRR abs/1810.04805 (2018). http://arxiv.org/abs/1810.04805
3. El Hamdani, R., Troussel, A., Houvenagel, C.: COLIEE case law competition task 1: the legal case retrieval task. In: Proceedings of the 6th Competition on Legal Information Extraction/Entailment. COLIEE'2019 (2019)
4. Gain, B., Bandyopadhyay, D., Saikh, T., Ekbal, A.: IITP@COLIEE 2019: legal information retrieval using BM25 and BERT. In: Proceedings of the 6th Competition on Legal Information Extraction/Entailment. COLIEE 2019 (2019)
5. Hayashi, R., Kano, Y.: Searching relevant articles for legal bar exam by Doc2Vec and TF-IDF. In: Proceedings of the 6th Competition on Legal Information Extraction/Entailment. COLIEE 2019 (2019)
6. Hoshino, R., Kiyota, N., Kano, Y.: Question answering system for legal bar examination using predicate argument structures focusing on exceptions. In: Proceedings of the 6th Competition on Legal Information Extraction/Entailment. COLIEE 2019 (2019)
7. Hudzina, J., Vacek, T., Madan, K., Tonya, C., Schilder, F.: Statutory entailment using similarity features and decomposable attention models. In: Proceedings of the 6th Competition on Legal Information Extraction/Entailment. COLIEE 2019 (2019)
8. Kano, Y., Kim, M.Y., Goebel, R., Satoh, K.: Overview of COLIEE 2017. In: Satoh, K., Kim, M.Y., Kano, Y., Goebel, R., Oliveira, T. (eds.) COLIEE 2017. 4th Competition on Legal Information Extraction and Entailment. EPiC Series in Computing, vol. 47, pp. 1–8. EasyChair (2017). https://doi.org/10.29007/fm8f. https://easychair.org/publications/paper/Fglr
9. Kim, M.Y., Goebel, R., Kano, Y., Satoh, K.: COLIEE-2016: evaluation of the competition on legal information extraction and entailment. In: International Workshop on Juris-Informatics (JURISIN 2016) (2016)
10. Kim, M.Y., Goebel, R., Satoh, K.: COLIEE-2015: evaluation of legal question answering. In: Ninth International Workshop on Juris-Informatics (JURISIN 2015) (2015)
11. Le, Q., Mikolov, T.: Distributed representations of sentences and documents. In: Proceedings of the 31st International Conference on International Conference on Machine Learning, ICML 2014, vol. 32, pp. II-1188–II-1196 (2014). JMLR.org. http://dl.acm.org/citation.cfm?id=3044805.3045025
12. Macdonald, C., McCreadie, R., Santos, R.L., Ounis, I.: From puppy to maturity: experiences in developing terrier. In: Proceedings of the SIGIR 2012 Workshop in Open Source Information Retrieval, pp. 60–63 (2012)

13. Madan, K., Hudzina, J., Vacek, T., Schilder, F., Custis, T.: Textual entailment using word embeddings and linguistic similarity. In: Proceedings of the 6th Competition on Legal Information Extraction/Entailment. COLIEE 2019 (2019)
14. Mi-Young, K., Rabelo, J., Goebel, R.: Statute law information retrieval and entailment. In: Proceedings of the 17th International Conference on Artificial Intelligence and Law. ICAIL 2019 (2019)
15. Mikolov, T., Sutskever, I., Chen, K., Corrado, G.S., Dean, J.: Distributed representations of words and phrases and their compositionality. In: Advances in Neural Information Processing Systems, pp. 3111–3119 (2013)
16. Nguyen, H.T., Tran, V., Nguyen, L.M.: A deep learning approach for statute law entailment task in COLIEE-2019. In: Proceedings of the 6th Competition on Legal Information Extraction/Entailment. COLIEE 2019 (2019)
17. Paulino-Passos, G., Toni, F.: Retrieving legal cases with vector representations of text. In: Proceedings of the 6th Competition on Legal Information Extraction/Entailment. COLIEE 2019 (2019)
18. Peters, M.E., et al.: Deep contextualized word representations. In: Proceedings of NAACL (2018)
19. Rabelo, J., Mi-Young, K., Goebel, R.: Combining similarity and transformer methods for case law entailment. In: Proceedings of the 17th International Conference on Artificial Intelligence and Law. ICAIL 2019 (2019)
20. Raiyani, K., Quaresma, P.: Keyword & machine learning based japanese statute law retrieval and entailment task at COLIEE-2019. In: Proceedings of the 6th Competition on Legal Information Extraction/Entailment. COLIEE 2019 (2019)
21. Rossi, J., Kanoulas, E.: Legal information retrieval with generalized language models. In: Proceedings of the 6th Competition on Legal Information Extraction/Entailment. COLIEE 2019 (2019)
22. Strohman, T., Metzler, D., Turtle, H., Croft, W.B.: Indri: a language-model based search engine for complex queries. In: Proceedings of the International Conference on Intelligent Analysis. Technical report (2005)
23. Tran, V., Nguyen, M.L., Satoh, K.: Building legal case retrieval systems with lexical matching and summarization using a pre-trained phrase scoring model. In: Proceedings of the 17th International Conference on Artificial Intelligence and Law. ICAIL 2019 (2019)
24. Wehnert, S., Hoque, S.A., Fenske, W., Saake, G.: Threshold-based retrieval and textual entailment detection on legal bar exam questions. In: Proceedings of the 6th Competition on Legal Information Extraction/Entailment. COLIEE 2019 (2019)
25. Yoshioka, M., Kano, Y., Kiyota, N., Satoh, K.: Overview of Japanese statute law retrieval and entailment task at COLIEE-2018. In: The Proceedings of the 12th International Workshop on Juris-Informatics (JURISIN2018), pp. 117–128. The Japanese Society of Artificial Intelligence (2018)
26. Yoshioka, M., Song, Z.: HUKB at COLIEE 2019 information retrieval task - utilization of metadata for relevant case retrieval. In: Proceedings of the 6th Competition on Legal Information Extraction/Entailment. COLIEE 2019 (2019)

An Agent-Based Model for Exploring Pension Law and Social Security Policies

Emilio Serrano[1(✉)] [iD] and Ken Satoh[2]

[1] Ontology Engineering Group, Department of Artificial Intelligence, Universidad Politécnica de Madrid, Madrid, Spain
`emilioserra@fi.upm.es`
[2] Principles of Informatics Research Division, NII (National Institute of Informatics), Tokyo, Japan
`ksatoh@nii.ac.jp`

Abstract. The increase in life expectancy and the decrease in birth rates pose a structural challenge for the pension systems of developed countries such as Japan and Spain. Pension law and social security system of these countries is complex. Moreover, describing or predicting the effects of changes in these laws is even more challenging. We contribute with an *agent-based model* (ABM) for computer-aided law education in this field. This model is a simplified representation of the complex reality of pension systems, to the point that the reality is more understandable and analytically manageable. The proposed model extends the wealth distribution scenario in the Sugarscape model, which is considered the first social simulation where the notion of modeling people was extended to consider entire cities. The proposed ABM encourages the exploration about different theories for the sustainability of pension systems through experimentation in a simple and controllable scenario. Experimental results indicate that a constant or increasing population of uniformly distributed ages is not enough to ensure the sustainability of pension systems as backbone of the welfare state. A Web version of model implementation as well as its source code, documentation, and extended experiments are available online.

Keywords: Pension law · Social security · Agent-based modeling · Agent-based social simulation · Multi-agent-based simulation

1 Introduction

Agent-based modeling (ABM) is a computational modeling paradigm based on describing agents' behaviors. An *agent* is an autonomous computational individual or object with particular properties and actions. ABM can be used to model and describe a wide variety of processes, phenomena, and situations, but especially *complex systems* [25]. Examples of complex systems are ecosystems, economies, immune systems, molecular systems, minds, stock market, and democratic government. ABM allows studying the global patterns that emerge in complex system from agents' local interactions and decisions.

© Springer Nature Switzerland AG 2020
M. Sakamoto et al. (Eds.): JSAI-isAI 2019, LNAI 12331, pp. 50–63, 2020.
https://doi.org/10.1007/978-3-030-58790-1_4

The public pension system is the backbone of the welfare state of a country and the intergenerational solidarity. The increase in life expectancy and the decrease in birth rates pose a structural challenge for the pension systems of developed countries. Japan was the world's most aged population in 2017 (33% aged 60 or over) [5]. Europe is expected to account for five of the ten most aged countries or areas in 2050. In the case of Spain, the problem is aggravated because the low average salary compared to Europe and the high unemployment rates of recent years.

We present an extension of the Sugarscape model [11] inspired by Spanish and Japanese laws for the pension system. This new model offers a simplified description of the complicated pension law and can serve as a *computer-aided law education system*. An online version of the model [21], which can be run in any Web browser, encapsulates this knowledge in an easily transferable way. Additionally, the model allows experimenting with changes in the law and pension policies in the controlled environment of the Sugarscape model, which is possibly the most studied artificial economy. Although these results are not necessarily extrapolatable to the Spanish or Japanese society, they serve as a proof-of-concept of possible scenarios that can result from different pension policies and demographic changes under the assumption of basic rules. Among others, experimental results indicate that, even with a constant population of uniformly distributed ages, the pension system can present sustainability problems if the labor market does not offer quality employment that improves the ratio between salary and average pension.

The remainder of the paper is structured as follows. Section 2 explores the related work. Section 3 summarizes the Spanish and Japanese pension law. Section 4 describes both the original Sugarcape model and the extension proposed here to study pension law and social security policies. Section 5 presents the model implementation and some of the main decisions involved in it. Section 6 presents experimental results from simulation runs and Sect. 7 discusses them. Finally, Sect. 8 concludes and give future work.

2   Related Work

There are several research work that study pension law and the sustainability of pension systems by ABM or other types of simulations. One of the most studied cases is precisely the Japanese society because it is one of the most aged populations in the world [17]. Murata and Arikawa [16] study the use of ABM to explain the effectiveness of the Japanese pension system under a variety of employment patterns instead of under a single model of family. Murata and Chen [17] evaluate the sustainability of the pension system under the condition of drastic demographic change and discuss the effectiveness of an agent-based approach to examine the pension law effect. Hirata et al. [12] propose a simulation using Equation-Based Modeling to study the policy of public pension finance in Japan, concluding the sum of premiums will be less than the sum of benefit payments to be paid. Lychkina and Morozova [15] propose agent-based models of the pension system of the Russian Federation designed to support government decision-making in the pension field. Silverman et al. [23] present an agent-based model of the aging UK population to examine the interaction between population change and the cost of social care in an aging population. Király and Simonovits [13], without a specific country in mind, apply the ABM approach to model the life-cycle savings when workers, who can be shortsighted or farsighted, contract voluntary pension plans. Epstein and Axtell [10] study by ABM the emergence of optimal behavior when deciding the retiring age in an artificial society composed of a few rational agents, a few random agents, and a majority of agents following imitation patterns.

These inspiring projects illustrate the potential of agent-based social simulation to study the challenging problem of achieving sustainable social security. We present, to the best of our knowledge, the first extension of the Sugarscape model [11] to study pension systems. Unlike the related work revised, this model is intended to be used for computer-aided law education. Furthermore, it also allows assessing the effects of pension law changes in a controlled and widely studied environment.

3 Pension Law

This section describes a summary of Spanish and Japanese pension law, which has been considered for the agent-based model presented in this paper.

3.1 Spanish Pension System

The state pension scheme is part of the Social Security system in Spain [4]. The pension system is financed by a 28.3% tax on salaries: 4.7% paid by the employee, and 23.6% paid by the employers.

The age for claiming a retirement pension is between 65 and 67 depending on the claimant's age and the contributions paid[1]. The amount of the pension depends on the "regulating base". This base is, roughly speaking, the average of the worker's gross salary for the last 21 years. The pension amount is 50% of this regulating base after paying contributions for 15 years. The more the worker contributes, the better the percentage to calculate the retirement pension amount. At the other end of the scale, a pension of 100% the regulating base requires paying contributions for 35 years[2].

In case of self-employment, there is a fixed rate depending on a contribution base. The employee chooses this base between a minimum and a maximum based on a series of conditions for age frames. From January 2019, self-employees pay a monthly premium between 283.30 and 1,221.03 euros.

Some of the current sustainability policies until 2027 includes: (1) increasing the years of contribution payment required to retire at 65; and, (2) increasing the years of work life considered for the calculation of the pension.

---

[1] The law also contemplates: (1) early retirement from the age of 60 with a reduction in benefits; and (2) partial retirement where part-time contracts are maintained.

[2] The average retirement pension in Spain is 15,942.5 euros per year in July 2019 [3].

3.2   Japanese Pension System

The National Pension is a public pension system participated by all persons aged 20 to 59 years who have an address in Japan, which provides benefits called the "Basic Pension" because old age, disability, or death [2]. All residents contribute to pension insurance.

Salaried workers under the age of 70 pay a percentage of their standard salary. As of September 2017, the premium for salaried workers is 18.30%, paid half by the employer and half by the employee [1]. Students, self-employed and unemployed persons of ages 20 to 59 pay a monthly flat-rate premium of 16,410 yen [2]. There are partial or full exemptions for contribution payments under certain conditions such as low income. Periods of full amount exemption also count for the calculation of the pension benefits. However, depending of the year of these exemption periods, they will count only one-third or one-half of full contribution paid periods.

The pension benefit is paid once the insured person is 65, unemployed, and if they have paid pension premiums for at least 10 years. The benefit amount depends on one's total contribution [1]. 780,100 yen per year is the full benefit amount based on 40 years of fully contributed coverage periods, considering the basic pension system. It should be noted that salaried workers will get the benefit more than people who pay only pension premiums for the basic pension system.

4   An Agent-Based Model to Study Pension Law

This section describes the Sugarscape model, and more specifically, the wealth distribution scenario that our contribution is based on. Then the extension of the model where a pension system is considered is detailed with its underlying economic assumptions.

4.1   Sugarscape Model and Wealth Distribution Scenario

The Sugarscape model was introduced by Epstein and Axtell in 1996 [11]. This model is considered the first "large scale model" (up to around 1K agents) and also the first model where the notion of modeling people was extended to consider entire cities [8]. The model is defined by: (1) agents or inhabitants; (2) an environment which is a two-dimensional grid where every cell can contain different amounts of sugar; and (3) rules governing the interaction of the agents with each other and the environment. The goal of Sugarscape is to understand the emergence of patterns, trends, and other characteristics observable in the society. This social simulation, through a number of scenarios, demonstrated that agents could emerge with a variety of characteristics and behaviors suggestive of a rudimentary society (e.g. death, disease, trade, health, culture, conflict, war) [8].

One of the most prominent Sugarscape scenarios is the wealth distribution model (described in chapter 2 of Epstein and Axtell's book [11]). This scenario provides a ground-up simulation of inequality in wealth, demonstrating how unequal distributions of wealth emerge through simple rules. NetLogo [24], a popular ABM environment, includes a sugarscape wealth distribution model implementation [14] whose GUI is shown in Fig. 1.

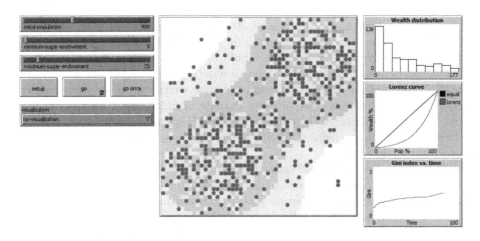

Fig. 1. Sugarscape wealth distribution model, NetLogo implementation [14]. (Color figure online)

In this Sugarscape scenario, a map is imported into the model with the maximum sugar available in each cell of the environment (more sugar is indicated in Fig. 1 with darker yellow). Initially agents are randomly distributed over the grid, and assigned a certain amount of sugar (with a minimum and maximum parameterizable value), an age, and a metabolic rate. At each time step, an agent checks its surrounding cells and moves to an unoccupied cell with the highest amount of sugar, eats all the sugar, consumes some of this sugar based on its metabolic rate, and thus accumulates wealth. An agent dies if it runs out of energy; otherwise, it dies when it reaches a certain age. Just as sugar represents the wealth of the real world, the movement of agents on the grid represents the search for this wealth that can motivate employment changes and migratory movements.

The simulation GUI displayed in Fig. 1 also shows relevant outputs to study the wealth distribution such as: a *histogram* of the agents' wealth (x-axis represents the sugar or wealth and y-axis represents the number of agents in the bin); the *Lorenz curve* (the percentage of agents is plotted on the x-axis, and the percentage of wealth these agents have is plotted on the y-axis); and, the *Gini index* (zero expresses perfect wealth equality, and 1 expresses maximal inequality).

4.2 Sugarscape Pension System Model and Economic Assumptions

This section describes an extension of the base model explained above to study pension law and social security.

The core of the extension is the agents' eating rule that dictates the agents' interaction with the environment. Algorithm 1 shows this rule in the base model. In each time-step, the agent a updates its sugar with its current sugar or wealth, subtracting its metabolism, and adding all available sugar in the position of the environment e that the agent occupies.

Algorithm 1. Sugar eating rule in Sugarscape model

$a_{sugar}(t+1) \leftarrow a_{sugar}(t) - a_{metabolism} + e_{sugar}(t, a_x, a_y)$

The model presented here updates this rule as described in Algorithm 2. This new rule considers: (1) a retirement age at which an agent stops collecting sugar; (2) a global pension piggy bank (or public pension fund, also known as a superannuation fund) p that retired agents use to eat and to which working agents contribute; (3) a percentage of pension taxes pt that is applied to the sugar collected by workers and that is saved in the pension piggy-bank p; and, (4) a flat-rate premium frp of sugar that working agents have to contribute to p if they have enough sugar saved.

Algorithm 2. Extended sugar eating and piggy bank rules

if $a_{age} < retirementAge$ then   ▷ a is a working agent
    $a_{sugar}(t+1) \leftarrow a_{sugar}(t) - a_{metabolism} + e_{sugar}(t, a_x, a_y) * (1 - pt/100)$
    $p_{sugar} \leftarrow e_{sugar}(t, a_x, a_y) * (pt/100)$ ▷ Taxes go to the piggy-bank
    if $a_{sugar}(t+1) > frp$ then   ▷ a can pay the fixed flat-rate premium
        $a_{sugar}(t+1) \leftarrow a_{sugar}(t+1) - frp$
        $p_{sugar} \leftarrow p_{sugar} + frp$
    end if
else   ▷ a is a retired agent
    if $p_{sugar} > a_{metabolism}$ then   ▷ a eats from the piggy-bank if possible
        $p_{sugar} \leftarrow p_{sugar} - a_{metabolism}$
    else   ▷ otherwise, a eats from its savings
        $a_{sugar}(t+1) \leftarrow a_{sugar}(t) - a_{metabolism}$
    end if
end if

This model behaves exactly as the base model with the following parameters values: a retirement age of 100 (agents in the base model can die between the 60 and the 100 time-steps); pension taxes of 0%; and, a flat-rate premium of 0. The extension only affects: the eating rule detailed in Algorithm 2; the move rule (retired agents stop moving since they do not collect sugar anymore); and the simulation initialization, where first agents receive a random age between 0 and 100 to avoid a great wave of retirement after a first generation of agents of the same age.

Besides the *Gini index* logged in the base model to study the wealth distribution, the model extension also contemplates other interesting outputs such as: the number of retired and working agents; the sugar accumulated in the pension piggy-bank; and the *agents in social exclusion*, meaning in this model those agents (working or retired) that die not because of their age but because of the lack of sugar necessary to live.

Simplicity is essential in ABM and models in general. Some simplifications and economic assumptions of this model are the following:

- All population is employed and contributes to the piggy bank except retirees.
- A minimum-to-live pension is contemplated. Retired agents only takes from the piggy bank enough sugar to live (their metabolic rate).
- As a result of the two previous assumptions, all agents have access to pensions independently of the amount or years of the contribution.
- One same policy is applied to the whole population: taxes in the form of salary percentage, flat-rate premium, or combination of these.
- The Sugarscape pension system, as the base model, considers a constant homogeneous population. Whenever an agent dies (either from starvation or old age), a new randomly initialized agent is created somewhere in the world with an initial sugar endowment.

These simplifications are designed for the education about pension laws in a controlled environment, i.e. the widely studied economy of the Sugarscape model. In addition, they present an optimistic scenario to study the effect of laws for improving the sustainability of pension systems.

5   Implementation

The Sugarscape pension system model described in Sect. 4.2 has been implemented in a social simulation using NetLogo [24]. NetLogo is an ABM language and development environment designed by Uri Wilensky at Northwestern University.

There is a large number of alternative ABM environments such as the MASON Multiagent Simulation Toolkit, the Repast Suite, or Mesa: Agent-based modeling in Python 3+. However, NetLogo is used in this research because its model library includes a canonical implementation of the Sugarscape wealth distribution model [14]. Other good reasons to use this framework are: (1) it allows quick prototyping; (2) simulations can be exported to HTML making easy to share the models; and, (3) its domain specific language reduces the gap between the modeler and the programmer. There are also some disadvantages associated with NetLogo. Newcomers to ABM may want to avoid the cost of learning a new language[3]. More importantly, NetLogo lacks modularity above the procedure and function level. This hinders researchers to use basic software engineering techniques to manage complex ABM models.

---

[3] NetLogo was designed in the spirit of the programming language Logo, which was first thought to teach LISP concepts.

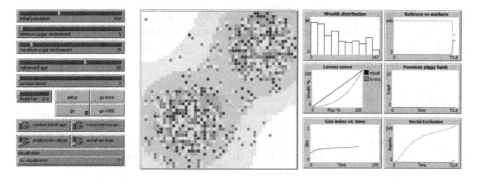

Fig. 2. Simulation GUI for the Sugarscape pension system model. (Color figure online)

A GitHub repository [20] has been created to allow the interested researcher to use, reproduce and extend the contributions presented here. The file *"Sugarscape Pension Law.nlogo"* can be loaded in the NetLogo environment providing the user with: a GUI for running the simulation, its source code, and the model documentation. The repository also includes: an HTML version of the model that can be loaded in a Web Browser without requiring the installation of NetLogo; CSV files with results from simulation runs; and R code to aggregate these results.

Figure 2 displays the simulation GUI. On the left, several sliders and switches allow changing the model parameters discussed in Sect. 4. On the right, a number of charts indicate main outputs of the simulations as the Gini index, the agents socially excluded, and the pension piggy-bank evolution. In the middle, the environment is represented with working agents in red, retired agents in blue, and the sugar available in a yellow-scale.

6   Experimental Results

Although the primary goal of the presented model is education about pension law, its use for experimentation is also possible. The simulation can be run repeatedly under slightly different conditions to observe the resultant changes in the Sugarscape artificial society.

The model simulation has been run 1280 times for 1000 time-steps. The different parameters values considered are as follows. A retirement age (ra) of 65, 67, or 70 is studied. An age of 100, meaning that agents do not get to retire, is also included to serve as a baseline. Pension taxes (pt) of 0%, 4.7%, 10%, or 28.3% of incomes are introduced following the Spanish pension law, see Sect. 3.1. A flat-rate premium (frp) worth 0, 0.1, 0.5 and 1 sugar units are also contemplated. Finally, two population sizes are considered 400 and 800 agents. Other simulation parameters in the base simulation [14] are fixed: agents receive a sugar endowment between 5 and 25 when they are born. The simulation is run ten times for each of these 128 parameters configuration, giving 1280 runs.

The logged output values include: gross domestic product (*gdp*), Gini coefficient (*gin*), number of agents in social exclusion (*se*), and number of retired agents socially excluded (*rse*). Finally, these values are aggregated using mean, standard deviation, and standard error.

Table 1. Extract of experimental results. 12 labeled experiments showing: retirement age (ra), pension taxes (pt), flat-rate premium (frp), gross domestic product (gdp), Gini coefficient (gin), number of agents in social exclusion (se), and number of retired agents socially excluded (rse). Output values (gdp, gin, se, and rse) display the mean of 10 execution with one configuration of the parameters values (population, ra, pt, and frp).

Population: 400

id	label	ra	pt	frp	gdp	gin	se	rse
1	best-gini	65	28.3	0.5	893.62	0.43	10.62K	0
2	worst-gini	70	0	1	898.74	0.56	5.45K	0
3	best-se	70	0	0	909.59	0.46	4.61K	673.5
4	worst-se	70	28.3	1	915.68	0.46	12.38K	0
5	balanced	65	10	0	870.74	0.44	4.95K	74.1

Population: 800

id	label	ra	pt	frp	gdp	gin	se	rse
6	best-gini	65	28.3	0.5	1.37K	0.34	26.57K	0
7	worst-gini	70	28.3	1	1.44K	0.61	34.86K	0
8	best-se	70	4.7	0.1	1.40K	0.46	13.05K	31.5
9	worst-se	70	28.3	1	1.44K	0.61	34.86K	0
10	balanced-1	70	0	0	1.42K	0.44	13.40K	2064.3
11	balanced-2	65	28.3	0	1.38K	0.39	20.79K	0.6
12	balanced-3	65	28.3	0.1	1.38K	0.38	22.30K	0

Table 1 shows 12 different experiments with the output data mean. The experiments are labeled and display the best and worst scenarios considering the Gini coefficient and the social exclusion for the two possible populations. Moreover, additional cases are introduced to seek a balance between these two measures. The simulation website [20], besides the simulation and experiments code, contains csv files with the 1280 experiments and its aggregated values with standard deviations and standard error.

The results show a GDP around 900 (units of sugar per year) for a population of 400 agents and around 1400 for a population of 800. Therefore, twice the population (an increase of 100%) does not produce double wealth (GDP only increases a 55%). In addition, at a lower retirement age, GDP is lower since there are more agents that stop collecting sugar.

Regarding the Gini coefficient, the population increase polarizes this value. A population of 400 has a value between 0.43 and 0.56 (experiments with ids 1 and

2), and a population of 800 presents values between 0.34 and 0.61 (experiments with ids 6 and 7). The lowest values (greater equality in the agents' wealth) are obtained for both populations with the earliest retirement considered (65 years), the highest pension taxes contemplated (28.3%), and an additional flat-rate premium for pensions which is the second-highest considered as parameter (0.5). However, the agents socially excluded with these policies are much more numerous than in the optimal cases (experiments 3 and 8).

The social exclusion for a population of 400 varies between 4K agents and 12K agents (experiments with ids 2 and 3). For a population of 800, this varies between 13K and 34K (experiments with ids 8 and 9). Therefore, a 100% increase in the population produces an 183% increase in social exclusion for the worst scenario, and an 181% increase for the best scenario. In addition, the fiscal policies for these better scenarios differ considerably in both populations. For a population of 400 agents, the retirement age is extended to the maximum considered (70 years) and there is no pension policy. This causes that, although it is possible to reduce social exclusion to the maximum (4.61K agents), a considerable number of these excluded agents correspond to pensioners (673.5). For a population of 800 agents, the lowest social exclusion is also achieved with a retirement age of 70 years, but here salary-based taxes and flat fees are combined with a pension tax rate of 4.7% and a flat-rate premium of 0.1.

Finally, experiments that seek to balance a low social exclusion and a low Gini coefficient are included in the results. For the population of 400, the experiment with id 5 offers a social exclusion 7% greater than the optimal case (id 3) and a Gini coefficient one point higher than the optimal case (id 1). For this balanced artificial society, the earliest possible retirement is considered (65 years), and the agents pay 10% of their earnings for the pension piggy bank. For the population of 800, this balance between a more egalitarian society in its wealth and little social exclusion seems more complicated. Three possible policies are provided (ids 10, 11, and 12). In one of them, id 11, a Gini index 5 points higher than the optimal case is achieved (id 6) and an increase in social exclusion by 59% with respect to the optimal case (id 8) is obtained. In this case, the model of taxes based on a percentage of income is used, although with the highest taxes considered (28.3%). In the experiment with id 12, an extra point in the Gini index is reduced by adding a flat-rate premium of 0.1, but it has a cost in social exclusion.

7   Discussion

As seen in the results, the effects of pension and social security legislation are complex to study even under an artificial society with simplistic behaviors. This motivates the use of computer-aided law education systems and decision support systems to study these laws and to evaluate their effects. Some conclusions that follow from the results presented are the following.

– Increasing the population means increasing wealth, and with it, the piggy bank of pensions. However, proportions matter. In an environment of limited resources, such as sugar in this model, doubling the population does not mean doubling wealth. Furthermore, doubling the population means increasing more than twice the social exclusion.

- High taxes produce a more equitable distribution of wealth and, therefore, a lower Gini coefficient. However, high taxes involve that many workers do not receive the necessary wealth to subsist, and therefore social exclusion is increased[4]. Moreover, since high social exclusion means that very few agents get to retire, this can give an unreal impression of sustainability of the pension system.

- Finding a balance between taxes high enough to sustain pensioners and taxes low enough to allow workers not to end up in social exclusion is not easy. In one of the populations studied, results close to the optimum are achieved with a 65-year retirement and a 10% pension tax payment. In this sense, the agents of this artificial society retire earlier and pay less taxes than Spanish and Japanese workers[5].

8   Conclusion and Future Work

The sustainability of pensions and social security is a matter of great importance in Japan and Spain. However, understanding these laws and the potential effects of their changes is very complex. We contribute with an *agent-based model* (ABM) for computer-aided law education in this field. This model is a simplified representation of the complex reality of pension systems, to the point that the reality is more understandable and analytically manageable.

The proposed ABM extends the wealth distribution scenario in the Sugarscape model [11], where wealth inequality emerges from agents' simple local interactions. Specifically, the eating rule of this model is modified so that the agents: pay taxes on the sugar collected following several schemes used in Spanish and Japanese law; and retire becoming pensionists when they reach a certain age. There is strong evidence that it is easier for students to learn the rules governing a single agent and then understand the system composed of many of these agents than it is to start with an aggregate description of, in this case, the pension system [7,25]. This makes ABM and the extension of existing simulations such as the SugarSape models a powerful tool for law education.

Beyond the educational value of this simulation, the proposed ABM encourages the exploration about different theories for the sustainability of pension systems through experimentation in a simple and controllable scenario. The experimental results show that pension system sustainability can be threatened even in optimistic scenarios considering a constant population of uniformly distributed ages and a minimum to live pension. In the experiments, a population

---

[4] In the model presented here, taxes are used exclusively for pensions. However, the implementation available online also allows experimenting with the use of tax revenue for social services.

[5] When considering the combination of taxes paid by employer and employee which, as explained, is 18.30% in Japan and 28.3% in Spain.

growth in an environment of limited resources produces a more unstable society with high rates of social exclusion. In Spain and Japan, this can be translated into the necessity of not only improving the ratio of workers to retirees, but also consider the ratio of average salary to average pension.

A Web version [21] of the model implementation as well as its source code, documentation, and extended experiments are available online to allow the interested researcher to use, reproduce and extend the contributions presented here [20].

Our main future work is the validation of the model by comparing the macro behaviors observed in the simulation with the macroeconomic variables of the countries studied, i.e. conducting an empirical output validation [19]. Additionally, the current implementation has extra parameters which have not been discussed here for the sake of shortness such as: considering social services to support social exclusion in agents of working age [22], releasing cell positions when agents retire to allow working agents to extract sugar from them, or considering a productivity decay because age [6].

The model can also be extended to more specific and descriptive scenarios (although at the cost of increasing its complexity) such as: different age distributions; variable population growths; more agents' profiles with different taxes; and, especially, intelligent policy changes during simulation. The use of deep learning [18] and deep reinforcement learning to decide policy changes during simulation runs could lead to AI-generated strategies for a more effective and sustainable social security. In this scheme, the policy reward structure will be defined based on an inverse of the social exclusion caused by a specific tax regime.

Finally, the specialized literature shows that learning with ABMs promotes better conceptual understanding than more traditional approaches [9]. However, it is interesting to study the best target audience, considering different students' backgrounds and different education levels, for the use of ABM as a technology to represent, understand, and study complex systems.

Acknowledgments. This research work is supported by the "Universidad Politécnica de Madrid" under the programs "Ayudas Dirigidas a Jóvenes Investigadores para Fortalecer sus Planes de Investigación" (2018), "Ayudas a PDI e Investigadores Doctores para realizar Estancias de Investigación Internacional" (2019), and "Ayudas de Viajes a Investigadores para solicitar proyectos ERCs" (2019). This work is also partially supported by JSPS KAKENHI Grant Number 17H06103.

References

1. HTM. Accounting, Payroll, HR, & Admin Services. http://bit.ly/2TEylpD. Accessed Sept 2019
2. Japan Pension Service. http://bit.ly/2MhWAt3. Accessed Sept 2019
3. Las pensiones en España, en datos. Datos actualizados el 25 de julio de 2019. http://bit.ly/2YUZKd2. Accessed Sept 2019
4. Social security of Spain. Ordinary Retirement. http://bit.ly/2MjslCb. Accessed Sept 2019

5. World population ageing 2017 highlights. Development department of economic and social affairs. United nations. http://bit.ly/2KDwWgi. Accessed Sept 2019

6. Bertoni, M., Brunello, G., Rocco, L.: Selection and the age - productivity profile. evidence from chess players. J. Econ. Behav. Organ. 110, 45–58 (2015). https://doi.org/10.1016/j.jebo.2014.11.011. http://www.sciencedirect.com/science/article/pii/S0167268114003023

7. Blikstein, P., Wilensky, U.: A case study of multi-agent-based simulation in undergraduate materials science education. In: ASEE Annual Conference and Exposition, Conference Proceedings, January 2006

8. Crooks, A., Malleson, N., Manley, E., Heppenstall, A.: Agent-Based Modelling and Geographical Information Systems: A Practical Primer. Spatial Analytics and GIS, SAGE Publications (2018). https://books.google.co.jp/books?id=ZPl6DwAAQBAJ

9. Dubovi, I., Lee, V.R.: Instructional support for learning with agent-based simulations: A tale of vicarious and guided exploration learning approaches. Comput. Educ. **142**, 103644 (2019). https://doi.org/10.1016/j.compedu.2019.103644. http://www.sciencedirect.com/science/article/pii/S0360131519301976

10. Epstein, J., Axtell, R.: Coordination in Transient Social Networks: An Agent-Based Computational Model of the Timing of Retirement, pp. 161–186. Russell Sage & Brookings Press, New York (1999)

11. Epstein, J.M., Axtell, R.: Growing Artificial Societies: Social Science from the Bottom Up. The Brookings Institution, Washington (1996)

12. Hirata, T., Nakamura, R., Ueda, M.: A simulation of the policy of public pension finance in Japan. Kawasaki J. Med. Welf. **13**, 127–136 (2008)

13. Király, B., Simonovits, A.: Saving and taxation in a voluntary pension system: Toward an agent-based model. IEHAS Discussion Papers MT-DP - 2016/6, Budapest (2016). http://hdl.handle.net/10419/144704

14. Li, J., Wilensky, U.: NetLogo Sugarscape 3 Wealth Distribution model (2009). http://ccl.northwestern.edu/netlogo/models/Sugarscape3WealthDistribution

15. Lychkina, N.N., Morozova, Y.A.: Agent based modeling of pension system development processes. In: 2015 SAI Intelligent Systems Conference (IntelliSys), pp. 857–862, November 2015. https://doi.org/10.1109/IntelliSys.2015.7361243

16. Murata, T., Arikawa, H.: Pension simulation with a huge number of agents. In: 2012 7th International Conference on Computing and Convergence Technology (ICCCT), pp. 1482–1487, December 2012

17. Murata, T., Chen, Z.: Agent-based simulation for pension system in japan. In: Murata, T., Terano, T., Takahashi, S. (eds.) Agent-Based Approaches in Economic and Social Complex Systems VII, pp. 183–197. Springer, Japan (2013). https://doi.org/10.1007/978-4-431-54279-7_1310.1007/978-4-431-54279-7_13

18. Serrano, E., Bajo, J.: Deep neural network architectures for social services diagnosis in smart cities. Future Gener. Comput. Syst. **100**, 122–131 (2019). https://doi.org/10.1016/j.future.2019.05.034. http://www.sciencedirect.com/science/article/pii/S0167739X19301918

19. Serrano, E., Iglesias, C.A.: Validating viral marketing strategies in Twitter via agent-based social simulation. Expert Syst. Appl. **50**, 140–150 (2016). https://doi.org/10.1016/j.eswa.2015.12.021

20. Serrano, E., Satoh, K.: Sugarscape, pension law and social security. https://github.com/emilioserra/SugarscapePensions. Accessed Sept 2019

21. Serrano, E., Satoh, K.: Sugarscape, pension law and social security. Online model. https://oeg4.dia.fi.upm.es/sugarscapepensionlaw. Accessed Sept 2019

22. Serrano, E., Suárez-Figueroa, M.C., González-Pachón, J., Gómez-Pérez, A.: Toward proactive social inclusion powered by machine learning. Knowl. Inf. Syst. **58**(3), 651–667 (2019). https://doi.org/10.1007/s10115-018-1230-x

23. Silverman, E., Hilton, J., Noble, J., Bijak, J.: Simulating the cost of social care in an ageing population (2013). https://doi.org/10.7148/2013-0689. http://eprints.gla.ac.uk/156294/

24. Wilensky, U.: Netlogo. http://ccl.northwestern.edu/netlogo/. Center for Connected Learning and Computer-Based Modeling, Northwestern University, Evanston, IL (1999). http://ccl.northwestern.edu/netlogo/

25. Wilensky, U., Rand, W.: An Introduction to Agent-Based Modeling: Modeling Natural, Social, and Engineered Complex Systems with NetLogo. The MIT Press, Cambridge (2015)

Automatic Extraction of Legal Norms: Evaluation of Natural Language Processing Tools

Gabriela Ferraro[1,2](✉), Ho-Pun Lam[1], Silvano Colombo Tosatto[1],
Francesco Olivieri[1], Mohammad Badiul Islam[1], Nick van Beest[1],
and Guido Governatori[1]

[1] Data61, CSIRO, Sydney, Australia
{gabriela.ferraro,brian.lam,silvano.colombotosatto,
francesco.olivier,badiul.islam,nick.vanbeest,
guido.governatori}@data61.csiro.au
[2] Australian National University, Canberra, Australia

Abstract. Extracting and formalising legal norms from legal documents is a time-consuming and complex procedure. Therefore, the automatic methods that can accelerate this process are in high demand. In this paper, we address two major questions related to this problem: (i) what are the challenges in formalising legal documents into a machine understandable formalism? (ii) to what extent can the data-driven state-of-the-art approaches developed in the Natural Language Processing (NLP) community be used to automate the normative mining process. The results of our experiments indicate that NLP technologies such as relation extraction and semantic parsing are promising research avenues to advance research in this area.

Keywords: Natural Language Processing · Automatic rule extraction · Legal norms · Evaluation

1 Introduction

Legal documents contain lots of information that needs to be interpreted and processed in order to decide whether an organisation's business processes are compliant with the regulations defined in such documents. Dealing with these regulations can be both costly and time consuming as it requires field experts to understand the legal aspects of the documentation concerning the required setting with respect to its interpretation and intent.

Having legal documents written into a format that could be automatically interpreted by machines would drastically reduce the cost associated with such process. However, in order to achieve that, it is first necessary to extract the set of legal norms from the legal documents and translate them into a machine understandable meaning representation, such as First-Order Logics (FOLs) or lambda calculus formulas, among others.

© Springer Nature Switzerland AG 2020
M. Sakamoto et al. (Eds.): JSAI-isAI 2019, LNAI 12331, pp. 64–81, 2020.
https://doi.org/10.1007/978-3-030-58790-1_5

Language technologies developed by the Natural Language Processing (NLP) community have been shown capable of dealing with some of the challenges of mining normative information from legal documents [7,9,33,39]. However, legal documents differ considerably from other types of documents with respect to their structure, sentence length, and other characteristics.

This paper aims to explain the problem of generating legal norms from legal documents, and to provide an investigation into the challenges of formalising legal norms from a NLP perspective. We also envision a holistic NLP system for legal norms generation from text, and outline some promising research avenues, connecting the requirements of legal norms to existing NLP research streams. Furthermore, we report some preliminary experiments on *neural semantic parsing* and *open relation extraction*, as they can be considered as an intermediate step towards automated generation of legal norms from legal documents.

2   Problems with Legal Documents

The process of acquiring knowledge from legal documents is usually considered as a process of writing norms or rules [29] that, to a certain extent, have basically a conditional structure like [17,31]:

$$r : \text{IF} \quad a_1, \dots, a_n \quad \text{THEN} \quad c \tag{1}$$

where r is the unique identifier of the rule, $a_1, \dots, a_n$ denote the *antecedent* representing the conditions (including the context(s) under which it is created) of applicability of the legal norm, and c denotes the *conclusion* representing the *desired consequence* (or the *normative effect*) of the legal norm. Notice here that legal norms can be unconditional, meaning that the antecedent of the rule can be *empty*. However, such legal norms may be deceptively ambiguous and limit the case of conditional legal norms in some situations [23].

Generating legal norms from legal documents is far from being trivial or intuitive. As discussed in [37], legal documents are technically so complex that even human lawyers are having difficulties understanding and applying it. Therefore, it is important to discuss some of the characteristics of legal documents that needs to be taken into account towards the automation of legal norms extraction. In this section, we present some of those characteristics and elucidate important challenges of generating legal norms.

2.1   Cross-referencing

Technically, a legal document is structured into different chapters, articles, sections and subsections, where each of these sections and/or subsections contain several sentences each has their own specific *goal(s)*, *objective(s)*, and *context(s)* (or *scope(s)*) in which the clauses are applicable. This modular nature of legislation allows legal drafters to focus on a particular aspect of legislation when drafting the document. Hence, referencing information from one section to another, or to other regulations, is not uncommon in legal documents. This is referred to as cross-referencing.

Cross-referencing can help to avoid ambiguity that may occur across different sections of the documents and can help to indicate whether a sentence is an elaboration, subordinate, or prevailing with respect to other sentences or definitions. They can also be used to confer a priority to reconcile potential conflicts by discarding existing goals or substituting alternative top-level goals [24]. In other words, cross-referencing defines the context of lexical units which should be taken into account when generating legal norms. Hence, identifying cross-references is an important task in mining legal norms as they define the context of linguistic utterance and can help to resolve referential and lexical ambiguities, which will be discussed below.

1.2 Natural ventilation – General
⋮

1.2.2 Natural ventilation of occupied spaces must be achieved by providing a net openable area of windows or other openings to the outside of no less than 5% of the floor area. The 5% floor area requirement does not apply to:
a) occupied spaces in Commercial <u>and</u> Industrial buildings where products listed in NZBC Clause G4.3.3 are generated (mechanical ventilation of these spaces is required), <u>and</u>
b) household units <u>and</u> accommodation units where there is only one external wall with opening windows (refer to Paragraph 1.3 for additional requirements if natural ventilation is used).

Fig. 1. Example of logical ambiguity, NZBC Clause G4 Ventilation (adopted from [25])

2.2   Ambiguity and Inconsistent Terminology

Drafters of legal documents try to avoid ambiguity and, ideally, produce a document that results in only one interpretation (e.g., avoid pronouns, avoid synonyms to refer to the same concept, add attributes to identify parties, use punctuation to define the scope of quantifiers, etc.). To avoid lexical ambiguity, legal documents usually include a glossary (sometimes referred to as Definitions) with the most important lexical items and their corresponding definitions.

However, as natural language is used to write the legislation, unintended ambiguities may arise. The most probable ambiguity is *referential ambiguity*, which occurs when a word or phrase has multiple meanings due to different restrictions/conditions. From a linguist point of view, the meaning of lexical units need to be *inferred from the context* in which they appear. However, in legal documents, in addition to the current (local) context, conditions related to the meaning of lexical units can be *inherited* from its parent statement(s), other document sections, and even from external documents via cross-referencing.

Logical ambiguity refers to the use of natural language that can be mapped to different logical interpretations [4]. Consider the fragment of legislation as shown in Fig. 1. Syntactically, the terms "commercial building" and "industrial building" in the first sub-condition, "household units" and "accommodation units" in the second sub-condition, and the two sub-conditions are connected using the conjunction term "and". However, logically (or semantically), the statement is in fact representing conditions to the four different types of building and should be represented using disjunction, i.e., *or*, in the legal norm.

Apart from the ambiguity problems just mentioned, the *inconsistent use of terminology* across different documents may also impact the reasoning process, even though they do not directly affect the generation of legal norms at the sentence level.

2.3   Sentence Complexity

In legal documents, sentences tend to be extremely long in comparison with sentences from other domains. The average number of lexical units in a sentence written in the English Wikipedia is about nineteen [38], while sentences from legal documents can have more than fifty units, as can be seen in Fig. 1.

Legal documents also tend to have a complex syntactic structure, in which coordinate and subordinate constructions are frequent. These pose a challenge to current NLP technologies, such as syntactic analysers and predicate-arguments extraction tools, which usually struggle to correctly capture the scope of coordinate conjunctions and the antecedent of subordinate phrases.

2.4   Normative Effects and Deontic Modalities

Legal documents typically contain normative information. Legal concepts such as *right, no right, privilege, duty, power, disability, immunity,* and *liability,* are important as they significantly affect the way that we interpret legislation. In the field of Artificial Intelligence & Law, capturing deontic modalities or behaviours such as *obligations, permissions,* and *prohibitions* are of major concern. These modalities can be considered as a sub-type of normative effects and should be identified and attached to legal norms when appropriate. A more comprehensive and updated list of legal-related normative effects can be found in [30].

3   Related Work

Algorithms developed by the NLP community have been used to model the process of extracting normative information from legal documents with certain success. [9] proposed an automated concept and norm extraction framework, by exploiting the use of a Juridical (Natural) Language Constructs (JLC) as an intermediate format between the legal texts and the formal model. In their approach, the JLC is essentially a set of patterns that can appear in the legal documents. Legal knowledge is identified and constructed using noun and verb phrase patterns that will later be transformed into formal rules. However, no evaluation of their automated approach has been reported in the paper.

[19, 26] proposed to convert sentences in Japanese into a logical representation using a rule-based approach over a morphological and dependency analysis. [39] presented a linguistic oriented rule-based approach to extract deontic rules from regulations and found that serious issues may appear when mapping thematic roles to syntactic positions. [3] described a technique to automatically extract semantic knowledge from legal texts. Instead of using pattern matching methods based on lexico-syntactic patterns, they proposed to adopt syntactic dependencies between terms extracted with a syntactic parser, which is also the approach used in [8], but with different kinds of information extracted. [12] developed a translation systems to learn the semantics of unknown words from syntactically similar words with known meanings, which is able to translate into a variety of formal language representations. As mentioned by the authors, their method needs to be tested with a bigger corpus.

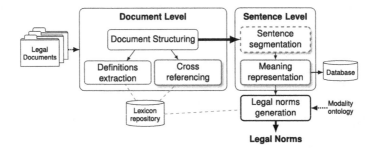

Fig. 2. Normative rules generation framework

Recently, [33] used the syntactic structures and hand-written rules to identify entities (*agent, action, condition, exception,* among others), which are relevant in legal knowledge representation, and can be useful for the automatic extraction of legal norms.

Although it would be valuable to compare the mentioned approaches to our proposal, an experimental comparison is not possible because of the lack of evaluation material. For example, none of the works mentioned above have released their evaluation data sets.

4   Normative Rules Generation Framework

Figure 2 depicts an overview of the process of generating normative rules as we have envisioned.[1] We have taken into account the characteristics of legal documents as well as normative rule requirements. The NLP related modules

---

[1] Here, the term *generation* is used in a loose way (normative rules can be generated or extracted or distilled or built, etc.), and is not used to refer exclusively to the text generation problem study by the Natural Language Generation community.

are highlighted so that it is easy to connect with the research avenues proposed in the next section.

As illustrated, the process is divided into Document Level and Sentence Level modules. The Document Level module reads a legal document (usually a pdf or XML file) as input and passes it to the Document Structuring module, which identifies the hierarchical structure of the document, such as sections, sub-sections, articles, and sentences.

The Document Structuring module also takes care of lexical aspects that need to be solved at the document level. As mentioned before, legal documents have a section in which the most important terms in the document are defined (i.e., the glossary). Thus, we envisioned the Definitions Extraction sub-module here will identify the terms and their corresponding definitions and store them in a lexical repository, which can be used at the later stage of the process, for disambiguation purposes.

The Sentence Level module takes the sentences and information identified at the Document Level module as input, and processes each sentence at a time. The core of this module is the Meaning Representation sub-module, which is used to identify the *predicate units* and their *arguments* in the sentence for the generation of the meaning representation. This module is method agnostic, which means it can be modelled in different ways, e.g., distilling predicates from syntactic trees or generating a logic formula using semantic parsing, among other possibilities (see Sect. 5). The output of this module should reflect the predicate units in a given sentence and is formalism agnostic. This allows choice between different formalisms, such as Abstract Meaning Representation (AMR) [2], Legal-RuleML [28], Process Compliance Language (PCL) [14], the "neo-Davidson" approaches [13], among others, as an intermediate formalism that capture all required information from the legal text, to ease the construction of legal norms at the later stage of the process. In addition, Fig. 2 depicts an optional sub-module called Sentence Segmentation that can be used to determine how a legal sentence should be divided into sub-sentences or clauses, so as to reduce its complexity for further process while preserving its meaning and context.

The output of the Meaning Representation module is then passed to the last module, i.e., Legal Norms Generation module, which generates the normative rules, with the associated modalities such as *obligation* and *permission*, in accordance with the requirements specified by the applications. It is also expected that the lexical terms used in the rules should be linked to the terms in the lexical repository (when possible) so that consistency across different rules can be maintained.

5   Research Avenues

This section outlines some promising avenues to advance research in normative rules generation. One of our focuses is on proposing research streams related to the meaning representation module depicted in Fig. 2, as it is the most challenging part in the whole normative rules generation process.

With new applications like this, evaluation can be a challenge in itself due to the lack of annotated data sets (i.e., sentences and their corresponding normative rules). Besides, this also impedes the possibility of using supervised machine learning, which is usually the preferred method for NLP. Fortunately, there are promising related techniques that can advance research in this area, which we are going to explore in this section.

Table 1. Example of semantic parsing as an intermediate steps towards the generation legal norms

	Example
Sentence	*A large building is any building with a net lettable area greater than* $300\,\mathrm{m}^2$
Logic formula	`lambda $0 (if (A large building: $0) then (is any building with a lettable area greater than ($0 300 m2)))`
Legal norm	*building, greaterThan(netLettableArea, 300) → largeBuilding*
Sentence	*For the purposes of subclause 2.4, a person is responsible for an individual if the person is a parent of the individual.*
Logic formula	`lambda $0 $1 (if (and (person:$0) (individual: $1) (parent of ($0 $1))) then (responsible for (for purpose of subclause 2.4 ($0 $1))))`
Legal norm	*subclause(2.4), parentOf(A, B) ⇒ₒ responsible(A, B)*

Sentence Complexity Reduction: As discussed in Sect. 2, sentences in legal domain tend to be long and considerably complex in structure, which leads to the question of whether it makes sense to reduce the sentence complexity as a pre-processing step to provide simpler sentences as input to normative rule generation.

Sentence complexity can be reduced in at least two ways: by applying some sort of intra-sentential segmentation and by applying simplification techniques. However, simplification techniques are not appropriate for parsing legal text since it involves lexical and grammatical modifications and there is a risk of changing meaning.

Sentences can be segmented, for example, into clauses [35]. This task usually involves two sub-tasks, clause boundary detection and clause type identification, and both can be modelled as classification problems.

Sentence segmentation should be applied in a conservative way, for instance by only segmenting sentences that are likely to struggle with later processing. The state-of-the-art methods for measuring sentence complexity are developed in the context of readability assessment—using lexical and sentence level features to build binary classifiers or regression algorithms [32,36]. In the context of normative rule generation, this is going to be a challenge, as measurement should be calculated based only on the grammatical complexity of sentences, disregarding the lexical aspects.

Semantic Parsing: Semantic parsing is the task of mapping sentences in natural language to a meaning representation, such as a logic formula. It can be seen as an intermediate step towards the generation of normative rules due to its predicate-argument structure, which can be used as building blocks for normative rule generation. Table 1 shows some example sentences written in natural language, their corresponding logic formula in lambda calculus (we follow the notation from [21]), and their corresponding normative rule represented using PCL [14].

Currently, the semantic parsing community is shifting from domain and meaning representation dependent approaches to more universal models using techniques such as transfer learning [10,18], multi-task learning [15,34], and data augmentation [16,20]. However, the data sets for semantic parsing are restricted at the moment to very specific domains such as geographical locations, fly booking system, and jobs, to just name a few, which contain only a small set of vocabularies (usually less than 100 words). As concluded by [18], the main limitation of applying transfer learning to semantic parsing is the domains of the data sets are considerable different. More importantly, the structures of the meaning representation proposed are simple and repetitive [11], which may not be sufficient to represent normative information in the legal domain. Hence, in addition to improving the efficiency and accuracy of semantic parsing, the challenge here is to develop more complex data sets with bigger sets of vocabularies, and a more diverse set of meaning representation structures that can cater the needs of representing legal information.

Open Relation Extraction: Relation extraction can be seen as a shallow semantic parsing analysis. In this context, *open* means that relations are not restricted to a set of relations defined beforehand, but to all possible relations. More concretely, open relation extraction focuses on capturing the verbal predicates and their arguments, and format them as tuples. Hence, it can be seen as a (shallow) meaning representation. Note that open relation extraction usually

Table 2. Example of relation extraction as an intermediate steps towards normative rules using OpenIE.

	Example
Sentence	*A large building is any building with a net lettable area greater than* $300\,\text{m}^2$
RE Tuples	'A large building', 'is building with', 'net lettable area greater than $300\,\text{m}^2$'
Normative rule	$building, greaterThan(netLettableArea, 300) \rightarrow largeBuilding$
Sentence	*For the purposes of subclause 2.4, a person is responsible for an individual if the person is a parent of the individual.*
RE Tuples	'For the purposes of subclause 2.4', 'a person', 'is responsible for an individual', 'if the person is a parent of the individual'
Normative rule	$subclause(2.4), parentOf(A, B) \Rightarrow_O responsible(A, B)$

focuses on verbal predicates (cf. the first sentence in Table 2, in which the predicative adjective *greater than* and its arguments is not captured by the relation extraction tool OpenIE [1]) and most methods are heavily depend on syntactic analysis. Thus, one of the main challenges of using relation extraction as an intermediate step towards normative rules generation is to have high quality syntactic parser outputs for complex sentences. Another possibility would be to explore approaches that combine sentence segmentation, syntactic analysis and relation extraction for complex sentences. Another research avenue would be to extend relation extraction to predicate nouns and adjectives. This is an interesting research direction, since not all nouns and adjectives are predicates.

6 Experiments

In this section, we present empirical results based on experiments in neural semantic parsing and relation extraction in the legal domain.

6.1 Neural Semantic Parsing Experiments

As discussed in Sect. 5, semantic parsing technologies can be used to generate meaning representations from which it is possible to distil normative rules. We have chosen to evaluate two models, namely: the sequence-to-sequence model proposed by [6], and the coarse-to-fine model proposed by [22], as described in more detail below:

Sequence-to-Sequence: This model [6] consists of an encoder and decoder with two different L-layer recurrent neural networks with long-short-term-memory (LSTM) units, which recursively process tokens one by one. A sentence in natural language x is encoded into a vector representation, and decoded into a sequence $y_1, \ldots, y_{|y|}$ that is learned conditioned on the encoded vector $p(y|x)$. Additionally, this approach can incorporate with an attention mechanism to integrate encoder-side information (also referred to as context version) for the current hidden state.

Coarse-to-Fine: In this model [22], the decoder process has two steps. In the first step, a decoder generates a sketch of the meaning representation, omitting arguments and variable names. Then, in the second step, a second decoder fills the missing details conditioned on the input and the sketch. As such, the sketches constrain the generation process. Thus, $p(y|x)$ is decomposed into a two stage generation which are realized as: $p(y|x) = p(y|x, a) \, p(a|x)$, where $a = a_1, \ldots, a_{|a|}$ is an abstract sketch representation of y.

The sequence-to-sequence approach can be considered as a vanilla model. Meanwhile, the coarse-to-fine model restricts the decoder by modelling the structure of the output meaning representations.

Table 3. Data sets splits and average length of input and output sequences (dash signs '-' indicates 'no data for those cells')

	ATIS	GEO	RegTech
Training set	4434	600	140
Development set	491	-	-
Test set	448	280	79
Total	5373	880	79
Avg. input length	10.6	7.3	26.75

Data Sets for Training Semantic Parsers

GEO. This is a standard semantic parsing benchmark which consists of a set of queries to a database of U.S. geography. The meaning representation of this data set is a lambda-calculus like formula (as in [6]) and values for variables such as *city, state, country, river* and *number* are identified beforehand. We used the splits provided by [6] in our experiments.

ATIS. This is another standard benchmark in semantic parsing which consists of queries to a flight booking system. Sentences are paired with lambda-calculus expressions and values for variables such as *date, time, city, aircraft code, airport, airline* and *number* are identified beforehand. We used the standard splits provided in the data set in our experiments.

RegTech.[2] We have developed this data set for evaluating the performance of semantic parsing in the legal domain. At the moment, the data set consists of 140 sentences extracted from regulations from New Zealand and Australia. Following the annotation schema of [6], sentences in the data set are paired with logical expressions that are used to indicate the scope of the predicates and their arguments. The annotations were carried out by annotators with a background in logic. Each annotator annotated a set of 10 sentences (without overlap). Next, two annotators reviewed the logical expressions, agreed on the best practises and produced a consistent final version of the data set.

Table 4. Examples of sentences written in natural language and their corresponding meaning representation for the three data sets

GEO	*what is the capital of the state with the largest population density?*
	`(capital:c (argmax $1 (state:t $1) (density:i $1)))`
ATIS	*is there ground transport available at the airport?*
	`(lambda $0 e (and (ground-transport $0) (from-airport $0 ap0)))`
RegTech	*a large building is any building with a net lettable area greater than* 300 m²
	`lambda $0 (if (a large building:$0) then (is any building with a lettable area greater than ($0 300m2)))`

---

[2] Available at: http://bitbucket.csiro.au/users/fer201/repos/regtech-dataset.

Information and examples of the data sets are shown in Tables 3 and 4, respectively.

Neural Semantic Parsing Settings. Semantic parsing is evaluated on accuracy, which is defined as the proportion of the input sentences that have an exact match with their gold standard logical form. Both models are trained on GPU with their default hyper-parameters.

6.2   Relation Extraction Experiments

We have chosen to evaluate the approach from OpenIE [1] due to its two promising features: (i) it is open to any relation (predicates), thus relations do not have to be defined in advance; (ii) it models long-range dependencies, thus is able to extract relations from long sentences which frequently appear in legal texts. The approach consists of two major steps. It first learns a classifier for splitting sentences into shorter utterances by traversing dependency parsed trees recursively. Subsequently, through the use of some natural logic, it tries to shorten these utterances into small clauses or compact sentences while maintaining the necessary context. Finally, it identifies *subject-verb-object* tuples with a traditional relation extraction approach.

Relation Extraction Settings. We run OpenIE off-the-shelf using Stanford CoreNLP with its default parameters. We have selected 78 sentences from the RegTech data set and obtained sets of tuples for each sentence. Since sentences in the RegTech data sets are pairs with logic representations rather than triplets, we cannot automatically compute the quality of the extracted tuples. Instead, we manually inspect the extracted triplets adopting the following criteria:

- Number of analysed sentences
- Number of tuples outputs
- Number of correct tuples: a tuple is considered correct if it is a predicate in the sentence and if its arguments (which explicitly appear in the sentence) are extracted as well
- All predicates are extracted (complete analysis): YES or NO
- Contained coordinated conjunctions: YES or NO

6.3   Semantic Parsing Evaluation Results

Table 5 shows the results of the semantic parsing experiments. We first verify the ability of the methods in analysing sentences of different complexity, assuming the sentence length is an indicator of sentence complexity (the longer the sentence, the more likely it is to contain complicated semantic structures). As already shown in Table 4, sentences in the legal domain (for example, in RegTech)) have an average input length that is significantly higher than sentences in standard semantic parsing data sets such as ATIS and GEO. Since the

Table 5. Semantic parsing evaluation on test sets (short sentences contained less than 10 tokens (<10 tokens) and long sentences contained 10 or more tokens (≥10 tokens))

	Sequence-to-sequence	Coarse-to-fine
ATIS (all)	83.03	86.83
ATIS (<10 tokens)	85.05	88.28
ATIS (≥10 tokens)	62.99	81.10
GEO (all)	83.57	88.93
GEO (<10 tokens)	92.09	89.47
GEO (≥10 tokens)	68.93	84.85
GEO (140)	29.28	29.86
RegTech (140)	18.28	18.42

Table 6. Examples of gold-standard formulas (GS) from RegTech and their corresponding predicted (P) formulas generated by the coarse-to-fine semantic parsing model

GS	`lambda $0 $1 $2 (and ((endorsing body or)` `(supplier of:$1))) then (must (be replaced by ($0 $1)))`
P	`lambda $0 $1 $2 (and ((endorsing body:$0)` `(supplier of:$1 (food:$2)) (must (<U> ($0 $1)))))`
GS	`lambda $0 (and ((claim:$0)) (must (not (refer to ($0` `prevention of (or ((disease) (disorder) (condition)))))))))`
P	`lambda $0 (and ((claim:$0)) (must (not (refer to ($0` `diagnosis of (or ((disease) (disorder) (condition)))))))))`

size of the RegTech) data set is small and potentially not sufficient to properly train a semantic parser, we evaluate the parsers performance on long sentences by splitting the ATIS and GEO test sets in two subsets: sentences containing less than 10 tokens and sentences with 10 or more tokens, respectively. For comparison, we also report the evaluation results with the full test sets: ATIS (all) and GEO (all). As expected, results shows considerable drops when parsing long sentences, The drop is more dramatic for sequence-to-sequence, which dropped about 20 points when parsing long sentences with ATIS (from 83.03 to 62.99), and about 14 points with GEO (from 83.57 to 68.99). The coarse-to-fine model is more resilient to long sentences, thus its performance is less hurt, dropping about 6 points with ATIS (from 86.83 to 81.1) and about 4 points with GEO (from 88.93 to 84.85). The experiments indicate that having a model that constrained its decoder with some kind of structure is preferable for the legal domain.

As mentioned, the size of RegTech is potentially too small to train a semantic parser. Results shows an accuracy of 18.28 for sequence-to-sequence, and a slightly better performance for coarse-to-fine with an accuracy of 18.42. For comparison, we report results on GEO trained only with 140 sentences that were randomly chosen. Results indicate that models trained with a limited amount

Table 7. Relation extraction evaluation results using the RegTech test set

	Counts	Percentage (%)
Total sentences	78	–
Analysed sentences	46	58.97
Triplets outputs	246	–
Correct triplets	166	67.48
Complete analysis	19	24.36
Contained coord. conjunctions	17	21.79

of data are not able to generalise well. A qualitative error analysis performed on the output of the semantic parsers trained with RegTech indicates that the models are able to correctly output the structure of the logic formulas, but failed to instantiate the appropriate vocabulary (cf. Table 6). We attribute this limitation to the vocabulary mismatch between the training and testing sets. The main take away from these experiments is that current technologies for semantic parsing are data hungry, and creating data sets for semantic parsing is not a trivial task.

In the ATIS and GEO data sets, values for in-domain variables e.g., city, airport, etc. are anonymised before training, thus the vocabulary size is reduced, making encoding and decoding simpler. Note that variables in RegTech are not anonymised. Consequently, the vocabulary size is bigger, which impacts the generalisation power of the model. Nevertheless, we argue that it is less costly to increase the size of RegTech and train a semantic parser, than investing in a syntax-based approach, which requires to manually annotate in-domain syntactic structures to re-train a syntax analyser and to write grammars to distil the rules from the trees.

6.4 Relation Extraction Evaluation Results

Overall, relation extraction is able to correctly identify many predicates from sentences in the RegTech data set. It also struggles to analyse some sentences, thus producing no tuples. Table 7 shows the experiments results for relation extraction when applied to RegTech. The OpenIE tool was able to extract predicates from 58.97% of the sentences. The results also show that OpenIE manages to analyse 21.79% of the sentences with coordinate phrases. This is not surprising, since OpenIE relies on automatic syntactic parsing, which is known to perform poorly with complex linguistics structures [5]. The tool extracted 246 predicates from which 67.48% are correct. Further assessment was done to evaluate whether all the predicates were extracted from a given sentence. The results show that for only 24.36 sentences (24.36%) all the predicates were extracted (cf., Table 7 'Complete analysis').

Table 8. Examples of natural language sentences from the RegTech data set and their tuples extracted using OpenIE

	Complete analysis
Input	*Toilet facilities for males must contain WC pans and basins and may contain urinals*
Tuples	toilet facility; contain; urinal
	toilet facility; must contain; WC pan
	toilet facility; must contain; basin
Input	*A urinal flushing system shall have the cistern outlet at least 450 mm above the sparge pipe and comply with Table 5*
Tuples	flushing system; shall have; cistern outlet at least 450 mm
	flushing system; comply with; Table 5
	Incomplete analysis
Input	*Flushing systems for sanitary fixtures shall use either cisterns or flushing valves*
Tuples	flush system; shall use either; cistern
Input	*This Verification Method can be used for housing, communal residential, communal non-residential and commercial buildings.*
Tuples	verification method; can; can used for housing
	No analysis
Input	*WC pans and basins are required in any building where people: a) live or are accommodated or b) work or c) eat food or drink on the premises or d) assemble*
Tuples	–
Input	*For determining the insulation requirements of the building envelope, buildings other than housing are classified as being either small or large.*
Tuples	–

Error Analysis. In the following, we summarised the OpenIE most salient errors when applied to the RegTech data set.

– **No output tuples**: the analysis of long and complicated sentences usually produce no output tuples. Sentences that were not parsed are usually long and contained itemised coordinate constructions, cf., Table 8 '*No analysis*'. We also found that the analysis of simple sentences in which a negation proceeds a verbal predicate produce no tuples, e.g., *This Standard does not apply to food that is intended for labelling.*

– **Prepositional phrases and noun post modifiers**: prepositional phrases and other noun post modifiers are not consistently analysed by OpenIE, cf., Table 8 '*Toilets facilities for males . . .*', in which '*for males*' is not output as an attribute of '*Toilets facilities*'. In contrast, from the text spanning '*cistern* *outlet at least* 450 mm *above the sparge pipe* ...', it manages to capture the first prepositional phrase ('*at least* 450 mm') that modifies the noun '*cistern outlet*', and fails to capture the second prepositional phrase '*above the sparge pipe*' as a modifier.

– **Modal verbs**: predicates with auxiliary modal verbs such as *must*, and *shall* are inconsistently analysed by OpenIE, e.g., for the sentence: *Flushing systems for sanitary fixtures <u>shall use</u> either cisterns or flushing valves*, one of the extracted tuple is: '*systems*'; '*use*'; '*flushing valves*'.

OpenIE relies on syntactic analysis. Thus, it is not surprising that it struggles to find the correct scope of prepositional phrases. Prepositions describe relations between terms, primarily about location, direction and time, and capture important content that should be available in a legal norm. This is a big challenge to syntax based approaches because of the well-known problem of attachment ambiguity, which is most commonly produced by prepositional attachment ambiguity. This happens when a prepositional phrase can be attached to a syntactic tree in more than one place. Similarly, syntactically analysing long and complex sentences is currently an open problem. This is mainly due to the treebanks used to train syntactic parsers, which mostly contained short sentences from news articles. This problem is likely to be alleviated by re-training a syntactic parser with in-domain sentences. The performance of OpenIE can also be boosted by reducing the complexity of the input sentences beforehand, for instance by applying a pre-process segmentation strategy, as proposed by [27].

In this paper, we did not address the problem of attaching modalities to the rules since that process can be considered as a separate problem. Nevertheless, we are aware that rules needs to be legally characterised with modalities to be useful for reasoning.

7   Conclusions and Future Work

This paper presents the task of generating normative rules from legal documents. Normative rules are executable statements generated from sentences written in natural language, which are used for reasoning. To attract research in this area, we have outlined some promising research avenues, connecting the requirements of normative rules to existing NLP research streams. One of the main challenges is how to produce an accurate meaning representation from complex sentences. We report some preliminary experiments on neural semantic parsing and open relation extraction, as they can be considered as an intermediate step towards the generation of normative rules. Results show that there is plenty of room for improvement. For future work, we plan to increase the RegTech data set, and to run experiments following the recommendations and new versions of semantic parsing benchmarks from [11].

References

1. Angeli, G., Johnson Premkumar, M.J., Manning, C.D.: Leveraging linguistic structure for open domain information extraction. In: Proceedings of the 53rd Annual Meeting of the Association for Computational Linguistics, ACL 2015, Beijing, China, pp. 344–354 (2015)
2. Banarescu, L., et al.: Abstract meaning representation for sembanking. In: Pareja-Lora, A., Liakata, M., Dipper, S. (eds.) Proceedings of the 7th Linguistic Annotation Workshop and Interoperability with Discourse, Sofia, Bulgaria, pp. 178–186, August 2013
3. Boella, G., Di Caro, L., Robaldo, L.: Semantic relation extraction from legislative text using generalized syntactic dependencies and support vector machines. In: Morgenstern, L., Stefaneas, P., Lévy, F., Wyner, A., Paschke, A. (eds.) RuleML 2013. LNCS, vol. 8035, pp. 218–225. Springer, Heidelberg (2013). https://doi.org/10.1007/978-3-642-39617-5_20
4. Breaux, T.D., Antón, A.I.: A systematic method for acquiring regulatory requirements: a frame-based approach. In: Proceedings of the 6th International Workshop on Requirements for High Assurance Systems, Pittsburg, PA, USA, September 2007
5. Burga, A., Codina, J., Ferraro, G., Saggion, H., Wanner, L.: The challenge of syntactic dependency parsing adaptation for the patent domain. In: Proceedings of ESSLLI-13 Workshop on Extrinsic Parse Improvement. EPI, Düsseldorf, Germany, August 2013
6. Dong, L., Lapata, M.: Language to logical form with neural attention. In: Erk, K., Smith, N.A. (eds.) Proceedings of the 54th Annual Meeting of the Association for Computational Linguistics, vol. 1: Long Papers, Berlin, German, pp. 33–43, August 2016
7. Dragoni, M., Villata, S., Rizzi, W., Governatori, G.: Combining natural language processing approaches for rule extraction from legal documents. In: Pagallo, U., Palmirani, M., Casanovas, P., Sartor, G., Villata, S. (eds.) AICOL 2015-2017. LNCS (LNAI), vol. 10791, pp. 287–300. Springer, Cham (2018). https://doi.org/10.1007/978-3-030-00178-0_19
8. Dragoni, M., Villata, S., Rizzi, W., Governatori, G.: Combining NLP approaches for rule extraction from legal documents. In: 1st Workshop on MIning and REasoning with Legal texts (MIREL 2016), Sophia Antipolis, France, December 2016
9. van Engers, T.M., van Gog, R., Sayah, K.: A case study on automated norm extraction. In: Gordon, T. (ed.) The 17th International Conference on Legal Knowledge and Information Systems, JURIX 2004, pp. 49–58. IOS Press, Amsterdam (2004)
10. Fan, X., Monti, E., Mathias, L., Dreyer, M.: Transfer learning for neural semantic parsing. In: Blunsom, P., et al. (eds.) Proceedings of the 2nd Workshop on Representation Learning for NLP, Rep4NLP 2017, Vancouver, Canada, pp. 48–56, August 2017
11. Finegan-Dollak, C., et al.: Improving text-to-SQL evaluation methodology. In: Gurevych, I., Miyao, Y. (eds.) Proceedings of the 56th Annual Meeting of the Association for Computational Linguistics, ACL 2018, Melbourne, Australia, pp. 351–360, July 2018
12. Gaur, S., Vo, N.H., Kashihara, K., Baral, C.: Translating simple legal text to formal representations. In: Murata, T., Mineshima, K., Bekki, D. (eds.) JSAI-isAI 2014. LNCS (LNAI), vol. 9067, pp. 259–273. Springer, Heidelberg (2015). https://doi.org/10.1007/978-3-662-48119-6_19

13. Gordon, A.S., Hobbs, J.R.: A Formal Theory of Commonsense Psychology: How People Think People Think, 1st edn. Cambridge University Press, New York (2017)
14. Governatori, G., Rotolo, A.: A conceptually rich model of business process compliance. In: Proceedings of the 7th Asia-Pacific Conference on Conceptual Modelling, APCCM 2010, ACS, Brisbane, QLD, Australia, pp. 3–12, January 2010
15. Herzig, J., Berant, J.: Neural semantic parsing over multiple knowledge-bases. In: Barzilay, R., Kan, M.Y. (eds.) Proceedings of the 55th Annual Meeting of the Association for Computational Linguistics, ACL 2017, Vancouver, Canada, pp. 623–628, July 2017
16. Jia, R., Liang, P.: Data recombination for neural semantic parsing. In: Erka, K., Smith, N.A. (eds.) Proceedings of the 54th Annual Meeting of the Association for Computational Linguistics, ACL 2016, Berlin, Germany, pp. 12–22, August 2016
17. Kelsen, H.: General Theory of Norms. Oxford University Press, Inc., Oxford (1991)
18. Kennardi, A., Ferraro, G., Wang, Q.: Domain adaptation for low-resource neural semantic parsing. In: MacKinlay, A., Piccardi, M. (eds.) Proceedings of the 17th Workshop of the Australasian Language Technology Association, ALTA 2019, Sydney, Australia, pp. 107–113 (2019)
19. Kimura, Y., Nakamura, M., Shimazu, A.: Treatment of legal sentences including itemized and referential expressions – towards translation into logical forms. In: Hattori, H., Kawamura, T., Idé, T., Yokoo, M., Murakami, Y. (eds.) JSAI 2008. LNCS (LNAI), vol. 5447, pp. 242–253. Springer, Heidelberg (2009). https://doi.org/10.1007/978-3-642-00609-8_21
20. Kočiský, T., et al.: Semantic parsing with semi-supervised sequential autoencoders. In: Su, J., Duh, K., Carreras, X. (eds.) Proceedings of the 2016 Conference on Empirical Methods in Natural Language Processing, EMNLP 2016, pp. 1078–1087. Association for Computational Linguistics, Austin, November 2016
21. Kwiatkowski, T., Zettlemoyer, L., Goldwater, S., Steedman, M.: Lexical generalization in CCG grammar induction for semantic parsing. In: Barzilay, R., Johnsn, M. (eds.) Proceedings of the 2011 Conference on Empirical Methods in Natural Language Processing, EMNLP 2011, Edinburgh, Scotland, UK, pp. 1512–1523, July 2011
22. Lapata, M., Dong, L.: Coarse-to-fine decoding for neural semantic parsing. In: Gurevych, I., Miyao, Y. (eds.) Proceedings of the 56th Annual Meeting of the Association for Computational Linguistics, ACL 2018, Melbourne, Australia, pp. 731–742, July 2018
23. Makinson, D.: On a fundamental problem of deontic logic. In: McNamara, P., Prakken, H. (eds.) Norms, Logics and Information Systems. New Studies in Deontic Logic and Computer Science, vol. 49, pp. 29–53. IOS Press, Amsterdam (1999)
24. Miall, H.: Emergent Conflict and Peaceful Change. Palgrave MacMillan, London (2007)
25. Ministry of Business, Innovation and Employment, New Zealand: New Zealand Building Code Clause G4 Ventilation: Acceptable Solutions and Verification Methods, 4th edn. (2017)
26. Nakamura, M., Nobuoka, S., Shimazu, A.: Towards translation of legal sentences into logical forms. In: Satoh, K., Inokuchi, A., Nagao, K., Kawamura, T. (eds.) JSAI 2007. LNCS (LNAI), vol. 4914, pp. 349–362. Springer, Heidelberg (2008). https://doi.org/10.1007/978-3-540-78197-4_33
27. Niklaus, C., Cetto, M., Freitas, A., Handschuh, S.: Transforming complex sentences into a semantic hierarchy. In: Proceedings of the 57th Annual Meeting of the Association for Computational Linguistics, Florence, Italy, pp. 3415–3427, July 2019

28. OASIS LegalRuleML TC: OASIS LegalRuleML (2013). http://www.oasis-open. org/committees/legalruleml. Accessed 7 Dec 2019

29. Popple, J.: A Pragmatic Legal Expert System. Dartmouth (1996)

30. Rubino, R., Rotolo, A., Sartor, G.: An OWL ontology of fundamental legal concepts. In: Proceedings of the 9th Annual Conference on Legal Knowledge and Information Systems, JURIX 2006, pp. 101–110. IOS Press, Amsterdam (2006)

31. Sartor, G.: Legal Reasoning: A Cognitive Approach to the Law, A Treatise of Legal Philosophy and General Jurisprudence, vol. 5. Springer, Berlin (2005)

32. Schwarm, S.E., Ostendorf, M.: Reading level assessment using support vector machines and statistical language models. In: Proceedings of the 43rd Annual Meeting on Association for Computational Linguistics, ACL 2005, Stroudsburg, PA, USA, pp. 523–530 (2005)

33. Sleimi, A., Sannier, N., Sabetzadeh, M., Briand, L., Dann, J.: Automated extraction of semantic legal metadata using natural language processing. In: The 26th IEEE International Requirements Engineering Conference, Banff, AB, Canada, pp. 124–135. IEEE, August 2018

34. Susanto, R.H., Lu, W.: Neural architectures for multilingual semantic parsing. In: Barzilay, R., Kan, M.Y. (eds.) Proceedings of the 55th Annual Meeting of the Association for Computational Linguistics, ACL 2017, Vancouver, Canada, pp. 38–44, July 2017

35. Tjong, E.F., Sang, K., Déjean, H.: Introduction to the CoNLL-2001 shared task: clause identification. In: Daelemans, W., Zajac, R. (eds.) Proceedings of the 2001 Workshop on Computational Natural Language Learning, ConLL 2001. Association for Computational Linguistics, Toulouse, July 2001

36. Vajjala, S., Meurers, D.: Readability-based Sentence Ranking for Evaluating Text Simplification. CoRR (2016). http://arxiv.org/abs/1603.06009

37. Wieringa, R.J., Meyer, J. J. C.: Applications of deontic logic in computer science: a concise overview. In: Meyer, J.J.C., Wieringa, R.J. (eds.) International Workshop on Deontic Logic in Computer Science, DEON 1993, Amsterdam, Netherlands, pp. 17–40, December 1993

38. Woodsend, K., Lapata, M.: WikiSimple: automatic simplification of wikipedia articles. In: Proceedings of the 25th AAAI Conference on Artificial Intelligence, AAAI 2011, San Francisco, CA, USA, pp. 927–932. AAAI Press, August 2011

39. Wyner, A.Z., Peters, W.: On rule extraction from regulations. In: Atkinson, K.M. (ed.) Proceedings of the 24th International Conference on Legal Knowledge and Information, JURIX 2011, Vienna, Austria, pp. 113–122. IOS Press, September 2011

AI-Biz 2019

Artificial Intelligence of and for Business (AI-Biz2019)

Takao Terano[1], Setsuya Kurahashi[2], and Hiroshi Takahashi[3]

[1] Chiba University of Commerce
[2] University of Tsukuba
[3] Keio University

1 The Workshop

In AI-Biz 2019 held on November 12, two excellent invited lectures and seven cutting-edge research papers were presented with a total of about 12 participants. The workshop theme focused on various recent issues in business activities and application technologies of Artificial Intelligence to them.

The first invited lecture was "Financial Data Analyses - Modeling of a Time-Series or a Multivariate Approach" by Prof. Goutam Chakraborty of Iwate Prefectural University, and head of the Intelligent Informatics laboratory, Department of the Software and Information Science. In his presentation, he discussed deterministic Chaos, often observed in financial time-series, and how to use its property to model the data. Besides, he showed how Recurrent Neural Network could be used for modeling and prediction of financial data.

The second invited lecture was "All you need is not money. - How to encourage posting contents on CGM? -" by Associate Professor, Dr. Fujio Toriumi of the University of Tokyo. In his presentation, he explained his agent-based model to confirm the effect of incentive systems which implemented to Consumer Generated Media (CGM) including monetary rewards. In several CGM, monetary incentive systems are often introduced to encourage providers. He also discussed whether the monetary are incentives encourage to post articles on CGM, or not.

The AI-Biz2018 was the fourth workshop hosted by the SIG-BI (Business Informatics) of JSAI. We believe the workshop was held successfully because of vast fields of business and AI technology. It includes for human capital, industry classifications, capturing mercurial customers, variable selection, organizational performance, traffic congestion, visualization of R&D project, credit risk, eco-cars, stock price prediction, and so on.

2 Papers

Twelve papers were submitted for the workshop, and seven of them were selected for oral presentation in the workshop (58% acceptance rate). After the workshop, they were reviewed by PC members again, and three papers were finally selected (25% acceptance rate). Followings are their synopses.

Masaya Abe and Kei Nakagawa implemented deep learning for multi-factor models to predict stock returns in the cross-section in the stock markets and investigated the performance of the method. The results showed that deep neural networks generally outperformed representative machine learning models all over the world. These results indicate that deep learning shows promise as a skilful machine learning method to predict stock returns in the cross-section.

Yoshihiro Nishi, Aiko Suge, and Hiroshi Takahashi constructed a news evaluation model utilizing GPT-2. The model evaluated news articles distributed to financial markets based on price fluctuation rates and predicted fluctuations in stock prices. They also added news articles generated by GPT-2 as data for analysis. News articles were classified through Long Short-Term Memory (LSTM). The results showed that the accuracy of the news evaluation model improved by generating news articles using a language generation model through GPT-2.

Hirotaka Yanada and Setsuya Kurahashi investigated relationships between performances of start-ups and external supports to them. They used a questionnaire survey with responses from 2,897 start-ups (as of the 1st survey) and adopted propensity score matching, which is one of the causal inference methods. These results suggest the potential for contributing to the performances by the proper combination of these supports, considering the characteristics of each type of external support.

3   Acknowledgment

As the organizing committee chair, I would like to thank the steering committee members, The members are leading researchers in various fields:

Reiko Hishiyama (Waseda University, Japan)
Manabu Ichikawa (National Institute of Public Health, Japan)
Yoko Ishino (Yamaguchi University, Japan)
Hajime Kita (Kyoto University, Japan)
Hajime Mizuyama (Aoyama Gakuin University, Japan)
Chathura Rajapaksha, University of Kelaniya, Sri Lanka
Masakazu Takahashi (Yamaguchi University, Japan)
Shingo Takahashi (Waseda University, Japan)
Takashi Yamada (Yamaguchi University, Japan).

The organizers would like to thank JSAI for financial support. Finally, we wish to express our gratitude to all those who submitted papers, steering committee members, reviewers, discussant and attentive audience. We are extremely grateful to all the reviewers. We would like to thank everybody involved in the sympodia organization that helped us in making this event successful.

Deep Learning for Multi-factor Models in Regional and Global Stock Markets

Masaya Abe[✉] and Kei Nakagawa

Nomura Assset Management Co., Ltd., Tokyo, Japan
masaya.abe.428@gmail.com

Abstract. Many studies have been undertaken with machine learning techniques to predict stock returns in terms of time-series prediction. However, from the viewpoint of the cross-sectional prediction with machine learning techniques, there are no examples that verify its profitability in regional and global stock markets. This paper implements deep learning for multi-factor models to predict stock returns in the cross-section in these stock markets and investigates the performance of the method. Our results show that deep neural networks generally outperform representative machine learning models all over the world. These results indicate that deep learning shows promise as a skillful machine learning method to predict stock returns in the cross-section.

Although deep learning performs quite well, it has significant disadvantages such as a lack of transparency and limitations to the interpretability of the prediction. Then, we present the application of layer-wise relevance propagation (LRP) to decompose attributes of the predicted return. By applying LRP to each stock and averaging them in a portfolio, we can determine which factor contributes to prediction. We illustrate which factor contributes to prediction in regional and global stock markets.

Keywords: Deep learning · Stock return prediction · Cross-section · Multi-factor model · Layer-wise relevance propagation

1 Introduction

Stock price predictability has been an important research theme both academically and practically. Various methods to predict stock prices have been studied. These methods can be roughly divided into time-series and cross-section analysis.

The first method analyzes past stock prices as time-series data and perform time-series analysis. The financial time-series analysis originally started from a linear model, such as the autoregressive (AR) model in which the parameters are uniquely determined [15]. As many nonlinear behaviors have been observed in actual financial time-series data, the generalized autoregressive conditional heteroscedasticity (GARCH) model [6] incorporating the time series structure into volatility has been used as one approach. In recent years, the GARCH model has been expanded to multivariate even for a large number of stocks [12,22].

© Springer Nature Switzerland AG 2020
M. Sakamoto et al. (Eds.): JSAI-isAI 2019, LNAI 12331, pp. 87–102, 2020.
https://doi.org/10.1007/978-3-030-58790-1_6

In addition, nonlinear models such as k-nearest neighbor [11], neural networks [28] and support vector machines [10] have been used for stock price predictions. These models not only strive to grasp economic implications such as market efficiency and non-arbitrage relationship but also strive to increase prediction accuracy practically. They especially try to grasp stock price fluctuations, that is, path-dependent patterns by trial and error. These approaches have attracted attention for improving computing capabilities in recent years.

The second method performs cross-section (regression) analysis using cross-sectional data such as corporate attributes. The attribute that explains the stock return revealed by a cross-section analysis is called a "factor" in the field of finance. Many empirical studies in finance have identified which stocks having attributes in the cross-section analysis relatively increase and which decrease in terms of return. The representative model that explains the cross-sectional stock returns is the Fama-French three-factor model [13,14]. They proposed that the cross-sectional structure of stock returns can be explained by three factors: beta (market portfolio), size (market capitalization), and value (price book-value ratio). Since then, many factors other than those in the Fama-French three-factor model were found one after another. As a result, [16] reported that over 300 factors were discovered until 2012. Moreover, most of these factors have been found in the last 10 years. Although the factors that investors should consider are rapidly increasing, it is not possible to simultaneously examine over 300 factors due to the curse of dimension.

Besides, a linear regression model is used because of easy statistical handling and the robustness of the result in the financial field. However, since the relationship between these factors and stock returns is complex [20], linear regression models have limited prediction accuracy.

As non-parametric cross-sectional stock prediction studies [2,25,26], they used deep learning to combine various factors targeting Japanese stock markets. They reported that the prediction accuracy and profitability can be improved by combining non-linearly using deep learning rather than simply combining various factors by linear regression. However, these studies are limited in Japanese stock markets.

In this study, we examine whether the effectiveness of stock return prediction in the cross-section using deep learning holds in each regional stock market (North America, Europe, and Asia Pacific) and global markets (aggregated all three regions) as well and whether there are regional differences. If the deep learning model that outperformed other models in the Japanese market works in the other markets, deep learning shows promise as a skillful machine learning method to predict stock returns in the cross-section in most stock markets.

Although deep learning performs quite well, it has significant disadvantages such as a lack of transparency and limitations to the interpretability of the prediction. Then, we present the application of layer-wise relevance propagation (LRP) [4] to decompose attributes of the predicted return. By applying LRP to each stock and averaging them in a portfolio, we can determine which factor contributes to prediction. We illustrate which factor contributes to prediction in regional and global stock markets.

Such robustness and reliability of the model are also important for practitioners in terms of accountability.

The remainder of the paper is organized as follows. Section 2 summarizes related works. Section 3 provides a brief description of the data and prediction methodology. Section 4 shows the empirical results of prediction with major regional and global stock indices. Section 5 tries to visualize what factors are considered important in each region and global stock markets. Section 6 concludes the paper.

2   Related Works

Many studies on stock return predictability using machine learning have been published. For example, [23,24] showed that the shape of stock price fluctuation is an important feature in the prediction of future prices. [23] proposed a method to predict future stock prices with past fluctuations similar to the current. They used the dynamic time warping method and the k^*-nearest neighbor [3] which outputs no classification model to predict major stock indices. Also, [24] extracted the representative price fluctuation patterns with k-Medoids clustering as feature values for prediction.

[29] created an automatic stock trading system in the Australian stock market. They used a neural network that decides when to buy or sell the stock. The inputs are four variables arising from the fundamental analysis: price earning ratio (PER), price book-value ratio (PBR), return on equity (ROE) and dividend payout ratio. The outputs are a strong signal that represents the expected returns of the predicted stock.

[8] investigated how to predict stock indices by using support vector machines (SVMs) to learn the relationship among several technical indicators such as several moving averages and the stock index price. They used the grid search method to optimize the SVM model parameters. The experimental results show that transforming the input data space of SVM can bring good performance in finance engineering.

[5,7] presented a review of the application of several machine learning methods in finance. In their survey, most of these were forecasts in terms of time series analysis. However, there is no paper that deals with the prediction method in terms of a multi-factor model.

In terms of the cross-section analysis, [20] discussed the use of multilayer feedforward neural networks for predicting stock returns within the framework of the multi-factor model. [2] extended this model to deep learning and investigated the performance of the method on the Japanese stock market. They showed that deep neural networks generally outperform shallow ones, and the best networks also outperform representative machine learning models.

These works are only for use as a return model, and the problem is that the viewpoint of a risk model is lacking. [26] proposed the application of LRP to decompose the attributes of the predicted return as a risk model. [25] extend this model to a time-varying multi-factor model with LSTM + LRP. However, they do not examine the influence on performance due to the approximation of LRP and not considering the time-dependency of factors.

From the above, these empirical studies are only targeting Japanese stock markets. This paper implements deep learning to predict stock returns in the cross-section in regional and global stock markets and investigates the performance of the method.

We also implement the layer-wise relevance propagation (LRP) [4] to decompose attributes of the predicted return. By applying LRP to each stock and averaging them in a portfolio, we can determine which factor contributes to prediction. We try to illustrate which factor contributes to prediction in global stock markets.

3   Data and Methodology

3.1   Data

We prepare the dataset for MSCI North America, MSCI Europe and Middle East, and MSCI Pacific Index constituents for each region (North America, Europe, and Asia Pacific). These MSCI indices comprise the large and mid-cap segments of regional stock markets made up of developed countries. MSCI World Index constituents are made up of these three regional index constituents for global markets (World). Each index is also often used as a benchmark for overseas institutional investors. We use the 20 factors listed in Table 1. These are used relatively often in practice. In fact, those factors are covered six among the seven categories of Deutsche Bank Quantitative Strategy [30]. The remaining one category, Size, is excluded because the universe we use does not include small caps. In calculating these factors, we acquire necessary data from Compustat, WorldScope, Thomson Reuters, I/B/E/S, and EXSHARE. Forecast data is obtained from Thomson Reuters Estimates and I/B/E/S Estimates (Thomson Reuters priority). Factors are calculated on a monthly basis (at the end of the month).

3.2   Problem Definition

We define the problem as a regression problem. For example, for stock i in index constituents at month T (end of month), 20 factors listed in Table 1 are defined by $\mathbf{x}_{i,T} \in \mathbb{R}^{20}$ as input values. The output value is defined by the stock return of next month, $r_{i,T+1} \in \mathbb{R}$. For data preprocessing, rescaling is performed so that each input value is from 0 to 1 by ranking each input value in ascending order by the stock universe at each time point and then dividing by the maximum rank value.

Similar rescaling is done for output values $r_{i,T+1}$, to convert to the cross-sectional stock returns (scores). Note that $\mathbf{x}_{i,T}$ and $r_{i,T+1}$ are assumed to be the

Table 1. List of factors.

No	Factor	Description
1	B/P	Net asset/Market value
2	E/P	Net profit/Market value
3	D/P	Dividend/Market value
4	S/P	Sales/Market value
5	CF/P	Operating cash flow/Market value
6	ROE	Net profit/Net asset
7	ROA	Net operating profit/Total asset
8	ROIC	Net operating profit after taxes/(Liabilities with interest + Net asset)
9	Accrual	-(Changes in current assets and liability-depreciation)/Total asset
10	Total asset growth rate	Change rate of total assets from the previous period
11	Current ratio	Current asset/Current liability
12	Equity ratio	Net asset/Total asset
13	Total asset turnover rate	Sales/Total asset
14	CAPEX growth rate	Change rate of CAPEX from the previous period
15	EPS revision (1 month)	1 month EPS revision
16	EPS revision (3 month)	3 month EPS revision
17	Momentum (1 month)	Stock returns in last month
18	Momentum(12–1 month)	Stock returns in the past 12 months except for last month
19	Volatility	Standard deviation of stock returns in the past 60 months
20	Skewness	Skewness of stock returns in the past 60 months

values after data preprocessing. This procedure is extended to using the latest N months rather than the most recent set of training data (one training set). We use the mean squared error (MSE) as the loss function and define MSE_{T+1} when training the model at $T + 1$ as follows:

$$\mathbf{MSE}_{T+1} = \frac{1}{K} \sum_{t=T-N+1}^{T} \sum_{i \in U_t} (r_{i,t+1} - f(\mathbf{x}_{i,t}; \boldsymbol{\theta}_{T+1}))^2 \qquad (1)$$

In Eq. (1), K is the number of all training examples. U_t is index constituents universe at t. $\boldsymbol{\theta}_{T+1}$ is the parameter calculated by solving Eq. (1) and makes the form of a function f.

3.3 Prediction Models

Our problem is to find a function f as a predictor to the stock relative return of next month $r_{i,t+1}$ as output variable given various factors $\mathbf{x}_{i,t}$ as input data.

Here, we use deep learning as the nonlinear function f. The largest advantage of deep learning is its capability to learn the nonlinear relationship between the factors and the stock returns.

We use a gradient boosting tree (GB), random forest (RF) and ridge regression (RR) model as comparison methods. Details are as listed below.

1. Deep Neural Network (DNN): Deep Neural Network is implemented with TensorFlow [1]. The hidden layers are $\{150 - 150 - 100 - 100 - 50 - 50\}$. The dropout rate for each layer is $(50\%-50\%-30\%-30\%-10\%-10\%)$. We use the ReLU function as the activation function, and Adam [18] for the optimization algorithm. Batch normalization [17] is applied to activation. The mini-batch size is set to 300 for each region and 1,000 for the world. For training the model, the network weights are updated until the average of the rank correlation coefficient between the predicted returns calculated by each training data set and the realized returns (ground truth) reaches 0.20. And those reached 0.16 are used for the initial network weights at the next point as sequential analysis. As for the starting point of the analysis, we initialize to generate the network weights from TensorFlow's function "tf.truncated_normal" set to mean "0" and standard deviation "$\sqrt{2/M}$" (M is the size of the previous layer).

2. Gradient Boosting Tree (GB): Gradient Boosting Tree is implemented with xgboost [9] with the class "XGBRegressor". For the hyperparameters, we set the max number of features("max_features") to 20, the number of trees ("n_estimators") to 500, and the depth of tree ("max_depth") to 3.

3. Random Forest (RF): Random Forest is implemented with scikit-learn [27] with the class "sklearn.ensemble.RandomForestRegressor". For the hyperparameters, we set the max number of features ("max_features") to 20, the number of trees ("n_estimators") to 500, and the depth of the tree ("max_depth") to 3.

4. Ridge Rigression (RR): Ridge Rigression is implemented with scikit-learn [27] with the class "sklearn.linear_model.Ridge". For the hyperparameters, we set the regularization strength ("alpha") to 1.

3.4   Training and Prediction

We train the model by using the latest 120 sets of training from the past 10 years. To calculate the prediction, we substitute the latest input values into the model after training has occurred. The cross-sectional predictive stock return (score) of stock i at time $T + 2$ is calculated from time $T + 1$ by Eq. (2) substituting $\mathbf{x}_{i,T+1}$ into the function $f(\cdot)$ in Eq. (2) with the parameter $\boldsymbol{\theta}^*_{T+1}$, where $\boldsymbol{\theta}^*_{T+1}$ is calculated from Eq. (1) with $N = 120$:

$$Score_{i,T+2} = f(\mathbf{x}_{i,T+1}; \boldsymbol{\theta}^*_{T+1}) \tag{2}$$

For example, to calculate the prediction score at January 2005 $(T + 2)$ from December 2004 $(T+1)$, the input values are the factors as of December 2004 $(T+$

1). The prediction model is updated by sliding one-month-ahead and carrying out a monthly forecast. The prediction period is from January 2005 to December 2018 (on a month-end basis). An illustration of the flow of the processing is shown in Fig. 1, which shows the relationship between prediction and training data at each time point.

3.5   Performance Measures

We construct two types of portfolio strategy comprising stock groups with the prediction scores. One is the long portfolio strategy that buys the top stocks with equal weighting aiming to outperform the average return of all stocks. The other is the long-short portfolio strategy that is a net-zero investment strategy that buys the top stocks with equal weighting and sells the bottom stocks with equal weighting to earn absolute returns. To form into the top and bottom stock groups, we make quintile (five) portfolios for each region and decile (ten) portfolios for the world.

The performance of these strategies is calculated monthly during the prediction period from January 2005 to December 2018. This is because most of the related studies forecast monthly [2,20,25,26]. For example, at the evaluation starting point January 2005 (Prediction: 1 set in Fig. 1), these measures are calculated from the prediction scores for January 2005 from December 2004 and the actual out-of-sample returns at January 2005.

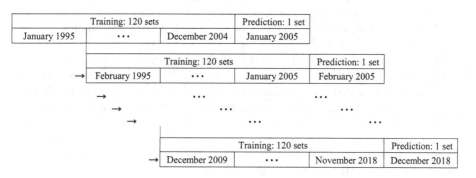

Fig. 1. Training-prediction set.

4   Experimental Results and Discussion

The performance summary of the long portfolio strategy (Long) and the long-short portfolio strategy (Long-Short) is Table 2. We evaluate annualized return (Return), the standard deviation of return (Risk), Return/Risk (R/R), and maximum drawdown (MaxDD)[1]. As for the long portfolio strategy, the return is the

---

[1] The rate of decline from the maximum return is called drawdown. The case with the largest drawdown is called the maximum drawdown and is usually used as a risk measurement.

excess return (Alpha) against the average return of all stocks, the risk is tracking error (TE) calculated as the standard deviation of Alpha, and Return/Risk is Alpha/TE called Information Ratio (IR). The bold numbers in the table represent the best values among the 4 patterns (DNN, GB, RF, and RR).

In this paper, we use RR as a baseline to test the difference in Return (resp. Alpha), Risk (resp. TE) ratio, and R/R (resp. IR) of other methods. Since we cannot assume equal variance for the test of Return (resp. Alpha) difference, we use the Welch method. We use the F-test for the test of Risk (resp. TE). The two-sided p-value for the null hypothesis $R/R_1 = R/R_2$ for the two R/R (resp. IR) can be written as:

$$2\Phi(-\frac{|R/R_1 - R/R_2|}{SE}) \tag{3}$$

$$SE = \sqrt{\frac{1}{T}(2(1-\rho) + 1/2(R/R_1^2 + R/R_2^2 - R/R_1 R/R_2 \rho^2))} \tag{4}$$

where $\Phi(x)$ denotes the cumulative density function of standard normal distribution and ρ denotes the correlation coefficient between returns of two portfolios [21].

Table 2 shows the long and the long-short portfolio strategy performance of DNN, GB, RF, and RR in North America, Europe, Asia Pacific, and World. The highest IR and R/R are DNN in all regions and the world, and DNN generally outperforms other methods in terms of Alpha and Return. In terms of Risk, TE, and MaxDD, DNN tends to be smaller than other methods, especially all Risks are statistically significant at the 0.01 level.

We focus on the results by region, we can see that the performance deteriorates in the order of Asia Pacific, Europe, and North America regardless of the prediction model. In general, it is said that the stock market liquidity decreases in the order of North America, Europe, and Asia Pacific, and the market efficiency decreases as with the previous study [19]. This is a typical example that shows the higher the market efficiency, the more difficult to earn returns. We also divide the performance period into two for robustness checks. Table 3 shows the first-half results from January 2005 to December 2011 and Table 4 shows the second-half results from January 2012 to December 2018. In the first half, DNN is the highest IR and R/R in Europe and Asia Pacific, while in the second half it is North America and World. The performance order in the three regions showed a strong trend in the first half.

5   Interpretation of Prediction Model

In the previous section, we confirmed that DNN is generally superior to GB, RF, and RR, but deep learning has significant disadvantages such as a lack of transparency and limitations to the interpretability of the prediction. Then, we present the application of layer-wise relevance propagation (LRP) to decompose attributes of the predicted return and determine which factor contributes to prediction. We introduce LRP [4] in the next section.

5.1   Layer-Wise Relevance Propagation

LRP is an inverse method that calculates the contribution of the prediction made by the network. The overall idea of decomposition is explained in [4]. Suppose the network has L layers, each of which is treated as a vector with dimensionality $V(l)$, where l represents the index of layers. Then, according to the conservation principle, LRP aims to find a relevance score $R_{i,d}$ for each vector element in layer l such that the following equation holds:

$$Score_{i,T+2} = \sum_{d \in V(L)} R_{i,d}^{(L)} = ... = \sum_{d \in V(l)} R_{i,d}^{(l)} = ... = \sum_{d \in V(1)} R_{i,d}^{(1)} \qquad (5)$$

Table 2. Long and Long-Short portfolio strategy performance of DNN, GB, RF, and RR in North America, Europe, Asia Pacific, and World. The out-of-sample period is from January 2005 to December 2018. The bold numbers in the table represent the best values among the 4 patterns (DNN, GB, RF, and RR). Significant out-performance of one of the two portfolios between RR and the others (in terms of the Sharpe ratio) is denoted by asterisks: *** denotes significance at the 0.01 level; ** denotes significance at the 0.05 level; * denotes significance at the 0.1 level.

North America									
Long	DNN	GB	RF	RR	Long-Short	DNN	GB	RF	RR
Alpha [%]	**1.16**	1.14	0.29	0.55	Return [%]	**2.96**	2.92	2.26	2.27
TE [%]	4.28***	**4.24***	5.04*	5.72	Risk [%]	**9.01***	10.00*	11.46	11.30
IR	**0.27**	0.27	0.06	0.10	R/R	**0.33**	0.29	0.20	0.20
MaxDD [%]	−19.41	**−14.25**	−20.62	−27.10	MaxDD [%]	−34.05	**−30.87**	−38.73	−42.10
Europe									
Long	DNN	GB	RF	RR	Long-Short	DNN	GB	RF	RR
Alpha [%]	**2.96**	1.99	1.53	2.56	Return [%]	6.48	5.59	4.39	**6.83**
TE [%]	3.80***	4.34***	4.61*	5.20	Risk [%]	**9.26***	11.17	12.43	11.88
IR	**0.78***	0.46	0.33	0.49	R/R	**0.70**	0.50	0.35	0.57
MaxDD [%]	**−8.39**	−14.68	−15.60	−16.98	MaxDD [%]	**−23.38**	−33.45	−35.77	−35.05
Asia Pacific									
Long	DNN	GB	RF	RR	Long-Short	DNN	GB	RF	RR
Alpha [%]	**4.08**	3.75	2.64	2.94	Return [%]	7.80	**8.52**	6.82	6.63
TE [%]	3.94**	4.67	5.32	4.65	Risk [%]	**6.65***	8.14	9.21	8.77
IR	**1.04***	0.80	0.50	0.63	R/R	**1.17***	1.05*	0.74	0.76
MaxDD [%]	**−5.74**	−9.71	−13.14	−11.43	MaxDD [%]	**−10.97**	−15.81	−20.57	−20.49
World									
Long	DNN	GB	RF	RR	Long-Short	DNN	GB	RF	RR
Alpha [%]	3.84	3.28	3.53	**3.85**	Return [%]	**8.33**	7.71	6.15	7.79
TE [%]	**3.75***	3.93**	4.25	4.54	Risk [%]	**7.55***	10.16	11.87	10.41
IR	**1.02**	0.83	0.83	0.85	R/R	**1.10***	0.76	0.52	0.75
MaxDD [%]	−9.13	−9.07	**−7.21**	−11.41	MaxDD [%]	**−20.82**	−23.64	−34.41	−28.39

Table 3. Long and Long-Short portfolio strategy performance of DNN, GB, RF, and RR in North America, Europe, Asia Pacific, and World. The out-of-sample period is from January 2005 to December 2011.

North America									
Long	DNN	GB	RF	RR	Long-Short	DNN	GB	RFR	RR
Alpha [%]	−0.54	**0.59**	−0.56	−0.42	Return [%]	−0.67	**2.19**	1.06	0.20
TE [%]	5.51***	**5.18*****	6.51	7.50	Risk [%]	**11.21****	11.63**	13.75	13.98
IR	−0.10	**0.11**	−0.09	−0.06	R/R	−0.06	**0.19**	0.08	0.01
MaxDD [%]	−18.83	**−12.54**	−20.24	−27.10	MaxDD [%]	−33.46	**−29.40**	−38.73	−42.10
Europe									
Long	DNN	GB	RF	RR	Long-Short	DNN	GB	RFR	RR
Alpha [%]	**4.33**	2.30	1.54	3.82	Return [%]	9.39	7.18	4.90	**11.10**
TE [%]	**4.05*****	4.54*	4.36**	5.38	Risk [%]	**9.96****	11.60	11.96	12.05
IR	**1.07**	0.51	0.35	0.71	R/R	**0.94**	0.62	0.41	0.92
MaxDD [%]	**−8.39**	−14.68	−15.60	−16.98	MaxDD [%]	**−23.38**	−33.45	−35.77	−35.05
Asia Pacific									
Long	DNN	GB	RF	RR	Long-Short	DNN	GB	RF	RR
Alpha [%]	**7.71**	6.24	5.39	5.99	Return [%]	**15.09**	13.94	12.40	12.22
TE [%]	**4.36**	4.65	5.69	4.71	Risk [%]	**7.36***	8.13	8.97	8.61
IR	**1.77**	1.34	0.95	1.27	R/R	**2.05***	1.71	1.38	1.42
MaxDD [%]	**−5.74**	−9.71	−13.14	−10.02	MaxDD [%]	**−10.97**	−15.81	−20.06	−17.93
World									
Long	DNN	GB	RF	RR	Long-Short	DNN	GB	RF	RR
Alpha [%]	4.23	4.87	4.46	**5.10**	Return [%]	9.56	**11.50**	7.89	10.71
TE [%]	4.59	**4.27**	4.90	4.82	Risk [%]	**9.02**	10.03	11.74	10.23
IR	0.92	**1.14**	0.91	1.06	R/R	1.06	**1.15**	0.67	1.05
MaxDD [%]	−9.13	−9.07	**−6.82**	−11.41	MaxDD [%]	**−20.82**	−23.64	−34.41	−28.39

Table 4. Long and Long-Short portfolio strategy performance of DNN, GB, RF, and RR in North America, Europe, Asia Pacific, and World. The out-of-sample period is from January 2012 to December 2018.

North America									
Long	DNN	GB	RF	RR	Long-Short	DNN	GB	RF	RR
Alpha [%]	**2.88**	1.70	1.15	1.52	Return [%]	**6.72**	3.65	3.46	4.38
TE [%]	**2.44****	3.06	2.94	3.05	Risk [%]	**5.98*****	8.13	8.67	7.82
IR	**1.18***	0.56	0.39	0.50	R/R	**1.12****	0.45	0.40	0.56
MaxDD [%]	**−2.22**	−3.51	−6.30	−6.12	MaxDD [%]	**−7.71**	−15.20	−18.24	−13.24

(*continued*)

Table 4. (*continued*)

Europe									
Long	DNN	GB	RF	RR	Long-Short	DNN	GB	RF	RR
Alpha [%]	1.61	**1.69**	1.53	1.31	Return [%]	3.64	**4.01**	3.88	2.71
TE [%]	**3.52****	4.15**	4.88	5.02	Risk [%]	**8.48****	10.78	12.96	11.67
IR	**0.46**	0.41	0.31	0.26	R/R	**0.43**	0.37	0.30	0.23
MaxDD [%]	−6.71	**−4.65**	−5.47	−6.79	MaxDD [%]	**−9.30**	−14.17	−15.50	−14.98

Asia Pacific									
Long	DNN	GB	RF	RR	Long-Short	DNN	GB	RF	RR
Alpha [%]	0.57	**1.32**	−0.04	−0.03	Return [%]	0.97	**3.35**	1.52	1.31
TE [%]	**3.19****	4.62	4.84	4.47	Risk [%]	**5.22****	7.94	9.27	8.74
IR	0.18	**0.29**	−0.01	−0.01	R/R	0.19	**0.42**	0.16	0.15
MaxDD [%]	**−5.44**	−6.59	−10.60	−11.43	MaxDD [%]	**−7.97**	−15.26	−20.57	−20.49

World									
Long	DNN	GB	RF	RR	Long-Short	DNN	GB	RF	RR
Alpha [%]	**3.45**	1.71	2.61	2.61	Return [%]	**7.11**	4.05	4.43	4.95
TE [%]	**2.68****	3.52**	3.48**	4.25	Risk [%]	**5.76****	10.26	12.06	10.59
IR	**1.29**	0.49	0.75	0.61	R/R	**1.24****	0.39	0.37	0.47
MaxDD [%]	**−2.31**	−6.54	−6.42	−6.86	MaxDD [%]	**−6.13**	−16.66	−22.23	−14.06

As we can see in Eq. (5), LRP uses the prediction score as the sum of relevance scores for the last layer of the network, and maintains this sum throughout all layers.

Here, we use a shallow neural network with one hidden layer ($L = 3$) that has three input factors, $\mathbf{x}_{i,T+1} \in \mathbb{R}^3$, as a toy example shown in Fig. 2 to easily understand. The network has a total of six units assigned to numbers from one to six, $d \in \{1, 2, 3, 4, 5, 6\}$. In the case of applying Eq. (5) to this example, we have the following equation:

$$Score_{i,T+2} = R_{i,6}^{(3)} = R_{i,5}^{(2)} + R_{i,4}^{(2)} = R_{i,3}^{(1)} + R_{i,2}^{(1)} + R_{i,1}^{(1)} \tag{6}$$

Furthermore, the conservation principle also guarantees that the inflow of relevance scores to one neuron equals the outflow of relevance scores from the same neuron. w_{pq} are network weights between neuron p at layer l and neuron q at layer $l + 1$. $z_{i,p}$ are output values from activation functions. $z_{i,pq}^{(l,l+1)}$ is the message sent from neuron q at layer $l+1$ to neuron p at layer l. In addition, $R_{i,d}^{(l)}$ is computed using network weights according to the equation below:

$$R_{i,p}^{(l)} = \sum_q \frac{z_{i,pq}^{(l,l+1)}}{\sum_k z_{i,kq}^{(l,l+1)}} R_{i,q}^{(l+1)}, z_{i,pq}^{(l,l+1)} = w_{pq} z_{i,p}^{(l)} \tag{7}$$

Therefore, LRP is a technique for determining which features in a particular input vector contribute most strongly to a neural network output.

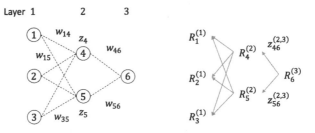

Fig. 2. LRP with toy example

5.2 LRP for Regional and Global Stock Markets

Here, we try to interpret the long-short portfolio based on the factor as of the August and September 2008. This is because we can see changes in model forecasts before and after the financial crisis.

Figures 3, 4, 5, and 6 shows which factor contributed to the prediction using LRP. The contribution of each factor calculated by LRP are the average of all stocks in the long-short portfolio. Before averaging, we normalized the contributions using z-score calculated by subtracting the mean and dividing them by the standard deviation in each stock. The contribution C_p^{DNN} is defined as follows:

$$C_p^{DNN} = \frac{1}{|L|} \sum_{i \in |L|} (z\text{-}score_p(R_{i,p}^{(1)})) - \frac{1}{|S|} \sum_{i \in |S|} (z\text{-}score_p(R_{i,p}^{(1)})) \qquad (8)$$

Here, $z\text{-}score_p$ calculates z-score. $|L|$ and $|S|$ denotes the number of stocks in the long and short portfolio. In all models, EPS Revision (1 month) contributes the most in September 2008. This is because EPS is a factor that contains the analyst's expectation of profit in the next fiscal year.

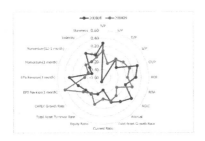

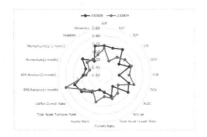

Fig. 3. LRP as of August and September 2008 in North America.

Fig. 4. LRP as of August and September 2008 in Europe.

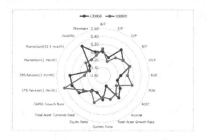

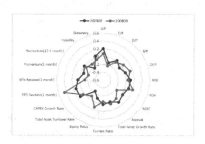

Fig. 5. LRP as of August and September 2008 in Asia Pacific.

Fig. 6. LRP as of August and September 2008 in World.

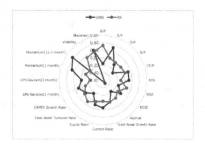

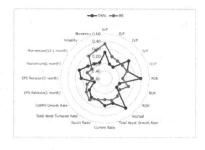

Fig. 7. The change in contributions between August and September 2008 in North America.

Fig. 8. The change in contributions between August and September 2008 in Europe.

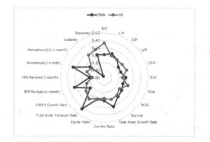

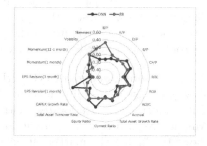

Fig. 9. The change in contributions between August and September 2008 in Asia Pacific.

Fig. 10. The change in contributions between August and September 2008 in World.

We also decompose which factors contributed to the predicted return of the RR models for comparing the change in contribution with the DNN models. The RR models are easier to decompose the predicted return to each factor than RF and GB models. The contribution C_p^{RR} is defined as follows:

$$C_p^{RR} = \frac{1}{|L|} \sum_{i \in |L|} (z\text{-}score_p(\beta_p x_{i,p})) - \frac{1}{|S|} \sum_{i \in |S|} (z\text{-}score_p(\beta_p x_{i,p})) \qquad (9)$$

Here, β_p denotes the regression coefficient of the factor and $x_{i,p}$ is the input factor. Figures 7, 8, 9, and 10 show the results of changes in the contribution of the DNN and RR models between August and September 2008. We confirm that the change is smaller than that of the DNN models. We can see that deep learning is flexibly changing positions after the financial crisis. We observe that the contribution of volatility declines significantly in North America and Asia Pacific in September 2008. This shows that each DNN model has become risk-averse by the market crash. On the other hand, the magnitude of change in Europe and World is smaller than other regions and the contribution of volatility is already low in August 2008. The financial crisis in 2008 was triggered by a major European financial institution in 2007 and spread to North America and the Asia Pacific.

Although these results are not so surprising, at least this study supports a well-known empirical fact that volatility plays a great role in financial markets. On the other hand, we need to deeply investigate why the other models performed worse as a future research.

6   Conclusion

In this paper, we implement deep learning to predict stock returns in the cross-section in regional and global stock markets and perform the empirical experiment.

Although deep learning performs quite well, it has significant disadvantages such as a lack of transparency and limitations to the interpretability of the prediction. Then, we present the application of layer-wise relevance propagation (LRP) to decompose attributes of the predicted return and we determine which factor contributes to prediction. Our conclusions are as follows:

- DNN is generally superior to GB, RF, and RR in all regions, so deep learning shows promise as a skillful machine learning method in global markets.
- The performance deteriorates in the order of Asia Pacific, Europe, North America regardless of the prediction model. This is a typical example that shows the higher the market efficiency, the more difficult to earn returns.
- We show which factor contributes to prediction using LRP before and after the financial crisis in 2008. This method is one of the solutions for the interpretation of the deep learning model which is a black box.

For future works, further experiments would be required to perform a statistical test to tell the difference between the DNN model and other nonlinear methods. We also analyze the cases of other forecast periods such as 1 week, 3 months, 6 months, and 1 year and compare the results among them to confirm the robustness of our results.

References

1. Abadi, M., et al.: TensorFlow: a system for large-scale machine learning. In: 12th {USENIX} Symposium on Operating Systems Design and Implementation ({OSDI} 16), pp. 265–283 (2016)
2. Abe, M., Nakayama, H.: Deep learning for forecasting stock returns in the cross-section. In: Phung, D., Tseng, V.S., Webb, G.I., Ho, B., Ganji, M., Rashidi, L. (eds.) PAKDD 2018. LNCS (LNAI), vol. 10937, pp. 273–284. Springer, Cham (2018). https://doi.org/10.1007/978-3-319-93034-3_22
3. Anava, O., Levy, K.: k*-nearest neighbors: from global to local. In: Advances in Neural Information Processing Systems, pp. 4916–4924 (2016)
4. Bach, S., Binder, A., Montavon, G., Klauschen, F., Müller, K.R., Samek, W.: On pixel-wise explanations for non-linear classifier decisions by layer-wise relevance propagation. PloS one **10**(7), e0130140 (2015)
5. Bahrammirzaee, A.: A comparative survey of artificial intelligence applications in finance: artificial neural networks, expert system and hybrid intelligent systems. Neural Comput. Appl. **19**(8), 1165–1195 (2010). https://doi.org/10.1007/s00521-010-0362-z
6. Bollerslev, T.: Generalized autoregressive conditional heteroskedasticity. J. Econom. **31**(3), 307–327 (1986)
7. Cavalcante, R.C., Brasileiro, R.C., Souza, V.L., Nobrega, J.P., Oliveira, A.L.: Computational intelligence and financial markets: a survey and future directions. Expert Syst. Appl. **55**, 194–211 (2016)
8. Chen, J.: SVM application of financial time series forecasting using empirical technical indicators. In: 2010 International Conference on Information, Networking and Automation (ICINA), vol. 1, pp. V1–77. IEEE (2010)
9. Chen, T., Guestrin, C.: XGBoost: a scalable tree boosting system. In: Proceedings of the 22nd ACM SIGKDD International Conference on Knowledge Discovery and Data Mining, pp. 785–794. ACM (2016)
10. Cortes, C., Vapnik, V.: Support-vector networks. Mach. Learn. **20**(3), 273–297 (1995). https://doi.org/10.1007/BF00994018
11. Cover, T.M., Hart, P., et al.: Nearest neighbor pattern classification. IEEE Trans. Inf. Theory **13**(1), 21–27 (1967)
12. Engle, R.F., Ledoit, O., Wolf, M.: Large dynamic covariance matrices. J. Bus. Econ. Stat. **37**(2), 363–375 (2019)
13. Fama, E.F., French, K.R.: The cross-section of expected stock returns. J. Finance **47**(2), 427–465 (1992)
14. Fama, E.F., French, K.R.: Common risk factors in the returns on stocks and bonds. J. Financ. Econ. **33**(1), 3–56 (1993)
15. Hamilton, J.D.: Time Series Analysis, vol. 2. Princeton University Press, Princeton (1994)
16. Harvey, C.R., Liu, Y., Zhu, H.:...and the cross-section of expected returns. Rev. Financ. Stud. **29**(1), 5–68 (2016)

17. Ioffe, S., Szegedy, C.: Batch normalization: accelerating deep network training by reducing internal covariate shift. arXiv preprint arXiv:1502.03167 (2015)
18. Kingma, D.P., Ba, J.: Adam: a method for stochastic optimization. arXiv preprint arXiv:1412.6980 (2014)
19. Kristoufek, L., Vosvrda, M.: Measuring capital market efficiency: global and local correlations structure. Physica A **392**(1), 184–193 (2013)
20. Levin, A.E.: Stock selection via nonlinear multi-factor models. In: Advances in Neural Information Processing Systems, pp. 966–972 (1996)
21. Memmel, C.: Performance hypothesis testing with the Sharpe ratio. Financ. Lett. **1**(1), 21–23 (2003)
22. Nakagawa, K., Imamura, M., Yoshida, K.: Risk-based portfolios with large dynamic covariance matrices. Int. J. Financ. Stud. **6**(2), 52 (2018)
23. Nakagawa, K., Imamura, M., Yoshida, K.: Stock price prediction with fluctuation patterns using indexing dynamic time warping and k^*-nearest neighbors. In: Arai, S., Kojima, K., Mineshima, K., Bekki, D., Satoh, K., Ohta, Y. (eds.) JSAI-isAI 2017. LNCS (LNAI), vol. 10838, pp. 97–111. Springer, Cham (2018). https://doi.org/10.1007/978-3-319-93794-6_7
24. Nakagawa, K., Imamura, M., Yoshida, K.: Stock price prediction using k-medoids clustering with indexing dynamic time warping. Electron. Commun. Jpn **102**(2), 3–8 (2019)
25. Nakagawa, K., Ito, T., Abe, M., Izumi, K.: Deep recurrent factor model: interpretable non-linear and time-varying multi-factor model. arXiv preprint arXiv:1901.11493 (2019)
26. Nakagawa, K., Uchida, T., Aoshima, T.: Deep factor model. In: Alzate, C., et al. (eds.) MIDAS/PAP -2018. LNCS (LNAI), vol. 11054, pp. 37–50. Springer, Cham (2019). https://doi.org/10.1007/978-3-030-13463-1_3
27. Pedregosa, F., et al.: Scikit-learn: machine learning in Python. J. Mach. Learn. Res. **12**(Oct), 2825–2830 (2011)
28. Rumelhart, D.E., Hinton, G.E., Williams, R.J., et al.: Learning representations by back-propagating errors. Cogn. Model. **5**(3), 1 (1988)
29. Vanstone, B., Finnie, G., Hahn, T.: Creating trading systems with fundamental variables and neural networks: the Aby case study. Math. Comput. Simul. **86**, 78–91 (2012)
30. Zoonekynd, V., LeBinh, K., Lau, A., Sambatur, H.: Machine learning in finance. In: Deutsche Bank Markets Research Report (2016). http://www.fullertreacymoney.com/system/data/files/PDFs/2017/October/20th/(Deutsche)%20Machine%20Learning%20in%20Finance.pdf

News Articles Evaluation Analysis in Automotive Industry Using GPT-2 and Co-occurrence Network

Yoshihiro Nishi[(✉)], Aiko Suge, and Hiroshi Takahashi

Graduate School of Business Administration, Keio University, Hiyoshi 4-1-1,
Kohoku-Ku, Yokohama-shi, Kanagawa-ken, Japan
nishi_yoshihiro@keio.jp

Abstract. News articles have great impacts on asset prices in the financial markets. Many attempts have been reported to ascertain how news influences stock prices. Stock price fluctuations of highly influential companies can have a major impact on the economy as a whole. In particular, the automobile industry is a colossal industry that leads the Japanese industry. However, the limitations in the number of available data sets usually become the hurdle for the model accuracy. In this study, we constructed a news evaluation model utilizing GPT-2. A news evaluation model is a model that evaluates news articles distributed to financial markets based on price fluctuation rates and predicts fluctuations in stock prices. We have added news articles generated by GPT-2 as data for analysis. Besides, we used a co-occurrence network analysis to review the overview of the news articles. News articles were classified through Long Short-Term Memory (LSTM). The results showed that the accuracy of the news evaluation model improved by generating news articles using a language generation model through GPT-2. More detailed analyses are planned for the future.

Keywords: Language generation · GPT-2 · Financial markets · Co-occurrence network · LSTM · Deep learning

1 Introduction

News articles are essential information about asset prices. News articles contain fundamental information and sentiment information. The content of news articles can be quantified to clarify the relationship between investor behavior and the stock market [2, 4, 5, 17, 18]. In the Japanese industry segment, automobiles are one of the major industries. Japan's automotive industry has high international competitiveness and accounts for about 50% of Japan's trade surplus [9]. Stock price fluctuations of major companies in the automobile industry may affect the entire Japanese economy. Attempts to analyze stock price fluctuations from news information have been made so far. However, the number and quality of news are limited because the analysis is based on actual events.

The limitations on the quality and number of news data may be solved by language generation technology. With the development of information technology, there is a growing interest in efforts to utilize various information in the financial field.

© Springer Nature Switzerland AG 2020
M. Sakamoto et al. (Eds.): JSAI-isAI 2019, LNAI 12331, pp. 103–114, 2020.
https://doi.org/10.1007/978-3-030-58790-1_7

Also, stock price fluctuations of major companies can sometimes have a significant impact on the economy as a whole. By using a language generation model that has learned a certain amount, it is possible to increase news data. Currently, several information technologies can generate news articles with high readability, as if it were historical, considering the context [14, 15].

The purpose of this study is to increase the data used for analysis by generating news articles and improve the accuracy of news evaluation. By creating a more accurate model, it is possible to accurately determine whether the news has a positive or negative effect on the stock price when the news articles are released in the market.

In this study, the analysis targets three major companies in the Japanese automobile industry. The analysis was conducted using Reuters News from 2014 to 2016 published on the stock market. As a result of generating news articles, adding it to the data set, and analyzing it, the accuracy of the analysis improved. The results of this study suggest that it is useful to use a language generation model as one of the methods for improving the accuracy of the model.

2   Related Work

The news distributed on the stock market has a great impact on stock prices. There have been many studies on the impact of news on stock prices. News articles contain fundamental information and sentiment information, suggesting that the information may be reflected in the price [2, 17, 18]. Several studies have analyzed the impact of news on stock prices using machine learning. News articles were categorized by naive Bayes classifiers and analyzed for relationships with stock prices [7]. Classification analysis using SVM was reported [4, 10, 16]. However, the limitations in the number of available data sets usually become the hurdle for the model accuracy. The number of data is a significant factor in improving the accuracy of these models. News used for analysis is document data, and in recent years there is a language generation model that generates documents.

Studies on document generation technology are actively conducted in the field of natural language processing [3]. There are studies on the generation of responses to questions and the generation of responses to utterances [1, 19]. Document generation technology has progressed year by year, and attempts have been made to generate a document as if a real person had written.

The purpose of this research is to generate high-precision news articles using the latest language generation model, GPT-2, and to increase the amount of data to improve the analysis accuracy of the news evaluation model. The comparative evaluation was performed by classification analysis using Long Short-Term Memory (LSTM) [8], which is a deep learning model.

3 Data

This study analyzes the Japanese automobile industry. The top three companies with the highest market capitalization (Toyota Motor Corporation, Honda Motor Co., Ltd., Nissan Motor Co., Ltd.) were defined as the main companies to be analyzed. This chapter describes market data and news data used for analysis.

3.1 Market Data

The acquired data includes information such as the transaction settlement price and the trading amount of each stock. High-frequency transaction data is large-scale data with a timestamp in microseconds. For the market data, a total of $1, 409, 901, 961$ tick data of the Japanese stock market from 2014 to 2016 is used. In this study, only the market data of three target companies (Toyota Motor Corporation, Honda Motor Co., Ltd., Nissan Motor Co., Ltd.) was acquired and analyzed.

3.2 News Data

The news data covers the headlines of news articles provided by Thomson Reuters. The text information of the distributed news data includes a headline and a text, and the headline is text data that summarizes essential contents in the text. Each news data has a timestamp of the date and time of distribution.

In this study, we acquired news articles of three target companies (Toyota Motor Corporation, Honda Motor Co., Ltd., Nissan Motor Co., Ltd.) for three years, from 2014 to 2016. Much of the news about the automotive industry is about market strategy and technology development. During the period, the Japanese automotive industry was focused on global expansion strategies and technological innovation [9]. Many strategies have been adopted that focus not only on the mature market in Japan but also on the global market, mainly in emerging countries. Besides, attention was paid to efforts aimed at improving the competitiveness of the entire Japanese automobile industry by cooperating in the cooperative area of each company. It can be said that in the financial market, news articles distribution related to such a series of activities was often performed.

Table 1 summarizes the number of news articles for each company. In this study, we used 2,259 English headlines that were traded for one minute before and after the news was distributed.

Table 1. The number of news data for each company

	Number of news articles
Toyota Motor Corporation	1,065
Honda Motor Co., Ltd.	587
Nissan Motor Co., Ltd.	607

4 Analysis Method

4.1 Co-occurrence Network Analysis of News Articles

Co-occurrence network analysis uses extracted edges to connect words with similar occurrence patterns [6]. News articles distributed in the financial markets are timely and include the main topics of companies during the period. We used a co-occurrence network to get information about topics in the news articles that were distributed.

We extracted vocabularies contained in articles distributed more than 50 times during the analysis period and calculated the co-occurrence relationship of each vocabulary using Jaccard coefficients. As for grouping, each vocabulary strongly connected was automatically detected and colored by modularity [11].

4.2 Overview of Analysis Using GPT-2

This section describes how to improve the accuracy of classification by generating news articles and increasing text data. The main procedure of the analysis method was shown in Fig. 1. In this study, we created news articles through GPT-2 using the acquired news headline. The data used news data and market data. For the market data, tick data (High-frequency transaction data) of the Japanese stock market from 2014 to 2016 used. For news data, we used Reuters news from 2014 to 2016. We vectorized news articles and performed classification analysis through LSTM.

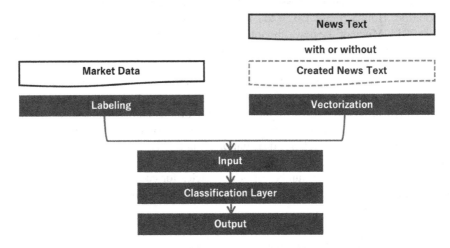

Fig. 1. Main procedure diagram of analysis in this study. Created news articles were generated based on the labeled news data and vectorized. After that, classification analysis is performed through LSTM and the analysis accuracy is calculated.

4.3   Labeling Based on Price Fluctuations

The news label (Positive or Negative) was made by the stock price fluctuation rates α [13]. In this study, binary classification performed. The formula for calculating the stock price fluctuation rate using news data and market data is (1). $\alpha > 0\%$ indicates the positive news article, and $\alpha < 0\%$ means the negative news article. The average stock price before or after news distribution was calculated, and the changing ratio gave α. We used market data to calculate stock price volatility and labeled the news articles.

$$
\begin{aligned}
Stock\ price\ &fluctuation\ rate\ (\%) \\
&= ((Average\ price\ 1\ min\ after\ news\ distribution) \\
&\quad - (Average\ price\ 1\ min\ before\ news\ distribution)) \\
&\quad / (Average\ price\ 1\ min\ before\ news\ distribution) \times 100
\end{aligned} \tag{1}
$$

Positive : $\alpha > 0\%$

Negative : $\alpha < 0\%$

4.4   News Articles Generation

In this study, we generated news articles based on labeled news data. The top five positive news and negative news with the highest rate of change in each year from 2014 to 2016 was used for sentence generation. The generated news articles were given the same label as the pre-generated news data and added to the data set [12]. GPT-2 was used for text generation. GPT-2 is a large-scale language generation model created by OpenAI, and has learned about 40 GB of text data in advance [14, 15].

Language Generation through GPT-2. In this study, GPT-2 is used as a language generation model. We used a model with 117 million parameters, which is a model of GPT-2 that is currently available. The GPT-2 model used is pre-trained based on 40 GB of text data. GPT-2 is a significant scale-up of GPT. The model used uses 8 billion parameters to train a dataset of 8 million web pages (40 GB) on a 48-tier network [15]. OpenAI reports in [14] that it has been able to learn the Transformer-based language model in advance and perform transfer learning for tasks such as sentence relationships, sentence similarity, and question answering, and update SOTA.

There is a limit to the number of news articles published in financial markets. Market data is also needed to determine how news articles affect stock prices. In principle, analysis cannot be performed on the impact of news on stock prices using only one of these data. Collecting data is time-consuming. An analysis using deep learning, it is said that the accuracy of analysis increases as the amount of data used for analysis increases. By generating sentences using the news data with labels, the number of news articles used for analysis can increase.

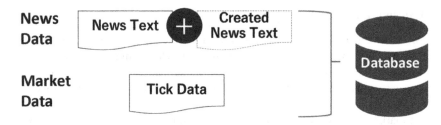

Fig. 2. Model 2 database diagram. In addition to the original news data, created news articles data were added.

Figure 2 shows the data stored in the database used in this study. In addition to news articles published in the real world, and stock price data (Tick data) traded in the real world, news articles (Created news text) generated by GPT-2 were stored. When the original news data sentence is entered, it will output a highly relevant sentence as a continuation sentence based on the input sentence. Figure 2 shows the data stored in the database used in this study. In addition to news articles published in the real world, and stock price data (Tick data) traded in the real world, news articles (Created news text) generated by GPT-2 were stored. When the original news data sentence is entered, it will output a highly relevant sentence as a continuation sentence based on the input sentence.

If the texts are generated, and the amount of data is increased, thereby improving the accuracy of classification, the generated text data can be used for analysis. Although it is difficult to replace the original news data entirely, the created news data can be used supplementary when the amount of data is insufficient. The cost of analysis is reduced, and analysis can be performed more quickly. When the investigation is conducted on an industry or company basis, there is a case where there is not enough news data, and the analysis cannot be performed smoothly. Using this method will counter the above problem.

4.5   Vectorization of News Data and Classification Through the LSTM Model

LSTM is a kind of RNN that learns time series data. LSTM extends RNN to enable long-term learning of dependencies [8]. News texts were converted with each index and embedded in 32 dimensions. LSTM layers were used for the classification model. The data set was divided into training data and test data using scikit-learn. 10% of the data set was used as test data.

A model with only original news data added to the data set is Model 1, and a model with created news articles added to the original news data is Model 2, and classification analysis is performed through LSTM. Classification accuracy was examined.

5   Results

As a result of the experiment, the accuracy of the model using created news articles slightly improved. In this study, we used Model 1 that used only the original news data and Model 2 that contained created news articles and compared the accuracy of the classification analysis of these two models.

5.1   Co-occurrence Network Analysis of News Articles

Figure 3 shows the co-occurrence network of news articles on Toyota Motor Corporation, Honda Motor Co., Ltd. and Nissan Motor Co., Ltd. from 2014 to 2016 used in the analysis. The color of the circle indicates the group containing each vocabulary. Each connected vocabulary was detected and colored by modularity. The size of the circle indicates the number of occurrences of each vocabulary. The dotted line indicates the co-occurrence relationship between groups, and the solid line indicates the co-occurrence relationship within the group. The Jaccard coefficient calculated the co-occurrence relation of each vocabulary, and the Jaccard coefficient displayed on the line. The higher the Jacquard coefficient, the stronger the co-occurrence relationship. In the acquired news articles, "NIKKEI" was a vocabulary mainly meaning the Nikkei Stock Average. A look at the co-occurrence shows that both good news and bad news for the market distributed. Also, Takata's airbag recall issue was frequently distributed during the analysis period from 2014 to 2016, indicating that Honda Motor Co., Ltd. and Toyota Motor Corporation were mainly involved in the recall issue.

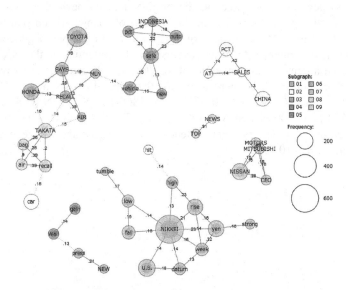

Fig. 3. News articles co-occurrence network diagram

5.2   Labeling Based on Stock Volatility

The news data was labeled using the formula of (1). The breakdown of the data set is shown in Table 2. The breakdown of positive and negative news in the dataset is shown in Table 2.

Table 2 shows positive and negative news from Toyota Motor Corporation as examples of labeling results. The news articles about "TOYOTA TO START SELLING NX COMPACT CROSSOVER SUV IN U.S. IN NOV, AIMS TO SELL 42,000 NX SUVS ANNUALLY IN U.S.-EXEC" has a positive effect on stock prices, the news articles about "TOYOTA MOTOR SAYS NO TRUTH TO REPORT ABOUT TIE-UP TALKS WITH SUZUKI MOTOR" has a negative effect on stock prices.

Table 2. Labeling of the original news articles

	Number of news articles	News article example
Positive	1,137	TOYOTA TO START SELLING NX COMPACT CROSSOVER SUV IN U.S. IN NOV, AIMS TO SELL 42,000 NX SUVS ANNUALLY IN U.S. -EXEC
Negative	1,122	TOYOTA MOTOR SAYS NO TRUTH TO REPORT ABOUT TIE-UP TALKS WITH SUZUKI MOTOR

5.3   News Articles Generation

We generated news articles based on the original labeled news data. The top five positive news and negative news with the highest rate of change in each year from 2014 to 2016 was used for sentence generation. Figure 4 is an example of generated news articles. The news sentence, "We are excited by the potential of the NX compact crossover as an alternative to conventional SUVs. The NX compact crossover allows for the introduction of… " was generated from the original news sentence "TOYOTA TO START SELLING NX COMPACT CROSSOVER SUV IN U.S. IN NOV, AIMS TO SELL 42,000 NX SUVS ANNUALLY IN U.S.-EXEC" distributed from Reuters News in 2014. The original sentence has 22 words, and the generated news article sentence has 410 words.

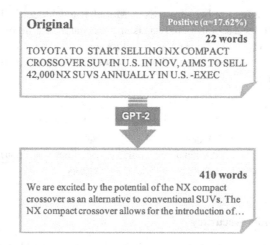

Fig. 4. Example of generated news articles. In this example, the created news article is generated based on positive news about Toyota Motor Corporation.

Created news articles generated based on positive news is assigned a positive label and produced based on negative news is assigned a negative label. The generated news articles were added to the Model 2 data set. Table 3 shows the breakdown of the created news articles. The same number of news articles were generated for each company.

Table 3. The number of news articles generated

	TOYOTA	HONDA	NISSAN
Positive	15	15	15
Negative	15	15	15

Table 4 is a breakdown of news data for Model 1 and Model 2. In Model 2, the number of data increases by the number of news articles generated. The ratio of positive news and negative news is about 50% each.

Table 4. Data set

	Model 1 (Original news only)	Created news articles#	Model 2 (Created news addition)
Positive	1,137	45	1,182
Negative	1,122	45	1,167

Table 5 compares the number of words in Model 1 and Model 2. The total number of parameters for Model 2 used for analysis is approximately 1.5 times the total number of parameters for Model 1. The model architecture used for the analysis is the same for Model 1 and Model 2. It can be seen that the amount of data used for the analysis of Model 2 is increasing.

Table 5. Model 1 and Model 2 total params

	Model 1 (Original news only)	Model 2 (Created news addition)
Total params	949,121	1,433,985

5.4   Result of Model Accuracy

Binary classification of news data was performed through LSTM. For both Model 1 and Model 2, the test data ratio is set to 10%. Table 6 is a breakdown of train data and test data of Model 1 and Model 2.

Table 6. The number of train data and test data

	Model 1 (Original news only)	Model 2 (Created news addition)
Train data	2,033	2,114
Test data	226	235

Table 7 shows the result of binary classification through LSTM. The accuracy of Model 2 using created news articles is improved compared to Model 1 using only original news data.

Table 7. Results of the LSTM model

	Model 1 (Original news only)	Model 2 (Created news addition)
Accuracy score	0.5176	0.5489

For additional verification, we randomly removed 45 positive original news and 45 negative original news from the Model 2 dataset. The number of data used in the analysis is 2,259, which is the same as Model 1. The total parameters for Model 2 were 1,427,329. The test data ratio is the same as 10%. Table 8 shows the result of binary classification through LSTM. As with Table 7, the accuracy of model 2 using created news articles is improved compared to model 1 using only the original news data.

Table 8. Results of additional validation LSTM model

	Model 1 (Original news only)	Model 2 (Created news addition)
Accuracy score	0.5176	0.5354

6 Conclusion

From this study, the accuracy of the news evaluation model improved by generating news articles using a language generation model through GPT-2. Besides, using the co-occurrence network, we were able to gain information on the topics of the news articles retrieved. The significance of this study is that a more precise news valuation model contributes to improved asset price valuation. When analyzing based on actual events, the number of data is limited. If the number of news data is limited, it may be possible to generate news articles and use them for analysis to improve accuracy.

When analyzing news articles that target multiple companies, there are several things to consider. For example, the news that Toyota Motor Corporation is doing well can be negative news for Honda Motor Co., Ltd. To further improve the accuracy of the analysis, it is necessary to analyze only a single company or consider other measures. Besides, it is necessary to consider stock price fluctuation factors from a macro perspective, such as foreign exchange, economic trends, investor market sentiment, etc. In this study, we confirmed the basic performance of the news evaluation model using data from 2014 to 2016. More detailed analyses are planned for the future.

References

1. Aishwarya, A., et al.: Visual question answering. In: Proceedings of the International Conference on Computer Vision (2015)
2. David, M.C., James, M.P., Lawrence, H.S.: What moves stock prices? J. Portfolio Manag. Spring **15**(3), 4–12 (1989)
3. Reiter, E., Robert, D.: Building Natural Language Generation Systems. Cambridge University Press, Cambridge (2000)
4. Fung, G.P.C., Yu, J.X., Lam, W.: News sensitive stock trend prediction. In: Chen, M.-S., Yu, P.S., Liu, B. (eds.) PAKDD 2002. LNCS (LNAI), vol. 2336, pp. 481–493. Springer, Heidelberg (2002). https://doi.org/10.1007/3-540-47887-6_48
5. Fung, G.P.C., Yu, J.X., Lam, W.: Stock prediction: integrating text mining approach using real-time news. In: Proceedings of the IEEE International Conference on Computational Intelligence for Financial Engineering, pp. 395–402 (2003)
6. Fruchterman, T., Reingold, E.M.: Graph drawing by force-directed. replacement. Softw. Pract. Exp. **21**, 1129–1164 (1991)
7. Gidófalvi, G.: using news articles to predict stock price movements. Department of Computer Science and Engineering, Technical report, University of California (2001)
8. Hochreiter, S., Schmidhuber, J.: Long short-term memory. Neural Comput. **9**(8), 1735–1780 (1997)
9. Ministry Economy, Trade and Industry.: 2014 Automobile Industry Strategy. METI working paper (2014) (in Japanese)

10. Mittermayer, M.A.: Forecasting intraday stock price trends with text mining techniques. In: Proceedings of the 37th Hawaii International Conference on System Sciences (2004)
11. Newman, M.E.: Modularity and community structure in networks. Proc. Natl. Acad. Sci. **103** (23), 8577–8582 (2006)
12. Nishi Y., Suge A., Takahashi H.: Text analysis on the stock market in the automotive industry through fake news generated by GPT-2. In: Proceedings of the International Workshop Artificial Intelligence of and for Business associated with JSAI International Symposia on AI 2019 (2019)
13. Takayama, L., Suge, A., Takahashi, H.: LSTM model for explaining the association between news data and stock price fluctuations. In: Proceedings of the 11th JSAI Special Interest Group on Business Informatics (2018)
14. Radford, A., Narasimhan, K., Salimans, T., and Sutskever, I.: Improving Language Understanding by Generative Pre-Training. Technical report, OpenAI (2018)
15. Radford, A., Wu, J., Child, R., Luan, D., Amodei, D., and Sutskever, I.: Language Models are Unsupervised Multitask Learners. Technical report OpenAI (2019)
16. Schumaker, R.P., Chen, H.: Textual analysis of stock market prediction using breaking financial news. Proc. ACM Trans. Inf. Syst. **27**, 1–19 (2009)
17. Tetlock, P.C.: Giving content to investor sentiment: the role of media in the stock market. J. Financ. **62**, 1139–1168 (2007)
18. Tetlock, P.C., Saar-Tsechansky, M., Macskassy, S.: More than words: quantifying language to measure firms' fundamentals. J. Financ. **63**(3), 1437–1467 (2008)
19. Zhang, R., Guo, J., Fan, Y., Lan, Y., Xu, J., Cheng, X.: Learning to control the specificity in neural response generation. In: Proceedings of the 56th Annual Meeting of the Association for Computational Linguistics, vol 1, pp. 1108–1117 (2018)

Research on the Usefulness of Start-Up Supports

Hirotaka Yanada[✉] and Setsuya Kurahashi[✉]

Graduate School of Business Sciences, University of Tsukuba, Tsukuba, Japan
hiroyana10@gmail.com,
kurahashi.setsuya.gf@u.tsukuba.ac.jp

Abstract. The purpose of this study is to investigate relationships between performances of start-ups and external supports to them. For the analysis, we used a questionnaire survey with responses from 2,897 start-ups (as of the 1st survey). As the analysis means, we adopted propensity score matching, which is one of the causal inference methods. First, after categorizing external supports and performances, and examining the effect of each support, only consulting information support was found to contribute to some performance improvement. Next, when we examined some external supports in combination with other supports, new causal effects such as significant growth in sales were confirmed by combining non-public and public funding supports. These results suggest the potential for contributing to the performances by the proper combination of these supports, considering the characteristics of each type of external support.

Keywords: Start-up company · External support · Variable structuring · Forward-backward stepwise selection method · Propensity score matching

1 Introduction

With the rapid advances in information technology, startups have increased in recent years, as represented by the so-called "fintech" that integrates finance and IT. A number of start-ups with innovative technologies and ideas have also grown remarkably in Japan as leaders in innovation. In addition, various external support activities for start-up companies have also received considerable attention. While there are many factors associated with improving a company's performance, external support is still one of the most important factors for startups as well as other long-standing companies. Researchers have reported a lot about start-up companies, studying the relevance between their characteristics and business performance. To the best of our knowledge, however, little attention has been given to the relevance between external support received by such start-up companies and their business performance as a performance enhancement factor. Recently in Japan, venture capital (VC) firms have provided start-up companies with generous support other than financial support. Such efforts aim, for example, to offer a right business environment for start-up companies assisting them in recruiting and providing them with offices so that start-up companies can concentrate on their business cultivation. There have been reported many attempts to support the

© Springer Nature Switzerland AG 2020
M. Sakamoto et al. (Eds.): JSAI-isAI 2019, LNAI 12331, pp. 115–127, 2020.
https://doi.org/10.1007/978-3-030-58790-1_8

growth of start-up companies (hereinafter, "start-ups") in order to increase their corporate value by getting their business on track.

2 Purpose of This Study

In this research, we analyze the relevance between external support and corporate performance using individual data collected by a panel survey. We take advantage of the benefit in covariate (cofounder) adjustments using propensity scores developed by Rosenbaum [1]. A total of nine indexes based on four categories are set as treatment variables for external support, and a total of four indexes are set as observational variables for performance. A propensity score is defined as a predictive probability for treatment variables where an observed covariate is conditioned. This approach adjusts cofounders by integrating several covariates into one variable. Many researchers agree that this approach is currently the most effective method in the field of observational study for approximating the observational study findings to the findings of the study based on random assignment experiments (Guo [2]; Hoshino et al. [3]).

Figure 1 shows the theoretical model based on these conditions mentioned above. The purpose of this research is, first of all, to estimate the causal effects (a total of 36 = 4 * 9) of external support based on nine indexes on performance enhancement in each of the four indexes using the above-mentioned individual data collected from start-up owners through a panel survey. Based on the results, it is also estimated whether there is a causal effect by combining some kinds of external supports.

3 Related Work

Growth is one of the representative indicators that symbolize a start-up's performance. There is a lot of research in the field of industrial organization theory and entrepreneurs regarding growth factors of companies. Based on a survey of enormous previous research, Storey [4] presented three frameworks "management resources," "company characteristics," and "management strategy" as growth factors for small and medium.

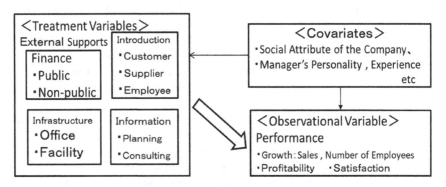

Fig. 1. A theoretical model of performance improvement of Start-ups.

This figure shows the theoretical model based on these conditions. Three factors including treatment variables (external supports), covariate (demography, personality, experience) and performance (observational variables) are related to performance improvement of start-ups.

enterprises. Among "management strategy" in particular, he focused on the four function "management training", "introduction of external shareholders", "planning" and "management staff procurement."

Lerner [5] dealt with the effect of the support policy in empirical research on the growth factors of enterprises. He analyzed the effect of US small business support policy "SBIR program" revealed that companies receiving government subsidies grew faster than other companies. However, this research is targeted not only to start-ups but also to SMEs as a whole.

In the research targeting Japan, Kutsuna [6] conducted a questionnaire survey targeting founded enterprises in Osaka City. It showed almost the same analysis result as Storey [4] mentioned above. In addition, Ejima [7] found the contribution of so-called entrepreneurial orientation (EO) to the growth (employment and sales) (Key et al. [8] and Madsen [9]). On the other hand, he noted that the policy support from the government and universities does not necessarily have the same effect depending on the specific policy measures and conditions. Also, he only pointed out the possibility of a mutually complementary relationship with a company's strategic attitude and organizational management factors. Furthermore, Okamuro et al. [10] revealed that there is a high possibility that companies that intend to expand the scale of business or companies that gained public subsidies at the start of the business will expand employment after that.

On the other hand, there are many studies that focus on relationships between managers and the surroundings as a factor for the success of start-ups. These studies show that the social capital of managers is as important as human capital for the success of start-up's. Human capital refers to the manager's abilities, education, and past experience, and is a unique quality of the manager. Social capital, on the other hand, refers to resources (information, knowledge, etc.) obtained through interaction with friends and acquaintances of managers, separately from human capital. Matsuda et al. [11] asked managers before and after starting their business about their consultants and their content, and presented analysis results supporting the above-mentioned views. More specifically, they report that successful managers are more likely than unsuccessful managers to receive consultation with an entrepreneur who has extensive networking and rich experiences, such as receiving introductions of excellent employees and business partners. Kazumi [12] defines a personal network, such as a network of managers, collaboration with people outside the company, or the selection of management teams, as a social network. In empirical research targeting managers, the top three networks used after starting business were "industry managers," "other industry managers," and "specialized human resources." In addition, "benefits from the network" were the most common, "support, advice and participation in management", followed by "introduction of business partners", etc., and showed analysis results consistent with the aforementioned views.

As described above, there are many studies on the growth factors of SMEs including start-ups, but the analysis target is limited to public financial support, such as subsidies, or vague concepts such as relationships with surrounding people around managers. These have limitations in practical contributions to the business. For startups, various support measures are actually taken in addition to subsidies. Therefore, it is meaningful to take a broader and more specific view of support and to examine the effects of each type of support. It is also important to consider the scale of a startup's performance not only by its growth potential, such as sales and employment, but also by expanding its scope.

Besides, examples of research that verified the effect of subsidies by comparing subsidy receiving companies with non-receiving companies include Okubo and Tomiura [13] and Czarnitzki and Delanote [14]. These all use propensity score matching. The advantage of using a propensity score is that the "covariate" as a set of leading variables that affect both the treatment and effect of interest in the analysis is aggregated into a single number, so the "curse of dimensionality" is overcome and matching is greatly facilitated. In this research as well, we adopt a propensity score matching method that can take advantage of the benefits mentioned above.

4   The Panel Survey on Business Start-Ups

As for the analysis that we conducted in our research, the Panel Data Research Center at Keio University provided us with the individual data of the Panel Survey on Business Start-ups entrusted by the Japan Finance Corporation Research Institute [15]. This survey was conducted on 2,897 client companies of Japan Finance Corporation, which started operation in 2006 (except for real estate firms). After 2006, setting December as the survey starting month, a total of five surveys were conducted ending in 2010. These were questionnaire surveys sent out by mail.

The number of valid respondents steadily decreased from 2,897 companies during the first survey and finally to 1,359 companies with the fifth and final survey. About two thirds of the organizational structures at the time of their founding were unincorporated enterprises. As for the gender of entrepreneurs, 83.8% were men with an average age of 41.9. The top 38.0% were in their 30 s. By industry, 15.2% were in the restaurant and lodging industry, followed by 14.5% in the service industries directed at individual consumers, 14.5% in the retail business, and 12.8% in the medical and welfare sector.

In addition to companies saying that they were not currently in business, this survey considered those companies with which the branches of TEIKOKU DATABANK, commissioned to collect the questionnaire sheets, and the Japan Finance Corporation Research Institute confirmed that they were not in business and to be closed. Judging from this, the ratio of companies closed by 2010 reached 15.2%, whereas those companies that continued their business until the end of 2010 reached 83.3%. By the close of the business year, 28.4% of the companies closed in 2008 (following the second or third year when their business started). The restaurant and lodging industry had the highest percentage, 23.2%.

5   The Method for Analyzing the Survey Data

This chapter refers to how various variables were structured from the initial data, and then explains the method for analyzing the relevance between external support and corporate performance. For the analysis, we narrowed down the samples into those (N = 1053) who responded to the survey in the final year and who seemed to be continuing their business at the end of that same year. Table 1 shows the summary table of the number of received support times of nine types.

5.1   Variable Structuring

The following four indexes described below are used for dependent variables as performance parameters. The first index is the growth index. This index is a continuous variable in units of 10 thousand yen and indicates monthly sales in the final business year. The second index is the same growth index that indicates the number of employees in the final business year, in units of the number of employees. The third index indicates the profitability in the final business year. This index is a binary variable, expressing "1 = black" or "0 = red." The fourth index indicates the overall satisfaction in the final business year. Specifically, this index is a five-point variable, expressing each point from "0 = Totally dissatisfied" through "4 = Totally satisfied."

As already mentioned, treatment variables express whether there is external support, and these variables are divided into a total of nine indexes from four different categories. In detail, the first category is funding which is categorized into the following two indexes based on the support source: public funding provided by a public institute and non-public funding received from other private networks. It is understood that the latter includes support from so-called private banks. The next category is the infrastructure support which is categorized into the following two indexes based on support targets: office or manufacturing equipment and facilities etc. The next category is the introduction support categorized into the following three indexes: the customer, the supplier, and the employee. The last category is the information support that is divided into two categories according to contents. Planning support that provides business plan instructions and advice, and consulting support that provides consulting services related to the entire foundation. With the above, a total of nine treatment variables have been set.

As for these categories, the survey asked about the use of these types of support in every 5-survey year. When using a build-up approach based on the number of uses of these supports, these treatment variables can be expressed using a six-point scale with 0 through 5 times. However, we need to binarize treatment variables in order to estimate propensity scores using the binary logit model. Table 1 shows that the variable distribution of the number of uses of each support varies, but the majority is biased toward 0 times. Therefore, use of binary variables, where treatment variables with 0 times are set to 0 (control group) and the other variables are set to 1 (treatment group), achieves a properly balanced distribution for the control group and the treatment group.

Table 1. Distribution of received times for each type of support (treatment)(%)

	0times	once	twice	3times	4times	5times	N
Public financial	57.9	20.3	10.8	6.3	3.6	1.1	1053
Non-public financial	43.8	39.5	11.6	4.0	0.9	0.2	1053
Offices inflastructure	80.1	16.8	2.7	0.4	0.0	0.0	1053
Facilities inflastructure	81.4	14.3	3.0	1.0	0.2	0.1	1053
Customer introduction	39.5	25.8	15.9	10.5	6.4	1.9	1053
Supplier introduction	53.7	26.7	11.9	5.0	1.8	0.9	1053
Employee introduction	75.1	17.2	5.2	1.6	0.8	0.1	1053
Planning information	47.2	34.1	11.0	5.7	1.5	0.5	1053
Consulting information	56.7	28.8	9.1	3.8	1.4	0.2	1053

Note: Distribution in sample used for later analysis

To estimate the propensity score, various covariates are obtained from the above data. In addition to demographic attributes such as manager's age, gender, educational background, etc., questions related to business experience, and attitude attributes related to corporate management, such as having confidence (5 items such as knowledge) and struggling (5 items such as marketing) were collected.

In this study, since the propensity score is calculated many times, the covariates that can be candidates are set as many as possible in the first stage. In each calculation, the covariates are narrowed down to the appropriate number for each propensity score.

5.2   Causal Relationship Between External Support and Performance: Propensity Score Matching

Based on the above-described framework, propensity scores are estimated by using logistic regression analysis based on the above-mentioned nine external support categories as dependent variables. As for score estimation, we use the forward-backward stepwise selection method to select appropriate covariates based on the AIC.

Propensity score matching is widely used in the field of observational study as a method for decreasing biases caused by observed covariates between the treatment group and the control group (Stuart [16]). The purpose of using this method is to estimate propensity scores from observed covariates and to create a matching sample with unbiased covariates between the groups using the estimated propensity scores. This pair-matching-based method selects and matches two samples with values in proximity to propensity scores in the treatment group and the control group and compares matched samples between both groups. There exist some methods for matching two samples from two groups. In this paper, we use the nearest neighbor matching using caliper 0.25 (1:1) based on statistical software, R, in order to estimate the average treatment effect for treated (ATT) of the treatment group. The result with a significant difference (under 5%) suggests the existence of the performance enhancement effect due to the proper external support.

After that, we pick up the external support that showed a significant effect by a single treatment and verify the effect when combined with other external support. For this purpose, it is necessary to estimate again propensity scores which are prediction probabilities of receiving supports by the combination, and then, propensity score matching is performed in the same method as in the case of single support. Then, we compare the effect with the case of support alone and examine the effective combination of supports and the characteristics of each support.

6 Analysis Results of the Causal Effects Using Propensity Score Matching

6.1 Estimating Propensity Scores

First, logistic regression analysis is estimated using nine types of external support as dependent variables to calculate the propensity score, which is the first step. Since the forward-backward stepwise selection method was used as described above, naturally, different variables were selected for each external support.

Table 2. C statistic when calculating propensity score per external support (AUC)

	Public financial	Non-public financial	Offices infla	facilities infla	Customer intro	Supplier intro	Employee intro	Planning inform	Consulting inform
c statistic	0.7545	0.6650	0.6539	0.7163	0.7203	0.7266	0.7561	0.6581	0.6320

Note:The c statistic is the fit index for the logistic regression model of propensity scores.

Table 2 shows the C statistic which is the fit index for the logistic regression model when propensity scores are calculated by an external support category. This index is a numerical value that indicates the degree where the condition "Strongly Ignorable Treatment Assignment" is satisfied. This value ranges from the minimum, 0.632, to the maximum, 0.756, which was confirmed to be of a decent level.

6.2 Causal Relationships Between Individual External Support and Performance

Then, we validate the treatment effects of each external support. As already mentioned, there are nine treatment variables as external supports and four dependent variables as performance indexes. Therefore, we conducted a total of 36 (= 9 * 4) propensity score matching sessions. Table 3 shows the results of analyzing these treatment effects. In each external support category, the average performance values were compared between the group with companies that received support (treatment group) and the group that received no support (control group). A statistically significant difference produced between both groups (ATT: Average Treatment effect for Treated) suggests that the relevant external support should be effective in enhancing the performance concerned.

In Table 3, most of the support did not show a statistically significant difference between the treatment and control groups, but some interesting results were observed.

The ATT for the profit and loss (profitability) status by consulting information support was 0.128 (p < 0.01). This indicates that the group of companies receiving information support with consultation increased the proportion of profit-earning companies approximately by 13% significantly.

In addition, at the level under a significant level of 5% (p < 0.05), the analysis confirmed that non-public funding support had negative effects in the profit and loss (profitability) status and the satisfaction level. Specifically, the group of companies that received non-public funding support decreased the proportion of profit earning approximately by 9% through receiving this support. The satisfaction level was also reduced approximately by 0.2 points (five-point scale). According to Sasaki et al. [17], if the dependence on borrowing (liabilities) increases and the interest payment level approaches the upper limit of the cash flow level, the likelihood of bankruptcy increases, and bankruptcy costs and financial distress costs occurs. The results of our study are consistent with that view. It can be also understood that the decline in satisfaction is considered to have declined as the profit/loss situation worsened.

Table 3. Verification of the effect of external support after propensity score matching This table provides inter-group differences (ATT; caliper = 0.25) and standard errors, and their statistical testing results.

N=1,053	Public funding(443)		Non-public funding(592)		Offices infla(209)		Facilities infla(196)		
	Difference	SE	Difference	SE	Difference	SE	Difference	SE	
Sales	56.574	88.679	56.065	77.555	-9.675	65.871	19.927	82.601	
Profitabilitu	-0.039	0.049	-0.093(**)	0.042	-0.067(*)	0.040	0.027	0.050	
Satisfaction	-0.081	0.092	-0.166(**)	0.084	-0.010	0.084	0.100	0.100	
N of Employee	1.153	0.991	0.583	0.777	-0.757	0.711	1.000	0.807	

	Customer intro(637)		Supplier intro(488)		Employee infla(262)		Planning Inform(556)		Consulting inform(456)	
	Difference	SE	Difference	SE	Difference	SE	Difference	SE	Difference	SE
Sales	111.520	79.222	14.985	63.445	10.500	94.154	-86.337	58.474	11.483	72.150
Profitabilitu	0.015	0.048	-0.059	0.042	-0.045	0.048	0.047	0.040	0.128(***)	0.039
Satisfaction	-0.066	0.096	-0.115	0.088	-0.189(*)	0.098	-0.021	0.083	0.055	0.080
N of Employee	1.206	0.825	-0.404	0.769	1.224	1.097	-1.46(*)	0.870	0.620	0.759

Note1: *:p < .10   ** p < .05   *** p < .01

Note2:Numbers in parentheses on the right side of the support name indicate the number of the treated

6.3   Causal Relationships Between Supports Combination and Performance

Up to this point, we have confirmed whether there is any performance improvement effect of each external support alone. The analysis in the previous section concludes that there is no significant positive effect other than consulting information support and no other support has a positive effect. However, it is rather unnatural that start-ups accept only one type of external support. In fact, it should be noted that the majority of companies surveyed in our data accept multiple supports. Therefore, focusing on non-public funding support and consulting information support, for which significant positive and negative effects were confirmed in the previous analysis, combining with other external supports, we verify how the significant effect changes in each performance.

First, the propensity scores are estimated using the same method as described in the previous analysis (15 times in total = other eight types of external support x 2−1). Here, it is a propensity score as a prediction probability of accepting both external supports to be combined. Then, the causal effect of accepting both external supports will be investigated. In other words, the companies that received the combination of external supports (treatment group) and the companies that did not receive them (control group) were matched, and the average causal effect ATT of the treatment group was estimated as in the previous analysis. As a result, if there is a significant difference (less than 5%), it can be considered that there is an effect of performance improvement by the combination of the external supports concerned.

Table 4 shows the results of an analysis of the treatment effects when another external support is added, focusing on the implementation of non-public funding support. The first thing that stands out is that, when combined with public funding support, a significant increase in monthly sales was confirmed at 5% level. On the other hand, the worsening of the profit and loss status was observed, as was the case with non-public funding support alone. In Addition, the increase in employees was also confirmed in combination with support for both infrastructures and customer introduction support respectively. From this, it is possible to interpret that the financial capacity and the expansion of operations by each combination of other supports can create new jobs. Further, when combined with customer introduction support, monthly sales increased significantly. From these results, it seems that non-public funding support tends to promote corporate growth in combination with other supports, while it

Table 4. Verification of the effect of each external support combined with **Non-public funding support** after propensity score matching [ATT; caliper = 0.25]

Inter-group differences (ATT) and standard errors, and their statistical testing results

N=1,053	Public funding(313)			Offices infla(128)		Facilities infla(118)		
	Difference	SE		Difference	SE	Difference	SE	
Sales	186.53 (**)	84.134		9.301	107.38	84.598	94.789	
Profitabilitu	-0.106(**)	0.047		-0.061	0.059	-0.080	0.063	
Satisfaction	-0.131	0.102		-0.051	0.112	0.1121	0.130	
N of Employee	1.9074 (*)	0.985		1.6043 (*)	0.969	2.050 (**)	1.007	

	Customer intro(361)		Supplier intro(283)		Employee infla(175)		Planning Inform(333)		Consulting inform(282)	
	Difference	SE	Difference	SE	Difference	SE	Difference	SE	Difference	SE
Sales	179.37 (**)	73.134	-11.887	70.86	-122.57	96.963	-46.495	68.119	57.262	76.874
Profitabilitu	0.011395	0.043	-0.0827 (*)	0.046	-0.093 (*)	0.053	-0.065672	0.041	0.0044833	0.044
Satisfaction	-0.095065	0.090	-0.0054854	0.097	-0.215(**)	0.106	-0.171(**)	0.080	0.045035	0.092
N of Employee	1.96(***)	0.719	0.14861	0.779	1.2743	1.346	0.2238	0.731	0.34937	0.997

Note1: *:p < .10 **p < .05 ***p < .01

Note2:Numbers in parentheses on the right side of the support name indicate the number of the treated

Notes3:The Non-public finance column shows the differences when only the support is provided alone.

seems to have a strong influence on the direction of worsening the profit and loss status. In addition, here, eight kinds of propensity scores were calculated, but it was confirmed that the C statistic was almost the same level as the calculated value of the support alone.

Next, Table 5 shows the results obtained by combining consulting information support with others. Looking at this result, although not as noticeable as when consulting information support was provided alone, when combined with planning information support, there was an effect of increasing management satisfaction approximately by 0.2 points (five-point scale) at a significance level of 5%. In addition, there were some observation results that were somewhat difficult to interpret, such as an increase in employees in combination with offices infrastructure support. It has been observed that unlike non-public funding, consulting information support, when combined with other external support, generally tends to increase stability and satisfaction over growth. Also, the C statistic when calculating propensity scores was not significantly different from the level of the calculated value of support alone.

The above confirms that combining each with other support may give different results than a single support showing a significant causal relationship.

Table 5. Verification of the effect of each external support combined with **Consulting information support** after propensity score matching [ATT; caliper = 0.25]

Inter-group differences (ATT) and standard errors, and their statistical testing results

N=1,053	Public funding(214)		Non-public funding(282)		Offices infla(110)		Facilities infla(103)		
	Difference	SE	Difference	SE	Difference	SE	Difference	SE	
Sales	99.251	83.732	57.262	76.874	164.23	105.94	110.63	118.08	
Profitabilitu	0.036134	0.050	0.0044833	0.044	0.040425	0.058	0.0036786	0.059	
Satisfaction	-0.177 (*)	0.101	0.045035	0.092	-0.066895	0.104	0.0038095	0.119	
N of Employee	1.642	1.238	0.34937	0.997	1.984 (**)	0.992	0.51015	1.011	
	Customer intro(316)		Supplier intro(252)		Employee infla(141)		Planning Inform(340)		
	Difference	SE	Difference	SE	Difference	SE	Difference	SE	
Sales	-21.413	59.394	-42.619	85.33	53.705	110.45	-5.8415	59.618	
Profitabilitu	0.043119	0.037	-0.011687	0.045	0.016022	0.058	0.0780(*)	0.043	
Satisfaction	0.07229	0.073	0.0030544	0.092	0.0049392	0.118	0.215 (**)	0.086	
N of Employee	0.059888	0.758	0.19343	0.891	1.8053	1.289	0.41324	0.814	

Note1: *:p < .10   ** p < .05   *** p < .01

Note2:Numbers in parentheses on the right side of the support name indicate the number of the treated

Notes3:The Consulting inform column shows the differences when only the support is provided alone.

6.4   Covariates Selection

In estimating each propensity score in the previous section, many covariates obtained from the survey data were used as independent variables, and whether or not the external support was accepted was used as a dependent variable (binary variable). And logistic regression analysis (forward-backward stepwise selection method) was performed on the subjects. As a result, the item adopted as an independent variable was

Table 6. Variable selection results after calculating propensity scores by logistic models

Covariate	Non-Public Funding (single)	Consulting Information (single)	Public+ Non-Public Funding	Non-Public Funding + Facilities	Non-Public Funding + Customer	Non-Public Funding + Employee	Non-Public Funding + Planning	Planning Information+ Office	Planning + Consulting Information
Industry dummies									
Construction		●	O***		●**		●**		●*
Manufacturing			O***	O***					
Information / communications			O***	●	O*	O**		O*	O*
Transportation			O***					●	
Wholesale business			O**						
Retail business			O*				●***		
Food and lodging			O***			O***			
Medical and welfare			O***		●*	O**		●**	O**
Education / learning support				●				●	
Individual services			O***						
Corporate services	●***						●**		
real estate				●					
Corporation dummy	O***		O***		O**	O***			
Venture dummy	O				O**		O**		
FC dummy			●**		●**				
Manager									
Sex(male:1,female:0)		●*	O						●**
Age	●**	●***		●**		●**	●**		●
Educational background								●*	
Management experience	O***	O**	O**				O*		
Business experience									
Married unmarried	●					●**			
Child presence						O			
Willingness to expand	●*	O***	O*	●					O**
Management awareness									
⟨Confidence⟩									
Knowledge	O				O***				
Marketing	●		O	●*					
Technology			●	O***					
Management	O**		O	O*	O*	O**		O*	
Network	O**	O***	O**	O**	O***	O**	O***	O**	O***
⟨Struggling⟩									
Marketing	●*	O*				●*			
Administration						O		O*	
Finance		O**		O***	O**	O*	O***		O***
Employee	O***	O**	O**		O**	O***	O***	O	O***
Fund	O**		O***		O**				
Survey first year results									
Monthly sales		O*							
number of employees						O***			●*
Profit	●**								
Satisfaction					O**		O*	O***	

· The covariates remaining as partial regression coefficients by stepwise forward selection method in the calculation of propensity scores
  for external support in which a significant (5% or less) causal relationship was recognized were indicated by O or ●.
· O indicates a positive coefficient, and ● indicates a negative coefficient.
· * Attached to the right side of O or ● indicates statistical significance of 1% (***), 5% (**), 10% (*), respectively.

determined as a covariate affecting the decision of each support acceptance, and the standard partial regression coefficient calculated in the process of logistic regression analysis was defined as the weight of the covariate.

Table 6 shows the covariates adopted as independent variables and the positive and negative of their standard partial regression coefficients when estimating the propensity score of external support (or a combination thereof) that showed a significant causal relationship.

In the table, the variable indicating the level of manager's confidence in the network was selected for all support items (or combinations), and the coefficients were all significantly positive. This result indicates that the greater the confidence in the network, the higher the probability of accepting the various supports (or combinations) described above that has a significant performance effect. In addition, for most effective support (or combinations), management confidence, financial and employees struggling, and the manager's age were selected as significant independent (explanatory) variables, with positive or negative coefficients, respectively.

7 Conclusion

In this study, we examined the causal relationship between various external supports and each performance for start-ups who responded to the panel survey. As a result of the analysis, it became clear that only consulting information support alone contributed to the improvement of the profit and loss situation. In addition, it was confirmed that non-public financial support reduces profit and loss conditions and managers' satisfaction. However, it is confirmed that sales and the number of employees significantly increase when public financial support and customer introduction support are combined. On the other hand, we could not find a combination that would improve profitability and satisfaction level. In addition, in the support (or combination of support) in which a significant causal effect was recognized, a variable indicating confidence in the network with the surroundings was always selected significantly. This suggests that the attitude of managers to actively accept support using their own networks is effective.

As mentioned earlier, much of the research on start-up performance has analyzed the usefulness of public funding, including subsidies, and in recent years, research focused on managers' network. However, external support for start-ups is being implemented in various ways besides public funding. So, are they really contributing to the startup's performance? And what kind of external support and what combination of support contributes to the startup's performance? Very little has been answered about these questions. This study fills these gaps, and it can be said that there are certain academic and practical contributions.

However, there are some issues left in this study. First, since the panel data used in this paper is targeted at start-ups that are financed by the Japan Finance Corporation, most of them are small businesses and there is a slight bias. Originally, if you can use data that includes many samples of emerging companies with innovative technologies and ideas as the driving force of innovation, it will be possible to analyze more precisely the actual situation of start-ups.

Another is the growth stage of startups. In this study, we analyze start-ups with the same corporate age since their establishment in 2006, controlling various factors that may affect the acceptance of each support. However, they consist only of observables. Even though the company ages are the same, if the growth speed of each company is various, start-ups that have different needs for external support at each growth stage are mixed, and the verification results of this study may have been affected. In this context, the results of this study must be interpreted with caution.

In the future, we hope that more meaningful research will be conducted on the characteristics of each support and their effective combination while complementing with various analytical methods, and contribute to the establishment of appropriate support methods for start-ups.

References

1. Rosenbaum, P.R., Rubin, D.B.: The central role of the propensity score in observational studies for causal effects. Biometrica **70**, 41–55 (1983)
2. Guo, S.Y., Fraser, M.W.: Propensity Score Analysis: Statistical Methods and Applications. Sage Publications, Thousand Oaks, CA (2010)
3. Hoshino, T., Okada, K.: Estimation of causal effects by covariate adjustment using propensity score and application in clinical medicine epidemiology pharmacology public health field. Health Med. Sci. **55**(3), 230–243 (2006). (in Japanese)
4. Storey, D.J.: Understanding the Small Business Sector. Thomson Learning, London (1994)
5. Lerner, J.: The government as venture capitalist: the long-run effects of the SBIR program. J. Bus. **72**, 285–318 (1999)
6. Kutsuna, K.: Management strategy of growth small and medium enterprises creating employment. Surv. Mon. Rep. Jpn. Financ. Corporation **523**, 12–19 (2004). (in Japanese)
7. Ejima, Y.: Growth factors for start-ups in Japan (1)(2). J. Osaka Univ. Econ. **61**(4), 49–64 (2010). (in Japanese)
8. Key, H.T., Nguen, T.T.M., NG, H.P.: The effects of entrepreneurial orientation and marketing information on the performance of SMEs. J. Bus. Ventur. **22**, 592–611 (2007)
9. Madsen, E.L.: The significance of sustained entrepreneurial orientation on performance of firms-a longitudinal analysis. Entrepreneurship Reg. Dev. **19**(2), 185–204 (2007)
10. Okamuro, H., Kato, M.: Determinants of employment growth and compositionchange in start-up companies. Financ. Rev. **112**, 8–25 (2013). (in Japanese)
11. Matsuda, N., Matsuo, Y.: Empirical Analysis on Success Factors of Entrepreneurs, RIETI Discussion Paper 13-J-064 (2013). (in Japanese)
12. Kazumi, M.: Entrepreneurship and social network-what is a network that helps to start a business? Jpn. Financ. Corporation **26**, 35–59 (2015). (in Japanese)
13. Okubo, T., Tomiura, E.: Industrial relocation policy, productivity and heterogeneous plants: evidence from Japan. Reg. Sci. Urban Econ. **42**(1–2), 230–239 (2012)
14. Czarnitzki, D., Delanote, J.: R&D policies for young SMEs: input and output effects. Small Bus. Econ. **45**(3), 465–485 (2015). https://doi.org/10.1007/s11187-015-9661-1
15. Japan Finance Corporation Research Institute.: Results of the new opening panel survey (2011). (in Japanese)
16. Stuart, E.A.: Matching methods for causal inference: a review and a look for ward. Stat. Sci. **25**(1), 1–21 (2010). https://doi.org/10.1214/09-sts313
17. Sasaki, K., Suzuki, H., Hanaeda, H.: Corporate capital structure and financing: analysis by survey of Japanese companies. J. Jpn Assoc. Manage. Financ. **35**(1), 22–28 (2015). (in Japanese)

LENLS 16

Logic and Engineering of Natural Language Semantics (LENLS) 16

Naoya Fujikawa

Graduate School of Arts and Sciences, The University of Tokyo
fjnaoya@gmail.com

Logic and Engineering of Natural Language Semantics (LENLS), which was started in 2005, is an annual international workshop on natural language semantics and pragmatics, and related discipline like philosophy of language, logic, artificial intelligence and computational linguistics. LENLS16 was held at JSAI-isAI 2019 from 10th to 12th November 2019.

LENLS 16 had 3 one-hour invited lectures and 21 thirty-minute submitted talks by selected by the program committee (including two online talks). The number of participants is about fifty.

The invited speakers were Sunwoo Jeong (Seoul National University), Paul Pietroski (Rutgers University), and Thomas Ede Zimmermann (Goethe-University Frankfurt). In her lecture titled 'The Effect of Prosody on Veridicality Inferences in Korean', professor Jeong pointed out that veridicality inferences concerning certain attitude verbs in Korean are valid only under certain prosody, and provided an analysis of prosodically-conditioned activity inferences in Korean attitude verbs based on local pragmatic reasoning involving alternatives. Professor Pietroski gave a lecture titled 'Types of Meanings: Two is Better than Too Many'. Emphasizing that natural language semantics is a study of human language, he critically examined the standard assumption in natural language semantics that there are infinitely many semantic types, and proposes an alternative research program where we begin with only two semantic types and add a new type if it is necessary. In his lecture titled 'Variables vs. Parameters in the Interpretation of Natural Language', professor Zimmermann compared two systems of logic that have been applied to semantic analysis of natural language, Montague's *IL* and *Ty*2 of two-sorted type theory. Even though their difference in whether they contain explicit reference and quantification over indices like possible worlds and times, it was argued that their differences are irrelevant to said applications. The submitted talks discussed a variety of topics in natural language semantics and pragmatics. The papers in the present volume represent a selection of the papers presented at the workshop. It is characteristic of LENLS to discuss the wide range of topics of natural language semantics and pragmatics from various theoretical perspectives. We hope to keep this to promote international researches in the semantics-pragmatics community.

Let me acknowledge some of those who helped with the workshop. The program committee and organizers, in addition to myself, were Elin McCready, Daisuke Bekki, Koji Mineshima, Alastair Butler, Yurie Hara, Magdalena Kaufmann, Yoshiki Mori, David Y. Oshima, Katsuhiko Sano, Osamu Sawada, Wataru Uegaki, Katsuhiko

Yabushita, Tomoyuki Yamada, Shunsuke Yatabe, and Kei Yoshimoto. The organizers would like to thank Emiko Naito for clerical support, Kei Yoshimoto and Hiroaki Nakamura and the JST CREST Programs "Advanced Core Technologies for Big Data Integration" for financial support, and JSAI International Symposia on AI (JSAI-isAI2019) sponsored by the Japan Society for Artificial Intelligence (JSAI) for giving us the opportunity to hold the workshop.

The Effect of Prosody on Veridicality Inferences in Korean

Sunwoo Jeong[(✉)]

Department of Linguistics, Seoul National University, Seoul, South Korea
sunwooj@snu.ac.kr

Abstract. Certain attitude verbs in Korean such as *al-* and *gieogha-* (standardly translated as 'know' and 'remember', respectively) may give rise to veridicality inferences, i.e., inferences that their propositional complements are true. These inferences arise systematically, but selectively. In particular, they arise only under certain prosody. When they do arise, they project through various entailment-canceling operators and are understood to be backgrounded, suggesting that they are presuppositional in nature. I characterize these patterns as *prosodically-conditioned factivity inferences.* I propose an analysis that can capture this systematic variation in factivity, which crucially occurs below the level of projection (i.e., variation within 'local contexts'). The analysis is in the vein of Abusch (2010) and Simons et al. (2017), in that it makes use of a general pragmatic reasoning process involving alternatives. I argue that asymmetries in meaning between the positive verbs (*al-* 'know', *gieokha-* 'remember') and their negative suppletive counterparts (*moreu-* 'not know', *ggameok-* 'forget') play an important role in deriving the prosodically-conditioned factivity inferences. In connection with this claim, I propose a new pragmatic principle that governs how alternatives come into contrast with each other. Via the activation of this principle, interpretations of verbs that are presuppositionally underspecified can obtain factive interpretations whenever their contrasting factive alternatives are activated.

Keywords: Veridicality · Factive presupposition · Attitude verbs · Prosody · Focus · Alternatives

1 Introduction

When attitude predicates such as *know, regret, remember, be right,* etc. in English take propositional complements, they standardly give rise to the inference that the embedded proposition is true, as shown in (1).

(1)   Wheein knows that Moonbyul went home.
       ⤳ Moonbyul went home.

I thank the organizers and the participants of LENLS16 for comments and feedback.

© Springer Nature Switzerland AG 2020

M. Sakamoto et al. (Eds.): JSAI-isAI 2019, LNAI 12331, pp. 133–147, 2020.
https://doi.org/10.1007/978-3-030-58790-1_9

This is known as a veridicality inference (White 2019, i.a.). When such an inference displays characteristics of a presupposition, such as projecting outside entailment-canceling operators (as shown in (2)) and being understood as 'backgrounded' in a given discourse, we call it a *factive* inference.

(2)   Wheein doesn't know that Moonbyul went home.
        ↝ Moonbyul went home.

The questions that arise are what the source(s) of these factive presuppositions are, and how they come about. Answers to them vary along a few key points: First, the inference may be argued to be directly encoded by a given expression or may be taken to arise systematically from compositional interactions between more abstract meanings of multiple expressions. In the former case, theories vary as to what the source expression is: verb (Hintikka 1962, Karttunen 1974), complement clause (Kiparsky and Kiparsky 1970), etc. In the latter case (e.g., Ozyildiz 2017), they vary as to what the relevant abstract meanings are, and how they compose. Alternatively, the inference may be argued to arise from general pragmatic process, possibly interacting with some conventional/semantic component (Abusch 2010, Abrusán 2011, i.a.). In this case, theories vary as to what the relevant pragmatic mechanism is (e.g., a general conversational implicature (Stalnaker 1977), a kind of scalar implicature (Chemla 2009, Romoli 2014), reasoning about at-issueness (Simons et al. 2010), etc.), and what kinds of conventionalized ingredients, if any, interact with pragmatics to derive the inference.

Against this backdrop, I present patterns of veridicality inferences in Korean that are likely to be factive in nature, but have certain characteristics that set them apart from how factivity is expressed in languages like English. In Korean, verbs such as *al-*, which native speakers standardly translate as *know* in English, give rise to veridicality inferences only under certain prosody (Lee To appear). A rough generalization is as follows: Veridicality inferences standardly arise when the matrix attitude verb is accentuated, as exemplified in (3). However, they do not arise when any element of the embedded clause is accentuated instead, as exemplified in (4). (Underlines henceforth mark prosodic prominence).

(3)   Solar-neun Moonbyul-i   noraeha-n-jul <u>án-da</u>
        Solar-NOM Moonbyul-NOM sing-PP-C   know-DEC

        ≈ 'Solar knows that Moonbyul sang.'
        ↝ Moonbyul sang.

(4)   Solar-neun Moonbyul-i   noraeha-n-<u>júl</u> an-da
        Solar-NOM Moonbyul-NOM sing-PP-C   know-DEC

        ≈ 'Solar believes (based on evidence) that Moonbyul sang.'
        ↛ Moonbyul sang.

When the veridicality inference does arise, as in (3), it is understood by a listener to be backgrounded, and persists even when the sentence is embedded under entailment canceling operators. In this sense, the inference appears to be *factive* in nature. However, the prosodic emphasis crucially needs to remain on the matrix verb in order to elicit these presuppositional behaviors. In sum, certain expressions in Korean appear to systematically give rise to factive inferences, but these inferences arise conditionally depending on the prosody.

These Korean data provide novel perspectives in pursuing the two questions regarding factive presuppositions outlined above. This is because, as Ozyildiz (2017) notes, previous work on factivity have focused primarily on dealing with variation at the level of *projection*. Consequently, they are not geared towards providing an explanation of systematic variation in factivity inferences in the absence of any entailment canceling operators (see however, Ozyildiz (2017) and Lee (2018)).

My aim in this paper is to engage with the two questions we started out with, namely, what the source(s) of factive presuppositions are, and how they come about, in light of the Korean factivity data, which I characterize as *prosodically conditioned factive inferences*.

To this end, I begin by clarifying the empirical landscape of veridicality inferences in Korean. I use this empirical background to delimit the range of data that will be the focus of my analysis. Given the wealth of factors that can have an effect on generating veridicality inferences in Korean (verbs, complementizers, complement clause type, prosody). I focus only on specific pairs verbs (*al-* 'to know', *moreu-* 'to not know', *gieokha-* 'to remember', *ggameok-* 'to forget') and a single complementizer (*jul*), in order to bring into relief the interaction between verbs and prosody and control for other factors that can potentially affect veridicality inferences.

I then propose an analysis that captures the *prosodically conditioned factive inferences* of these verbs and the complementizer *jul*. The analysis is in the vein of Abusch (2010) and Simons et al. (2017), and crucially makes use of a general pragmatic reasoning process involving alternatives. Prosody is argued to enter into the picture by generating different focus alternatives, which systematically constrain the discourse salient alternatives that are targeted by the pragmatic component.

In order to extend the alternative-based pragmatic account of factive presupposition to capture the Korean data, I argue that asymmetries in meaning between the positive verbs (*al-* 'know', *gieokha-* 'remember') and their negative counterparts (*moreu-* 'not know', *ggameok-* 'forget') play an important role, and propose a new principle that governs how alternatives come into contrast with each other. Via the activation of this principle, interpretations of verbs that are presuppositionally underspecified can come to obtain factive interpretations only when the contrasting factive alternatives are activated via focus prosody.

2   The Empirical Landscape

In this section, I present a brief overview of factors that can affect the patterns of verdicality inferences in Korean. My aim here is to navigate through various types of complementizers, complement clauses, and attitude verbs, in order to identify a pocket of empirical space that highlights the interaction between verbs and prosody that is of interest to this paper. A comprehensive overview of the interplay between verbs and complementizers in generating factive inferences is provided in Lee (2018). An analysis of Turkish factive inferences, again with an emphasis on verb and complementizer interaction, is provided in Ozyildiz (2017).

2.1 Complementizers

It has been noted that in languages like Korean, Turkish, Hungarian, etc., types of complementizers systematically affect factive inferences (Ozyildiz 2017, Lee 2018, i.a.). For instance, when an attitude verb combines with an embedded clause headed by a nominal complementizer *geot* in Korean, inferences about the truth of the propositional complements arise without exception, irrespective of prosody. Furthermore, these veridical inferences project, and behave like presupposition.

(5)   Solar-neun Moonbyul-i noraehan-geot-eul an-da
      Solar-NOM Moonbyul-NOM sang-NC know-DEC
      ≈ 'Solar knows (the fact) that Moonbyul sang.'

      ↝ Moonbyul sang.

Crucially, when the CP is headed by *geot*, factive inference arises regardless of the choice of attitude verbs. For example, the inference arises not only when *geot* combines with verbs such as *al-* 'know'[1], but also when it combines with other verbs such as *saengakha-* 'think' and *mit-* 'believe', which are standardly translated as non-factives and do not give rise to veridical inferences in other linguistic contexts. Korean patterns are unlike Turkish in this respect. In the case of Turkish, the nominal complementizer gives rise to factivity inferences, but only when combined with certain types of attitude verbs.

(6)   Solar-neun Moonbyul-i noraehan-geot-eul mitneun-da
      Solar-NOM Moonbyul-NOM sang-NC believe-DEC
      ≈ 'Solar believes (the fact) that Moonbyul sang.'

      ↝ Moonbyul sang.

Previous work have often remarked on the close connection between nominalization morphology and factivity (Moulton 2009, Kastner 2015, Hanink and Bochnak 2017 i.a.). Based on this, we may conclude that in examples like (5)–(6), the complementizer *geot*, one way or another, functions as an independent source of the observed factive inference. As we are concerned primarily with verb/prosody interactions in generating factive inferences, we will set these examples outside the scope of our discussion.

---

[1] Though *al-* will be shown not to lexically encode factivity, for the time being, I will maintain the standard translation 'know' as its gloss. This is partly because the attitudinal relations it picks out are epistemic in nature rather than merely doxastic; see Sect. 2.2 for more discussion.

The situation is different, however, for other types of Korean complementizers. In particular, when a CP is headed by the complementizer *go* or the complementizer *jul*, veridicality inferences do not always arise. These patterns are summarized in (7)–(8).

(7)   Solar-neun Moonbyul-i noraeha-ess-da-go an-da
       Solar-NOM Moonbyul-NOM sang-PAST-DEC-C know-DEC
       ≈ 'Solar believes (based on evidence) that Moonbyul sang.'

       ?⤳ Moonbyul sang.

(8)   Solar-neun Moonbyul-i noraeha-n-jul an-da
       Solar-NOM Moonbyul-NOM sang-PP-C know-DEC
       ≈ 'Solar believes (based on evidence) that Moonbyul sang.'

       ?⤳ Moonbyul sang.

The complementizer *go* has a quotative flavor and can combine with a wide rage of attitude verbs. It embeds a clause which is fully inflected in mood. The complementizer *jul* combines with a more restricted range of attitude verbs: it is used primarily with *al-* 'know' and *moreu-* 'not know', but occasionally also with verbs such as *gieokha-* 'remember', *ggameok-* 'forget', and *yaegyeonha-* 'predict'. As we will see in more detail below, sentences with embedded clauses headed by *go* and *jul* may systematically obtain factive inferences, but only when combined with certain types of attitude verbs and only under certain prosody.

The upshot of the section is this. Sentences involving certain complementizers such as *geot* appear to always derive factive inferences. This indicates that complementizers can function as an independent source of factivity. Cases involving other complementizers such as *go* or *jul* however, do not reliably generate factive inferences. This indicates that when the inferences do arise in such cases, their sources must trace back to factors other than (just) complementizers. As we will see shortly, the key factors in these cases amount to verb type and prosody.

2.2 Verbs

One factor that appears to determine whether factive inferences arise from embedded clauses with complementizers like *go-* and *jul-* is verbs. When *go-* and *jul-* combine with attitude verbs such as *al-* 'to know', and *gieokha-* 'to remember', factive inferences may reliably emerge, depending crucially on prosody (see Sect. 2.3). When they combine with verbs like *saengakha-* 'think' and *mit-* 'believe', however, factive inferences do *not* arise, regardless of prosody. In short, it is impossible to obtain a factive inference from examples such as (10), while such an inference may arise from examples such as (9), depending on prosodic conditions.

(9)   Solar-neun Moonbyul-i noraeha-ess-da-go an-da
       Solar-NOM Moonbyul-NOM sang-PAST-DEC-C know-DEC
       ≈ 'Solar believes (based on evidence) that Moonbyul sang.'

       ?⤳ Moonbyul sang.

(10)   Solar-neun Moonbyul-i noraeha-ess-da-go mitneun-da
        Solar-NOM Moonbyul-NOM sang-PAST-DEC-C believe-DEC
        ≈ 'Solar believes that Moonbyul sang.'

        ↛ Moonbyul sang.

This suggests that the ways in which verbs such as *al-* 'know' and *gieokha-* 'remember' are interpreted play a role in deriving factive inferences.

At this point, it is worth noting that the verb *al-* encodes something more than mere doxastic relations denoted by non-factive attitudinal verbs such as 'think' and 'believe'. This may come off as a bit surprising. Given that even within 'local contexts'[2], *al-* doesn't always give rise to factive inferences, 'believe' may seem like a suitable first approximation of *al-*, since 'believe' is often treated as a non-factive counterpart of 'know'.

However, even when used non-factively, *al-* calls for a state in which the agent comes to form a belief about p based on having obtained some knowledge-formulating evidence about the truth of p. The use of *al-* can be non-factive in the sense that this evidence may turn out to be misguided. Nevertheless, the presence of such evidence is necessarily presumed by the use of *al-*, unlike in the case of 'believe'. For instance, (9) can be felicitously used in a scenario whereby Solar hears from the tour manager that Moonbyul sang at a concert, and concludes that this was indeed the case. But (9) cannot be used in a scenario whereby Solar believes that Moonbyul sang simply because she thinks that all rappers inevitably end up singing during the last leg of the tour. One would need to use the verb *mit-* in such case (Ozyildiz (2017) considers analogous contrasts in Turkish).

Put differently, verbs such as *saengakha-* 'think' and *mit-* 'believe' appear to tap into doxastic accessibility relations, whereas verbs such as *al-* appear to tap into some kind of extended epistemic accessibility relations which govern beliefs/knowledge formed based on 'conclusive' or 'sufficient' evidence (conclusive/sufficient from the point of view of the agent). As a shorthand for epistemic relations along this line, which do not encode factivity and appear to be associated *al-*, I will henceforth use $\mathcal{K}$. Likewise, I will use $\mathcal{M}$ as a shorthand for the relations denoted by *gieokha-*, which is translatable to 'remember', but without the associated factive inference. I will also provisionally assume that $\mathcal{K}$ and $\mathcal{M}$ provide adequate glosses for *al-* and *gieokha-*, respectively, as examples like (9)–(10) suggest that factivity is likely not hard-wired into the semantics of these verbs but rather derived systematically.

To summarize, we conclude that verbs such as *al-* '$\mathcal{K}$' and *gieokha-* '$\mathcal{M}$' contribute some meaning component that can come to derive the factive inferences, while likely not directly encoding factivity. In contrast, verbs such as *mit-* and *saengakha-* do not appear to contribute any analogous factivity-deriving meaning components. In the remainder of the paper, we focus on the former type of verbs: *al-* '$\mathcal{K}$' and *gieok-* '$\mathcal{M}$' and their negative counterparts, and examine

---

[2] This isn't a theory-neutral term, but I will use it informally to refer to linguistic contexts that do not introduce the issue of projection.

their interaction with prosody. As emotive factives combine with a completely different range of complementizers and clausal structures, they will not be our concern here.

2.3 Prosody: Generalizations

Sentences containing the verbs mentioned above, namely, *al-* '$\mathcal{K}$' and *gieok-* '$\mathcal{M}$', may systematically give rise to the inference that the embedded complements are true, even in the absence of nominal complementizers like *geot*. However, these inferences do not always arise.

The generalization is this: Veridicality inferences arise when the matrix attitude verb bears the nuclear pitch accent (henceforth NPA), as exemplified in (3) and (11). However, they do not arise when any element of the embedded clause bears the primary accent instead, as exemplified in (4) and (12). In the case of (4), the complementizer bore the NPA. In the case of (12), the embedded subject bears it instead. In neither cases do veridical inferences arise. In fact, for both (4) and (12), listeners often obtain enriched, anti-veridical inferences that the propositional complements are false (e.g., the inference that in fact, Moonbyul did not sing, for (12)).

(11)   Solar-neun Moonbyul-i noraehan-jul án-da
        Solar-NOM Moonbyul-NOM sang-PP-C know-DEC
        ≈ 'Solar knows that Moonbyul sang.'

        ↝ Moonbyul sang.

(12)   Solar-neun Móonbyul-i noraehan-jul an-da
        Solar-NOM Moonbyul-NOM sang-PP-C know-DEC
        ≈ 'Solar believes (based on evidence) that Moonbyul sang.'

        ↝̸ Moonbyul sang.

As mentioned earlier, When the veridicality inferences do arise, as in (3) and (11), they appear to be *factive* in the sense that they project, i.e., persist even when the sentences are embedded under entailment canceling operators. Example (13) demonstrates this. Even when the clause is embedded under the *eojjeomyeon ... molla* 'perhaps...' construction, the factive inference survives, as long as the NPA remains on the matrix verb.

(13)   Eojjeomyeon Solar-neun Moonbyul-i noraehan-jul ál-jidomo-la
        Perhaps Solar-NOM Moonbyul-NOM sang-PP-C know-perhaps-DEC
        ≈ 'Perhaps Solar knows that Moonbyul sang.'

        ↝ Moonbyul sang.

The last point is important. The prosodic emphasis (i.e., the NPA) crucially needs to remain on the matrix verb to elicit these presuppositional behaviors. If it is shifted, the factive inference goes away.

In sum, in the absence of factive complementizers like *geot*, sentences with verbs such as *al-* '$\mathcal{K}$' and *gieokha-* '$\mathcal{M}$' obtain factive inferences only when the verbs themselves are accented (receive the NPA). Interestingly, similar prosodic generalizations have been drawn for Turkish (Ozyildiz 2017), and for English (Beaver 2010, Tonhauser 2016, and Simons et al. 2017). In the case of English however, the generalization is drawn at the level of projection (i.e., accent on the matrix verb increases the likelihood that the factive presupposition will *project*), whereas the one drawn here governs factivity variation within 'local contexts' as well. Despite the subtle differences, there appears to be a robust and thus likely non-accidental connection between the presence of prosodic emphasis on attitude verbs and the presence of factive inference regarding their clausal complements. This state of affairs calls for a cross-linguistically generalizeable explanation, which would likely have to tap into a common mechanism via which prosody manages meaning.

3   Towards an Analysis

The previous section presented data which suggest that interactions between certain attitude verbs and prosody give rise to systematic variation in factive inferences, even in the absence of any entailment canceling operators. How can we capture this prosody-dependent patterns of factive inferences? As mentioned earlier, most accounts dealing with variation in factivity cannot by themselves resolve this question, because they are concerned primarily with variation at the level of projection. For instance, analyses which explain the presence/absence of factive inferences based on the distinction between local vs. global accommo-dation cannot be used to capture the current data (Heim 1983, Van der Sandt 1992, i.a.), as the variation examined here all occurs within local contexts. Like-wise, analyses which capture the presence/absence of factive inferences based on general pragmatic principles cannot apply straightforwardly to the present data, as they also focus primarily on capturing variation in projection. Nevertheless, I will show that the analysis I develop here is in the spirit of these pragmatic analyses, which crucially posit a general pragmatic process that makes use of a discourse salient alternative set. Explanations using alternative sets provides a natural pathway via which prosody can enter into the picture. This is because it is widely accepted that prosody marks focus, and focus in turn systematically constrains pragmatic alternatives.

The core pragmatic process I posit in my analysis is most analogous to the ones proposed in Abusch (2010) and Simons et al. (2017). However, I claim that in order to be able to extend this line of account to capture systematic factivity variation within 'local contexts', we need an additional principle which governs how alternatives contrast with each other. I argue that this principle is motivated by discourse pragmatics (Stalnaker 1977). Furthermore, I claim that asymmetries in meaning within pairs of attitude verbs play a crucial role in how this proposed principle comes to have an interpretive effect. In sum, the basic ingredients of my analysis are as in (14)–(16):

(14)   Prosody (NPA) marks focus, and focus constrains relevant pragmatic alternatives

(15)   There exists a general pragmatic reasoning process which gives rise to the presupposition that the disjunction of these alternatives is true

(16)   Alternatives of attitudinal predicates that feed into the above pragmatic process cannot contrast along more than one semantic dimension.

I now go over each component of the analysis in more detail.

3.1   Focus and Pragmatic Alternatives

We begin with the standard assumption that prosody, in particular, the place-ment of nuclear pitch accent (NPA), determines focus and that focus gener-ates alternatives (Rooth 1992, i.a.). For instance, the ordinary vs. focus seman-tic values of expressions such as *Moonbyul* would be as in (17-a) and (17-b), respectively.

(17)   a. $[\![\text{Moonbyul}]\!]^o = \text{MOONBYUL}$
       b. $[\![\text{Moonbyul}]\!]^f = \{x \mid x \in D_e\}$
            $= \{\text{MOONBYUL, WHEEIN, HWASA, SOLAR} \ldots\}$

Via point-wise functional application, the focus semantic values we obtain for the two sentences we examined in (11) and (12), which contrast in prosody and factive inferences, are as in (18-a) and (19-a), respectively.

(18)   Solar-neun Moonbyul-i noraehan-jul [an$_F$]-da
       Solar-NOM Moonbyul-NOM sang-PP-C know-DEC

       a. $[\![(18)]\!]^f = \{p : \text{Solar } R \text{ that Moonbyul sang}\}$
            $= \{$ Solar *al-* that Moonbyul sang, Solar *moreu-* that Moonbyul sang, Solar *gieokha-* that Moonbyul sang, $\ldots\}$
       b. $\text{ALT}_{(18)} = \{$ Solar *al-* that Moonbyul sang, Solar *moreu-* that Moon-byul sang $\}$

(19)   Solar-neun [Moonbyul$_F$]-i noraehan-jul an-da
       Solar-NOM Moonbyul-NOM sang-PP-C know-DEC

       a. $[\![(19)]\!]^f = \{p : (\text{Solar } al\text{- that}) x \text{ sang}\}$
            $= \{$ (Solar *al-* that) Moonbyul sang, (Solar *al-* that) Hwasa sang, (Solar *al-* that) Wheein sang $\ldots\}$
       b. $\text{ALT}_{(19)} = \{$ (Solar *al-* that) Moonbyul sang, (Solar *al-* that) Hwasa sang $\}$

The set of focus alternatives of a given expression φ are indiscriminate in that it includes all elements that are of the same semantic type as φ. Therefore, it is standardly assumed that discourse salient alternatives, whether they be conceptualized as Question Under Discussions (QUDs; Roberts 1996, Ginzburg 1996, i.a.) or other objects, are subsets of focus alternatives, as constrained further by context and other factors. Let us henceforth refer to this context-sensitive alternative set of φ as ALT_φ, and following Simons et al. [2017], posit that ALT_φ is a contextually determined non-empty, non-singleton subset of $[\![\varphi]\!]^f$ which includes φ itself.

Furthermore, let us posit that the ALT set derived from focused verbs such as *al-* '$\mathscr{K}$' and *gieokha-* '$\mathscr{M}$' always includes their suppletive negative counterparts *moreu-* 'not know' and *ggameok-* 'forget', as exemplified in (18-b). This assumption is motivated in part by the native speakers' intuition that *al-/moreu-* and *gieokha-/ggameok-* are often evoked as pairs, such that the use of one automatically makes the other discourse salient.

3.2   The Pragmatic Component

A strain of work which aims to provide a pragmatic account of (factive) presupposition posits a pragmatic process which targets these alternative sets. The general idea goes as follows. Certain expressions, including focus (e.g., (18), (19), (21)) and questions (under Hamblin-style denotations; e.g., (20)) contribute alternative sets, which interact with context to produce ALT. One way or another, listeners reason pragmatically that the disjunction of the elements in ALT, i.e., $\vee$ALT is presupposed (i.e., under the Stalnakerian view, is entailed by the context set).

(20)   Who sang?

     a. $\mathrm{ALT}_{(20)}$ = { Moonbyul sang, Solar sang, Wheein sang ... }

     b. $\leadsto$ Someone sang

(21)   [Moonbyul]$_F$ sang

     a. $\mathrm{ALT}_{(20)}$ = { Moonbyul sang, Solar sang, Wheein sang ... }

     b. $\leadsto$ Someone sang

Questions such as (20) and sentences such as (21) are therefore predicted to generate a (defeasible) existential presupposition in (20-b) and (21-b).

Abusch's implementation of this general idea, realized under the dynamic semantics framework, is as follows: if ψ embeds a clause φ which introduces ALT_φ, then the local context of φ entails the disjunction of ALT_φ. In comparison, Simons et al. (2017)'s implementation, which focuses on capturing variation in presupposition projection, links ALT_φ with the notions of QUD and at-issueness. It is roughly as follows: a factive presupposition φ projects iff the current Question Under Discussion (QUD), as indicated by focus, entails φ. And a question entails φ if a disjunction of its elements (i.e., possible answers to the question) entails φ. As difference in focus indicates difference in QUD, the analysis predicts that projection may vary depending on prosody.

The two accounts diverge regarding the question of what the source and the nature of ALT is. According to Abusch (2010), ALT can reduce to QUD, but may also be a lexically determined alternative set that can operate at a local level. According to Simons et al. (2017), the relevant ALT that generates the pragmatic inference is always the QUD, because fundamentally, at-issueness is what governs projection (an inference projects iff it is not at-issue, i.e., iff it is entailed by the QUD).

Here, we will not go into much detail about the nature of ALT, as the data examined here do not involve complex filtering/compositional phenomena that may tease apart the predictions of the two accounts. All that matters for us is that ALT is a contextually salient alternative set determined systematically by focus.

Can we adopt this line of '∨ALT' analysis to capture the Korean data? To be able to answer this, we first need to determine if $[\![al\text{-}]\!]^o$ and $[\![al\text{-}]\!]^f$ encode factivity. This is beginning to sound suspiciously circular, so let me elaborate. If $[\![al\text{-}]\!]^o$ does not encode factivity, as defined in (22), then we correctly predict that sentences such as (19) do not give rise to factive inferences. In (19), focus alternatives of Moonbyul combine point-wise with ordinary semantic value (22) of al- to generate (19-a), and subsequently the ALT set in (19-b). Given (22), ∨ALT amounts to: $\mathscr{K}_w$(Solar, Moonbyul sang) ∨ $\mathscr{K}_w$(Solar, Hwasa sang). This only results in the presupposition that Solar knows that someone sang, but does not result in any factive inference.[3]

(22) $[\![al\text{-}]\!]^o = \lambda p.\lambda x.\lambda w.\mathscr{K}_w(x, p)$

(23)   Working analysis – to be discarded
        $[\![(18)]\!]^f = \{\ \mathscr{K}_w(S, p) \wedge p,\ \neg\mathscr{K}_w(S, p) \wedge p,\ \dots\}$
        where S = Solar, p = Moonbyul sang

So far so good. However, in order to be able to predict that cases like (18) do systematically give rise to factive inferences, we additionally need to posit that when al- is interpreted as an element of an alternative set ALT, it (as well as other alternatives in the set) somehow contributes factivity. Put differently, we need to assume that the *focus* semantic value of al- collects relational functions R, all of which encode factivity, resulting in alternatives such as (23). With this assumption, correct predictions emerge. In (18), focus alternatives of al- go through composition in the usual fashion to generate (18-a), and subsequently the ALT set in (18-b). Given (23), ∨ALT amounts to: ($\mathscr{K}_w$(Solar, Moonbyul sang) ∧ (Moonbyul sang)) ∨ (¬$\mathscr{K}_w$(Solar, Moonbyul sang) ∧ (Moonbyul sang)). This results in the observed factive inference that Moonbyul sang.

But the assumption outlined in (23) seems stipulative and unmotivated. Why would verbs like al- contribute factivity only when it is evaluated as a part of the alternative set, but not when it is evaluated in the ordinary semantic domain?

Rather than try to answer this question, I will instead argue that verbs like al- do not encode factivity, regardless of whether they are interpreted as alternatives or not. Instead, the factive inference gets introduced via an independent principle which governs how alternatives contrast with each other.

3.3   Asymmetry in Attitude Predicates

Before getting into what this interpretive principle is, I first highlight certain semantic properties of attitude verbs that function as alternatives to verbs like al- '$\mathscr{K}$' and *gieokha-* '$\mathscr{M}$'. Recall that al- and gieokha- have salient negative counterparts *moreu-* 'not know' and *ggameok-* 'forget'.

---

[3] For ease of exposition, I encode the factive inferences conjunctively as in Stalnaker (1977), though additional considerations may favor alternative renditions.

It turns out there is an interesting asymmetry among these pairs. Predicates such as *moreu-* and *ggameok-*, denoting negative attitudinal relations between an agent and a proposition, do appear to lexically encode factivity, unlike their positive counterparts.

For one, veridicality inferences arise for sentences containing these verbs irrespective of prosody, as exemplified in (24) and (25). The latter in particular demonstrates that even when the NPA falls on an element of the embedded clause, we obtain the veridicality inference.[4] Likewise for *ggameok-* 'forget'.

(24)   Hwasa-neun Wheein-i gan-jul <u>móreun-da</u>
        Hwasa-NOM Wheein-NOM left-PP-C notknow-DEC
        ≈ 'Hwasa doesn't know that Wheein left.'

        ⤳ Wheein left.

(25)   Hwasa-neun <u>Whéein-i</u> gan-jul moreun-da
        Hwasa-NOM Wheein-NOM left-PP-C not-know-DEC
        ≈ 'Hwasa doesn't know that Wheein left.'

        ⤳ Wheein left.

In sum, the veridical inferences arising from verbs *moreu-* and *ggameok-* are not prosody-dependent. Furthermore, these inferences project across entailment-canceling operators, suggesting that they are factive in nature. Based on this, I conclude that there exists a lexical semantic asymmetry, such that *al-* does not encode factivity, but *moreu-* does. Likewise, *gieokha-* does not encode factivity, but *ggameok-* does.

I won't try to answer why such an asymmetry exists in the first place. But I will show that this lexical asymmetry in factivity among contrasting attitudinal verbs generative interesting interpretive consequences, combined with the principle I propose below.

3.4   Derivation from Alternatives

The final piece of the analysis is a new interpretive principle, which I characterize as follows.

(26)   **Unidimensional Heterogeneity of Alternatives**
        Elements of a discourse salient set of alternatives ALT that enter into the disjunctive pragmatic inference ∨ALT can vary only along a single semantic dimension.

Specifically, in the context of attitude predicates, I propose that the constraint above amounts to the following:

---

[4] Prosody/focus does have the predicted effect in the sense that (25) additionally gives rise to the presupposition that someone left (or that Hwasa doesn't know that someone left). But crucially, the inference about the truth of the complement also arises in both (24) and (25).

(27)   Attitudinal predicates in ALT can contrast with each other in only one
of the two following semantic dimensions:

    a.   relation between proposition p and agent x's mental state
    b.   relation between proposition p and the actual world

The semantics of attitude verbs may conventionally encode both (27-a) and
(27-b), or just (27-a). The verb *moreu-* specifies both ($\neg\mathscr{K}$ relation between x
and p, and $w \in p$ relation between w and p), whereas *al-* specifies only the former
($\mathscr{K}$ relation between x and p), and is underspecified with regards to whether
$w \in p$ (i.e., whether p is true).

When *al-* is not focused, as in (19), the ALT set introduces contrasts between
alternatives which observe (26), as elements in (19-b) vary only along the identity
of the subject (Moonbyul or Hwasa). Furthermore, as the relevant contrasts
evoked by ALT do not involve contrasts between attitude verbs, the verb *al-*
merely obtains the lexical, non-factive interpretation.

When *al-* is focused however, as in (18), the ALT set is predicted to be as
follows, based on the asymmetrical lexical semantics of *al-* and *moreu-* proposed
in Sect. 3.3:

(28) $\text{ALT}_{(18)} = \{\,\mathscr{K}_w(S,p),\ \neg\mathscr{K}_w(S,p) \wedge p\,\}$

Without pragmatic enrichment, the elements in this set cannot be used to
generate the $\vee$ALT inference, as they violate (26): the two elements may potentially contrast in both (27-a) and (27-b) dimensions of meaning. As the (27-a)
and (27-b) aspects of *moreu-* is already fixed, and as the (27-a) aspect of *al-*
already contrasts with that of *moreu-*, the only way for a listener to interpret
the sentence while observing (26) is to enrich and saturate the lexically underspecified (27-b) dimension of *al-* meaning with $p = 1$ (such that it agrees with,
i.e., does not contrast with the (27-b) dimension of *moreu-*). Consequently, *al-* in
$\text{ALT}_{(18)}$ is in effect interpreted as $\mathscr{K}_w(S,p) \wedge p$. Via the general pragmatic process outlined in Sect. 3.2, we obtain the observed factive inference that Moonbyul
sang, as $\vee$ALT $= (\mathscr{K}_w(\text{Solar, Moonbyul sang}) \wedge (\text{Moonbyul sang})) \vee (\neg\mathscr{K}_w(\text{Solar,}$
Moonbyul sang) $\wedge$ (Moonbyul sang)).

The principle proposed in (26) is motivated pragmatically. Stalnaker [1977]
was the first to recognize an interpretive constraint that is somewhat along this
vein. As a way of analyzing the factive presupposition of *know*, he notes as
follows: if a speaker were to assert that x knows that P where the truth of P is
in doubt or dispute, he would be 'saying in one breath something that could be
challenged in two different ways', thus leaving unclear 'whether his main point
was to make a claim about the truth of P, or to make a claim about the epistemic
situation of x' (Stalnaker 1977: 206).

The motivation behind the principle in (26) is similar in spirit to Stalnaker
(1977)'s claim above, but differs crucially in the following respect: The current analysis predicts that the drive to convey a single dimension of meaning
comes into force only when the associated expression enters into active contrast
with alternatives (i.e., only when the expression is ALT-generating). This makes

intuitive sense, because under many views of how alternatives function in the discourse, such as Simons et al. (2017), ALT-generating property is considered to be closely associated with the 'at-issue' status of a given meaning (i.e., something is at-issue if it is ALT-generating).

Put differently, ALT is a way of representing information-structural differences of a given sentence. Via ALT, information-structurally salient aspects of a sentence enters into contrast with unsaid alternatives. When such a contrast is evoked, it would be functionally useful to adopt certain interpretive strategies to ensure that the core contrast that is at-issue can be *uniquely* identified by the listener. Otherwise, there would be multiple potential contrasts that could be at issue, which would burden the listener. The constraint in (26) can be construed as one possible trigger for such interpretive strategies.

4   Looking Ahead

In this paper, I've focused on a particular type of variation in factive inferences, which I characterized as prosodically conditioned factive inferences. I've provided an analysis of this variation. It remains an open question if the analysis proposed here can extend to cover analogous data involving other complementizers, e.g., *go*. Before answering this however, perhaps the next step to take at this point is to obtain clearer empirical data on whether *go* and *jul* display comparable prosody-sensitivity, or if there exists subtle differences between the two. A controlled experiment gathering patterns of veridical inferences in Korean across a wide range of verbs, complementizers, and prosody is currently underway (Jeong 2020).

References

Abrusán, M.: Predicting the presuppositions of soft triggers. Linguist. Philos. **34**(6), 491–535 (2011)

Abusch, D.: Presupposition triggering from alternatives. J. Semant. **27**(1), 37–80 (2010)

Beaver, D.: Have you noticed that your belly button lint colour is related to the colour of your clothing. In: Presuppositions and Discourse: Essays Offered to Hans Kamp, vol. 21, p. 65 (2010)

Chemla, E.: Presuppositions of quantified sentences: experimental data. Nat. Lang. Semant. **17**(4), 299–340 (2009)

Ginzburg, J.: Dynamics and the semantics of dialogue. In: Seligman, J., Westerståhl, D. (eds.) Language, Logic, and Computation. CSLI Lecture Notes, vol. 1, pp. 221–237. CSLI, Stanford (1996)

Hanink, E., Bochnak, M.R.: Factivity and two types of embedded clauses in Washo. In: Proceedings of North East Linguistic Society (NELS), vol. 47, pp. 65–78 (2017)

Heim, I.: On the projection problem for presuppositions. Form. Semant. Ess. Read., 249–260 (1983)

Hintikka, J.: Knowledge and Belief: An Introduction to the Logic of the Two Notions. Cornell University Press, Ithaca (1962)

Jeong, S.: Prosodically conditioned factive inferences in Korean: an experimental study. To appear at Semantics and Linguistic Theory 30 (2020)

Karttunen, L.: Presupposition and linguistic context. Theor. Linguist. **1**(1–3), 181–194 (1974)

Kastner, I.: Factivity mirrors interpretation: the selectional requirements of presuppositional verbs. Lingua **164**, 156–188 (2015)

Kiparsky, P., Kiparsky, C.: Fact. In: Bierwisch, M., Heidolph, K.E. (eds.) Progress in Linguistics. Mouton, The Hague (1970)

Lee, C.: Non-factive alternants of the attitude verb 'know' in Korean, Turkish, and Hungarian. J. Natl. Acad. Sci. Repub. Korea **58**(1), 37–85 (2018)

Lee, C.: Syntactic/Semantic Structures and Cognition. Hankookmunhwasa (to appear)

Moulton, K.: Natural selection and the syntax of clausal complementation. Ph.D. thesis, UMass Amherst (2009)

Ozyildiz, D.: Attitude reports with and without true belief. In: Semantics and Linguistic Theory, vol. 27, pp. 397–417 (2017)

Roberts, C.: Information structure in discourse: towards an integrated formal theory of pragmatics. In: OSU Working Papers in Linguistics, vol. 49 (1996)

Romoli, J.: The presuppositions of soft triggers are obligatory scalar implicatures. J. Semant. **32**(2), 173–219 (2014)

Rooth, M.: A theory of focus interpretation. Nat. Lang. Semant. **1**(1), 75–116 (1992)

Van der Sandt, R.A.: Presupposition projection as anaphora resolution. J. Semant. **9**(4), 333–377 (1992)

Simons, M., Tonhauser, J., Beaver, D., Roberts, C.: What projects and why. In: Semantics and Linguistic Theory 20 (SALT 20), pp. 309–327 (2010)

Simons, M., Beaver, D., Roberts, C., Tonhauser, J.: The best question: explaining the projection behavior of factives. Discourse Process. **54**(3), 187–206 (2017)

Stalnaker, R.: Pragmatic presuppositions. Semantics and Philosophy, pp. 135–148. New York University, New York (1977)

Tonhauser, J.: Prosodic cues to presupposition projection. In: Semantics and Linguistic Theory, vol. 26, pp. 934–960 (2016)

White, A.S.: Lexically triggered veridicality inferences. In: Under Review for Handbook of Pragmatics (2019)

Semantic Types: Two Is Better Than Too Many

Paul M. Pietroski[(⊠)]

Rutgers University, New Brunswick, NJ 08091, USA
paul.pietroski@rutgers.edu

Abstract. In studies of linguistic meaning, it is often assumed that the relevant expressions exhibit many semantic types: <e> for entity denoters; <t> for truth-evaluable sentences; and the non-basic types <α, β> such that <α> and <β> are types. Expressions of a type <α, β>—e.g., <e, t> or <<e, t>, <<e, t>, t>—are said to signify functions, from things of the sort associated with expressions of type <α> to things of the sort associated with expressions of type <β>. On this view, children acquire languages that are importantly like the language that Frege invented to study the foundations of arithmetic. I think this conception of human linguistic meaning overgenerates wildly, even distinguishing—as we should—competence from performance. I sketch an alternative, defended elsewhere, to illustrate a broader point: when offering theories of natural languages, we shouldn't be surprised if vocabulary designed for other purposes is inadequate, and attention to relevant phenomena motivates a spare semantic typology.

Keywords: Meaning · Typology · Overgeneration

1 Introduction

It seems obvious that 'dog' and 'cat' have distinct meanings that are somehow instances of the same type, while 'dog' and 'every' have meanings of different types. Likewise, it seems obvious that 'every brown dog' and 'some gray cat' have distinct meanings of the same type, but not so for the meanings of 'every brown dog' and 'barked at noon'. Though even if we assume that words and phrases have meanings that exhibit various semantic types, it isn't clear which taxonomy we should adopt when offering theories of meaning for the spoken or signed languages that human children naturally acquire. For various reasons, it has become common to assume that these languages are like Frege's [14–16] invented language—his *Begriffsschrift*—whose expressions exhibit endlessly many semantic types that can be characterized recursively in terms of truth and denotation. I advocate a sparer typology. But my main point is methodological: if the goal is to describe natural phenomena, we should posit semantic types cautiously.

1.1 Some Terminology and Background

Humans regularly acquire languages of a special sort. These languages—let's call them Slangs—have expressions that may be spoken or signed. These expressions are also

© Springer Nature Switzerland AG 2020

M. Sakamoto et al. (Eds.): JSAI-isAI 2019, LNAI 12331, pp. 148–163, 2020.
https://doi.org/10.1007/978-3-030-58790-1_10

meaningful, syntactically structured in distinctive ways, and generable by creatures like us. So let's think of Slangs as expression-generating procedures; cp. Chomsky's [9] talk of "I-languages," which is implicit in his earlier [4–7] characterization of syntactic structure in terms of how strings of "formatives" can be derived via certain generative procedures. If we adopt the idealization that for each Slang, there is a set whose elements are all and only the expressions generated by that Slang, then we can say that each Slang determines a set of expressions that is an "E-language" in Chomsky's sense. In principle, distinct I-languages might generate the same expressions. But there may be no actual examples of Slangs that are extensionally equivalent in this sense.

It can be useful, heuristically or pedagogically, to start with a conception of languages as sets of expressions. Though like most words, 'language' is polysemous. So theorists should be open to describing Slangs as procedures that can be biologically instantiated, instead of insisting that English is a set of strings; cp. [24, 25]. One can choose to focus on the sets that are the alleged extensions of Slangs. But like Chomsky, I don't think these sets constitute an interesting domain of inquiry; and I don't think it's explanatory to describe them, along with extensions of various invented procedures, as special cases of languages in a broad sense. In any case, my focus is on Slangs and the human capacity to acquire and use these procedures, which generate expressions that are meaningful and pronounceable in ways that invite empirical investigation.[1]

I assume that the expressions generated by a Slang connect meanings of some kind with pronunciations that are associated with vocal or manual gestures. This leaves room for debate about what pronunciations (or "phonological interpretations") are, and how they are related to (i) perceptible events like acoustic vibrations or bodily movements and (ii) the capacities/representations that speakers use to produce and classify such events. Likewise, theorists can disagree about how the meanings in questions are related to shared environments and human psychology. But whatever these meanings are, Slangs connect them with pronunciations in human ways.

These ways of connecting meanings with pronunciations allow for endlessly many examples of homophony, subject to substantive constraints. The constraints are valuable clues for inquirers trying to discover which types Slang expressions exhibit. In this context, I want to review some familiar points that are often ignored.

The pronunciation of 'bank' (a.k.a. /bæŋk/) can be used to express more than one word meaning, and likewise for the pronunciation of 'drew' (a.k.a. /dru/). Put another way, the lexical items of English include some homophones that link their distinct meanings to /bæŋk/ and some homophones that link their distinct meanings to /dru/. So

---

[1] Thomason [32] urged a different project in which linguistics—or at least studies of syntax and semantics—would be developed as a branch of mathematics ("Montague Grammar"), without focusing on properties of human languages/procedures that are "merely psychologically universal." But as Chomsky remarks [8, pp. 29–30], if the envisioned enterprise is to be evaluated in terms of the interesting theorems that have emerged, it hasn't been a great success; and one wouldn't expect to find mathematicians (e.g., David Hilbert) describing physicists as being unduly concerned with the "merely physical" properties of the universe. Similarly, insisting on a "general semantics" that covers Slangs and also sundry invented languages that meet certain stipulated conditions (see [24]) may be like insisting on a "general biology" that is not limited to living things but also covers logically possible animals like unicorns and dragons. Such a project might lead to describing actual animals in ways that are less than ideal for purposes of actual biology.

the pronunciation of (1) is shared by at least four strings of lexical items that correspond to the four sentence meanings indicated with (1a–1d), in which superscripted symbols are used to distinguish homophonous lexical items.

$$\textit{a sheriff drew his gun near the bank} \qquad (1)$$

A sheriff near a $^\$$bank $^\circ$drew a gun. (1a)

A sheriff near a $^{\approx}$bank $^\prime$drew a gun. (1b)

A sheriff near a $^\$$bank $^\circ$drew a gun. (1c)

A sheriff near a $^{\approx}$bank $^\prime$drew a gun. (1d)

There are finitely many cases of lexical homophony.[2] But as Chomsky [4, 6] stressed, there are endlessly many cases of constructional homophony. For example, 'an aim' and 'a name' have the same phonological formatives. So larger phrases like 'horse with an aim' and 'horse with a name' pair their distinct meanings with a shared pronunciation. Moreover, a single string of lexical items can be comprehensible in distinct ways that correspond to distinct sentential meanings. Consider string (2), which can be understood in the three ways indicated with (2a–2c).

$$\textit{a woman saw a man reading in the library} \qquad (2)$$

A woman saw a man who was reading in the library. (2a)

A woman saw a man do some reading in the library. (2b)

A woman saw a man while she was reading in the library. (2c)

These three meanings reflect different ways of combining the lexical items in (2)—and more specifically, the ways in which 'reading in the library' can combine with 'man', 'a man', or 'saw a man'. Though for present purposes, the details are less important than the point that examples of homophony provide anchors for talk of meanings.

Whatever meanings are, three of them can be expressed with string (2). By contrast, string (3) has only the meaning indicated with (3b).

$$\textit{this is the library a woman saw a man reading in} \qquad (3)$$

---

[2] And they are usually arbitrary. The meanings expressed with /bæŋk/ could be expressed, as in many languages, with lexical items that have distinct pronunciations. The polysemous word 'window' seems to have a meaning that supports related "subsenses," which can be used to talk about certain openings in walls or framed panes of glass that fill such openings. But even if polysemy is open-ended, the number of subsenses is presumably finite for each speaker.

This is the library such that a woman saw a man who was reading in it. #   (3a)

This is the library such that a woman saw a man do some reading in it.   (3b)

This is the library such that a woman saw a man while she was reading in it. #   (3c)

Neither (3a) nor (3c) can be used to paraphrase an available "reading" of (3). Similarly, while (4) can be understood in two ways that we might indicate with 'ready to dine' and 'fit to be eaten', (5) and (6) are unambiguous; cp. 'eager to dine' and 'easily eaten'.

$$the\ duck\ is\ ready\ to\ eat \tag{4}$$

$$the\ duck\ is\ eager\ to\ eat \tag{5}$$

$$the\ duck\ is\ easy\ to\ eat \tag{6}$$

So even if we initially describe languages as sets of grammatical strings of lexical items, a good specification of what a Slang generates must specify all and only the relevant pronunciation-meaning (π-μ) pairs. Given a list of lexical items, it's easy to describe a procedure that generates every string—and hence, every meaningful string—that can be formed from these items. But if some such procedure generates (3) and (4), it will also generate gibberish like (7) and (8).

$$this\ a\ reading\ the\ is\ saw\ library\ a\ in\ woman\ man \tag{7}$$

$$eat\ to\ is\ duck\ the\ ready \tag{8}$$

Moreover, suppose we discovered a procedure that generates all and only the sentential strings of English words. Since endlessly many of these strings are homophonous, we would want to know why each of them has the meaning or meanings that it has, but no others. As we'll see, this can motivate appeal to a semantic typology that limits the candidate lexical and phrasal meanings.

1.2 Slangs: Descriptions and Explanations

For any given Slang, S, specifying a procedure that generates all and only the π-μ pairs generated by S would be a monumental task. But this is not a license for inquirers to focus on this task and ignore how Slangs generate π-μ pairs. One can't stipulate that the primary—initial, or any—scientific task in this vicinity is to specify grammars that are extensionally equivalent to Slangs. There may not be an independently specifiable notion of extensional equivalence, much less one that is illuminating. Moreover, when characterizing Slangs, inquirers need to balance the goals of describing attested π-μ pairs and explaining the absence of alternatives; cp. Chomsky's [6, 7] discussion of adequacy conditions for proposed grammars. There are several related points here.

First, we don't know what meanings are. So in assessing whether or not a proposed model of a Slang pairs certain sentential strings with interpretations of the right sort—truth values, sets of worlds, structured propositions, mental representations of some kind, or whatever—we should consider insights obtained from attempts to model how Slangs generate what they generate.[3] Second, even if we adopt a particular conception of meanings and assume that each Slang determines a certain set of π-μ pairs, proposed models won't determine this set. Extensional inadequacy will be the norm for the foreseeable future, at least with regard to many details. But absent reasons for thinking that some proposed procedures are on the right track, we have no clear sense of what it is for models to have extensions that are roughly equivalent to a target set with boundlessly many elements not yet specified. Third, if the goal is to describe Slangs as the natural objects they are, we shouldn't restrict attention to π-μ pairs that are actually produced; probing in other ways, via designed experiments, may well be valuable. In general, we shouldn't arbitrarily prioritize observations of any kind. As in other domains on inquiry, we have to discover what is theoretically important.[4]

Describing Slangs as procedures that generate certain π-μ pairs is certainly useful, and for many purposes, more productive than describing Slangs as cognitive resources that have a certain biologically instantiated recursive character that we don't yet understand. But we shouldn't conclude that the essential properties of Slangs are captured by any extensionally equivalent procedures, and that describing "further" properties of Slangs is theoretically optional. If the goal is to describe Slangs, and not merely to mimic their alleged extensions, then descriptive adequacy seems to require far more than extensional equivalence—especially if we tentatively assume a particular conception of sentence meanings (e.g., as mappings from contexts to sets of worlds).

For example, just as speakers have intuitions regarding how pronunciations are related—think of rhyme and alliteration—they have analogous intuitions regarding meanings. Chomsky [4, 6] highlighted question-answer pairs like (9) and (10).

$$\textit{can the birds that sing softly fly fast} \qquad (9)$$

$$\textit{the birds that (do) sing softly can fly fast} \qquad (10)$$

Note that (9) cannot be understood as the yes-no question corresponding to (11).

$$\textit{the birds that can sing softly (do) fly fast} \qquad (11)$$

Declarative sentences also seem to exhibit relations of implication. Consider (12–15).

---

[3] For example, if π-μ pairs are generated in structure-dependent ways involving transformations (but no context-sensitive operations of inversion), that is relevant; see, e.g., [4–6].

[4] One can define a task of describing certain facts (e.g., those concerning apparent motions of celestial bodies from a certain vantage point) without regard to other facts (e.g., those concerning the motions of terrestrial pendula and balls rolling down inclined planes, or correlations between tides and phases of the moon). But whatever the value of such tasks, they shouldn't be confused with the goal of explaining natural phenomena. History suggests that this goal is hindered by trying to define the relevant explananda in advance, but that when studying Slangs, it's easy to slide into behavioristic stipulations that restrict attention to data that is accessible in certain ways.

$$a\ red\ bird\ sang\ proudly \tag{12}$$

$$a\ bird\ sang\ proudly \tag{13}$$

$$a\ red\ bird\ sang \tag{14}$$

$$a\ bird\ sang \tag{15}$$

Prima facie, (12) implies (13) and (14), each of which implies (15). But the conjunction of (13) and (14) doesn't imply (15); see, e.g., [13, 33]. This pattern is systematic and exhibited by examples like (16–19), despite the Carrollian nouns, verbs, and modifiers.

$$a\ slithy\ tove\ gimbled\ in\ the\ wabe \tag{16}$$

$$a\ tove\ gimbled\ in\ the\ wabe \tag{17}$$

$$a\ slithy\ tove\ gimbled \tag{18}$$

$$a\ tove\ gimbled \tag{19}$$

So just as an adequate grammar for English mustn't overgenerate meanings for (9), it mustn't overgenerate implications for (12–15). Of course, examples like (20)—which implies neither (21) nor (22)—must also be accommodated.

$$a\ fake\ diamond\ was\ allegedly\ stolen \tag{20}$$

$$a\ diamond\ was\ allegedly\ stolen \tag{21}$$

$$a\ fake\ diamond\ was\ stolen \tag{22}$$

But if the task is to describe Slangs and what they generate, then examples like (12–19) tell against the hypothesis urged by Lewis [24]: intuitions of implication reflect what speakers know about specific lexical meanings (e.g., 'red' and 'proudly', as opposed to 'fake' and 'allegedly'); 'bird' and 'red bird' are not instances of logically related types, much less types in virtue of which the grammatical modifier 'red' is understood to be restrictive; likewise for 'sang' and 'sang proudly'. Instead of generalizing from (20–22) in this apparently retrograde way, we can these cases as special despite their superficial similarity to (12–14).[5]

Put another way, it's not enough for a theory to associate the pronunciations of (12–14) with sets of worlds Σ^{12}, Σ^{13}, and Σ^{14} such that Σ^{13} and Σ^{14} are non-exhaustive subsets of Σ^{12}. If competent speakers understand the modifiers in (12) as restrictive, then a descriptively adequate grammar needs to account for this. More generally, such a

---

[5] Compare 'easy/eager to please' and 'persuaded/expected John to leave'; see [6, 7]. Note that 'I persuaded him that he should leave' is fine, unlike 'I persuaded that he should leave'. But 'I expected that he would leave' is fine, unlike 'I expected him that he should leave'.

grammar has to generate the right π-μ pairs in the right way. If this requires deriving the π-μ pair corresponding to the interrogative (9) as a transformation of the π-μ pair corresponding to (10), then there is no point in pretending otherwise by defining some weaker notion of adequacy. Similarly, if (12) is understood as some kind of existential generalization akin to (12a), then there is no point in pretending otherwise.

$$\exists x \exists e[Bird(x) \ \& \ Red(x) \ \& \ PastSingingBy(e,x) \ \& \ DoneProudly(e)] \tag{12a}$$

Examples like (23)—which can be understood as (23a) or (23b), but not as (23c)—provide independent support for Davidsonian event analyses.

$$a \ boy \ saw \ a \ man \ with \ a \ spyglass \tag{23}$$

$$\text{A boy saw a man who had a spyglass.} \tag{23a}$$

$$\text{A boy saw a man by using a spyglass.} \tag{23b}$$

$$\text{A boy saw a man and had a spyglass.} \qquad \# \tag{23c}$$

The string 'saw a man with a spyglass' can be grammatically structured in two ways that correspond to (23a) and (23b), which can be regimented as (23a') and (23b'), with 'PSBO' abbreviating the semantically triadic predicate 'PastSeeingByOf'.

$$\exists e \exists x \exists y[Boy(x) \ \& \ PSBO(e,x,y) \ \& \ Man(y) \ \& \ Had\text{-}A\text{-}Spyglass(y)] \tag{23a'}$$

$$\exists e \exists x \exists y[Boy(x) \ \& \ PSBO(e,x,y) \ \& \ Man(y) \ \& \ Done\text{-}With\text{-}A\text{-}Spyglass(e)] \tag{23b'}$$

But this highlights the question of why human speakers of English cannot understand (23) as having the unattested meaning (23c), which can be regimented as (23c').

$$\exists e \exists x \exists y[Boy(x) \ \& \ PSBO(e,x,y) \ \& \ Man(y) \ \& \ Had\text{-}A\text{-}Spyglass(x)] \tag{23c'}$$

If the meaning of the verb is semantically triadic, we want to know why (23) has the two meanings it does have, as opposed to others. One suggestion is that while the verb meaning is eventish, it turns out to be semantically dyadic in the way indicated with regimentation (23b''), where 'PSO' abbreviates 'PastSeeingOf'; see [28], drawing on [21, 29, 30] among others.

$$\exists x \exists e \exists y[Woman(x) \ \& \ AgentOf(e,x) \ \& \\ PSO(e,y) \ \& \ Man(y) \ Had\text{-}A\text{-}Spyglass(y)] \tag{23b''}$$

But if this is correct, it highlights the question of why speakers fail to understand 'see' triadically. (As usual, and as desired, replies beget queries.)

One possible answer is that speakers acquire particular grammars in accord with a Universal Grammar that precludes supradyadic expressions, including any of the Fregean type <e, <e, <e, t≫>; see [28] for elaboration and defense. Of course, one can reject any such proposal and say that at least in principle, verbs can be triadic, tetradic, pentadic, etc. But this is also a hypothesis about Slangs, as is the claim that human Universal Grammar doesn't preclude expressions of type $\ll e, <e, t\gg, \ll e, t>, t\gg$.

In short, a fact about (23)—viz., that it is two but not three ways ambiguous—can, perhaps surprisingly, be germane to questions concerning the semantic typology of Slang expressions. More generally, for any given Slang, theorists face the task of formulating a grammar that generates the right π-μ pairs without overgenerating; and once we consider relations of implication, it becomes clear that there are many ways to overgenerate. Upon reflection, this highlights the real task of describing the procedures that humans actually acquire as examples of the "internalized grammars" that we can naturally acquire, given ordinary courses of experience, by virtue of having an innate endowment that lets us acquire and use expression-generating procedures of a certain sort. And to carry out this task, we need to discover the relevant sort; see Chomsky [7].

We can't stipulate that Slangs are procedures of a kind that suits the purposes of logicians. Likewise, we can't stipulate that Slangs connect pronunciations with meanings of Fregean types. We don't know what meanings are, and so unsurprisingly, we don't know what types they exhibit. But one familiar idea is very implausible.

2 Unwanted Recursion

Given at least one semantic type, the recursive and Fregean principle (RF) implies that there are boundlessly many such types.

$$\text{if } <\alpha> \text{ and } <\beta> \text{ are types, so is } <\alpha, \beta> \qquad \text{(RF)}$$

This might seem innocuous, given that a Slang can generate endlessly many π-μ pairs in the (innocuous) sense that a finitely specified theory can generate endlessly many theorems. But while any expression of English can be part of another, even though there are limits on the size of expressions that can actually be produced by human minds, it doesn't follow there are endlessly many *types* of expressions or expression meanings. On the contrary, given available evidence regarding constraints on how Slangs generate what they generate, I think we should be deeply skeptical of (RF) and try to replace it with an account that posits a small number of semantic types —perhaps as few as two.

2.1 Apparent Overgeneration[6]

It's worth noting that given two basic semantic types, just a few iterations of (RF) yields many, many more. Consider, in the usual way, an initial domain consisting of some entities (e.g., the natural numbers) and two truth values, T and ⊥.

Given such a domain, we can say that $<e>$ and $<t>$ are types that constitute Level Zero of a hierarchy whose next level includes four types: $<e, e>$; $<e, t>$; $<t, e>$; and $<t, t>$; where each of these types corresponds to a class of functions from things of some

---

[6] Some of this section is drawn, with slight modifications, from [27] and [28].

Level Zero sort to things of some Level Zero sort. Put another way, Level Zero is exhausted by the two basic types <e> and <t>, which can be described as <0> types. Level One is exhausted by the four <0> types. The next level includes all and only the new types that can be formed from those at the two lower levels: eight <0, 1> types, including <e, <e, t>> and <t, <t, e≫; eight <1, 0> types, including <<e, e>, e>> and <<t, t>, t>; and sixteen <1, 1> types, including <<e, e>, <e, e>> and <<e, t>, <t, t≫. So at Level Two, there are thirty-two types, each corresponding to a class of functions. (Compare the "iterative conception" of the Zermelo-Frankl sets, as discussed by [B].)

At Level Three, there are the 1408 new types that can be formed given those at the three lower levels: sixty-four <0, 2> types, including <e, <e, <e, t>>>; sixty-four <2, 0> types, including <<e, <e, t>>, t>; one-hundred-and-twenty-eight <1, 2> types, including <<e, t>, <<e, t>, t>>; one-hundred-and-twenty-eight <2, 1> types, including <<e, <e, t>>, <e, t>>; and one-thousand-and-twenty-four <2, 2> types, including the Fregean type <<e, <e, t>>, <e, <e, t>>>. Level Four has more than two million types: <e, <e, <e, <e, t>>>> and 5631 more <0, 3> or <3, 0> types; 11,264 <1, 3> or <3, 1> types; 90,112 <2, 3> or <3, 2> types; and 1,982,464 <3, 3> types. Let's not worry about Level Five, at which there are more than 5×10^{12} types.

My concern is not merely that endlessly many Fregean types, including the vast majority of those below Level Five, are unattested in actual Slangs. I grant that endlessly many types are too abstract for our limited memories, and that many types like <t, <e, <t, e>>> correspond to functions that we wouldn't want words for. But as Frege showed, some of the types at Levels Three and Four seem fine.

Let 'et' abbreviate '<e, t>' and consider the Level Three type <<e, et>, t>. Expressions of type <e, et> indicate functions like $\lambda y.\lambda x.Predecessor(x, y)$—i.e., $\lambda y.\lambda x.T$ if x is the predecessor of y, and $\perp$ otherwise; such functions map entities onto functions from entities to truth values.[7] Expressions of type <<e, et>, t> thus indicate functions that map functions like $\lambda y.\lambda x.Predecessor(x, y)$ onto truth values. Frege showed how to use such expressions to encode judgments about certain properties of first-order dyadic relations. For example, $\lambda y.\lambda x.Predecessor(x, y)$ isn't transitive, but $\lambda y.\lambda x.Precedes(x, y)$ is. This judgment can be encoded with (24).

$$\sim \textbf{TRANS}[\lambda y.\lambda x.\textbf{Predecessor}(x, y)] \& \textbf{TRANS}[\lambda y.\lambda x.\textbf{Precedes}(x, y)] \qquad (24)$$

Fregean languages also support abstraction over relations. The function $\lambda D.TRANS(D)$ maps $\lambda y.\lambda x.Precedes(x, y)$ to T and $\lambda y.\lambda x.Predecessor(x, y)$ to $\perp$. Correlatively, one can encode relational thoughts about relations—e.g., the thought that precedence is the transitive closure (or "ancestral") of the predecessor relation—in a logically perspicuous way, instead of using phrases like 'the predecessor relation' and

---

[7] Hence, **Predecessor**(2, 3) is a truth value, even if 'Predecessor(3)' denotes a number. Likewise, **Prime**(2) is a truth value, even if 'Prime(2)' does not denote a truth value but instead has a Tarskian satisfaction condition. In this sense, expressions of type <e, t> are relational, even if they also count as monadic; they indicate mappings from entities to truth values, highlighted here with boldface. In this sense, $\lambda x.Predecessor(x)$ and $\lambda x.$**Prime**(x) are on a par with regard to arity/adicity. If only for simplicity, I ignore Frege's [16] talk of Functions/Concepts being *unsaturated* and use lambda expressions to talk about denotable functions as in [12].

nominalizations like 'precedence'. Indeed, as Frege showed, the real power of his logic is revealed with expressions of the Level Four type <<e, et>, <<e, et>, t>> as in (25).[8]

$$\text{ANCESTRAL}-\text{OF}[\lambda y.\lambda x.\textbf{Precedes}(x, y), \lambda y.\lambda x.\textbf{Predecessor}(x, y)] \qquad (25)$$

Frege thought he was offering a novel way of representing relations among relations. He thought he had to invent a new kind of language to allow for sentences with constituents of type <<e, et>, <<e, et>, t>>. But one can hypothesize that Slangs already allow for expressions of types <e> and <t>, and that our linguistic competence supports acquisition of words that exhibit more abstract types as characterized by (RF).

$$\text{if } <\alpha> \text{ and} <\beta> \text{ are types, so is } <\alpha, \beta> \qquad (RF)$$

In which case, perhaps our capacities to acquire and combine words support generation of sentences like (24) and (25), which might be pronounced like (24a) and (25a); where 'transit' and 'ancest' would be words of types <<e, et>, t> and <<e, et>, <<e, et>, t>>.

> Predecessor doesn't transit, but precede transits.   (24a)

> Precede ancests predecessor.   (25a)

But if this brave hypothesis is correct, one wants to know why humans don't—and apparently can't—acquire such words.

One can say that we lack the cognitive resources needed to abstract and store expressions of certain types. As an analogy, one might note that the grammatical and not especially long sentence 'the rats the cats the dogs chased chased ate the cheese' sounds like gibberish, presumably because memory limitations make it impossible for us to parse multiple center embeddings; cp. [4, 11]. But my concern is not that merely that some coherent Fregean types below Level Five seem to be unavailable as semantic types. My worry is more is that humans can, and with a little help often do, grasp the thoughts indicated with formalism like (24) and (25). So why can't we pronounce these thoughts directly, with words like 'transits' and 'ancests', if Slangs permit expressions of types like <<e, et>, t> and <<e, et>, <<e, et>, t>>? These types don't seem especially arcane, or hard to grasp, compared to <e, et> and <et, <et, t>>.

2.2 Ungrammatical Abstraction

Here is another way of indicating the concern, drawing on [3]. Relative clause abstraction on the subject or object of (26), as in (27–28), is easy. So why isn't (29) equally available, with the italicized phrase construed as a relative clause of type <<e, et>, t>?

---

[8] Note that the function $\lambda \textbf{D}'.\lambda \textbf{D}.\textbf{ANCESTRAL-OF}(\textbf{D}, \textbf{D}')$ is like $\lambda \textbf{D}.\textbf{TRANSITIVE}(\textbf{D})$ in being second-order, but also like $\lambda y.\lambda x.\textbf{Predecessor}(x, y)$ in being dyadic. By contrast, the function $\lambda \textbf{D}.\textbf{ANCESTRAL}(\textbf{D})$ maps $\lambda y.\lambda x.\textbf{Predecessor}(x, y)$ to $\lambda y.\lambda x.\textbf{Precedes}(x, y)$.

$$the\ plate\ outweighs\ the\ knife \tag{26}$$

$$the\ plate\ is\ something\ which\ outweighs\ the\ knife \tag{27}$$

$$the\ knife\ is\ something\ which\ the\ plate\ outweighs \tag{28}$$

$$^*outweighs\ is\ something\ which\ the\ plate\ the\ knife \tag{29}$$

One can say that 'something' or 'which' imposes a type restriction. But then why can't we have a type-appropriate analog like 'somerelat whonk the plate the knife'? And why can't we use 'Precedes is something that three four' to convey, perhaps in a grammatically imperfect way, that $\lambda y.\lambda x.Precedes(x, y)$ is a relation that three bears to four?

Similar questions arise with regard to quantificational determiners. It is often said that words like 'every' and 'most', as in (30), are instances of type $\langle et, \langle et, t\rangle\rangle$.

$$every\ dog\ saw\ most\ of\ the\ cats \tag{30}$$

The familiar idea is that modulo niceties regarding tense and agreement, a determiner combines with an "internal" argument of type $\langle e, t\rangle$ and an "external" argument of the same type, much as transitive verb can combine with two arguments of type $\langle e\rangle$. In explaining this idea to students, one might say that the types $\langle e, et\rangle$ and $\langle et, \langle et, t\rangle\rangle$ are both instantiations of the abstract pattern $\langle\alpha, \langle\alpha, t\rangle\rangle$. But so is $\langle\langle e, et\rangle, \langle\langle e, et\rangle, t\rangle\rangle$. So if some human words are of type $\langle e, et\rangle$, and the space of possible Slang semantic types is characterized by (RF), what precludes words of type $\langle\langle e, et\rangle, \langle\langle e, et\rangle, t\rangle\rangle$? Even if *verbs* cannot be examples of this type, one wants to know why humans can't naturally use Slangs to form expressions like (31); where 'Ancestral predecessor' is a complex constituent of type $\langle\langle e, et\rangle, t\rangle$.

$$Ancestral\ predecessor\ precede \tag{31}$$

This bolsters other reasons for suspecting that phrases like 'every dog' are not instances of the Fregean type $\langle et, t\rangle$. One difficulty for this view is that (32) cannot be understood as an expression of type $\langle t\rangle$ according to which every dog barked today.

$$every\ dog\ which\ barked\ today \tag{32}$$

But if 'which barked today' is of type $\langle e, t\rangle$, why can't it combine with 'every dog' to yield the following sentential meaning: every dog (is one which) barked today? Why is (32) unambiguous and understood only as a quantifier in which 'dog' is modified by the relative clause? One can say that for some syntactic reason, 'every' cannot take a relative clause as its external argument and must instead combine with a smaller clause of the same semantic type. But the issue runs deeper.

We can specify the meaning of (32) as follows: for every dog, there was an event of it barking today. And we can posit a syntactic structure in which 'every dog' raises, leaving a trace of displacement, so that the external argument of 'every' is a sentential expression akin to 'it barked today'. But if such an expression is of type $\langle t \rangle$, then we need another assumption to maintain that 'every' is of type $\langle et, \langle et, t \rangle\rangle$.

Heim and Kratzer [18] are admirably explicit about this. On their view, (32) has the form shown in (32a), with the indexed trace interpreted like a bound pronoun.

$$\left[\left[\text{every}_{\langle et, \langle et, t \rangle\rangle}\, \text{dog}_{\langle et \rangle}\right]_{\langle et, t \rangle}\left[1\left[t_1\,\text{barked today}\right]_{\langle t \rangle}\right]_{\langle et \rangle}\right]_{\langle t \rangle} \qquad (32a)$$

The bare index is a syncategorematic element that combines with the original sentence, thereby converting an expression of type $\langle t \rangle$—from which 'every dog' has moved—into an expression of type $\langle et \rangle$.[9] Like Heim and Kratzer, I think we need to posit a syncategorematic operation of abstraction, corresponding to Tarski-style quantification over ways of assigning values to indices; see [28]. So my concern is not that they posit indices that are not instances of a Fregean type. But I do worry that (32a) posits an element that effectively converts the external/sentential argument of 'every' into a relative clause, thereby effacing the contrast with the internal/nominal argument, even though quantificational determiners cannot take relative clauses as external arguments.

Given that (32) cannot be understood as a sentence, it seems odd to say that (32a) is the grammatical form of a sentence in which 'every dog' combines with an expression whose meaning is that of the relative clause 'which barked today'. One can insist that 'every' abhors relative clauses, yet still maintain that (i) 'every' indicates a relation that is exhibited by functions of the sort indicated with relative clauses, and (ii) the apparently sentential argument of 'every' gets converted into something that looks like a relative clause. But even if this position is coherent, it seems strained.

With these points in mind, let's return to the absence of expressions that would exhibit the Level Four type $\langle\langle e, et\rangle, \langle\langle e, et\rangle, t\rangle\rangle$. Perhaps some cognitive limitation inhibits abstractions like $\lambda D'.\lambda D.\textbf{ANCESTRAL-OF}(\textbf{D}, \textbf{D}')$ without precluding expressions of types like $\langle et, \langle et, t \rangle\rangle$ and $\langle e, et\rangle$. But even if this ancillary hypothesis is correct, the Level Four types also include $\langle et, \langle et, \langle et, t \rangle\rangle\rangle$ and $\langle e, \langle e, \langle e, \langle et\rangle\rangle\rangle\rangle$.

If these types are also unattested in Slangs, one wants to know why. It's not hard to imagine triadic determiners like 'trink', which could combine with three monadic predicates as in (33) to yield a meaning like that of (33a) or (33b).

$$\textit{trink dogs cats are brown} \qquad (33)$$

$$\text{The brown dogs outnumbered the brown cats.} \qquad (33a)$$

$$\text{There are some brown dogs or brown cats.} \qquad (33b)$$

---

[9] The index is not posited as an expression of type $\langle t, et \rangle$; but neither is the displaced element in [which$_1$ [t$_1$ ran quickly]$_{\langle t \rangle}$]$_{\langle et \rangle}$. Heim and Kratzer posit a rule according which: if a sentence S contains a trace with index i and combines with a copy of i, the result is an expression of type $\langle e, t \rangle$; and relative to any assignment A, $i^\wedge$S indicates a function that maps each entity e to **T** iff S denotes **T** relative to the minimally different assignment A* that assigns e to i.

It's even easier to imagine "tri-transitive" verbs that could appears in sentences like (34), with the following meaning: a man sold a woman a car for a dollar.[10]

$$\text{a man sald a woman a car a dollar} \tag{34}$$

We can, it seems, form a concept of selling whose adicity exceeds that of a corresponding concept of giving. A seller gets something back as part of the exchange. So why can't we introduce a semantically tetradic verb, akin to the concept SOLD(X, Y, Z, w)? Why do we need prepositional phrases like 'for a dollar' if verbs can be of instances of the Fregean type <e, <e, <e, <et>>>>?

2.3 The Initially Plausible Eight

One can speculate that some cognitive limitation precludes expressions of any semantic types from above Level Three. But if the number of plausibly attested types is small, why appeal to (RF) and the requisite performance limitations, as opposed to a short list?

$$\text{if } <\alpha> \text{ and } <\beta> \text{ are types, so is } <\alpha, \beta> \tag{RF}$$

One might start with <e> and <t> from Level Zero; <e, t> and <t, t> from Level One; <e, et> and <et, t> from Level Two; <e, <e, et>> and <et, <et, t>> from Level Three. Perhaps there are good empirical reasons for adding a few more. But there are also motivations for shortening this initial list of eight semantic types.

We've already seen some reasons for doubting that quantificational determiners like 'every' are instances of type <et, <et, t>> and that phrases like 'every dog' are instances of type <et, t>.[11] With regard to <t, t>, it can be tempting to analyze the negations in 'is not red' and 'may not be red' as sentential. But such analyses are not attractive empirically; see [19, 22]. Given [31], one can eschew appeal to truth values and <t> as a semantic type—treating closed sentences as predicates that are satisfied by everything or nothing—unless <t> is needed to introduce higher types via some principle like (RF); see [26] for related and helpful discussion. So instead of describing monadic/dyadic/triadic predicates in terms of relations to truth values, one might simply posit basic types <M>, <D>, and <T>. Complete sentences can be described as "polarized" expressions that are special cases of type <M>; see [28].

This provides independent motivation for describing proper nouns as special cases of nouns that are instances of type <M>, as opposed to expressions of a special type <e>. In my view, predicative conceptions of names are both viable and attractive; see,

---

[10] For these purposes, let's not worry about the indefinite descriptions. Suppose that 'sald' would be of type <e, <e, <e, <et>>>> and not the Level Five type <et, <et, <et, <et, t>>>>. For these purposes, let's also ignore adverbial modification and the need for an event variable.

[11] See [28] for further discussion, a treatment of quantificational determiners as plural monadic predicates, and the puzzles presented by "conservativity" if we say that words like 'every' and 'most' express second-order relations exhibited by first-order monadic predicates.

e.g., [2, 17, 20, 21]. More generally, I think there are very few reasons—apart from habit and convenience—for positing <e> or <t> as semantic types.

It's less controversial that we can and probably should do without appeal to semantically triadic predicates. In Sect. 1.2, I offered one reason for eschewing such predicates in connection with possible construals of (23).

$$a\ boy\ saw\ a\ man\ with\ a\ spyglass \qquad (23)$$

But to take a simpler example, children can presumably acquire triadic concepts like BETWEEN(X, Y, Z), FORMED-A-TRIO(X, Y, Z), etc. So if Slangs are relevantly like Frege's *Begriffsschrift*, one might have expected 'between' to indicate a triadic concept and appear in sentences like (35). But instead, we circumlocute and use (36), as if Slangs abhor lexical items of type <e, <e, et≫.

$$a\ cat\ betweens\ a\ dog\ a\ barn \qquad (35)$$

$$a\ cat\ is\ between\ a\ dog\ and\ a\ barn \qquad (36)$$

In light of [1, 10, 21, 23], the verbs in ditransitive constructions like (37)

$$a\ woman\ gave\ a\ dog\ a\ bone \qquad (37)$$

can be analyzed as dyadic predicates, as suggested by (38) and (39).

$$a\ woman\ gave\ a\ bone\ to\ a\ dog \qquad (38)$$

$$a\ bone\ was\ given\ to\ a\ dog\ by\ a\ woman \qquad (39)$$

So perhaps we should make do with appeal to monadic and dyadic predicates, taking these to be instances of two basic types, <M> and <D>. In [28], I show how to cover the usual range of textbook cases and more with this spare typology and some principles for constructing complex monadic concepts from a stock of initial concepts that are monadic or dyadic. The two basic principles are unsurprising: combining two expressions of type <M> yields a third that is understood as a conjunction; combining an instance of <D> with an instance of <M> yields an instance of <M> that corresponds to whatever *bears the dyadic relation to something* that meets the monadic condition.

Phrases, including 'a woman' and 'gave a dog a bone', can then be described as expressions that connect their pronunciations with monadic concepts whose constituents are monadic or dyadic; where these constituents include both representations of events and thematic relations like being-the-agent-of. Complete sentences and relative clauses can be described as special cases of using one expression of type <M> to make another, via grammatical operations that correspond to ways of constructing special (i.e., polarized or de-polarized) monadic concepts from simpler constituents. Perhaps to achieve descriptive adequacy, we will need to posit a few additional types and/or syncategorematic operations. But so long as the additions are minimal and plausibly constrained, this seems preferable to positing endlessly many types, only a few of which are needed or wanted. If the goal is to discover the semantic typology exhibited by Slang expressions, then we shouldn't start by assuming $<e>$, $<t>$, and (RF).

$$\text{if } <\alpha> \text{ and } <\beta> \text{ are types, so is } <\alpha, \beta> \qquad \text{(RF)}$$

Instead, we can start by asking which types seem to be independently motivated, and then ask how our initial list should be revised in light of further data and methodological reflection. If the net result is that we posit less as inquiry proceeds (cp. [10]), that is a good sign, not a cause for dismay.[12]

References

1. Baker, M.: Thematic roles and grammatical categories. In: Haegeman, L. (ed.) Elements of Grammar, pp. 73–137. Kluwer, Dordrecht (1997)
2. Burge, T.: Reference and proper names. J. Philos. **70**, 425–439 (1973)
3. Chierchia, G.: Topics in the syntax and semantics of infinitives and gerunds. Dissertation, University of Massachusetts, Amherst, MA (1984)
4. Chomsky, N.: Syntactic Structures. Mouton, The Hague (1957)
5. Chomsky, N.: On certain formal properties of grammars. Inf. Control **2**, 137–167 (1959)
6. Chomsky, N.: Current Issues in Linguistic Theory. Mouton, The Hague (1964)
7. Chomsky, N.: Aspects of the Theory of Syntax. MIT Press, Cambridge (1965)
8. Chomsky, N.: Rules and Representations. Columbia University Press, New York (1980)
9. Chomsky, N.: Knowledge of Language. Praeger, New York (1986)
10. Chomsky, N.: The Minimalist Program. MIT Press, Cambridge (1995)
11. Chomsky, N., Miller, G.A.: Introduction to the formal analysis of natural languages. In: Luce, R., et al. (eds.) Handbook of Mathematical Psychology, vol. 2, pp. 269–321. Wiley, New York (1963)
12. Church, A.: The Calculi of Lambda Conversion. Princeton University Press, Princeton (1941)
13. Davidson, D.: The logical form of action sentences. In: Rescher, N. (ed.) The Logic of Decision and Action. University of Pittsburgh Press, Pittsburgh (1967)
14. Frege, G.: Begriffsschrift. Louis Nebert, Halle (1879). English translation. In: van Heijenoort, J. (ed.) From Frege to Gödel: A Source Book in Mathematical Logic, 1879–1931. Harvard University Press, Cambridge (1967)
15. Frege, G.: Die Grundlagen der Arithmetik. Wilhelm Koebner, Breslau (1884). In: Austin, J.: English Translation the Foundations of Arithmetic. Basil Blackwell, Oxford (1974)
16. Frege, G.: Function and concept (1892). In: Geach, P., Black, M.: Translations from the Philosophical Writings of Gottlob Frege. Blackwell, Oxford (1980)
17. Fara, D.: Names are predicates. Philos. Rev. **124**, 59–117 (2015)
18. Heim, I., Kratzer, A.: Semantics in Generative Grammar. Blackwell, Oxford (1998)
19. Horn, L.: A Natural History of Negation. Chicago University Press, Chicago (1989)
20. Katz, J.: Names without bearers. Philos. Rev. **103**, 1–39 (1994)

---

[12] My thanks to the participants, and especially to Naoya Fujikawa, for helpful discussions both during and after the conference.

21. Kratzer, A.: Severing the external argument from its verb. In: Rooryck, J., Zaring, L. (eds.) Phrase Structure and the Lexicon, pp. 109–137. Kluwer, Dordrecht (1996)
22. Laka, I.: On the Syntax of Negation. Garland, New York (1994)
23. Larson, R.: On the double object construction. Linguist. Inq. **19**, 335–391 (1988)
24. Lewis, D.: General semantics. Synthese **22**, 18–67 (1970)
25. Montague, R.: Formal philosophy. Yale University Press, New Haven (1974)
26. Partee, B.: Do we need two basic types? In 40–60 Puzzles for Manfred Krifka (2006). http://www.zas.gwz-berlin.de/40-60-puzzles-for-krifka
27. Pietroski, P.: Semantic typology and composition. In: Rabern, B., Ball, D. (eds.) The Science of Meaning, pp. 306–333. Oxford University Press, Oxford (2018)
28. Pietroski, P.: Conjoining Meanings: Semantics Without Truth Values. Oxford University Press, Oxford (2018)
29. Schein, B.: Events and Plurals. MIT Press, Cambridge (1993)
30. Schein, B.: Events and the semantic content of thematic relations. In: Preyer, G., Peters, G. (eds.) Logical Form and Language, pp. 91–117. Oxford University Press, Oxford (2002)
31. Tarski, A.: The semantic conception of truth. Philos. Phenomenol. Res. **4**, 341–375 (1944)
32. Thomason, R.: Introduction to Formal Philosophy. Yale University Press, New Haven
33. Taylor, B.: Modes of Occurrence. Blackwell, Oxford (1985)

Variables vs. Parameters in the Interpretation of Natural Language

Jan Köpping and Thomas Ede Zimmermann[✉]

Goethe-Universität, Frankfurt am Main, Germany
koepping@em.uni-frankfurt.de, T.E.Zimmermann@lingua.uni-frankfurt.de

Abstract. This paper compares two systems of functional type logic that have been applied to the analysis of meaning composition in natural language: Montague's Intensional Logic *IL* and its extensional substratum *Ty2* of two-sorted type theory. The two systems differ in their treatment of reference and quantification over indices (like possible worlds or times): whereas the denotations of *IL*-formulae (*inter alia*) depend on indices as parameters, their *Ty2*-counterparts contain explicit free and bound variables for them. Building on earlier results, it is argued that, appearances to the contrary, the two systems are largely equivalent; that any differences in expressivity are irrelevant to said applications; and that the equivalence also extends to variations of the systems that make use of multiple indices (as in mixed systems of modal and temporal interpretation) or additional dimensions (as in standard accounts of context dependence).

Keywords: Variable binding · Parameters · Parameterization

1 Introduction

Two variants of functional type logic have been used widely in linguistic semantics: Montague's Intensional Logic *IL* [20] and its extensional substratum *Ty2* of two-sorted type theory (cf. [9, p. 58ff.]). The two systems differ in their treatment of reference and quantification over indices (like possible worlds or times): whereas the denotations of *IL*-formulae (*inter alia*) depend on indices as parameters, their *Ty2*-counterparts contain explicit free and bound variables for them. Yet although the latter proves to be both more flexible and better-behaved in logical derivations, the expressive gap between the two systems is far less dramatic than in comparable systems of modal logic and their predicate logic counterparts. In fact, it has been argued that, as far as applications to compositional semantics

---

The first two sections are based on [32] and cover the material the second author presented at his invited LENLS lecture; the results in the third section had also been hinted at in that presentation, but were only obtained by a joint effort of both authors well after the LENLS conference. We would like to thank the LENLS audience for an interesting discussion following the presentation and the editors for providing an opportunity to publish our work.

© Springer Nature Switzerland AG 2020
M. Sakamoto et al. (Eds.): JSAI-isAI 2019, LNAI 12331, pp. 164–181, 2020.
https://doi.org/10.1007/978-3-030-58790-1_11

are concerned, *IL* and *Ty2* cover the same ground [30,32]. In this paper we will briefly review these arguments and then extend the results supporting them.

Section 2 introduces *IL* and *Ty2* from the point of view of the theory of extension and intension [2,7,20]; the exposition presupposes some familiarity with at least one of these systems and its application to compositional semantics. The differences between them and their impact on linguistic applications are addressed in Sect. 3. Section 4 widens the perspective by passing from sets of possible worlds to parameterized indices (as in [25] and [21]), thereby generalizing the results of the previous section; moreover, it is shown that the same results persist once Kaplan's [14] standard two-dimensional account of context-dependence is integrated.

2   Explicit Variables vs. Implicit Indices

This section introduces the two type-logical systems to be compared, *IL* and *Ty2*. Since the former derives its motivation chiefly in terms of the theory of extension and intension whose limitations the latter has been claimed to overcome, we will start with a brief survey of that general framework, concentrating on those aspects that are most relevant for its type-logical reconstruction.

2.1   Extension and Intension

The basic architecture of the theory of extension and intension [2,7] has it that each expression of a language gets assigned two semantic values: its extension, which relates the expression with the (mostly extra-linguistic) objects in the world, and its intension, which accounts for its contribution to informational content. Starting out from the *basic* (or 'saturated') extensions that coincide with the individual referents of nominal expressions and the truth values of declarative sentences, the extensions of all other expressions are taken to be their contributions to the extensions of larger expressions in which they occur and determined by a heuristic strategy that identifies these contributions with functions assigning the extensions of sister constituents to those of the common mother constituent [6]. As a case in point, the extension of the main predicate of a sentence comes out as a *characteristic* function that assigns to any individual, taken as the (basic) extensions of its subject, the truth value of the ensuing sentence, which again happens to be its (basic) extension; by iterating the same heuristics, the extension of a transitive verb may be identified with a function that assigns characteristic functions, taken as the (derived) extensions of the ensuing predicate to individuals, taken as the (basic) extensions of their objects; moreover, if the extension of a count noun (like *table*) is identified with that of the corresponding predicate nominal (*is a table*), the extension of a quantifying nominal (like *every table*) comes out as a function from characteristic functions to truth values; and the extension of a determiner as a Curried (or 'Schönfinkeled') binary relation between [characteristic functions of] sets of individuals; etc. (cf. [11, p. 13ff.]). The heuristics is non-deterministic in that the extensions obtained by it depend on the grammatical environments (or 'syntactic constructions') it is applied to; thus, the extensions of quantifiers could also be determined as their contributions to the extensions of predicates whose direct object positions they occupy ([32, p. Sec. 2.1]). Moreover, and more importantly, when applied to a particular construction, the procedure requires the extension of the mother constituent to depend on the extension of the sister constituent – which it does not always do. In particular, as famously observed in [7], in propositional attitude reports, the embedded clause does not contribute its truth value to the extension of the ensuing predicate: that two sentences are materially equivalent does not mean that they are believed, wished, ... to be true by the same subjects. To make up for this deficiency, the contribution a sister expression makes to the extension of its mother in such *intensional* environments in which replacing it by a co-extensional alternative does not necessarily preserve the extension of the mother, is identified with its *intension*. Using double bars to indicate extensions and a circumflex for the intension, we thus have:

(1)   *Fregean heuristics*   cf. [6, 7]

$$\|X\| = \begin{cases} \text{that function } f \text{ such that, for any possible sister node } Y: \\ f(\|Y\|) = \|X\ Y\|, \text{ if such a function } f \text{ exists;} \\ \text{that function } g \text{ such that, for any possible sister node } Y: \\ g(\|Y\|^{\wedge}) = \|X\ Y\|, \text{ otherwise.} \end{cases}$$

For the rest of this paper it will be crucial that the intension of an expression is identified with a (set-theoretic) function mapping the variation of its extension across a space of possible worlds, times, situations, or (most generally) *indices*. Hence, though the strategy underlying (1) is Fregean, the tactics are (broadly) Carnapian.[1]

There is no guarantee that Frege's heuristics will eventually cover the whole language. For one thing, it requires all constructions to be either extensional or intensional, thus allowing for potential substitution problems with intensions; following semantic tradition, we will ignore this complication here and refer to the pertinent literature, including [27,28]. Apart from hyper-intensionality, the Fregean heuristics may fail for lack of suitable environments in which the extensions of daughter nodes can be determined; again we will ignore the embarrassment, trusting that in the event, scholarly ingenuity will come to the rescue, as in the case of count nouns indicated above. Still, in the absence of other cues, (1) turns out to be a powerful and helpful tool in developing an account of meaning composition for a given language. Indeed, the constructions that serve to determine the extensions of daughter constituents given those of mother and sister, automatically come out as being compositionally interpretable in terms of functional application: the mother's extension is obtained by applying one daughter's extension to the contribution of the other daughter(s) – i.e., the extension or intension, depending on whether the construction is intensional.

---

[1] With the variability of the underlying Logical Space of possibilities, the intensions are generalizations of Kripke's [17] possible worlds, as propagated in [19].

The remaining constructions may turn out to be somewhat recalcitrant, though, and require special attention. A case in point are the infamous quantifying objects ([11, p. 178ff.]), which require either syntactic maneuvering (like Quantifier Raising) or a sophisticated ('*in situ*') combination of the extensions involved. At the end of the day, one should thus reckon with three ways of compositionally interpreting syntactic constructions, as represented by the following samples and using familiar notational devices:[2]

(2)   a.   If P is a sentence predicate and Q is its quantificational subject, then:
$$\|Q\ P\| = \|Q\|(\|P\|).$$

        b.   If V is a clause-embedding verb and S is its complement, then:
$$\|V\ S\| = \|V\|(\|S\|^{\wedge}).$$

        c.   If V is a transitive verb and Q is its quantificational object, then $\|V\ Q\|$ is that function f such that, for any individual x:
$$\|V\ Q\| = [\lambda x.\ \|Q\|(\lambda y.\ \|V\|(y)(x))].$$

2.2 *IL* and *Ty2*

In [20], *IL* was introduced as a framework for describing compositional semantics within the theory of extension and intension. The guiding idea is that every (underlying structure of an) English expression gets assigned a type-logical formula that denotes its extension. Given the set-up in the previous sub-section, three kinds of extensions may be distinguished: the basic extensions of sentences and referring nominals; the functional extensions obtained by Frege's heuristics (1) in extensional environments; and the intensions that act as *ersatz* extensions of intensional arguments. This distinction motivates the following type hierarchy that will serve as an index set for the formulae of *IL*:

(3)   *Definition*

        a. $t \in IT$; $e \in IT$;

        b. $(a, b) \in IT$ whenever $a \in IT$ and $b \in IT$;

        c. $(s, a) \in IT$ whenever $a \in IT$.

In (3), t, e, and s are fixed set-theoretic objects (but no pairs) whose names are mnemonic for *truth value*, *entity*, and *sense* [or *Sinn*]; pairs (a, b) indicate (total) function spaces from a-type extensions to b-type extensions, whereas pairs (s, a) stand for functions from a Logical Space of possible worlds (or other indices) to type-a-extensions. For all logical purposes, e and s indicate arbitrary domains and may thus be thought of as distinct sorts of individuals, determining a family

---

[2] The λ-operator indicates functional abstraction: $[\lambda x.\dots\ x\ \dots]$ is that function f that assigns $\dots\ u\ \dots$ to any u in its domain D (which is left implicit); given the set-theoretic account of functions we thus have:

$$[\lambda x.\dots\ x\ \dots]\ =\ \{(u, v)|u \in D\ \&\ v = \dots\ u\dots\}.$$

$(D_a)_{a \in IT}$ in the way indicated. In particular, the models and assignments of IL (as well as those of $Ty2$) will depend on two arbitrary non-empty sets D_e and D_s that we take to be fixed until further notice. The hierarchy of extensions, which covers the intensions as special cases (of types (s, b)) may then be defined in the obvious way, where $D_t = \{0, 1\}$; we leave filling in the straightforward details to the reader's imagination.

The formulae (or *terms*) of IL form a family $(IL_a)_{a \in IT}$, where any $\alpha \in IL_a$ denotes an object of type a. The atomic terms are constants and variables, which also form families $(Con_a)_{a \in IT}$ and $(Var_a)_{a \in IT}$. The members of the sets Var_a are all of the form v_n^a where n is a natural number and the usual distinctness and disjointness conditions apply. The sets Con_a depend on a given selection or *signature* (which we will not bother to define), with the proviso that $Con_a = \emptyset$ if a is not of the form (s, b). An *interpretation* function F assigns to each constant $c \in Con_a [= Con_{(s,b)}]$ an extension $F(c) \in D_{(s,b)}$; similarly, a *variable assignment* is a function g from $\bigcup_{a \in IT} Var_a$ to $\bigcup_{a \in IT} D_a$, where $g(x) \in D_a$ whenever $x \in Var_a$.

Starting with the basic type-a-terms $Con_{(s,a)} \cup Var_a \subseteq IL_a$ (for each $a \in IT$), IL-formulae are then formed by five formation rules: *application*, forming $\alpha(\beta) \in IL_b$ from $\alpha \in IL_{(a,b)}$ and $\beta \in D_a$; *abstraction*, forming $(\lambda x.\beta) \in IL_{(a,b)}$ from $x \in Var_a$ and $\beta \in IL_b$; *identity*, forming $(\alpha = \beta) \in IL_t$ from $\alpha, \beta \in IL_a$; *cup*, forming $(^\vee\beta) \in IL_a$ from $\beta \in IL_{(s,a)}$; and *cap*, forming $(^\wedge\beta) \in IL_{(s,a)}$ from $\beta \in IL_a$. While the first three operations are familiar from extensional functional type logic [3, 12] and receive their usual interpretation in IL, the two additional operators manipulate the index w on which the denotation of any IL-formula depends (apart from a model M and an assignment g): $[\![(^\vee\beta)]\!]^{M,g,w} = [\![\beta]\!]^{M,g,w}(w)$; and $[\![(^\wedge\beta)]\!]^{M,g,w} = \lambda w'. [\![\beta]\!]^{M,g,w'}$. Hence cup and cap respectively express application to, and abstraction from, the implicit index. A further means of expressing application to the index in IL is by using a constant $c \in Con_{(s,a)}$; by the above formation rules, $c \in IL_a$ and thus denotes an extension of type a: $[\![c]\!]^{M,g,w} = F(c)(w)$. This unusual treatment of constants is motivated by semantic applications, which need not concern us here.[3]

Due to the identity operation and the unlimited order of quantifiable variables, the expressive power of IL exceeds that of languages of predicate logic of any finite order. In particular, all Boolean connectives as well as existential and universal quantification over objects of any (intensional) type can be defined using the above means of expression. (4-a) is a straightforward schematic definition of universal quantification over variables x of arbitrary types $a \in IT$; (4-b) shows how to express negation in IL (where $p \in Var_t$); in (4-c) conjunction is defined by applying Leibniz's Principle to the pair $(1,1)$ (where $\mathfrak{p}, \mathfrak{q} \in Var_t$ and $R \in Var_{(t,(t,t))})^4$; and (4-d) gives an account of (unrestricted) necessity as truth at all indices:

---

[3] Following [20], the sets $Con_{(s,b)}$ are usually referred to as Con_b, which we feel is confusing (given their interpretation) and moreover leads to complications when it comes to comparing IL and $Ty2$.

[4] See [20, p. 387] and [9, p. 15] for other, less transparent ways of defining conjunction.

(4)   a. $(\forall x)\varphi := ((\lambda x.\varphi) = (\lambda x.(x = x)))$
       b. $[\neg\varphi] := (\varphi = (\forall \mathfrak{p})\ \mathfrak{p})$
       c. $[\varphi \wedge \psi] := (\lambda \mathfrak{p}.(\lambda \mathfrak{q}.((\lambda R.\ R(\mathfrak{p})(\mathfrak{q})) = (\lambda R.\ R(R = R)(R = R)))))(\phi)(\psi)$
       d. $\Box\varphi := ([{}^{\wedge}\varphi] = [{}^{\wedge}(\forall x)\ (x = x)])$

In [20], *IL* was avowedly designed so as to refute certain logical laws like Existential Generalization that are traditionally associated with extensionality. As a consequence, *IL*-terms do not even obey the laws of λ-conversion in their usual form: if the extension of the argument β depends on the index and the variable x occurs within the scope of the cap operator (which creates an intensional context by abstracting from the index), the constellation $(\lambda x.\alpha)(\beta)$ need not be equivalent to the result $\alpha[x/\beta]$ of replacing free x in α by β, even in the absence of any (other) variable clash. (As usual, *logical equivalence* of *IL*-terms is understood as co-designation across arbitrary models, indices, and assignments.) Hence a restricted version of β-conversion, as formulated in [9, p. 19], is called for to cope with constellations of this kind. As it turns out, though, the ensuing λ-reduction mechanism loses the diamond property ([8, p. 323]) for reasons to be come apparent in the next subsection. These findings reveal that a certain amount of wariness is in order when dealing with *IL*. Its explicit counterpart *Ty2*, to which we now turn, fares much better in this respect.

As will be demonstrated in Sect. 3.1, *IL* can be construed as a notational variant *IL** of a fragment of the language of extensional type theory with two sorts of individuals. *Ty2* is defined in a most straightforward way. To begin with, the set *2T* of *two-sorted types* is obtained by closing the set $\{e, s, t\}$ under pairing:

(5)   *Definition*

       a. $t \in \mathit{2T};\ e \in \mathit{2T};\ s \in \mathit{2T};$
       b. $(a, b) \in \mathit{2T}$ whenever $a \in \mathit{2T}$ and $b \in \mathit{2T}$.

Hence $\mathit{IT} \subsetneq \mathit{2T}$; in particular, *IT* contains neither s nor any types of the form (a, s) as members, but *2T* does. The atomic terms of *Ty2*, then, are families $(\mathit{Var}_a)_{a \in \mathit{2T}}$ and $(\mathit{Con}_a)_{a \in \mathit{2T}}$. The *Ty2*-variables are defined in analogy to (and extension of) the *IL*-variables. In general, (the signatures for) the *Ty2*-constants do not come with any restrictions; however, unless explicitly stated (in Sect. 3.3), we will only consider *Ty2*-signatures that meet the requirement that $\mathit{Con}_a = \emptyset$ if a is not of the form (s, b), where $b \in \mathit{IT}$. Still, *Ty2* differs from *IL* in that the variables and constants behave in a parallel fashion: $\mathit{Var}_a \cup \mathit{Con}_a \subseteq \mathit{Ty2}_a$ for any $a \in \mathit{2T}$. Starting from these atomic terms, *Ty2*-formulae are constructed by the three operations of application, abstraction, and identity, which are of course generalized to all of *2T*. Models and variable assignments are defined in the obvious way, and so are the denotations of *Ty2*-formulae depending on them – and only them: given a *Ty2*-model M and an assignment g (both based on given sets D_a and D_s), the denotation $[\![\alpha]\!]^{M,g} \in D_a$ whenever $a \in \mathit{2T}$ and

$\alpha \in Ty2_a$. Given this set-up, it is readily seen that the law of β-conversion holds in $Ty2$ and that the λ-reduction process possesses the diamond property.

3   Comparing Expressive Power

3.1   The Basic Picture

In $Ty2$ no implicit index parameter, cup or cap operators are needed because the rôle of the index may be played by the (fixed) variable v_0^s. Thus, IL-terms of the forms $(^\vee \alpha)$ and $(^\wedge \alpha)$ correspond to $Ty2$-formulae of the forms $\alpha^*(v_0^s)$ and $(\lambda v_0^s. \alpha^*)$, respectively, provided that α corresponds to α^*. Moreover, as an IL-formula denoting its extension, a constant $c \in Con_{(s,b)}$ corresponds to the (complex) $Ty2$-formula $c(v_0^s)$.[5]

(6)   *Theorem* ([9, p. 61])
    Whenever $a \in IT$ and $\alpha \in IL_a$, there is a $Ty2$-formula α^* such that, for any IL-model M with interpretation F, any IL-assignment g based on the same sets D_e and D_s, and any $w \in D_s$:
    $[\![\alpha]\!]^{M,g,w} = [\![\alpha^*]\!]^{M^*,g^*}$,
    where M^* is any $Ty2$-model (based on D_e and D_s) with interpretation F^* such that $F \subseteq F^*$, and g^* is any $Ty2$-assignment (based on D_e and D_s) such that $g \subseteq g^*$ and $g^*(v_0^s) = w$.

Given this correspondence, the *-image of IL turns out to be equivalent to the family $(IL_a^*)_{a \in IT}$ of those $Ty2$-formulae all of whose sub-terms are of types in $IT^+[:= IT \cup \{s\}]$ and that do not contain any (free or bound) variables of type s other than v_0^s.[6] The correspondence also reveals why the restricted version of λ-reduction in IL lacks the diamond property: in a constellation $(\lambda x.\alpha)(\beta)$, the conflict between free occurrences of v_0^s in β and of x in the scope of a λv_0^s-prefix within α cannot be resolved by renaming, because IL (understood as a sub-language of $Ty2$) lacks any other variables of type s.

In view of (6), $Ty2$ is at least as expressive as IL. And in an obvious sense it is strictly more expressive: formulae of types outside IT cannot be equivalent to (the *-image of) any IL-formula; neither can, in general, be formulae that contain constants or free variables of non-IT-types (apart from v_0^s, that is).[7] However, such formulae are arguably outside the intended application of IL, since they make reference to objects outside the theory of extension and intension [30]; we will return to this question in Sects. 3.2 and 3.3. But there are also $Ty2$-terms that do not so obviously lie outside the range of IL, viz. those that are themselves of IT-types, do not contain any offensive free variables or constants, but do contain bound variables alien to IL. Here are two cases in point (where the superscript on the first occurrence of a variable indicates its type):

---

[5] It ought to be mentioned that there is every reason to believe that Montague had been aware of Theorem (6), given the very design of IL.

[6] In fact, it *is* almost that fragment, except for a little twist concerning constants occurring without index argument; cf. [30, p. 75].

[7] Tautologies are among the obvious exceptions.

(7)   a. $(\lambda v_1^s. \, (v_1^s = v_0^s))$
      b. $(\forall f^{(s,s)})(\forall v_0^s) \, (f(v_0^s) = v_0^s)$

Though (7-a) is a term of type $(s,t)[\in IT]$ and its only free variable is v_0^s, it is not the *-counterpart of any *IL*-formula, because it contains v_1^s as a bound variable. Similarly, (7-b) is a closed formula of type $t[\in IT]$, but it contains $f \in Var_{(s,s)}$ as a bound variable. Yet while neither of these two formulae directly corresponds to a *-counterpart, they are equivalent to the *-counterparts of the following two *IL*-terms, as the reader is invited to verify:[8]

(8)   a. $(\lambda F^{((s,t),t)}. \, (\wedge \, ((\lambda p^{(s,t)}. \, (^\vee p)) = F))) \, (\lambda p. \, (^\vee p))$
      b. $(\forall \mathfrak{p}^t) \, [(\mathfrak{p} = (\exists \mathfrak{p}) \, \mathfrak{p} \vee \mathfrak{p} = (\forall \mathfrak{p}) \, \mathfrak{p})]$

As it turns out, the equivalences between (7) ad (8) are not accidental: neither the use of bound multiple index variables nor quantification over objects outside the *IT*-hierarchy increases the expressivity of *IL*. In order to formulate this result, we first introduce some notation and terminology that will come in handy for the generalizations addressed in Sect. 4:

(9)   *Definition*
      a. $(IL_a^+)_{\in IT^+}$ is that fragment of *Ty2* that contains only (free or bound) variables of types $a \in IT^+$.
      b.   For any $a \in IT^+$, $Ty2_a^-$ is the set of all $\alpha \in Ty2_a$, satisfying:
            if $x \in Var_a$ occurs freely in α, then $a \in IT^+$.

Hence IL^+ is like IL^* except that it also allows for multiple index variables; and $Ty2^-$ is like *Ty2*, except that it requires offensive variables to be bound. In particular, (7-a) $\in IL_{(s,t)}^+$ and (7-b) $\in Ty2_t^-$. We then have, for any $a \in IT$:

(10)   *Theorem* ([30])
      a.   If $\alpha \in IL_a^+$ and v_0^s is the only free variable of type s in α, then there exists an equivalent $\alpha^- \in IL_t^*$.
      b.   For any $\alpha \in Ty2_a^-$ there is an equivalent $\alpha^+ \in IL_a^+$.
      c.   If $\alpha \in Ty2_a^-$ and v_0^s is the only free variable of type s in α, then there is some $\beta \in IL_a$ such that α is equivalent to β^*.

According to (10-c), which follows from the other two parts and (6), the only expressivity difference between *IT* and *Ty2* concerns terms that are either themselves of outside *IT* or contain free variables (or constants) that are. (10-a) can be proved by a procedure that is somewhat reminiscent of the elimination of λ-bound variables in combinatory logic; the reformulation (8-a) of (7-a) gives a

---

[8] *Hint:* (7-a) and (8-a) boil down to a cardinality condition on D_s; and the *-counterpart of (8-b) is:

$(\lambda F^{((s,t),t)}. \, (\lambda v_0^s. \, (\lambda p^{(s,t)}. \, (p(v_0^s) = F)))) \, (\lambda p.p(v_0^s)).$

clue as to how this procedure works.[9] The proof of (10-b) involves coding by type-shifting and crucially turns on the highly restricted occurrences of (bound) non-IT-variables in $Ty2^-$, as established in:

(11)   *Lemma* ([30, p. 67])
         If $a \in IT^+, b \in 2T \backslash IT^+, \alpha \in Ty2_a^-$ and $\beta \in Ty2_b^-$ is a sub-term of α such that there are no $c \in 2T \backslash IT^+$ and $\gamma \in Ty2_c^-$ of which β is a sub-term, then:
         either β contains a free variable alien to IL^+ or β is of the form $(\lambda x.\gamma)$.

(11) means that the only positions for maximal non-IL^+-terms within $Ty2_a^-$-formulae are to the left and right of '='. This observation dramatically simplifies the type coding needed to establish (10-b); and it will carry over to the more complex situation to be encountered in Sect. 4.1. For the proofs of (10) and (11), we refer the interested reader to [30] and briefly discuss the impact of these results for the applications of functional type logic to linguistic semantics.

3.2   Multiple Index-Dependence

It has been argued that the theory of extension and intension is inadequate when it comes to *generalized de re* constellations in which a constituent in a multiply embedded intensional environment appears to contribute neither its extension nor its intension to the extension of its mother constituent ([1,23], and many others). The simplified *Ty2*-translation (12-b) of a natural reading of (12-a), according to which Billy's alleged suspicion concerns the majority of those objects that Sue takes to be plush toys, is a case in point:

(12)   a.   Sue believes that Billy suspects that **most plush toys are former pets**.
         b. $\text{SB}(v_0^s)\,(\lambda v_1^s.\ \text{BS}(v_1^s)\,(\lambda v_2^s.\ \underline{\text{MOST}(\text{PT}(v_1^s))(\text{FP}(v_2^s))}))$

The boldface clause in (12-a) apparently matches the underlined part of the formula (12-b), which contains two index-variables and thus does not seem to correspond to an extension of that clause at any single index; as a consequence, abstracting from neither index derives its intension. Hence the theory of extension and intension ought to give way to a more liberal account involving multiple index dependence, or so it seems.

There are, however, two known strategies to reconcile readings like (12-b) with the theory of extension and intension. The first is to fiddle around with the syntactic structure of (12-a) by allowing the noun *plush toys* to take scope over the embedding operator. (13-a) indicates the amount of re-bracketing

---

[9] The classic elimination algorithm from [4, p. 189] cannot be applied directly because it outputs terms of types outside IT^+. Thanks are due to Oleg Kiselyov for bringing up the question during the discussion following the LENLS presentation.

needed for a compositional analysis along the lines of (13-b), which is equivalent to (12-b):[10]

(13)   a.   Sue believes that [[plush toys]$_t$ Billy suspects that most t are former pets].

b. $\text{SB}(v_0^s)\ (\lambda v_1^s.(\lambda P.\ \text{BS}(v_1^s)\ (\lambda v_2^s.\ \text{MOST}(P)(\text{FP}(v_2^s))))(\text{PT}(v_1^s)))$

We leave the details to be figured out by the reader and move on to the second possibility of accounting for (12) without leaving the theory of extension and intension. It derives its inspiration from the architecture of multiple intensional embedding frequently attributed to [7] (*pace* [22]), which employs the full *hierarchy of intensions* to account for the interpretation of expressions A whose extensions are of any type $a \in IT$: if A is in an extensional position, its contribution will be of type a; when it gets embedded by an intensional operator that is itself in an extensional position, its contribution is of type (s, a); however, when the intensional operator is itself in an intensional position, A makes a contribution of type $(s, (s, a))$; etc. In other words, the rank of A's contribution on the intensional hierarchy reflects its degree of (intensional) embedding. In particular, the contribution of the boldface clause in (12-a) would be a *propositional concept* of type $(s, (s, t))$, i.e., a truth value depending on two indices – just like the denotation of the underlined formula in (12-b). Now, although this type assignment in itself does not answer the question of how the embedded clause expresses this propositional concept rather than some other one (cf. [5, p. 136]), it may be taken as a guiding principle from which a compositional account of (12) can be developed. However, since the technical details of this procedure are rather involved, we must refer the interested reader to [31].

3.3   Non-intensional Types

The types outside IT appear to be irrelevant to compositional semantics because there seems no place for them within the framework sketched in Sect. 2.1. However, even if there are no expressions whose extension is a function of a type $a \in 2T \backslash IT$, such functions may still play a rôle in semantic analysis. Stalnaker's [26] 'closeness' account of conditionals is a case in point; it naturally gives rise to a lexical decomposition of the subordinator *if* as a relation between two propositions (taken as sets of possible worlds):

(14) $\|if\|^w (p, q)\ =\ \chi_w(p) \in q$

Relative to a possible word w, the (choice) function χ selects the closest world at which a given proposition is true. The meta-linguistic description in (14) directly translates into a *Ty2*-translation of *if*:

---

[10] The syntactic variable t indicates the surface position from which the underlying noun *plush toys* has been moved and corresponds to the λ-bound *Ty2*-variable P in (13-b). See [10, p. 199f.] for an early formulation (and a different motivation) of such an analysis.

(15) $(\lambda p^{(s,t)}. (\lambda q^{(s,t)}. q(\chi'(p)(v_0^s))))$,

where χ' is a constant denoting the result of Currying χ. Obviously, for (15) to be well-formed, χ' needs to be of type $((s,t),(s,s))$ – which lies outside IT. Equally obviously, though, an alternative $Ty2$-account (16) of (15) would involve (a constant denoting) the *graph* $\chi^* \in Con_{((s,t),(s,(s,t)))}$ of (the function denoted by) χ':

(16) $(\lambda v_0^s. (\lambda p^{(s,t)}. (\lambda q^{(s,t)}. (\exists v_1^s) [q(v_1^s) \wedge \chi^*(p)(v_0^s)(v_1^s)])))$

Given that $((s,t),(s,(s,t))) \in IT$, the $Ty2$-formula (16) is IL-expressible, by (10). Of course, the interpretation of χ^* would still have to be restricted so as to guarantee that it denotes the graph of a choice function. So with the addition of suitable meaning postulates, the use of the offending constant may be avoided.[11] In this way replacing indices by their singleton sets (which is at the heart of the move from functions to their graphs) can always come to the rescue when offending constants threaten to obstruct IL-expressibility.

4   Adding Parameters and Dimensions of Reference

4.1   Splitting Up the Index: Parameterization

While it is quite common to identify the set of objects D_s with the set of possible worlds familiar from modal logic (cf. [20]), the index might stand for other extension-determining parameters like temporal instants or intervals; so interpreted, IL may be understood as a (higher order) temporal logic. Moreover, the fact that there is only one implicit index parameter in IL and just one sort of variables of type s in $Ty2$ does not imply that the very entities represented are simple. In fact, they could be inherently complex, thus simultaneously reflecting a multitude of dependencies on, say, worlds and times (cf. [21]). This may be captured by identifying D_s with $W \times T$. IL's cap and cup operators $((^\wedge\alpha)$ and $(^\vee\alpha))$ as well as $Ty2$'s $(\lambda v_n^s.\alpha)$ and $\alpha(v_n^s)$ then abstract from and apply to pairs of worlds and times simultaneously. Hence, IL's $\Box\varphi$ would literally stand for "necessarily always φ". But this does not mean that there is no way to define quantification over one parameter only. To this end, one may assume that there are dedicated constants (of type $(s,(s,t))$) that receive an interpretation so that they are only dependent on one of the two parameters in question. For example, a constant $\sim_w$ could be introduced that, applied to two indices consecutively, yields truth iff the indices coincide on their time parameter. With the help of this constant (which is similar to the notion of x-variant know from the interpretation of variable binding), quantification over the world component alone can be achieved. And by similar means, quantification over times alone is possible as well. Since the specific nature of the indices are of no concern to its proof, this way of splitting up the index does not interfere with the result in (10),

---

[11] χ', too, would have to be subjected to a meaning postulate in order to make sure it denotes a choice function χ, i.e. that $w \in \chi(p)$ whenever $p \neq \emptyset$.

which continues to hold when restricted to IL-/$Ty2$-models whose domains D_s and interpretations of constants like $\sim_w$ are as indicated. By the same token, Gallin's translation procedure (6) also remains unaffected. Certainly, this strategy of splitting up indices may be generalized from worlds and times to any (finite) number of components. Let us, for further reference, call the ensuing version of IL that is restricted to models with structured indices and additional $\sim$-constants as $IL^\times$.

There is another, more general way of implementing parameterization. Instead of adding more structure to the domain D_s, one could also introduce further (index) *sorts* into the language. More specifically, IL could be endowed with another pair of operators similar to $(^\wedge \alpha)$ and $(^\vee \alpha)$ which represented abstraction from, and application to, an additional temporal index parameter apart from the original one which may in turn be reserved for possible worlds. The resulting language could then be translated into a *three-sorted* type logic, where the familiar cap and cup operators are translated as before and, in a similar fashion, the newly introduced operators are translated in the same way but making use of variables of the newly introduced sort. Even more generally, many-sorted variants of the above languages can roughly be described in parallel to IL and $Ty2$ above: given a finite set $\Sigma = \{s_1, \ldots, s_n\}[\not\ni e, t]$, the set of intensional types is the smallest set IT such that (17-a) and (17-b) hold, while the set of (many-sorted) types is the smallest set MT such that (18-a) and (18-b) hold:

(17)   a. $\{e, t\} \subseteq \text{IT}$;
        b. $(a, b) \in \text{IT}$ whenever $a \in \text{IT} \cup \Sigma$ and $b \in \text{IT}$.

(18)   a. $\{e, t\} \cup \Sigma \subseteq \text{MT}$;
        b. $(a, b) \in \text{T}$ whenever $a, b \in \text{MT}$.

(17) and (18) generalize the definitions (3) and (5) of IT and $2T$, respectively. The definitions of the many-sorted variants of intensional logic (IL) and type logic (Tyn) also run parallel to those in Sect. 2.2. The signatures on which the sets of constants depend need to be slightly adapted so that the general form of types of constants needs to be $(s_1, \ldots (s_n, a) \ldots)$, and the interpretation function has to be extended to match the newly defined constants involving any of the sorts s_k to the appropriate domains featuring the respective D_{s_k}. Also, IL's variable assignments can be adapted, as can be the first three formation rules *application*, *abstraction* and *identity*. As suggested above, there are separate cap and cup operators for each index sort in IL. In general, the cap operators can be written as $(\lambda_s.\beta)$ (which are of type (s, a) if $s \in \Sigma$ and $\beta \in \text{IT}_a$) while cup operators may be denoted by $\beta(_s)$ (of type a if $\beta \in \text{IT}_{(s,a)}$, for any $s \in \Sigma$); thus, the original $(^\wedge \beta)$ and $(^\vee \beta)$ are given new syntactic shapes. Finally, setting up the many-sorted type logic Tyn is even more straightforward since the main difference from $Ty2$ consists in the availability of (denumerably many) more variables (of types in Σ). Apart from that, the formation rules are the same. Also, the definitions of assignment functions, domains, models, and denotations of Tyn terms proceed in the same way. It should be noted that $IL^\times$ may be faithfully embedded into IL by translating the operators $^\wedge$ and $^\vee$ as pairs (or,

more generally: sequences) of the corresponding $IL^{\times}$-operators coming in a fixed ('canonical') order.

Given this setup, it turns out that the strategy of [30] for proving the near-reversibility (10) of Gallin's translation (6) carries over straightforwardly as well. To begin, the fragments IL$^+$, IL*, and Tyn$^-$ can be defined from IL and Tyn in quite the same way as IL^+, IL^*, and $Ty2^-$ are obtained from IL and $Ty2$ above. Instead of having to keep an eye on variables of type s, however, one needs to watch all variables of all types in Σ simultaneously: IT$^+$ is IT $\cup$ Σ; IL$^+$ is a language like IL but with infinitely many variables for each with one variable for each of the (finitely many) $s \in \Sigma$; IL* is a language based on the same types as IL$^+$ but with only one variable v_0^s per $s \in \Sigma$; and finally, Tyn$^-$ is that set of Tyn-formulae whose only free variables are of types in IT$^+$ (compare (9)). The close parallelism in the construction guarantees a straightforward adaption of (10). As the reader is invited to verify, the proof in [30] can be adapted from IL and $Ty2$ to IL and Tyn, basically by generalizing predications about type s to universal quantifications over members of Σ:

(19)   *Theorem*
   a.   If $\alpha \in \mathtt{IL}_a^+$ and there is at most one free variable v_0^s per type $s \in \Sigma$ in α, then there exists an equivalent $\alpha^- \in \mathtt{IL}_t^*$.
   b.   For any $\alpha \in \mathtt{Tyn}_a^-$ there is an equivalent $\alpha^+ \in \mathtt{IL}_a^+$.
   c.   If $\alpha \in \mathtt{Tyn}_a^-$ and for any $s \in \Sigma$, v_0^s is the only free variable of that type s in α, then there is some $\beta \in \mathtt{IL}_a$ such that α is equivalent to β^*.

4.2   Adding Contexts: Two-Dimensionalism

This section briefly sketches how languages like IL, IL, or $Ty2$ and Tyn can be enriched by a second dimension [13,14], which must not be confused with the above dissection of single indices into components to distinguish operators that act on different domains. Rather, the technique of *double indexing* is meant to capture differences between operators on the same domain. The temporal adverb *now* is a case in point. Though it does not seem to have any effect on the truth conditions when occurring in extensional positions, as in (20), it is not redundant in intensional environments, given that (21-a) does not have the same truth conditions as (21-b):

(20)   a.   It is raining.
        b.   It is raining now.

(21)   a.   I learned last week that there would be an earthquake.
        b.   I learned last week that there would now be an earthquake.

(20) suggests that the time denoted by *now* is the same as that denoted by the index at which the entire sentence is evaluated; (21) suggests that the temporal index quantified over by the (relative) future operator *would* should not affect the temporal index denoted by *now*. To reconcile the two suggestions, a second

dimension on top of the index – the *context* – is added as an evaluation parameter and reserved for the denotations of *context-dependent* locutions such as *now* and its modal and spatial cognates *actually* and *here*. Intuitively, the context represents the situations *in* which an expression is used to say something *about* (or *of*) the situations represented by the index. In order to capture the redundancy effect observed in (20), the truth-conditions of un-embedded sentences may then be determined by taking them to be about the situation in which they are uttered. These short remarks must suffice as a background to the type-logical formalization to follow.

Using *IL* as a basis, the contextual dimension c is just carried along, so that the value of any context-dependent (sub-) expression can be retrieved locally. In particular, the interpretation of variables and constants remains as unaffected as that of abstraction and application. This also holds for *IL*'s means of index-manipulation, cap and cup, which are confined to the dimension of indices, represented by i: $[\![(^\vee\beta)]\!]^{M,g,c,i} = [\![\beta]\!]^{M,g,c,i}(i)$; and $[\![(^\wedge\beta)]\!]^{M,g,c,i} = \lambda i'. [\![\beta]\!]^{M,g,c,i'}$. The denotations of two-dimensional *IL*-formulae thus depend on *points of reference* (c, i), but can also be evaluated at contexts c only, provided they are represented by the index at a corresponding *diagonal* point (c, i_c).[12] As to context-dependent expressions like *now*, *actually*, *here*, etc., *IL* can only handle them in a rather roundabout fashion, since their manipulation of one out of several parameters has to be represented by quantification over the full index; see [16, Sec. 2.2] for details. But even such operators do not *shift* the context c in that their value at a given point of reference (c, i) never depends on the denotation of their argument at points (c', j) where $c \neq c'$. The language thus conforms to Kaplan's infamous *Ban on Monsters*.[13] As a consequence, the context may be represented in (the two-dimensional version of) *Ty2* by a variable which, like the index variable v_0^s may occur freely, but unlike it, must not be bound. Again, we refer the interested reader to [16] for further details and move on to the parameterization strategy introduce in the previous subsection.

Turning to IL, then, where the index $i = (i_1, \ldots, i_n)$ is split into several components, the context $c = (c_1, \ldots, c_n)$ follows suit.[14] To avoid notational clutter, we will for the rest of this paper stick to the case $n = 2$ with index types ω and τ, where contexts c and indices i are world-time pairs, whence $c = (w_c, t_c)$, and similarly for i. Then the application of *now* and *actually* just amounts to the manipulation of one of the index sorts:

---

[12] The exact nature of the representation relation between contexts and indices varies across different versions of two-dimensional semantics and need not concern us here.

[13] Cf. [15, p. 510], where the ban is presented as a descriptive observation on English and related languages. The more natural interpretation, following [18], takes it to be a defining criterion for context-dependence: unlike indices, contexts comprise those denotation-determining factors that cannot be shifted.

[14] Here we slightly simplify matters: contexts are usually taken to contain more components than indices (cf. [14]); alternatively, they may be taken to be fully specified (utterance) situations (cf. [18]). In any case, these complications are orthogonal to our concerns.

(22)   a. $[\text{NOW } \alpha]^{M,g,(w_c,t_c),(w_i,t_i)} = [\![\alpha]\!]^{M,g,(w_c,t_c),(w_i,t_c)}$
        b. $[\text{ACT } \alpha]^{M,g,(w_c,t_c),(w_i,t_i)} = [\![\alpha]\!]^{M,g,(w_c,t_c),(w_c,t_i)}$

It may be noted in passing that the equations in (22) do not require α to be of type t and could thus also be used as analyses of adjectives like *current* or *actual*, where α stands for nominal extensions of type (e,t). In fact, if we avail ourselves to these operators for any type in IT, going two-dimensional will preserve the relation between IL and Tyn as regards expressive power; we will refer to the two-dimensional version of IL that includes the operators in (22) as IL-2d. More specifically, the two context components may be represented in Tyn by variables w^* and t^*, in addition to the index variables t_0 and w_0 that generalize the unidimensional v_0^s. The Gallin translation (6) then extends to the operators in (22) by putting: $[\text{NOW } \alpha]^* = (\lambda t_0.\ \alpha^*)(t^*)$, and similarly for ACT; as a consequence, w_0 and t_0 remain the only bound index variables in the *-image. To prove the reverse translation, where $a \in \text{IT},$[15] we first observe that for any $\alpha \in \text{Tyn}_a^-$ whose free index-variables are among those mentioned two sentences ago, the term

$$(\lambda w_0.(\lambda t_0.(\lambda w^*.(\lambda t^*.\ \alpha)))) \in \text{Tyn}_{(\omega,(\tau,(\omega,(\tau,a))))}^-$$

satisfies (19-c) and is thus equivalent to the Gallin translation β^* of some $\beta \in \text{IL}_{(\omega,(\tau,(\omega,(\tau,a))))}$. It is then easy to see that the formula

$$(\lambda f^{(\omega,(\tau,a))}.\ \text{ACT NOW}(f_{(\omega)}(_\tau)))(\beta_{(\omega)}(_\tau)) \in \text{IL-2d}_{(\omega,(\tau,(\omega,(\tau,a))))}^+$$

is equivalent to the starting point α.

4.3   Remarks on Backwards-Looking Operators

The results in the previous two sub-sections have repercussions on the extension of intensional type logic by so-called *backwards-looking operators* that have been proposed as formal counterparts to certain anaphoric locutions like the final word of a classic example from [24, p. 343]:

(23)   Every man who ever supported the Vietnam war believes now that one day he will have to admit that he was an idiot then.

It should first be noted that the interpretation of (23) requires the kind of index-splitting described in Sect. 4.1: the noun *idiot* needs to be evaluated relatively to a world quantified over by the attitude verb *admit* and a time quantified over by the temporal adverb *ever*. Here is a simplified Tyn-formalization of a straightforward reading of (23), where index-arguments of constants are listed as subscripts to increase readability:

---

[15] The reasoning runs parallel to the proof Corollary (50b) in [16, Sec. 2.6]; see the next sub-section for this connection.

(24) $(\forall x)[\text{Man}_{w_0,t_0}(x) \rightarrow (\forall t_1)[t_1 < t_0$
         $\rightarrow \text{Bel}_{w_0,t^*}(x)(\lambda w_1.\ (\exists t_2 > t_0)\ \text{Adm}_{w_1,t_2}(x)(\lambda w_2.\ \text{Idi}_{w_2,t_1}(x)))]]$

Due to the presence of *now* in the main clause, (23) calls for a two-dimensional framework – thence the t^* indicating at which time the main predicate is evaluated.[16] However, the final *then* in (23) poses an additional problem, beyond parameter-splitting and two-dimensionality: neither does it relate back to the context time denoted by t^*, nor is it captured by the 'local' evaluation time(s) introduced by *would* and indicated by the bound variable t_2; rather, *then* relates to the times quantified over by *ever* in the relative clause and denoted by t_1. In other words, the temporal anaphor calls for another dimension beyond context and index. In fact, given its flexibility – co-reference with t_2 is only one of the many ways of construing *then* in (23) – a multitude of dimensions appears to be required to cover its full range of readings, viz. one for each potential antecedent (temporal) operator in whose scope the relevant occurrence of *then* is located.

Backwards-looking operators have been designed to capture precisely this referential flexibility. For reasons of space, we cannot go into the – notoriously messy – interpretive details, and refer to the literature starting with [24]. In [16], the semantic account of [29] has been adapted for integration into a two-dimensional intensional type-logic with split indices, along the lines of the first paragraph of Sect. 4.1 above. There the operators take the form Я_r^l (where l and r are natural numbers), and are subject to the following interpretative clause (= [16, (42h)]):

(25) $[\![\text{Я}_r^l \varphi]\!]^{M,(w_c,t_c),\rho,n,g} = [\![\varphi]\!]^{M,(w_c,t_c),\rho[n+1/(\rho(l)_1,\rho(r)_2)],n+1,g}$

In (25), the index is replaced by a sequence ρ of world-time pairs keeping track of 'local' indices introduced by other operators and the additional parameter n measures the depth of intensional embedding. Hence Я_r^l shifts the evaluation index of its argument to a pair consisting of the world bound by the operator of depth l and the time bound by the operator of depth r.

As the choice of the variable 'φ' in (25) suggests, the backwards-looking operators only embed formulae of type t. This is so because the $Ty2$-translation of terms of the form $\text{Я}_r^l \varphi$ need to make explicit reference to the two components of the index, which they can only do by way of a side condition to be conjoined to the rest of the translation. However, once $IL^\times$ gives way to IL, the operators in (25) can be simplified and generalized to arbitrary types. As a case in point, the pertinent reading of *then* needed for (23) would come out as follows:

(26) $[\![\text{Я}_k^\tau \alpha]\!]^{M,(w_c,t_c),(\rho_\omega,\rho_\tau),n,g} = [\![\alpha]\!]^{M,(w_c,t_c),(\rho_\omega,\rho_\tau[n+1/(\rho_t(k))]),n+1,g}$

As in the previous subsection, ω and τ are the (index) types of worlds and times and α stands for IL-2d terms of arbitrary types $a \in IT$. As a result of splitting up the indices into separate sorts, backwards-looking operators à la (26) only

---

[16] The (contextual) truth conditions of (23) are captured by equating index time t_0 and context time t^* in (24), which still need to be kept apart to account for embedded occurrences of (23).

target one index type at a time, which is why they can do with one numerical subscript. For the same reason the sequences ρ of world-time pairs in (25) need to give way to pairs of sequences ρ_ω and ρ_τ of worlds and times. Apart from these cosmetic changes, (25) and (26) are completely parallel. But, of course, (26) is unselective as regards the types of its arguments.

In [16] it was shown that the addition of backwards-looking operators as in (25) does not increase the expressivity of *IL-sentences*, i.e. terms of type t.[17] However, the equivalence does not seem to extend to formulae of other types $a \in IT$. The reason for this embarrassment lies in the fact that the two-dimensional operators NOW and ACT need to be combined with terms of type t – like those in (25), and for analogous reasons. However, since no such restriction holds once index components are represented by types (cf. (22) above), we are now in a position to establish a stronger expressivity result (where *YIL* is the result of extending IL-2d with backwards-looking operators along the lines of (26)):[18]

(27)   *Theorem*
        For any $\alpha \in YIL_a$ (where $a \in IT$), there is a $\beta \in IL_a$ such that for any $M, (w_c, t_c), \rho_\omega, \rho_\tau,$ and g:
        $[\![\alpha]\!]^{M,(w_c,t_c),(\rho_\omega,\rho_\tau),0,g} = [\![\beta]\!]^{M,(w_c,t_c),(\rho_\omega(0),\rho_\tau(0)),g}$.

References

1. Bäuerle, R.: Pragmatisch-semantische Aspekte der NP-Interpretation. In: Faust, M., Harweg, R., Lehfeldt, W., Wienold, G. (eds.) Allgemeine Sprachwissenschaft, Sprachtypologie und Textlinguistik, pp. 121–131. Narr, Tübingen (1983)
2. Carnap, R.: Meaning and Necessity. University of Chicago Press, Chicago (1947)
3. Church, A.: A formulation of the simple theory of types. J. Symb. Log. **5**(2), 56–68 (1940)
4. Curry, H.B., Feys, R.: Combinatory Logic, vol. I. North-Holland Publishing Company, Amsterdam (1958)
5. Davidson, D.: On saying that. Synthese **19**, 130–146 (1968)
6. Frege, G.: Function und Begriff. Pohle, Jena (1891)
7. Frege, G.: Über Sinn und Bedeutung. Zeitschrift für Philosophie und philosophische Kritik NF **100**(1), 25–50 (1892)
8. Friedman, J., Warren, D.S.: λ-normal forms in an intensional logic for English. Studia Logica **XXXIX**(2–3), 311–324 (1980)
9. Gallin, D.: Intensional and Higher-order Modal Logic. North-Holland Pub. Company, Amsterdam (1975)
10. Groenendijk, J., Stokhof, M.: Semantic analysis of WH-complements. Linguist. Philos. **5**(2), 175–233 (1982)

---

[17] Apart from that a further result was proved to the effect that denotational equivalence holds across all types at diagonal points; obviously, this result is also covered by (27).

[18] The 'Y' stands for 'Yanovich' on whose account [29] of backwards-looking operators (25) and (26) are based.

11. Heim, I., Kratzer, A.: Semantics in Generative Grammar. Blackwell Publishers Ltd., Oxford (1998)

12. Henkin, L.: A theory of propositional types. Fundamenta Mathematicae **52**(3), 323–334 (1963)

13. Kamp, H.: Formal properties of "now". Theoria **37**, 227–273 (1971)

14. Kaplan, D.: On the logic of demonstratives. J. Philos. Log. **8**, 81–98 (1979)

15. Kaplan, D.: Demonstratives. An essay on the semantics, logic, metaphysics and epistemology of demonstratives and other indexicals. In: Almog, J., Perry, J., Wettstein, H. (eds.) Themes from Kaplan, pp. 481–563. Oxford University Press, Oxford (1989)

16. Köpping, J., Zimmermann, T.E.: Looking backwards in type logic. Inquiry (forthcoming)

17. Kripke, S.A.: Semantical considerations on modal logic. Acta Philosophica Fennica **16**, 83–94 (1963)

18. Lewis, D.K.: Index, context, and content. In: Kanger, S., Öhman, S. (eds.) Philosophy and Grammar, pp. 79–100. Reidel, Dordrecht (1980)

19. Montague, R.: Pragmatics. In: Klibansky, R. (ed.) Contemporary Philosophy. Volume I: Logic and the Foundations of Mathematics, pp. 102–122. La Nuova Italia Editrice, Florence (1968)

20. Montague, R.: Universal Grammar. Theoria **36**(3), 373–398 (1970)

21. Montague, R.: The proper treatment of quantification in ordinary English. In: Hintikka, J., Moravcsik, J., Suppes, P. (eds.) Approaches to Natural Language, pp. 221–242. Reidel, Dordrecht (1973)

22. Parsons, T.: Frege's hierarchies of indirect senses and the paradox of analysis. In: French, P., Uehling, T., Wettstein, H. (eds.) Midwest Studies in Philosophy VI: The Foundations of Analytic Philosophy, pp. 37–57. University of Minnesota Press, Minneapolis (1981)

23. Percus, O.: Constraints on some other variables in syntax. Nat. Lang. Semant. **9**(1), 173–229 (2000)

24. Saarinen, E.: Backwards-looking operators in tense logic and in natural language. In: Hintikka, J., Niiniluoto, I., Saarinen, E. (eds.) Essays on Mathematical and Philosophical Logic, pp. 341–367. Reidel, Dordrecht (1979)

25. Scott, D.: Advice on modal logic. In: Lambert, K. (ed.) Philosophical Problems in Logic, pp. 143–173. Reidel, Dordrecht (1970)

26. Stalnaker, R.: A theory of conditionals. In: Rescher, N. (ed.) Studies in Logical Theory, pp. 41–55. Blackwell, Oxford (1968)

27. Stalnaker, R.: The problem of logical omniscience, I. Synthese **89**, 425–440 (1991)

28. Stalnaker, R.: The problem of logical omniscience, II. In: Context and Content, pp. 255–273. Oxford University Press, Oxford (1999)

29. Yanovich, I.: Expressive power of "now" and "then" operators. J. Log. Lang. Inf. **24**(1), 65–93 (2015)

30. Zimmermann, T.E.: Intensional logic and two-sorted type theory. J. Symb. Log. **54**(1), 65–77 (1989)

31. Zimmermann, T.E.: Fregean compositionality. In: Ball, D., Rabern, B. (eds.) The Science of Meaning, pp. 276–305. Oxford University Press, Oxford (2018)

32. Zimmermann, T.E.: Representing intensionality: variables vs. parameters. In: Gutzmann, D., Matthewson, L., Meier, C., Rullmann, H., Zimmermann, T.E. (eds.) The Wiley Blackwell Companion to Semantics. Oxford, Wiley (forthcoming)

From Discourse to Logic with Stanford CoreNLP and Treebank Semantics

Alastair Butler[✉]

Faculty of Humanities and Social Sciences, Hirosaki University,
Bunkyo-cho 1, Hirosaki-shi 036-8560, Japan
ajb129@hirosaki-u.ac.jp

Abstract. This paper describes combining the parsing of Stanford CoreNLP with the transformations of Treebank Semantics to realise a system for taking raw text as input to reach logical representation output. The analysis converts tree content into the structures of a formal language which is then processed against a locally constrained global calculation. The calculation resolves the interpretation, including the accessibility of antecedents for pronouns and definites, but, most in particular, it is the system that decides predicate valency through self-regulation of the calculation to ensure results from a minimum of explicit input.

Keywords: Logical representation · Treebank annotation · Analysis conversion · Predicate valency · Antecedent accessibility

1 Introduction

This paper describes combining the parsing of Stanford CoreNLP with the transformations of Treebank Semantics to realise a system for taking raw text as input to reach logical representation output. Section 2 sketches creating parsed structure from raw text using the Stanford CoreNLP server. Section 3 adds the ability to normalise parsed data to the format Treebank Semantics expects as input. Section 4 details the command line tools of Treebank Semantics that obtain semantic representations. Section 5 illustrates the treatment of a complex sentence. Section 6 is a summary for the paper.

The described method builds on the approach of Butler (2015), sharing the formal language of Scope Control Theory (SCT) as the pivotal intermediate component. What is new are the interfaces that surround the SCT calculation. These interfaces include the resulting XML output, but more in particular the method of normalisation for taking input syntactic structure. The expectation

This paper benefited from the comments of two anonymous reviewers, from the participants of LENLS16, from Naoya Fujikawa, and from discussions with Vance Gwidt and Hiroaki Nakamura, all of whom are gratefully acknowledged. This research was supported by the NINJAL Parsed Corpus of Modern Japanese (NPCMJ) project funded by the National Institute for Japanese Language and Linguistics (NINJAL), and by the Japan Society for the Promotion of Science (JSPS), Kakenhi Project 19K00541.

© Springer Nature Switzerland AG 2020
M. Sakamoto et al. (Eds.): JSAI-isAI 2019, LNAI 12331, pp. 182–196, 2020.
https://doi.org/10.1007/978-3-030-58790-1_12

of normalised input provides a common point of interface for accepting parsed data from essentially any source format and for any natural language, provided there is enough information about word class, constituency, functional role, and named entity information (a basis for resolving anaphoric relations), illustrated here with the Stanford CoreNLP parser.

2   Parsing with Stanford CoreNLP

We first need a way to get from raw text input to data that is syntactically parsed. One way to do this is to use the Stanford CoreNLP on-line parser (Manning et al. 2014) available at:

`http://corenlp.run`

In addition to a web interface for browser interaction, we can make command line server submissions.

Distributed with `ts_parse` (http://www.compling.jp/ajb129/ts_parse.html), the wrapper script `parse_english_xml_corenlp` takes raw text input as part of a pipeline and, through a call of `wget`, sends this text input to the CoreNLP server, returning the result as output for the pipeline. For example, (2) shows how analysis for (1) is placed into the file `example.xml`. (Note: XML output seen with `cat` in (2) is abbreviated to show only the content used here in postprocessing.)

(1)   John smiled.

(2)

```
$ echo John smiled. | parse_english_xml_corenlp > example.xml
$ cat example.xml
<root>
  <document>
    <sentences>
      <sentence id="1">
        <tokens>
          <token id="1">
            <word>John</word>
            <lemma>John</lemma>
            <POS>NNP</POS>
            <NER>PERSON</NER>
          </token>
          <token id="2">
            <word>smiled</word>
            <lemma>smile</lemma>
            <POS>VBD</POS>
            <NER>O</NER>
          </token>
          <token id="3">
            <word>.</word>
```

```
    <lemma>.</lemma>
    <POS>.</POS>
    <NER>O</NER>
  </token>
</tokens>
<parse>(ROOT (S (NP (NNP John)) (VP (VBD smiled)) (. .)))
</parse>
<dependencies type="basic-dependencies">
  <dep type="root">
    <governor idx="0">ROOT</governor>
    <dependent idx="2">smiled</dependent>
  </dep>
  <dep type="nsubj">
    <governor idx="2">smiled</governor>
    <dependent idx="1">John</dependent>
  </dep>
  <dep type="punct">
    <governor idx="2">smiled</governor>
    <dependent idx="3">.</dependent>
  </dep>
</dependencies>
</sentence>
</sentences>
</document>
</root>
```

Such output contains skeleton constituency tree encodings that are easy to extract, notably, from the content of the `<parse>` node of (2). More specifically, we can see that the parse tree follows the annotation scheme of the Penn Treebank (Bies et al. 1995), only without any functional tags to mark grammatical role. Traces and other zero elements are also absent from parse tree results.

A look elsewhere at the overall XML parse information reveals that some functional information is available from the gathered dependencies. In addition, packaged with word tokens, there is named entity (NER) information available. With `process_xml_corenlp`, such information can be integrated into the parse tree, as in (3).

(3)

```
$ cat example.xml | process_xml_corenlp --id example --lemma > example.psd
$ cat example.psd
( (IP-MAT (NP-SBJ;{PERSON} (NPR John)) (VBD smile) (PU .)) (ID 1_example;EN))
```

The output from (3) can be seen as the graphical tree (4).

(4)

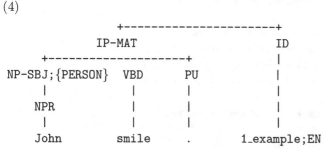

```
                    +---------------------+
            IP-MAT                         ID
    +-------------------+                  |
NP-SBJ;{PERSON}  VBD        PU             |
    |             |         |              |
   NPR            |         |              |
    |             |         |              |
  John          smile       .      1_example;EN
```

With (4), we have a tree that conforms to the Treebank Semantics Parsed
Corpus annotation scheme (TSPC; http://www.compling.jp/ajb129/tspc.html).
This can require substantial alterations to how syntactic information is encoded
(made with Tsurgeon, a pattern-action language for altering trees; Levy and
Andrew 2006), but is essentially preserving of the information content available
from the CoreNLP parse. For our running example, we see that -SBJ is integrated to the noun phrase. Also, available named entity information ;PERSON is
added to the noun phrase.

3   Normalisation

The parsing seen with (2) and (3) produces a language-specific syntactic analysis
of the source text. With normalisation the goal is to preserve the information
encoded in syntactic structures but express that information with a reduced
number of language neutral structures and categories. With normalisation, we
reach a syntactic analysis that is suitable for sending on to the Treebank Semantics command line tools for reaching a meaning representation analysis.

The full inventory of tags available for encoding normalised trees is as follows:

Construction Marker Tags.

```
ACT       - invoke or supplement an operation
CONN      - connective
PROP      - propositional relation
ROLE      - grammatical role
SORT      - sort information for discourse referent
```

Part-of-speech tags

```
ADX       - adjective/adverb
N         - noun
NPR       - proper name
PRO       - pronoun
Q         - quantifier
VB        - main predicate
WH        - WH word
```

Syntactic tags

```
ADXP    - adjective/adverb phrase
CONJP   - conjunction phrase
CP-QUE  - types the clause as a question
CP-REL  - types the clause as a relative clause
CP-THT  - types the clause with a complementiser
IML     - intermediate clause level (occurs with CONJP)
IP-CTL  - control clause
IP-CTL2 - control clause for external subject
IP-MAT  - matrix clause
IP-SUB  - non-control clause
NP      - noun phrase
PP      - projection for grammatical role or subordinate conjunction
```

We have seen with (3) how to reach parsed trees presented with the TSPC annotation scheme. To reach normalised trees, we process with parse_modify, as in (5).

(5)
```
$ cat example.psd | parse_modify > example.norm
$ cat example.norm
( (IP-MAT (ACT past) (PP (ROLE ARG0) (NP (SORT PERSON) (NPR John))) (VB
smile)) (ID 1_example;EN))
```

The returned content of example.norm can be seen with the graphical tree (6).

(6)

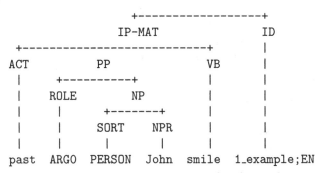

```
                        +------------------+
                        IP-MAT              ID
        +---------------------------+        |
     ACT          PP                VB       |
      |     +----------+            |        |
      |   ROLE         NP           |        |
      |     |     +--------+        |        |
      |     |   SORT     NPR        |        |
      |     |     |       |         |        |
    past  ARG0  PERSON  John      smile  1_example;EN
```

Normalisation regularises structure and reduces the inventory of tag labels. This includes redistributing information from basic grammatical categories into offset elements. Thus, the NP-SBJ tag is changed to NP, which is placed under a PP projection that contains (ROLE ARG0) to retain the contribution of -SBJ. This generalises so that all arguments become PP projections with role information. Also, a SORT node is created to carry the PERSON information offset from NP-SBJ;PERSON.

Also note that VBD (past tense verb) is changed with normalisation to VB. The otherwise lost tense information is retained with the offset (ACT past) at the clause level. Because (ACT past) has a set scope contribution (that is, below all arguments and modifiers, and immediately above the verb), it is of no consequence where in the clause it is placed.

4   Treebank Semantics Command Line Tools

We can now consider using the Treebank Semantics command line programs (available from http://www.compling.jp/ajb129/ts.html).

4.1   Obtaining a Normalised Prolog Expression

The first step is to convert a normalised tree into a normalised Prolog expression. This is achieved by sending normalised trees through start_ts, as in (7).

(7)

```
$ cat example.norm | start_ts
sent('1_example', local(['ARG0'], npr(c('PERSON', 'John'), 'ARG0',
past('.event', verb('.event', x('EVENT', 1), 'smile', ['ARG0']))))).
```

This creates a Prolog term expression that follows the basic constituency of (6), while adding functors

- npr/3 to capture the contribution of a noun phrase with a proper name, that manifests as the discourse referent (entity constant) c('PERSON', 'John');
- past/2 to retain past tense information through a '.event' binding; and
- verb/4 to capture the content of the main verb of the source clause by providing the discourse referent (event variable) x('EVENT', 1) as content for a '.event' binding, together with the content for a 'smile' predicate that selects an 'ARG0' argument.

4.2   How Was the Normalised Prolog Expression Built?

We might wonder how the normalised Prolog expression was assembled from the normalised syntactic tree that was taken as input. To find out, we can use start_ts with the --detail command line switch. Here is how the normalised Prolog expression for our running example was built:

(8)

```
$ cat example.norm | start_ts --detail
=========================
NP-in:
  (SORT PERSON) (NPR John)
-------------------------
NP-out:
  (NP npr(c('PERSON', 'John'), _X_, _E_)_LOCAL_)
=========================
PP-in:
  (ROLE ARG0) (NP npr(c('PERSON', 'John'), _X_, _E_)_LOCAL_)
-------------------------
PP-out:
  (PP-NP-ENTITY npr(c('PERSON', 'John'), 'ARG0', _E_)_LOCAL_'ARG0')
=========================
IP-MAT-in:
  (ACT past) (PP-NP-ENTITY npr(c('PERSON', 'John'), 'ARG0', _E_)_LOCAL_'ARG0')
(VB smile)
-------------------------
IP-MAT-out:
  (IP-MAT-FACT npr(c('PERSON', 'John'), 'ARG0', past('.event', verb('.event',
x('EVENT', 1), 'smile', ['ARG0'])))_LOCAL_'ARG0')
=========================
```

4.3 Obtaining a Semantic Representation

The next step is to obtain semantic representations derived from the evaluation of normalised Prolog expressions. At the start of the calculation, there is a collection of discourse referents which are read from the normalised input. For our running example, this is the entity constant c('PERSON', 'John'), and the event variable x('EVENT', 1).

Discourse referents are ultimately destined to be bound by operations of closure (e.g., "exists") in the overall resulting logical expression, or left free in the case of constants. The operations of closure are themselves either reflexes of quantification instructions from the normalised input, or arise because there is discourse closure. During the runtime of the calculation, the collected discourse referents are released as content for argument slots of predicates that populate the resulting logical expression. The exact makeup of arguments (valency) for a given predicate is typically left unspecified by the input. At the point in the calculation when the predicate is reached, the availability of accessible discourse referents is established. The predicate's sensitivity to what is accessible determines the arguments for the predicate.

Calculation of an output is achieved by adding run_tsxml to the pipeline, as follows:

(9)

```
$ cat example.norm | start_ts | run_tsxml
<tsxml>
    <top id="1_example">
        <quant name="exists">
            <bound><term sort="EVENT" id="1"/></bound>
            <connect name="and">
                <pred name="past">
                    <at role="h"><term sort="EVENT" id="1"/></at>
                </pred>
                <pred name="smile">
                    <at role="EVENT"><term sort="EVENT" id="1"/></at>
                    <at role="ARG0"><term sort="PERSON" id="John"/></at>
                </pred>
            </connect>
        </quant>
    </top>
</tsxml>
```

Semantic representations are presented with an XML format that has the virtue of being easily transformed to other formats. As the foundation for considering inference, we can—inspired by Blackburn and Bos (2003) and, more in particular, Kiselyov (2018)—transform to representations in the format of TPTP (Thousands of Problems for Theorem Provers; Sutcliffe 2009)—that is, to a representation format suitable for being submitted to theorem provers or model builders. With our running example, we reach TPTP output by further processing with tsxml_to_text, as follows:

(10)

```
$ cat example.norm | start_ts | run_tsxml | tsxml_to_text --tptp
fof(ex1Example,axiom,(
    ? [EVENT1] :
    ( isIn(EVENT1,past) & isIn(EVENT1,smile)
    & arg0(EVENT1) = personSortJohn ) )).
```

4.4   Seeing Steps in the Semantic Calculation

The program run_tsxml undertakes and completes a semantic calculation all in one go, returning only the XML output. To gain insight into how the calculation works, we need to further expose stages involved. For reasons of space, we limit discussion here to what is needed for our running example. For a full description, the interested reader is referred to the documentation that accompanies the Treebank Semantics distribution.

The internal stages of run_tsxml involve several tasks of changing input from a higher level formal language (in the sense of being close to the original parsed form) to a lower level formal language (in the sense of being close to the end logical formula output). This starts from normalised Prolog expressions as seen produced with (7) in Sect. 4.1. From such initial Prolog expressions, there is transformation into Prolog expressions of an intermediate language—the Scope Control Theory (SCT) language of Butler (2015).

With this change to the SCT language, expressions rapidly grow in size with the complexity of the sentence/discourse. While output is sent to a single line, one quick way to achieve a more readable output is to place the content on multiple lines with `sed 's/ \([^ ]*\)/\n\1/g'`. We can take a look at the transformation of our running example into an intermediate Prolog SCT expression with `run_tsterm -2`, as follows:

(11)

```
$ cat example.norm | start_ts | run_tsterm -2 | sed 's/ \([^ ]*\)/\n\1/g'
head('exists',
.('@e',
.('.event', []))),
body(.('@e',
.('.event', []))),
namely(c('PERSON', 'John'), '@e',
mov('@e', 'ARGO',
rel([], [], '',
.(namely(x('EVENT', 1), '.event',
rel([], [], 'smile',
.(at(t('.event'), 'EVENT'),
.(at(t('ARGO'), 'ARGO'), [])))),
.(bodyClimb('.event',
rel([], [], 'past',
.(at(t('.event'), 'h'), [])), []))))))))
```

With (11) the high-level functors of (7) (`npr/3`, `past/2`, and `verb/4`) are replaced by combinations of

- `namely/3`, which adds its discourse referent to the information state as part of the assignment made to the binding name given with its second parameter;
- `mov/3`, which is an operation to transfer the assignment of a discourse referent; e.g., for the creation of a local binding.
- `rel/4`, which assembles predicate relations, and (dynamic) connective relations;
- `at/2`, which encodes role information to realise an argument;
- `t/1`, which constructs a terminal binding; and
- `bodyClimb/2`, which marks conditions, that await integration into the containing expression at higher coindexed instances of `body/2`.

Moreover all content is placed under a `head/3` and `body/2` structure that creates existential closure for the entire discourse, where:

- `head/3` brings about a quantificational closure (`'exists'`, etc.) and is indexed to collect `x/2` discourse referents, and

– `body/2` is indexed to collect coindexed `headClimb/3` content.

Having reached an SCT expression, the system next performs a calculation to derive an expression in a target language. The result of this further stage can be seen with **run_tsterm -3**, as follows:

(12)

```
$ cat example.norm | start_ts | run_tsterm -3 | sed 's/ \([^ ]*\)/\n\1/g'
head('exists',
.('@e',
.('.event', [])),
.(x('EVENT', 1), []),
body(.('@e',
.('.event', [])),
rel('',
.(rel('smile',
.(at(x('EVENT', 1), 'EVENT'),
.(at(c('PERSON', 'John'), 'ARG0'), []))),
.(bodyClimb('.event',
rel('past',
.(at(x('EVENT', 1), 'h'), []))), [])))))
```

With (12) we can see a representation that essentially has the form of a Discourse Representation Structure (DRS; Kamp and Reyle 1993), with **head/4** to declare the top box, which is binding the discourse referent x('EVENT', 1), and **body/2** to declare the bottom box which collects conditions.

Further calculation of the target language expression to realise the description for a predicate logic expression is achieved with **run_tsterm -4**, as follows:

(13)

```
$ cat example.norm | start_ts | run_tsterm -4 | sed 's/ \([^ ]*\)/\n\1/g'
quant('exists',
.(x('EVENT', 1), []),
rel('',
.(rel('past',
.(at(x('EVENT', 1), 'h'), [])),
.(rel('smile',
.(at(x('EVENT', 1), 'EVENT'),
.(at(c('PERSON', 'John'), 'ARG0'), []))), []))))
```

Having reached the description of (13) using the target language—that is, a Prolog term—the final step is to convert the result into the XML format, seen achieved already with **run_tsxml** in Sect. 4.3.

5   A More Interesting Example

The example we have considered so far, (1), is a very simple sentence. To illustrate wider applicability, this section considers the Bach-Peters sentence (14)

(Bach 1970; Karttunen 1971). Notably, (14) allows for an interpretation in which (i) *it* is understood to refer to the same individual as the entity *the MIG that chased him*, and (ii) *him* is coreferential with the subject *the pilot who shot at it*.

(14)   The pilot who shot at it hit the MIG that chased him.

With the Stanford CoreNLP parser and the further processing of Sect. 2, we reach the parse tree of (15).

(15)

```
 1 ( (IP-MAT (REF;{ENTITY} *)
 2            (NP-SBJ;{PERSON} (D;{DEF} The)
 3                            (N pilot)
 4                            (IP-REL (NP-SBJ (WPRO who))
 5                                    (VBD shot)
 6                                    (PP-DIR (P-ROLE at)
 7                                            (NP;{ENTITY} (PRO it)))))
 8            (VBD hit)
 9            (NP-OB1;{ENTITY} (D;{DEF} the)
10                            (N MIG)
11                            (IP-REL (NP-SBJ (WPRO that))
12                                    (VBD chased)
13                                    (NP-OB1;{PERSON} (PRO him))))
14            (PU .))
15   (ID 120_samples_BUFFALO;EN))
```

Note (15) includes (REF;ENTITY *) at the discourse initial position of line 1. This is an accommodated antecedent for the pronoun (NP;ENTITY (PRO it)) at line 7, which otherwise has no accessible antecedent.

With the normalisation of Sect. 3, we reach the structure of (16).

(16)

```
 1 ( (IP-MAT (ACT past)
 2            (PP (ROLE *)
 3                (NP (SORT ENTITY)))
 4            (PP (ROLE ARG0)
 5                (NP (SORT PERSON)
 6                    (ACT DEF)
 7                    (N pilot)
 8                    (CP-REL (IP-SUB (ACT past)
 9                                    (PP (ROLE ?e)
10                                        (NP *T*))
11                                    (PP (ROLE ARG0)
12                                        (NP (WH who)))
13                                    (VB shot)
14                                    (PP (ROLE DIR_at)
```

```
15                                          (NP (SORT ENTITY)
16                                              (PRO it)))))))
17          (VB hit)
18          (PP (ROLE @e)
19              (NP (SORT ENTITY)
20                  (PRO *DEF*)))
21          (PP (ROLE ARG1)
22              (NP (ACT DEF)
23                  (N MIG)
24                  (CP-REL (IP-SUB (ACT past)
25                                  (PP (ROLE ?e)
26                                      (NP *T*))
27                                  (PP (ROLE ARG0)
28                                      (NP (WH that)))
29                                  (VB chased)
30                                  (PP (ROLE ARG1)
31                                      (NP (SORT PERSON)
32                                          (PRO him)))))))))
33   (ID 120_samples_BUFFALO))
```

(REF;ENTITY *) in line 1 of (15) expands to (PP (ROLE *) (NP (SORT ENTITY))) in lines 2–3 of (16). This in turn will be converted (following Sect. 4.1) to Prolog expression content (17), where __E__ is a place holder for the rest of the matrix clause content.

```
(17)  some( '.e',
             x( 'ENTITY',1)
             ,
             local( .( 'h',[])
                    ,
                    pred( '',[]))
             ,'*',__E__)
```

Conversion to (17) creates x('ENTITY',1) as a discourse referent that '*' immediately makes accessible as a referent of the discourse context. pred('',[]) reflects the lack of further restriction for the created antecedent.

Also note the contribution of the relative pronoun 'who' of line 4 in (15), which expands to (PP (ROLE ARG0) (NP (WH who))) in lines 11–12 of (16). This is converted (following Sect. 4.1) to Prolog expression content (18), with some/5 to open an 'ARG0' binding over the remaining clause content __E__. Moreover, (WH Who) of (16) gives '?e' to state that the created discourse referent x('ENTITY',2) is under question. There is no other content to the noun phrase, giving pred('',[]) as the empty restriction.

```
(18)  some( '?e',
           x( 'ENTITY',2)
           ,
           local( .( 'h',[])
                  ,
                  pred( '',[]))
           ,'ARG0',__E__)
```

Content (18) is the typical contribution of a WH-phrase as found in a WH-question. That is, (18) functions to introduce a new discourse referent that is marked to be placed under question. Yet, within the context of (14), the WH phrase needs to function as a relative pronoun, so rather than introduce a completely new discourse referent, its contribution should rather be the maintenance of a binding inherited from the noun phrase that is brought through to the relative clause as a local 'ARG0' (subject) binding. This change in role is accomplished by lines 9–10 of (16), namely (PP (ROLE ?e) (NP *T*)), which expands into the Prolog expression content of (19), with __E__ as a place holder to take the content of (18).

```
(19)  mov( 'T','?e',
           wipe( '?e',__E__))
```

Having (19) prepares the ground for the relative pronoun by providing an instruction to integrate the binding that will correspond to the binding for the head of the relative clause. This head binding is picked up with 'T' (having been placed there by operations induced by CP-REL of line 8 of (16)) and moved to the '?e' name. There is also a wipe/2 instruction that serves to eliminate from the calculation the next '?e' introduced element. As a consequence, the discourse referent of (18), namely x('ENTITY',2), will have no presence in the final calculated result.

This trick of a created discourse referent having its contribution "wiped away" and replaced holds true of the second relative pronoun in lines 27–28 of (16), but it also holds true for the definite noun phrase introduced at line 22. This is because the line 22 noun phrase is preceded by lines 18–20. Lines 18–20, namely (PP (ROLE @e) (NP (SORT ENTITY) (PRO *DEF*))), contain PRO to create a discourse referent that is resolved to an accessible ENTITY antecedent. Because of (ROLE @e), this discourse referent created by PRO is used to supplant the discourse referent of the next occurring definite, to thereby establish a link between the noun phrase *the MIG that chased him* and the preceding *it* by virtue of both having been anaphorically resolved to the discourse referent of the accommodated REF in line 1 of (15).

Following Sect. 4, that is, conversion to a Prolog term, semantic calculation, and then conversion to a TPTP formula expression, we are able to reach (20).

(20)

```
fof(ex120SamplesBUFFALO,axiom,(
    ? [PERSON9,ENTITY3,ENTITY7,EVENT13,EVENT4,EVENT10,PERSON6,ENTITY1]  :
      ( isIn(EVENT13,past)
      & isIn(EVENT10,past)
      & isIn(EVENT4,past)
      & PERSON9 = PERSON6
      & isIn(ENTITY7,mig)
      & isIn(EVENT10,chased)
      & arg1(EVENT10) = PERSON9
      & arg0(EVENT10) = ENTITY7
      & ENTITY3 = ENTITY1
      & isIn(PERSON6,pilot)
      & isIn(EVENT4,shot)
      & dirAt(EVENT4) = ENTITY3
      & arg0(EVENT4) = PERSON6
      & ENTITY7 = ENTITY1
      & isIn(EVENT13,hit)
      & arg1(EVENT13) = ENTITY7
      & arg0(EVENT13) = PERSON6 ) )).
```

Following creation of (20), the result can be still further processed, e.g., with the Clause Normal Form translation procedure of FLOTTER (Nonnengart et al. 1998), which includes skolemisation to distill the dependencies to those visualised in Fig. 1.

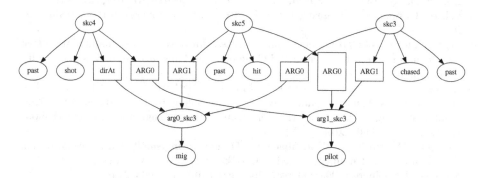

Fig. 1. Dependencies visualisation of (20)

6   Summary

The semantic analysis sketched in Sect. 4 is a language-independent system that converts tree content into the structures of a formal language which is then processed against a locally constrained global calculation. Outputs of the calculation are logic based meaning representations. The calculation makes reference to a changing information state that manages the availability of collected discourse referents over an entire discourse (although for reasons of space only two examples, both as single sentences, could be demonstrated). This information state holds content to resolve the interpretation, including the accessibility of antecedents for pronouns and definites constrained by named entity information, but more pervasively the support for determining predicate valency. In this way, the parse information obtained from Stanford CoreNLP is found to be sufficient for automatically obtaining rich semantic representations.

References

Bach, E.: Pronominalization. Linguist. Inq. **1**, 121–122 (1970)

Bies, A., Ferguson, M., Katz, K., MacIntyre, R.: Bracketing guidelines for Treebank II style Penn Treebank project. Technical report MS-CIS-95-06, LINC LAB 281. University of Pennsylvania Computer and Information Science Department (1995)

Blackburn, P., Bos, J.: Computational Semantics. Theoria **13**, 27–45 (2003)

Butler, A.: Linguistic Expressions and Semantic Processing: A Practical Approach. Springer, Heidelberg (2015). https://doi.org/10.1007/978-3-319-18830-0

Kamp, H., Reyle, U.: From Discourse to Logic: Introduction to Model-theoretic Semantics of Natural Language, Formal Logic and Discourse Representation Theory. Kluwer, Dordrecht (1993)

Karttunen, L.: Definite descriptions with crossing coreference: a study of the bach-peters paradox. Found. Lang. **7**, 157–182 (1971)

Kiselyov, O.: Transformational semantics on a tree bank. In: Arai, S., Kojima, K., Mineshima, K., Bekki, D., Satoh, K., Ohta, Y. (eds.) JSAI-isAI 2017. LNCS (LNAI), vol. 10838, pp. 241–252. Springer, Cham (2018). https://doi.org/10.1007/978-3-319-93794-6_17

Levy, R., Andrew, G.: Tregex and Tsurgeon: tools for querying and manipulating tree data structure. In: 5th International Conference on Language Resources and Evaluation (2006)

Manning, C.D., Surdeanu, M., Bauer, J., Finkel, J., Bethard, S.J., McClosky, D.: The stanford CoreNLP natural language processing toolkit. In: Proceedings of the 52nd Annual Meeting of the Association for Computational Linguistics: System Demonstrations, pp. 55–60 (2014)

Nonnengart, A., Rock, G., Weidenbach, C.: On generating small clause normal forms. In: Kirchner, C., Kirchner, H. (eds.) CADE 1998. LNCS, vol. 1421, pp. 397–411. Springer, Heidelberg (1998). https://doi.org/10.1007/BFb0054274

Sutcliffe, G.: The TPTP problem library and associated infrastructure: the FOF and CNF parts, v3.5.0. J. Autom. Reason. **43**(4), 337–362 (2009)

Even More Varieties of Conventional Implicatures: Paratactically Associating Intonation, Particles and Questions

Yurie Hara[1]([envelope])(iD) and Mengxi Yuan[2](iD)

[1] Hokkaido University, Sapporo, Hokkaido, Japan
hara@imc.hokudai.ac.jp
[2] Jinan University, Guangzhou, Guangdong, China
mengxiyuan49@hotmail.com

Abstract. This paper proposes a new composition rule for discourse particles and prosodic morphemes that paratactically-associate with the main text. Furthermore, the data and analyses support the framework of inquisitive semantics since the morphemes at issue often embed both declarative and interrogative clauses.

Keywords: Intonation · Particles · Expressives · Conventional implicatures · Compositional semantics · Inquisitive semantics · Clause types · Paratactic association

1 Introduction

Discourse particles and prosodic morphemes often give rise to secondary meanings in addition to the meanings computed from the main text to which they attach. For instance, in Osaka Japanese, when a *wh*-question is uttered with a sentence-final particle *nen* with final fall '$\downarrow$/L%' as in (1),[1] the sentence seems to express two meanings. One is a plain question 'What are you going to eat?' and the other is the speaker's irritation:

(1)   nani taberu nen$\downarrow$
        what eat   NEN
        'What are you going to eat?!' (You have to decide now!)

In the literature on the interpretation of prosodic morphemes (Bartels 1999; Gunlogson 2003) and discourse particles, it has been tacitly assumed that the morpheme/particle is somehow attached to the entire sentence and projects an expressive meaning independent of the meaning of the host sentence. This paper

---

[1] See Ikeda (2001) for ToBI labelling of prosody in Osaka Japanese.

This project is supported by JSPS Kiban (C) "Semantic-Pragmatic Interfaces at Left Periphery: a neuroscientific approach" (18K00589) awarded to the first author.

© Springer Nature Switzerland AG 2020
M. Sakamoto et al. (Eds.): JSAI-isAI 2019, LNAI 12331, pp. 197–213, 2020.
https://doi.org/10.1007/978-3-030-58790-1_13

offers a more concrete compositional analysis of prosody and particles by introducing a new composition rule that instructs how to interpret paratactically-associated expressive morphemes.

Another hallmark of prosodic morphemes and particles is that they often attach to both declarative and interrogative clauses. As an illustration, the same Osaka Japanese *nen↓* can be attached to a declarative as in (2).

(2)   konban furansu ryoori taberu nen↓.
       tonight France cuisine eat   NEN
       'I'll eat French cuisine tonight.'

The linguistic data and analyses offered in the current paper provide new evidence for the framework of inquisitive semantics (Ciardelli et al. 2019), which can deal with declaratives and interrogatives uniformly as a set of propositions.

This paper is structured as follows: Sect. 2 presents our main proposal and briefly reviews the framework of inquisitive semantics. In particular, we propose to add a new compositional rule for conventional implicatures, PARATACTIC ASSOCIATION, which is applied to the discourse particles and prosodic morphemes that are paratactically associated to the root clause. In Sect. 3, we show how the interpretations of the morphemes at issue can be derived using PARATACTIC ASSOCATION in the framework of inquisitive semantics. Section 4 concludes the paper.

2   Proposal and Theoretical Background

This section presents two theoretical frameworks that are crucial to the semantic analysis of particles and intonation in question. First, we present a new type system for expressives, namely $\mathcal{L}_{CI}^{+S,PA}$, which enables us to compute paratactically associated expressions. Second, the framework of inquisitive semantics is briefly introduced to see how declaratives and interrogatives are given the same semantic type as a set of propositions.

2.1   Syntax and Composition of Paratactic Association, $\mathcal{L}_{CI}^{+S,PA}$

We propose that discourse particles and intonational morphemes are paratactically associated (Lyons 1977; Bartels 1999) to the main sentence. Syntactically, a prosodic morpheme or particle β is paratactically associated (indicated by '$\otimes$') to the head α of the root clause, as depicted in (3).

(3)   Syntactic representation of paratactic association

$$C_{\text{ROOT}}$$
$$|$$
$$\alpha \otimes \beta$$

Meanings that arise from intonation and particles are often analyzed as expressives or conventional implicatures (Potts 2005a,b; Hara 2006; McCready 2008; Potts 2012, among others). To assign a composition rule that corresponds to the structure in (3), this paper augments McCready's (2010) $\mathcal{L}_{CI}^{+S}$ type system for conventional implicatures, since the behaviors of linguistic items discussed in the current paper are different from that of expressive expressions discussed in Potts (2005b) in several respects. The composition rule for expressives/conventional implicatures proposed by Potts (2005b), CI APPLICATION, consists of two components, one is a functional application which returns an expressive meaning $\alpha(\beta) : \tau^c$ and the other which is an identity function that returns the same at-issue content $\beta : \sigma^a$. The two expressions are conjoined by •, which is a metalogical operator that combines expressions of different types. Furthermore, the expressive part of the conjunction is saturated, i.e., of type t^c.

(4)   CI APPLICATION

$$\beta : \sigma^a \bullet \alpha(\beta) : \tau^c$$

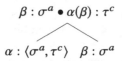

$$\alpha : \langle \sigma^a, \tau^c \rangle \quad \beta : \sigma^a$$

To see why CI APPLICATION is not suitable for the meaning composition of particles and intonation, consider the following example of standard Japanese. The sentence-final auxiliary *daroo* induces the speaker's bias toward the prejacent proposition as in (5).

(5)   Marie-wa   nomu daroo
       Marie-TOP drink DAROO
       Marie drinks, probably/I bet.

If we employed CI APPLICATION to *daroo* and a sentence it attaches to, it would return an illicit interpretation where the expressive content expresses a weaker meaning of the at-issue content, i.e., '*p* and probably *p*'.[2]

Thus, we adopt and modify McCready's (2010) $\mathcal{L}_{CI}^{+S}$ to give semantics to the structure proposed in (3). $\mathcal{L}_{CI}^{+S}$ is an extension of Potts' (2005b) $\mathcal{L}_{CI}$ obtained by adding *shunting types* to the system. Expressions with shunting types shunt the meaning tier from at-issue to expressive, thereby generate expressive contents only without yielding at-issue ones. More concretely, when the function is of shunting type then the following rule is used instead of CI APPLICATION.

(6)   SHUNTING-TYPE FUNCTIONAL APPLICATION (McCready's (2010) R7)

$$\alpha(\beta) : \tau^s$$

$$\alpha : \langle \sigma^a, \tau^s \rangle \quad \beta : \sigma^a$$

---

[2] See Hara (2006) for more discussions.

Now, we propose a new system $\mathcal{L}_{CI}^{+S,PA}$, which is obtained by adding the following type specification (7) and composition rule (8), PARATACTIC ASSOCIATION, to $\mathcal{L}_{CI}^{+S}$.[3]

(7)   A shunting product type
          If σ and τ are shunting types for $\mathcal{L}_{CI}^{+S,PA}$, then $\sigma \times \tau$ is a shunting product type for $\mathcal{L}_{CI}^{+S,PA}$.

(8)   PARATACTIC ASSOCIATION

$$\lambda\chi.\alpha(\chi){\blacklozenge}\beta(\chi) : \langle\sigma, \tau \times \upsilon\rangle$$

$$\lambda\chi.\alpha(\chi) : \langle\sigma, \tau\rangle \quad \lambda\chi.\beta(\chi) : \langle\sigma, \upsilon\rangle$$

The PARATACTIC ASSOCIATION (8) merges two functions into one by abstracting over the argument type of the two functions. $\blacklozenge$ is another metalogical operator that combines expressions of different types. Unlike $\bullet$, however, each conjunct can be unsaturated, thus can interact with other expressions in the composition. The resulting function, $\lambda\chi.\alpha(\chi){\blacklozenge}\beta(\chi)$, is combined with an at-issue expression χ of type σ^a by McCready's SHUNTING-TYPE FUNCTIONAL APPLICATION (6) and outputs a pair of shunting-type expressions $\alpha(\chi){\blacklozenge}\beta(\chi)$ of type $\tau^s \times \upsilon^s$.

In summary, discourse particles and intonational morphemes that are paratactically associated to the main sentence are semantically composed by the PARATACTIC ASSOCIATION (8). The expression that results from the composition is a pair of shunting-type expressions.

2.2   Uniform Treatment of Declaratives and Interrogatives

As we will see in Sect. 3, many particles and prosodic morphemes can attach to both declarative and interrogative sentences. Inquisitive semantics is a suitable framework to analyze these items because if declaratives and interrogatives have the same semantic type, these items that embed them do not need to be ambiguously defined.

Inquisitive Semantics. In inquisitive semantics, both declarative and interrogative sentences are treated as issues, which are downward closed sets of propositions, which in turn are sets of possible worlds:

(9)   a.   A proposition p is a set of possible worlds, i.e., $p \subseteq \mathcal{W}$.
          b.   An *issue* $I \subseteq \wp(\mathcal{W})$ is a non-empty, downward closed set of propositions.

---

[3] See Appendix A.1 and McCready (2010, 51–53) for the full type system of $\mathcal{L}_{CI}^{+S}$.

In other words, whether it is a declarative or an interrogative, a sentence is a set of sets of possible worlds of type $\langle\langle s,t\rangle, t\rangle$ (abbreviated as T in the following to avoid clutter).

Furthermore, the set of all possible worlds where φ is true is called the truth set of φ ($\text{TS}(\varphi)$) and it is obtained by taking a union of the sentence:

(10) $\text{TS}(\varphi) := \bigcup[\![\varphi]\!]$

To semantically distinguish declaratives and interrogatives, the notion of possibilities is introduced. The possibilities for a sentence φ are the maximal propositions in $[\![\varphi]\!]$:

(11) $\text{POSSIBILITY}(\varphi) := \{p \mid p \in [\![\varphi]\!] \text{ and there is no } q \in [\![\varphi]\!] \text{ such that } p \subset q\}.$

In case of a declarative clause, the set only contains a single maximal element, i.e., it is a singleton set, $|\text{POSSIBILITY}(\varphi)| = 1$, while in case of an interrogative, $|\text{POSSIBILITY}(\varphi)| \geq 2$.

To illustrate, let us see how a disjunction, a polar interrogative and a *wh*-interrogative are semantically composed.[4] First of all, a simple declarative sentence such as *Marie drinks* is a downward closed set of propositions, written $\{|\text{Marie drinks}|\}^{\downarrow}$.

(12) $[\![\textbf{Marie drinks}]\!]$ = $\{p \mid \text{Marie drinks in every } w \in p\}$ =
$\{|\text{Marie drinks}|\}^{\downarrow} = [\![\alpha]\!]$

In the following illustrations, we use $[\![\alpha]\!]$ for a denotation of *Marie drinks*.

Second, to compose a disjunction sentence like *Marie drinks or Bill eats*, we take union of two downward closed sets of propositions. Thus, the disjunction sentence is also a downward closed set of propositions. The set has two maximal propositions, 'Marie drinks' and 'Bill eats'.

(13) $[\![\textbf{Marie drinks or Bill eats}]\!] = [\![\alpha]\!] \cup [\![\beta]\!]$

Third, a polar interrogative is obtained by combining a declarative sentence with the question feature [Q]. In English, [Q] is realized by the auxiliary at Spec CP moved by the Subject-Aux inversion as in (14).

---

[4] See Ciardelli et al. (2017) for the fully compositional system for inquisitive semantics.

(14)

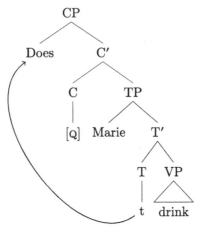

We assume that [Q] is an interrogative operator $\langle ? \rangle$ proposed by Roelofsen and Farkas (2015). In order to define the semantics of $\langle ? \rangle$, the semantics of sentential negation needs to be defined as follows:

(15) $[\![\neg\varphi]\!] := \{p \mid p \cap q = \emptyset \text{ for all } q \in [\![\varphi]\!]\}$

Following Roelofsen and Farkas (2015), $\langle ? \rangle$ is defined conditional on the status of its sister sentence. If its sister sentence φ is a declarative, that is, it is a singleton set of propositions, $\langle ? \rangle$ takes a union of $[\![\varphi]\!]$ and $[\![\neg\varphi]\!]$. If φ is already an interrogative sentence, i.e., contains multiple maximal propositions, it returns the same interrogative sentence.

(16)   a. $[\![\langle ? \rangle]\!] \in D_{\langle T, T \rangle}$

   b. $[\![\langle ? \rangle \varphi]\!] := \begin{cases} [\![\varphi]\!] \cup [\![\neg\varphi]\!], & \text{if } |\text{POSSIBILITY}(\varphi)| = 1 \\ [\![\varphi]\!], & \text{if } |\text{POSSIBILITY}(\varphi)| \geq 2 \end{cases}$

Thus, the polar interrogative, *Does Mary drink?* is also a union of two downward closed sets of propositions:

(17) $[\![\textbf{Does Mary drink}]\!] = [\![\alpha]\!] \cup [\![\neg\alpha]\!]$

Finally, we assume that a *wh*-interrogative has the following structure in (18). The *wh*-pronoun agrees with [Q] at C.

(18)

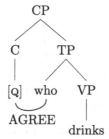

The *wh*-clause denotes a downward closed set of propositions as in (19-a). This set then combines with ⟨?⟩ but it is not a singleton set so it returns the same set as in (19-b).

(19)   a. $[\![$**who drinks**$]\!]$ = $\{p|\exists x \in D_e.x$ is human & x drinks in every $w \in p\}$
        b. $[\![\langle?\rangle$**who drinks**$]\!]$ = $\{p|\exists x \in D_e.x$ is human & x drinks in every $w \in p\}$

In short, in inquisitive semantics, both declarative and interrogative clauses are issues, i.e., downward closed sets of propositions of type $\langle\langle s, t\rangle, t\rangle = T$.

Inquisitive Epistemic Logic. A brief introduction to Inquisitive Epistemic Logic (IEL; Ciardelli and Roelofsen (2015)), which includes a treatment of modal operators, is in order, since the linguistic phenomena considered in this paper include a Japanese modal auxiliary *daroo*, which can embed both declaratives and interrogatives.

In classical epistemic logic, each agent is associated with an information state $\sigma_a(w)$ that encodes the information that is available to the agent a at w. In IEL, each agent is associated with an inquisitive state $\Sigma_a(w)$ that encodes the issues that are entertained by a at w. The standard information state $\sigma_a(w)$ can be obtained by taking a union of the inquisitive state:

(20) $\sigma_a(w) := \bigcup \Sigma_a(w).$

Now, we define the two modal operators in IEL, K and E. When K is applied to a declarative φ, it is concurrent with the knowledge operator in standard epistemic logic. That is, $K_a\varphi$ denotes a set of propositions p such that φ is true everywhere in a's information state at w for any $w \in p$. When φ is an interrogative, $K_a\varphi$ denotes a set of propositions p such that the issue represented by φ is resolved by a's information state at w for any $w \in p$.

(21) $[\![K_a\varphi]\!]$ = $\{p|$ for any $w \in p, \sigma_a(w) \in [\![\varphi]\!]\}$

When the entertain operator E applies to φ, $E_a\varphi$ denotes a set of propositions where φ is supported by any information state in a's inquisitive state at w for any

$w \in p$. Intuitively, $E_a\varphi$ states that once the issues entertained by a are resolved, the issue represented by φ will be resolved as well:

(22) $[\![E_a\varphi]\!] = \{p|$ for any $w \in p, \Sigma_a(w) \subseteq [\![\varphi]\!]\}$

Now, as can be seen, both K and E can embed both declaratives and interrogatives. Furthermore, one fact about the relation between K and E is crucial to the current paper. If the embedded sentence φ is a declarative, i.e., $|\text{POSSIBILITY}(\varphi)| = 1$, $E_a\varphi$ is equivalent to $K_a\varphi$ (see Ciardelli and Roelofsen 2015).

(23)   For any declarative φ and agent a, $[\![K_a\varphi]\!] = [\![E_a\varphi]\!]$

This equivalence can be shown as follows:[5]

(24)   Suppose $|\text{POSSIBILITY}(\varphi)| = 1$. Then, $[\![\varphi]\!] = \{q|q \subseteq \text{TS}(\varphi)\}$.

$$
\begin{aligned}
[\![E_a\varphi]\!] &= \{p|\text{for any } w \in p, \Sigma_a(w) \subseteq [\![\varphi]\!]\} \\
&= \{p|\text{for any } w \in p, \Sigma_a(w) \subseteq \{q|q \subseteq \text{TS}(\varphi)\}\} \\
&= \{p|\text{for any } w \in p, \bigcup \Sigma_a(w) \subseteq \text{TS}(\varphi)\} \\
&= \{p|\text{for any } w \in p, \sigma_a(w) \in [\![\varphi]\!]\} \\
&= [\![K_a\varphi]\!]
\end{aligned}
$$

2.3   Interim Summary

We have presented two frameworks necessary to analyze the semantics of discourse particles and prosodic morphemes. We first have proposed a new type system $\mathcal{L}_{CI}^{+S,PA}$ which enables the semantic composition to output a pair of shunting-type expressives. Second, we have sketched how declaratives and interrogatives are uniformly treated as downward closed sets of propositions in inquisitive semantics. In other words, both have the same semantic type, $\langle\langle s,t\rangle, t\rangle = T$. Moreover, IEL has two modal operators K and E which can embed both declaratives and interrogatives.

3   Deriving the Interpretations

This section shows how the two systems introduced in the previous section can derive the meanings that arise from particles and prosodic morphemes. The linguistic phenomena considered are: Osaka Japanese sentence-final particle *nen↓*, standard Japanese sentence-final auxiliary *daroo* with a rising contour, and Final Fall in English and Mandarin.

---

[5] This exposition is inspired by Uegaki and Roelofsen (2018). See also Ciardelli and Roelofsen (2015); Hara (2019).

3.1   Osaka Japanese *nen↓*

Osaka Japanese has a sentence-final particle *nen↓* which has to be uttered with falling tone L%.[6] Hara and Kinuhata (2012) claim that *nen↓* is an assertion marker since the implicit subject of (2), repeated here as (25) has to be the speaker and rendering (25) into a *yes-no* question by attaching a rising intonation (↑/LH%) results in ungrammaticality as in (26).

(25)   konban furansu ryoori taberu nen↓.
        tonight France cuisine eat   NEN
        'I'll eat French cuisine tonight.'

(26)   *konban furansu ryoori taberu nen↑.
        tonight France cuisine eat   NEN
        Intended: 'Will you eat French cuisine tonight?'

Interestingly, however, *nen↓* can be attached to *wh*-interrogatives (though they still need to be uttered with falling intonation) and the constructions have emotive/discourse effects. In uttering (1), repeated here as (27), the speaker sounds irritated after waiting for the addressee to decide for a long time (n.b., it is still an information-seeking question).

(27)   nani taberu nen↓
        what eat   NEN
        'What are you going to eat?!' (I've waited enough!)

(28) can only be interpreted as a rhetorical question.

(28)   dare-ga   anta sodate-t-en↓
        who-NOM you raise-PAST-NEN
        'Who raised you up?!' (Obviously, I did.)

To account for the data, we make two proposals: 1. *Nen↓* is a complex lexical entry which is composed of phonemic segments /nen/ and prosodic segment (L%/↓). In other words, *nen↑* does not exist in the Osaka Japanese lexicon, hence (26) is ungrammatical. 2. *Nen↓* is an expressive morpheme which takes an at-issue set of propositions (T^a) and returns an expressive set of propositions (T^s), which denotes that one of the propositions in the set is true:

(29)   a. $[\![\textbf{nen } \downarrow]\!] \in D_{\langle T^a, T^s \rangle}$
        b. $[\![\varphi \textbf{ nen } \downarrow]\!] := \{p|$ for some $q \in [\![\varphi]\!] : w \in q$ for every $w \in p\}$

Thus, when *nen↓* attaches to a declarative as in (2), its argument is a downward closed set which contains a single maximal proposition p, $\{p\}^{\downarrow}$. Thus, it simply asserts that the embedded proposition is true as depicted in (30).

---

[6] There is a phonological variant *en* after the past-tense morpheme *d/t* as in (28).

(30)

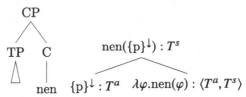

Turning to *wh*-interrogatives with *(n)en↓*, as discussed above, a *wh*-pronoun agrees with a question feature [Q] at C:

(31)

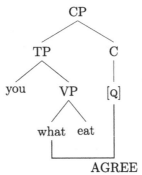

Furthermore, when [Q] occupies the root C, it renders an at-issue interrogative to an expressive one (32).

(32)   a. $[\![Q_{\text{ROOT}}]\!] \in D_{\langle T^a, T^s \rangle}$
        b. $[\![Q_{\text{ROOT}}]\!] = \lambda\varphi.\varphi$

The syntactic and composition trees of (27) are given in (33). *Nen↓* paratactically associates with this root [Q], therefore the two expressive morphemes are combined by PARATACTIC ASSOCIATION (8), which yields a function that takes an at-issue meaning and returns a pair of expressive meanings, $\{p, q, r, ...\}^{\downarrow} \blacklozenge \text{nen}\downarrow(\{p, q, r, ...\}^{\downarrow})$. Thus, it projects a question meaning and at the same time asserts that at least one of the propositions denoted by the interrogative clause is true.

(33)

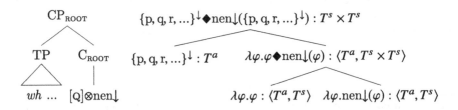

In (27), therefore, the speaker is urging the addressee to answer the question by asserting that one of the answers is true. In (28), the speaker knows which answer is true.

In short, Osaka Japanese sentence-final particle *nen↓* is a complex lexical entry that is composed of phonetic segments /nen/ and prosodic segment (L%/↓). *Nen↓* is paratactically associated with the root clause, which denotes a set of propositions. When it attaches to a declarative, which is a singleton set of propositions, it yields an expressive meaning that the embedded proposition is true. When it attaches to an interrogative, which is a non-singleton set of propositions, it yields a pair of meanings; one is the ordinary question at the expressive tier and the other is an expressive meaning that one of the propositions is true. The latter gives rise to a discourse/emotive effect because the questioner is asking a question at the same time as claiming that one of the answers is true.

3.2   Japanese Rising *Daroo*

Hara (2018) observed that a Japanese sentence-final auxiliary modal *daroo* has an intricate interaction with clause types and prosody. In particluar, a declarative that ends with a modal auxiliary *daroo* and a rising contour LH%/↑ yields an interpretation similar to a tag question as in (34).[7]

(34)   Marie-wa   nomu daroo↑
       Marie-TOP drink DAROO
       'Marie drinks, right?'

Hara (2018, 2019) analyzes *daroo* as an expressive entertain modality anchored to the speaker E_{SP} in inquisitive epistemic logic discussed in Sect. 2.2. As defined in (22), $E_{SP}\varphi$ means that if the issues entertained by SP are resolved, the issue φ is resolved too. As shown in (24), furthermore, when it is attached to a declarative φ, it indicates the speaker's bias toward φ:[8]

(35)   a. $[\![\textbf{daroo}]\!] \in D_{\langle T^a, T^s \rangle}$
       b. $[\![\varphi\,\textbf{daroo}]\!] = E_{SP}(\varphi)$
            If $|\text{POSSIBILITY}(\varphi)| = 1$, $[\![E_{SP}(\varphi)]\!] = [\![K_{SP}(\varphi)]\!]$

Furthermore, ↑ is analyzed as an expressive polar question marker which denotes the interrogative operator defined above in (16).

---

[7] See Venditti (2005) for the ToBI labelling for standard Japanese.

[8] The reported intuition for *daroo*, namely, the bias toward the prejacent, is apparently weaker than the semantics of K. For the purpose of this paper, the proposal in line with Karttunen (1972) and Kratzer (1991) is adopted. The bare assertion α and its modalized one α-*daroo* are in pragmatic competition. The modalized α-*daroo* claims that α is true everywhere in the speaker's information state while the bare assertion α claims that α is true in the actual world. Thus, by asserting α-*daroo*, the speaker implicates that she has a reason not to assert α.

(36) a. $[\![\uparrow]\!] \in D_{\langle T^a, T^s \rangle}$
      b. $[\![\uparrow]\!] = \lambda\varphi.\langle?\rangle\varphi$

The syntactic and composition trees are given in (37). The two shunting-type morphemes are combined by PARATACTIC ASSOCIATION (8), which yields a function that takes an at-issue meaning and returns a pair of expressive meanings. As a result, (34) has two independent meanings, the speaker's bias toward the single maximal proposition in $[\![\alpha]\!]$ ($[\![E_{\mathrm{SP}}(\alpha)]\!] = [\![K_{\mathrm{SP}}(\alpha)]\!]$) and her question $[\![\langle?\rangle\alpha]\!] = [\![\alpha]\!] \cup [\![\neg\alpha]\!]$.

(37)

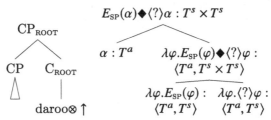

Furthermore, *daroo* can embed morphologically marked interrogatives. The resulting construction expresses a self-addressing question as in (38).

(38)   Marie-wa   nomu daroo   ka
         Marie-TOP drink DAROO Q
         'I wonder if Marie drinks.'

The meaning derivation of (38) can be straightforwardly accounted for in the current framework. As shown in (39), *daroo* simply occupies the C_{ROOT} position without any prosodic morpheme, thus it takes its sister interrogative clause as its argument. There is no paratactic association involved in the construction, thus the SHUNTING-TYPE FUNCTIONAL APPLICATION projects one expressive meaning $E_{\mathrm{SPKR}}\langle?\rangle\alpha$. Since $\langle?\rangle\alpha$ is an interrogative ($|\mathrm{POSSIBILITY}(\langle?\rangle\alpha)| = 2$), the entertain operator E in $E_{\mathrm{SPKR}}\langle?\rangle\alpha$ remains as it is, yielding the interpretation that the speaker entertains whether α is true or not.

(39)

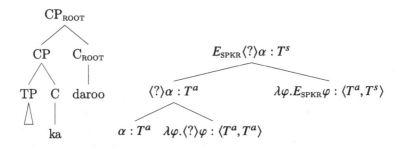

As can be seen, the final auxiliary *daroo* can embed both declaratives and interrogatives and it does not need to be ambiguously defined, which supports the uniform approach for declaratives and interrogatives (see Hara 2018, 2019).[9]

3.3   Final Fall in English and Mandarin

Zimmermann (2000) treats English Final Fall (H*L-L%/↓) in disjunction declaratives like (40) as a closure operator which applies to a list in that it indicates that all and only items in the list have the "property in question".

(40)   A: Which tube stations are one stop from Oxford Circus?
       B: Piccadilly Circus, Bond Street, Tottenham Court Road, Green
            Park, Warren Street, Regent's Park ↓

Biezma and Rawlins (2012) claim that the falling contour that accompanies alternative questions like (41) is the same closure operator as the one in (40), since they "offer unbiased choices" between the alternatives. We can derive the same interpretation by treating ↓ as an expressive closure operator defined in (42) based on Biezma and Rawlins (2012).

(41)   Do you want iced tea, coffee, or lemonade↓

(42) $[\![↓]\!] = [\![\text{Closure}]\!] \in D_{\langle T^a, T^s \rangle}$,
       $[\![\varphi ↓]\!] = [\![\text{Closure}(\varphi)]\!] := \{p | (\text{SalAlts} = \varphi)$ or $(\text{SalAlts} = \emptyset)$ in every
       $w \in p\}$,
       where SalAlts is the set of propositional alternatives that are salient in
       the context of interpretation.

The [Q] (defined in (32)) and ↓/Closure are paratactically-associated as shown in (43). (41) raises a question $\{i, c, l\}^↓$ and expresses that all the alternatives are salient.

(43)

CP$_{\text{ROOT}}$ $\{i, c, l\}^↓ \blacklozenge \text{Closure}(\{i, c, l\}^↓) : T^s \times T^s$

CP   C$_{\text{ROOT}}$ $\{i, c, l\}^↓ : T^a$ $\lambda\varphi.\varphi \blacklozenge \text{Closure}(\varphi) : \langle T^a, T^s \times T^s \rangle$

$[Q] \otimes ↓$ $\lambda\varphi.\varphi : \langle T^a, T^s \rangle$ $\lambda\varphi.\text{Closure}(\varphi) : \langle T^a, T^s \rangle$

Mandarin A-not-A questions like (44) that end with Final Fall (L%/↓) seem to express a similar meaning, since they can be used only when the context is unbiased, i.e., both alternatives (p and ¬p) are equally salient (see also Yuan and Hara 2013).

---

[9] Uegaki and Roelofsen (2018) offer a similar analysis of *daroo* using inquisitive epistemic logic, which makes different predictions. See Hara (2019) for the comparison.

(44)   Ni he-bu-he   jiu↓
      you drink-not-drink wine
      'Do you drink wine or not?'

In short, Final Fall contour in English and Mandarin can be attached to both declaratives and interrogatives. In case of interrogatives, the contour is paratactically associated to the question feature at C_{ROOT} and the construction denotes a pair of expressive meanings, one is an alternative question and the other expresses that all the alternatives are salient ones in the discourse.

4 Conclusion

We have proposed a new type system $\mathcal{L}_{CI}^{+S,PA}$ that includes the PARATACTIC ASSOCIATION rule. $\mathcal{L}_{CI}^{+S,PA}$ can provide compositional analyses of expressive meanings that arise from prosodic morphemes and particles. Moreover, a wide range of cross-linguistic data show that prosodic morphemes and particles can embed both declaratives and interrogatives, which calls for a semantic platform that can uniformly deal with different clause types.

A   Formal system of McCready's (2010) $\mathcal{L}_{CI}^{+S}$ plus Paratactic Association Rule

A.1 $\mathcal{L}_{CI}^{+S}$

(45)   Types for $\mathcal{L}_{CI}^{+S}$

    a. e^a, t^a, s^a are basic at-issue types for $\mathcal{L}_{CI}^{+S}$.

    b. e^c, t^c, s^c are basic CI types for $\mathcal{L}_{CI}^{+S}$.

    c. e^s, t^s, s^s are basic shunting types for $\mathcal{L}_{CI}^{+S}$.

    d.   If σ and τ are at-issue types for $\mathcal{L}_{CI}^{+S}$, then $\langle \sigma, \tau \rangle$ is an at-issue type for $\mathcal{L}_{CI}^{+S}$.

    e.   If σ is an at-issue type for $\mathcal{L}_{CI}^{+S}$ and τ is a CI type for $\mathcal{L}_{CI}^{+S}$, then $\langle \sigma, \tau \rangle$ is a CI type for $\mathcal{L}_{CI}^{+S}$.

    f.   If σ is an at-issue type for $\mathcal{L}_{CI}^{+S}$ and τ is a shunting type for $\mathcal{L}_{CI}^{+S}$, then $\langle \sigma, \tau \rangle$ is a shunting type for $\mathcal{L}_{CI}^{+S}$.

    g.   If σ and τ are shunting types for $\mathcal{L}_{CI}^{+S}$, then $\langle \sigma, \tau \rangle$ is a shunting type for $\mathcal{L}_{CI}^{+S}$.

    h.   If σ and τ are at-issue types for $\mathcal{L}_{CI}^{+S}$, then $\sigma \times \tau$ is an at-issue product type for $\mathcal{L}_{CI}^{+S}$.

    i.   If σ and τ are at-issue types for $\mathcal{L}_{CI}^{+S}$ and ζ and υ are shunting types for $\mathcal{L}_{CI}^{+S}$, then $\sigma \times \zeta$, $\langle \sigma, \tau \rangle \times \zeta$, $\sigma \times \langle \tau, \zeta \rangle$ and $\sigma \times \langle \zeta, \upsilon \rangle$ are mixed types for $\mathcal{L}_{CI}^{+S}$.

    j.   If σ, τ and ζ are at-issue types for $\mathcal{L}_{CI}^{+S}$ and υ is a shunting type for $\mathcal{L}_{CI}^{+S}$, then $\langle \sigma, \tau \rangle \times \langle \zeta, \upsilon \rangle$ is a mixed type for $\mathcal{L}_{CI}^{+S}$.

k.   The full set of types for $\mathcal{L}_{CI}^{+S}$ is the union of the at-issue types, the CI types and the shunting types for $\mathcal{L}_{CI}^{+S}$.

(46)   Rules of proof in $\mathcal{L}_{CI}^{+S}$

(R1)

$$\frac{\alpha : \sigma}{\alpha : \sigma}$$

(R2)

$$\frac{\alpha : \langle \sigma^a, \tau^a \rangle \quad \beta : \sigma^a}{\alpha(\beta) : \tau^a}$$

(R3) Predicate Modification

$$\frac{\alpha : \langle \sigma^a, \tau^a \rangle \quad \beta : \langle \sigma^a.\tau^a \rangle}{\lambda \chi.\alpha(\chi) \wedge \beta(\chi) : \langle \sigma^a.\tau^a \rangle}$$

(R4) CI application

$$\frac{\alpha : \langle \sigma^a, \tau^c \rangle \quad \beta : \sigma^a}{\beta : \sigma^a \bullet \alpha(\beta) : \tau^c}$$

(R5)

$$\frac{\beta : \sigma^a \bullet \alpha : \tau^c}{\beta : \sigma^a}$$

(R6)

$$\frac{\alpha : \sigma}{\beta(\alpha) : \tau}$$

(where β is a designated feature term)

(R7)

$$\frac{\alpha : \langle \sigma^a, \tau^s \rangle \quad \beta : \sigma^a}{\alpha(\beta) : \tau^s}$$

(R8)

$$\frac{\alpha \blacklozenge \beta : \langle \sigma^a, \tau^a \rangle \times \langle \sigma^a, v^s \rangle \quad \gamma : \sigma^a}{\alpha(\gamma) \blacklozenge \beta(\gamma) : \tau^a \times v^s}$$

(R9)

$$\frac{\alpha \blacklozenge \beta : \sigma^a \times t^s}{\alpha : \sigma^a \bullet \beta : t^s}$$

A.2 $\mathcal{L}_{CI}^{+S,PA}$

The formal system of $\mathcal{L}_{CI}^{+S,PA}$ is identical to that of $\mathcal{L}_{CI}^{+S}$ except that the following type specification and proof rule are added:

(47)   A shunting product type
        If σ and τ are shunting types for $\mathcal{L}_{CI}^{+S,PA}$, then $\sigma \times \tau$ is a shunting product type for $\mathcal{L}_{CI}^{+S,PA}$.

(R10) Paratactic Association

$$\frac{\lambda \chi.\alpha(\chi) : \langle \sigma, \tau \rangle \quad \lambda \chi.\beta(\chi) : \langle \sigma, v \rangle}{\lambda \chi.\alpha(\chi) \blacklozenge \beta(\chi) : \langle \sigma, \tau \times v \rangle}$$

References

Bartels, C.: The Intonations of English Statements and Questions. Garland Publishing, New York (1999)

Biezma, M., Rawlins, K.: Responding to alternative and polar questions. Linguist. Philos. **35**, 361–406 (2012)

Ciardelli, I., Groenendijk, J., Roelofsen, F.: Inquisitive Semantics. Oxford Surveys in Semantics and Pragmatics, OUP Oxford (2019). ISBN 9780192546388, https:// books.google.co.jp/books?id=a8d-DwAAQBAJ

Ciardelli, I., Roelofsen, F., Theiler, N.: Composing alternatives. Linguist. Philos. **40**, 1–36 (2017)

Ciardelli, I.A., Roelofsen, F.: Inquisitive dynamic epistemic logic. Synthese **192**(6), 1643–1687 (2015)

Gunlogson, C.: True to Form: Rising and Falling Declaratives as Questions in English. Routledge, New York (2003)

Hara, Y.: Japanese discourse items at interfaces. Ph.D. thesis, University of Delaware, Newark, DE (2006)

Hara, Y.: *Daroo* as an entertain modal: an inquisitive approach. In: Fukuda, S., Kim, M.S., Park, M.J., Cook, H.M. (eds.) Japanese/Korean Linguistics, vol. 25, CSLI Publications (2018)

Hara, Y.: *Daroo* ka↑: The interplay of deictic modality, sentence type, prosody and tier of meaning (2019). https://semanticsarchive.net/Archive/jA5ZWZhN/, semantics Archive

Hara, Y., Kinuhata, T.: Osaka Japanese *nen*: one-sided public belief and paratactic association. Sprache und Datenverarbeitung: International Journal for Language Data Processing, pp. 49–70 (2012)

Ikeda, Y.: A proposal for ToBI labelling of Osaka dialect. Master's thesis, Nara Institute of Science and Technology (2001)

Karttunen, L.: Possible and must. In: Kimball, J. (ed.) Syntax and semantics, vol. 1, Seminar Press (1972)

Kratzer, A.: Modality. In: von Stechow, A., Wunderlich, D. (eds.) Semantics: An International Handbook of Contemporary Research, pp. 639–650. de Gruyter, Berlin (1991)

Lyons, J.: Semantics. Cambridge University Press, Cambridge (1977)

McCready, E.: What man does. Linguist. Philos. **31**(6), 671–724 (2008)

McCready, E.: Varieties of conventional implicature. Semant. Pragmat. **3**(8), 1–57 (2010). https://doi.org/10.3765/sp.3.8

Potts, C.: Lexicalized intonational meaning. In: Kawahara, S. (ed.) UMOP 30: Papers on Prosody, pp. 129–146. GLSA, Amherst, MA (2005a)

Potts, C.: The Logic of Conventional Implicatures. Oxford Studies in Theoretical Linguistics. Oxford University Press, Oxford (2005b), [Revised 2003 UC Santa Cruz PhD thesis]

Potts, C.: Conventional implicature and expressive content. In: Maienborn, C., von Heusinger, K., Portner, P. (eds.) Semantics: An International Handbook of Natural Language Meaning, vol. 3, pp. 2516–2536. Mouton de Gruyter, Berlin (2012). this article was written in 2008

Roelofsen, F., Farkas, D.F.: Polarity particle responses as a window onto the interpretation of questions and assertions. Language **91**(2), 359–414 (2015)

Uegaki, W., Roelofsen, F.: Do modals take propositions or sets of propositions? Evidence from Japanese darou. In: Proceedings of SALT 28 (2018)

Venditti, Jennifer, J.: The J-ToBI model of Japanese intonation. In: Jun, S.A. (ed.) Prosodic Typology, pp. 172–200. Oxford University Press, Oxford (2005)

Yuan, M., Hara, Y.: Questioning and asserting at the same time: the L% tone in A-not-A questions. In: Aloni, M., Franke, M., Roelofsen, F. (eds.) Proceedings of the 19th Amsterdam Colloquium, pp. 265–272 (2013)

Zimmermann, T.E.: Free choice disjunction and epistemic possibility. Nat. Lang. Seman. **8**, 255–290 (2000)

Towards a Unified, Semantically-Calculable and Anti-lexicalistic Analysis of Various Anaphoric Expressions Using "Stacked" Continuations

Noritsugu Hayashi[✉]

The University of Tokyo, Tokyo, Japan
hayashi@phiz.c.u-tokyo.ac.jp

Abstract. This paper takes an initial step to boil down the notion of (anti-)locality (or Binding Conditions A and B) of anaphoric expressions into semantic and morphological formalisms. Inspired by [15], this paper proposes a substructure internal to NPs which mirrors the verb cartography. This mirroring tree constitutes a stacked continuation which takes all the verbal heads one by one from the bottom to the root of the sentence. The tree can then be broken down to a part of a covert reflexivizer and the remaining dummy parts, the latter being filled with overt anaphoric morphemes. This treatment of anaphoric NPs enables a compositional analysis of complex anaphors (which tend to be local) and is subsumed under an established semantics and anti-lexalistic morphology. This paper also discusses more complex cases of multiple anaphors, verbal syncretism and non-c-commanding antecedents.

Keywords: Anaphora · Anti-locality · Continuation · Morphology

1 Problems

Anaphoric expressions have been a central issue in the history of (contemporary) theoretical linguistics ([8] inter alia). One would expect a theory that addresses all of the issues below[1]:

(1) a. Description of anti-locality. Some anaphors are under locality conditions (e.g. *himself*) and some under anti-locality constraints (e.g. *him*). A theory should predict their different distributions in sentences.

---

[1] I mean *anaphor(ic)* here as a general term for anaphoric expressions. For *anaphors* that are obligatorily locally bound, the term *reflexive* is used instead.

Thanks Prof. Yoshiki Mori, Mr. Shinya Okano and Ms. Jane Middleton for suggestive data and comments. My thanks also go to all who give me suggestions at the venue of LENLS 16.

© Springer Nature Switzerland AG 2020
M. Sakamoto et al. (Eds.): JSAI-isAI 2019, LNAI 12331, pp. 214–230, 2020.
https://doi.org/10.1007/978-3-030-58790-1_14

b. Semantic analysis of complex anaphors. Some anaphors are morphologically complex (e.g. *her-self* in English, *zich-zelf* in Dutch). A theory should analyze them on the morphemic basis and establish a way to integrate the meaning of the parts into a whole.

c. Self-contained description. The fundamental semantic function of anaphors (i.e. establishing a dependency between two arguments in a sentence) should be attributed to no linguistic modules other than the semantic (the LF) component.

Various proposals have been made since, but none of them seems to be free from problems. [19] and [20] seem to satisfy (1) to the greatest extent. They assign to anaphoric morphemes different functions: Pronouns (e.g. *him*) and those of ϕ-deficiency (called SE-anaphors; e.g. *zich*) are both variables which are made to find their antecedents within domains in different sizes. On the other hand, SELF-anaphors are local reflexivizers which are made favored over other non-SELF anaphoric expressions. It is then predicted that SELF-anaphors are allowed only in exactly local co-referential configurations, and so is accordingly complementary distribution of SELF-anaphors and pronouns, suppose that there is an economic constraint that favors SELF-anaphors over other non-SELF anaphoric expressions. Their framework thus satisfies (1a). However, the means of anaphoric linkage they use (1c) is controversial. [10] points out that it is not quite apparent that ϕ-feature sharing (in terms of [17]) of deficient anaphors is ever conceptually related to co-reference. Moreover, in the empirical domain, there are some instances in other languages that ϕ-features are hard to be assumed to involved in the process of co-reference (e.g. *zibun*) and some cannot be assumed at all (e.g. anaphors to accusative experiences in Slavic languages; [16]). [21], which makes use of the framework of *Distributed Morphology* [5] to address the substitution of pronouns for reflexives (e.g. the German *mich/mich* vs. *es/sich*), also ends up resorting to ϕ-feature sharing just like [20].

[7] directly refers to structural conditions in lexicalizing constraints on reflexives and pronouns, which will be later found to be akin to my proposal. However, it does not seem to provide morphological analyses of *himself* after all.

[11] (along with her subsequent works) develops a variable-free semantics observing direct compositionality, satisfying (1c). However, the (near) complementary distributions of pronouns and reflexives are waiting for a clearer account. The Principle B effect (disallowing locally co-referring pronouns) can apparently be attributed to a confined denotation of local predicates [12], but as she admits, "one still needs to account for the distribution of reflexives" [14], violating (1a) and (1b). Neither does [24] satisfy either (1a) or (1b), who proposes an index-free semantics and "pied-piping" reflexives and pronouns which affect whole VPs and Ss in situ and turn them into larger pied-piping anaphors.

2   Anti-lexicalistic Considerations

Incidentally, some trending anti-lexicalist morphological theories ([5,6,9, 22] among others) are looking into the internal structures of nominals.

Among those is [15], who proposes the internal hierarchy for (anaphoric) NPs (2). She observes a cross-linguistic fact that the types of anaphoric expressions (reflexive/logophoric/exophoic) correlate to their inner morphologies.[2] Reflexives take (2) as a whole (ANAPHOR) while (exophoic) pronouns take only subnodes thereof (namely, the EXOPHOR or the PRONOUN subtree).[3] Their morphological realizations are also in accordance to (2); an anaphoric expression is either realized by a combination of morphemes each of which occupies the terminal nodes in (2) or a morphological syncretism under the *ABA-constraint [4], which necessitates this hierarchial and (at the same time) linear arrangement.

Each node on (2) of [15] wants a pure semantics in order to meet (1c). Obviously, the ANAPHOR head has a function which could be informally paraphrased like "the antecedent must be local" and the LOGOPHOR head could be described as something like "the antecedent must be inside the sentence and the anaphor must be bound by it". However, this informality defies (1c). This paper aims to fill this gap, particularly

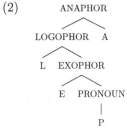

the semantic gap lying in the (anti-)locality condition, which is ascribed to the (non-)existence of the ANAPHOR head.

3   The Idea: "Stacked Up" Continuations

I will propose a theoretical alternative which satisfies all criteria in (1) and incorporates the morphological fine structure (2).

It is well known that a (delimited) continuation ([1,3] inter alia) can force a scope relation between two syntactic objects in the course of derivation. In this regard, anaphoric expressions are "scope-takers" which scope just over their antecedents. Another ingredient we need for capturing (anti-)locality is a tracker tracking the whole path from an anaphor to its antecedent. This can be made by

---

[2] In this connection, [18]'s quote that "compound reflexives [...] are usually clause bound while non-compound reflexives can frequently be long distance bound" is to be recalled.

[3] In [15], both LOGOPHORs and EXOPHORs refer to intra-sentential long-distance anaphors. The difference between them lies in that LOGOPHORs are bound by their antecedents (generating sloppy interpretations) while EXOPHORS are strictly interpreted. PRONOUNs are inter-sentential anaphors.

However, [15]'s author has recently abandoned the LOGOPHOR/EXOPHOR distinction and unified them to DIAPHORs because the same interpretive alternation is also found in ANAPHORs (personal communication). That is, The sloppy/strict reading alternation is orthogonal to structural distances of anaphoric relations (but nevertheless it has some interactions with choices between ANAPHORs and DIAPHORs). I am not going to incorporate this change of hers in this paper, but it is worth noting that the LOGOPHOR/EXOPHOR distinction should be addressed in other ways than stacked-up continuations, which is exempt from being explained here.

stacking a series of continuations each of which targets a superjacent predicate (or head). In a formal perspective, it amounts to a type constructor (or a functor on the category of the syntactic categories) applied to NP, written as $\uparrow$ (NP), defined as below:[4,5]

$$\uparrow (NP) = (\cancel{RootP} \to RootP) \circ \ldots \circ (\cancel{CP} \to \ldots)$$
$$\circ\, (\cancel{TP} \to (TP \to CP) \to \cancel{CP})$$
$$\circ\, (\cancel{VP} \to (VP \to T') \to NPsbj \to \cancel{TP})$$
$$\circ\, ((NP \to VP) \to \cancel{VP})$$
$$= (NP \to VP)$$
$$\to (VP \to T') \to NPsbj$$
$$\to (TP \to CP) \to \ldots \to RootP$$
$$= V^0 \to T^0 \to NPsbj \to C^0 \to \ldots \to Root^0 \to RootP$$

This brutal stacking of continuations is then mirrored into the internal fine structure of an NP exemplified as (3) and (4). Morpho-lexical fusion (at both PF and LF) takes place there. I postulate a reflexivization function with a null phonological realization $\emptyset$ *spanning* from the top down to somewhere in the mirroring tree. What fills the residue are *self* and *him*, which are assigned vacuous semantic functions made up by functional compositions of trivial *unit functions* of atomic continuations. I further assume that *self* can only occupy the upmost C, and that *him* anchors to the bottom of an NP expanding and spanning freely up to the second highest V. The dashed arrows in the tree diagrams represent this flexibility and the middle vertical lines show the actual range of spanning in the particular cases. Note that *self* and *him* do not have any semantic import. Rather, they mark boundaries between an area inside of which $\emptyset$ is effective and an outside area.

(3)

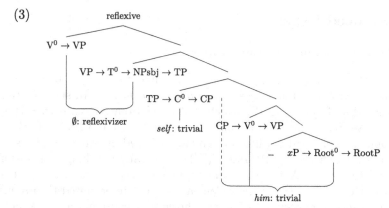

---

[4] Note that $T' = NPsbj \to TP$.
[5] A fixed verbal cartography is necessary for deciding what are stacked in $\uparrow$, which will be given later as (17) .

(4)

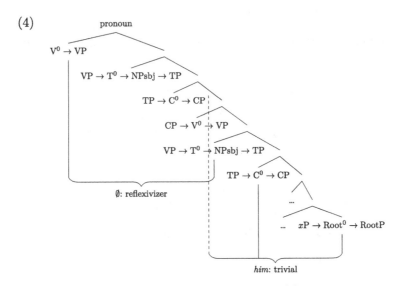

Such a theory and lexicon meets all criteria of (1) and is compatible to (2). For (1a), it reproduces the anti-locality of *him* and the locality of *himself*. This results from the particular English lexicon which gives no room for *self* to occupy in (4) with the reflexivizer $\emptyset$ being so large that it already subsumes the upmost C. It also provides a combinatorial calculation of *him*, *self* and the reflexivizer $\emptyset$ (1b), which is just another functional composition targeting at reflexivization functions and unit functions. Besides, as for (1c), the semantics of complex anaphors does not require any further levels other than LF, just in the same way as [11]. Finally, it is notable that the proposed structure (3) and (4) give a semantics for [15]'s (2).

4 Advanced Issues

4.1 Type-Constructor Transformers

To deal with simultaneous occurrences of multiple anaphors, $\uparrow$ must be generalized and reformulated as a *type-constructor transformer*. In such a situation, anaphoric NPs of type $\uparrow$ (NP), which is derived from NP with the type constructor $\uparrow$, are readily applied to plain predicates (such as VP and T') but fails to be applied to predicates which are already affected by other anaphors earlier in derivation (such as $\uparrow$ (VP) and $\uparrow$ (T')). Generally speaking, a transformed category $X(a)$, where X is an arbitrary type-constructor and a a type is independent of the original a and their elements are not interrelated by any means. Hence, for a second occurrence of an anaphoric type constructor $\uparrow$ in a sentence, it is necessary for $\uparrow$ to deal with not only vanilla categories but also with those already transformed and affected by another $\uparrow$ (or any other type-constructors). Our definition of $\uparrow$ is therefore so modified that it simultaneously takes a type a *and* a type constructor F as its arguments. This will enable us to obtain not only continuational types targeting plain predicates (5a) but also those targeting predicates of derived types. A new definition of $\uparrow$ is formulated as (5b) below:

(5) a. $\uparrow_{id} (NP) = (NP \to VP) \to (VP \to T') \to NP \to (TP \to CP) \to \ldots$

  b. $\uparrow_F (NP) = (F(NP) \to F(VP)) \to (F(VP) \to F(T'))$
$$\to NP \to (F(TP) \to F(CP)) \to \ldots$$

The following is an instantiation of (5b) where $F = \uparrow_{id}$.

$$\uparrow_{\uparrow_{id}} (NP) = (\uparrow_{id} (NP) \to \uparrow_{id} (VP)) \to (\uparrow_{id} (VP) \to \uparrow_{id} (T')) \to NP$$
$$\to (\uparrow_{id} (TP) \to \uparrow_{id} (CP)) \to \ldots$$

4.2 On Being a Functor (Transformer)

We are expected to take a further step to consider whether $\uparrow$ is a functor (or $\uparrow_F$ is a functor transformer).[6] A mapping from a "family" of syntactic categories to another one, F,[7] is qualified as a *functor* if and only if

- for any $f : A \to B$ in the domain of F, there is a counterpart $\langle \$ \rangle_F(f) :$ $F(A) \to F(B)$ in the range of F, and
- for any $f : A \to B$ and $g : B \to C$, $\langle \$ \rangle_F(g \circ f) = \langle \$ \rangle_F(g) \circ \langle \$ \rangle_F(f)$.

The first condition is easily met by recognizing $F(A) = (A \to B) \to (B \to C) \to$ $\ldots$ and then postulating that $\langle \$ \rangle_F(f) = \lambda a_{F(A)}. a(f)$. The second one is, on the other hand, not so straightforward in this case. The problem is that the same type of arguments, namely reflexivizers, cannot be applied to both $\langle \$ \rangle_F(g \circ f)$, which requires a $(A \to C) \to \uparrow (C)$, and a $\langle \$ \rangle_F(g) \circ \langle \$ \rangle_F(f)$, which calls for an $\uparrow (A)$ $(= (A \to B) \to (B \to C) \to \uparrow (C))$. We need an adjustment on the side of $\langle \$ \rangle_F(g \circ f)$ which converts a reflexivizer $(A \to B) \to (B \to C) \to \uparrow (C)$ into another one of type $(A \to C) \to \uparrow (C)$. The difficulty lies exactly here. Since $g \circ f : A \to C$ cannot be distinguished from other functions (i.e. predicates) of the same type which is not made from functional composition, there are no obvious ways of decomposing a given function $h : A \to C$ into its "ingredients", $h_1 : A \to B$ and $h_2 : B \to C$, in order to apply *one by one* to a stacked continuation $a : \uparrow (A) = (A \to B) \to (B \to C) \to \uparrow (C)$. By the same token, a function which takes an $A \to B$ and an $B \to C$ cannot be readily transformed to a function taking an $A \to C$ as its argument because there is no evident way to designate the result when the argument of type $A \to C$ is not made from a functional composition of an $A \to B$ and a $B \to C$.

---

[6] In this subsection I will concentrate on $\uparrow$ as a functor. The argumentation in the following can be extended to $\uparrow_F$ as a functor transformer, where F is a functor such that $F(A \to B) = A \to F(B)$.

[7] Properly speaking, I mean a self-mapping on the category (of syntactic categories).

Does It Linguistically Matter? Yes. The following consideration is in favor of commencing the inquiry. Anti-lexalistic morphology occasionally *fuses* contiguous head nodes into a single phonological unit. English finite verbs, such as *knew*, can be construed as amalgams of V^0, v^0 and T^0 which are divorced into *did* and *know* in negative declarative and interrogative sentences.[8] *Knew* can be taken to be a phonological form paired with a functional composition of V^0, v^0 and T^0

(3)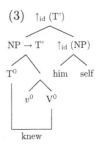

predicates, which are of type $(NP \to \mathcal{V\!P}) \to (\mathcal{V\!P} \to v\!\mathcal{P}) \to (v\!\mathcal{P} \to NP \to TP)$. Such complex predicates are embedded in syntactic derivations illustrated by (6).[9] Taking into consideration that it is statically underdetermined whether or not morphological syncretisms take place in the course derivation, $\uparrow$ should be capable of being applied to both the simple V^0 and the complex $T^0 \circ v^0 \circ V^0$.

Conversion of Reflexivizers. As is already said above, there is basically no means of decomposition of a function of type $A \to C$ to a pair of $A \to B$ and $B \to C$ functions (namely, an inverse of functional composition), and it is for this very reason that a fragment of a stacked continuation (of type $(A \to B) \to (B \to C) \to C$) cannot be readily applied to composed predicates of type $(A \to C)$. Nevertheless, this problem can be circumvented as far as only *reflexivizers* are concerned. A reflexivizer is meant to be a composition of atomic continuations which tampers the remaining arguments of the predicate it applies to but leaves anything else as it is. That is, a reflexivizer has a λ-term in a form like $\lambda f. \lambda g. \ldots \lambda r. \ldots \ldots (\ldots (g(f(r)))r)$, where $f : A \to B$ and $g : B \to C$ are predicates to which the continuation is applied without any modification, r represents a specifier in somewhere above which is bound by the innermost argument of f. To focus on reflexivizers amounts to picking out particular elements belonging to a type and considering a subtype of it.

For $f : A \to B$ and $g : B \to C$, we have $\langle \$ \rangle_\uparrow (f) = \lambda a. a(f)$, $\langle \$ \rangle_\uparrow (g) = \lambda b. b(g)$ and $\langle \$ \rangle_\uparrow (g \circ f) = \lambda x. x(g \circ f)$, where a, b, x are of type $\uparrow (A)$, $\uparrow (B)$ and a composed $(A \to C) \to \uparrow (C)$, respectively. Suppose further that a, b and x are reflexivizers. Especially, $a = \lambda f. \lambda g. \ldots \lambda r. \ldots \ldots (\ldots (g(f(r)))r)$. The composition $(\langle \$ \rangle_\uparrow (g) \circ \langle \$ \rangle_\uparrow (f))(a) = (af)g$ is expanded with a, resulting in

$$(\langle \$ \rangle_\uparrow (g) \circ \langle \$ \rangle_\uparrow (f))(a) = (\lambda a. a(g \circ f))(\lambda h. \ldots \lambda r. \ldots \ldots (\ldots (hr))r),$$

---

[8] This spares us covert head postulates. One can also sublimate my covert reflexivizer $\emptyset$ by incorporating it into predicates.

[9] Note that this kind of functional compositions are what [23] proposes for the framework of *Nanosyntax*, dubbed *merge-XP*, the least preferred way of merging T^0 with $v^0 \circ V^0$, which involves the exact same tree structuring as the verb part of (6).

We can find a new reflexivizer there, namely $\lambda h. \ldots \lambda r. \ldots \ldots \ldots (\ldots (hr))r$. Based on this we can postulate a reflexivizer converter $\sim^C_{A,B}:\uparrow (A) \rightarrow ((A \rightarrow C) \rightarrow\uparrow (C))$ such that

$$(7) \quad \sim^C_{A,B} (a) = \lambda h. \ldots \lambda r. \ldots \ldots (\ldots (hr))r.$$

Finally, we elaborate the definition of $\langle\$\rangle_\uparrow$ so that it can deal with cases of functional composition; that is,

$$(8) \quad \langle\$\rangle_\uparrow(h)(a) = (\sim^C_{A,B} (a))h$$

where $h : A \rightarrow C$ and $a : \uparrow (A) = (A \rightarrow B) \rightarrow (B \rightarrow C) \rightarrow \ldots$.

and $\langle\$\rangle_\uparrow(g \circ f) = \langle\$\rangle_\uparrow(g) \circ \langle\$\rangle_\uparrow(f)$ is therefore made to hold.

4.3   Non-c-commanding Antecedents

Non-c-commanding antecedents as in (9) and (10) pose at least two questions to the proposal made here. How can it be made possible to establish an anaphoric (and moreover, a binding) relation between an anaphor and an antecedent which does not c-command it? And how can this kind of anaphoric relations be incorporated into the internal structure of anaphoric expressions (2), given that there seems to be a variation between languages where English excludes the ANAPHOR variants *himself* and *itself* in (9) while Japanese uses the same ANAPHOR *zibun* in (11)?[10]

(9)   cited from [3]

    a.   Everyone$_i$'s mother think he$_i$'s a genius.

    b.   Someone of every city$_i$ hates it$_i$.

(10)   (Geach's donkey anaphora)

    Every farmer [who owns a donkey$_i$] beats it$_i$.

(11)   a.   (non-c-commanding (local?) antecedent)

      [dono otokonoko-no heya]-ni-mo   [zibun-no syasin]-ga   aru.
      which boy-GEN   room-in-ever self-GEN picture-NOM exist

      'In every boy$_i$'s room there's a picture of self$_i$.'

    b.   (c-commanding local antecedent)

      [dono otokonoko]-ni-mo [zibun-no syasin]-ga   aru.
      which boy-DAT-ever   self-GEN picture-NOM exist

      'Every boy$_i$ has a picture of self$_i$.'

    A possible solution to the first question is to "explicitly" mention "binding side effects" from the subject NPs to the TPs "in the lexical entry" of anaphors, which is nearly same as, but runs just in the opposite direction of, [2] and [3, p. 101]. In the following derivation, the binding effect of *every city* is represented by the upmost two continuation layers of the NP. Taking this, the pronoun *it* tries to catch this non-c-commanding antecedent quantifier by explicitly mentioning

---

[10] This is pointed by [15]'s author which is discussed in her forthcoming paper.

the binding side effect with the upmost two continuation layers of the T'. After merging and a series of lowering, we obtain the correct binding result, as shown on the topmost node.[11,12]

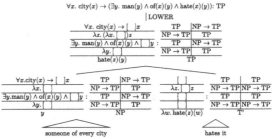

The LOGOPHOR *it* above does more than just catch its antecedent; it anticipates a series of quantifier-r elated continuations (with the two occurrences of

$$\frac{TP \quad | \quad TP}{NP \to TP | NP \to TP}$$

on the VP, or $\mathcal{C}_1$ for short) and after the binding to the sub-

ject NP, the resulting TP is wrapped by two occurrences of $\dfrac{TP \quad | NP \to TP}{NP \to TP \quad | \quad TP}$

($\mathcal{C}_2$ for short), which are readily eliminated to establish the scope of the quantifiers. Note that we need to manually do these somewhere in the middle of the derivation to establish the scope of those quantifiers, which motivates the insertion of lowering functions to the internal structure of anaphoric NPs.[13] This lowering can be encoded as heads in (2) as illustrated below:

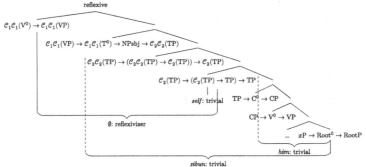

If we shift *self* to the second $\mathcal{C}_2$ lowering head, it will mark the boundary of the covert reflexivizer. The non-c-commanding antecedent *every city* in (9b)

---

[11] Note that the direction of the continuation combination is changed from left-to-right to right-to-left here. The consequence is that phenomena other than anaphors such as wh-superiority should be reconsidered.

[12] Lowering $\dfrac{TP|NP \to TP}{NP \to TP}$ to a TP appears to compromise [2]'s account for crossover effects. However, the problem will not happen in our theory because in our theory anaphors must find their antecedents upwards.

[13] The reason that I do not make use of the nature of being a functor transformer (in Sect. 4.1) lies here. The apparent algebra of type $(\uparrow_{\mathcal{C}_2}(A) \to \uparrow_{id}(A))$, which is made from the $\mathcal{C}_2$'-algebra (of type $\mathcal{C}_2(A) \to A$), will take effect only at RootP.

requires the reflexivizer[14] to be large enough to span over that lowering head, *self* being excluded. On the other hand, reflexivizers getting bound by whole subject NPs (hence making a c-command relation) will leave the second lowering head vacuous[15] and therefore allow *self* to fill it. *Zibun* in (11) has a wider left boundary, showing no alternation regarding to (non-)c-commanding antecedents.

5   Conclusion

In this paper I explored a morphological analysis that observes all of the criteria in (1), Sect. 1. Inspired by anti-lexicalistic works such as [15] (in Sect. 2), I proposed in Sect. 3 a novel way of analyzing anaphoric expressions. The semantic import of anaphoricity is driven by a composition of stacked continuations which tries to look up all the upward heads (predicates). On the other hand, the role of overt phonology is to fill the contentless residue of abovementioned reflexivizers. The proposal is extended to the case of multiple anaphors (Sect. 4.1), predicate syncretism (Sect. 4.2) and non-c-commanding antecedents (Sect. 4.3).

The proposal leaves much room for further theoretical investigation. How this analysis deals with intersentential anaphors, backward anaphors and the strict/sloppy distinction (see also Footnote 3)? A formal representation theory of discourse seems to be necessary for the first two. Another question is whether this theory observes [13]'s *Type 3 Compositionality*. It might be too optimisitic to just assume a fixed verbal cartography (as in Footnote 5), which is advocated by many since 1990s, to address this question.

6   Implementation

On the basis of the Lambek calculus with the directionalities of the exponentials / and \ ignored and collapsed into a neutral $\rightarrow$ for explanatory simplicity, we first construct the internal structure of a NP. The following operators and functor transformers on the collection of syntactic categories $\{V^0, V', VP, T^0, T', TP, N^0, N', NP, \dots\}$ are defined. Let

- $a, b, c, \dots, x, y, z$ represent type constants and type variables of $\mathcal{SynCat}$,
- for any head $x^0 \in \mathcal{SynCat}$, $x^{(k)}$ refers to the k-th bar level of x^0 and xP to the maximal projection of x^0,
- F an arbitrary functor.

---

[14] Its semantic import is $\lambda p_V. \lambda p_T. \lambda e_{NP}. \lambda p_{l_1}. \lambda p_{l_2}. (p_{l_2} \circ p_{l_1})$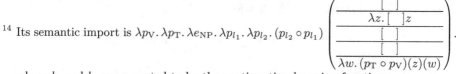

where l_1 and l_2 are expected to be the continuation lowering functions.

[15] It is because that the reflexivizer $\lambda p_V. \lambda p_T. \lambda e_{NP}. \lambda p_{l_1}. p_{l_1}$ $\left(\frac{[\ \ ]}{\frac{\lambda z.[\ \ ]z}{\lambda w. (p_T \circ p_V)(z)(w)}} \right)$

does not involve the second layer of the continuations.

6.1   The Type Constructor Transformer

We define:

(12)   the function $\mathrm{pred}(a\mathrm{P})$,

$$\mathrm{pred}(a\mathrm{P}) = b^{(i-1)} = a\mathrm{P} \to r_i\mathrm{P} \to \ldots \to r_n\mathrm{P} \to b\mathrm{P}$$

where $a\mathrm{P} \neq \mathrm{RootP}$, which tells the "selector" selecting $a\mathrm{P}$, namely, some projection of b^0 according to a particular given cartography, with its residue arguments $r_i\mathrm{P}, \ldots, r_n\mathrm{P}$ remaining unsaturated (see the tree to the right), the function $\mathrm{pred}^+(a\mathrm{P})$,

$$\mathrm{pred}^+(a\mathrm{P}) = b^{(i)} = r_i\mathrm{P} \to \ldots \to r_n\mathrm{P} \to b\mathrm{P},$$

the function $\mathrm{nextPh}(a\mathrm{P}) = b\mathrm{P}$,

(13)   the superjacent continuation of $a\mathrm{P}$ ($\neq \mathrm{RootP}$), $\ast_F(a\mathrm{P})$,

$$\ast_F(a\mathrm{P}) = F(\mathrm{pred}(a\mathrm{P})) \to \ast_F(\mathrm{pred}^+(a\mathrm{P}))$$

defined via $\ast_F$ recursively:

$$\ast_F(a \to b) = a \to \ast_F(b)$$
$$\ast_F(b\mathrm{P}) = F(b\mathrm{P})$$

and

(14)   the stacked continuation of $a\mathrm{P}$, a sequence of functional compositions like:

$$\uparrow_F(a\mathrm{P}) = \begin{cases} (F(\mathrm{nextPh}(a\mathrm{P})) \to\uparrow_F (\mathrm{nextPh}(a\mathrm{P}))) \circ \ast_F(a\mathrm{P}) & \\ (= (F(b\mathrm{P}) \to\uparrow_F (b\mathrm{P})) \circ \ast_F(a\mathrm{P})), & a\mathrm{P} \neq \mathrm{RootP} \\ F(\mathrm{RootP}), & a\mathrm{P} = \mathrm{RootP} \end{cases}$$

$$\uparrow_F(a \to b) = a \to\uparrow_F(b)$$

6.2   The Functor Transformer

$\uparrow_F$ is a functor transformer such that for $f : a\mathrm{P} \to b$,

$$\langle \$ \rangle_{\uparrow_F} f = \lambda e.\,(\sim^b_{a\mathrm{P},b} e)(f) = \lambda e.\, e(f)$$

of type $\uparrow_F(a) \to\uparrow_F(b)$, where $a\mathrm{P}$ is the innermost argument of b. The reflexivizer converter $\sim$ is defined in the same way as (7) in Sect. 4.2.

(7)
$$\sim_{x,y}^{z}(l) = \lambda h. \ldots \lambda r. \ldots . \ldots (\ldots (hr))r$$

where l is an arbitrary reflexivizer $\lambda f. \lambda g. \ldots \lambda r. \ldots . \ldots (\ldots (g(f(r)))r)$,
and f, g, h are of types $x \to y, y \to z, x \to z$, respectively.

For predicates $h = g \circ f$ that is made from a composition of other atomic predicates $f : a \to b$ and $g : b \to c$, $\langle \$ \rangle_{\uparrow_F} h$ is defined in a similar way:

$$\langle \$ \rangle_{\uparrow_F} h = \langle \$ \rangle_{\uparrow_F} (g \circ f) = \lambda e. (\sim_{a,b}^{c} e)(f)$$

Theorem 1. $\uparrow_F$ *is a well-defined functor transformer.*

Proof. For arbitrary $f : x \to y$ and $g : y \to z$ and an reflexivizer $l = \lambda f. \lambda g. \ldots \lambda r. \ldots . \ldots (\ldots (g(f(r)))r)$ of type $\uparrow_F (x) = (x \to y) \to (y \to z) \to \ldots$, the following holds:

$(\langle \$ \rangle_{\uparrow_F}(g) \circ \langle \$ \rangle_{\uparrow_F}(f))(l)$

$= (\lambda f. \lambda g. \ldots \lambda r. \ldots . \ldots (\ldots (g(f(r)))r))fg$

$= \ldots \lambda r. \ldots . \ldots (\ldots (\ldots (g(f(r)))r))$

$= \ldots \lambda r. \ldots . \ldots (\ldots (\ldots (g \circ f(r)))r)$

$= (\lambda h. \ldots \lambda r. \ldots . \ldots (\ldots (hr))r)(g \circ f)$

$= (\lambda a. a(g \circ f))(\lambda h. \ldots \lambda r. \ldots . \ldots (\ldots (hr))r)$

$= (\lambda a. a(g \circ f)) \sim_{x,y}^{z} (l)$

$= (\lambda a. \sim_{x,y}^{z} (a)(g \circ f))(l)$

$= \langle \$ \rangle_{\uparrow_F}(g \circ f)(l)$

This equation is diagramed to the right.

6.3   Unit Functions

We further define a *unit function* $\mu^{a \uparrow_F} : F(a) \to \uparrow_F (a)$:
(15)
$$\mu_{\uparrow_F}^{aP}(x) = \begin{cases} (\mu_{*_F}^{RootP} \circ \ldots \circ \mu_{*_F}^{bP} \circ \mu_{*_F}^{aP})(x), & x = aP \neq RootP \\ id, & x = RootP \\ \mu_{\uparrow_F}^{b} \circ x, & x = a \to b \end{cases}$$

via $\mu_{*_F}^{aP} : F(aP) \to *_F(aP) = F(aP) \to F(pred(aP)) \to \cdots \to F(bP)$:

(16) $\mu_{*_F}^{aP}(x) = \lambda p_b. \lambda r_i. \ldots \lambda r_n. (((p_b a)r_1) \ldots)r_n$

Theorem 2. *Suppose that a self-functor F on $\mathcal{S}yn\mathcal{C}at$ has a unit function μ_F and for any exponential type $aP \to pred(aP)$, $F(aP \to pred(aP)) = aP \to F(pred(aP))$. Then $\mu_{\uparrow_F}^{aP} \circ \mu_F$ is also a unit function for maximal projections in $\mathcal{S}yn\mathcal{C}at$, i.e. it is a (partial) natural transformation $1 \to \uparrow_F$ on $\mathcal{S}yn\mathcal{C}at$.*

Proof. The diagram whose commutativity to be proven is:

$$
\begin{array}{ccccc}
aP & \xrightarrow{\ \mu_F\ } & F(aP) & \xrightarrow{\ \mu_{\uparrow_F}^{aP}\ } & \uparrow_F(aP) \\[2pt]
{\scriptstyle f}\Big\downarrow & & {\scriptstyle \langle\$\rangle_F(f)}\Big\downarrow & & {\scriptstyle \langle\$\rangle_{\uparrow_F}(\langle\$\rangle_F(f))}\Big\downarrow \\[2pt]
\mathrm{pred}(aP) & \xrightarrow{\ \mu_F\ } & F(\mathrm{pred}(aP)) & \xrightarrow[\ \mu_{\uparrow_F}^{\mathrm{pred}(aP)}\ ]{} & \uparrow_F(\mathrm{pred}(aP))
\end{array}
$$

The left part is given. For the right part, take an arbitrary predicate g of type $F(aP) \to F(\mathrm{pred}(aP))$. Note that the arbitrary g is of the same type as is $\langle\$\rangle_F f$ in the diagram above. Let b and $r_i, \dots, r_n \in \mathcal{SynCat}$ be such that $\mathrm{pred}(aP) = F(b^{(i-1)}) = r_i \to \dots r_n \dots \to F(bP)$. The following hold:

$$
\mu_{\uparrow_F}^{aP} = \mu_{*_F}^{\mathrm{RootP}} \circ \dots \circ \mu_{*_F}^{bP} \circ \mu_{*_F}^{aP}
$$

$$
= \lambda a.\, \lambda p_b.\, \lambda r_i.\, \dots \lambda r_n.\, \mu_{*_F}^{\mathrm{RootP}} \circ \dots \circ \mu_{*_F}^{bP}((((p_b a)r_i)\dots)r_n)
$$

$$
= \lambda a.\, \lambda p_b.\, \lambda r_i.\, \dots \lambda r_n.\, \mu_{\uparrow_F}^{bP}((((p_b a)r_i)\dots)r_n)
$$

$$
(\langle\$\rangle_{\uparrow_F}(g)) \circ \mu_{\uparrow_F}^{aP}
$$

$$
= (\lambda e.\, e(g)) \circ (\lambda a.\, \lambda p_b.\, \lambda r_i.\, \dots \lambda r_n.\, \mu_{\uparrow_F}^{bP}((((p_b a)r_i)\dots)r_n))
$$

$$
= \lambda a.\, (\lambda e.\, e(g))(\lambda p_b.\, \lambda r_i.\, \dots \lambda r_n.\, \mu_{\uparrow_F}^{bP}((((p_b a)r_i)\dots)r_n))
$$

$$
= \lambda a.\, \lambda r_i.\, \dots \lambda r_n.\, \mu_{\uparrow_F}^{bP}((((ga)r_i)\dots)r_n)
$$

On the other hand:

$$
\mu_{\uparrow_F}^{b} \circ (\langle\$\rangle_{\uparrow_F}(g)) = \mu_{*_F}^{\mathrm{RootP}} \circ \dots \circ \mu_{*_F}^{bP} \circ g
$$

$$
= \mu_{*_F}^{\mathrm{RootP}} \circ \dots \circ \mu_{*_F}^{bP} \circ (\lambda a.\, \lambda r_i.\, \dots \lambda r_n.\, ((((ga)r_i)\dots)r_n))
$$

$$
= \lambda a.\, \lambda r_i.\, \dots \lambda r_n.\, \mu_{*_F}^{\mathrm{RootP}} \circ \dots \circ \mu_{*_F}^{bP}((((ga)r_i)\dots)r_n)
$$

$$
= \lambda a.\, \lambda r_i.\, \dots \lambda r_n.\, \mu_{\uparrow_F}^{bP}((((ga)r_i)\dots)r_n)
$$

6.4 The Verbal Cartography

(17)   [CP [TP NPsbj [VP [...[CP [TP [VP V NPobj]]]]]]]

where $\mathrm{Root}^0 =$ upmost C^0

It is assumed that subjects are base-generated at the specifiers of T^0s'. Besides, small-V^0s are opted out and cases of double objects are ignored. All of these are merely for avoiding unnecessary confusion in explanation.

6.5   The Template of Lexical Entries

(18)   a. $\emptyset$: anchoring to the NP-root, downward syncretism extending any-where,

$$\lambda p_{F(\mathrm{V})}. \; ... \; \lambda p_{F(x)}. \, \lambda e_{\mathrm{NP}}. \, p_{F(\mathrm{V})}(... \, (p_{F(\mathrm{V})} \, e_{\mathrm{NP}}))e_{\mathrm{NP}}$$

(a reflexivizer)

b. *self*: anchoring to the upmost C, no syncretism, $\mu_{*_F}^{\mathrm{TP}}$

c. *him*: anchoring to the bottom, upward syncretism extending elasti-cally up to the second highest V,

$$\mu_{*_F}^{\mathrm{RootP}} \circ \; ... \; \circ \mu_{*_F} \circ \; ...$$

It is noted that the "left end" of the compositional chain varies in different anaphors, but nevertheless the chain is composed of a *finite* number of μ_{*_F}'s.

7   Sample Derivations of English *him/himself*

7.1   The Lexicon

English has the exact lexicon as is specified in (18). Putting them in terms proof theory, we have:

The English anaphors *him* and *him + self* etc. result from (18) above:

Reflexives

Pronouns

7.2 A Simple Sentence with a Reflexive

A simple sentence with a reflexive anaphor (such as (19)) is derived in the following way:

(19)   John hates himself.

$$
\begin{array}{c}
\text{John} \\
\text{john} \\
\text{NPsbj}
\end{array}
\quad
\dfrac{
\dfrac{
\dfrac{
\begin{array}{c}
\text{(fused to the right)} \\
\lambda p_{VP}.\,\lambda e_{NPsbj}.\,\text{present}(p_{VP}e_{NPsbj}) \\
\hline
VP \to NPsbj \to TP
\end{array}
\;\;
\dfrac{
\dfrac{
\begin{array}{c}
\text{hates} \\
\text{hate} \\
NPobj \to VP
\end{array}
\;(\$)\;
\dfrac{
\begin{array}{c}
\text{himself} \\
\lambda p_V.\,\lambda p_T.\,\lambda e_{NP}.\,\lambda p_C.\,p_C(p_T(p_V e_{NP})e_{NP})
\end{array}
}{\uparrow_{id}(NPobj)}
}{\lambda e_{\uparrow_{id}(NP)}.\,e_{\uparrow_{id}(NP)}(\text{hate})}
}{\lambda p_T.\,\lambda e_{NP}.\,\lambda p_C.\,p_C(p_T(\lambda e_{NP}.\,\text{hate}\,e_{NP}e_{NP})e_{NP})}
}{\lambda p_{VP}.\,p_{VP}(\lambda p_{VP}.\,\lambda e_{NPsbj}.\,\text{present}(p_{VP}e_{NPsbj}))}
\;(\$)
}{\lambda e_{NP}.\,\lambda p_C.\,p_C(\text{present}(\text{hate}\,e_{NP}e_{NP}))}
}{\lambda p_C.\,p_C(\text{present}(\text{hate john john}))}
$$

If the syncretism of the predicate *hates* is taken into account (Sect. 4.2), the derivation would be:

(complex derivation for the syncretism case, with labels "hates / present ∘ hate", "himself", and "John john NPsbj")

7.3 A Complex Sentence with a Reflexive and a Pronoun

A complex sentence with a reflexive anaphor *and* a pronoun like (20) can be also obtained.

(20)   John$_i$ said that he$_i$ hates himself$_i$.

First the embedded clause is made up:

(complex derivation for the embedded clause, with labels "that id CP", "he", and "hates himself")

The derivation continues until the whole sentence is then built up as follows:

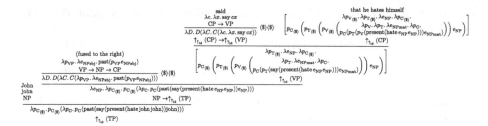

References

1. Barker, C.: Continuations and the nature of quantification. Nat. Lang. Seman. **10**, 211–242 (2002)
2. Barker, C., Shan, C.C.: Donkey anaphora is in-scope binding. Semant. Pragmatics **1**(1), 1–46 (2008). https://doi.org/10.3765/sp.1.1
3. Barker, C., Shan, C.C.: Continuations and Natural Language. Oxford University Press, Oxford (2014)
4. Bobaljik, J.D.: Universals in Comparative Morphology: Suppletion, Superlatives, and the Structure of Words. MIT Press, Cambridge (2012)
5. Bobaljik, J.D.: Distributed morphology. In: Aronoff, M. (ed.) Oxford Research Encyclopedia of Linguistics. Oxford University Press, Oxford (2017)
6. Caha, P.: The nanosyntax of case. Ph.D. thesis, University of Tromsø (2009)
7. Cann, R., Kempson, R., Marten, L.: The Dymamics of Language: An Introduction. Elsevier, San Diego (2005)
8. Chomsky, N.: Lectures on Government and Binding: The Pisa Lectures. Foris, Dordrecht (1981)
9. Halle, M., Marantz, A.: Distributed morphology and the pieces of inflection. In: Kenneth Hale, Keyser, S.J. (eds.) The View from Building 20: Essays in Linguistics in Honor of Sylvain Bromberger, pp. 111–176. MIT Press, Cambridge (1993)
10. Hicks, G.: The Derivation of Anaphoric Relations. John Benjamins, Amsterdam (2009)
11. Jacobson, P.: Towards a variable free semantics. Linguist. Philos. **22**(2), 117–185 (1999)
12. Jacobson, P.: Direct compositionality and variable free semantics: the case of 'Principle B' effects. In: Barker, C., Jacobson, P. (eds.) Direct Compositionality, pp. 191–236. Oxford University Press, Oxford (2007)
13. Jacobson, P.: Direct compositionality. In: Hinzen, W., Machery, E., Werning, M. (eds.) The Oxford Handbook of Compositionality. Oxford University Press, Oxford (2012)
14. Jacobson, P.: Pauline Jacobson's Papers on Variable Free Semantics: Annotated (Partial) Bibliography (2019). available at Sematic Archives
15. Middleton, J.: Everyone left the room, except the logophor: *ABA patterns in pronominal morphology. In: Olomouc Linguistcs Colloquium 2018 Book of Abstracts, pp. 108–109. Palacký University Olomouc, Olomouc, Czech (2018)
16. Nikolaeva, L.: The secret life of pronouns. Ph.D. thesis, MIT (2014)
17. Pesetsky, D., Torrego, E.: The syntax of valuation and the interpretability of features. In: Karimi, S., Samiian, V., Wilkins, W.K. (eds.) Phrasal and Clausal Architecture: Syntactic derivation and interpretation. In honor of Joseph E. Emonds, pp. 262–294. Linguistik Aktuell 101, John Benjamins, Amsterdam (2007)

18. Pica, P.: On the nature of the reflexivization cycle. In: Proceedings of NELS 17, pp. 483–500. GLSA, Amherst, MA (1987)
19. Reinhart, T., Reuland, E.: Reflexivity. Linguist. Inq. **24**(4), 657–720 (1993)
20. Reuland, E.: Anaphora and Language Design. MIT Press, Cambridge (2011)
21. Rooryck, J., Wyngaerd, G.V.: Dissolving Binding Theory. Oxford University Press, Oxford (2011)
22. Starke, M.: Nanosyntax: a short primer to a new approach to language. Nordlyd **36**(1), 1–6 (2009). https://doi.org/10.7557/12.213
23. Starke, M.: Complex left branches, spellout, and prefixes. In: Baunaz, L., De Clercq, K., Haegeman, L., Lander, E. (eds.) Exploring Nanosyntax, pp. 239–249. Oxford University Press, Oxford (2018)
24. Szabolcsi, A.: Combinatory grammar and projection from the lexicon. In: Sag, I., Szabolcsi, A. (eds.) Lexical Matters, pp. 241–268. CSLI Lecture Notes 24, CSLI, Stanford, CA (1992)

Lambek Grammars as Second-Order Abstract Categorial Grammars

Oleg Kiselyov$^{(\boxtimes)}$ (ID) and Yuya Hoshino

Tohoku University, Sendai, Japan
oleg@okmij.org

Abstract. We demonstrate that for all practical purposes, Lambek Grammars (LG) are *strongly* equivalent to Context-Free Grammars (CFG) and hence to second-order Abstract Categorial Grammars (ACG). To be precise, for any Lambek Grammar LG there exists a second-order ACG with a second-order lexicon such that: the set of LG derivations (with a bound on the 'nesting' of introduction rules) is the abstract language of the ACG, and the set of yields of those derivations is its object language. Furthermore, the LG lexicon is represented in the abstract ACG signature with no duplications. The fixed, and small, bound on the nesting of introduction rules seems adequate for natural languages. One may therefore say that ACGs are not merely just as expressive as LG, but strongly equivalent.

The key is the algebraic description of Lambek Grammar derivations, and the *avoidance* of the Curry-Howard correspondence with lambda calculus.

Keywords: Lamkek grammar · Context-free grammar · Pentus construction · ACG

1 Introduction

Expressing a Lambek Grammar (LG) as an Abstract Categorial Grammar (ACG) is a sort of a problem that on the surface is either impossible or trivial, with unfolding subtleties and depth – the problem that just does not go away. Lambek Grammar with its directional types is based on logic with directional implications without any exchange rule. In contrast, ACG uses ordinary arrow types, and its underlying implicative fragment of multiplicative linear logic is commutative. No matter what tricks one may play, the fundamental distinction inevitably comes to haunt us, as Kubota and Levine [8] and Moot [9] have claimed: "The best approximations that we can obtain all suffer from overgeneration because non-commutativity is insufficiently enforced." [9, §7.2]. In fact, analyzing right-node raising in an ACG formalism without directional types while avoiding overgeneration has been posed as a challenge to the first author by Yusuke Kubota at ESSLLI 2013.

© Springer Nature Switzerland AG 2020
M. Sakamoto et al. (Eds.): JSAI-isAI 2019, LNAI 12331, pp. 231–243, 2020.
https://doi.org/10.1007/978-3-030-58790-1_15

On the other hand, the problem seems trivial: as Pentus showed [10], any LG is weakly equivalent to a context-free grammar (CFG), and CFGs are trivially representable as ACGs [3]. Weak equivalence means that the two grammars generate the same set of strings. The correspondence of derivations is a different, and subtle matter, investigated by Kanazawa, Salvati [4,6], De Groote [1] and others [12]. The latest result is De Groote's construction of an ACG that reproduces both derivations and the yields of an LG [1]. However, that ACG is third order, and still suffers from redundancies that arise in Pentus-like constructions. Furthermore, the paper [1] notes that the strong equivalence of ACG and LG cannot be guaranteed in every case.

Our contribution is the general strong equivalence of LG and ACG:

Theorem 1. *For any LG and the natural number n, there exists a second-order ACG with a second-order lexicon whose abstract language is all and only LG derivations of the distinguished type of hyp-rank n (to be defined below) and whose object language is the yields of those LG derivations. The LG lexicon enters the ACG signature with no duplications, let alone exponential explosions.*

As a corollary, we answer the Kubota challenge. As another corollary,

Corollary 1. *For any LG and the natural number n, there exists a context-free grammar (CFG) whose parses are all and only start-type LG derivations of hyp-rank n. (In fact, CFG parse trees are LG derivation trees, written 'upside down'.)*

The paper presents the construction of the CFG and ACG from an LG and argues, in Sect. 5, that the hyp-rank qualification is irrelevant in practice. The key is the algebraic approach to LG derivations and ACG and avoiding the Curry-Howard correspondence. We do *not* regard directional types as function (arrow) types.

The structure of the paper is as follows. The next section reminds Lambek calculus and grammars and introduces their different but provably equivalent presentation, which is easier to characterize algebraically. Section 3 gives an unconventional, algebraic presentation of second-order abstract categorial grammars. The algebraic presentation immediately relates ACG with LG derivations, leading to the main result of the paper. The strong equivalence of ACG and LG means the absence of overgeneration. Section 3.1 explicates the reason preventing the overgeneration, and, on the concrete examples from Moot [9] and the Kubota challenge, demonstrates the descriptive adequacy of second-order ACGs. In Sect. 4 we examine related work, in particular, [1]. We also show how our presentation of LG avoids the most difficult issues in the Pentus construction [10]. Section 5 discusses hyp-rank and the algebraic presentation of LG.

2   Lambek Grammars, Derivations, and Algebras

First we recall the needed definitions of Lambek calculus and grammar, define the hyp-rank and introduce the running example. Section 2.1 later presents the variation, the calculus LA, and its algebraic characterization.

A grammar is a description of a language, that is, of a set of finite strings built from a finite fixed set of 'words' (so-called alphabet). We write ϵ for the empty string and $+$ for string concatenation. In Lambek Grammars (LG) – and type logical grammars that followed – the string building rules are expressed through a deductive system. In the case of LG, the deductive system is the (associative) Lambek calculus L presented below, in the Gentzen-style natural deduction form (from [11, §2.2.2]).

$$
\begin{array}{llll}
\text{Primitive types } P & ::= & s, n, np \\
\text{Types} & A, B, C & ::= & P \mid A\backslash B \mid B/A \\
\text{Environments} & \Gamma, \Delta & ::= & A \mid A, \Gamma \mid \Gamma, A \\
\text{Judgements} & \Gamma \vdash A
\end{array}
$$

$$
\frac{\Delta \vdash B/A \quad \Gamma \vdash A}{\Delta, \Gamma \vdash B} /e \qquad\qquad \frac{\Gamma, A \vdash B}{\Gamma \vdash B/A} /i
$$

$$
\frac{\Gamma \vdash A \quad \Delta \vdash A\backslash B}{\Gamma, \Delta \vdash B} \backslash e \qquad\qquad \frac{A, \Gamma \vdash B}{\Gamma \vdash A\backslash B} \backslash i
$$

$$
\frac{}{A \vdash A} Var
$$

The formulas of L are called syntactic types, for which we use the metavariables A, B, and C. They are inductively built from the primitive types s, n, and np using the left- and right- slashes. As the convenient abbreviation, vp stands for $np\backslash s$, tv for vp/np, det for np/n, rel for $(n\backslash n)/(s/np)$ and pp for $n\backslash n$. The metavariables Γ and Δ stand for an environment: a non-empty sequence of types. Furthermore, $A, (B, C)$ and $(A, B), C$ represent the same environment; an environment is hence just a linear sequence of types. Besides associativity, there are no other (structural) rules about the environments; in particular, there is no exchange rule: the order of types in an environment is significant. We define a partial order on types $A \prec B$ (pronounced: 'A is a subformula of B') as $A \prec A$, and $A \prec B/C$, $A \prec B\backslash C$ whenever $A \prec B$ or $A \prec C$. We say A is a subformula of a collection of types if it is a subformula of some type in the collection. As an example of L, Fig. 1 shows the derivation of the judgement $det, n, rel, np, tv, vp \vdash s$.

A grammar based on L – Lambek Grammar (LG) – is a tuple $(\mathcal{L}_L, A_s)$ of the lexicon and the *initial type* (which is often s). The lexicon $\mathcal{L}_L$ defines the alphabet of the grammar and assigns to each word of the alphabet the corresponding L type. Figure 2 shows the sample lexicon, also to be denoted by $\mathcal{L}_L$.

A non-empty string $w_1 \ldots w_n$ (where w_i is a word of the alphabet) is in the language of the grammar $(\mathcal{L}_L, A_s)$ just in case the judgement $A_1, \ldots, A_n \vdash A_s$ is derivable in L, where A_i is the type assigned by $\mathcal{L}_L$ to w_i. The derivation in Fig. 1 thus shows that the language of the grammar $(\mathcal{L}_L, s)$ includes the string "The book that John read vanished," which will be our running example.

$$\cfrac{det \vdash det \quad \cfrac{n \vdash n \quad \cfrac{rel \vdash rel \quad \cfrac{\cfrac{np \vdash np \quad \cfrac{tv \vdash tv \quad np \vdash np}{tv, np \vdash vp} \backslash e}{\cfrac{np, tv, np \vdash s}{\cfrac{np, tv \vdash (s/np)}{rel, np, tv \vdash pp} /e}} /i}{\cfrac{n, rel, np, tv \vdash n}{}} \backslash e}{det, n, rel, np, tv \vdash np} /e}}{\cfrac{det, n, rel, np, tv, vp \vdash s}{}} \qquad vp \vdash vp \quad \backslash e$$

Fig. 1. Gentzen-style, natural deduction derivation in L

John : np book : n the : det that : rel read : tv vanished : vp

Fig. 2. The LG lexicon $\mathcal{L}_L$ for the running example

The derivation in Fig. 1 contains a number of hypotheses (on the left-side of the turnstile), only one of which is discharged, by the introduction rule. The maximum number of to-be-discharged hypotheses in any judgement of a derivation is called the *hyp-rank* of the derivation. (The derivation in Fig. 1 hence has the hyp-rank one).

2.1 The Calculus LA

To conveniently view Lambek derivations as an algebra, and to later relate them to ACG, we give a different but provably equivalent presentation of L and LG, to be called LA. The only differences from L are the addition of marks . to the environment and a different treatment of the lexicon. The new syntax of the environment is:

$$\Gamma, \Delta ::= . \mid A \mid A, \Gamma \mid \Gamma, A$$

We write $\bullet$ for a sequence of one or more consecutive marks ., and $\breve{\Gamma}$, $\breve{\Delta}$ for a possibly empty mark-free sequence of types.

The grammar based on the calculus (also to be called LA) adjoins to LA a set of axioms – the LA lexicon $\mathcal{L}_A$ – and designates one of the types as initial (usually, s). $\mathcal{L}_A$ is a different presentation of the LG lexicon: the mapping of a word to a type is written as an axiom, whose name is the word and whose conclusion is the corresponding type. If w is a word in $\mathcal{L}_A$, we write $\mathcal{L}_A(w)$ for its type; the notation extends to sequences of words. Shown below are three (for the sake of space) axioms of $\mathcal{L}_A$ that correspond to $\mathcal{L}_L$ of the running example:

$$\cfrac{}{. \vdash np} john \qquad \cfrac{}{. \vdash n} book \qquad \cfrac{}{. \vdash tv} read$$

The mark thus 'marks the place' of a lexical entry axiom in the derivation. Figure 3 gives the LA derivation for the running example.

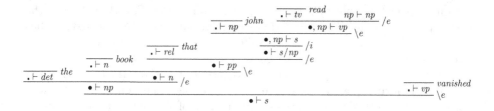

Fig. 3. Sample derivation in LA

If t is an LA derivation (tree), its *fringe* $\mathcal{F}(t)$ is a string of words naming the axioms that appear in its derivation. It is inductively defined as follows:

- if t is an axiom named w, $\mathcal{F}(t)$ is w;
- if t is a Var axiom $A \vdash A$, $\mathcal{F}(t)$ is ϵ
- if the last rule in t is $\backslash i$ or $/i$ with the premise t', then $\mathcal{F}(t)$ is $\mathcal{F}(t')$;
- if the last rule in t is $\backslash e$ or $/e$ with the premises t_1 and t_2, then $\mathcal{F}(t)$ is $\mathcal{F}(t_1) + \mathcal{F}(t_2)$.

A non-empty string $w_1 \ldots w_n$ is said to belong to the language of an LA grammar with the lexicon $\mathcal{L}_A$ and the initial type A_s just in case there is an LA derivation of $\bullet \vdash A_s$ whose fringe is $w_1 \ldots w_n$.

The notion of *normal derivations* in LA is the same as in L [11, §2.8], as should be clear from the strong equivalence shown below. That is, an LA derivation is called normal if it does not contain an introduction rule for the type B/A or $A \backslash B$, immediately followed by the rule that eliminates A. As in L, LA derivations can always be normalized [11, §2.8]. Therefore, we restrict our attention to normal derivations only. Also like in L, normal LA derivations enjoy the subformula property: any type that appears within a normal derivation $\Gamma \vdash A_s$ is a subformula of Γ, A_s or the set of lexicon types.

2.2 Strong Equivalence of LG and LA Grammars

Proposition 1. *If t is an LA derivation of $\check{\Gamma}, \bullet, \check{\Delta} \vdash A$ (given the lexicon $\mathcal{L}_A$), then there exists the L derivation $\check{\Gamma}, \mathcal{L}_A(\mathcal{F}(t)), \check{\Delta} \vdash A$.*

The proof is an easy induction on the structure of t. Indeed,

- If t is an axiom $\bullet \vdash A$ named w, the corresponding L judgement is $A \vdash A$, which is the Var axiom of L.
- If the last rule of t is $/i$ with the conclusion $\check{\Gamma}, \bullet, \check{\Delta} \vdash B/A$, its premise must be $\check{\Gamma}, \bullet, \check{\Delta}, A \vdash B$ (whose derivation is to be called t'). By the inductive hypothesis, there exists an L derivation $\check{\Gamma}, \mathcal{L}_A(\mathcal{F}(t')), \check{\Delta}, A \vdash B$, which can then be extended with the $/i$ rule to $\check{\Gamma}, \mathcal{L}_A(\mathcal{F}(t)), \check{\Delta} \vdash B/A$ (keeping in mind that $\mathcal{F}(t) = \mathcal{F}(t')$).

- Suppose the last rule of t is $/e$ with the conclusion $\check{\Gamma}, \bullet, \check{\Delta} \vdash B$ and the premises t_1 and t_2. There are three cases to consider. In the first, t_1 has the form $\check{\Gamma}, \bullet \vdash B/A$ and t_2 has the form $\bullet, \check{\Delta} \vdash A$. Applying the inductive hypothesis to both and then $/e$ gives $\check{\Gamma}, \mathcal{L}_A(\mathcal{F}(t)), \check{\Delta} \vdash B$, keeping in mind that $\mathcal{F}(t) = \mathcal{F}(t_1) + \mathcal{F}(t_2)$. In the second case, t_1 has the form $\Gamma_1 \vdash B/A$ and t_2 has the form $\check{\Gamma}_2, \bullet, \check{\Delta} \vdash A$ where Γ_1 is unmarked and non-empty. Then t_1 is the ordinary L derivation, using no axioms of $\mathcal{L}_A$, with no marks in its environment and with the empty fringe. We reach the conclusion by applying the induction hypothesis to t_2 only, and then the $/e$ rule to get the final L derivation. The remaining case is symmetrical.
- The cases of $\backslash e$ and $\backslash i$ as the last rules of t are symmetrical.

Proposition 2. *If $\Gamma \vdash A$ is derivable in L, then there exists a lexicon $\mathcal{L}_A$ and an LA derivation t of $\check{\Gamma}, \bullet, \check{\Delta} \vdash A$ such that $\check{\Gamma}, \mathcal{L}_A(\mathcal{F}(t)), \check{\Delta}$ is Γ.*

Consider an L derivation of $\Gamma \vdash A$ where Γ, which must be non-empty, is $A_1, \ldots, A_n$. Each type A_i must come from a Var axiom $A_i \vdash A_i$ that is used at some point in the derivation. Pick from Γ a non-empty consecutive sequence of types $A_k, A_{k+1}, \ldots, A_l$ with $l > k$, and build the lexicon $\mathcal{L}_A$ with the axioms $\bullet \vdash A_i$ named by distinct words w_i, where $i = k..l$. For each such A_i we replace the Var axiom that introduced that A_i into Γ with the corresponding axiom from $\mathcal{L}_A$ – replacing the corresponding occurrences of A_i with $\bullet$. It is easy to see that the result is the valid LA derivation with the fringe whose types are $A_k, A_{k+1}, \ldots, A_l$.

The easy corollary from the two propositions is that LG and LA describe the set of strings: they are weakly equivalent. The examination of the proofs lets us conclude the stronger result: LG and LA derivations for the same string have the same shape, and differ only in the 'kind' of some of their axioms, Var vs. lexicon. Thus LG and LA are *strongly equivalent*. We may thus speak of LA derivations as Lambek grammar derivations.

2.3   The Algebra of LA Derivations

One may regard the derivation trees like those in Fig. 3 as a multi-sorted algebra, to be called $\mathcal{ALC}_{D_1}$. Its carrier sets are LA derivations; Fig. 4 shows the signature Σ_{AL_1} of the operations. (Notably, it includes the lexicon $\mathcal{L}_L$, without any duplications: see the first column of Fig. 4.) There, $\langle \bullet, np; vp \rangle$, etc. is the notation for *atomic* sorts (that is, types); although angular brackets, commas, semicolons might suggest an internal structure, it is only for the convenience of the reader. In the formalism, the whole complicated symbol denotes an atomic type (sort) without any separately interpreted components.

The carriers of $\mathcal{ALC}_{D_1}$ are LA derivations with no more than one dischargeable np hypothesis at a time. The construction of $\mathcal{ALC}_{D_n}$ for derivations of any other fixed hyp-rank is analogous. For example, the general $\mathcal{ALC}_{D_2}$ adds to $\mathcal{ALC}_{D_1}$ the operations such as $\langle \bullet; tv \rangle \rightarrow \langle np, \bullet, np; np \rangle \rightarrow \langle np, \bullet, np; vp \rangle$ and $\langle \bullet; tv \rangle \rightarrow \langle \bullet, np, np; np \rangle \rightarrow \langle \bullet, np, np; vp \rangle$. There are many such operations, but

their number is finite (see below). We can build an algebra whose carriers are all
LA derivations with no restrictions; it will have an infinite number of operations:
all instances of a finite set of schematic operations (which are the restatement
of the LA inference rules).

john	: $\langle \bullet; np \rangle$	evp : $\langle \bullet; np \rangle \rightarrow \langle \bullet; vp \rangle \rightarrow \langle \bullet; s \rangle$
book	: $\langle \bullet; n \rangle$	enn : $\langle \bullet; n \rangle \rightarrow \langle \bullet; pp \rangle \rightarrow \langle \bullet; n \rangle$
the	: $\langle \bullet; det \rangle$	edp : $\langle \bullet; det \rangle \rightarrow \langle \bullet; n \rangle \rightarrow \langle \bullet; np \rangle$
that	: $\langle \bullet; rel \rangle$	etv : $\langle \bullet; tv \rangle \rightarrow \langle \bullet; np \rangle \rightarrow \langle \bullet; vp \rangle$
read	: $\langle \bullet; tv \rangle$	ehtv : $\langle \bullet; tv \rangle \rightarrow \langle np; np \rangle \rightarrow \langle \bullet, np; vp \rangle$
vanished	: $\langle \bullet; vp \rangle$	hnp : $\langle np; np \rangle$
		ehvp : $\langle \bullet; np \rangle \rightarrow \langle \bullet, np; vp \rangle \rightarrow \langle \bullet, np; s \rangle$
		irnp : $\langle \bullet, np; s \rangle \rightarrow \langle \bullet; s/np \rangle$
		erel : $\langle \bullet; rel \rangle \rightarrow \langle \bullet; s/np \rangle \rightarrow \langle \bullet; pp \rangle$

Fig. 4. The signature Σ_{AL_1}

Let $\mathbb{L}_n$ be the language of an LA grammar whose derivations have the hyp-
rank n. The hyp-rank is the bound on the nesting of the introduction rules –
or, the bound on the length of Γ of any judgement used in a derivation. The
hyp-rank does not limit the total number of the introduction (or, elimination,
for that matter) rules that may occur in a derivation. Therefore, $\mathbb{L}_n$ is generally
infinite. Nevertheless, all its derivations can be performed with a finitely many
instances of inference rules. Indeed, if t is a normal derivation $\bullet \vdash A_s$, all types of
all judgements within t are subformulas of A_s or the types of the lexicon. Therefore, the set of distinct types appearing within all (potentially infinite many)
derivations for $\mathbb{L}_n$ is finite. Furthermore, each judgement within a derivation has
no more that n hypotheses. Therefore, the total number of distinct judgements,
and hence the distinct instances of inference rules, within all derivations of $\mathbb{L}_n$
is also finite.

It is easy to see $\mathcal{AL}_{D_1}$ is an initial algebra of the signature Σ_{AL_1}, and hence
represents all and only the LA (and correspondingly, LG) derivations of the given
lexicon (with a single dischargeable np hypothesis).

One may view Σ_{AL_1} as a CFG. For example, the type of the operation
'evp' may be viewed as the production $\langle \bullet; s \rangle \rightarrow \langle \bullet; np \rangle \langle \bullet; vp \rangle$. The grammar is
almost in Chomsky Normal Form (it would be in CNF if we substitute-out the
productions that correspond to the unary rule 'irnp').

3   ACG, Algebraically

We now define an algebraic ACG: a subset of second-order ACGs [2,5], and relate
it with LA. An algebraic ACG $\mathcal{G}$ is a quadruple of two algebraic signatures Σ_A
(called 'abstract') and Σ_O (called 'object'), a morphism $\mathcal{L}$ (called lexicon) and a
sort s of the abstract signature called 'the distinguished type'. $\mathcal{L}$ is a morphism

from an initial algebra of Σ_A to the initial algebra of Σ_O that commutes with Σ_A's operations. Let $\mathcal{I}(\mathcal{G})$ be the word algebra of Σ_A. Its carrier of the sort s is called the abstract language generated by $\mathcal{G}$. The object language of $\mathcal{G}$ is the image of the abstract language by $\mathcal{L}$.

In the original De Groote's definition of ACG [2], the abstract language is taken to be the set of all closed linear lambda terms of the type s built over a (generally higher-order) signature. In the simplest second-order ACG, the signature is algebraic. Furthermore, a *normal* lambda term of the primitive type s over such signature has no lambda-abstractions. Thus our algebraic ACG fits with the original second-order ACG definition.

In the following, let $\mathcal{G}$ be a particular algebraic ACG whose abstract signature is Σ_{AL_1}, the object signature is the string signature defined below, and the distinguished type is s. The zero-arity operations of Σ_{AL_1} are precisely the LG lexicon, Fig. 2; the other operations are determined by the hyp-rank and the set of lexicon categories – both of which are small, in natural languages. The abstract language of $\mathcal{G}$ is, by definition, the set of terms, such as

```
evp(edp(the, enn(book,
  erel(that, irnp(ehvp(john, ehtv(read,hnp))))))), vanished)
```

which is an encoding of the LG derivation in Fig. 1. Since $\mathcal{I}(\mathcal{G})$ is also an initial algebra and hence isomorphic to $\mathcal{AL}_{D_1}$, the abstract language of $\mathcal{G}$ represents all and only derivations of LG (with the hyp-rank restriction).

The string signature has only one sort: string. Its constants are john and book, etc., for each lexical item (Fig. 2), plus ϵ and $+$. The morphism from $\mathcal{I}(\mathcal{G})$ is defined in Fig. 5. (In conventional ACG terms, the lexicon can be called second-order.) In particular, $\mathcal{L}$ maps the abstract language term above to (the + (book + (that + (ϵ + (john + (read + ϵ)))))) + vanished. It is easy to see the morphism computes the fringe of the LA derivation tree: in other words, it computes the yield of the corresponding LG derivation.

$$\mathcal{L}(\text{john}) \mapsto \text{john} \qquad \mathcal{L}(\text{hnp}) \mapsto \epsilon \qquad \mathcal{L}(\text{irnp}(x)) \mapsto \epsilon + \mathcal{L}(x)$$
$$\mathcal{L}(\text{evp}(x,y)) \mapsto \mathcal{L}(x) + \mathcal{L}(y)$$

Fig. 5. The lexicon $\mathcal{L}$: the mapping from $\mathcal{I}(\mathcal{G})$ to the string language. Only the representative mappings are shown. The others are analogous.

3.1   The Absence of Overgeneration

We have just demonstrated that an algebraic ACG describes the same language as the corresponding LG of a fixed hyp-rank and hence does not overgenerate. Since overgeneration is a serious problem in (naive) ACGs [9], let us discuss how it could arise and how it is prevented in algebraic ACGs. We use concrete examples from [9] and the Kubota challenge.

We start with one of the examples from [9, §7.2]: sentences with adverbs. The base sentence is "John hit Mary", which is in the language of $\mathcal{G}$ (after adding to Σ_{AL_1} the lexical entries mary: $\langle \bullet; np \rangle$ and hit: $\langle \bullet; tv \rangle$). The corresponding abstract term is evp(john, etv(hit,mary)). After adding "deliberately" with the syntactic type vp/vp, "John deliberately hit Mary" should become recognizable. It does indeed, after the following additions to Σ_{AL_1}:

$$\text{deliberately} : \langle \bullet; vp/vp \rangle \qquad \text{evpvp} : \langle \bullet; vp/vp \rangle \to \langle \bullet; vp \rangle \to \langle \bullet; vp \rangle$$

of which only the first is the lexical entry. The LG derivation is represented by the abstract term evp(john, evpvp(deliberately,etv(hit,mary))).

The challenge itself is avoiding overgeneration. Moot shows in [9] that a naive ACG generates not just the above sentence but also "John deliberately Mary hit" and "Mary John hit deliberately". Let us see how the former could come about. The signature Σ_{AL_1} has no combinators to combine 'mary' with 'hit'. We can introduce a np hypothesis and build irnp(ehvp(mary,ehtv(hit,hnp))) of the sort $\langle \bullet; s/np \rangle$ – similar to the analysis of "john read" in our running example. In the naive ACG this term has the type indistinguishable from vp (which is $np\backslash s$), and hence can be combined with 'deliberately' and then with 'john', leading to the overgenerated sentence. Such derivation is, however, impossible in $\mathcal{G}$: the sort $\langle \bullet; s/np \rangle$ is different from $\langle \bullet; vp \rangle$; the combination with 'deliberately' is not possible. The second overgeneration example by Moot is also not derivable in $\mathcal{G}$.

Thus although ACGs do not have directional types, the overgeneration can still be prevented, if directional syntactic types such as $np\backslash s$ are mapped to atomic ACG types (viz., $\langle \bullet; np\backslash s \rangle$) rather than function types. The key, hence, is avoiding the Curry-Howard correspondence, prominently present in other approaches [1,4]. Using rich set of atomic types does *not* imply duplicating lexical entries: Σ_{AL_1} uses just as many lexical entries as the corresponding LG lexicon.

The Kubota challenge is analyzing right-node-raising such as "John loves and Bill hates Mary" without overgeneration. The original sentence is recognized by $\mathcal{G}$ after adding (besides the obvious lexical entries for 'bill', 'loves' and 'hates'):

and   : $\langle \bullet; (rn\backslash rn)/rn \rangle$ eandr : $\langle \bullet; (rn\backslash rn)/rn \rangle \to \langle \bullet; rn \rangle \to \langle \bullet; rn\backslash rn \rangle$

eandl : $\langle \bullet; rn \rangle \to \langle \bullet; rn\backslash rn \rangle \to \langle \bullet; rn \rangle$ esnp   : $\langle \bullet; rn \rangle \to \langle \bullet; np \rangle \to \langle \bullet; s \rangle$

(we write rn for s/np.) Here is the derivation

```
esnp(eandl(irnp(ehvp(john, ehtv(loves,hnp)))),
       eandr(and, irnp(ehvp(bill, ehtv(hates,hnp))))), mary)
```

Crucially, "*Mary John loves and Bill hates" is not recognizable: $\langle \bullet; s/np \rangle$ is different from $\langle \bullet; vp \rangle$ as explained earlier, and the only combinator that accepts the arguments of the types $\langle \bullet; s/np \rangle$ and $\langle \bullet; np \rangle$ takes them in the shown order.

4   Related Work

The most closely related is the work by De Groote [1]. His approach is based on a Pentus-like construction connecting LG and CFG, Kanazawa and Salvati's characterization of that construction [6], a novel method of interpreting LG lexicon as linear lambda terms, and lexicalization of second-order ACGs [7,13].

To clearly see the differences between De Groote's and our approaches, let us take the running example of [1]: "Every man who loves some woman loves every woman." It is recognized by LG in a hyp-rank–zero derivation with the following lexicon

$$\text{man}: n \qquad \text{woman}: n \qquad \text{some}: det \qquad \text{every}: det \qquad \text{loves}: tv \qquad \text{who}: pp/vp$$

(The lexicon shown in [1, Fig. 1] has an extra entry for 'whom' that is not used in the running example.)

The most insightful is the comparison of our algebraic ACG with the intermediate result of De Groote's derivation, which he dubs $LDER$: see Fig. 6. The differences show already in the abstract signature: $LDER$ is larger, reflecting the fact that Pentus-like constructions produce (highly) redundant grammars. (Even though $LDER$ relied on a particular case of the Pentus construction with less redundancy than the general case). The most significant differences are in the lexicon. The $LDER$ lexicon is clearly third order, producing lambda-terms. Our lexicon is second order, and outputs strings (the yield of the grammar). The final result [1, Figs. 12 and 13] also has the second-order string lexicon, but a *third-order* ACG.

One of the most difficult parts of the Pentus proof [10] is demonstrating that an L derivation $A_1, \ldots, A_n \vdash A_{n+1}$ for an arbitrary n can be constructed, using only the cut rule, from the derivations of $A_1, \ldots, A_m \vdash A_{m+1}$ where m is only 1 or 2. Limiting the number of hypotheses in all judgements of L to, say, two, limits the length of strings in the LG language also to two. In LA, however, the number of marks . (collapsed into •) does not count for the purpose of hyp-rank. Therefore, we may impose the hyp-rank 2 and still generate an infinite set of strings. In fact, as we argue below, the hyp-rank of two or three may be sufficient as far as natural languages are concerned. Therefore, LA side-steps the main difficulty of the Pentus construction.

Moot's [9] is the comprehensive study of type logical grammars, naive ACG and lambda-grammars from the point of view of multiplicative linear logic. It catalogs the overgeneration and the descriptive inadequacy of lambda-grammars and naive ACGs. Incidentally, Moot introduced what amounts to our hyp-rank 1 restriction, under the name 'strict separation'. Thus hyp-rank is a generalization of strict separation. Since we eschew the Curry-Howard correspondence for directional types, we also forsake the direct semantic or intuitionistic linear logic interpretation for $\mathcal{AL}_D$ derivations. (Syntax-semantics interface is out of scope for the present paper.)

Kanazawa [4] describes a radically different approach to preventing overgeneration and ensuring the descriptive adequacy of ACGs, based on so-called syntactic features represented by regular constraints, and tree automata that

Abstract signature, [1]

prod$_0$: $<det>$ → $<n>$ → $<np>$
prod$_1$: $<tv>$ → $<np>$ → $<np>$ → $<s>$
prod$_2$: $<pp/vp>$ → $<vp>$ → $<n>$ → $<n>$
prod$_4$: $<tv>$ → $<np>$ → $<vp>$
prod$_7$: $<det>$ → $<n/np>$ → $<np/np>$
prod$_8$: $<pp/vp>$ → $<tv>$ → $<n>$ → $<n/np>$
prod$_9$: $<tv>$ → $<np/np>$ → $<tv>$
man   : $<n>$

Abstract signature, this paper

edp : $\langle \bullet; det \rangle \to \langle \bullet; n \rangle \to \langle \bullet; np \rangle$
evp : $\langle \bullet; np \rangle \to \langle \bullet; vp \rangle \to \langle \bullet; s \rangle$
etv : $\langle \bullet; tv \rangle \to \langle \bullet; np \rangle \to \langle \bullet; vp \rangle$
enn : $\langle \bullet; n \rangle \to \langle \bullet; pp \rangle \to \langle \bullet; n \rangle$
esrel : $\langle \bullet; pp/vp \rangle \to \langle \bullet; vp \rangle \to \langle \bullet; pp \rangle$

man : $\langle \bullet; n \rangle$

other lexical entries elided   other lexical entries elided

Object signature, [1]

man,woman : n
some,every : $n \to np$
loves   : $np \to np \to np$
who   : $(np \to s) \to n \to n$

Object signature, this paper

man,woman,some,every,loves,who : *string*
$+$: *string* → *string* → *string*

Lexicon, [1]

prod$_0$:= $\lambda xy. \, xy$
prod$_1$:= $\lambda xyz. \, xyz$
prod$_2$:= $\lambda wxy. \, w(\lambda z. \, xz)y$
prod$_8$:= $\lambda vwxy. \, v(\lambda z. \, wyz)x$

. . .

man := man

. . .

Lexicon, this paper

$\mathcal{L}(\text{edp}(x,y)) \mapsto \mathcal{L}(x) + \mathcal{L}(y)$
$\mathcal{L}(\text{evp}(x,y)) \mapsto \mathcal{L}(x) + \mathcal{L}(y)$
$\mathcal{L}(\text{etv}(x,y)) \mapsto \mathcal{L}(x) + \mathcal{L}(y)$
$\mathcal{L}(\text{enn}(x,y)) \mapsto \mathcal{L}(x) + \mathcal{L}(y)$
$\mathcal{L}(\text{esrel}(x,y)) \mapsto \mathcal{L}(x) + \mathcal{L}(y)$
$\mathcal{L}(\text{man})$ $\mapsto$ man

. . .

Fig. 6. Comparison of the ACG grammar *LDER* of [1] and the algebraic ACG of the present paper, for the running example of [1]. The *LDER* grammar is cited from Figs. 4–7 of [1], after removing the unused entry for 'whom' and adjusting the notation.

capture those constraints. Nevertheless, there is surprising a similarity: his marking of atomic types by features is similar in spirit to our atomic types like $\langle \bullet, np; s \rangle$ that 'mark', so to speak, the type s with the hypothetical environment containing np.

Retoré and Salvati [12], like us, are interested if ACGs could 'faithfully' represent categorical formalisms, that is, their derivations. There are also many similarities in technical details: our calculus LA and the treatment of lexical entries is similar to the calculus used in their paper, modulo associativity. However, Retoré and Salvati study the non-associative Lambek calculus whereas we use the associative one. Mainly, underlying [12] is the linear lambda calculus. We, in contrast, rely on the algebraic approach and specifically avoid lambda-terms.

5   Discussion

Our approach of representing LGs as algebraic ACGs relies on hyp-rank: the fixed upper bound on the number of not-yet-discharged hypotheses that can appear at any single time in any branch of an L derivation. This section discusses the theoretical significance and the practical insignificance of the hyp-rank. We also say a few words about the development and motivations of the LA calculus.

We should stress that the hyp-rank concerns only those hypotheses of an L derivation that are discharged by the introduction rules in that derivation. The hypotheses that persists until the end (i.e., correspond to the lexicon of LG) do not count towards the hyp-rank. Thus the hyp-rank in no way restricts the size of the LG lexicon. Furthermore, the hyp-rank counts not the total number of hypotheses in a derivation – not the total number of introduction rules – but their maximum number along any single derivation branch. If one branch introduces a hypothesis and then discharges it with an introduction rule, and so does another, independent branch, the hyp-rank of each branch and of the merged derivation is one.

From the practical point of view, the hyp-rank can be disregarded. Whatever large or infinite may be the set of strings in a natural language, one may expect that recognizing it requires only a bounded, and rather small, number of hypotheses. The success of CCG in parsing natural languages lends credit to this assertion: CCG rules such as composition and lifting are derivable in LG with only one, local assumption. Thus the core CCG (AB grammar plus composition, lifting and associativity) corresponds to LG derivations of hyp-rank one.

From the point of ACG, the fixed hyp-rank qualification can be lifted if one allows polymorphic ACG signatures. On the other hand, it is interesting to investigate classes of context-free languages recognizable by LGs of a given hyp-rank.

The LA calculus was originally developed for a different project: to give some automation to the field of type-logical grammars. The goal is to use the facilities of programming languages to not only mechanically verify the derivations, but also to easily compose them from already checked parts, to reuse in new projects, to develop libraries of derivations and regression testing suites – and to conveniently display derivations and produce figures for papers.

We have used the automation in the present paper. We have embedded LA calculus in OCaml and used the embedding to mechanically check the derivation in Fig. 3 and produce the LaTeX code for Figs. 1 and 3. In fact, the former was produced from the latter by implementing the proof of Proposition 1, which is constructive and can be taken as an algorithm.

6   Conclusions

We have thus demonstrated the strong equivalence of LGs and algebraic ACGs, by exhibiting the construction of an algebraic ACG for a given LG and the hyp-rank. The abstract language of this ACG is the set of LG derivations of the given hyp-rank and the object language is the set of yields of those derivations – with no blow-up in the lexicon.

Contra Moot [9], we conclude that although ACG lack directional types, they are just as descriptively adequate as Lambek Grammars. Thus ACG may, after all, be rightly called categorial grammars.

In the future work we would like to extend our ACG construction to other type logical grammars, such as Hybrid TLG (HTLG).

Acknowledgments. We thank Yusuke Kubota for his inspiring challenge. The comments by Richard Moot and the anonymous reviewers are gratefully acknowledged.
This work was partially supported by JSPS KAKENHI Grant Number 17K00091.

References

1. De Groote, P.: Lambek categorial grammars as abstract categorial grammars. In: LENLS 13. Logic and Engineering of Natural Language Semantics 13, Tokyo, Japan, October 2016. https://hal.inria.fr/hal-01412795

2. de Groote, P.: Towards abstract categorial grammars. In: ACL, pp. 148–155 (2002). http://www.aclweb.org/anthology/P01-1033

3. de Groote, P., Pogodalla, S.: On the expressive power of abstract categorial grammars: representing context-free formalisms. J. Logic Lang. Inform. **13**(4), 421–438 (2004)

4. Kanazawa, M.: Syntactic features for regular constraints and an approximation of directional slashes in abstract categorial grammars. In: Kubota, Y., Levine, R. (eds.) Proceedings for ESSLLI 2015 Workshop 'Empirical Advances in Categorial Grammar' (CG 2015), pp. 34–70. University of Tsukuba and Ohio State University (2015). https://makotokanazawa.ws.hosei.ac.jp/publications/approx_proc.pdf

5. Kanazawa, M., Pogodalla, S.: Advances in abstract categorial grammars: language theory and linguistic modeling. Lecture Notes, ESSLLI 09, Part 2, July 2009. http://www.loria.fr/equipes/calligramme/acg/publications/esslli-09/2009-esslli-acg-week-2-part-2.pdf

6. Kanazawa, M., Salvati, S.: The string-meaning relations definable by Lambek grammars and context-free grammars. In: Morrill, G., Nederhof, M.-J. (eds.) FG 2012-2013. LNCS, vol. 8036, pp. 191–208. Springer, Heidelberg (2013). https://doi.org/10.1007/978-3-642-39998-5_12

7. Kanazawa, M., Yoshinaka, R.: Lexicalization of second-order ACGs. Technical report, NII, July 2005. https://www.nii.ac.jp/TechReports/public_html/05-012E.html

8. Kubota, Y., Levine, R.: Against ellipsis: arguments for the direct licensing of 'non-canonical' coordinations. Linguist. Philos. **38**(6), 521–576 (2015)

9. Moot, R.: Hybrid type-logical grammars, first-order linear logic and the descriptive inadequacy of lambda grammars, 26 May 2014. https://hal.archives-ouvertes.fr/hal-00996724

10. Pentus, M.: Lambek grammars are context free. In: Proceedings of the Eighth Annual Symposium on Logic in Computer Science (LICS 1993), pp. 429–433 (1993). https://doi.org/10.1109/LICS.1993.287565

11. Retoré, C.: The logic of categorial grammars: lecture notes. Technical report RR-5703, INRIA, September 2005. https://hal.inria.fr/inria-00070313

12. Retoré, C., Salvati, S.: A faithful representation of non-associative Lambek grammars in abstract categorial grammars. J. Logic Lang. Inform. **19**(2), 185–200 (2010)

13. Yoshinaka, R., Kanazawa, M.: The complexity and generative capacity of lexicalized abstract categorial grammars. In: Blache, P., Stabler, E., Busquets, J., Moot, R. (eds.) LACL 2005. LNCS (LNAI), vol. 3492, pp. 330–346. Springer, Heidelberg (2005). https://doi.org/10.1007/11422532_22

Tying Free Choice in Questions to Distributivity

Filipe Hisao Kobayashi$^{(\boxtimes)}$ and Vincent Rouillard

Massachusetts Institute of Technology, Cambridge, MA 02139, USA
{filipek,vincents}@mit.edu

Abstract. The idea that *wh*-phrases can quantify over generalized quantifiers emerged following two main observations: (i) disjunctive answers to modalized questions lead to free choice inferences if the *wh*-phrases's restrictor is plural and (ii) questions with collective predicates do not lead to uniqueness presuppositions. Such proposals, however, fail to derive the connection between (i-ii) and plurality. We propose a novel analysis in which (i-ii) are derived via the presence of an existential distributivity operator. By tying these phenomena to distributivity, our analysis is able to establish the desired connection to plurality.

Keywords: Question semantics · Free choice · Distributivity · Exhaustification

1 Introduction

The semantics literature has seen growing discussion on the topic of free choice in *wh*-interrogatives [1,5,16–19]. It has been noted that questions like (1-a) can receive disjunctive answers such as (1-b) which carry free choice inferences.[1]

(1)   a.   Q: Which books are we required to read?
       b.   A: The French books or the Russian books.
          ↝ ◇we read only the French books ∧
            ◇we read only the Russian books

A popular analysis of these facts involves assuming that *wh*-items have the option of quantifying over generalized quantifiers. In the case above, this allows *which books* to quantify over an existential quantifier ranging over books which scopes below the universal modal. This in turn allows us to apply familiar theories of implicature calculation to get the free choice inference.

It has also been noted that the free choice effects discussed above do not arise when the restrictor of the *wh*-phrase is singular. The disjunctive answer in (2-b) to the question in (2-a) leads to ignorance rather than free choice.

---

[1] Free choice generally describes an inference drawn from $\Diamond A \vee B$ that $\Diamond A \wedge \Diamond B$. Here, however, following previous literature on the data in (1), we also use it to describe the stronger inference from $\Box A \vee B$ to $\Box A \vee B \wedge \neg \Box A \wedge \neg \Box B$, which entails that both only A and only B are possible.

© Springer Nature Switzerland AG 2020
M. Sakamoto et al. (Eds.): JSAI-isAI 2019, LNAI 12331, pp. 244–257, 2020.
https://doi.org/10.1007/978-3-030-58790-1_16

(2)   a.   Q: Which book are we required to read?
      b.   A: The French book or the Russian book.
         $\not\leadsto$ $\Diamond$ we only read the French book $\land$
          $\Diamond$ we only read the Russian book

The interaction between free choice and number has been left largely unexplored in the literature. We propose to establish this link by discussing a new account of free choice in interrogatives which involves the presence of a covert existential distributivity operator [2]. We show that this move allows us to derive free choice for plural *wh*-interrogatives, whilst deriving no such inference for the singular case. Furthermore, we show that this does not result in bad predictions for other data that have served as motivation for higher-order quantification, namely the lack of a uniqueness presupposition in (3).

(3)   Which students formed a group?
      does not presuppose: $\exists!x[\mathsf{students}(x) \land \mathsf{formed\text{-}a\text{-}group}(x)]$

We show that under the assumptions that (i) questions are felicitous when the exhaustified set of their answers forms a partition on the context [7], and (ii) the exhaustification of alternatives involves a step which allows us to assert some of those alternatives [3], we can derive the lack of uniqueness of (3).

    The use of a distributivity operator to derive free choice establishes a natural connection between the presence of this inference in plural *wh*-interrogatives and its absence in their singular counterparts. Furthermore, as we will show, restrictions on the kind of generalized quantifiers *wh*-items quantify over are naturally derived from our proposal. We therefore argue that our proposal offers a number of advantages over the view that *wh*-items quantify over generalized quantifiers, both on conceptual and empirical grounds.

2   Background

Following [8,10], we assume questions to denote the set of their answers, as shown in (4).[2] The question denotation in (4-c) is compositionally derived from the LF in (4-b), where the interrogative complementizer **?** denotes [10]'s proto-question operator and the *wh*-phrase an existential quantifier, as in (5). We call denotations like (4-c) a question's answer-set.

(4)   a.   Who arrived?
      b. λp who λ_x [**?** p] [x arrive]
      c. $[\![(\text{4-b})]\!] = \{\mathsf{arrive}(x) \mid \mathsf{human}(x)\}$
(5)   a. $[\![\text{who}]\!] = \lambda f_{et}.\ \exists x \in \mathsf{human} : f(x)$
      b. $[\![?]\!] = \lambda p_{st}.\lambda q_{st}.\ p = q$

---

[2] For ease of exposition, we use set-theoretic notation for question denotations. We could have equivalently written (4-c) as $[\lambda p_{st}.\ \exists x \in \mathsf{human}_w : p = \lambda w'.\ \mathsf{arrive}_{w'}(x)]$. We furthermore suppress intensional details.

The question in (4-a) presupposes that someone arrived. To derive this, we follow [4] in assuming interrogatives to fall within the scope of a covert answer-hood operator ANS. The LF schema for (4-a) should, therefore, be represented as (6). We adopt a version of [7]'s formulation of ANS, shown in (7), in which ANS takes a question denotation as its argument and ouputs the set of its exhaustified answers (i.e., its Exh-answer-set) only if this set partitions the context set C. In (7), we take C to be a parameter on $[\![\cdot]\!]$, but we supress it from the definitions to follow[3].

(6)   ANS $[\ \lambda_p$ who $\lambda_x\ [\ ?\ p\ ]\ [\ x$ arrive $]\ ]$

(7) $[\![\text{ANS}]\!]^C = \lambda Q_{stt} : \text{Partition}(Q, C). \{\text{Exh}(q) \mid q \in Q\}$
        where $\text{Partition}(Q, C)$ iff $\{\text{Exh}_Q(q) \cap C \mid q \in Q\}$ partitions C

Exhaustification is assumed to proceed as proposed by [3], where, in order to exhaustify a proposition p with respect to a set of alternatives Q, one must first determine two sets. The set of *innocently excludable* alternatives of p given Q is the the maximal set of elements of Q that can be consistently negated if p is true, while the set of *innocently includable* alternatives of p given Q is the maximal set of elements of Q that can be consistently asserted if p is true and its innocently excludable alternatives are false. Exhaustification of p given Q thus consists in negating all of its innocently excludable alternatives and asserting all of its innocently includable alternatives. A semi-formal definition of these procedures is given in (8).

(8) $\text{Exh}_Q(p) := \forall q \in Q[q \in \text{IE}_Q(p) \to \neg q] \wedge \forall q \in Q[q \in \text{II}_Q(p) \to q]$

   a. $\text{IE}_Q(p) = \bigcap\{C' \subseteq C : C'$ is a maximal subset of C s.t.
                                    $\{\neg p : p \in C'\} \cup \{p\}$ is consistent$\}$

   b. $\text{II}_Q(p) = \bigcap\{C'' \subseteq C : C''$ is a maximal subset of C s.t.
                          $\{r : r \in C''\} \cup \{p\} \cup \{\neg q : q \in \text{IE}_Q(p)\}$ is consistent$\}$

We derive (4-a)'s presupposition that someone left in the following way. Due to ANS, (6) will only be defined if the pointwise intersection of the Exh-answer-set of (4-c) with the context set C induces a partition on C. This is shown in (9), where we assume that human $= \{a, b\}$[4]. To illustrate how exhaustification works, in (10) we show the exhaustification of a singular alternative of (4-c).

---

[3] Let A be a set and $B \subseteq \mathcal{P}(A)$, we say B partitions/induces a partition on A iff $A = \bigcup B \wedge \{C \cap C' \mid C, C' \in B\} = \{\emptyset\} \wedge \emptyset \notin B$.

[4] Note that, given that *arrive* is distributive, a$\oplus$b is equivalent to a $\wedge$ b.

The exhaustification of the plural alternative a⊕b is vacuous, given that it is the strongest alternative in the set[5].

(9) $\{\mathsf{Exh}_{(4\text{-}c)}(q) \mid q \in (4\text{-}c)\} = \{\mathsf{Exh}_{(4\text{-}c)}(\mathsf{a}), \mathsf{Exh}_{(4\text{-}c)}(\mathsf{b}), \mathsf{Exh}_{(4\text{-}c)}(\mathsf{a}\oplus\mathsf{b})\}$
$= \{\mathsf{a} \wedge \neg\mathsf{b}, \mathsf{b} \wedge \neg\mathsf{a}, \mathsf{a}\oplus\mathsf{b}(= \mathsf{a} \wedge \mathsf{b})\}$

(10)   a. $\mathsf{IE}_{(4\text{-}c)}(\mathsf{a}) = \{\mathsf{b}, \mathsf{a}\oplus\mathsf{b}\}$
        b. $\mathsf{II}_{(4\text{-}c)}(\mathsf{a}) = \{\mathsf{a}\}$
        c. $\mathsf{Exh}_{(4\text{-}c)}(\mathsf{a}) = \mathsf{a} \wedge \neg\mathsf{b}$

The set in (9) will impose a partition on C only if (i) for each proposition p in (9), there is at least one world in C in which p is true, (ii) for each world in C, there is a proposition p in (9) such that p is true in that world. Therefore, if there is a single world in the context set in which no one has arrived, the presupposition of ANS will not be satisfied, as no proposition in (9) is true in that world. Therefore, the current system correctly predicts (4-a) to presuppose that someone arrived.

3   Higher-Order Quantification in Questions

3.1   Free Choice

[16,17] is to our knowledge the first to discuss the presence of free choice effects in complex *wh*-interrogatives. In the presence of a universal modal, disjunctive answers to plural complex *wh*-interrogatives lead to a free choice inference.

(11)   a.   Q: Which books are we required to read?
        b.   A: The French books or the Russian books.
              ⤳ ◇we read only the French books ∧
              ◇we read only the Russian books

If we follow standard assumptions and take *which books* to quantify over regular individuals, it becomes difficult to derive free choice from the utterance of the disjunctive answer in (11-b). To see this, consider the Exh-answer-set to (11-a) in (12-b), where we assume *books* denotes the set in (12-a).

(12)   a. $[\![\text{books}]\!] = \{\mathsf{f}, \mathsf{r}, \mathsf{f} \oplus \mathsf{r}\}$
        b. $\left\{ \begin{array}{l} \square \text{ we read } \mathsf{f} \wedge \Diamond \neg \text{ we read } \mathsf{r}, \\ \square \text{ we read } \mathsf{r} \wedge \Diamond \neg \text{ we read } \mathsf{f}, \\ \square \text{ we read } \mathsf{f} \wedge \square \text{ we read } \mathsf{r} \end{array} \right\}$

---

[5] The inclusion of the alternative a⊕b in $\mathsf{IE}_{(4\text{-}c)}(a)$ depends on whether we take $\neg(a\oplus b)$ to mean $\neg(a \wedge b)$ or $\neg(a \vee b)$. Although logically it should be the former, the natural language sentence *A and B didn't arrive* seems to be interpreted as the latter (a phenomenon known as homogeneity, which will be discussed below). Nothing in the above analysis depends on which of these is the right answer: if $\neg(a \oplus b) = \neg(a \wedge b)$, it will be vacuously included to $\mathsf{IE}_{(4\text{-}c)}(a)$; if $\neg(a \oplus b) = \neg(a \vee b)$, it won't be either in $\mathsf{IE}_{(4\text{-}c)}(a)$ or $\mathsf{II}_{(4\text{-}c)}(a)$, and therefore won't affect the final result.

While this question is well-formed insofar as it partitions the context, it is not clear how any answer should lead to free choice here. In fact, none of them is compatible with the desired inference. The free choice effect of disjunctive answers such as (11-b) is derivable if we assume the disjunction to take narrow scope below the modal. This can be achieved if we provide a meaning for *which books* such that it can quantify over generalized quantifiers (GQs). More specifically, we can assume the *wh*-phrase can quantify over generalized disjunctions of individuals rather than quantifying over individuals proper.

(13) $[\![\text{which books}]\!] = \lambda P_{((et)t)t}.\exists \Pi \in \{\lambda f_{et}.\ \exists x \in X : f(x) \mid X \subseteq \text{books}\} :$
        $P(\Pi)$

The answers in (12-b), prior to the application of ANS, can be interpreted using the LF schema in (14-a), where *which books* binds a variable of type $(et)t$, which itself binds a type e variable. This in turn denotes the set of propositions described in (14-b).[6]

(14)   a. λ_p which books λ_Π [? p] [$\Box \Pi_{(et)t} \lambda_x$ [we read x_e]]

        b. $\left\{ \begin{array}{l} \Box \text{ we-read}(f), \\ \Box \text{ we-read}(r), \\ \Box \text{ we-read}(f \oplus r), \\ ①\Box \text{ we-read}(f) \vee \text{we-read}(r) \end{array} \right\}$

The answer in (11-b) can be taken to correspond to the proposition in ①. Once the ANS operator is applied to the set in (14-b), each of its members is exhaustified relative to the others. The answer in ① is entailed by every member of (14-b). Furthermore, each member of (14-b) is innocently excludable relative to ①, and will as a result be negated. The exhaustified meaning of ① will be the one in (15), which entails the free choice inference.

(15) $\text{Exh}_{(14\text{-b})}(\Box \text{ we-read}(f) \vee \text{we-read}(r)) =$
        $(\Box \text{ we-read}(f) \vee \text{we-read}(r)) \wedge \neg \Box \text{ we-read}(f) \wedge \neg \Box \text{ we-read}(r) \Rightarrow$
        $(\Diamond \text{ we-read}(f) \wedge \neg\text{we-read}(r)) \wedge (\Diamond \text{ we-read}(r) \wedge \neg\text{we-read}(f))$

3.2   Collective Predicates

Questions involving collective predication, such as (16-a), allow for answers where multiple groups were formed.

(16)   a.   Q: Which students formed a group?
        b.   A: Al and Bob, and Bob and Carl.

[18] notes that if we assume *which students* to range over individuals, we predict answers such as (17-b) to be unavailable. Let (17-a) be the contextually relevant set of students. We predict (16-a) to denote (17-b) before the application of ANS.

---

[6] The following are equivalent:
   $\Box \exists x \in \{f, r\} : \text{we-read}(x) \equiv \Box \text{ we-read}(f) \vee \text{we-read}(r)$.

(17)   a. $[\![$students$]\!] = \{$a, b, c, a$\oplus$b, a$\oplus$c, b$\oplus$c, a$\oplus$b$\oplus$c$\}$

     b.
$$\left\{\begin{array}{l} \text{formed-group(a}\oplus\text{b)}, \\ \text{formed-group(a}\oplus\text{c)}, \\ \text{formed-group(b}\oplus\text{c)}, \\ \text{formed-group(a}\oplus\text{b}\oplus\text{c)} \end{array}\right\}$$

Given the collective nature of the predicate *formed a group*, the alternatives in (17-b) are logically independent from one another. As a result, ANS will presuppose that a unique group was formed. Indeed, the partition on the context created through the application of Exh on each member of (17-b) will only contain propositions in which exactly one group was formed. This is because given the logical independence of the alternatives in (17-b), all those distinct from the prejacent are negated.

    This problem can be avoided if we once again assume that complex *wh*-interrogatives have the option to range over GQs. More specifically, we can avoid uniqueness inferences if we assume that *which students* can range over generalized conjunctions of students.

(18) $[\![$which students$]\!] = \lambda P.\, \exists \Pi \in \{\lambda f. \forall x \in X : f(x) \mid X \subseteq \text{students}\}\, :\, P(\Pi)$

Assuming for (16-a) a structure similar to (14-a), we obtain the following set of alternatives.

(19)
$$\left\{\begin{array}{c} \text{formed-group(a}\oplus\text{b)}, \\ \text{formed-group(a}\oplus\text{c)}, \\ \vdots \\ \text{formed-group(a}\oplus\text{b)} \wedge \text{formed-group(a}\oplus\text{c)}, \\ ②\text{formed-group(a}\oplus\text{b)} \wedge \text{formed-group(b}\oplus\text{c)}, \\ \vdots \end{array}\right\}$$

The application of ANS to (19) will yield a partition of the context. The proposition in ② can be taken to correspond to the answer in (16-b). Once exhaustified, it will negate all innocently excludable alternatives in (19), generating the meaning in (20), which states that a$\oplus$b and b$\oplus$c each formed a group, and that nobody else did.

(20) $\text{Exh}_{(19)}(\text{formed-group(a}\oplus\text{b)} \wedge \text{formed-group(b}\oplus\text{c)}) =$
      $\text{formed-group(a}\oplus\text{b)} \wedge \text{formed-group(b}\oplus\text{c)} \wedge$
          $\neg\exists x \in \{\text{a}\oplus\text{c}, \text{a}\oplus\text{b}\oplus\text{c}\} : \text{formed-group}(x)$

3.3   Problems

Assuming that *wh*-items can quantify over GQs runs into a number of problems. On the one hand, it has been pointed out that modalized complex *wh*-interrogatives with singular restrictors do not lead to free choice inferences when answered with a disjunction of atomic books.

(21)   a.   Q: Which book are we required to read?
        b.   A: The French book or the Russian book.
              $\not\rightarrow \Diamond$ we read the French book $\land \Diamond$ we read the Russian book

A free choice effect is predicted to arise if we allow for *which book* to quantify over generalized disjunctions of atomic books. To avoid this, one must stipulate that this sort of higher-order quantification is reserved for *wh*-items with plural restrictors.

A further problem with the account so far presented is in the choice of quantifiers over which complex *wh*-interrogatives can range. We have proposed that these items can range over at least generalized disjunctions and generalized conjunctions. However, the theory so far presented suggests that they cannot always range over both. Consider the case of collective predicates, repeated below.

(22)   Which students formed a group?

Let us assume for *which students* the lexical entry in (23), where the phrase ranges over both generalized conjunctions and disjunctions of students.

(23)   a. $[\![\text{which students}]\!] = \lambda P.\exists Q \in (\text{23-b}) : P(Q)$
        b. $\{\lambda f. \exists x \in X : f(x) \mid X \subseteq \text{student}\} \cup$
              $\{\lambda f. \forall x \in X : f(x) \mid X \subseteq \text{student}\}$

The set of answers denoted by (22) will contain propositions formed through all the disjunctions and conjunctions of students. However, such an answer set will fail to partition the context, resulting in undefinedness given our semantics for ANS.[7] To see this, consider the exhaustified meanings of the sentences in (24).

(24)   a. $\text{Exh}_{[\![(22)]\!]}(\text{formed-group}(a\oplus b) \lor \text{formed-group}(b \oplus c)) =$
              $(\text{formed-group}(a\oplus b) \lor \text{formed-group}(b\oplus c)) \land$
              $\neg \text{formed-group}(a\oplus c) \land \neg \text{formed-group}(a\oplus b\oplus c) \land$
              $\neg(\text{formed-group}(a\oplus b) \land \text{formed-group}(b\oplus c))$

        b. $\text{Exh}_{[\![(22)]\!]}(\text{formed-group}(a\oplus b)) =$
              $\text{formed-group}(a\oplus b) \land \neg \text{formed-group}(a\oplus c) \land$
              $\neg \text{formed-group}(b\oplus c) \land \neg \text{formed-group}(a\oplus b\oplus c)$

The intersection of the propositions in (24-a) and (24-b) is non-empty, hence no partition of the context can be made from a set which contains both. We must therefore assume an ambiguity for complex *wh*-interrogatives insofar as they can be taken to denote either generalized disjunctions or generalized conjunctions of individuals. This leads into a further problem with the proposal, namely what restrictions exist on the type of quantifiers over which complex *wh*-phrases can

---

[7] This problem only arises if the meaning assumed for ANS is that of [7]. It will not arise if we follow [4] and assume ANS to presuppose only that there is within the question denotation a maximally informative true answer.
$[\![\text{ANS}]\!] = \lambda Q_{(st)t} : \exists! p \in Q[p(w) \land \forall q \in Q[q(w) \to p \subseteq q]]. Q.$

in principle range. Spector notes that the set of GQs over which complex *wh*-phrases can range must be restricted to at least upward-monotone quantifiers. This is due to the fact that allowing for downward-monotone quantifiers would make it possible for (25-a) to be answered by prohibitions.

(25)   a.   Q: Which books are we required to read?
        b.   A: #None of the French books.
              $\not\rightsquigarrow \Box\neg$we-read(f)

Summarizing, assuming that *wh*-phrases can quantify over GQs forces us to make three stipulations. On the one hand, we must assume this type of quantification to be available only when the restrictor of the *wh*-item is singular. We must further stipulate that *wh*-items are ambiguous with respect to whether they quantify over generalized disjunctions or conjunctions. Finally, we must assume that these items cannot quantify over downward-monotone quantifiers.

4   A Novel Approach

Higher-order readings of questions are tied to plurality: the first phenomenon, free choice, is only observed with plural *wh*-interrogatives, whereas the second, lack of uniqueness, occurs with collective predication. In this section, we offer a novel account of these readings that derives their connection with plurality, rather than stipulating it. The resulting account furthermore allows us to stick with the standard assumption that *wh*-items are quantifiers that range over individuals.

We argue that the source of higher-order readings of questions can be explicated by (i) the presence of an existential distributivity operator [2], and (ii) the possibility of binding the cover restricting this operator by an existential quantifier. These two assumptions are independently motivated.

The first ingredient in our proposal, a covert existential distributivity operator, was proposed by [2] to account for homogeneity effects. These are illustrated in (26): distributivity is interpreted as a universal quantifier in positive sentences, but as an existential in negative ones.[8]

(26)   a.   Henry and Rico are Italian.
              $\rightsquigarrow$ *Both* Henry and Rico are Italian.
        b.   Henry and Rico aren't Italian.
              $\rightsquigarrow$ *Neither* Henry nor Rico are Italian.

[2] proposes an implicature account of the effects in (26). The proposal is that the covert distributivity operator is lexically weak: it denotes an existential

---

[8] Although it is possible that in (26-b) negation takes scope below the distributive quantifier, [11] shows that, in at least some cases, this is not a possible line of argumentation: *No boy read his books* is interpreted as implying that there isn't a single boy who read *any* of his books. Given that the definite description *his books* is bound by the negative generalized quantifier *no boy*, it must be interpreted in its scope, and, therefore, under the scope of negation.

quantifier, as shown in (27). However, in upward entailing environments, it can be exhaustified into a universal quantifier.

(27) $[\![\exists\text{-}\mathrm{DIST}_C]\!] = \lambda x_e.\lambda f_{et} : \mathsf{Cov}(C, x).\ \exists x' \in C : x' \leq x \wedge f(x')$
         where $\mathsf{Cov}(C, x)$ iff $x = \bigoplus C$

The strengthening of $\exists\text{-}\mathrm{DIST}_C$ is possible due to the exhaustification procedure presented in Sect. 2 coupled with certain assumptions about the alternatives of sentences involving distributivity. We present a rough rendition of [2]'s analysis of (26-a). This sentence is associated with the LF in (28), where a covert exhaustification operator takes scope over the sentence (see [6]). In (28-a) we have the denotation of the prejacent and in (28-b) the set of its alternatives. A crucial property of the set of alternatives in (29-b) is that it is not closed under conjunction, which results in the set of innocently excludable alternatives being empty. Given that all of the prejacent's alternatives are innocently includable, they are all asserted, giving rise to universal quantification.

(28)   [$\mathrm{EXH}_{\mathrm{ALT}(\phi)}$ [$_\phi$ [Henry and Rico $\exists\text{-}\mathrm{DIST}_C$] italian]]

(29)   a. $(\exists x \leq \mathsf{h}\oplus\mathsf{r} : \mathsf{italian}(x)) = \mathsf{italian}(\mathsf{h}) \vee \mathsf{italian}(\mathsf{r})$
         b. $\mathrm{ALT}(\phi) = \{\mathsf{italian}(\mathsf{h}) \vee \mathsf{italian}(\mathsf{r}), \mathsf{italian}(\mathsf{h}), \mathsf{italian}(\mathsf{r})\}$

(30)   a. $\mathsf{IE}_{\mathrm{ALT}(\phi)}(\mathsf{italian}(\mathsf{h}) \vee \mathsf{italian}(\mathsf{r})) = \emptyset$
         b. $\mathsf{II}_{\mathrm{ALT}(\phi)}(\mathsf{italian}(\mathsf{h}) \vee \mathsf{italian}(\mathsf{r})) = \mathrm{ALT}(\phi)$
         c. $\mathsf{Exh}_{\mathrm{ALT}(\phi)}(\mathsf{italian}(\mathsf{h}) \vee \mathsf{italian}(\mathsf{r})) = \mathsf{italian}(\mathsf{h}) \wedge \mathsf{italian}(\mathsf{r})$

Note that the same will not happen in negative sentences: since the prejacent, $\neg(\mathsf{italian}(\mathsf{h}) \vee \mathsf{italian}(\mathsf{r}))$, is the strongest alternative, exhaustification is vacuous. The contrast in (26) is thus naturally captured in this framework.

The second ingredient in our analysis is the assumption that the cover that serves as the restrictor of the covert distributivity operator can be existentially quantified over. [14], who defended an analysis of distributivity that crucially relied on pragmatically given covers, argues against such a possibility. Nonetheless, [14]'s proposal seems too strong. First, it requires speech participants to have full knowledge regarding the organization of the objects in the world, and most of the time this is not the case (see [13,15] for discussion). Furthermore, there are cases in which covers do seem to be existentially quantified over. Among such cases we note the command in the first half of (31), where it is irrelevant how the subject is distributed over the VP (i.e., which cover is fed to the distributivity operator) so long as there is one such cover.[9]

(31)   You three need to fix these bikes, and I don't care who fixes which.

---

[9] A reviewer points out that (31) is actually an instance of cumulativity, and should thus be handled by [12]'s ∗-operator. However, the ∗-operator can be seen as nothing more than universally quantifying over elements of an existentially quantified cover. Thus, we believe that, rather than having a lexical opposition between ∗ and $\exists$-DIST, we could simply have the latter, with the option of sometimes existentially quantifying over it.

We now have the tools to present our analysis of higher-order readings in questions. We first discuss free choice readings, then collective readings.

4.1   Free Choice

We propose the LF schema in (32-b) as representing the question in (32-a), where (i) ∃-DIST is stranded under the scope of the modal and (ii) existential closure over covers scopes above ?.

(32)   a.   Which books are we required to read?
       b.   ANS$[\lambda_p \exists \lambda_C$[which books$\lambda_x$[$?p$][require[$\exists$-DIST$_C x$]$\lambda_y$[you read y]]]]

The meaning assigned to the prejacent of ANS is shown (33-a), which can in fact, be equivalently written as (33-b).

(33)   a. $\{\Box \exists x' \in C : x' \leq x \land \text{we-read}(x') \mid \text{books}(x) \land \text{Cov}(C, x)\}$

       b. $\left\{ \begin{array}{l} \Box \text{ we-read}(f), \\ \Box \text{ we-read}(r), \\ \Box \text{ we-read}(f \oplus r), \\ \Box \text{ we-read}(f) \lor \text{we-read}(b), \end{array} \right\}$

In order to obtain the simple sentence $\Box$ we-read(f), we need only assume that, in (33-a), the value of x is f and that of C, $\{f\}$. This is shown in (34). We can similarly obtain the proposition $\Box$ we-read(r) if we take x takes r as a value with C denoting $\{r\}$.[10] The conjunctive alternative is obtained in a similar fashion: in (35), x and C take $f \oplus r$ and $\{f \oplus r\}$ as values, respectively.

(34) $\Box \exists x' \in \{f\} : x' \leq f \land \text{we-read}(x') \equiv \Box \text{ we-read}(f)$

(35) $\Box \exists x' \in \{f \oplus r\} : x' \leq f \oplus r \land \text{we-read}(x') \equiv \Box \text{ we-read}(f \oplus r)$

Remember that the issue faced by standard approaches to the meaning of *wh*-questions was that the proposition denoted by *We are required to read the French books or the Russian books*, where disjunction takes scope below the necessity modal, was absent from the question denotation. As shown in (36), our approach does not have this problem, as this proposition can be obtained by taking x to have $f \oplus r$ as a value and C, $\{f, r\}$.

(36) $\Box \exists x' \in \{f, r\} : x' \leq f \oplus r \land \text{we-read}(x') \equiv \Box \text{ we-read}(f) \lor \text{we-read}(r)$

(36) is in fact equivalent to the question set one obtains under the GQ analysis. However, a number of stipulations made under that analysis are derived here. ∃-DIST, being an existential quantifier, will restrict the set of answers to upward entailing quantifiers, and, furthermore, account for the plural-singular

---

[10] We can also get these simple alternatives through other means. For example, if x takes $f \oplus r$ as a value and C takes $\{f, f \oplus r\}$, then the resulting proposition is $\Box$ we-read(f) $\lor$ we-read(f $\oplus$ r), which, due to the fact that *read* is lexically distributive, is equivalent to $\Box$we-read(f). We can reason similarly about r and $\{r, f \oplus r\}$.

asymmetry. Indeed, given that complex *wh*-phrases restricted by singular nouns only range over singularities, $\exists$-DIST will apply vacuously. In other words, no disjunctive answers are predicted to be available, and thus we predict the lack of free choice inferences with singular restrictors.

4.2 Collective Predicates

We assign for a question like (37-a) the set of of alternatives in (37-b). This question set can be simplified to (37-c) by the same procedure described above. This set differs from the one predicted in a GQ theory insofar as it does not contain conjunctive answers such as "formed-group($a \oplus b$) $\wedge$ formed-group($a \oplus c$)", where multiple groups were formed.

(37) a. Which students formed a pair?

  b. $\{\exists x' \in C : x' \leq x \wedge \text{form-group}(x') \mid \text{students}(x) \wedge \text{Cov}(C, x)\}$

  c. $\left\{ \begin{array}{l} \text{form-group}(a \oplus b), \\ \text{form-group}(a \oplus b), \\ \text{form-group}(b \oplus c), \\ \text{form-group}(a \oplus b \oplus c), \\ \text{form-group}(a \oplus b) \vee \text{form-group}(a \oplus c), \\ \text{form-group}(a \oplus b) \vee \text{form-group}(a \oplus c), \\ \text{form-group}(a \oplus c) \vee \text{form-group}(b \oplus c), \\ \vdots \end{array} \right\}$

  where $[\![\text{students}]\!] = \{a, b, c, a \oplus b, a \oplus c, b \oplus c, a \oplus b \oplus c\}$

While it may appear as though this account fails to predict the lack of a uniqueness presupposition for (37-a), this is not so. Given that exhaustification is built into the semantics of the ANS operator, and given that conjunctive answers are absent from the set in (37-b), we predict disjunctive answers to become conjunctions after the application of ANS. As shown in the discussion of [2]'s account of distributivity, exhaustifying disjunctive alternative with respect to a set not closed under conjunction will give rise to conjunctive propositions. For example, an answer such as $a \oplus b \vee b \oplus c$ will take on a conjunctive meaning following the application of ANS. We therefore do not predict a uniqueness presupposition to arise in questions involving collective predication.[11]

(38) a. $\text{IE}_{(37\text{-b})}(a \oplus b \vee a \oplus c) = \{q \in (37\text{-b}) \mid a \oplus b \not\Rightarrow q \wedge a \oplus c \not\Rightarrow q\}$

  b. $\text{II}_{(37\text{-b})}(a \oplus b \vee a \oplus c) = (37\text{-b}) - \text{IE}_{(37\text{-b})}(a \oplus b \vee a \oplus c)$

  c. $\text{Exh}_{(37\text{-b})}(a \oplus b \vee a \oplus c) = a \oplus b \wedge a \oplus c \wedge \neg b \oplus c \wedge \neg a \oplus b \oplus c$

---

[11] Note that the conclusion from this section are not confined to our analysis of higher order readings of questions. It in fact is arguing against the necessity of having generalized conjunction in the question denotation of interrogatives given that one can access conjunctive readings via a more sophisticated procedure of exhaustification.

4.3   A Possible Issue

Our analysis − as in the case for GQ theories − seems to make bad predictions for a sentence like (39-a). If this sentence had the LF in (39-b), its question denotation would be the set in (39-c), which is equivalent to (39-d) if books = $\{a, b, a \oplus b\}$. Pointwise exhaustification of (39-d) yields the set in (40), which is unable to partition context set. The presupposition of ANS is thus not satisfied.

(39)   a.   Which books arrived?
       b.   ANS $[\lambda_p \exists \lambda_C$ which books $\lambda_x [\, ? \, p\,] [\,[\, \exists\text{-DIST}_c \, x\,] \lambda_y [\, y$ was sold $]]]$
       c. $\{\exists x' \in C : x' \leq x \wedge \text{arrive}(x) \mid \text{books} \wedge \text{Cov}(C, x)\}$
       d. $\{\text{arrive}(a), \text{arrive}(b), \text{arrive}(a) \vee \text{arrive}(b), \text{arrive}(a \oplus b)\}$

(40) $\{\text{arrive}(a) \wedge \neg\text{arrive}(b), \text{arrive}(b) \wedge \neg\text{arrive}(a), \text{arrive}(b) \wedge \text{arrive}(a),$
       $(\text{arrive}(a) \vee \text{arrive}(b)) \wedge \neg(\text{arrive}(a) \wedge \text{arrive}(b))\}$

The problem with the question denotation in (39-d) is the presence of disjunctive alternatives: once these are ignored, pointwise exhaustification of the question set of (39-a) is once again able to partition a context. The source of these alternatives is the presence of an existential quantifier in the question nucleus. Removing the existential quantifier from the question nucleus would thus also remove these alternatives from the question set. We see at least three different ways of doing this.

We could in principle say that the presence of $\exists$-DIST is optional. This solution is however problematic: if $\exists$-DIST was optional, we would expect homogeneity effects be so as well, which is not the case. Another solution would be to allow $\exists$-DIST to take scope outside the question nucleus. This solution would be equivalent to simply not having $\exists$-DIST in the sentence. Yet another approach would be to have EXH in the question nucleus − it would exhaustify $\exists$-DIST into a universal quantifier, and thus also eliminate disjunctive alternatives from the question set.

5   Conclusion

We have shown that assuming the presence of a covert existential distributivity operator allows us to derive the free choice effects of questions with universal modals in them, as well as the lack of uniqueness in questions involving collective predication.

Our proposal allows us to derive why singular *wh*-interrogatives differ from their plural counterparts insofar as that they do not generate free choice effects. We believe that to account for this difference in terms of the interaction between the number of the *wh*-item's restrictor and a distributivity operator is a natural path to follow.

Our analysis finally derives why, under the GQ view, it was necessary to restrict the domain of higher-order quantifiers to upward monotone GQs. This follows from the fact that the answers to questions are obtained via the presence of an existential quantifier in the question nucleus.

We take this work to provide new insight into the semantics of *wh*-interrogatives by incorporating new developments in the semantics of plurality. We do not believe the relationship between these two fields of study to be accidental. The semantics of interrogatives and plurality constitute areas of research which have seen fruitful development come from analyses involving exhaustification [2,7]. The main insight of the present work is to establish a firm connection between plurality and questions through the intermediary of exhaustification.

We should note that the claim that higher-order readings of questions are tied to plurality has been recently disputed. [9] have found cases, such as (41), in which a question with a singular *wh*-item and a possibility modal can take disjunctive answers. The disjunction in (41-b) seems to scope below the possibility modal and trigger a free choice inference.

(41)   a.   Q: Which letter could we add to *fo_m* to make a word?
        b.   A: *a* or *r*.
              $\leadsto \Diamond$ we add $a \wedge \Diamond$ we add r

Our analysis cannot extend to such data because we take higher-order readings to arise via the presence of a distributive operator in the question nucleus, which is in turn licensed by a plural *wh*-item. We therefore leave this puzzle unresolved. Nonetheless, we do not believe (41) to support a GQ analysis of higher-order readings, since it seems that questions with singular *wh*-items can only give rise to such readings if the question has a possibility modal (as we have seen above, the same cannot be done if the question has a necessity modal). Therefore, GQ analyses still suffer from an overgeneration problem.

Acknowledgements. We are grateful to Patrick D. Elliott, Danny Fox and Roger Schwarzschild for useful conversations. We would also like to thank the audiences at LENLS 16 and MIT's LF Reading Group as well as two anonymous reviewers.

References

1. Alonso-Ovalle, L., Rouillard, V.: Number inflection, Spanish bare interrogatives, and higher-order quantification. In: Proceedings of the 49th Annual Meeting of the North East Linguistic Society (NELS 49) (2019)
2. Bar-Lev, M.E.: Free choice, homogeneity, and innocent inclusion. Ph.D. dissertation, Hebrew University of Jerusalem (2018)
3. Bar-Lev, M.E., Fox, D.: Universal free choice and innocent inclusion. In: Burgdorf, D., Collard, J., Maspong, S., Stefánsdótir, B. (eds.) Semantics and Linguistic Theory (SALT), vol. 27, pp. 95–115 (2017). https://doi.org/10.3765/salt.v27i0.4133
4. Dayal, V.: Locality in WH Quantification: Questions and Relative Clauses in Hindi. Kluwer Academic Publishers, Dordrecht (1996). https://doi.org/10.1007/978-94-011-4808-5
5. Elliott, P.D., Nicolae, A., Sauerland, U.: Who and what do who and what range over cross-linguistically. Ms (2018). https://patrl.keybase.pub/papers/whoAndWhatMs.pdf

6. Fox, D.: Free choice and the theory of scalar implicatures. In: Sauerland, U., Stateva, P. (eds) Presupposition and Implicature in Compositional Semantics, pp. 71–120. Palgrave Macmillan, London (2007). https://doi.org/10.1057/9780230210752_4

7. Fox, D.: Partition by exhaustification: comments on Dayal 1996. In: Sauerland, U., Solt, S. (eds.) Proceedings of Sinn und Bedeutung 22:1, ZASPiL 60, Leibniz-Centre General Linguistics, Berlin, pp. 403–434 (2018)

8. Hamblin, C.L.: Questions in Montague English. Found. Lang. **10**, 41–53 (1973)

9. Hirsch, A., Schwarz, B.: Singular which, mention-some, and variable scope uniqueness. In: Blake, K., Davis, F., Lamp, K., Rhyne, J. (eds.) Proceedings of Semantics and Linguistic Theory (SALT) 29, Linguistic Society of America, pp. 748–767 (2019)

10. Karttunen, L.: Syntax and semantics of questions. Linguist. Philos. **1**, 3–44 (1977). https://doi.org/10.1007/BF00351935

11. Križ, M.: Aspects of homogeneity in the semantics of natural language. Ph.D. dissertation, University of Vienna, dissertation (2015)

12. Link, G.: The logical analysis of plurals and mass terms: a lattice theoretical approach. In: Bauerle, R., Schwarze, C., von Stechow, A. (eds.) Meaning, Use and Interpretation of Language, pp. 303–323. de Gruyter, Berlin (1983)

13. Malamud, S.A.: The meaning of plural definites: a decision-theoretic approach. Semant. Pragmat. **5**, 1–58 (2012). https://doi.org/10.3765/sp.5.3

14. Schwarzschild, R.: Pluralities. Kluwer Academic Plublishers, Dordrecht (1996). doi: 10.1007/978-94-017-2704-4

15. Schwarzschild, R: Homogeneity, unpublished lecture notes for 24.979, Spring 2018, MIT (joint class with Danny Fox and Irene Heim) (2018)

16. Spector, B.: Modalized questions and exhaustivity. In: Friedman, T., Ito, S. (eds.) Proceedings of the 18th Semantics and Linguistic Theory Conference, pp. 282–299. CLC Publications, Ithaca (2007). https://doi.org/10.3765/salt.v17i0.2962

17. Spector, B.: An unnoticed reading for wh-questions: quantified elided answers and weak islands. Linguist. Inquiry **34**, 677–686 (2008). https://doi.org/10.1162/ling.2008.39.4.677

18. Xiang, Y.: Interpreting questions with non-exhaustive answers. Ph.D. dissertation, Harvard University (2016)

19. Xiang, Y.: Higher-order readings of wh-questions. In prep (2020)

On the Semantic Concept
of Logical Consequence

Hidenori Kurokawa[✉]

Kanazawa University, Kakuma, Kanazawa 920-1192, Japan
hidenori.kurokawa@gmail.com

Abstract. In this paper, we give a groundwork for the foundations of the semantic concept of logical consequence. We first give an opinionated survey of recent discussions on the model-theoretic concept, in particular Etchemendy's criticisms and responses, alluding to Kreisel's squeezing argument. We then present a view that in a sense the semantic concept of logical consequence irreducibly depends on the meaning of logical expressions but in another sense the extensional adequacy of the semantic account of first-order logical consequence is also of fundamental importance. We further point out a connection with proof-theoretic semantics.

Keywords: Logical consequence · Model-theoretic semantics · Natural language

1 Introduction

What is it to give a formal semantics of natural language? The traditional view in the semantics of natural language may be to give the truth condition of a sentence of natural language. This, in turn, is partly because by doing this we can give an account of a certain inferential relationship among sentences. E.g., one can see what conclusion can or cannot be drawn from certain sentences.

In such a semantic endeavor, it is a substantial problem which concept of logical consequence (we abbreviate this as "l.c.") we take to be the basis for our semantic studies of natural language. But our pre-theoretical concept of l.c. already appears to diverge; hence, we need to first discuss what data our account should be based on. Some take the pre-theoretical concept for our account of l.c. to be: it is impossible that the premises are true and the conclusion is false; however, others do: no argument with the same logical form has true premises and the false conclusion; yet others take the combination thereof (p. 366, [13]).[1]

To theorize these pre-theoretical concepts, the two major formal accounts of the semantic concept of l.c. have been proposed: 1. the **substitutional** account;

---

[1] In the following we often switch the terms i) "l.c." and ii) "logical truth or validity" as a special case. The difference never affects our philosophical points.

© Springer Nature Switzerland AG 2020
M. Sakamoto et al. (Eds.): JSAI-isAI 2019, LNAI 12331, pp. 258–275, 2020.
https://doi.org/10.1007/978-3-030-58790-1_17

2. the **model-theoretic** account. Quine, an advocate of 1, gives a formal substitutional account. For any sentence φ and a set of sentences Γ of a given language $\mathcal{L}$, we define an interpretation J (based on an appropriate substitution function) for $\mathcal{L}$ and define the notion of "truth in the interpretation J" (φ is true in J if the result of substitution φ^J is *truth simpliciter*). The substitutional consequence is defined: φ is a (substitutional) consequence of Γ if φ is true in each interpretation J in which all sentences in Γ are true.[2] On the other hand, Tarski, the founder of 2 states that X is a consequece of $\mathfrak{K}$ if "every model of the class $\mathfrak{K}$ [of sentences] is at the same time a model of the sentence X [27]."[3] The idea that the concept of l.c. can be identified with the model-theoretic concept of it is often considered to be a "thesis," i.e., **Tarski's thesis**: φ is an intuitive semantic (logical) consequence of Γ if and only if, for all model (structure) $\mathfrak{M}$, $\mathfrak{M} \models \Gamma$ lmplies $\mathfrak{M} \models \varphi$. The left side is an intuitive notion, so one cannot prove this as a theorem but needs to state it as a thesis like Church's thesis.

The difference between these accounts may be highly relevant to the semantics of natural language. When adopting the substitutional account, the central notion is *truth simpliciter*, and one can consider only the absolute truth condition of a sentence. In the model-theoretic one, the concept of consequence is based on *truth in a model*, and we need to take into consideration *truth conditions with respect to a model* (cf. [24]). Thus, in the two accounts, one considers different sorts of "truth conditions" to determine consequence relations.[4]

In this paper, we give an opinionated survey of the semantic concept of l.c. We take up two problems raised in [17] and criticisms of the accounts in [7,8]. Discussing these issues, we present a view that there is a sense in which the semantic concept of l.c. irreducibly depends on the meaning of logical expressions.

2   Criticisms of the Accounts

We discuss criticisms of the model-theoretic account of l.c., McGee's problems and Etchemendy's criticisms, one of which overlaps with one of the former. McGee's problems are: a) the reliability problem; b) the contingency problem. a) goes: "it is by no means obvious that being true in every model is any guarantee that a sentence is true [17]." The problem arises because "models" in Tarski's thesis are all sets but the extant entire universe of mathematics may not be

---

[2] This is obviously condensed. For details, see, e.g., [6].

[3] It may sound misleading to quote this sentence from [27], for the concept of "model" is in [27] is significantly different from the currently standard one since Tarski's does not seem to allow domain variations. We handle the issue later.

[4] Glanzberg [11] discusses the issue of what sort of "truth conditions" we consider in different schools of the semantics of natural language. According to him, Davidsonians consider the absolute notion of truth condition, Montagovians initially considered the one based on "truth in a model" but these days they also use the absolute notion.

identified with a set (presumably a proper class).[5] b) is "what sentences are valid ought not to be a matter of contingent fact, and Tarski's thesis would appear to make it so (p. 273, [17])." b) is essentially the same as one of Etchemendy's coming next.

Etchemendy's point can be summarized: "Tarski's analysis involves a simple, conceptual mistake: confusing the symptoms of logical consequence with their cause (p. 264, [8])." The extensional adequacy of the account is "at least as problematic as the conceptual adequacy of the analysis," although the critique "is not aimed at model-theoretic techniques, properly understood [8]."

Etchemendy begins his discussion by classifying semantics into the two kinds: representational and interpretational. The former fixes the meaning of expressions in a given sentence and considers possible worlds in which the sentence is true or not, but the latter modifies interpretations of expressions in the sentence (it becomes true or false depending on interpretations). E.g., concerning a situation in which a sentence "Snow is white" is false, representational semantics considers, say, a possible world in which snow is black, while interpretational semantics considers an interpretation where "white" means black.

Based on this distinction, Etchemendy argues that the essence of Tarski's account of l.c. can be explained as follows. First, expressions in a given sentence are divided into the two sorts: one is "fixed terms" and the other is "variable terms" (not "variables"). The former are expressions which behave like logical constants and hence fixed. The latter are expressions whose interpretations can be varied. Then Tarski's original account of validity is not much different from: given a set of fix terms $\mathfrak{F}$ in a given sentence, say S, a sentence is logically true if it is true under all substitutions of (the variables replacing) the variable terms. Note that this is essentially the substitutional account. But, on this account, there is a possibility that, due to the poverty of the object language, a sentence clearly invalid may be artificially judged to be valid; hence, Tarski modifies the definition by using satisfaction. Despite its use of satisfaction, Etchemendy takes such a model-theoretic account to be "interpretational," which is essentially the same as the substitutional account to the extent that it explains l.c. by *the ordinary universal quantification* (over all satisfactions). He claims that this account cannot explain the notion of "necessity" involved in the concept of l.c.

This interpretational version of model-theoretic account (we call it "the I-model-theoretic account") that Etchemendy takes to be given in [27] is importantly different from the currently standard model-theoretic account. The latter not only considers all satisfactions but variations of domains (of quantifications) over all non-empty sets, whereas the I-model-theoretic account does not explicitly deal with domain variations and is apparently a fixed-domain account. Besides, Etchemendy even thinks that the I-model-theoretic account

---

[5] The problem has been aware of, e.g., "Mathematics as a whole – this is the lesson of the set theoretic antinomies – is not a structure itself, i.e., an object of mathematical investigation, nor is it isomorphic to one ([1], p. 7)."

is not congenial to the idea of domain variations.[6] But still he seems to take Tarski to reduce the representational aspects of semantics to the interpretational ones by the I-model-theoretic account. This introduces complications in handling Etchemendy's criticisms of the model-theoretic account because this is not based on the standard one. However, we keep discussing the I-model-theoretic account to examine Etchemendy's criticisms for a few reasons. It may be controversial both whether Etchemendy's interpretation of Tarski [27] is accurate or not[7] and whether Etchemendy's presentation accurately represents the standard model-theoretic account or not. But it does not matter much since there is a way of assimilating domain variations without explicitly talking about it, i.e., taking a relativization of quantifier by a monadic predicate in the language. Moreover, as we will see, his particular criticism forces us to consider domain variations by the construction in his case. Thus, if there is any substantial philosophical divergence between the I-model-theoretic account and the standard model-theoretic one, it cannot rest merely on the fact one takes the variable-domain account and the other does not, but on more substantial issues of how to understand l.c.

Etchemendy admits that Tarski's I-model-theoretic account provides a necessary condition for the concept of logical truth relativized w.r.t. $\mathfrak{F}$, but he claims that the account fails to give a sufficient condition for logical truth. He gives concrete arguments against the (I-) model-theoretic account to show this. We present two of them. In one, Etchemendy claims that it is ultimately difficult to make a distinction between the model-theoretic view and a view often criticized by the view. In the other, he argues that the account may fail to guarantee the extensional adequacy, in particular it overgenerates, i.e., generating more sentences as logical truths than our pre-theoretic concept allows.

1) Etchemendy argues that the foregoing account of l.c. is problematic when it comes to talking about quantifiers, since taking a quantifier to be either a fixed term or a variable term produces a problem. E.g., in the former case, if we take the equality symbol to be logical and hence in $\mathfrak{F}$, then $\exists x \exists y (x \neq y)$ would be a logical truth, which is absurd. But if we take "something" to be simply a variable term (to make the argument simpler, adopting Etchemendy's suggestion, i.e. taking "some" to be fixed and "thing" to be a variable term), then the inference (1) "Able Lincoln was president. Therefore something was president" may turn out to be invalid, provided we take "thing" to denote the class of dogs. This is invalid since the subcollection of the individuals over which the existential quantifier ranges is disjoint from that of humans. He then argues that, to avoid such cases, Tarski's view needs to adopt a maneuver called **cross-term restriction**. This is to put some constraints on our interpretations of two expressions often based on semantic categories. E.g., "Abe Lincoln" and "something" are so constrained that the interpretation of the former is in the latter. Any cross-term restriction has an effect of excluding some interpretations; hence, a cross-term restriction is similar

---

[6] Indeed, Etchemendy states, "it is hard to understand why in the semantics for first-order languages we vary the domain of quantification (p. 290, [8])."

[7] We do not go into historical issues here.

to meaning postulates. Meaning postulates are considered by model-theorists not to be determining logical truth, since they make the determination of logical truth circular. E.g., "If Abe Lincoln was president, then Abe Lincoln was an elected official" is not a logical truth, but if this case looks valid, this would be only because we exclude all the models invalidating this by appealing to the specific interpretations of pertinent expressions. But advocates of interpretational semantics criticizing meaning postulates while using cross-terms restrictions would be question begging since there is no in-principle distinction between the two.

This may be one of the strongest points in [7]. Indeed, in the I-model-theoretic account, there is no principled way of both excluding quantifiers from fixed terms *and* keeping valid the foregoing case of inference without appealing to the cross-term restriction; hence, using the restriction and criticizing meaning potulates is incoherent.

2) The second criticism is concerned with the size of the world. Let us consider

i) σ_2: $\exists x \exists y (x \neq y)$, σ_3: $\exists x \exists y \exists z (x \neq y \land y \neq z \land z \neq x)$, $\cdots$
σ_n: $\exists x_1 \exists x_2 \exists x_3 \ldots \exists x_n (x_1 \neq x_2 \land x_2 \neq x_3 \land \ldots)$

If $\exists$, $\neq$ are in $\mathfrak{F}$, then they would be logically true, to which practically nobody would agree. First, one can easily see how to falsify these formulas. Second, the truths of these depend on the size of the world, although the logical truth should not depend on the size of the world (this ought to be carefully examined).

The implausibility of the claim of the logical truth of i) is due to taking both $\exists$ and the equality symbol to be fixed terms. Indeed, both may well be variable terms. But we present Etchemendy's argument which fixes only equality.[8]

To fix i), Etchemendy first takes the negation of each of the σ_n sentences.

ii) $\neg\sigma_2$: $\neg\exists x \exists y (x \neq y)$, $\neg\sigma_3$: $\neg\exists x \exists y \exists z (x \neq y \land y \neq z \land z \neq x)$, etc.

He treats $\exists$ as a variable term and introduces an *existential quantifier variable* E, whose satisfaction domain consists of various subcollection of the universe.[9]

iii) $\forall E[\neg\sigma_2(\exists/E)]$: $\forall E \neg Ex Ey (x \neq y)$
$\forall E[\neg\sigma_3(\exists/E)]$: $\forall E \neg Ex Ey Ez (x \neq y \land y \neq z \land z \neq x)$, etc.

For each n, iv) $\forall E[\neg\sigma_n(\exists/E)]$ claims that every subcollection of the universe contains fewer than n objects. On the I-model-theoretic account: if the universe is finite, then the account tells us that $\neg\sigma_2$, $\neg\sigma_3$, $\ldots$ are logically true; if the universe is infinite, then the account tells us that none of these is logically true.

---

[8] The second weakness can be fixed by avoiding equality and by using any relation symbol s.t. (*) that R is transitive and irreflexive implies that there exists x for all y s.t. $\neg R(x, y)$. The negation of (*) has only infinite models. But we keep using equality.

[9] This is a kind of relativization, but we universally quantify over relativizations.

Then Etchemendy argues as follows. $\neg\sigma_n$ is indeed not (usually counted as) logically true. But this is only because iv) is false, i.e., there are more than n objects in the universe. Nothing in the (standard or I-) model-theoretic account can assure that this is not logically true by any purely logical ground, but the logical status of iv) depends on a non-logical feature (the size of the universe), i.e., the axiom of infinity. Hence, the definition does not capture "the ordinary concept of logical truth" and gives no internal guarantee of the extensional adequacy.

Note that the example is so chosen as to show that his point is also valid for the variable-domain account. In the example, the idea of variable-domain is incorporated in terms of E. So what is at issue is the size of the universe out of which each domain is taken. Hence, the variable-domain account and the fixed-domain one make no substantial difference. Anyways, on the model-theoretic account the logical status of a sentence depends on extralogical facts. The upshot is that there is no guarantee that the account does not overgenerate. Etchemendy claims an overgeneration can happen if there is a substantive generalization – generalization making a substantive claim of the world.[10]

After these critiques are given, Etchemendy's alternative view is stated as: "a sentence is *logically* true if it is true *solely by virtue of the meaning of the logical vocabulary it contains* (p. 103, [7])." Endorsing this point enables him to take the representational view and to explain how the notion of necessity is involved in l.c. He claims that the representational view "makes perfectly good sense of model-theoretic practice – much better sense, in fact, than the Tarskian view (p. 286, [8])." The idea is: "[t]he set-theoretic structures that we construct in giving a model-theoretic semantics are meant to be mathematical models of logically possible ways the world ... might be or might have been [8]."[11] This suggests that he criticizes the *traditional* model-theoretic (both I-model-theoretic and standard) account to the extent that the one is essentially reducible to the substitutional one, also called quantificational.

Instead of criticizing the techniques in model theory, he gives an *alternative* view of model-theoretic account. Etchemendy endorses a view that the logical truth of a sentence in an object language ultimately has its source in the metatheory by appealing to an observation (due to Carnap): "if the truth of a sentence follows logically from the recursive definition of truth for the language in which it occurs, then that sentence must be logically true." Consider: (1) Lincoln was president or Lincoln was not a president. To establish its logical truth, one can

---

[10] He adds that the issue of the choice of logical constants is red herring, for the dependence on extralogical facts can arise even when all expressions are "logical constants," e.g., $\forall x\forall y\forall P(Px \rightarrow Py)$. This is true in a world with essentially one object.

[11] In [8], Etchemendy emphasizes that Kripke semantics is a good case of representational semantics. However, he elsewhere suggests that there is a severe limitation in representational semantics. "$2+2 \neq 4$ (p. 62, [7])" is easy to make sense in interpretational semantics but makes no sense in representational one (since mathematical truth is a necessary truth). This can be a reason why interpretational semantics is also needed in addition to the representational view. See Sect. 3, Sect. 4.

start from an elementary logical truth of the metatheory: (M) For any f, either f satisfies 'xP' or f does not satisfy 'xP.' From this, by the recursive clause for 'not' and 'or' in the definition of satisfaction, it follows: (2) For any f, f satisfies 'xP or not xP.' By the closure principle: "[i]f a universally quantified sentence is logically true, then all of its instances are logically true as well," this is sufficient to show that (1) is logically true. The moral is that "the fact that the above demonstration requires no appeal external to the semantics of the language and the logic of the metatheory provides us with a genuine assurance, quite independent of Tarski's account, of the logical truth of the associated universal closure (2) (p. 140, [7])."[12] The source of logical truth is claimed to be the recursive clauses in the logic of the metatheory, not ordinary universal quantifications.

3   Critical Assessments of the Criticisms

Here we give critical assessments of the criticisms. We first give a survey of the extant discussions on l.c., most of which directly handles Etchemendy's second criticism, and then move on to presenting our own view. Before going into concrete cases, let us give some caveats on general points. One is about one's goal. Etchemendy uses the phrase "conceptual analysis" but is not clear about the adequacy conditions for the concept of l.c.,[13] while some critiques aims for only "the extensional adequacy." Such a difference of pursued goals may raise complications in the assessments of the arguments. Another is the scope of one's argument. Depending on which logic one has in mind, e.g., first-order, higher-order, etc., one may have different conclusions, and this affects an evaluation of a view. Most critiques confine their discussions to classical first-order logic, but Etchemendy puts no limitation in his general conceptual discussions, in which first-order logic is merely a special case satisfying some desirable properties.

3.1   Prawitz's Anticipation of Etchemendy's Critiques

We first discuss Prawitz's [19] neglected criticism of the model-theoretic account, which anticipates Etchemendy's. Prawitz reconstructs Tarski's account as follows. Let $A(c_1, \ldots, c_n)$ and $B(c_1, \ldots, c_n)$ be sentences where $c_1, \ldots, c_n$ stand for the nonlogical constants in A and B, and let $A(c_1, \ldots, c_n)$ and let $A(v_1, \ldots, v_n)$ and $B(v_1, \ldots, v_n)$ be the open formulas obtained by replacing the constants c_i by variables of v_i. Then $B(c_1, \ldots, c_n)$ is a logical consequence of $A(c_1, \ldots, c_n)$ iff

(1) every assignment or model satisfying $A(v_1, \ldots, v_n)$ satisfies $B(v_1, \ldots, v_n)$, or

(2) $(\forall v_1 \in D_1) \ldots (\forall v_n \in D_n)(A(v_1, \ldots, v_n) \rightarrow B(v_1, \ldots, v_n))$ is true regardless of how *independent* (not determined by fixing the range of quantifers) domains are chosen.

---

[12] Schurz [23] also claims that the intensions of logical terms are determined by the recursive truth definition.

[13] He does not explain the phrase "the ordinary concept of logical truth," either.

(1) is closer to Tarski's original (Etchemendy's I-model-theoretic) version, and (2) relativizes quantifiers, which can be an alternative to domain variations.

Prawtiz observes that "I think that there is no doubt that ... the material equivalence asserted between logical consequence and (1) [is] correct ..." but "the analysis does not go very far" and argues as follows. i) Suppose A and B are sentences (e.g., in predicative second order logic) without descriptive [non-logical] constants. Then (2) says only that B is a l.c. of A if and only if $A \to B$ is true. Then, there is no way of considering "a variation of descriptive constants" in Tarski's account (cf. footnote 10). ii) " [A]nalysis makes no distinction between logical sentences (containing only logical constants) and factual sentences (containing also descriptive constants)." Hence, a logical sentence is logically true just in case it is true in the same sense as factual sentences are true. So "no analysis is made of the necessity involved in logical truth" nor "the *ground* for a universal truth like (2)." Prawitz argue for bringing in the notions of proof to fix this. It is notable that his points substantially overlap with Etchemendy's.

3.2   The Extensional and Intensional (Conceptual) Adequacy

Etchemendy appears to claim that the dependence on the size of the universe shows that the model-theoretic account is wrong since i) whether or not a sentence follows from premises should not depend on extralogical facts; ii) due to the dependence of nonlogical facts we have no guarantee that the account does not overgenerate. One can find the following objections in the literature: a) showing that there is a fallacy in Etchemendy's argument; b) showing that dependence on extralogical facts is not enough to show that the conceptual analysis is defective; c) showing that the dependence on extralogical facts does not occur; d) giving a justification for the claim that the account does not overgenerate. We will discuss not a)[14] but b), c), d). In discussing d), we focus on a method of *proving* that a logic with a complete formal proof system is extensionally correct: **Kreisel's squeezing argument.**

3.2.1   With Kreisel's Squeezing Argument

Kreisel [14] gives the squeezing argument in order to illustrate the role of intuitive concepts in foundational studies under the methodological concept "informal rigour." First, for any first-order formula φ, let us write $D(\varphi)$ for "φ is formally derivable (in a given system of formal rules)," $V(\varphi)$ for "φ is valid in all set-theoretic structures" (model-theoretically valid) and $Val(\varphi)$ for "φ is intuitively valid," which means that φ is true in arbitrary (not necessarily set-theoretic) "structures."[15] Then we postulate the two principles: (1): $D(\varphi) \to Val(\varphi)$; (2): $Val(\varphi) \to V(\varphi)$. (1) expresses intuitive soundness. (2) states that intuitive validity implies set-theoretic validity because a formula valid in all structures is valid in all set-theoretic ones. Then we have $(*)$ $V(\varphi) \to D(\varphi)$, which is simply

---

[14] [12,26], etc. analyze fallacies in his argument. We omit these partly because we have reason to reject his claim even if we find no alleged fallacy in the argument.

[15] We omit the details of the complicated background of this notion of Val.

Gödel's completeness theorem. By the principle (1), (2) and (∗), we can establish: $Val(\varphi) \leftrightarrow D(\varphi) \leftrightarrow V(\varphi)$.

This shows that, under some natural assumptions, the completeness theorem is sufficient to establish the co-extensiveness of the model-theoretic validity and the intuitive validity. Kreisel's main motivation to give the "proof" is to argue that from the viewpoint of "informal rigour" even our intuitive concept may have a precise characterization. But Kreisel's squeezing argument has been adapted by philosophers of logic, who have their own purposes, as follows.

i) Assuring that validity implies truth. Recall that the reliability problem has been raised because there is no reason why the actual world itself is a structure or a set, and if we define the concept of validity as "truth in all structures," then it would be unclear whether even a valid sentence is true (simpliciter). However, by Kreisel's squeezing argument, as far as first-order logic is concerned, the established equivalence between Val and V can assure that if a sentence is invalidated by something too large to be a set, then there is a set-size structure invalidating it. By taking the contrapositive, if the actual mathematical world can be identified with one of "class-size structures," then the sentence being valid, i.e., having no set-theoretic countermodel of it, suffices to show that the sentence is true simpliciter. Hence, Kreisel's squeezing argument can give a solution to the reliability problem.[16]

ii) Preventing overgeneration. Etchemendy himself modified the squeezing argument to show that, although there is no conceptual guarantee that the traditional model-theoretic account does not overgenerate (in fact, he argues that the second-order logic overgenerates by using the case of the continuum hypothesis (CH)), first-order logic does not overgenerate. Etchemendy modifies Kreisel's argument as follows. Kreisel identifies the intuitive validity Val with truth in all "structures." However, once the identification is lifted, the latter makes (2) correct, but the former makes (2) "dubious." Thus, Etchemendy introduces a new predicate LTr, meaning "intuitive notion of logical truth" with the principle: (1′) $D(\varphi) \to LTr(\varphi)$ (intuitive soundness). By (1′), (2) and $V(\varphi) \to D(\varphi)$ (completeness), we can prove $V(\varphi) \to LTr(\varphi)$ (p. 149, [7]). Hence, even the traditional model-theoretic account does not overgenerate for first-order l.c.

iii) Accommodating modality. Both Shapiro and Hanson appear to adapt Kreisel's squeezing argument to accommodate "modality" involved in the pre-theoretical characterization of l.c. Thus we explain their cases in a uniform scheme. First, they both take the issue of modality (necessity) involved in the concept of l.c. very seriously. Accordingly, they adopt the combined pre-theoretic concept mentioned in Sect. 1: it is impossible that the premises are true and the conclusion is false by the form of the argument. Then Shapiro [24] adopts a *blended* view, combining Etchemendy's representational and interpretational view, which means taking the combination of the views, i.e., i) fixing the language and considering possible worlds and ii) considering reinterpretation of all non-logical expressions. Hanson [13] takes three factors: necessity; generality; a priority to be properly treated in any satisfactory account of l.c. Second, at

---

[16] There are some other solutions, e.g. Boolos' in [3] and McGee's [17].

least in [13, 24, 25], they focus on first-order logic as a paradigmatic case. Third, they define the standard, precise model-theoretic l.c. $\Gamma \models \varphi$ with no explicit mention of modality; hence, they "accommodate" modality, i.e., the modality is represented by structures and "reduced" to them. Fourth, adapting Kreisel's squeezing argument, both Shapiro and Hanson aim for obtaining only extensional adequacy.[17]

iv) Characterizing the primitive concept of consequence. Field thinks that the genuine l.c. is neither (standard) model-theoretic nor proof-theoretic and should be treated as a primitive concept. The traditional soundness and completeness theorems "merely connect two different notions (p. 62, [9])," but we need to show that the model theory (also the proof theory) is sound and complete with respect to the primitive concept. Kreisel's squeezing argument tells us how to use completeness to characterize the primitive concept.

Let $\Gamma \Rightarrow B$ mean that the argument from Γ to B is logically valid in the "primitive" sense. Let Γ be a set of sentences and B be a sentence of a particular fixed language. Then we can state the following properties of $\Rightarrow$.

(P-Sound) [Genuine Soundness of the proof theory]: if $\Gamma \vdash_S B$ then $\Gamma \Rightarrow B$.
(P-Comp) [Genuine Completeness of the proof theory]: if $\Gamma \Rightarrow B$ then $\Gamma \vdash_S B$.
(M-Sound) [Genuine Soundness of the model theory]: if $\Gamma \models_M B$ then $\Gamma \Rightarrow B$.
(M-Comp) [Genuine Completeness of the model theory]: if $\Gamma \Rightarrow B$ then $\Gamma \models_M B$.

Formal soundness and completeness theorems can be formulated as follows: (FST) if $\Gamma \vdash_S B$ then $\Gamma \models_M B$; (FCT) if $\Gamma \models_M B$ then $\Gamma \vdash_S B$. In this setting, one can reconstruct Kreisel's squeezing argument and more.

a) P-sound, M-comp, FST: $\Gamma \vdash_S B \Leftrightarrow \Gamma \models_M B \Leftrightarrow \Gamma \Rightarrow B$.
b) M-sound, P-comp, FCT: $\Gamma \vdash_S B \Leftrightarrow \Gamma \models_M B\Gamma \models_M B\Gamma \Rightarrow B$.

a) is essentially a reconstruction of Kreisel's squeezing argument. By this equivalence, Field's primitive consequence can be proven to at least extensionally coincide with the two traditional concepts of l.c., whereas b) is pointless since M-soundness is not obvious for the same reason why $V(\varphi) \to Val(\varphi)$ was not.

3.2.2   Without Kreisel's Squeezing Argument

Critiques argue that Etchemendy's claim that his argument shows that we can't ensure to avoid overgeneration is mistaken. The first two disagree with Etchemendy's understanding of the traditional model-theoretic account.

i) Conceptual considerations. MacFarlane [16] considers a modified version of Etchemendy's argument, using a case of modal finitist, who believes (n-fin): "there could not be an infinite number of objects." She can consistently assert (n-fin) and (*) in footnote 8 is not logically true. But she cannot consistently assert (n-fin) and (*) is not true in all models. Therefore, logical truth and

---

[17] Shapiro takes modality involved in l.c. to be a "logical modality" given with respect to the isomorphism property (a necessary condition for a logical term). But Hanson's modality is not particularly "logical."

truth in all models are not identical. MacFarlane argues against this by claiming that this is based on the hidden assumption: "[t]he semantic value of an expression depends only on its meaning and the state of the world (p. 9, [16])," and this does not support the conclusion. Indeed, the semantic value of a term is determined by the two items "only against the background of a specification of the term's semantic category (p. 10, [16])." To specify this means to specify "the range of possible semantic values" by our sortal concepts. "Provided that our sortal concepts themselves do not rule out an infinite number of instances, there is a sense in which there can be an infinite number of possible semantic values for singular terms (p. 11, [16])." Hence, even the modal finitist cannot assert both (n-fin) and "(*) is logically true" solely on a logical ground.

ii) **Informal proofs.** According to **Garcia-Carpintero**, the model-theoretic account of l.c., as he understands it, is different from the quantificational account, since it involves a *semantic* theory for the logical particles (cf. [5] for a similar point). The *partial semantic theory* gives us a syntactic formation of sentences and semantically "determine[s] the truth conditions of complex sentences" (p. 115, [10])." "*Relative to that partial semantic theory* [10]," one can say that logical truth (truth in virtue of the meanings of expressions) is a truth in all *preformal models*. Here a *preformal model* means: "a possible set of logical values such that expressions belonging to the same logical category as the nonlogical expressions in the sentence or argument could have those values [10]," where logical values are, roughly, the semantic properties contributing the determination of truth condition of a sentence. Then Garcia-Carpintero informally proves: a sentence being true in virtue of the meaning of logical constants is equivalent to being true in all preformal models. From his viewpoint, set theory is not a core part of the partial semantic theory that describes preformal models but "only a tool to give us a more precisely defined sense of 'model' (p. 121, [10])." The semantics already "involves the existence of an infinite preformal model [10]."

iii) **The entanglement of logic and mathematics.** Purporting to show that the ground for a sentence being logically true may not be purely logical, **Parsons** argues that Etchemendy demands too much, when he does: "if a sentence is not logically true, this has to be by virtue of statements that are logical truths (p. 158 [18])." Parsons says that he doesn't see how this demand can be satisfied, no matter what one's criterion of logical truth is. The reason is quite general. "Given a sentence A, the statements 'A is logically true' and 'A is not logically true' are neither of them logical truths on the usual criteria, for a rather trivial reason: they depend on the existence of the sentence A and of the elements making up its structures, as well as its truth-conditions [18]" These are matters of logic, broadly speaking, but, since Etchemendy endorses "the ontological minimalism of logical truth," Parsons doesn't "see how one could show a sentence not logically true without appeal to extra-logical facts [18]" and concludes that Etchemendy's case is not sufficient to show that we have no guarantee that there is no overgeneration. (cf. p. 151, [24], for a similar point.)

4   Some Reflections on Logical Consequence

In the final section, we both take stock of our discussions and present our own view of the concept of l.c.[18] First of all, we are pessimistic about obtaining a uniform view of the concept of l.c. throughout various contexts. Hence, the discussions on the semantic concept of l.c. should be given by distinguishing the contexts in a two-dimensional manner: I) Adequacy; II) Scope. The distinction concerning I) is made between 1) the intensional and 2) the extensional adequacy. The distinctions concerning II) are made in the hierarchy of logics.

Concerning the intensional (conceptual) adequacy, we require that the semantic concept of l.c. satisfy more conditions than mere extensional adequacy. E.g., we take the modal intuition of it to be heeded. Also, the semantic concept of l.c. should take into account the necessity and the formality of the consequence due to the meaning of logical expressions. To be intensionally adequate, our account should take the pre-theoretic concept to be the combined version in Sect. 1: it is impossible that premises are true but the conclusion is false due to the form of the argument. According to this view, the substitutional account, which can at most give an extensionally adequate account due to its use of truth simpliciter, does not respect this pre-theoretic concept. Consider $\exists x \exists y (x \neq y)$ again. If we take $\neg$, $=$, $\exists$ to be logical expressions, this would be logically true, although it is obviously not.[19] Indeed, it is easily conceivable that there is a "possibility" that there is only one object in the domain of quantification. Considering variable domains is close to considering "possible" situations in which there are things of different cardinalities. Hence, concerning the fundamental viewpoint, we are inclined to share with Prawitz and Etchemendy the view that the quantificational account of l.c. does not explain the modal feature of l.c. (see Sect. 2, Sect. 3). Logical necessity (or justification) should be caused via the "guarantee" of the truth of the conclusion raised by the connection between the premises and the conclusion by virtue of the meaning of the (logical) expressions.[20]

Let us additionally note that we are in partial agreement with some views presented in Sect. 3. First, when we consider l.c., it is necessary to adopt a conceptual framework in which two independent dimensions, explained by Etchemendy as representational/interpretational, can be taken into account (cf. [24,28], see footnote 11).[21] Secondly, we take the pre-theoretic concept to be neither proof-theoretic nor (standard) model-theoretic, the latter of which must be not a pre-theoretically given datum, but a result of theorization, although they are

---

[18] Due to the limited space, we often state our points without detailed arguments.

[19] One might immediately object that $=$ is not a logical symbol. However, such a change's raising significant difference would already make dubious the robustness of the view. Also, from an intensional viewpoint, it is out of the question whether we can extensionally accommodate this pre-theoretic concept by a subsitutional account.

[20] L.c. can be a special case of "analytic" consequence. A system of transformation rules which transforms an atomic formula to another can be taken to give an analytic consequence. Formal systems of logic are often conservative extensions thereof (cf. [21]).

[21] We refrain from entirely agreeing with Etchemendy and Shapiro about the details.

often conflated in logic. Both model-theoretic and proof-theoretic views may work together to characterize both of the concepts.

Besides, Etchemendy's point on the cross-term restriction (among his two arguments) is well-taken. To this extent, we do not consider that the I-model-theoretic (quantificational) account is completely intact. However, these do not imply that his overgeneration argument is convincing. The argument needs to be examined carefully. Etchemendy's view is that since the conceptual analysis given in the account is wrong, ultimately the account may get the extension of l.c. wrong, unless we use a kind of squeezing argument to save the account. We argue both that Etchemendy's argument to show the lack of extensional adequacy, based on conceptual considerations, is dubious and that, concerning the extensional adequacy w.r.t. first-order logic, there is reason to be content with an argument given independently of Etchemendy's. In order to argue this way, we need to make clear in which context we give our argument, i.e., which logic in the hierarchy of logics is at issue. Hence, we now handle the distinctions of scope. We have hardly any problem about propositional logic.[22] But Etchemendy's argument related to the cross-term restriction suggests that first-order quantifiers be treated carefully, since the interpretation is varied over every non-empty domain, despite their being "(logical) constants."[23] In addition to this, second-order logic has yet other numerous meta-logical differences from first-order logic. Thus, putting aside propositional logic, we make only a distinction between first-order and second-order logic. Then, combined with the distinction concerning the adequacy, we have four combinations: i) first-order/extensional; ii) first-order/intensional; iii) beyond first-order/extensional; iv) beyond first-order/intensional. In the literature, nobody takes iii), the others take i) or ii), and Etchemendy seems to be the only one taking iv). He criticizes the model-theoretic account in an unlimited scope, i.e., first- and second-order logic in terms of intensional adequacy, even claiming that in both cases it may get their extensions wrong, but we mainly focus on first-order logic.

We recapitulate the structure of Etchemendy's second argument. 1. Suppose a situation in which the universe of sets is finite. 2. People in the finite universe ("finitists") may take a non-logical truth in our sense to be true in all models. 3. But the case of non-logical truth is not logically true (in our sense), since it is false in some infinite model. 4. Hence, logical truth and truth in all models cannot be conceptually identified (intensional inadequacy). 5. In fact, our identification of logical truth with truth in all models is made possible only by the axiom of infinity, but it is a non-logical fact that the axiom holds. 6. No extensional correctness is guaranteed due to an extra-logical fact (extensional inadequacy?). 7. But the extensional adequacy of the account of logical truth is guaranteed by the help of a (sound) proof system and completeness for first-order logic. The traditional model-theoretic account of logical truth for second-order logic, where

---

[22] Even this may not be entirely unproblematic. There is an issue called "non-categoricity" in propositional logic first pointed out by Carnap [4].

[23] This point seems to be underrated (see [23]), although this is not unnoticed, e.g., Enderton's textbook treats quantifiers as "parameters [24]."

completeness fails, is indeed extensionally inadequate (overgeneration), since CH or its negation is a logical truth in second-order logic (cf. [14]).

Let us give a tentative examination of the argument only for the case i), i.e., without going into the case of CH. First, in general, it is unclear whether we should appeal to such a "counterfactual" situation to discuss the intensional adequacy. Secondly, the steps from 2 to 4 depends on a tacit assumption that our concept of "logic" is at least common both to ourselves and the "finitists." But this needs to be independently argued. Third, Etchemendy claims that the step 5, i.e., our model-theoretic account of logical truth depends on an extra-logical fact (the axiom of infinity), suggests that the conceptual analysis is defective, but he does not explicitly give a condition for the intensional adequacy of an account to succeed. Fourth, note that the completeness theorem itself actually depends on the infinity of the universe of sets in the meta-theory, so if only the finite universe is available to the "finitist," then it would be unclear whether one can coherently appeal to Etchemendy's modified squeezing argument to guarantee the extensional adequacy of the I-model-theoretic account of first-order l.c.[24]

We are now discussing what we can be sure of. Unlike Etchemendy, most authors take (i) and think that we should be content with an extensionally adequate account of classical first-order logic, and there seems to be an almost uniform agreement that the model-theoretic (however conceived) account of l.c. of it is extensionally adequate. Kreisel's squeezing argument plays a major role in this agreement.

We will give quick comments on Kreisel's squeezing argument in this context. Let us first remind the reader of why we care about the semantic concept of l.c. at all. At least in the traditional viewpoint, proof theoretic systems are for provability; the model-theoretic concept of l.c. is primarily for proving unprovability or independence.[25] This role of the model-theoretic concept is still technically fundamental, and the extensional adequacy is sufficient for this. This has an important effect on the debate between the substitutional and the model-theoretic view. If one confines her attention only to the extensional adequacy of the model-theoretic account of l.c. of first-order logic, then Kreisel's squeezing argument can go further. Combined with the extensional equivalence between Val and V, Kreisel's equivalence in [15]: $V(\varphi) \leftrightarrow V^\omega(\varphi) \leftrightarrow V^a$, where V^ω stands for "valid in all countable models" and V^a stands for "valid in all arithmetic interpretations," establishes the co-extensionality of Val and the other validities. The former equivalence is based on Löwnheim-Skolem theorem and the latter on Hilbert-Bernays arithmetized completeness theorem. In particular, the latter uses the notion of "substitution" of formulas in the language of arithmetic. Thus, as far as first-order logical truth and the extensional adequacy are at issue, there is no substantial difference between the substitutional and

---

[24] Etchemendy addresses the issue (p. 275, footnote 6, [8]), saying that the finitist overgenerates. But there may be a further problem: the use of the axiom of infinity in proving completeness makes Etchemendy's squeezing argument circular.

[25] This roughly means that logical truth corresponds to a lack of counterexample.

the model-theoretic view (however conceived).[26] In general, showing the extensional adequacy of an account of first-order l.c. by a convincing argument is a significant contribution. Kreisel's ingenious squeezing argument gives a kind of "proof" of Tarski's thesis for first-order logic and deserves credit for that. More specifically, to a) The reliability problem; b) The contingency (overgeneration) problem, Kreisel's squeezing argument can give solutions, concerning the extensional adequacy of first order l.c., no matter what one's background motivation is (see Sect. 3). Even Etchemendy uses a variant of Kreisel's argument to prevent overgeneration for first-order logic. We take these to be evidence for the claim that the issue of the concept of l.c. is pretty much settled for the extensional adequacy w.r.t. first-order logic and to this extent we should be content with the result given by Kreisel's argument. This does not mean that the point of Kreisel's squeezing argument consists in to secure the "faulty" analysis of quantificational account. It shows that it is possible to establish the extensional adequacy by using an extensive variety of semantic methods. Hence, it is not necessarily fruitful nor feasible to criticize the extensional inadequacy of an account among them by arguing that it is inadequate.

Still, some critiques are engaged in the debate on the intensional adequacy of the model-theoretic account of first-order l.c., i.e., Sect. 3.2.2 (ii). They try to give informal proofs or conceptual observations that the model-theoretic account of first-order l.c. is even intensionally adequate. MacFarlane's and Garcia-Carpintero (Sect. 3) contend that we can "require" the (possible) existence of infinitely many objects to falsify a sentence on a purely logical ground. Their strategy is to undermine the step 5 of the foregoing summary of Etchemendy's argument, i.e., to show that there is no conceptual gap between logical truth and truth in all models. However, Parsons has a different view of this. Grounds for a sentence being logically true may not be purely logical but this is not sufficient to show that the model-theoretic account of first-order l.c. overgenerates because it is unclear that the dependence on extralogical (mathematical) facts is a good reason for overgeneration.

The arguments given by MacFarlane and Garcia-Carpintero presented in Sect. 3 show that there is something more in the model-theoretic concept than those reducible to the substitutional (or quantificational) account. Although Etchemendy appears to think otherwise, the concept of truth by virtue of the meaning of logical expressions seems not to be incompatible with fulfilling a sort of ontological requirement (especially when one shows that a sentences is invalid). Their arguments look convincing to this extent. But it is another issue whether or not their views *completely* capture intensional aspects of the model-theoretic concept. It is yet another issue whether their view is correct or Parsons' view is correct as a reason why Etchemendy's argument against the extensional

---

[26] Quine's substitutional view in [20] is based on the Hilbert-Bernays arithemtiized completeness theorem. There is a subtlety on the issue of compactness. See [2,6].

adequacy of the model-theoretic account is wanting,[27] although either of these seems to give a sufficient ground for the claim that Etchemendy's contention of overgeneration needs to be reconsidered. However, we leave these issues open.

Whereas Etchemendy criticizes the traditional model-theoretic account as an quantificational one and proposes an alternative view and MacFarlane and Garcia-Carpintero take "the model-theoretic" concept to have something more than that, their ultimate views are not very different (see [8] footnote 20) though certainly not identical. Be that as it may, in our current understanding, the intensional aspects of the concept of l.c. is far from being settled. Indeed, we can describe our current situation as: we are in agreement with Prawitz and Etchemendy on the fundamental view, but we consider Etchemendy's particular argument to be problematic; hence, although the extensional adequacy of a variety of accounts of first-order l.c. is settled, anything beyond that is still widely open, e.g., the intensional adequacy of a semantic account of first-order l.c. We consider investigations of it to be carried out by focusing on the meaning of expressions and along the line suggested by Etchemendy on the logic of the metatheory,[28] i.e., the logical power of a logical expression is conferred to it via the recursive clause for the expression in Tarskian inductive characterization of satisfaction.

We then point out a connection between this idea and proof-theoretic semantics. Interestingly, one can find a similar idea in proof-theoretic semantics. Sambin et al. [22] suggest a general scheme of introducing the logical constants called **the principle of reflection**. E.g.,"The common explanation of the truth of a compound proposition like $A\&B$ is that $A\&B$ is true if and only if A is true and B is true." More schematically, they claim that for any connective $\circ$, "[i]n our terms, a connective $\circ$ between propositions, like $\&$ above, reflects at the level of object language a *link* between assertions in the meta-language. (*link* is an expression for a meta-linguistic device corresponding to $\circ$.) The equivalence "A $\circ$ B true if and only if A true *link* B true," which we call *definitional equation* for $\circ$, "gives all we need to know about it. A $\circ$ B is semantically defined as that proposition which, when asserted true, behaves exactly as the compound assertion A true *link* B true. The inference rules for $\circ$ are derived in a system for $\circ$ by using reflexivity $\varphi \vdash \varphi$ and transitivity (cut) for $\vdash$ (we eliminate cut afterwards). We say that $\circ$ is introduced by the principle of reflection. E.g., for $\otimes$, from the definitional equation $\Gamma, A \otimes B \vdash \Delta$ iff $\Gamma, A, B \vdash \Delta$, we derive

$$L \otimes : \frac{\Gamma, A, B \vdash \Delta}{\Gamma, A \otimes B \vdash \Delta} \qquad R \otimes : \frac{\Gamma \vdash A, \Delta \qquad \Gamma' \vdash B, \Delta'}{\Gamma, \Gamma' \vdash A \otimes B, \Delta, \Delta'}.$$

[27] This issue is not simple, since those who argue that the infinity of a domain can be equipped on purely logical ground consider only first-order logic. To invalidate a formula in first-order language, we only need a countable model (see V^ω). But things are more complicated in second-order logic, since falsifying a sentence in the language of second-order logic may require staggering ontology (p. 151, [24]). For second-order logic, Parsons' entanglement view is more reasonable.

[28] The concept is so fundamental that it may be difficult to reduce it to something more fundamental.

The similarity of these ideas may suggest that the idea of reflecting the metatheory by the theory in the object language is worth further investigating. Perhaps, there is a convergence between these ideas.

References

1. Bernays, P.: Schematic korrespondenz und die idealisierten strukturen (English translation: schematic correspondence and idealized structures, bernays project). Dialectica, pp. 14–25 (1970). www.phil.cmu.edu/projects/bernays/
2. Boolos, G.: On second-order logic. J. Philos. **72**(16), 509–527 (1975)
3. Boolos, G.: Nominalist platonism. Philos. Rev. **94**(3), 327–344 (1985)
4. Carnap, R.: Formalization of Logic. H. U. Press, Cambridge (1943)
5. Chihara, C.: Tarski's thesis and the ontology of mathematics. In: Schirn, M. (ed.) The Philosophy of Mathematics Today, pp. 157–172. Clarendon Press (1998)
6. Eder, G.: Boolos and the metamathematics of quine's definitions of logical truth and consequence. Hist. Philos. Log. **37**(2), 170–193 (2016)
7. Etchemendy, J.: The Concept of Logical Consequence. HUP (1990)
8. Etchemendy, J.: Reflections on consequence. In: Patterson, D. (ed.) New Essays on Tarski and Philosophy, pp. 263–299. Oxford University Press, Oxford (2008)
9. Field, H.: What is logical validity? In: Caret, C.R., Hjortland, O.T. (eds.) Foundations of Logical Consequence. Oxford University Press, Oxford (2015)
10. García-Carpintero, S.: The grounds for the model-theoretic account of the logical properties. Notre Dame J. Form. Log. **34**(1), 107–131 (1993)
11. Glanzberg, M.: Logical consequence and natural language. In: Caret, C., Hjortland, O. (ed.) Foundations of Logical Consequence, pp. 71–120. OUP (2015)
12. Gómez-Torrente, M.: Logical truth and Tarskian logical truth. Synthese **117**(3), 375–408 (1998)
13. Hanson, W.H.: The concept of logical consequence. Philos. Rev. **106** (1997). https://doi.org/10.2307/2998398
14. Kreisel, G.: Informal Rigour and completeness proofs. In: Lakatos, I. (ed.) Problems in the philosophy of mathematics. North Holland, Amsterdam (1967)
15. Kreisel, G.: What have we learnt from Hilbert's second problem? In: Mathematical developments arising from Hilbert problems (Proceedings of Symposia in Pure Mathematics). AMS (1976)
16. MacFarlane, M.: What is modeled by truth in all models? (2000). Unpublished preprint presented at the 2000 Pacific Division APA
17. McGee, V.: Two problems with Tarski's theory of consequence. Proc. Aristot. Soc. **92**(1), 273–292 (1992)
18. Parsons, C.: Some consequences of the entanglement of logic and mathematics. Ref. Rat. Phenomenol. **2**, 153–178 (2013)
19. Prawitz, D.: Remarks on some approaches to the concept of logical consequence. Synthese **62**, 153–171 (1985)
20. Quine, W.: Philosophy of Logic, 2nd edn. Harvard University Press, Cambridge (1986)
21. Read, S.: Formal and material consequence. J. Philos. Log. **23**(3), 247–265 (1994)
22. Sambin, G., Battilotti, G., Faggian, C.: Basic logic: reflection, symmetry, visibility. J. Symb. Log. **65**(3), 979–1013 (2000)
23. Schurz, G.: Tarski and Carnap on logical truth: or: what is genuine logic? Vienna Circ. Inst. Yearb. **6**, 77–94 (1999)

24. Shapiro, S.: Logical consequence: models and modality. In: Schirn, M. (ed.) The Philosophy of Mathematics Today, pp. 131–156. Clarendon Press (1998)
25. Shapiro, S.: Logical consequence, proof theory, and model theory. In: Oxford Handbook of Philosophy of Mathematics and Logic (2005)
26. Soames, S.: Understanding Truth. Oxford University Press, Oxford (1998)
27. Tarski, A.: On the concept of following logically translated by Magda Stroinska and David Hitchcock. Hist. Philos. Log. **23**(3), 155–196 (2002)
28. Zimmermann, T.: Model-theoretic semantics. In: Heusinger, K.v., C.M., Portner, P. (eds.) Handbook of Semantics, vol. 1, pp. 762–802. De Gruyter (2011)

Reasoning with an (Experiential) Attitude

Kristina Liefke[✉]

Institute for Linguistics, Goethe University Frankfurt, Frankfurt am Main, Germany
Liefke@lingua.uni-frankfurt.de

Abstract. This paper gives a compositional semantics for attitude reports with nominal, gerund, and that-clause complements that captures the intuitive entailment relations between these reports (e.g. Ida sees/imagines a penguin diving ⇒ Ida sees/imagines a penguin). These relations are identified through the familiar diagnostic tests. We observe that entailments that are licensed by counterfactual attitude verbs (here: imagine) are largely different from the entailments between veridical vision reports that are described in (Barwise 1981). To capture this difference, we give a non-clausal syntax for gerund attitude reports and assign factive clausal complements a different semantics from non-factive and gerund complements. The resulting account captures the entailment patterns of imagination and vision reports without assuming special axioms in the lexical semantics of see or imagine. On our account, the 'logic' of the above reports thus falls directly out of their semantics.

Keywords: Perception reports · Imagination reports · Selectional flexibility · Entailment patterns · Predication theory · Situation semantics

1 Introduction

Research on mental attitude reports has traditionally focused on reports of propositional attitudes (see [18,37]; cf. [12]). The latter are sentences with a clausal complement (e.g. (1)) that have at least one of the following properties (see [46, p. 516]): (i) the complement's constituent expressions resist the truth-preserving substitution by a co-referential or truth-conditionally equivalent expression (i.e. *referential opacity [= non-transparency]*), (ii) the complement's constituent DPs lack existential import (i.e. *non-actuality*), and (iii) the complement's constituent existential DPs allow for a non-specific reading (i.e. *non-specificity*). The above properties are all exemplified in (1):

I thank three anonymous referees for valuable comments on an earlier version of this paper. The paper has profited from discussions with Sebastian Bücking, Kai von Fintel, Carla Umbach, & Ede Zimmermann. The research for this paper is supported by the German Research Foundation (via Ede Zimmermann's grant ZI 683/13-1).

© Springer Nature Switzerland AG 2020
M. Sakamoto et al. (Eds.): JSAI-isAI 2019, LNAI 12331, pp. 276–293, 2020.
https://doi.org/10.1007/978-3-030-58790-1_18

(1) Ida believes [$_{CP}$that there is [$_{DP}$a unicorn] in her garden]

    ⇏ a. Ida believes [$_{CP}$that there is [$_{DP}$a griffin] in her garden]

    ⇏ b. There is [$_{DP}$a unicorn] of which Ida believes [$_{CP}$that it is in her garden]

    ⇏ c. There are (actual/real-world) unicorns

In particular, on its *de dicto*-reading, (1) neither commits the attributor of the attitude to the existence of unicorns (i.e. (1) does not entail (1c); see (ii)) nor does it attribute to Ida the belief that there is a <u>particular</u> unicorn in her garden (i.e. (1) does not entail (1b); see (iii)) or that there is a griffin in her garden[1] (i.e. (1) does not entail (1a); see (i)).

The above properties are also exemplified by attitude reports with a nominal (i.e. direct object) complement (e.g. (2)). In virtue of their matrix verb's selection behavior, such reports are sometimes called *objectual attitude reports* (see [12]).

(2) Ida is searching [$_{DP}$a unicorn]

    ⇏ a. Ida is searching [$_{DP}$a griffin]

    ⇏ b. There is [$_{DP}$a unicorn] which Ida is searching

    ⇏ c. There are (actual/real-world) unicorns

Many objectual attitude reports (incl. (2)) even lack a clausal equivalent. On the level of syntax, this is due to the DP-bias of their matrix verbs, s.t. the combination of these verbs with a clausal complement (e.g. (3)) is ungrammatical:

(3) *Ida is searching [$_{CP}$that [$_{DP}$a unicorn] ...]

On the level of semantics, the lack of a clausal equivalent is due to the fact that many objectual attitude reports are intuitively not equivalent to the result of extending their direct object DP to a full CP (see [12,13,47], *pace* [37]). In particular, as regards (2), Ida may not be searching for a unicorn that exemplifies any particular property, but only for a *unicorn* (cf. [13, p. 829]). In this case, even the grammatical fix of (3), i.e. (4), is false and, hence, not equivalent to (2).

(4) Ida is searching [$_{PP}$for [$_{DP}$a unicorn that ...]]

The above prevents the obtaining of entailment relations of the form in (5), where 'V' and 'N' stand proxy for an intensional attitude verb and a common noun, respectively:

(5) a. Ida Vs [$_{CP}$that [$_{DP}$an N] ...] ⇒ b. Ida Vs [$_{DP}$an N]

The above notwithstanding, entailments of the form of (5) are well-attested (see (6)). Such entailments involve reports with a DP/CP-neutral matrix verb whose complements describe a directly witnessed situation or event (see [17,41]).

---

[1] This last possibility relies on the non-existence of unicorns and griffins in the actual world, such that the set of unicorns and the set of griffins are the same set (i.e. ∅).

(6)   a. Ida imagines [$_{CP}$that [$_{DP}$a unicorn] is cantering in her garden]
    ⇒ b. Ida imagines [$_{DP}$a unicorn]

To capture the direct experiential nature of the actions that are described by these verbs, we call these verbs *experiential attitude verbs*.[2] They include counterfactual attitude verbs (e.g. imagine, dream), epistemic verbs (e.g. remember, notice), and perception verbs (e.g. see, hear). We will use the term *same-type attitude reports* to describe pairs of experiential attitude reports with the same matrix verb that have grammatically different complements (e.g. a DP and a CP; see (6)).

The report in (6) illustrates the selectional flexibility of imagine between nominal and that-clause complements. However, experiential attitude verbs also combine with gerund complements[3] (see, e.g., (7a)) and license entailments from reports with this kind of complement (e.g. (7)):

(7)   a. Ida imagines [$_{DP}$a unicorn] cantering in her garden
    ⇒ b. Ida imagines i. [$_{DP}$a unicorn] / ii. [$_{CP}$that [$_{DP}$a unicorn] is cantering ...]

This paper focuses on entailment relations between same-type attitude reports like the above. Our discussion of these relations will proceed in two steps: the first part of the paper (Sect. 2) uses the familiar diagnostic tests (i.e. non-cancellability, non-reinforceability) to identify the intuitive entailment relations between same-type attitude reports. The second part (Sect. 3, 4) models these relations by assuming that the grammatically different complements in these reports are uniformly interpreted as propositions/propositionally coded situations.

Notably, for veridical vision reports (i.e. reports with factive uses of see), many of the above entailments have already been identified in early situation semantics (see [3]; cf. [2,4,8]). Our paper improves upon these results by capturing them in a standard compositional semantic framework, by extending them to other experiential attitude verbs (esp. imagine), and by dispensing of designated lexical semantic axioms. This extension is particularly important since different verbs (see vs. imagine) license different entailments, as we will see below.

2   Testing for Entailments

To investigate entailment relations between same-type attitude reports, we consider representative instances of each of the grammatically different 'types' of attitude reports from Sect. 1. These include reports with a nominal complement (see A, below; cf. (6b)), reports with a gerund complement (see C; cf. (7a)), and

---

[2] In linguistic semantics, the term *experiential attitude* only appears in the handout version of [41]. Anand [1] calls the relevant attitudes *imagistic attitudes*.

[3] Higginbotham [16, p. 120] has pointed out that imagine – unlike see – does not accept bare infinitival complements. In view of this fact, we focus on gerund complements.

reports with a that-clause complement (see F; cf. (6a)).[4] To test for the intensionality of the embedded DP in these reports (see [46, p. 516]), we further consider variants of gerund reports that replace the restrictor of the embedded DP with an extensionally equivalent expression (here: Antarctic flightless bird, see D; cf. (1a), (2a)), that force a specific reading of the embedded DP (see E; cf. (1b), (2b)), and that modify the restrictor of the embedded DP by the adjective real-world, or actual (see B; cf. (1c), (2c)). Our use of reports D and E follows [3, pp. 376–377] (see [8, pp. 246–248]). Our use of B is inspired by the veridicality of vision reports (see [3, p. 376]; cf. [8, pp. 248–249]) and by the considerations in [12, p. 63 ff.].

A.   Ida i. imagines / ii. sees [a penguin]

B.   Ida i. imagines / ii. sees [a real-world penguin] (diving into the sea)

C.   Ida i. imagines / ii. sees [a penguin] diving into the sea

D.   Ida i. imagines / ii. sees [an Antarctic flightless bird] diving into the sea

E.   There is [a penguin] which Ida i. imagines / ii. sees diving into the sea

F.   Ida i. imagines / ii. sees that [a penguin] is diving into the sea

For A–F, we identify thirty interesting pairs of attitude reports (see Table 1). These pairs exclude identity pairs (marked '≡'). To test the interesting pairs for entailments, we use the familiar diagnostic tests (see [6]; cf. [14]). These include the non-cancellability of entailments (see Test 1, below) and the non-reinforceability of entailments (Test 2, below):

Test 1 (non-cancellability) *If* $X \Rightarrow Y$ *is an entailment, then 'X, but (it is) not (the case that) Y' is a contradiction in any context.*   (see [3])

Test 2 (non-reinforceability) *If* $X \Rightarrow Y$ *is an entailment, then 'X and, specifically, Y' is redundant/semantically deviant.*

(see [28, pp. 672–673]; cf. [19])

By applying the above tests to the interesting pairs of attitude reports, we yield the entailment judgements in Table 1.[5] This table distinguishes different kinds (or 'types') of entailments: apart from *general* entailments (marked '⇒'), the pairs of reports from Table 1 also exemplify *lexical* entailments, i.e. entailments whose validity depends on the matrix attitude verb. The latter include entailments that only hold for (pairs of) imagination reports – but not for (pairs of) vision reports – ($\Rightarrow / \not\Rightarrow$), and entailments that only hold for vision reports – but not for imagination reports – ($\not\Rightarrow / \Rightarrow$).

---

[4] To allow for minimal pairs of reports, we mark the complement in F for progressive aspect. For the same reason, we include the material in round brackets in B when B is contrasted with a gerund or clausal report.

[5] For a color version of the table, please consult the online copy of this paper.

Table 1. Entailments between same-type attitude reports.

	A	B	C	D	E	F
A	≡	⇏/⇒	⇏	⇏	⇏	⇏
B	⇒	≡	(⇒)	⇏/⇒	⇏/⇒	⇒/⇏
C	⇒	⇏/⇒	≡	⇏/⇒	⇏/⇒	⇒/⇏
D	⇏/⇒	⇏/⇒	⇏/⇒	≡	⇏/⇒	⇏
E	⇒	⇏/⇒	⇒	⇏/⇒	≡	⇒/⇏
F	⇏	⇏	⇒/⇏	⇏	⇏	≡

Class 1   Class 2   Class 3   Class 4   Class 5   Class 6

Table 1 identifies a total of 26 valid entailments (see the colored cells): nine for the imagine- and seventeen for the see-cases. Of these entailments, five are general (**Class 1:** B–C/E ⇒ A, B/E ⇒ C). Twelve entailments hold only for vision reports (see **Classes 2–4**, below); four hold only for imagination reports (**Class 5**: B–C/E ⇒ F; **Class 6**: F ⇒ C). Of the entailments that hold only for vision reports, four hold in virtue of DP-actuality (**Class 2:** A/C–E ⇒ B), seven hold in virtue of DP-transparency (**Class 3:** B–C/E ⇒ D, D ⇒ A–C/E), and three in virtue of DP-specificity (**Class 4:** B–D ⇒ E). Our tests thus confirm the entailment judgements for vision reports from [3].

To facilitate future reference, we copy an example of each class below:

(8)   a. C: Ida imagines/sees [a penguin] diving into the sea   (**Class 1**)
    ⇒ b. A: Ida imagines/sees [a penguin]

(9)   a. A: Ida i. imagines / ii. sees [a penguin]   (**Class 2**)
    b. B: Ida ⇏ i. imagines / ⇒ ii. sees [a real-world penguin]

(10)   a. C: Ida i. imagines / ii. sees [a penguin] diving into the sea   (**Cl. 3**)
    b. D: Ida ⇏ i. imagines /
        ⇒ ii. sees [an Antarctic flightless bird] diving into the sea

(11)   a. C: Ida i. imagines / ii. sees [a penguin] diving into the sea   (**Cl. 4**)
    b. E: There is [a penguin] which Ida ⇏ i. imagines /
        ⇒ ii. sees diving into the sea

(12)   a. C: Ida i. imagines / ii. sees [a penguin] diving into the sea   (**Cl. 5**)
    b. F: Ida ⇒ i. imagines / ⇏ ii. sees that [a penguin] is diving …

(13)   a. F: Ida i. imagines / ii. sees that [a penguin] is diving …   (**Cl. 6**)
    b. C: Ida ⇒ i. imagines / ⇏ ii. sees [a penguin] diving into the sea

The above shows that veridical see licenses largely different entailments from imagine: while the DP a penguin shows an *extensional* behavior in nominal and gerund complements of see (s.t. see licenses the entailments in (9)–(11)), it shows an *intensional* behavior in the complements of imagine (s.t. imagine does <u>not</u>

license these entailments). Conversely, while gerund imagination reports entail the result of replacing their complement with its that-clause variant (i.e. they are *epistemically positive* in the sense of [3,9]; see (12)), gerund vision reports do <u>not</u> validate this entailment (i.e. they are *epistemically neutral*).

The rest of this paper provides a uniform semantics for imagination and vision reports that captures the above behavior. The provision of such a semantics is challenged by the fact that nominal, gerund, and that-clause complements of experiential attitude verbs are typically assigned different semantic types[6] (i.e. *se* [or $s((s(et))t)$], *s*, and *st*, respectively; see [12,30,41]), that gerund complements are commonly analyzed as syntactic constituents (see [3,17,41]), and that entailments like (12) are blocked on the basis of syntactic form (see [3,4,24]). The first two facts disable the obtaining of entailments between different-category complements (see (8)) and the easy manipulation of the scope of the embedded DP (see (11.ii)), respectively. The last fact makes it difficult to explain the different entailment patterns in (12).

In particular, situation semantics captures the non-entailment in (12.ii) (i.e. C.ii $\nRightarrow$ F.ii) by associating gerund (or bare infinitival) complementation with the *directness* of the attitude report, by associating that-clause complementation with the *indirectness* of the report, and by assuming that inferences from direct to indirect attitude reports are generally invalid (see [3,24]). However, this move also predicts that C.i $\nRightarrow$ F.i, *contra* the relevant finding in Table 1.

3   Proposal and Background

We propose to solve the above problems by adopting a three-part strategy. This strategy involves (i) the same-type interpretation of nominal, gerund, and that-clause complements (along the lines of [43]), (ii) the assumption of a non-clausal syntax for gerund attitude reports (along the lines of [45]), and (iii) the use of a different semantics for the factive and the non-factive complementizer (see [23]). Parts (i) and (iii) help us capture the entailment relations between gerund and nominal respectively between gerund and that-clause reports (see (8), (12)–(13)). Part (ii) gives us a better handle on the scope of the embedded DP in such reports (i.e. it helps us explain the difference between (9.i)–(11.i) and (9.ii)–(11.ii)).[7]

3.1   The Semantics of Veridical Vision Reports

To capture the extensional behavior of the DP subject in the complement of veridical vision reports (see (9.ii)–(11.ii)), we adopt Williams' [45] predication theory of DP-predicate sequences (see Part (ii), above; cf. [38,39]). The latter is a non-clausal syntax that analyzes the gerund in B–E as a non-constituent

---

[6] In what follows, we use a partial variant, TY_2^3, of Gallin's type logic TY_2 with basic types for individuals (type e), situations (type s), and (partial) truth-values (type t). Functions from objects of type α to objects of type β are written '$(\alpha\beta)$', or '$\alpha\beta$'.

[7] We thus contradict van der Does' claim that "no semantical reason has been found to reject Small Clauses" (see [8, p. 246]).

element of a ternary branching VP of the form [V DP XP]. The occurrences of
see and imagine in B–E thus take two complements, i.e. a gerund VP predicate
(here: diving into the sea; labelled 'XP') and a direct DP object (here: a penguin)
that c-commands this predicate. In predication theory, a rule of predication co-
indexes the XP with its c-commanding DP, thus indicating that the DP serves
as the syntactic subject of the XP predicate. The predication-theoretic analysis
of C.ii is given in (14):

(14)   Ida [$_{VP}$sees [$_{DP}$a penguin]$_i$ [$_{XP}$diving into the sea]$_i$]

(14) suggests that the DP a penguin is the external argument of a maximal
projection of X that is not c-commanded by the head of the XP. Since there
is, thus, no need for a subject position inside the XP, the co-indexed DP and
XP need not form a syntactic constituent, i.e. they are not clausal (see [29, p.
45]). This analysis differs from Barwise's [3,4] 'S[mall] C[lause]'-account of such
constructions (see the analysis of C.ii in (15); see [8,41]) and from the standard
analysis of attitude reports with finite that-clause complements, whose matrix
verbs select for a single CP complement (see the analysis of F.ii in (16)):

(15)   Ida [$_{VP}$sees [$_{SC}$[$_{DP}$a penguin] [$_{XP}$diving into the sea]]]

(16)   Ida [$_{VP}$sees [$_{CP}$that [$_{TP}$[$_{DP}$a penguin] [$_{VP}$was diving into the sea]]]]

To capture the extensional behavior of the embedded DP in veridical vision
reports (see (9.ii)–(11.ii)) and the predication relation between the DP and the
XP in the complement of these reports (see (14)), we assign 'DP XP'-taking
occurrences of see the semantics in (17).[8] This semantics interprets see as a
relation between an evaluation situation (in (17): k [resp. i]), an event (e),
an agent (z), and a situation/visual scene (represented by a set of situations,
$f_e(\lambda j. P_j(y))$).

(17) $[\![\text{see-DP XP}]\!]^i = \lambda \mathcal{Q} \lambda P \lambda z [\mathcal{Q}_i(\lambda k \lambda y (\exists e)[see_k(e, z, \underbrace{f_e(\lambda j. P_j(y))})])]$

(a set of situations that codes) z's visual scene in k

Our use of a (coded) situation-argument is motivated by the observations in [41]
(cf. [3,17,44]). These include the observation that the 'DP XP'-sequence in C.ii
allows the truth-preserving substitution by a DP of the form a situation/event in
which [$_{TP}$] (see (18); cf. [44]), that the verb see in this report can be modified by
an 'experiential' modifier like in vivid / lifelike detail (see (19); cf. [41, p. 148]), and
that this report implies the truth of a sentence (i.e. (20)) that reports the agent's
direct witnessing of the event described by the complement (see [41, p.147]):

---

[8] We hereafter adopt the following naming convention for variables: x, y, z are variables
over individuals; i, j, k are variables over situations (or events); e is an event variable;
p, q are variables over propositions (type st). P, Q are variables over type-$s(et)$ properties (incl. XP-denotations). $\mathcal{Q}$ is a variable over type-$s((s(et))t)$ quantifiers (i.e.
DP-denotations). A function's simultaneous application to a sequence of arguments
indicates successive application in the reverse order of these arguments ('Currying').
Index arguments will be written in subscript.

(18)   a. Ida sees [$_{DP}$a penguin]$_i$ [$_{XP}$diving into the sea]$_i$

≡ b. Ida sees [$_{DP}$*a visual scene* in which a penguin is diving into the sea]

(19)   Ida sees [$_{DP}$a penguin] diving into the sea *in vivid/lifelike detail*

(20)   Ida sees (= perceptually witnesses) a penguin diving into the sea

In (17), f is a subset selection function that chooses a subset from a given set of situations λj [...] in dependence on a parameter, e, for the described attitudinal/perception event (here, z's seeing in k; cf. [11]). For e the agent's seeing event in k, this subset represents the visual scene that the agent perceives in e. Our use of *sets of* situations (rather than of a single situation) is motivated by the fact that – in contrast to visual scenes – imagined situations are often <u>not</u> anchored in a particular world or time, and by the possibility of representing non-anchored situations by sets of isomorphic [= qualitatively identical] situations (see [22, p. 667]; cf. [10, p.136]). The latter are situations in which exactly the same propositions are true (resp. false). We will see below that the propositional interpretation of gerund complements facilitates the modelling of (8) and (12)–(13).

We have suggested above that the parameterizing event constrains the function f. In particular, we assume that, when it is parameterized by a seeing event, f selects from the set denoted by $\lambda j.\, P_j(y)$ (a subset representing) a situation to which the agent uniquely bears a visual acquaintance relation (in the sense of [7, 20, 25]). For (17), this relation is given, somewhat informally, in (21):

(21) $\lambda k \lambda z \lambda j$ [j is in z's field of vision in k]

The compositional interpretation of C.ii is given in Fig. 1:[9]

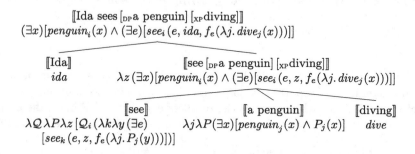

Fig. 1. Compositional semantics for C.ii.

Note that (17) interprets the XP at (each member, j, of the set of situations that codes) z's perceived visual scene. This interpretation captures the informational asymmetry between the (extensionally behaved) DP and the (intensionally

---

[9] Since none of the relevant differences between A–E turns on the aspectual properties of the verb, we here neglect aspect.

behaved) XP in gerund vision reports (see [2]): in contrast to (10), the substitution of the XP by an extensionally equivalent expression is intuitively invalid:

(22)   a. C.ii: Ida sees a penguin [diving into the sea]

      b. In the actual world, any penguin who is diving into the sea switches to anaerobic metabolism

$\not\Rightarrow$ c. Ida sees a penguin [switching to anaerobic metabolism]

Our previous considerations have focused on the interpretation of gerund reports. To give the semantics for nominal occurrences of see (e.g. A.ii), we use Stephenson's observation that the direct object DPs in such reports are also interpreted as situations (s. [41, p. 156]). The semantics of nominal see in (23) enables this interpretation.[10] This semantics differs from (17) only in dropping the argument place for the XP. To compensate for the absence of the property (P) that is denoted by the XP, we replace 'P' by a situation-relative existence predicate, E (see [26, p. 117 ff.]). The compositional interpretation of A.ii is given in Fig. 2.

(23) $[\![\text{see-DP}]\!]^i = \lambda \mathcal{Q} \lambda z [\mathcal{Q}_i (\lambda k \lambda y (\exists e)[see_k (e, z, f_e(\lambda j. E_j(y)))])]$

$$[\![\text{Ida sees } [_{\text{DP}}\text{a penguin}]]\!]$$
$$(\exists x)[penguin_i(x) \wedge (\exists e)[see_i (e, ida, f_e(\lambda j. E_j(x)))]]$$

$[\![\text{Ida}]\!]$	$[\![\text{see } [_{\text{DP}}\text{a penguin}]]\!]$
ida	$\lambda z (\exists x)[penguin_i(x) \wedge (\exists e)[see_i (e, z, f_e(\lambda j. E_j(x)))]]$

$[\![\text{see}]\!]$ $[\![\text{a penguin}]\!]$

$\lambda \mathcal{Q} \lambda z [\mathcal{Q}_i (\lambda k \lambda y (\exists e)[see_k (e, z, f_e(\lambda j. E_j(y)))])]$ $\lambda j \lambda P (\exists x)[penguin_j(x) \wedge P_j(x)]$

Fig. 2. Compositional semantics for A.ii.

The use of E in (23) is inspired by Parsons' *Hamlet ellipsis*-account of depiction and imagination reports (see [35, pp. 375–376]). This account analyzes the direct object DP in such reports as the result of eliding the XP being there from an embedded 'DP XP'-sequence (for A.ii: from a penguin being there (see (24b)):

(24)   a. Ida $[_{\text{VP}}$sees $[_{\text{DP}}$a penguin$]]$

  $\equiv$ b. Ida $[_{\text{VP}}$sees $[_{\text{DP}}$a penguin$]$ $[_{\text{XP}}$being there$]$ (in her visual scene)$]$

In fact, the full adoption of Parsons' account – on which the embedded DP in (24a) is an elliptical clause – would even allow us to avoid postulating a separate lexical entry for DP-taking see. However, this adoption would lead us to wrongly

---

[10] (23) is reminiscent of Montague's [33] interpretation of extensional verbs like find:

(†) $[\![\text{find-DP}]\!]^i = \lambda \mathcal{Q} \lambda z [\mathcal{Q}_i (\lambda k \lambda y. find_k (z, y))]$.

predict that (25) is ambiguous between a reading where **yesterday** modifies the matrix verb, **see** (i.e. (25a)), and a reading where **yesterday** modifies the implicit predicate, **be there**, in the verb's complement (i.e. (25b); cf. [12, p. 63 ff.]).

(25)   Ida saw [$_{DP}$a penguin] yesterday

   ≡ a. Ida's seeing of a penguin occurred yesterday

   ≢ b. $^{??}$Ida saw yesterday's being(-there) of a penguin

By assuming that (24a) is only *equivalent* to (24b) (see [27]), we avoid this prediction.

   We assume that clausal occurrences of **see** have (a close variant of) the familiar semantics, in (26). According to this semantics, clausal **see** presupposes the factivity of its complement. In (26), the factivity presupposition (underlined) on the clausal complement of **see** is written after a colon.

(26) $[\![\text{see-CP}]\!]^i \; = \; \lambda p : \underline{p_i}.\lambda z (\exists e)[see_i(e, z, p)]$

The factivity presupposition of **see** is supported by the observation that the negation of a clausal vision report still entails the truth of the embedded clause:

(27)   a. <u>Ida does not see [that a penguin is diving into the sea]</u>

   ⇒ b. A penguin is diving into the sea

   Our interpretation of **see** assumes that the factivity presupposition is triggered by the factive verb itself (for this view, see [5,40]), rather than by the embedded clause (see, e.g., [21,23]). This assumption is motivated by the observation that this presupposition is shared by vision reports like A.ii [≡ (24b)] or C.ii whose complement lacks a clausal analysis.

   Arguably, to capture the factivity presupposition of nominal and gerund occurrences of **see**, one would need to replace (17) and (23) by the semantics in (28) and (29), respectively. However, to keep our semantics as simple as possible, we here use (17) and (23) instead.

(28) $[\![\text{see-DP XP}]\!]^i = \lambda Q \lambda P : \underline{Q_i(P)}.\, \lambda z\, [Q_i (\lambda k \lambda y (\exists e)[seek_k(e, z, f_e(\lambda j. P_j(y)))])]$

(29) $[\![\text{see-DP}]\!]^i \quad = \lambda Q : \underline{Q_i(E)}.\, \lambda z\, [Q_i (\lambda k \lambda y (\exists e)[seek_k(e, z, f_e(\lambda j. E_j(y)))])]$

   We close this section with an observation about the polysemy of **see**: our lexical entries in (17) (cf. (23)) and (26) suggest that **see** is polysemous[11] between an experiential (i.e. (17)) and a 'propositional' use (26). This polysemy captures Barwise and Perry's distinction between direct [≈ experiential] and indirect [≈ propositional] perception reports. It is inspired by Dretske's [9] distinction between epistemic [≈ propositional] and non-epistemic [≈ experiential] perception.

   We will show below that, by following Niiniluoto's assumption that **imagine** only has an experiential use (see [34], *pace* [36,41]), we straightforwardly capture the validity of C.i ⇒ F.i and F.i ⇒ C.i (see (12), (13)). This assumption follows the intuition that – given the essential experiential nature of imagination – we cannot have indirect evidence about imaginary situations or events.

---

[11] Since these lexical entries have a common semantic core, **see** is not ambiguous.

3.2   The Semantics of Imagination Reports

We have observed in Sect. 2 that imagination reports show a different entailment behavior from veridical vision reports. This behavior includes the *intensional* interpretation of the embedded DP in imagination reports. To capture this interpretation, we assume that the DP is interpreted *inside* the scope of imagine. Since we assume a non-clausal syntax for gerund attitude reports, we can then capture the entailment pattern of imagine in either of two ways:

The first way lies in the lexical decomposition of imagine into '■ to see', where ■ is an intensional operator. On this account, 'DP XP'-taking occurrences of imagine receive the semantics in (30):

(30) $[\![\text{imagine-DP XP}]\!]^i$
$= \lambda Q \lambda P \lambda z [\blacksquare_i(z, \lambda j. Q_j(\lambda k \lambda y (\exists e)[see_k(e, z, f_e(\lambda l. P_l(y)))]))]$

The above is reminiscent of Quine's [37] interpretation of seek as try to find (see (31); cf. [33, pp. 264, 267]), where try contributes the intensional operator:

(31) $[\![\text{seek-DP}]\!]^i = \lambda Q \lambda z [try_i(z, \lambda j. Q_j(\lambda k \lambda y. find_k(z, y)))]$

However, because of its similarity to (31), the semantics in (30) also inherits the challenges of this interpretation. These include the difficulty of specifying the identity of the intensional operator for some verbs[12] and of finding a suitable lexical decomposition of these and other verbs (see [31, pp. 177]). The specification of ■ is required by the need to assign a distinct semantics to verbs (e.g. imagine, visualize, and hallucinate) that all suggest a lexical decomposition in terms of see.

We avoid the above problems by adopting instead the semantics for imagine in (32). This semantics interprets imagine as a lexical primitive that takes scope over its DP complement. The interpretation of imagine in (32) follows Montague's [32] interpretation of seek (see [30]), in (33):

(32) $[\![\text{imagine-DP XP}]\!]^i = \lambda Q \lambda P \lambda z (\exists e)[imagine_i(e, z, f_e(\lambda j. Q_j(P)))]$

(33) $[\![\text{seek-DP}]\!]^i = \lambda Q \lambda z [seek_i(z, Q)]$

Following the above interpretation strategy, transitive occurrences of imagine are interpreted as a DP-low-scope version of (23) (in (34)). To capture the essential experiential nature of imagination,[13] we interpret clausal imagine as a relation to a coded situation, rather than to a classical proposition (see our elaborations above). The relevant entry is given in (35):

(34) $[\![\text{imagine-DP}]\!]^i = \lambda Q \lambda z (\exists e)[imagine_i(e, z, f_e(\lambda j. Q_j(E)))]$

(35) $[\![\text{imagine-CP}]\!]^i = \lambda p \lambda z (\exists e)[imagine_i(e, z, f_e(p))]$

---

[12] This is particularly problematic in view of competing philosophical analyses of imagination, like imagine seeing, seeming to see, and pretending (to oneself) to see.

[13] This nature is supported by the observation (corroborated by a corpus study by Carla Umbach) that even reports like F.i allow for experiential modification (see (‡)):

(‡)   Ida *vividly* imagines that a penguin is diving into the sea.

Note that, in contrast to see, imagine does not presuppose the factivity of its complement. The absence of the factivity presupposition in (35) captures the fact that imagination is a counterfactual attitude (i.e. we can also imagine what is *not* there). We will return to this point in the next section.

4   Capturing the Entailments

With our entries for see and imagine in place, we can now show that our proposed semantics captures the different entailment patterns from Sect. 2:

4.1   Modelling Classes 2–4: DP-Extensionality Entailments

Our semantics for 'DP XP'-taking occurrences of see (in (17)) ensures that the interpretation of the embedded DP subject in vision reports is specific (i.e. the quantifier that is denoted by the DP lies outside the scope of see) and referentially transparent (i.e. the restrictor of the DP is interpreted at the evaluation situation i). In virtue of this fact, gerund vision reports are always interpreted *de re*:

(36) $[\![C.ii]\!]^i_{de\ dicto'} \equiv [\![$Ida sees $[_{DP}$a penguin$]\,[_{XP}$diving into the sea$]]\!]^i$
$= (\exists x)[penguin_i(x) \wedge (\exists e)[see_i(e, ida, f_e(\lambda j.\,dive_j(x)))]]$
$\equiv (\lambda P(\exists x)[penguin_i(x) \wedge P_i(x)])$
$\qquad (\lambda k\lambda x_1(\exists e)[see_k(e, ida, f_e(\lambda j.\,dive_j(x_1)))])$
$= [\![C.ii]\!]^i_{de\ re} \equiv [\![$[a penguin] $[\lambda_1$ [Ida sees t_1 $[_{XP}$diving into the sea$]]]]\!]^i$

In particular, as a result of the DP's transparent interpretation, the restrictor, i.e. penguin, admits substitution *salva veritate* by an extensionally equivalent expression (here: by the complex noun Antarctic flightless bird, in (37); see **Class 3.ii**) and allows for a truth-preserving modification by the adjective real-world (in (39); see **Class 2.ii**). The latter uses the interpretation of real-world in (39), where w_i is a variable for the world that is associated with the evaluation situation (i):

(37)   a. $[\![C.ii]\!]^i \equiv [\![$Ida sees $[_{DP}$a penguin$]\,[_{XP}$diving into the sea$]]\!]^i$
$= (\exists x)[penguin_i(x) \wedge (\exists e)[see_i(e, ida, f_e(\lambda j.\,dive_j(x)))]]$
b.   (Ext) $(\forall x)[penguin_i(x) \leftrightarrow antarctic\text{-}flightless\text{-}bird_i(x)]$
$\Leftrightarrow$ c. $[\![D.ii]\!]^i \equiv [\![$Ida sees [an Antarctic flightless bird] diving into the sea$]\!]^i$
$= (\exists x)[antarctic\text{-}flightless\text{-}bird_i(x) \wedge (\exists e)[see_i(e, ida, f_e(\lambda j.\,dive_j(x)))]]$

(38) $[\![$real-world $[_N\ ]]\!] = \lambda P\lambda j\lambda x\,[P_j(x) \wedge E_{w_i}(x)]$

(39)   a. $[\![C.ii]\!]^i = (\exists x)[penguin_i(x) \wedge (\exists e)[see_i(e, ida, f_e(\lambda j.\,dive_j(x)))]]$
$\Leftrightarrow$ b. $[\![B.ii]\!]^i \equiv [\![$Ida sees [a real-world penguin] diving into the sea$]\!]^i$

As a result of the specific interpretation of the DP a penguin, C.ii is equivalent to the report E.ii (see (42); **Class 4.ii**). Our proof of this equivalence uses the semantics of the relativizer which from (40) (see [15, p. 82 ff.]). The predicate be there is interpreted through the existence predicate E (see (41)):

(40) $[\![\text{which}]\!] = \lambda Q \lambda P \lambda j \lambda y \, [P_j(y) \wedge Q_j(y)]$

(41) $[\![\text{be there}]\!]^i \equiv [\![\text{exist}]\!]^i = \lambda \mathcal{Q} \, [\mathcal{Q}_i (\lambda j \lambda y. \, E_j(y))]$

Together, the above enable the compositional interpretation of E.ii in (42b):

(42) a. $[\![\text{C.ii}]\!]^i = (\exists x)[penguin_i(x) \wedge (\exists e)[see_i(e, ida, f_e(\lambda j. \, dive_j(x)))]]$

$\Leftrightarrow$ b. $[\![\text{E.ii}]\!]^i \equiv [\![\text{There is } [_{\text{DP}}\text{a penguin}] \text{ which Ida sees } [_{\text{XP}}\text{diving} \ldots]]\!]^i$

$\equiv [\![\text{there is}]\!]^i ([\![\text{a}]\!] ([\![\text{which}]\!] ([\![\text{penguin}]\!], \lambda_1. [\![\text{Ida sees } t_1 \text{ dive}]\!])))$

$= \lambda \mathcal{Q} \, [\mathcal{Q}_i (\lambda j \lambda y. \, E_j(y))] (\lambda k \lambda P (\exists x)[penguin_k(x) \wedge$
$(\exists e)[see_k(e, ida, f_e(\lambda l. \, dive_l(x))) \wedge P_k(x)]])$

Note: A more standard, i.e. 'clausal' version of (17) (in (43); cf. (15)) may try to capture (9.ii)–(11.ii) by interpreting the complement in C.ii as a syntactic constituent (see the S[mall] C[lause] in (43)) and by adopting the quantifier exportation rule **DP-Exp** (cf. [4, p. 182]) as an axiom in the lexical semantics of see:

(43) $[\![\text{see } [_{\text{SC}}[_{\text{DP}} \,] [_{\text{XP}} \,]]]\!]^i = \lambda p \lambda z (\exists e)[see_i(e, z, f_e(p))]$

(44) (**DP-Exp**) $(\forall P)(\forall Q)(\forall z)(\forall e)[see_i(z, f_e(\lambda j \exists x. P_j(x) \wedge Q_j(x))) \rightarrow$
$(\exists y)[P_i(y) \wedge see_i(z, f_e(\lambda j. Q_j(y)))]]$

However, because of the order-insensitivity of conjunction, this rule wrongly predicts that the embedded predicate in C.ii (i.e. diving into the sea) likewise has an extensional interpretation (*contra* (22); cf. [2,8]). The difficulty of finding a weaker variant of **DP-Exp** that avoids this prediction – and the ease of capturing (9.ii)–(11.ii) through (17) – provides support for our non-clausal analysis.

In contrast to our semantics for 'DP XP'-taking see, our semantics for 'DP XP'-taking imagine (in (32)) allows for the possibility that the embedded DP subject receives a non-specific and referentially opaque interpretation. As a result, the *de dicto*-reading of C.i (i.e. Ida imagines a penguin diving; in (45a)) has a different interpretation from the report's *de re*-reading (see (45b)). The identification of E.i (i.e. There is a penguin which Ida imagines diving) with the *de re*-reading of C.i (see (45b)) then captures the non-entailment from C.i to E.i (**Class 4.i**):

(45) a. $[\![\text{C.i}]\!]^i_{de \; dicto} \equiv [\![\text{Ida imagines } [_{\text{DP}}\text{a penguin}] [_{\text{XP}}\text{diving into the sea}]]\!]^i$
$= (\exists e)[imagine_i(e, ida, f_e(\lambda j \exists x. \, penguin_j(x) \wedge dive_j(x)))]$

$\not\Rightarrow$ b. $[\![\text{C.i}]\!]^i_{de \; re} \equiv [\![[\text{a penguin}] [\lambda_1 [\text{Ida imagines } t_1 [_{\text{XP}}\text{diving} \ldots]]]]\!]^i$
$= (\exists x)[penguin_i(x) \wedge (\exists e)[imagine_i(e, ida, f_e(\lambda j. \, dive_j(x)))]]$

$= [\![\text{E.i}]\!]^i = [\![\text{there is}]\!]^i ([\![\text{a}]\!] ([\![\text{which}]\!] ([\![\text{penguin}]\!], \lambda_1. [\![\text{Ida imagines } t_1 \text{ dive}]\!])))$

The opaque interpretation of the embedded DP in the *de dicto*-reading of C.i (see (45a)) blocks the entailment to D.i (i.e. Ida imagines an Antarctic flightless bird diving; see (46); **Class 3.i**) and B.i (i.e. Ida imagines a real-world penguin diving; see (47); **Class 2.i**):

(46) a. $[\![C.i]\!]^i_{de\ dicto} = (\exists e)[imagine_i\,(e, ida, f_e(\lambda j\,\exists x.\,penguin_j(x) \wedge dive_j(x)))]$

　　　b. (Int)　　　　$(\exists j)(\exists x)[penguin_j(x) \wedge \neg antarctic\text{-}flightless\text{-}bird_j(x)]$

$\not\Rightarrow$ c. $[\![D.i]\!]^i_{de\ dicto} \equiv [\![Ida\ imagines\ [_{DP}an\ Antarctic\ flightl.\ bird]\ [_{XP}diving]]\!]^i$
　　　　$= (\exists e)[imagine_i\,(e, ida, f_e(\lambda j\,\exists x.\,antarctic\text{-}flightless\text{-}bird_j(x) \wedge dive_j(x)))]$

(47) a. $[\![C.i]\!]^i_{de\ dicto} = (\exists e)[imagine_i\,(e, ida, f_e(\lambda j\,\exists x.\,penguin_j(x) \wedge dive_j(x)))]$

$\not\Rightarrow$ b. $[\![B.i]\!]^i_{de\ dicto} \equiv [\![Ida\ imagines\ [a\ real\text{-}world\ penguin]\ [_{XP}diving\ \ldots]]\!]^i$
　　　　$= (\exists e)[imagine_i\,(e, ida, f_e(\lambda j\,\exists x.\,(penguin_j(x) \wedge \underline{E_{\boldsymbol{w_i}}(x)}) \wedge dive_j(x)))]$

4.2　Modelling Class 1: Propositional-to-Nominal Entailments

We have pointed out in Sect. 3.1 that, in virtue of our interpretation of transitive occurrences of see (cf. (23)), our semantics assigns to nominal vision reports the same interpretation as to the result of enriching the object DP in these reports with the XP being there (see (24)). Our interpretation of transitive occurrences of imagine gives rise to the same kind of equivalence. For imagine, this equivalence is captured below:

(48)　$(\forall Q)(\forall z)[[\![\text{imagine-DP}]\!]^i(Q)(z) \equiv [\![\text{imagine-DP XP}]\!]^i(Q)(E)(z)]$

(4.2) enables the obtaining of entailment relations between imagination reports with gerund and nominal complements. In particular, the entailment in (8) (cf. **Class 1**) is supported by the fact that being a penguin (in a situation) is a more general property than being a penguin who is diving into the sea (in this situation) (see (49b)). The entailment further relies on the intuitive parthood principle ($\subseteq$) and on the upward-monotonicity, M$\uparrow$, of the complement of imagine:

(49)　a.　$[\![C.i]\!]^i_{de\ dicto} = (\exists e)[imagine_i\,(e, ida, f_e(\lambda j\,\exists x.\,penguin_j(x) \wedge dive_j(x)))]$

　　　b.　(Gen)　　　$(\forall j)(\forall x)[(penguin_j(x) \wedge dive_j(x)) \rightarrow penguin_j(x)]$

　　　c.　$(\subseteq)$　　　$(\forall p)(\forall q)[p \subseteq q \rightarrow (\forall e.\,f_e(p) \subseteq f_e(q))]$

　　　d.　$\underline{(M\uparrow)}$ $(\forall p)(\forall z)(\forall e)[imagine_i(e,z,p) \rightarrow (\forall q.\,p \subseteq q \rightarrow imagine_i(e,z,q))]$

$\Rightarrow$ e.　$[\![A.i]\!]^i_{de\ dicto} \equiv [\![Ida\ imagines\ [a\ penguin]]\!]^i$
　　　　$= (\exists e)[imagine_i\,(e, ida, f_e(\lambda j\,\exists x.\,penguin_j(x)))]$

4.3　Modelling Classes 5–6: Positivity- & Experientiality-Entailments

We have seen in Sect. 2 that only imagine – but not see – licenses the replacement of its gerund complements by their that-clause variants (see (12)). To block the entailment from C.ii to F.ii (i.e. Ida sees that a penguin is diving into the sea), we follow Kratzer's [23] assumptions that that is ambiguous between the propositional complementizer, i.e. that$_P$, and the factive complementizer, i.e. that$_F$, and that clause-taking occurrences of factive verbs (incl. see) select for clauses with the factive complementizer. Kratzer assumes that that$_F$ receives the interpretation in (50). Given a simple variant of her analysis of exemplification (see [22, pp. 660–661], [24, Sect. 6]), this interpretation can be formalized as (51), where $\leq$ is a partial (i.e. spatio-temporal/informational inclusion-)ordering on situations:

(50) $\lambda p \lambda j \, [exemplify\,(p, j)]$

(51) $[\![that_F]\!] \;=\; \lambda p.\, \Pi\,(p),$ where $\Pi := \lambda q \lambda j \, [q_j \wedge (\forall k.(q_k \wedge k \leq j) \rightarrow k = j)]$

In virtue of (51) and the lexical entry for clausal see (in (26)), the *de re*-reading of F.ii receives the interpretation in (52c). This interpretation asserts the obtaining of the seeing relation between Ida and the set of facts [= minimal situations] in which a particular real-world penguin is diving into the sea. Since visual scenes typically do <u>not</u> represent isolated facts, the scene that serves as the argument of C.ii will likely not be a member of this set.[14] The non-inclusion of the set, $f_e(\lambda j.\, dive_j(x))$, that codes this scene in the set $\Pi(\lambda j.\, dive_j(x))$ (see (52b)) then captures the non-validity of C.ii $\Rightarrow$ F.ii (see **Class 5.ii**).[15]

(52)   a. $[\![C.ii]\!]^i \;=\; (\exists x)\,[penguin_i(x) \wedge (\exists e)\,[see_i\,(e, ida, f_e(\lambda j.\, dive_j(x)))]]$
   b. $(\forall x)(\forall e)(\exists k)\,[f_e(\lambda j.\, dive_j(x))(k) \wedge \neg\Pi\,(\lambda j.\, dive_j(x))(k)]$

$\not\Rightarrow$ c. $[\![F.ii]\!]^i_{de\ re} \equiv [\![\,[\text{a penguin}]\,[\lambda_1\,[\text{Ida sees }[_{CP}\text{that } t_1 \text{ is diving} \ldots]]]]\!]^i$
      $= (\exists x)\,[penguin_i(x) \wedge (\exists e)\,[see_i\,(e, ida, \Pi\,(\lambda j.\, dive_j(x)))]]$

The non-inclusion of the set $\Pi\,(\lambda j.\, dive_j(x))$ in the set $f_e(\lambda j.\, dive_j(x))$ explains the non-validity of the entailment in the other direction (see **Class 6.ii**).

Since it is non-factive, imagine selects for the propositional complementizer $that_P$. When combined with the lexical entry for clausal imagine (see (34)), the semantics of $that_P$ (in (53)) captures the validity of C.i $\Rightarrow$ F.i, as desired (see (54) for the *de dicto*-case).

(53) $[\![that_P]\!] \;=\; \lambda p \lambda j \, [p_j]$ (i.e. $that_P$ is semantically vacuous)

(54)   a. $[\![C.i]\!]^i_{de\ dicto} = (\exists e)\,[imagine_i\,(e, ida, f_e(\lambda j \exists x.\, penguin_j(x) \wedge dive_j(x)))]$
   b. $(M\!\uparrow)\;(\forall p)(\forall z)(\forall e)\,[imagine_i(e, z, p) \rightarrow (\forall q.\, p \subseteq q \rightarrow imagine_i(e, z, q))]$

a. $\Leftrightarrow$ c. $[\![F.i]\!]^i_{de\ dicto} \equiv [\![\text{Ida imagines }[\text{that a penguin is diving into the sea}]]\!]^i$

Since the semantic arguments of the occurrences of imagine in C.i and F.i are, in fact, identical, the entailment in the other direction is also valid (see **Class 6.i**).

---

[14] The latter is the case if Ida's perceived visual scene includes information beyond the fact that the penguin is diving into the sea, e.g. that the penguin has a black face and/or that its feet are covered in dirt.

[15] Alternatively, one could try to capture this non-validity by combining (51) with a see-variant of (35). However, the resulting account would counterintuitively interpret the complement in F.ii as a single fact (with a specific spatio-temporal location in w_i), rather than as a sets of facts (with different spatio-temporal locations in w_i). Since this account would further need to explain C.ii $\not\Rightarrow$ F.ii through the (dubious) non-inclusion of the fact $f_e(\Pi(\lambda j.\, dive_j(x)))$ in the situation, $f_e(\lambda j.\, dive_j(x))$, of which this fact is true, we refrain from adopting this account.

5   Outlook

We expect that the proposed semantics can be straightforwardly extended to capture the entailment properties of other experiential attitude verbs (e.g. remember, hallucinate) that cut across the entailment patterns of see and imagine. This is achieved by combining the intensional interpretation of the embedded DP subject in (32) and (34) with the selection for factive clauses like (51) (for remember) and by assigning this DP a specific, but referentially opaque interpretation through Szabó's [42] rule of split raising (for hallucinate).

References

1. Anand, P.: Suppositional projects and subjectivity. In: Michigan Linguistics and Philosophy Workshop, pp. 1–22 (2011)
2. Asher, N., Bonevac, D.: How extensional is extensional perception? Linguist. Philos. 8(2), 203–228 (1985)
3. Barwise, J.: Scenes and other situations. J. Philos. 78(7), 369–397 (1981)
4. Barwise, J., Perry, J.: Situations and Attitudes. MIT Press, Cambridge (1983)
5. Beaver, D., Geurts, B.: Presupposition, Stanford Encyclopedia of Philosophy: Summer. In: Zalta, E.N. (ed.) 2011 edn. (2011). https://plato.stanford.edu/archives/sum2011/entries/presupposition
6. Blome-Tillmann, M.: Conversational implicatures (and how to spot them). Philos. Compass 80(2), 170–185 (2013)
7. Cresswell, M.J., von Stechow, A.: De re belief generalized. Linguist. Philos. 5(4), 503–35 (1982)
8. van der Does, J.: A generalized quantifier logic for naked infinitives. Linguist. Philos. 14(3), 241–294 (1991)
9. Detske, F.: Seeing and knowing. Mind 79, 281–287 (1970)
10. Fine, K.: Properties, propositions, and sets. J. Philos. Logic 6, 135–191 (1977)
11. von Fintel, K.: Quantifier domain selection and pseudo-scope. In: Handout from a Talk at the Cornell Conference on Theories of Context Dependency (1999). http://mit.edu/fintel/fintel-1999-cornell-context.pdf
12. Forbes, G.: Attitude Problems: An Essay on Linguistic Intensionality. Oxford University Press, Oxford and New York (2006)
13. Grzankowski, A.: Limits of propositionalism. Inquiry 57(7-8), 819–838 (2016)
14. Grice, H.P.: Logic and conversation. In: Cole, P., Morgan, J.L. (eds.) Syntax and Semantics III: Speech Acts, pp. 41–58. Academic Press, New York (1989)
15. Heim, I., Kratzer, A.: Semantics in Generative Grammar, Blackwell Textbooks in Linguistics, vol. 13. Blackwell, Malden and Oxford (1998)
16. Higginbotham, J.: The logic of perceptual reports: an extensional alternative to situation semantics. J. Philos. 80(2), 100–127 (1985)
17. Higginbotham, J.: Remembering, imagining, and the first person. In: Barber, A. (ed.) Epistemology of Language, pp. 496–533. Oxford University Press, Oxford (2003)
18. Hintikka, J.: Semantics for propositional attitudes. In: Davis, J.W., et al. (eds.) Philosophical Logic, pp. 21–45. Reidel, Dordrecht (1969)
19. Horn, L.R.: On the Semantic Properties of the Logical Operators in English. Chicago University Press, Chicago (1972)

20. Kaplan, D.: Quantifying in. Synthese **19**(1–2), 178–214 (1969)
21. Kiparsky, P., Kiparsky, C.: Fact. In: Bierwisch, M., Heidolph, K.E. (eds.) Progress in Linguistics: A Collection of Papers, pp. 143–73. Mouton, The Hague (1970)
22. Kratzer, A.: Facts: particulars or information units? Linguist. Philos. **25**(5-6), 655–670 (2002)
23. Kratzer, A.: Decomposing attitude verbs. Hebrew University of Jerusalem, Handout (2006). https://semanticsarchive.net/Archive/DcwY2JkM/attitude-verbs2006.pdf
24. Kratzer, A.: Situations in natural language. In: Zalta, E.N., (ed.) Stanford Encyclopedia of Philosophy: Summer 2019 (edn) (2019). https://plato.stanford.edu/entries/situations-semantics/
25. Lewis, D.: Attitudes de dicto and de se. Phil. Rev. **88**(4), 513–543 (1979)
26. Liefke, K.: A single-type semantics for natural language. Dissertation, Tilburg Center for Logic and Philosophy of Science, Tilburg (2014)
27. Liefke, K.: Saving Hamlet ellipsis. In: Loukanova, R. (ed.) Logic and Algorithms in Computational Linguistics 2018 (LACompLing2018). SCI, vol. 860, pp. 17–43. Springer, Cham (2020). https://doi.org/10.1007/978-3-030-30077-7_2
28. Liefke, K., Werning, M.: Evidence for single-type semantics - an alternative to e/t-based dual-type semantics. J. Semant. **35**(4), 639–685 (2018)
29. Lundin, K.: Small clauses in Swedish: towards a unified account. Dissertation, Lund University, Lund (2003)
30. Moltmann, F.: Intensional verbs and quantifiers. Nat. Lang. Sem. **5**(1), 1–52 (1997)
31. Montague, R.: On the nature of certain philosophical entities. The Monist **41**, 159–194 (1969)
32. Montague, R.: Universal grammar. Theoría **36**(3), 373–398 (1970)
33. Montague, R.: The proper treatment of quantification in ordinary English. In: Hintikka, J. (ed.) Approaches to Natural Language, pp. 221–242. Reidel, Dordrecht (1973)
34. Niiniluoto, I.: Imagination and fiction. J. Semant. **4**(3), 209–222 (1985)
35. Parsons, T.: Meaning sensitivity and grammatical structure. In: Chiara, M.L.D., Doets, K., Mundici, D., Van Benthem, J. (eds.) Structures and Norms in Science. SYLI, vol. 260. Springer, Dordrecht (1997). https://doi.org/10.1007/978-94-017-0538-7_22
36. Peacocke, C.: Implicit conceptions, understanding and rationality. Philos. Issues **9**, 43–88 (1998)
37. Quine, W.V.: Quantifiers and propositional attitudes. J. Philos. **53**(5), 177–187 (1956)
38. Rothstein, S.: The Syntactic Forms of Predication. Dissertation, MIT, Cambridge (1983)
39. Schein, B.: Small clauses and predication. Syntax Semant. **28**, 49–76 (1995)
40. Schlenker, P.: Be articulate: a pragmatic theory of presupposition projection. Theoret. Linguist. **34**, 157–212 (2008)
41. Stephenson, T.: Vivid attitudes: centered situations in the semantics of 'remember' and 'imagine'. In: Proceedings of SALT XX, pp. 147–160 (2010)
42. Szabó, Z.G.: Specific, yet opaque. In: Aloni, M., Bastiaanse, H., de Jager, T., Schulz, K. (eds.) Logic, Language and Meaning. LNCS (LNAI), vol. 6042, pp. 32–41. Springer, Heidelberg (2010). https://doi.org/10.1007/978-3-642-14287-1_4
43. Theiler, N., Roelofsen, F., Aloni, M.: A uniform semantics for declarative and interrogative complements. J. Semant. **35**(3), 409–466 (2018)

44. Umbach, C., Hinterwimmer, S., Gust, H.: German 'wie'-complements: Manners, methods and events in progress. Forthcoming in Natural Language and Linguistic Theory. http://www.carla-umbach.de/publications/UmbachHinterwimmerGust_wie-complements.Dec2019.draft.pdf
45. Williams, E.S.: Against small clauses. Linguist. Inquiry **14**(2), 287–308 (1983)
46. Zimmermann, T.E.: Unspecificity and intensionality. In: Féry, C., Sternefeld, W. (eds.) Audiatur Vox Sapentiae, pp. 524–543. Akademie Verlag, Berlin (2001)
47. Zimmermann, T.E.: Painting and opacity. In: Freitag, W., Rott, H., Sturm, H., Zinke, A. (eds.) Von Rang und Namen, pp. 427–453. Mentis, Münster (2016)

A Choice Function Analysis of *Either* in the *Either/or* Construction

Mioko Miyama[✉] [iD]

Nagoya University of Commerce and Business, Nisshin, Aichi, Japan
mioko_miyama@nucba.ac.jp

Abstract. In this paper, I propose an analysis that covers both the wide scope *or* reading of the *either/or* construction and the availability of Alternative Question and Yes/No Question readings, namely a hybrid of an ellipsis analysis and a choice function analysis of *either*. After presenting two sets of data, I introduce two hybrid analyses that combine an ellipsis analysis and a choice function analysis. The two differ from each other in terms of the item that introduces the choice function variable: in the first analysis, the disjunction particle *or* introduces the choice function variable while in the second analysis, *either* has that semantic role. It is demonstrated that the two analyses both account for the *either/or* construction data, whereas only the second hybrid analysis, in which *either* introduces the choice function variable, explains the Alternative Question and Yes/No Question data. Finally, I review another account proposed in previous research, namely the focus alternative semantics analysis, and point out its problems.

Keywords: *Either/or* construction · Alternative questions · Choice functions

1 The Data

As noted in [1] as a problematic case and discussed in [2] in more detail, when disjunction is combined with certain kinds of elements in a sentence the sentence is (at least) two-ways ambiguous:

(1) The department is looking for a phonologist or a phonetician. (cf. [1])
    a. $[\![$ look for $]\!]$ ($[\![$ a phonologist or a phonetician $]\!]$) (d)   (narrow scope)
    b. $[\![$ look for $]\!]$ ($[\![$ a phonologist $]\!]$) (d) $\vee$ $[\![$ look for $]\!]$ ($[\![$ a phonetician $]\!]$) (d)
                                                     (wide scope)

There are two *de dicto* readings of *or* in relation to the intentional predicate. The narrow scope *or de dicto* reading is in (1a), and under this reading the department would be satisfied by finding either a phonologist or a phonetician. The "problematic"

I am indebted to Akira Watanabe, Noriko Imanishi, Christopher Tancredi, audience at LENLS 16, and two anonymous reviewers for helpful comments and suggestions. All remaining errors are my own. This study was supported by Grant-in-Aid for Young Scientists (#18K12414) from the Japan Society for the Promotion of Science, to which I am grateful.

© Springer Nature Switzerland AG 2020
M. Sakamoto et al. (Eds.): JSAI-isAI 2019, LNAI 12331, pp. 294–308, 2020.
https://doi.org/10.1007/978-3-030-58790-1_19

de dicto reading, which I am interested in, is described in (1b). On this reading, the department does not yet necessarily have a specific candidate in mind. They do already have in mind which of the two types of specialist they are going to look for, but the speaker forgot which it was. This reading becomes clearer when continued with "… but I don't know which." Thus, the overall meaning is as if the disjunction is connecting two propositions, taking widest scope, even though the indefinite in each disjunct takes narrow scope. This is called the "wide scope *or*" reading in [2].

[3] observes that the possible readings of a sentence change when *either* comes into the structure. He states a generalization:

(2) [3]'s generalization (from [4]):
   a. In *or* coordinations without *either*, as well as in *either…or…* coordinations with *either* undisplaced, the scope of *or* is confined to those positions where *either* can potentially appear.
   b. When *either* is displaced it specifies the scope of *or* to be at that displaced position.

(2a) is based on the assumption that the base position of *either* is next to the left edge of the Disjunction Phrase (DisjP). Thus, when *either* is adjacent to the DisjP all three readings are available (3), whereas when *either* floats to a higher position the narrow scope *or* de dicto reading disappears (4). Note that sentences with *either* floated higher than that in (4) behave in the same way as (4).

(3) Mary is looking for (either) a maid or a cook.
   a. $[\![\text{look for}]\!] ([\![\text{a maid or a cook}]\!]) (m)$ (narrow scope)
   b. $[\![\text{look for}]\!] ([\![\text{a maid}]\!]) (m) \lor [\![\text{look for}]\!] ([\![\text{a cook}]\!]) (m)$ (wide scope)
(4) Mary is either looking for a maid or a cook.
   a. $*? [\![\text{look for}]\!] ([\![\text{a maid or a cook}]\!]) (m)$ (narrow scope)
   b. $[\![\text{look for}]\!] ([\![\text{a maid}]\!])(m) \lor [\![\text{look for}]\!] ([\![\text{a cook}]\!]) (m)$ (wide scope)

[4] and [5] report data which at first glance look like an exception to [3]'s generalization, where disjunction can take wide scope over an island as in (5) but *either* cannot appear out of the island as in (6). In (5), *or* can take either narrow or wide scope with respect to *if*. Note that *either* can appear inside the island and the disjunction can take narrow or wide scope with respect to *if* as in (7). ((5) and (6) are taken from [4]).

(5) If Bill praises Mary or Sue then John will be happy.
   a. If Bill praises Mary then John will be happy and if Bill praises Sue then John will be happy. (narrow scope)
   b. If Bill praises Mary then John will be happy or if Bill praises Sue then John will be happy. (wide scope)
(6) *Either if Bill praises Mary or Sue then John will be happy.
(7) If Bill praises either Mary or Sue then John will be happy. (^{OK}NS/^{OK}WS)

The fact that sentences with *either* inside an island do have wide scope *or* readings as in (7) conforms to the generalization in (2a), since sentences with *either* in its base position can have the scope of *or* higher than the surface position of *either*. In contrast, it goes against the generalization in (2b), since floated *either* does not mark the exact scope of *or* but allows the scope of *or* to be in a higher position.

To sum up, [3]'s generalization in (2) states that (i) in sentences with no *either* or with *either* in its base position, *or* can take both narrow scope and wide scope, while (ii) in sentences with floated *either*, only the wide scope *or* reading is available. We have also reviewed additional data reported by [4] and [5], in which *or* can take scope over an island but *either* cannot overtly appear outside the island.

Lastly, consider (8). An interrogative sentence with a DisjP without *either* is ambiguous between an Alternative Question (AltQ) and a Yes/No Question (YNQ) as in (8a). Once *either* comes in, however, an AltQ reading is no longer available and the sentence is unambiguously a YNQ regardless of the position of *either*, as shown in (8b, c).

(8)   Availability of question readings and the position of *either*
   a. Did John see a maid or a cook? (AltQ/YNQ)
   b. Did John see either a maid or a cook? (*AltQ/YNQ)
   c. Did John either see a maid or a cook? (*AltQ/YNQ)

In the rest of this paper, I propose an analysis that accounts for the wide scope *or* reading of the *either/or* construction and the availability of AltQ/YNQ readings introduced above. In Sect. 2, I first introduce two hybrid analyses that combine an ellipsis analysis and a choice function analysis. The two differ from each other in terms of the item that introduces the choice function variable: in the first analysis, the disjunction particle *or* introduces the choice function variable while in the second analysis, *either* has that semantic role. It is demonstrated that the two analyses both account for the *either/or* construction data, whereas only the second hybrid analysis, in which *either* introduces the choice function variable, explains the AltQ/YNQ data. I thus eventually propose a hybrid analysis of an ellipsis analysis and a choice function analysis of *either*. In Sect. 3, I review a previous study and point out its problems. Section 4 concludes.

2   Proposal

2.1   Two Hybrid Analyses

I first introduce two possible analyses combining an ellipsis analysis and a choice function analysis, and examine the wide scope *or* data. Both of the analyses combine an ellipsis analysis, and a choice function analysis in which an item introduces a choice function variable and the wide scope *or* reading is obtained through Existential Closure of the choice function variable.

The first hypothesis is that *or* introduces a choice function variable (cf. [5, 6]) and *either* only has a syntactic role of marking the left edge of the first disjunct (cf. [7]). The choice function variable that *or* introduces takes the set of disjuncts, the denotation of the DisjP, as its argument and the position of Existential Closure determines the scope position of *or*. With the work of *either*, it is guaranteed that the scope position of *or* is never lower than the position of *either*, since *either* determines the size of the DisjP.

Let us look at the examples. In sentences with no *either* or with *either* in its base position (9) (= (3)), where there is an ambiguity between narrow scope and wide scope *or*, no ellipsis is involved in the derivation of the examples. Thus there are multiple possible positions for Existential Closure which correspond to the multiple possible scope positions of *or*.

(9) Ambiguous between NS and WS *or*
    a. Mary is looking for a maid or a cook.
    b. Mary is looking for either a maid or a cook.
      ○ [∃f] Mary is looking for [∃f] PRO to FIND f({a maid, a cook}) (cf. [8])

In sentences with floated *either* as in (10), where the wide scope *or* reading is forced, *either* marks the left edge of the first disjunct and ellipsis is involved in the derivation. Since the choice function variable is introduced with the disjunction, Existential Closure is restricted to a position above the DisjP. With this analysis, we can account for the fact that only the wide scope *or* reading is available in the sentences.

(10) Unambiguous: only WS *or*
    a. Mary is either looking for a maid or ~~looking for~~ a cook (= (4)).
      ○ ∃f. Mary is f({looking for a maid, looking for a cook})
    b. Mary either is looking for a maid or ~~is looking for~~ a cook.
      ○ ∃f. Mary f({is looking for a maid, is looking for a cook})
    c. Either Mary is looking for a maid or ~~Mary is looking for~~ a cook.
      ○ ∃f. f({Mary is looking for a maid, Mary is looking for a cook})

The second hypothesis is that *either* introduces a choice function variable and *or* forms a set of disjuncts that serves as its argument. The claim that a DisjP denotes the set of its disjuncts is not new (cf. [9] among others). I adopt a compositional semantics of DisjP with the denotation of *or* in (11). (For detailed discussion, see Sect. 3.2).

(11) $[\![\,or\,]\!]^{w,g} = \lambda x_{<s,\sigma>} \cdot \lambda y_{<s,\sigma>} \cdot \{[\![\,x\,]\!]^{w}, [\![\,y\,]\!]^{w}\}$
(12) $[\![\,a\ maid\ or\ a\ cook\,]\!]^{w,g} = \{[\![\,a\ maid\,]\!]^{w}, [\![\,a\ cook\,]\!]^{w}\}$

Or has a set-forming function as its denotation. It takes two arguments of the same type and forms a set of them. The result of combining *or* with the disjuncts is the set of the disjuncts, as in (12).

The second version of the hybrid analysis can equally capture the facts in (9) and (10) since, as we can observe from the data, the position where the choice function variable is placed coincides with the overt position of *either*. In this analysis, we assign *either* the semantic work of introducing the choice function variable, as in (13). To get this to work out formally, I analyze this as involving a covert operator coindexed with *either*, whose sole semantic work is to modify the assignment function g so that it assigns to its index a choice function variable f_i, as in (14).

(13) $[\![\,either_i\,]\!]^{w,g} = g(i)$

(14) $[\![\,Op_i\,[either_i\ DisjP]\,]\!]^{w,g} = [\![\,either_i\ DisjP\,]\!]^{w,\,g[i \to f_i]}$, where $f_i \in D_{Chf}$ is a choice function $Chf(f_i)$ iff for all P in $dom(f_i)$: $f_i(P) \in P$

With the items, the NS reading of the sentence with *either* in its base position is derived as in (15) and the WS reading of the sentence with floated *either* is derived as in (16).

(15) Mary is looking for [$_{TP}$ PRO TO FIND [$_{XP}$ Op$_i$ either$_i$ [$_{DisjP}$ a maid or a cook]]].

$[\![XP]\!]^{w,g} = [\![either_i\ DisjP]\!]^{w,\,g[i \to f_i]} : f_i \in D_{Chf}$

   a. $= [\![either_i]\!]^{w,\,g[i \to f_i]} \left([\![DisjP]\!]^{w,\,g[i \to f_i]} \right) : f_i \in D_{Chf}$

             $= f_i (\{a\ maid\ in\ w, a\ cook\ in\ w\}) : f_i \in D_{Chf}$

   b. $[\![TP]\!]^{w,g} = \lambda w. \exists f_i.\ Chf\,(f_i)\ \&\ Mary\ to\ find\ f_i\,(\{a\ maid\ in\ w, a\ cook\ in\ w\ a\ maid\ in\ w, a\ cook\ in\ w\})\ in\ w$

   c. $[\![(15)]\!]^{w,g} = \lambda w'.\ Mary\ is\ looking\ for\ [\lambda w.\ \exists f_i.\ Chf(f_i)\ \&\ Mary\ to\ find\ f_i(\{a\ maid\ in\ w, a\ cook\ in\ w\})\ in\ w] in\ w'$

(16) Mary is [$_{XP}$ Op$_i$ either$_i$ [$_{DisjP}$ looking for PRO TO FIND a maid or looking for PRO TO FIND a cook]].

$[\![XP]\!]^{w,g} = [\![either_i\ DisjP]\!]^{w,\,g[i \to f_i]} : f_i \in D_{Chf}$

   a. $= [\![either_i]\!]^{w,\,g[i \to f_i]} ([\![DisjP]\!]^{w,\,g[i \to f_i]}) : f_i \in D_{Chf}$

           $= f_i(\{\lambda w'.\ \lambda x.\ x\ is\ looking\ for\ [\lambda w.\ Mary\ to\ find\ a\ maid\ in\ w]\ in\ w',$

           $\lambda w'.\ \lambda x.\ x\ is\ looking\ for\ [\lambda w.\ Mary\ to\ find\ a\ cook\ in\ w]\ in\ w'\}):$

           $f_i \in D_{Chf}$

   b. $[\![(16)]\!]^{w,g} = \lambda w''.\ \exists f_i.\ Chf\,(f_i)\ \&\ f_i(\{\lambda w'.\ \lambda x.\ x\ is\ looking\ for\ [\lambda w.\ Mary\ to\ find\ a\ maid\ in\ w]\ in\ w',\ \lambda w'.\ \lambda x.\ x\ is\ looking\ for\ [\lambda w.\ Mary\ to\ find\ a\ cook\ in\ w]\ in\ w'\})(w'')(Mary)$

So far, the first and the second hypotheses both account for the set of data examined. In order to tease apart the two hypotheses, I consider AltQ and YNQ data in the next section.

2.2   AltQ/YNQ Data Distinguish Hybrid Analyses

In this section, I turn to AltQ and YNQ data. As for the semantics of AltQs and YNQs, it is assumed here that the Question (Q) operator existent in the CP level in interrogatives has a different denotation in the two constructions. For AltQs, I adopt [10]'s *wh* operator that moves to take CP scope and leaves its restrictor in situ.[1]

[10]'s claim is that there is a *wh* operator (and/or the Q morpheme in C) that moves to the CP domain and takes CP scope while its trace is interpreted as a choice function variable. An AltQ (17a) has the LF representation in (17b). They propose that the Q operator and the *wh* operator in AltQs have the denotations in (18). The *wh* operator combined with the index does the work of rewriting the assignment function.

(17) AltQ example and its LF representation
    a. Did John drink coffee or tea?
    b. [$_{CP}$ wh i [$_{C'}$ Q [$_{IP}$ John drank [t$_i$ coffee or tea]]]] (cf. [10])
(18) Denotations of items

---

[1] Another, often cited, analysis of the semantics of AltQs is [11]'s analysis that makes use of focus alternative semantics. I take up the analysis in Sect. 3.

a. $\llbracket Q \rrbracket = \lambda q_{st}.\, \lambda w.\, \lambda p_{st}.\, p = q$

b. $\llbracket wh \rrbracket^{w,g} = \lambda R_{<Chf,\, <s,\, <st,\, t>\, >\, >}\, \lambda w.\, \lambda p.$
$[\exists f.\, Chf(f)\, \&\, R(f)(w)(p)]$, where $f \in D_{Chf}$

The derivation of (17b) proceeds as in (19) in the notation adopted here. The DisjP denotes a set of the disjuncts and the trace of the *wh* operator is taken to be a choice function variable that takes that set as its argument.

(19)   Derivation of (17b)

a. $\llbracket t_i \text{ coffee or tea} \rrbracket^{g[i \to f_i]} = f_i(\{coffee, tea\})$

b. $\llbracket IP \rrbracket^{w,\, g[i \to f_i]} = \lambda w'.\, \text{John drank } f_i(\{coffee, tea\}) \text{ in } w'$

c. $\llbracket C' \rrbracket^{w,\, g[i \to f_i]} = \lambda w.\, \lambda p.\, p = \lambda w'.\, \text{John drank } f_i\, (\{coffee, tea\}) \text{ in } w'$

d. $\llbracket CP \rrbracket^{w,g} = \lambda w.\, \lambda p.\, \exists f_i.\, Chf(f_i)\, \&\, p = \lambda w'.\, \text{John drank } f_i(\{coffee, tea\}) \text{ in } w'$

For YNQs, I assume that there is a distinct Q operator that derives a YNQ reading when the denotation of the IP in a question is a single proposition. This Q operator has a special semantic denotation which takes a single proposition and gives back the set of it and its negation as the question interpretation as in (20).[2] With this operator in the CP level, the interpretation of a YNQ (21a) is as in (21b). The Q operator takes the proposition denoted by the IP, and the meaning of the whole sentence is the set of the proposition and its negation, successfully deriving the YNQ reading.

(20) $\llbracket Q_{YNQ} \rrbracket^{w,g} = \lambda p.\, \{\lambda w.\, p(w),\, \lambda w.\, \neg p(w)\}$

(21)   A YNQ and its denotation

a. Q_{YNQ} Did John come?

b. $\llbracket (21a) \rrbracket^{w,g} = \{\lambda w.\, \text{John came in } w,\, \lambda w.\, \neg\text{John came in } w\}$

Let us now proceed to the discussion of whether the two hybrid analyses can handle the AltQ/YNQ data (8), repeated in (22).

(22)   Availability of question readings and the position of *either*

a. Did John see a maid or a cook? (AltQ/YNQ)

b. Did John see <u>either</u> a maid or a cook? (*AltQ/YNQ)

c. Did John <u>either</u> see a maid or a cook? (*AltQ/YNQ)

According to the first version of the hybrid analysis, there is no difference between (22a–c) in that the IPs in all of the sentences denote a single proposition. This is because of the choice function variable introduced by *or*, which is present in all of the sentences. The choice function variable takes the set denoted by the DisjP and gives back a single member of the set, and thus the denotation of the IP ends up as a single proposition. We can derive the YNQ reading for these sentences with the Q operator

---

[2] There are several other lines of research regarding the semantics of YNQs. [12], for example, takes the assumption that the denotation of a YNQ is a singleton set of its literal meaning (declarative meaning) as in (i).

(i) [[Can Jack come to tea]] = {Jack can come to tea}

Here, however, I maintain the simplest idea that questions denote the set of their possible answers and adopt the semantics of the YNQ operator in (20).

for YNQs in (20). For (23), which is the LF representation of (22b) with an overt *either* in its base position, the Q operator takes the proposition that the IP denotes and gives back the set of it and its negation, as in (24). The same account applies to the availability of the YNQ reading in (22a) and (22c).

(23) Q_{YNQ} John saw either a maid or a cook

(24) $[\![(23)]\!]^{w,g} = \{\lambda w.\ \exists f.\ \text{John saw } f(\{\text{a maid, a cook}\}) \text{ in } w, \lambda w.\ \neg\exists f.\ \text{John saw}$
$f(\{\text{a maid, a cook}\}) \text{ in } w\}$

However, the first version of the hybrid analysis cannot derive the AltQ reading in (22a). Making use of the *wh* operator that moves to take CP scope and whose trace is interpreted as a choice function variable (18) will give rise to two choice function variables in the LF structure of (22a): one originating from the *wh* operator and another from *or*. Once one of the two variables takes the set of the disjuncts as its argument, the result is a single member that the other variable is unable to operate over.

For example, consider example (17a) repeated in (25), whose underlying structure is as in (17b) repeated in (25a). If we combine this structure with the first version of the hybrid analysis, the denotation of the DisjP is as in (25b), where *or* introduces a choice function variable that takes as its argument the set of the disjuncts.

(25)   Did John drink coffee or tea?
   a. [$_{CP}$ wh i [$_{C'}$ Q [$_{IP}$ John drank [t_i coffee or tea]]]]
   b. $[\![\text{coffee or tea}]\!]^{w,g} = \lambda w.\ f\ (\{\text{coffee in } w, \text{tea in } w\})$

It is clear that (25b) cannot be the argument of the choice function variable introduced in the position of the trace of the *wh* operator, since (25b) is a single semantic interpretation that is not a set. It is impossible to derive the AltQ interpretation of (25) with the first version of the hybrid analysis.

How about the second version of the hybrid analysis? I take there to be two possible structures for (22a): *either* being completely absent and *either* being covert. When there is a covert *either* adjacent to the DisjP in (22a), the structure is identical to (22b), analyzed in (24) above. The existence of *either* accounts for the availability of the YNQ reading in (22a–c) in a way similar to (24). The second version of the hybrid analysis also successfully obtains the AltQ reading of (22a) with the Q operator and the *wh* operator in (18). Since *either* is absent, the only choice function variable in the structure is the one originating from the *wh* operator. The computation thus proceeds in exactly the same manner as (19):

(26)   Did John see a maid or a cook? (= (22a))
   a. [cp Wh i [c' Q [ip John saw [t_i a maid or a cook]]]]

   b.
$$[\![CP]\!]^{w,g} = [\![Wh]\!]^{w,g}\ ([\![i\,C']\!]^{w,g})$$
$$= [\![Wh]\!]^{w,g}\ \left(\lambda f_i.\ [\![C']\!]^{w,g[i \to f_i]}\right)$$
$$= [\![Wh]\!]^{w,g}\ \left(\lambda f_i.\ [\![Q]\!]^{w,g[i \to f_i]}\right)\ \left([\![IP]\!]^{w,g[i \to f_i]}\right)$$
$$= [\![Wh]\!]^{w,g}(\lambda f_i.\ [\![Q]\!]^{w,g[i \to f_i]}\ (\lambda w'.\ \text{John saw } f_i(\{\text{a maid, a cook}\}) \text{ in } w'))$$
$$= [\![Wh]\!]^{w,g}(\lambda f_i.\lambda w.\ \lambda p.\ p = \lambda w'.\ \text{John saw } f_i(\{\text{a maid, a cook}\}) \text{ in } w')$$
$$= \lambda w.\ \lambda p.[\exists f_i.\ \text{Chf}(f_i)\ \&\ p = \lambda w'.\ \text{John saw } f_i(\{\text{a maid, a cook}\}) \text{ in }$$
$$w'] : f_i \in D_{\text{Chf}}$$

Now it has been shown that the second version of the hybrid analysis, namely the ellipsis analysis + the choice function analysis of *either*, accounts for both the wide scope *or* reading data and the AltQ/YNQ data.

3 Comparison with Other Analysis

3.1 The Focus Alternative Semantics Analysis

[11] investigate the semantics of AltQs based on the focus alternative semantics of [13] and comment on the role of *either* in the *either/or* construction.

The basic idea of focus alternative semantics is that focused items have two semantic values: an ordinary semantic value and a focus semantic value. For example, in sentence (27), the focused item *John* has its ordinary denotation as its ordinary semantic value (27a) and a set of alternatives (of the same semantic type) as its focus semantic value (27b). A sentence that has a focused item in it also has an ordinary semantic value (27c) and a focus semantic value (27d), which is a set of propositions in which the position of the focused item varies according to the focus semantic value of the focused item.

(27) $[John]_F$ left.

    a. $[\![John_F]\!]^o = John$

    b. $[\![John_F]\!]^f = \{John, Bill, Amelie, \ldots\}$

    c. $[\![John_F \, left]\!]^o = \lambda w. \, John \, left \, in \, w$

    d. $[\![John_F \, left]\!]^f = \{p: p = \lambda w. \, x \, left \, in \, w \mid x \in D\}$

             $= \{\lambda w. \, John \, left \, in \, w, \lambda w. \, Bill \, left \, in \, w, \lambda w. \, Amelie \, left \, in \, w, \ldots\}$

Building on the idea that *either* is focus-sensitive [11, 14, 15] propose that *either* operates over the focus semantic value of its sister, just like focus-sensitive items like *only* do, as we see immediately below. Their denotation of *either XP* is in (28), where *either* is proposed to be a focus sensitive operator that takes its sister DisjP as its argument as in (29) and gives rise to "closure" as in (30) (note that this denotation is primarily aimed to capture the "epistemic" reading of *or* discussed in [16] among others).

(28) $[\![either \, XP]\!]^o = for \, all \, q \, in \, [\![XP]\!]^f : \, may \, q \, \& \, \neg \exists p \, \big[for \, all \, q \, in \, [\![XP]\!]^f : \, p \cap q$

    $= \{\} \, \& \, may \, p]$

(29) $[\![either \, it \, is \, raining \, or \, it \, is \, snowing]\!]^o = may \, r \, \& \, may \, s \, \& \, \neg \exists p \, [p \cap r = \{\} \, \& \, p$

    $\cap \, s = \{\} \, \& \, may \, p]$

(30) Either it is raining or it is snowing. $\approx$ It is possible that it is raining and it is possible that it is snowing and there are no other relevant possibilities.

In order to support the claim that focus-sensitive items such as *only* access the focus alternatives of their sister, [11] present an analysis based on focus alternative semantics to account for intervention effects in AltQs. *Only*, a focus-sensitive item, has the semantics in (31).

(31) $[\![\,only\ \phi\,]\!]^o = \left[\lambda w.\ \text{for all p such that } p(w) = 1 \& p \in [\![\,\phi\,]\!]^f\right] (p = [\![\,\phi\,]\!]^o)$

(31) means that of all the alternative propositions introduced by the focus semantic value of the sister of *only*, the only true one is the ordinary semantic value of the sister. Thus in the sample sentence (32), the overall meaning is equivalent to (32b).

(32) $[\![\,\text{Only John}_F\ \text{left}\,]\!]^o$

a. $= \lambda w.\ [\text{for all p such that } p(w) = 1 \& p \in \{\lambda w.\ x\ \text{left in } w\ |\ x \in D\}]\,(p = \{\lambda w.\ \text{John left in } w\})$

b. $= \lambda w.\ [\text{for all x such that x left in } w]\,(x = \text{John})$

[11] present data like (33a, b) to show that *only* gives rise to intervention effects in AltQs. When *only* structurally intervenes between the DisjP and the Q operator in the CP layer, an AltQ reading is unavailable.

(33) Intervention effects of *only*

a. ? Did John or Susan introduce Sue to only Mary$_F$?

b. ?* Did only Mary$_F$ introduce Sue to Bill or to Tom?

According to [11], the Q operator in *wh*-Questions takes the focus semantic value of its sister and makes it the ordinary semantic value of the whole sentence as in (34).[3]

(34) Two semantic values of *wh*-Questions

a. $[\![\,Q\,\phi\,]\!]^o = [\![\,\phi\,]\!]^f$

b. $[\![\,Q\,\phi\,]\!]^f = \{[\![\,Q\,\phi\,]\!]^o\}$

[11] argue that this Q operator derives the AltQ reading of (35) (although they argue against the idea that AltQs are a kind of *wh*-Question).

(35) Did the program execute or the computer crash?

$= [_{CP}\ Q\ [_{DisjP}\ [\text{the program executed}]\ \text{or}\ [\text{the computer crashed}]]]$ (cf. [11])

[11] further claim that the ordinary semantic value of a DisjP is the union of the disjuncts while the focus semantic value is the set of the disjuncts. Based on [17]'s analysis, [11] argue for an ordinary semantic value in (36a) and a focus semantic value in (36b) for the DisjP in the AltQ in (36).[4]

---

[3] Note that this semantics for *wh*-Questions and AltQs does not account for the AltQ/YNQ data discussed in the previous section, under either the first or the second version of the hybrid analysis. If we adopt the semantics in (34) in the first hybrid analysis, the choice function variable is closed via Existential Closure and the IP always denotes a single proposition. The semantics of the question would be the singleton set of this proposition. However, this is not the intended AltQ reading. A similar problem arises if we adopt (34) for the second hybrid analysis too.

[4] According to [17], the denotation of *or* is set-theoretic union in both (36a) and (36b). In (36a), *or* takes the ordinary semantic value of the disjuncts, in this case two propositions, and gives back their union. This is equivalent to the meaning in (36a), a set of worlds where the program executed or the computer crashed. In (36b), on the other hand, *or* takes the focus semantic value of the disjuncts,

(36) Did [$_\text{DisjP}$ the program execute or the computer crash]?
  a. $[\![\,\text{DisjP}\,]\!]^{\circ} = \lambda w.$ the program executed in w or the computer crashed in w
  b. $[\![\,\text{DisjP}\,]\!]^{f} = \{\lambda w.$ the program executed in w, $\lambda w.$ the computer crashed in w$\}$

By combining the denotation of DisjPs with that of the Q operator in *wh*-Questions, the AltQ reading of (35) is obtained. From (34a), the ordinary semantic value of the interrogative (35) is the focus semantic value of the DisjP, i.e. (36b). Based on previous research that analyzes the semantic denotation of questions as the set of their possible answers (cf. [18]), this is equivalent to the AltQ interpretation.

Now let us proceed to the discussion of how *only* intervenes between the DisjP and the Q operator. For (33b), [11] assume a (simpified) underlying structure (37), in which the DisjP has two VPs as disjuncts. Then, the denotation of the DisjP is the set of the denotations of the disjuncts as in (38) and the DisjP combines with *Mary*, which is the associate of *only* and carries a Focus intonation. The result is as in (39). After that, *only* makes use of the two semantic values to derive the semantics in (40). With the semantic work of the Q operator in (34), the overall interpretation of the whole sentence results in (41). Since this is not an AltQ interpretation, [11] account for the intervention effects of *only* in AltQs.

(37) Q [$_\text{XP}$ only [$_\text{IP}$ Mary$_\text{F}$ [$_\text{DisjP}$ [introduce Sue to Bill] or [~~introduce Sue~~ to Tom]]]]?
(38) Denotation of DisjP
  a. $[\![\,\text{DisjP}\,]\!]^{\circ} = \lambda x.\, \lambda w.$ x introduces Sue to Bill in w or x introduces Sue to Tom in w
  b. $[\![\,\text{DisjP}\,]\!]^{f} = \{\lambda x.\, \lambda w.$ x introduces Sue to Bill in w, $\lambda x.\, \lambda w.$ x introduces Sue to Tom in .w$\}$
(39) Denotation of IP
  a. $[\![\,\text{IP}\,]\!]^{\circ} = \lambda w.$ Mary introduces Sue to Bill in w or Mary introduces Sue to Tom in w
  b. $[\![\,\text{IP}\,]\!]^{f} = \{\lambda w.$ x introduces Sue to Bill in w, $\lambda w.$ x introduces Sue to Tom in w $|$ x $\in$ D$_e\} = \{\lambda w.$ Mary introduces Sue to Bill in w, $\lambda w.$ Jane introduces Sue to Bill in w , $\lambda w.$ Mary introduces Sue to Tom in w, $\lambda w.$ Amy introduces Sue to Tom in w, . . .$\}$
(40) Denotation of XP
  a. $[\![\,\text{XP}\,]\!]^{\circ} = \lambda w.$ [for all p such that p(w) = 1 & p $\in \{\lambda w.$ x introduces Sue to Bill in w, $\lambda w.$ x introduces Sue to Tom in w $|$ x $\in$ D$_e\}$] (p = $\lambda w.$ Mary introduces Sue to Bill in w or Mary introduces Sue to Tom in w)
  b. $[\![\,\text{XP}\,]\!]^{f} = \{\,[\![\,\text{XP}\,]\!]^{\circ}\,\}$
(41) $[\![\,(37)\,]\!]^{\circ} = \{\,[\![\,\text{XP}\,]\!]^{\circ}\,\}$

(Footnote 4 continued)
namely two singleton sets, and gives back their union. This is equivalent to (36b), a set of the focus semantic values of the disjuncts. Here I use the original analysis of [17] in (36), and not the version of [11] in which the focus semantic value of a DisjP is a set containing the two ordinary meanings of the disjuncts.

Thus, adopting focus alternative semantics enables us to account for the semantics of *only* and the intervention effect it induces in AltQs, and [11] suggest extending this analysis to *either*.

There are, however, problems in the analysis. I discuss them next.

3.2 Problems of the Focus Alternative Semantics Analysis

The focus alternative semantics analysis faces several difficulties when we try to explain the data introduced in the previous section. I first describe an empirical problem, and then move on to theoretical problems.

The first problem is that the analysis makes a wrong prediction for the scope of disjunction. Recall that, as repeated below, (42a) is ambiguous between wide scope and narrow scope *or* readings whereas (42b–d) only have a wide scope *or* reading.

(42)   Narrow and wide scope *or*
      a. Mary is looking for either a maid or a cook.
      b. Mary is either looking for a maid or looking for a cook.
      c. Mary either is looking for a maid or is looking for a cook.
      d. Either Mary is looking for a maid or Mary is looking for a cook.

According to the denotation in (28), *either* makes use of the focus semantic value of its sister and gives back an ordinary semantic value. We thus have no way to get the wide scope *or* reading of (42a). Claiming that *either* projects up the focus semantic value is not a possible move, taking into consideration AltQ/YNQ data:

(43)   Availability of question readings and the position of *either*
      a. Did John see a maid or a cook? (AltQ/YNQ)
      b. Did John see either a maid or a cook? (*AltQYNQ)
      c. Did John either see a maid or a cook? (*AltQ/YNQ)

According to [11], the AltQ reading available for sentences like (43a) comes from the focus semantic value that projects up to the TP level and is lifted to the ordinary semantic value by the work of the covert Q operator in the C position. Given that the AltQ reading is unavailable when *either* comes in, it is clear that *either* does not pass up the focus semantic value of its sister node but closes the alternatives in the position it occupies. It thus seems difficult to explain the availability of the wide scope *or* reading available for sentences with *either* adjacent to the DisjP by giving *either* some semantic role related to focus.

Aside from the empirical problem, the focus alternative semantics analysis in the form introduced in the previous section has a theoretical problem in the semantics of the DisjP and *only*. Consider again the derivation of (37) in (38)–(41) above. Two problems exist in this derivation. First, the ordinary semantic value of the XP shown in (40) means that, of all p such that p is true and p is a member of the focus semantic value of the IP (a set of propositions of the form $\lambda w.\ x\ introduces\ Sue\ to\ Bill\ in\ w$ or of the form $\lambda w.\ x\ introduces\ Sue\ to\ Tom\ in\ w$, where x is a focus alternative to *Mary*), the only true one is the proposition $\lambda w.\ Mary\ introduces\ Sue\ to\ Bill\ in\ w\ or\ Mary\ introduces\ Sue\ to\ Tom\ in\ w$. However, note that in the focus semantic value of the IP, there are the propositions $\lambda w.\ Mary\ introduces\ Sue\ to\ Bill\ in\ w$ and $\lambda w.\ Mary\ introduces\ Sue$

to Tom in w. These propositions are presupposed to be false according to the semantics of *only*, since they are not equal to the proposition that is asserted to be true, $\lambda w.$ *Mary introduces Sue to Bill in w or Mary introduces Sue to Tom in w*. Thus, for the disjoined proposition to be true, at least one of its disjuncts has to be true, but the given semantics requires both disjuncts to be false. This renders (37) necessarily false. Although (37) is a degraded example, it is not intuitively necessarily false. It is easy to see that the problem lies at least in part in the semantics of *only* itself and the problem is carried over to acceptable sentences.

Following [19], we can avoid this problem by modifying the semantics of *only* to make use of entailment (cf. [20]):

(44) $\llbracket \text{only } \phi \rrbracket^{\circ} = \lambda w. \forall p \left[p(w) = 1 \, \& \, p \in \llbracket \phi \rrbracket^{f} \right] (p \supseteq \llbracket \phi \rrbracket^{\circ}) : \llbracket \phi \rrbracket^{\circ} = 1$

I next turn to the second problem of (38)–(41). Adopting the revised interpretation of *only* in (44), the ordinary semantic value of the XP shown in (40) means that, of all p such that p is true and p is a member of the focus semantic value of the IP (a set of propositions of the form $\lambda w.$ *x introduces Sue to Bill in w* or of the form $\lambda w.$ *x introduces Sue to Tom in w*, where x is a focus alternative to *Mary*), the only true one(s) is entailed by the proposition $\lambda w.$ *Mary introduces Sue to Bill in w or Mary introduces Sue to Tom in w*. However, neither the proposition $\lambda w.$ *Mary introduces Sue to Bill in w* or the proposition $\lambda w.$ *Mary introduces Sue to Tom in w* is entailed by the proposition $\lambda w.$ *Mary introduces Sue to Bill in w or Mary introduces Sue to Tom in w* (and in fact, there is no such proposition in the focus semantic value of IP that is entailed by $\lambda w.$ *Mary introduces Sue to Bill in w or Mary introduces Sue to Tom in w*). Thus there is no p which is a member of the focus semantic value of the IP and, at the same time, is entailed by the ordinary semantic value of IP, and the semantics in (40) then comes out true only if nobody introduced Sue to Bill and nobody introduced Sue to Tom. This difficulty, which still exists when the revised denotation of *only* is adopted, arises from the semantics of DisjPs, in which the ordinary semantic value is not a member of the focus semantic value.

Notice that this problem is avoided by adopting the compositional semantics of DisjPs proposed in this paper. I have proposed that *or* has a set-forming function. In its ordinary semantic value, *or* takes two arguments of the same type and forms a set of them as in (45a). Its focus semantic value is a singleton set of this function, as in (45b).

(45)   Compositional semantics of DisjPs
   a. $\llbracket \text{or} \rrbracket^{g, \circ} = \lambda x_{\sigma}. \lambda y_{\sigma}. \{x, y\}$
   b. $\llbracket \text{or} \rrbracket^{g, f} = \{\lambda x_{\sigma}. \lambda y_{\sigma}. \{x, y\}\}$

With this semantics, the semantics of sentence (46) can be computed fully compositionally with the semantics of *either* in the present proposal. On the assumption that subjects reconstruct at LF in their base position, inside the VP, the LF representation has *John* below *only* and covert *either* in its base position.[5]

---

[5] Note that there is another, perhaps a more salient reading, in which John only saw Bill, among other candidates, or John only saw Sue, among other candidates, but the speaker forgot which John

(46) John only saw Bill$_F$ or Sue$_F$. = Only [$_{IP}$ John saw [$_{XP}$Op$_i$ either$_i$ Bill$_F$ or Sue$_F$]].

The ordinary semantic value is the result of applying the choice function introduced by *either* to the set of disjuncts, as in (47a). The focus semantic value is the result of combining a singleton set of a choice function, which is the focus semantic value of *either*, and the set of the sets of the alternatives of the disjuncts, which is the focus semantic value of the DisjP, via pointwise function application. This is shown in (47b). The alternatives of the focus semantic value expand up to the IP level, resulting in (48b). Notice that *either* and Op are necessarily above the DisjP to resolve a type mismatch that would occur without them when *saw* combines with the DisjP.

(47) Denotation of XP

    a. $[\![\,\mathrm{XP}\,]\!]^{g[i\to f_i],o} = f_i(\{\mathrm{Bill, Sue}\})$: $f_i \in D_{Chf}$

    b.

        $[\![\,\mathrm{XP}\,]\!]^{g[i\to f_i],f} = \{f(A): f \in \{f_i\}$ & $A \in \{\{x,y\} \mid x \in [\![\,\mathrm{Bill_F}\,]\!]^{g,f}$ and $y \in [\![\,\mathrm{Sue_F}\,]\!]^{g,f}\}\}: f_i \in D_{Chf}$

(48) Denotation of IP

    a. $[\![\,\mathrm{IP}\,]\!]^{g[i\to f_i],o} = $ John saw $f_i(\{\mathrm{Bill, Sue}\})$: $f_i \in D_{Chf}$

    b.

        $[\![\,\mathrm{IP}\,]\!]^{g[i\to f_i],f} = \{$John saw x: x $\in \{f(A): f \in \{f_i\}$ & $A \in \{\{x,y\} \mid x \in [\![\,\mathrm{Bill_F}\,]\!]^{g,f}$ and $y \in [\![\,\mathrm{Sue_F}\,]\!]^{g,f}\}\}\}: f_i \in D_{Chf}$

Now the revised denotation of *only* with entailment in (44) comes into the structure. The interpretation of (46) is given in (49), assuming that Existential Closure of the choice function variable takes place above the whole proposition. This means that, for a particular way of picking out a value from a pair of disjuncts, every true sentence of the form *John saw A or B* using that way of picking values is entailed by the result of using that way of picking values in *John saw Bill or Sue*. This is the intended reading.

(49) $[\![\,(46)\,]\!]^{g[i\to f_i],o} = \exists f_i. f_i \in D_{Chf}$ and for all p such that p(w) = 1 & p $\in$ {John saw

    x: x $\in$ {f(A): f $\in$ {f$_i$} & A $\in \left\{\{x,y\} \mid x \in [\![\mathrm{Bill_F}]\!]^{g,f}$ and $y \in [\![\mathrm{Sue_F}]\!]^{g,f}\right\}\}\}$: p

    $\supseteq$ John saw $f_i(\{\mathrm{Bill, Sue}\})$

(Footnote 5 continued)

actually saw. This reading falls out from the present analysis by assuming that the covert *either* floats up to a higher position and (46) can have the LF representation in (i).

    (i) Op$_i$ either$_i$ [John only saw Bill$_F$ or John only saw Sue$_F$]

From the discussion in this section, it is clear that the present claim not only covers most of the data but also has theoretical advantages over [11]'s claim reviewed in the previous section.[6]

4 Conclusion

In this paper, I have investigated in detail the semantics of the *either/or* construction and AltQs in English. It has been shown that the proposed analysis, namely a hybrid analysis of an ellipsis analysis and a choice function analysis of *either*, accounts for the availability of the wide scope *or* reading and the distribution of AltQ/YNQ readings in English.

References

1. Partee, B., Rooth, M.E.: Generalized conjunction and type ambiguity. In: Bäuerle, R., Schwarze, C., von Stechow, A. (eds.) Meaning, Use, and Interpretation of Language, pp. 360–383. Walter de Gruyter, Berlin (1983)
2. Rooth, M.E., Partee, B.: Conjunction, type ambiguity, and wide scope 'or'. In: 1st West Coast Conference on Formal Linguistics, Stanford, CA, pp. 353–362 (1982)
3. Larson, R.K.: On the syntax of disjunction scope. Nat. Lang. Linguist. Theory **3**(2), 217–264 (1985). https://doi.org/10.1007/BF00133841
4. Winter, Y.: On some scopal asymmetries of coordination. In: Bennis, H., Everaert M., Reuland, E. (eds.) Interface Strategies: Proceedings of the Colloquium, pp. 387–405. KNAW, Royal Netherlands Academy of Arts and Sciences, Amsterdam (2000)
5. Schlenker, P.: Scopal independence: a note on branching and wide scope readings of indefinites and disjunctions. J. Semant. **23**(3), 281–314 (2006). https://doi.org/10.1093/jos/ffl005
6. Winter, Y.: Flexibility Principles in Boolean Semantics: The Interpretation of Coordination, Plurality, and Scope in Natural Language. MIT Press, Cambridge (2001)
7. Schwarz, B.: On the syntax of either ... or. Nat. Lang. Linguist. Theory **17**(2), 339–370 (1999). https://doi.org/10.1023/A:1006046306942
8. Larson, R., den Dikken, M., Ludlow, P.: Intensional transitive verbs and abstract clausal complementation (1997). http://semlab5.sbs.sunysb.edu/~rlarson/itv.pdf. Accessed 20 Oct 2019
9. Alonso-Ovalle, L.: Disjunction in alternative semantics. Ph.D. dissertation, University of Massachusetts (2006)
10. Romero, M., Han, C.: Focus, ellipsis and the semantics of alternative questions. In: Beyssade, C., Bonami, O., Hofherr, P.C., Corblin, F. (eds.) Empirical Issues in Formal Syntax and Semantics, vol. 4, pp. 291–307. Presses Universitaires de Paris Sorbonne, Paris (2003)

---

[6] It seems, however, that the intervention effect of *only* cannot be obtained without a focus alternative semantics for questions. Since, as noted in footnote 3, a focus alternative semantics for questions does not account for AltQ/YNQ data, this point remains as a problem. I leave this point for future research.

11. Beck, S., Kim, S.-S.: Intervention effects in alternative questions. J. Comp. German. Linguist. **9**(3), 165–208 (2006). https://doi.org/10.1007/s10828-006-9005-2

12. Büring, D.: On D-trees, beans, and B-accents. Linguist. Philos. **26**(5), 511–545 (2003). https://doi.org/10.1023/A:1025887707652

13. Rooth, M.E.: A theory of focus interpretation. Nat. Lang. Semant. **1**(1), 75–116 (1992). https://doi.org/10.1007/BF02342617

14. Hendriks, P.: 'Either' as a focus particle (2003). http://www.let.rug.nl/hendriks/papers/either03.pdf. Accessed 20 Oct 2019

15. Den Dikken, M.: Either-float and the syntax of co-or-dination. Nat. Lang. Linguist. Theory **24**, 689–749 (2006). https://doi.org/10.1007/s11049-005-2503-0

16. Zimmermann, T.E.: Free choice disjunction and epistemic possibility. Nat. Lang. Semant. **8**(4), 255–290 (2000). https://doi.org/10.1023/A:1011255819284

17. von Stechow, A.: Focusing and background operators. In: Werner, A. (ed.) Discourse Particles: Descriptive and Theoretical Investigations on the Logical, Syntactic and Pragmatic Properties of Discourse Particles in German, pp. 37–84. John Benjamins, Amsterdam (1991)

18. Hamblin, C.L.: Questions in montague English. Found. Lang. **10**(1), 41–53 (1973)

19. Krifka, M.: Focus and presupposition in dynamic interpretation. J. Semant. **10**(4), 269–300 (1993). https://doi.org/10.1093/jos/10.4.269

20. van Rooij, R., Schulz, K.: Only: meaning and implications. In: Aloni, M., Butler, A., Dekker, P. (eds.) Questions in Dynamic Semantics, pp. 193–223. Elsevier, Amsterdam (2007)

Anticipative and Ethic Modalities: Japanese *Hazu* and *Beki*

Lukas Rieser[(⊠)]

Tokyo University of Agriculture and Technology, Fuchu, Japan
lukasjrieser@gmail.com

Abstract. The Japanese modals *hazu* and *beki* respectively correspond to alleged weak epistemic and deontic necessity readings of English *ought*. I propose a novel analysis of weak necessity as **generic** as opposed to the **individual** modality of both strong necessity and possibility modals, using ingredients from extant analysis of modality in a possible-world framework. On my view, the modal flavor of *hazu* is **anticipative**, replacing the epistemic modal base with a circumstantial one, that of *beki ethic*, differing from deontic modality in that its replaces individuated with idealistic norms. Both share the absence of agent-variables in the conversational background, which distinguishes them from individual modals. I conclude that the view from Japanese with its articulated and unambiguous modal inventory explains the strong/weak necessity distinction better than extant analyses.

Keywords: Modality · Weak necessity · Japanese

1 How to Say OUGHT (and MUST) in Japanese

In this section, I show that the Japanese modals *hazu* and *beki* are unambiguous correspondents to epistemic and deontic readings of English weak necessity modals. Summarizing some relevant points from the discussion on weak necessity in English, I argue that the usual labels are at best partially correct as on my view, *hazu* and *beki* are neither "weak" in terms of the strength of necessity they encode, nor actually epistemic/deontic in flavor.

1.1 Weak (vs. Strong) Necessity Modals

English *should* and *ought* (*to*) have been labeled "weak necessity" modals to capture empirical contrasts with their "strong" counterparts *must* and *have to*. I henceforth write MUST for strong, OUGHT for weak necessity modals in English, glossing over possible differences between lexical variants. Both MUST and OUGHT are ambiguous between epistemic and deontic readings, as in these examples:

(1)   Alex {must/has to} be home by now.

(2)   Alex {should/ought to} be home by now.

© Springer Nature Switzerland AG 2020
M. Sakamoto et al. (Eds.): JSAI-isAI 2019, LNAI 12331, pp. 309–324, 2020.
https://doi.org/10.1007/978-3-030-58790-1_20

MUST in (1) is ambiguous between an epistemic reading, on which it conveys a speaker assumption that Alex is home by now, and a deontic reading on which Alex has an according obligation. OUGHT in (2) shows the same ambiguity, with the difference that there is more room for the actual situation to differ—on the epistemic reading, the degree of speaker conviction is perceived as lower, on the deontic reading, the obligation as less binding. To reflect observations like this, the two readings of OUGHT have been labeled "weak epistemic necessity" and "weak deontic necessity" (henceforth also WEN, WDN), as opposed to the corresponding strong necessity readings of MUST (henceforth also SEN, SDN).

1.2 Epistemic MUST and OUGHT in Japanese

The epistemic readings of English (1) and (2) are translated to Japanese in (3) and (4) with the unambiguously epistemic *nichigainai* (corresponding to MUST) and *hazu* (corresponding to OUGHT).

(3)   Alex-wa imagoro kaet-teiru   nichigainai.
       PN-TOP now   return-RES.NPST MOD
       "Alex {must/has to} be home by now."

(4)   Alex-wa imagoro kaetteiru   hazu da.
       PN-TOP now   return-RES.NPST MOD COP
       "Alex {should/ought to} be home by now."

The lack of epistemic/deontic ambiguity in modern Japanese (except for some highly marginal cases) is well-documented, *cf.* Narrog [11], and holds for both strong and weak necessity modals. I maintain that due to this lack of ambiguity, Japanese allows for a clearer view on basic modal flavors than English. Below, I summarize some points from the literature on WEN, showing that issues raised w.r.t. OUGHT also apply to *hazu*, and outline my view on its modal flavor.

Strength and Entailment Patterns. The label "weak" for OUGHT has been motivated by the claim that it is logically weaker, and hence entailed by, its "strong" counterpart MUST, *cf.* Horn [3]. On this view, weak epistemic necessity OUGHT must entail the epistemic possiblity (henceforth also EP) modal MAY[1], so that an entailment pattern {MUST ⊃ OUGHT ⊃ MAY} holds. If this is on the right track, the straightforward assumption on a Kratzer/Lewis-style view of modality as quantification over possible worlds would be that this reflects quantificational entailment—reducing {SEN ⊃ WEN ⊃ EP} to a parallel entailment pattern of quantifiers over possible worlds {all ⊃ most ⊃ some}.

There are, however, numerous counterexamples to this "traditional" entailment view of WEN. Copley [2], for instance, provides example (5), shown alongside its Japanese translation in (6).

---

[1] Written for English *may* and *might*, ignoring differences.

(5)   The beer {#must/should/#may} be cold by now, but it isn't.

(6)   Biiru-wa imagoro hie-tei-ru...
       beer-TOP by_now cool-RES-NPST
            ...{#nichigainai/hazu da/#kamoshirenai} ga, hie-tei-nai.
            MOD   MOD   COP MOD   but cool-RES-NEG

(5) and (6) show that in both English and Japanese, alleged WEN-modals are compatible with a speaker belief that their prejacent is false, in contrast to their SEN and EP counterparts. This is to say that the entailment pattern {SEN ⊃ WEN ⊃ EP} cannot be right, as the acceptability of alleged WEN-modals *should* and *hazu* would have to entail that of the logically weaker EP-modals *may* and *kamoshirenai*.[2]

Furthermore, the compatibility of the (weak) necessity claim of *should* and *hazu* with a speaker belief that its prejacent is false suggests that these modals are either interpreted differently from SEN and EP, or that they are not epistemic modals after all. Below, I discuss two solutions that have been proposed in the literature and outline my own view on *hazu*.

Weakness as Non-factual Interpretation. A first line of analyses attempts to salvage an epistemic modal analysis of OUGHT with universal quantification by making additional assumptions on its evaluation. Copley [2] analyses OUGHT as an epistemic necessity modal conveying that its prejacent holds at the epistemically most plausible worlds, but, in contrast to MUST, does not make a claim that the actual world is among them.

Okano and Mori [13] analyze Japanese *hazu* in a similar spirit, building on Silk [15] to propose that *hazu* does not require "acceptability conditions" for the epistemic necessity claim to be part of the common ground. Rather, *hazu* updates the modal base with such conditions before making its claim, explaining how WEN-claims are not necessarily factual.

In an update of [15], Silk [16] proposes that the premises on which the speaker judges epistemic necessity are verified against the actual world in the case of OUGHT, but not MUST, a purely interpretational difference. Thus, the speaker can felicitously make an epistemic necessity claim while knowing some premise of it to be false, also covering plain counterfactual cases like (5).

OUGHT as a Normality Modal. Another way to explain the apparent weakness of OUGHT without weaker quantification is to abandon the view that it is an epistemic modal altogether, thus allowing for counterfactual claims, and stipulate the existence of a root modal flavor with properties observed from alleged weak epistemic readings.

Yalcin [19] implements a suggestion from von Fintel and Iatridou [18] that the alleged epistemic reading of OUGHT represents a root modal flavor with a "normality" ordering source. This ordering source differs from a deontic one in that it orders worlds not by compliance with rules or norms, but by whether or

---

[2] For space, I ignore the possiblity to explain the badness of EP as an implicature.

not they are expected relative to an information state. Thus, OUGHT conveys that its prejacent holds at maximally normal worlds and thus represents an expected state of affairs or outcome, but is not sensitive to whether the prejacent is included in the information state this expectation relies on.

***Hazu* as an Anticipative Modal.** I analyze *hazu* as a root modal, more in line with the second camp, first and foremost based on the assumption that modal flavors realized with separate lexical items in Japanese are distinct not only in the way they are evaluated against the conversational background. However, rather than a distinctive "normality" ordering, I propose that the ordering source of *hazu* is plain and simple stereotypical, as has been proposed for (strong) epistemic necessity modals like MUST, but coupled with a circumstantial, rather than epistemic, modal base to yield a flavor I label **anticipative**.

With an analysis of *hazu* as circumstantial/stereotypical modal, I do not argue against any of the analytical decisions in previous analyses of WEN as root modals—it is entirely possible that an analysis of root stereotypical modality requires some or all of the refinements proposed by Yalcin [19] for "normality". I do claim, however, that *hazu* (if not necessarily WEN modals in other languages) represents a basic modal flavor, rather than one derived from, and thus likely more complex than others, and that it is worth pursuing the most simple assumption that this flavor is a combination of a modal base and ordering source also found in other modals rather than an ordering unique to *hazu*.

1.3   Deontic MUST and OUGHT in Japanese

Things appear less complex for deontic than epistemic OUGHT, as the question of (counter)factuality does not arise as acutely—neither a weaker nor a stronger obligation is incompatible with non-compliance. Example (7) comparing *ought* and *must* from von Fintel and Itariadou [18], along with a Japanese translation with the correspondents *beki* and *-nakerebanaranai* in (8), illustrates intuitions on strength of obligation.

(7)   Everybody ought to wash their hands, employees must.

(8)   Minna-wa   te-o   arau beki da ga,...
       everyone-TOP hand-ACC wash MOD COP but

                    ...jugyooin-wa   kanarazu   arawa-nakerebanaranai.
                    employees-TOP without_fail wash-MOD

The question is how WDN differs from SDN to be interpreted as a less binding obligation if weaker quantification is not the right path of analysis, as shown for the epistemic readings of OUGHT and MUST. Below, I discuss some observations from the literature and outline my view on Japanese *beki*.

Weaker Context-Dependence. Silk [16] analyzes deontic OUGHT parallel to its epistemic reading, citing the following examples, where (9-a) and (9-b) are setups which influence the felicity of the modals appearing in (10). The context is one in which the question is whether to fight for one's country, or to care for one's ailing mother, and (11) shows a Japanese translation.

(9)   a.   Family is very important.
       b.   Family is most important—more important than country.

(10)   I agree. You {ought to/must} tend to your mother.

(11)   Un, haha-no   kaigo-o   {suru-beki da/shi-nakerebanaranai}.
        yes mom-GEN care-ACC do-MOD   COP   do-MOD

Silk reports that OUGHT is preferred for setup (9-a), MUST for (9-b), and takes this as support for an analysis that OUGHT does not require premises to be checked against the actual situation—in the deontic case, this means conflicting obligations do not need to be weighted against each other. For (10), OUGHT is thus preferred when only the importance of family is considered, whereas MUST is preferred when the relevant conflicting norms (family vs. country) have been weighed and family came out on top. In Japanese, however, *beki* is intuitively preferred in both cases, raising the possibility that this factuality effect is linked to deontic/epistemic ambiguity in English.

Subjectivity in WDNs. As for the norms typically associated with *beki*, Moriya and Horie [10] provide (12), shown here with an English translation (13) in which OUGHT and MUST behave parallel to their Japanese counterparts.

(12)   Nihon-de-wa   kuruma-wa hidari-gawa-o...
        Japan-LOC-TOP car-TOP   left-side-ACC
                        ...too- {??-ru-beki   da/-ranakerebanaranai}.
                        pass   NPST-MOD COP

       MOD

(13)   In Japan, cars {??should / must} drive on the left.

On Moriya and Horie's view, *-nakerebanaranai* is used when an obligation, here to drive on the left, is due to external factors, whereas *beki* conveys a personal evaluation of the speaker, making it more subjective. Hence, in the case of rules such as traffic laws, *beki* is dispreferred (as is *should* in the English translation). This differs from Silk's view on MUST and OUGHT, on which there is no qualitative difference between the rules in the background of the respective modals, but rather in whether or not all actually applicable rules are considered.

***Beki* as an Idealistic Modal.** My view on *beki* differs from both of the afore-mentioned in that I take the norms it applied to be qualitively different from that of deontic *-nakerebanaranai*, but not necessarily less subjective. I take *-nakerebanaranai*, like MUST, to convey obligations resulting from the application of rules to an individual case, and *beki* obligations based on generic ideals, such as ethic norms, that are universally applicable. In (11), *beki* is preferred because the norms in the conversational background are ethic principles, whereas in (12)

-nakerebanaranai is preferred because the application of traffic laws and the resulting obligation depend on the individual case. *Beki* on my view is thus neither weak nor deontic in the sense of individual obligations.

Recall that I the genericity of *hazu* is a result of the circumstantial modal base not requiring individual beliefs to be taken into account. What sets generic *beki* apart from its individual counterpart, on the other hand, is not its circumstantial modal base, but the lack of individual application of rules in the ordering source. I label *beki*'s ordering source **idealistic**, its modal flavor in combination with a circumstantial base **ethic**, based on typical uses like (11).

1.4   Interim Summary

Summing up, I propose that the shared quality between the two OUGHT correspondents *hazu* and *beki* is (negatively defined) genericity—in the case of *hazu*, the absence of an agent-specific epistemic modal base, in the case of *beki*, the absence of individual rule-application in the ordering source.

The classification of necessity modals proposed so far summarized in the table below along with their labels from the literature on English and proposed flavors in Japanese, showing that the deontic and epistemic readings of English MUST and OUGHT have unambiguous correspondents in Japanese.

		English		Japanese			
label	(flavor)	OUGHT	MUST	*hazu*	*beki*	*nichigainai*	*-nakerebanaranai*
SEN	(epistemic)	–	✓	–	–	✓	–
SDN	(deontic)	–	✓	–	–	–	✓
WEN	(anticipative)	✓	–	✓	–	–	–
WDN	(ethic)	✓	–	–	✓	–	–

In the next section, I propose an analysis of *beki* and *hazu* as **generic** modals, as opposed to the **individual** modals *nichigainai* and *-nakerebanaranai*. Whether or not this analysis is (fully) applicable to the deontic and epistemic readings of OUGHT and MUST remains an open question.

Crucially for what follows, there is not only no deontic/epistemic ambiguity, but also no apparent morhpological or historical link between alleged strong and weak necessity modals in Japanese, *cf.* [10,11], making an analysis that differentiates between them in interpretation only or derives weak modals as variants of their strong counterparts less obviously attractive than in English.

2   Analysis

The common feature of *hazu*, *beki*, and (alleged) weak necessity OUGHT, is their situational independence. My analysis attempts to capture this as generic modality, where genericity is implemented as a lack of agent-reference in the conversational background of generic modals. In this section, I first discuss what I take to be the modal flavors of *hazu* and *beki*, then sketch a formalization for this within a Kratzer/Lewis-style model of modal meaning as quantification over possible worlds. I do not claim that this model is in principle advantageous over other analyses of modality, but maintain that genericity ("weakness") needs to be sufficiently accounted for in any analysis, and that my proposal can achieve this using only building blocks from the analysis of individual ("strong") modals.

2.1 *Hazu*: Anticipative Modality

Combining a circumstantial modal base parallel to deontic modals with a stereotypical ordering source as has been proposed for epistemic modals under the label of human necessity (*cf.* [1,4]) *hazu* encodes what I label "anticipative" modality from the frequent use of *hazu* anticipating a typical course of events or outcome, see for instance (6). I avoid a label on the lines of "circumstantial human necessity" in order to make clear that my perspective on circumstantial modality is rather different from that sometimes exemplified by physical necessities like sneezing (which is not typically encoded in a separate lexeme).

Stereotpyical vs. Normal Ordering. Amending an intermediate-quantification analysis of OUGHT within a possible-world framework by simply replacing the epistemic modal of MUST with a circumstantial one while retaining the stereotypical ordering source is a rather obvious option. Indeed, Yalcin [19] discusses but dismisses this option, arguing that one would expect other modals, like MUST, to take a WEN reading as well in the light of systematic modal ambiguity in English. This would make MUST triply ambiguous between epistemic/stereotypical, circumstantial/deontic, and circumstantial/stereotypical necessity, the last reading being unavailable.

I have two points to make in defense of my proposal. First, assuming the WEN reading of OUGHT is actually circumstantial/stereotypical like *hazu*, it is a root, rather than epistemic reading, and assuming its WDN interpretation is actually circumstantial/idealistic like *beki* (see discussion below), it is not deontic either. This means that the usual deontic/epistemic ambiguity observed for MUST might not be applicable to OUGHT. Second, even if the proposed analysis does not work for English, it can still be applicable to Japanese, considering that they do not show epistemic/deontic ambiguities, and that the Japanese correspondents of MUST and OUGHT are not only seperate lecixal items, but also differ formally, as the former are verbal, the latter nominal predicates, favoring an analysis on which they constitute separate classes individual vs. generic modals.

Gradability and Modal Necessity. Lassiter [7] argues more generally against the analysis of OUGHT as a normalcy modal that Yalcin proposes, as the latter involves universal quantification, but OUGHT appears to be gradable (if more clearly so on its deontic reading). However, this does not apply to Japanese *hazu* or *beki*, neither of which are readily modifiable in the same way, as the Japanese translation of Lassiter's example shows:

(14)   Bill ought very much to be home by now.

(15)   Bill-wa ima (??totemo/ ??hontoo-ni) ie-ni   iru {hazu/ beki} da.
         PN-TOP now   very   really   home be MOD MOD COP

In sum, it seems reasonable to assume that *hazu* encodes an independent modal
flavor not merely derivative of epistemic necessity, and circumstantial/stereo-
typical is a straightforward choice for this, also in terms of connecting *hazu* to
beki. I implement this assumption in this section and return to interpretational
differences between epistemic and anticipative necessity arising from the different
nature of epistemic and circumstantial modal bases in Sect. 3.

2.2 *Beki*: Ethic Modality

While anticipative *hazu* differs from its epistemic counterpart in modal base,
beki differs from its deontic counterpart in ordering source. It thus shares the
circumstantial modal base with *hazu*, but combined with an ordering source
encoding universal standards or behavioral ideals. While the label "ethic" stems
from *beki*s typical use conveying behavioral norms, see (8), it should be noted
that the ideals in the conversational background are not always behavioral, as
the following example from Nishiyama [12][3] shows:

(16)   Yoru-wa   shizuka de_aru beki-da.
         night-TOP quiet   COP   MOD-COP
         "The night should be quiet."

What this example conveys is that, ideally, nights are quiet. While there must
be some generic standards for nights in the background here, behavioral norms
are not obviously involved. To include such cases, I label the ordering source of
beki "idealistic" (even though it could be argued that best worlds according to
an ordering represent some type of ideal in any case).

External Bouletic vs. Ethic Modality. Matthewson and Truckenbrodt [8]
propose another way to capture the generic version of deontic modality, analyzing the modal flavor of German *soll* (cognate to English "shall") as "external bouletic", that is bouletic modality where the relevant wishes are not the
speaker's. Their observations do, however, not carry over to Japanese, where an
entirely different construction is used for this type of modality, as in (17).

(17)   Kaet-te   hoshii.   (18)   Kae-ru   beki da.
         return-CONT want   return-NPST MOD COP
         "I want you to go home."   "You ought to go home."

Summing up, the Japanese data suggests it is reasonable to introduce a
generic counterpart to deontic modality. First and foremost, this directly reflects
the intuition that *beki*, in contrast to *-nakerebanaranai*, expresses general norms

---

[3] Who is concerned with phenomena completely orthogonal to the discussion here.

rather than specific rules. Additionally, it relates *hazu* and *beki* in a straight-forward way, as the only difference between the two is the ordering source—the normality of *hazu* is descriptive, or anticipative on its typical use, whereas that of *beki* is prescriptive, or ethical on its typical use. Note that the ideal-istic ordering source can also be thought of as intermediate between deontic and stereotypical—it is concerned with (behavioral) norms like the former, and with states of affairs that can (ideally) be expected like the latter, rather than prescriptively correct ones.

2.3 Formalization

In this section, I sketch a formalization of *hazu* and *beki*, along with their coun-terparts encoding (strong) necessity, *nichigainai* and *-nakerebanaranai*. The cru-cial point is how the respective modals differ from each other, without strongly defending a possible-world view of modality. The analysis builds on a Kratzer-Lewis framework of modality, as developed in Kratzer [4–6].

Epistemic and Circumstantial Modal Bases. The difference between an epistemic and a circumstantial modal base that is most relevant to the observa-tions and analysis in this paper is that the former, but not the latter represents the beliefs of, and is therefore interpreted relative to, a contextually resolved agent (usually the speaker). $\mathcal{E}^{w,x}$ is the epistemic modal base, defined as the set of worlds doxastically accessible to agent x at world w. In contrast, the cir-cumstantial modal base $\mathcal{C}^w$ is not dependent on an agent (I leave the question of what worlds this modal base selects open, see also Thomas [17] for relevant discussion).

Stereotypical Ordering Source. The stereotypical ordering source S par-tially orders worlds according to assumptions that can be reasonably made from the modal base. Essentially, this is an order of worlds by normalcy in light of the relevant beliefs or circumstances. The best stereotypical worlds are therefore those in which most reasonable expectations are satisfied. A stereotypical order-ing source crucially does not involve an agent variable and is therefore generic. These definitions in place, the denotations for anticipative *hazu* and epistemic *nichigainai*, taking a prejacent proposition φ, are given below. The operator BEST is taken from Portner [14], returning the set of best worlds relative to a modal base f, an ordering source g, a world w, and, where applicable, an agent x, under the limit assumption.

(19) $[\![hazu(\varphi)]\!]^w = \forall w' \in \text{BEST}(\mathcal{C}^w, \mathsf{S}) : w' \in [\![\varphi]\!] \leftrightarrow \text{BEST}(\mathcal{C}^w, \mathsf{S}) \subseteq [\![\varphi]\!]$

(20) $[\![nichigainai(\varphi)]\!]^{w,x} =$
   $= \forall w' \in \text{BEST}(\mathcal{E}^{w,x}, \mathsf{S}) : w' \in [\![\varphi]\!] \leftrightarrow \text{BEST}(\mathcal{E}^{w,x}, \mathsf{S}) \subseteq [\![\varphi]\!]$

Anticipative *hazu* with its circumstantial modal base conveys that its prejacent is true at all the most stereotypical, or normal, worlds out of those worlds in which the relevant circumstances hold. In other words, the set of φ-worlds is a superset of the best anticipative, *i.e.* most normal or expected worlds. *Nichigainai* has a similar meaning, but the epistemice modal base introduces an agent x to whose beliefs the interpretation is relative. This makes the *nichigainai* nongeneric, which has consequences for what kind of inference the modal is compatible with—the conclusions expressed by *nichigainai* can be highly subjective both in terms of premises and in terms of conjecture processes, whereas those conclusions expressed by *hazu* must by default be more objective in the sense of being shared across agents.

Deontic and Idealistic Ordering Sources. For the ethic modal *beki*, I propose an ideal ordering source I, which, in contrast with a stereotypical ordering source, does not involve predictions via normality, but rather encodes generic norms directly. In cases where *beki* is used to express normative behavioral expectations, idealistic ordering can be straightforwardly related to deontic ordering as in *-nakerebanaranai*. The deontic ordering source D^x encodes specific rules, which, crucially, need to be applied to an agent x in order to return a set of the best worlds. One could argue that it is not just an agent, but rather a situation that the rules are applied to, but this should be taken care of by the circumstantial modal base, which provides the circumstances relevant to the individual case. Below, denotations of the two modals applied to a prejacent φ are shown.

(21) $[\![beki(\varphi)]\!]^w = \forall w' \in \text{BEST}(\mathcal{C}^w, \mathsf{I}) : w' \in [\![\varphi]\!] \leftrightarrow \text{BEST}(\mathcal{C}^w, \mathsf{I}) \subseteq [\![\varphi]\!]$

(22) $[\![\text{-}nakerebanaranai(\varphi)]\!]^{w,x} =$
$= \forall w' \in \text{BEST}(\mathcal{C}^w, \mathsf{D}^x) : w' \in [\![\varphi]\!] \leftrightarrow \text{BEST}(\mathcal{C}^w, \mathsf{D}^x) \subseteq [\![\varphi]\!]$

On this view, the interpretation of *beki* is agent-independent, *i.e.* generic, which is in contrast to *-nakerebanaranai* in that the latter encodes rules or norms that vary in applicability to a specific agent. The difference between the ordering sources D^x and I should be more substantial than just specification to a subject to an agent or forgoing this, however, as rules that apply generically would be different in nature from rules the application of which has different consequences on an individual basis.

Note that *beki* looks quite similar to *hazu* with the difference of the respective ordering sources S and I. This is as intended: the difference between anticipative and ethic modality is, by example of the typical uses shows that they both encode expectations, which are descriptive and prescriptive, respectively. The former are more closely linked to the actual world in that they describe its typical state, potentially given some premises, which straightforwardly links them to epistemic modality, as such descriptive expectations arguably form the bulk of our beliefs. I touch on this point and some other consequences of this proposal briefly in the final section below.

2.4   Interim Summary

The analysis proposed in this section replaces the strong/weak label devised for the English necessity modals MUST and OUGHT with a distinction I label generic/individual based on the empirical differences between Japanese *hazu* and *beki* on the one hand and *nichgainai* and *-nakerebanaranai* on the other. Each of the four modals has a distinct modal flavor, and a modal is generic by definition when there is no agent variable individuating either the modal base or the ordering source. The table below summarizes the proposal.

modal	type	flavor	base f	source g
nichigainai	ind.	epistemic	epist. $(\mathcal{E}^{x,w})$	ster. (S)
-nakerebanaranai	ind.	deont.	circ. $(\mathcal{C}^w)$	deont. (D^x)
hazu	gen.	anticipative	circ. $(\mathcal{C}^w)$	ster. (S)
beki	gen.	ethic	circ. $(\mathcal{C}^w)$	ideal. (I)

3   Discussion and Outlook

Recall that on my proposal, generic modality is negatively defined by the absence of an agent variable within the conversational background. In this sense, both *hazu* and *beki* are generic in the same way. Individual modality, on the other hand, is characterized by the presence of an agent variable, the locus of which makes *nichgainai* and *-nakerebanaranai* individual in different ways. Whereas the situational dependence of epistemic *nichigainai* stems from the restriction of the modal base by the agents beliefs, what makes deontic *-nakerebanaranai* individual is the application of the relevant norms to a specific agent. In this way, the notion of "individuality" as implemented in the present analysis can be understood as a more fine-grained version of "strength" of modal necessity.

There are, however, some additional differences in the evaluation of generic and individual modals in Japanese not immediately apparent from the formal analysis. I discuss some of these for epistemic/anticipative and deontic/ethic modals below, before briefly touching an additional pair of, namely bouletic (and hence agent-specific and individual) *-tai* and its generic counterpart *tsumori*.

3.1   Grounds for Anticipative and Epistemic Necessity Claims

In the formalization proposed above, the difference between epistemic and anticipative necessity lies only in the modal base, which in the case of the former are the speaker's beliefs, in the case of the latter the relevant circumstances. This is not a mere difference between an agent-specific set of premises and a more general one, but there is a deeper, qualitative distinction in the type grounds for and type of conjecture that leads to epistemic and anticipative necessity claims. While formal implementation of such effect remains for further research, I discuss some of these distinctions below.

Conjecture and the Modal Base. To illustrate how genericity influences the type of conjecture behind necessity claims, consider an additional example from Silk [16]:

(23)   Where are the color pencils?
    a.   They {should/must} be in the drawer with the crayons.
    b.   Kureyon-to   onaji hikidashi-ni aru {hazu da/nichigainai}.
        caryone-with same drawer-in   be   MOD COP   MOD

Silk reports that assuming the speaker normally puts the pencils in the drawer, but sometimes misplaces them on the shelf, *should* is preferred in absence of evidence, but *must* when, for instance, the speaker has evidence that the crayons are not on the shelf. This contrast comes out with Japanese *nichigainai*, but not so with *hazu*—that is, the epistemic modal is dispreferred when the speaker is making an assumption based on what can generally be expected, which on my analysis is the core function of anticipative *hazu*.

This leads to the question of whether and how the two types of conjecture observed by Silk can be differentiated by the ordering source of the respective modal, which is the only difference between *nichigainai* and *hazu* on my analysis. I propose that the choice of modal base has a two-fold effect. First and more obviously, it influences the premises on which conjecture is based—in the case of *nichigainai*, it is the speaker's individual beliefs or knowledge, in the case of *hazu* the premises are treated as generally accessible, such as information in the common ground, explaining why *nichigainai* is dispreferred when the speaker is not conjecturing based on individual knowledge. Second, the conjecture process itself differs, too, as in the case of *hazu*, the only rules by which to reach a necessity claim are those of stereotypicality encoded in the ordering source, whereas with *nichigainai*, an entirely separate internal reasoning process by the speaker can occur within the modal base.

Individuality, Genericity and Evidentiality. The qualitative difference in circumstantial and epistemic grounds for necessity claims links to observations concerning an alleged evidential meaning component of *hazu*, as in the following example from McCready and Asher [9], in which the speaker makes a claim about the next day's weather based on observing the sky.

(24)   Ashita   ame-ga   fu-ru   {nichigainai/??hazu da}.
        tomorrow rain-NOM fall-NPST   MOD   MOD COP
        "Tomorrow it will rain."

They report that *hazu* in (24) would be acceptable only if the speaker were a 75-year-old farmer that can infallibly predict the weather by observing the sky. This, in turn, leads them to conclude that *hazu* requires direct and clear evidence for the prejacent, where the directness of evidence depends on an agent's abilities to derive accurate judgments from it. Okano and Mori [13], on the other hand, report that *hazu* in the same example becomes good when adding an overt clause stating the grounds for the necessity claim, such as "because clouds are low and winds are strong". They take this as compatible with their claim that *hazu* differs from *nichigainai* in that it involves dynamic update of acceptability conditions, in this case grounds for a necessity claim.

In addition to these apparently conflicting observations, there are cases like (25), where *hazu* is used to make an (anticipative) necessity claim without any evidence whatsoever involved, uttered to generally reassure the addressee that things will work out fine.

(25)   Kitto daijoobu {??nitigainai / na hazu da}
         surely okay   MOD   COP MOD COP
         "I'm sure it'll be fine."

I take this to support the view that *hazu* is not primarily sensitive to evidence, but rather to the type of grounds for the necessity claim and whether or not purely stereotypical reasoning is involved. In the case of (23), the epistemic modal *nichigainai* is dispreferred when the necessity claim is only based on normalcy, while *hazu* can be used in the evidential case when all information is generally accessible. This is also one way to license *hazu* in (24), as Okano and Mori note that a causal relative clause makes the premises for the necessity claim common ground. Even without this additional clause, the conjecture in (24) is within the domain of what can generally be assumed for a 75-year-old farmer, whereas *nichigainai* indicating a subjective evaluation process is generally preferred. Finally, in (25) no conjecture grounded in epistemic knowledge takes place whatsoever, but the general expectation is that things will be fine for an optimistic speaker.

Stacking Modal Bases. There is evidence for a sharp distinction between epistemic and anticipative modalities in Japanese from cases where they occur stacked. While this may not a highly productive phenomenon, presumably due to the relative complexity of the reasoning processes it represents, examples like the following are possible, in contrast to English:

(26)   a.   ??It might be the case that John should be home by now.
         b.   Jon-wa   imagoro kaet-tei-ru   hazu kamoshirenai.
               John-TOP by_now return-RES-NPST MOD MOD

The Japanese is example should be acceptable in contexts where the question under discussion is what can be reasonably assumed about John's whereabouts, judging which in turn depends on individual beliefs and reasoning. Why such examples are worse in English remains as an open question, but could have to do with systematic ambiguity making utterances like (26-a) exceedingly hard to process.

3.2   Ethical Necessity and Individuality

In ethic necessity modals, the role of the circumstantial modal base is rather different than in deontic necessity, as the relevant circumstances for deontic ordering are necessarily dependent on the agent subject to the rules in question. This poses an additional question how the ordering source feeds back into the modal base by co-determining which circumstances are relevant, another point that requires further investigation.

Generic vs. Individual Norms.   Rather than deriving the weak/strong contrast in terms of quantification or additional conditions of evaluation in the weak case, the current proposal directly reflects observations on OUGHT also made by von Fintel and Iatridou [18] illustrated by examples (7) and (8). Ethical necessity is based on rules that apply, in principle, to everyone, while deontic necessity encodes regulations that apply specifically. The differentiation is by no means trivial, but there is a clear intuition that it exists and, as I argue, linguistic forms corresponding to each type of rules. Therefore, I would argue that finding a formalization that incorporates this distinction is the extent of what linguistics can do, the identification of what makes a rule ethic might be a metaphysical problem best left to philosophy.

An illustration of a rather clear deontic/ethic distinction that brings out the difference between unchangeable and generic norms are legal decisions. Whereas examples of deontic necessity frequently involve legal rules (such as the example cited above for driving on the left in Japan), in cases where a judicial ruling is in question, SHOULD and *beki* are used.[4]

(27)   Muazai-ga   iiwatas-areru   beki da.
       innocence-NOM hand_down-PASS MOD COP
       "An innocent verdict should be handed down."

The ethic modal is preferred here not because the norms of the law are somehow less binding for judges (which would be a consequence of weak-modal analyses of SHOULD), but rather because the decision to be made is to be measured against the behavior of an ideal judge, which, ideally, will yield the same decision in any case. While the difference between an idealistic and a deontic ordering source can seem somewhat blurry, it is clear in this case.

3.3   Genericity in Bouletic/Teleological Modality

Looking at (alleged) epistemic and deontic modals alone, the present analysis is but one option to account for the strong/weak distinction they exhibit that happens to fit well with the Japanese data. In addition to the pairs *nichigainai/hazu* and *-nakerebanaranai/beki*, there is a corresponding pair including the (on my view individual) bouletic/teleological modal *-tai* and its generic counterpart *tsumori*. This pair has no direct correspondent in English and provides

---

[4] Example found in online news quoting defense lawyers.

evidence in favor of a individual/generic rather than a strong/weak distinction, thus favoring an analysis on the lines proposed here. Consider the following example of -*tai*/*tsumori*.

(28) Iki-tai   kedo, iku tsumori-wa nai.
      go-MOD but   go MOD-CTOP exist.NEG
      "I want to go, but I am not planning to."

This resembles cases of *hazu* like the counterfactual example (6), with the difference that the individual necessity claim is positive, the generic one negated. Assuming that the modal base for generic *tsumori* is circumstantial, what ordering source would allow for this use?

One possibility that comes to mind is that *tsumori* is a kind of hybrid between *beki* and *hazu*—roughly, -*tai* could be circumstantial/bouletic much like *want*, whereas *tsumori* is the behavioral equivalent of *hazu*, predicting not normal states of affairs but normal behaviors, which in turn connects it to ethic *beki*.

This would mean that with -*tai*, the necessity claim depends on the speaker's wishes in the conversational background, but is detached from the actual outcome, whereas with *tsumori*, the necessity claim requires things to typically play out according to the speaker's intentions. This makes *tsumori* more teleological than bouletic, as it conveys a typical outcome of intentions rather than the realization of individual wishes or goals. To illustrate, consider a variant of (11) featuring *tsumori*:

(29) a. They {should/must be} be in the drawer with the crayons.
      b. Kureyon-to   onaji hikidashi-ni aru {hazu da / nichigainai}.
          caryone-with same drawer-in   be   MOD COP MOD
      c. ... hikidashi-ni {ire-teiru   tsumori da / ??ire-ta-katta}.
          drawer-in   insert-RES MOD   COP   insert-MOD.PST

The only difference between *tsumori* and *hazu* is that the stereotypical outcome does not depend on intentions in the latter. *Tsumori* here conveys that, given the behavioral preferences of the speaker, the crayons can now reasonably be assumed to be in the drawer as a result.

4 Conclusion

I have proposed a novel analysis of strong and weak necessity based on observations from modals in Japanese, replacing the strong/weak distinction with an individual/generic one, where genericity is defined as the absence of agent-reference in the conversational background. I have analyzed *hazu* as anticipative (generic version of epistemic), *beki* as ethic (generic version of deontic), and suggested that *tsumori* is likely a generic version of bouletic modality. A full analysis of the latter and more detailed discussion and formalization of the interpretational effects arising from combinations of specific modal bases and ordering sources remain for future work.

References

1. Cariani, F., Kaufmann, M., Kaufmann, S.: Deliberative modality under epistemic uncertainty. Linguist. Philos. **36**(3), 225–259 (2013)
2. Copley, B.: What should "should" mean? (2006). https://halshs.archives-ouvertes. fr/halshs-00093569, Language Under Uncertainty Workshop, Kyoto University, January 2005
3. Horn, L.: A Natural History of Negation. University of Chicago Press, Chicago (1989)
4. Kratzer, A.: The notional category of modality. In: Words. Worlds, and Contexts, New Approaches to Word Semantics, pp. 38–74. Walter de Gruyter, Berlin (1981)
5. Kratzer, A.: Modality. In: Semantics: An International Handbook of Contemporary Research, pp. 639–650. Walter de Gruyter, Berlin (1991)
6. Kratzer, A.: Modals and Conditionals. Oxford University Press, Oxford (2012)
7. Lassiter, D.: Graded Modality: Qualitative and Quantitative Perspectives. Oxford University Press, Oxford (2017)
8. Matthewson, L., Truckenbrodt, H.: Modal flavour/modal force interactions in German: soll, sollte, muss and müsste. Linguistische Berichte **255**, 4–57 (2018)
9. McCready, E., Asher, N.: Modal subordination in Japanese: dynamics and evidentiality. Univ. Pennsylvania Working Pap. Linguist. **12**(1), 20 (2006)
10. Moriya, T., Horie, K.: What is and is not language-specific about the Japanese modal system? A comparative and historical perspective. In: Japanese Modality. Exploring its Scope and Interpretation, pp. 87–114. Palgrave Macmillan (2009)
11. Narrog, H.: Modality in Japanese: The Layered Structure of the Clause and Hierarchies of Functional Categories. John Benjamins, Amsterdam (2009)
12. Nishiyama, K.: Adjectives and the copulas in Japanese. J. East Asian Linguist. **8**(3), 183–222 (1999)
13. Okano, S., Mori, Y.: On CG management of Japanese weak necessity modal *Hazu*. In: Murata, T., Mineshima, K., Bekki, D. (eds.) JSAI-isAI 2014. LNCS (LNAI), vol. 9067, pp. 160–171. Springer, Heidelberg (2015). https://doi.org/10.1007/978-3-662-48119-6_12
14. Portner, P.: Modality. Oxford University Press, Oxford (2009)
15. Silk, A.: Modality, weights, and inconsistent premise sets. In: Proceedings of Semantics and Linguistic Theory, vol. 22, pp. 43–64 (2012)
16. Silk, A.: Weak and strong necessity modals: on linguistic means of expressing "a primitive concept ought". In: Meaning, Decision, and Norms: Themes from the Work of Allan Gibbard (forthcoming)
17. Thomas, G.: Circumstantial modality and the diversity condition. In: Proceedings of Sinn und Bedeutung, vol. 18, pp. 433–455 (2014)
18. Von Fintel, K., Iatridou, S.: How to say ought in foreign: The composition of weak necessity modals. In: Guéron, J., Lecarme, J. (eds.) Time and Modality, pp. 115–141. Springer, Berlin (2008). https://doi.org/10.1007/978-1-4020-8354-9_6
19. Yalcin, S.: Modalities of normality. In: Charlow, N., Chrisman, M. (eds.) Deontic Modality, pp. 230–255. Oxford University Press (2016)

The Ambiguity of Tense in the Japanese Mirative Sentence with *Nante/Towa*

Osamu Sawada[1(✉)] and Jun Sawada[2]

[1] Department of Linguistics, Kobe University,
1-1 Rokkodai-machi, Nada-ku, Kobe 657-8501, Japan
`sawadao@lit.kobe-u.ac.jp`
[2] Department of Japanese Language and Literature, Aoyama Gakuin University,
4-4-25 Shibuya, Shibuya-ku, Tokyo 150-8366, Japan
`juns0807@cl.aoyama.ac.jp`

Abstract. This paper investigates the ambiguity of tense in the Japanese mirative sentence with *nante/towa*. Unlike an English sentence exclamative (e.g., *(Wow), John won the race!*), a Japanese sentence with *nante/towa* has a property of ambiguity with regard to tense. When *nante* or *towa* is combined with a proposition that contains the so-called non-past form *ru*, the sentence can be ambiguous between a non-past (future/present) reading and a past reading. This fact is surprising because the non-past form *ru* can never be used for describing a past event. We argue that the ambiguous interpretation of *nante/towa* comes from the conventional implicature of *nante/towa*. Unlike an English sentence exclamation (Rett 2011), the Japanese *nante/towa* takes a "tenseless" proposition p (i.e., *ru* does not specify a tense) and conventionally implies that (i) p is settled (i.e., p is/was true or predicted to be true) and (ii) the speaker had not expected that p. We will also consider the case where p + *nante/towa* is embedded under a surprising predicate and claim that both the embedded and non-embedded *nante/towa* can be analyzed in a uniform way, suggesting that the embedded *nante/towa* clause is an instance of a main clause phenomenon (rather than a relative tense phenomenon).

Keywords: Mirativity · Exclamativity · (Embedded) *nante/towa* · Tense · Ambiguity · Main clause phenomenon

We are very grateful to Naoya Fujikawa, Hideki Kishimoto, Yusuke Kubota, Elin McCready and the audience and reviewers of LENLS 16 for their valuable comments and suggestions. Parts of this paper were also presented at Functional Categories and Expressive Meaning at Universitat Autònoma de Barcelona and the linguistics meeting at Kobe University and we thank the audiences for their valuable comments and discussions. This study is based on work supported by JSPS KAKENHI Grant (18K00531 and 16K16845) and the NINJAL collaborative research project 'Cross-linguistic Studies of Japanese Prosody and Grammar'. All remaining errors are of course our own.

© Springer Nature Switzerland AG 2020
M. Sakamoto et al. (Eds.): JSAI-isAI 2019, LNAI 12331, pp. 325–340, 2020.
https://doi.org/10.1007/978-3-030-58790-1_21

1   Introduction

This paper investigates the interpretation of the Japanese mirative expressions *nante/towa* with special reference to tense specification. In English there is a sentence exclamative like (1):

(1)   (Wow,) John won the race! (Rett 2011: 430)

Rett (2011) claims that in English sentences, exclamations like that in (1) express that a particular proposition has violated the speaker's expectation and proposes an illocutionary force operator for an exclamation that is a function from propositions to expressive speech acts, as in (2b) (s_C stands for the speaker, w_C and t_C stand for the world and a time of utterance):

(2)   a. $p = \lambda w : \text{won}_w(\text{john}, \iota x \, [\text{race}_w \, (x)])$
       b. E-FORCE (p), uttered by the s_C, is appropriate in a context C if p is salient and true in the w_C. When appropriate, E-FORCE(p) counts as an expression when the s_C had not expected that p.
           (Rett 2011: 430)

In (1) E-FORCE takes the proposition "John won the race" and expresses that the speaker had not expected John to win the race. Japanese also has a sentence exclamative:

(3)   John-ga   kat-ta!
       John-NOM win-PST
       'John won!'

In this paper we will focus on another kind of Japanese mirative expressions *nante/towa* that also trigger an exclamative meaning. An interesting point of *nante/towa* is that they have a property of ambiguity with regard to tense. When *nante* or *towa* is combined with a proposition that contains a non-past tense form *ru*, the sentence can be ambiguous between a non-past (future/present) reading and a past reading (NON.PST=non-past, MIR=mirative):

(4)   Taro-ga   paatii-ni ku-ru-{nante/towa}.
       Taro-NOM party-to come-NON.PST-MIR/MIR

       a. Future reading: Taro is going to come to the party!
       b. Past reading: Taro came to the party!

In the future reading, the speaker is surprised about the scheduled plan that Taro will come to the party; whereas in the past reading, the speaker is surprised that Taro came to the party. The fact that there is a past reading in (4) is surprising because the *ru*-form is usually considered a non-past tense form that represents the present (when it attaches with a stative verb) or the future (when it attaches with a non-stative verb). If we delete *nante/towa* in (4), the sentence has only a future reading:

(5) Taro-ga   paatii-ni ku-ru.
     Taro-NOM party-to come-NON.PST
     Future reading: Taro is going to come to the party.

The contrast between (4) and (5) becomes clearer if we add temporal adverbs *kinou* 'yesterday' and *ashita* 'tomorrow'. *Kinou* 'yesterday' cannot co-occur in the simple *ru*-form sentence, but it can occur within the *ru*-form sentence if *nante/towa* is added:

(6) {Ashita   /*kinou}   Taro-ga   paatii-ni ku-ru.
     Tomorrow /yesterday Taro-NOM party-to come-NON.PST
     'Taro will come to the party tomorrow/*yesterday.'

(7) {Ashita   / kinou}   Taro-ga   paatii-ni ku-ru-{nante/towa}.
     Tomorrow / yesterday Taro-NOM party-to come-NON.PST-MIR/MIR

     a. Future reading: Taro is going to come to the party tomorrow!
     b. Past reading: Taro came to the party yesterday!

What is the meaning of the mirative *nante/towa*? Why is it that the sentence with *nante/towa* can be ambiguous in terms of tense? What is the difference between the English sentence exclamatives and the Japanese mirative *nante/towa*?

In this paper we will argue that *nante/towa* are an illocutionary force operator that takes a "tenseless" proposition p and conventionally implies that (i) the at-issue proposition p is "settled" (i.e., p is/was true or predicted to be true) and (ii) the speaker had not expected that p. We then claim that the information of tense in the at-issue proposition is specified via the adjustment to the conventional implicature (CI) of *nante/towa*. If p is interpreted as true at the CI, then the event described by p is interpreted as a past (or a present) event; if p is predicted to be true in the CI, then the event described by p is a future event.

Interesting point is that *nante/towa* can be embedded under a "surprising predicate" and has the same property of ambiguity with regard to tense:

(8) Taro-ga   paatii-ni ku-ru-{nante/towa}   odoroki-da.
     Taro-NOM party-to come-NON.PST-MIR/MIR surprising-PRED

     Future reading: It is surprising that Taro is going to come to the party!
     Past reading: It is surprising that Taro came to the party!

We will argue that the analysis of non-embedded *nante/towa* and the embedded *nante/towa* can be analyzed in a uniform way. Namely, the embedded *nante/towa* clause is an instance of a main clause phenomenon.

The phenomenon of *nante/towa* suggests there is a rich interaction between at-issue meaning and CI (pragmatics). The pragmatic (CI) intrusion into "what is said" occurs in the phenomenon *nante/towa*. This paper provides a new perspective for the semantics-pragmatics interface.

2   Some Empirical Facts About the Japanese *Nante/Towa*

2.1   Tense System of Japanese

This section introduces the basic properties of the Japanese tense system and clarifies the difference between the basic Japanese tense system and the tense interpretation of the sentence with *nante/towa*. It is standardly assumed in the literature that Japanese has two basic forms for tense, the *ru*-form (non-past form) and the *ta*-form (past form).

Let us first consider the interpretation of *ru*-form. When the *ru*-form is used with a stative verb, it has a present interpretation; however, if the *ru*-form is used with a non-stative predicate, it usually has a future interpretation:

(9)

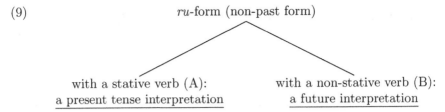

(10) is the example of the *ru*-form with a stative verb and (11) is the example of the *ru*-form with a non-stative verb:

(10)   (Present, with a stative verb)(=A)

    Konnnani ryouri-ga   a-ru.
    This much cuisine-NOM exist-NON.PST

    'There are so many dishes.'

(11)   (Future, with a non-stative verb)(=B)

    Ashita   Taro-ga   paatii-ni ku-ru.
    Tomorrow Taro-NOM party-to come-NON.PST

    'Taro will come to the party tomorrow.'

Next, let us consider the *ta*-form. Basically, *ta* is consistently interpreted as past with both stative and non-stative verbs.[1]

(12)

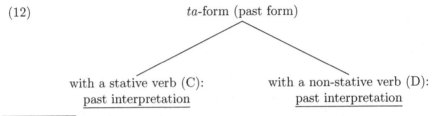

---

[1] There are also what is called a present perfect use of *ta*, in addition to a regular past use; however, we will not go into detail in this paper regarding the present perfect use.

The following are examples of *ta*-sentences (type C and D):

(13)   (Past, with a stative verb) (=C)

    Annnani   ryouri-ga   at-ta.
    That much cuisine-NOM exist-PST

    'There were so many dishes.'

(14)   (Past, with a non-stative verb)(=D)

    Kinou   Taro-ga   paatii-ni ki-ta.
    Yesterday Taro-NOM party-to come-PST

    'Taro came to the party yesterday.'

Now let us consider the interpretation of *nante/towa*. When a stative verb + *ru* is combined with *nante/towa*, there can be both a present interpretation and a past interpretation:

(15)   (Stative verb + *ru*, with *nante/towa*)

    a. Konnani   ryouri-ga   a-ru-{nante/towa}.
       This much cuisine-NOM exist-NON.PST-MIR/MIR

       'There are so many dishes!' (present reading)

    b. Annnani   ryouri-ga   a-ru-{nante/towa}.
       That much cuisine-NOM exist-NON.PST-MIR/MIR

       'There were so many dishes!' (past reading)

The sentences above are not ambiguous because of the meaning of the degree modifiers. *Annna* 'that much' is recognitional (retrospective), and the degree is anchored to the past, while *konna* 'this much' is deictic (spatial) and the degree is anchored to the current time.

When a non-stative verb + *ru* is combined with *nante/towa*, the sentence can have both future and past interpretations:

(16)   (Non-stative verb + *ru*, with *nante/towa*)

    a. Ashita   asa   6-ji-ni   Taro-ga   koko-ni
       Tomorrow morning 6-o'clock-to Taro-NOM here-to
       ku-ru-{nante/towa}.
       come-NON.PST-MIR/MIR

       'Taro will come here at 6 a.m. tomorrow!' (future reading)

    b. Kinou   asa   6-ji-ni   Taro-ga   koko-ni
       Yesterday morning 6-o'clock-to Taro-NOM here-to
       ku-ru-{nante/towa}.
       come-NON.PST-MIR/MIR

       'Taro came here at 6 a.m. yesterday!' (past reading)

As shown in (15b) and (16b) if *nante/towa* is added, "a stative verb/non-stative verb + *ru*" can have a past interpretation. This suggests that the interpretation of tense with *nante/towa* is quite different from the interpretation of tense without *nante/towa*. How can we explain these facts?

2.2   The Mirative Property of *Nante/Towa*

Based on the above empirical facts, this section considers the meaning of *nante/towa*. Similar to English exclamative sentence like (1), *nante/towa* expresses a meaning of mirativity. According to DeLancey (1997: 369–370), mirativity refers to "the linguistic marking of an utterance as conveying information which is new or unexpected to the speaker." Further, according to Aikhenvald (2012: 437), across languages, the "mirative" encompasses the following values, each of which can be defined with respect to the speaker, the audience (or addressee), or the main character: (i) sudden discovery, sudden revelation, or realization; (ii) surprise; (iii) unprepared mind; (iv) counterexpectation; (v) new information (See also Aikhenvald (2004)).

The following contrast supports that the sentence with *nante/towa* conveys a mirative meaning (surprise/counterexpectation):

(17)   (Federer is a world-class tennis player)

    a. Roger Federer-ga   make-ru-{towa/nante}.
        Roger Federer-NOM lose-NON.PST-MIR/MIR

        'Roger Federer lost!'

    b. # Roger Federer-ga   kat-su-{towa/nante}.
          Roger Federer-NOM win-NON.PST-MIR/MIR

        'Roger Federer won!'

Pragmatically, it would be surprising for Roger Federer to lose, while it is not surprising for Federer to win.

Descriptively, we propose that the mirative *nante/towa* has a following pragmatic function:

(18)   The pragmatic function of the mirative *nante/towa* (Descriptive): The Japanese *nante/towa* takes a "non-tensed" proposition p and conventionally implies that (i) p was true/is true or predicted to be true and (ii) the speaker had not expected that p.

Strictly speaking, there seems to be a slight difference between *nante* and *towa* in meaning. Namely, *nante* is more emotional than *towa* in that *nante* additionally implies that it is hard for the speaker to accept p (although it is/was true or expected to be true). In this paper we will set aside this subtle difference. The meaning of *nante/towa* is a conventional implicature (CI) and independent of "what is said" (Grice 1975; Potts 2005, 2007; McCready 2010; Gutzmann 2011; Sawada 2010, 2018). This idea is supported by the fact that a denial cannot target the speaker's attitude of surprise.

Note, however, that since the at-issue proposition in the *nante/towa* sentence (with the *ru*-form) can be ambiguous between future and past readings, the denial alone is not enough for signaling in what sense the listener is objecting to the speaker's utterance:

(19) A: John-ga   paatii-ni ku-ru-{nantet/towa}.
          John-NOM party-to come-NON.PST-MIR/MIR

      'John is going to come to the party!/John came to the party!'
      (CI: The speaker has not expected that John is going to come/came to the party.)

      B: Iya sore-wa   nani-ka-no   machigai-da.
          No, that-TOP what-KA-GEN mistake-PRED.

      'No, that's some kind of mistake.'

It is possible that A is talking about a future event, but B is objecting to a past event.[2] To convey B's intention of denial, it is necessary to add information after a denial:

(20) (Future reading)

      A: John-ga   paatii-ni ku-ru-{nante/towa}.
          John-NOM party-to come-NON.PST-MIR/MIR

      'John is going to come to the party!'

      B: Iya sore-wa   nani-ka-no   machigai-da. John-wa   ko-nai-yo.
          No that-TOP what-KA-GEN mistake-PRED John-TOP come-NEG-Prt

      'No, that's some kind of mistake. John will not come to the party.'

(21) (Past reading)

      A: John-ga   paatii-ni ku-ru-{nante/towa}.
          John-NOM party-to come-NON.PST-MIR/MIR

      'John came to the party!'

      B: Iya sore-wa   nani-ka-no   machigai-da. Kare-wa
          No, that-TOP what-KA-GEN mistake-PRED. He-TOP
          ko-nakat-ta-yo.
          come-NEG-PST-Prt

      'No, that's some kind of mistake. He didn't come to the party.'

---

[2] This kind of ambiguity never arises in the English sentence exclamation. As the following example shows, the use of a simple denial is enough to deny A's assertion:

(i) A: (Wow,) John won the race!

     B: No, that's not true.

The utterance of an English sentence exclamation can count as an assertion of the denoted proposition *p* in addition to having an illocutionary force of exclamation (Rett 2011) and the tense of the assertion is fixed.

3   The Semantics of *Nante/Towa* (Non-embedded)

Now let us analyze the meaning of *nante/towa* in a formal way based on the following example:

(22)   Taro-ga   paatii-ni ku-ru-{nante/towa}.
       Taro-NOM party-to come-NON.PST-MIR/MIR

   a. Future reading: Taro is going to come to the party!
   b. Past reading: Taro came to the party!

In the previous section we claimed that the Japanese *nante/towa* takes a "non-tensed" proposition p and conventionally implies that p was true/is true or predicted to be true and the speaker had not expected that p. We consider that this can be formalized based on the notion of "settledness" (Superscript a stands for an at-issue type, and superscript c stands for a CI type):

(23)   a. $p = \lambda t \lambda w.$ Taro-come-to-the-party at t in w
       b. [[nante/towa]]: $\langle\langle i^a, \langle s^a, t^a\rangle\rangle, t^c\rangle = \lambda p.p$ is SETTLED in w_C and s_C had not expected that p

Here we define the notion of SETTLED as follows:

(24) p is SETTLED iff
       a. p is true sometime before t_0 or,
       b. p is true at t_0 or,
       c. p is predicated to be true sometime after t_0

Compositionally, *nante/towa* is combined with the "non-tensed" proposition via Potts' (2005) CI application in (25), as shown in (26):

(25)   CI application (Potts 2005: 65)

$$\beta : \sigma^a$$
$$\bullet$$
$$\alpha(\beta) : \tau^c$$
$$\overset{\frown}{\alpha : \langle \sigma^a, \tau^c \rangle \quad \beta : \sigma^a}$$

(26)

$$\lambda t \lambda w.\ \text{Taro-come-to-the-party at } t \text{ in } w:$$
$$\langle i^a, \langle s^a, t^a\rangle\rangle$$
$$\bullet$$
$$\text{nante/towa } (\lambda t \lambda w.\ \text{Taro-come-to-the-party at } t \text{ in } w): t^c$$

$\lambda t \lambda w.$ Taro-come-to-the-party at t in w: C
$\langle i^a, \langle s^a, t^a\rangle\rangle$ nante/towa: $\langle\langle i^a, \langle s^a, t^a\rangle\rangle, t^c\rangle$

Note that here the "non-tensed" proposition is an argument of *nante/towa*, but at the same time, the non-tensed proposition is passed up to the higher level as an at-issue meaning (above •).

How is the tense information specified in the at-issue dimension? Syntactically, *nante/towa* is a speech act operator placed at C (i.e., above TP). We claim that the information of tense in the at-issue proposition is specified via the adjustment to the CI. If it is interpreted that p was true sometime before the utterance time in the CI level, then the event described by p is interpreted as a past event in the at-issue dimension, and if it is interpreted that p is expected to be true in the CI, then the event described by p is a future event in the at-issue dimension.

For example, (27) is the situation where the at-issue proposition was interpreted to be true in the past in the CI dimension:

(27) (Logical structure of (22), past interpretation)

Taro-came-to-the party in w_C: t^a

(= tensed via the adjustment to the CI)

•

nante/towa ($\lambda t \lambda w$. Taro-come-to-the-party at t in w): t^c

$\lambda t \lambda w$. Taro-come-to-the-party at t in w: C
$\langle i^a, \langle s^a, t^a \rangle \rangle$ nante/towa: $\langle \langle i^a, \langle s^a, t^a \rangle \rangle, t^c \rangle$

We consider that this can be viewed as a new kind of pragmatic intrusion into "what is said" (CI-intrusion into "what is said").

4   The Embedded *Nante/Towa*

4.1   The Interpretation of Embedded *Ru* with *Nante/Towa*

Interestingly, a *nante/towa* clause can be embedded under certain kinds of predicates such as *odoroki-da* 'is surprising' and *shiji-rare-nai* 'can't believe':[3]

---

[3] The fact that *nante/towa* clause in (28) is syntactically embedded is supported by the fact that unlike the non-embedded *nante* like (i), the sentence final particle *yo* cannot be added after *nante/towa*, as in (ii):

(i) (Non-embedded)

Taro-ga   paatii-ni ku-ru-{nante/towa}-yo.
Taro-NOM party-to come-NON.PST-MIR/MIR-Prt

Future reading: Taro is going to come to the party!
Past reading: Taro came to the party!

(ii) (Embedded)

(28)   a. (Watashi-ni-wa) [Taro-ga   paatii-ni
            I-to-TOP   Taro-NOM party-to
            ku-ru-{nante/towa}]   odoroki-da.
            come-NON.PST-COMP.MIR/COMP.MIR surprising-PRED

   Future reading: It is surprising for me that Taro is going to come to
   the party!
   Past reading: It is surprising for me that Taro came to the party!

        b. (Watashi-wa) [Taro-ga   paatii-ni
            I-to-TOP   Taro-NOM party-to
            ku-ru-nante/towa]   shinji-rare-nai.
            come-NON.PST-COMP.MIR/COMP.MIR believe-can-NEG

   Future reading: I can't believe that Taro is going to come to the
   party!
   Past reading: I can't believe that Taro came to the party!

In this case the mirative *nante/towa* syntactically functions as a complementizer. Interestingly, similarly to the non-embedded *nante/towa*, the embedded *nante/towa* has both a future reading and a past reading (relative to the utterance time).[4]

The phenomenon that the meaning of the embedded *nante/towa* clause can be ambiguous between a future reading and a past reading is surprising when the system of embedded tense in Japanese is considered. It is well known that in

---

Watashi-ni-wa [Taro-ga   paatii-ni
I-to-TOP   Taro-NOM party-to
ku-ru-{nante/towa}-(*yo)]   odoroki-da.
come-NON.PST-COMP.MIR/COMP.MIR-Prt surprising-PRED

Future reading: It is surprising to me that Taro is going to come to the party!
Past reading: It is surprising to me that Taro came to the party!

[4] The existence of ambiguity can be confirmed by the test of denial:

(i)   A: Taro-ga   paatii-ni ku-ru-{nante/towa}
           Taro-NOM party-to come-NON.PST-COMP.MIR/COMP.MIR
           shinji-rare-nai.
           believe-can-NEG

       Future reading: I can't believe that Taro is going to come to the party!

       B: Iya sore-wa   nani-ka-no   machigai-da.   Kare-wa ko-nai-yo.
           No that-TOP what-KA-GEN mistake-PRED He-TOP come-NEG-Prt

       'No, that's some kind of mistake. He will not come to the party.'

(ii)   A: Taro-ga   paatii-ni ku-ru-{nante/towa}
           Taro-NOM party-to come-NON.PST-COMP.MIR/COMP.MIR
           shinji-rare-nai.
           believe-can-NEG

       Past reading: I can't believe that Taro came to the party!

Japanese, the *ru*-form (non-past tense form) in a subordinate clause is "relative" (Comrie 1985) in that its tense is determined from the perspective of the time of the matrix clause (e.g., Mihara 1992; Ogihara 1995, 1996; Kubota et al. 2009) (Or, we can say that *ru* can be "bound" by the tense in the matrix clause (Kusumoto 1999, 2005)). For example, in (29), the embedded event is interpreted as a future event in the past and in (30), the embedded event is interpreted as a past event that occurred at the same time as the event described by the main clause (= simultaneous interpretation):

(29)   (Regular embedded *ru*-form, with a non-stative verb)

Mary-wa   [Taro-ga   paatii-ni ku-ru-to]   it-ta.
Mary-TOP Taro-NOM party-to come-NON.PST-that say-PST

'Mary said that Taro would come to the party.' (relative future reading)

(30)   (Regular embedded *ru*-form, with a stative verb)

John-wa   [Mary-ga   i-ru-to]   it-ta.
John-TOP Mary-NOM BE-NON.PST-that say-PST

'John said that Mary was there.' (simultaneous reading only)

The fact that (29) is not interpreted as future relative to the utterance time is corroborated by the fact that it is possible to say "but, actually she didn't come" after the sentence.[5]

How can we analyze the difference between the usual embedded tense of Japanese and the embedded *nante/towa*? We claim that the embedded *nante/towa* clause can be analyzed in the same way as the non-embedded *nante/towa*. The embedded *nante/towa* clause can be analyzed as an embedded speech act (i.e., a main clause phenomenon), and the *ru*-form (non-past tense form) in the embedded clause is independently interpreted from the main clause. This means that we can use the same lexical item for *nante/towa* for the embedded case as well:

(31)   a. $p = \lambda t \lambda w.$ Taro-come-to-the-party at t in w
       b. [[nante/towa]]: $\langle\langle i^a, \langle s^a, t^a \rangle\rangle, t^c \rangle = \lambda p.p$ is SETTLED in w_C and s_C had not expected that p

---

B: Iya sore-wa   nani-ka-no   machigai-da.   Kare-wa
    No, that-TOP what-KA-GEN mistake-PRED.   He-TOP
    ko-nakat-ta-yo.
    come-NEG-PAST-Prt

'No, that's some kind of mistake. He didn't come to the party.'

---

[5] However, in (29) it seems that there is also a reading where the embedded *ru* is interpreted relative to the utterance time. We will put this issue aside.

Recall that we define the notion of SETTLED as follows:

(32) p is SETTLED iff

   a. p is true sometime before t_0 or,

   b. p is true at t_0 or,

   c. p is predicated to be true sometime after t_0

Compositionally, just like the non-embedded *nante/towa*, the embedded *nante/towa* is combined with a non-tensed proposition via Potts' CI application. Namely, the tense information of the proposition in the at-issue dimension (above •) is adjusted to the interpretation of the CI meaning (a past reading or a future reading). The tense-adjusted proposition is then combined with *shira-nakat-ta* 'didn't know' or *odoroki-da* 'surprising' that has a factive presupposition. Figure (33) shows the past reading of (28a):

(33)   (The past reading of (28a))

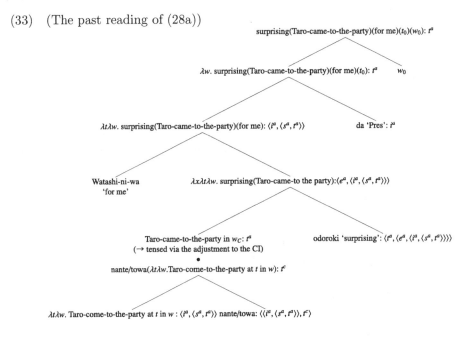

5   *Nante/Towa* with a Tensed Proposition

In this paper we have solely focused on examples where *nante/towa* co-occurs with a proposition with the *ru*-form (non-past form). However, actually, *nante/towa* can also combine with a tensed proposition that has the *ta*-form (past tense form), as well:

(34)   Taro-ga   paatii-ni ki-ta-{nante/towa}.
       Taro-NOM party-to come-PST-MIR/MIR

       Past reading: Taro came to the party!

Semantically, the above sentence is similar to the past reading in the *nante/towa* sentence with the *ru*-form:

(35) Taro-ga   paatii-ni ku-ru-{nante/towa}.
      Taro-NOM party-to come-NON.PST-MIR/MIR
      Past reading: Taro came to the party!

However, it is important to point out that there is a slight difference between the two patterns. *Nante/towa* with the *ta*-form sounds more indirect than *nante/towa* with the *ru*-form. Intuitively, the *ta*-form is used with *nante/towa* in a situation in which the speaker heard indirectly that Taro came to the party or in which s/he is recalling the past event of Taro having come to the party. By contrast, *nante/towa* with *ru* is neutral regarding the indirectness of information. It can be used in the situation in which a speaker directly experienced the event, but it can also be used in the situation in which the speaker heard indirectly that Taro came to the party or in which s/he is recalling the past event. We consider that *nante/towa* with the *ta*-form is more marked than *towa/nante* with the *ru*-form in that the past event is construed as an indirect remote event and cannot predicate about the utterance situation. It seems possible to explain this based on Horn's (1984) division of pragmatic labor: Unmarked expressions are generally used to convey unmarked messages. Compositionally, the fact that mirative *nante/towa* can take a tensed proposition (a proposition having a past tense) suggests that we need to posit another lexical entry for *nante* and *towa*.

6 Note on the Deontic Use of the Mirative *Nante/Towa*

Finally, let us consider the examples of the mirative *nante/towa* that have a deontic flavor. The mirative *nante/towa* can be used in a deontic context (to convey "should not *p*"):[6]

(36) a. (Non-deontic reading)
          Shushoo-ga   jinin-suru-{nante/towa}.
          Prime minister-NOM resignation-do-MIR/MIR

          'The prime minister resigned/is going to resign!'

      b. (Deontic reading)
          Shushoo-ga   anna hatsugen-o   suru-{nante/towa}.
          Prime minister-NOM such statement-ACC do-MIR/MIR

          'The prime minister made such a statement!' (The prime minister should not say something like that.)

(37) a. (Non-deontic reading)
          Shushoo-ga   jinin-suru-{nante/towa} shinji-rare-nai.
          Prime minister-NOM resignation-do-MIR/MIR believe-can-NEG

---

[6] We thank Naoya Fujikawa for the valuable comments and discussion.

'I can't believe that the prime minister resigned/is going to resign!'

b. (Deontic reading)

Shushoo-ga   anna hatsugen-o   suru-{nante/towa}
Prime minister-NOM such statement-ACC do-MIR/MIR
shinji-rare-nai.
believe-can-NEG

'I can't believe that the prime minister made such a statement!'

Unlike the (a) sentences, the (b) sentences have a deontic meaning. For example, in (36b), we can glean the deontic meaning that the prime minister should not say something like that. Should we consider that the deontic reading arises from a different semantic mechanism? We consider that both the (a) sentences (=non-deontic) and the (b) sentences have the same mirative meaning/CI (i.e. p is unexpected), and the deontic meaning is pragmatically derived via context. The deontic interpretation arises because there is an expectation that the prime minister should make a good remark. One piece of supporting evidence for the idea that the deontic meaning is pragmatic comes from the fact that the deontic meaning does not arise if we posit a different context. For example, if we replace *shushoo* 'prime mister' with Taro, then a deontic reading does not arise:

(38) (Context: We know that Taro is not good at presenting his own ideas, but today he made an excellent remark in the meeting.)

a. (Non-deontic reading)

Taro-ga   anna hatsugen-o   suru-{nante/towa}.
Taro-NOM such statement-ACC do-MIR/MIR

'Taro made such a statement!'

b. (Non-deontic reading)

Taro-ga   anna hatsugen-o   suru-{nante/towa}
Taro-NOM such statement-ACC do-MIR/MIR
shinji-rare-nai.
believe-can-NEG

'I can't believe that Taro made such a statement!'

7   Conclusion

This paper investigated the meaning and use of the Japanese mirative expressions *nante/ towa*. We observed that when *nante* or *towa* is combined with a proposition that contains the so-called non-past form *ru*, the sentence can be ambiguous between a future/present reading and a past reading. We explained the ambiguous interpretation of *nante/towa* based on the implicature of *nante/towa*. Namely, the Japanese *nante/towa* takes a "tenseless" proposition p (i.e., *ru* does not specify a tense) and conventionally implies that (i) p is settled (i.e., p is/was true or predicted to be true) and (ii) the speaker had not expected that *p*. In this paper we also looked at the case where *p* + *nante/towa* is embedded under a surprising predicate and showed that we can analyze both the embedded and non-embedded *nante/towa* in a uniform way, suggesting that the embedded *nante/towa* clause is an instance of a main clause phenomenon.

The phenomenon of *nante/towa* is theoretically important in that the phenomenon strongly shows that there is a rich interaction between at-issue meaning and CI (pragmatics). In the literature, CI and at-issue meanings are logically and compositionally independent of each other. An at-issue proposition is part of "what is said" in the sense of Grice (1975), while CI is not part of "what is said." However, in the phenomenon of *nante/towa*, the tense of at-issue proposition is influenced by the CI triggering expression *nante/towa*. This can be viewed as a new kind of pragmatic intrusion into "what is said" (CI-intrusion into "what is said").

Finally, let us consider the following fundamental question: Why is it that *nante/towa* takes a tenseless proposition (and allows multiple interpretations with regard to tense)? We suggest that the ambiguous property of mirative *nante/towa* regarding tense can be explained naturally by assuming that *nante/towa* was developed from a complementizer. As discussed in the paper, Japanese is a relative tense language in that the *ru*-form (non-past tense form) in a subordinate clause is "relative" (or tenseless), meaning that its tense is determined from the perspective of the time of the matrix clause (e.g., Mihara 1992; Ogihara 1996; Kubota et al. 2009) or *ru* is 'bound' by the tense in the matrix clause (Kusumoto 1999, 2005):

(39)   (The regular embedded tense, with the *ru* form)

Anotoki,   Taro-wa   [Jiro-ga   ku-ru-to-wa]
That time Taro-TOP Jiro-NOM come-Non.PST-that-TOP
iwa-nakat-ta.
say-NEG-PST

'At that time, Taro didn't say that Jiro would come to the party.' (But actually, he came.)

Both the regular embedded *ru*-form and the *ru*-form in the mirative *nante/towa* clause do not specify tense. It seems reasonable to consider that the mirative *nante/towa* retains the property of relative tense (non-tensed property). In future research, we would like to consider other relative tense languages, such as Korean, and check whether a similar mirative phenomenon can be observed in these languages.

References

Aikhenvald, A.Y.: Evidentiality. Oxford University Press, Oxford (2004)
Aikhenvald, A.Y.: The essence of mirativity. Linguist. Typol. **16**, 435–486 (2012)
Comrie, B.: Tense. Cambridge University Press, Cambridge (1985)

DeLancey, S.: Mirativity: the grammatical marking of unexpected information. Linguist. Typol. **1**, 33–52 (1997)

Grice, H.P.: Logic and conversation. In: Cole, P., Morgan, J. (eds.) Syntax and Semantics, vol. 3, Speech Acts, pp. 43–58. Academic Press, New York (1975)

Gutzmann, D.: Expressive modifiers & mixed expressives. In: Bonami, O., Hofherr, C.P. (eds.) Empirical Issues in Syntax and Semantics, vol. 8, pp. 123–141 (2011)

Horn, L.R.: Toward a new taxonomy for pragmatic inference: Q-based and R-based implicatures. In: Schiffrin, D. (ed), Meaning, Form, and Use in Context, pp. 11–42. Georgetown University Press, Washington (1984)

Kubota, Y., Lee, J., Smirnova, A., Tonhauser, J.: On the cross-linguistic interpretation of embedded tenses. In: Proceedings of Sinn und Bedeutung, vol. 13, pp. 307–320 (2009)

Kusumoto, K.: Tense in embedded contexts. Ph.D. thesis, University of Massachusetts, Amherst (1999)

Kusumoto, K.: On the quantification over times in natural language. Nat. Lang. Seman. **13**, 317–57 (2005). https://doi.org/10.1007/s11050-005-4537-6

McCready, E.: Varieties of conventional implicature: evidence from Japanese. Seman. Pragmat. **3**, 1–57 (2010)

Mihara, K.: Jisei Kaishaku to Tougo Genshou. Kuroshio Publishers, Tokyo (1992)

Potts, C.: The Logic of Conventional Implicatures. Oxford University Press, Oxford (2005)

Potts, C.: The expressive dimension. Theoret. Linguist. **33**, 165–197 (2007)

Ogihara, T.: The semantics of tense in embedded clauses. Linguist. Inq. **26**, 663–679 (1995)

Ogihara, T.: Tense, Attitudes, and Scope. Kluwer Academic Publishers, Dordrecht (1996)

Rett, J.: Exclamatives, degrees and speech acts. Linguist. Philos. **34**(5), 411–442 (2011). https://doi.org/10.1007/s10988-011-9103-8

Sawada, O.: Pragmatic aspects of scalar modifiers. Ph.D. Dissertation, University of Chicago (2010)

Sawada, O.: Pragmatic Aspects of Scalar Modifiers: The Semantics-Pragmatics Interface. Oxford University Press, Oxford (2018)

Equative *hodo* and the Polarity Effects
of Existential Semantics

Eri Tanaka[1](✉) ⓘ, Kenta Mizutani[1] ⓘ, and Stephanie Solt[2] ⓘ

[1] Osaka University, 1-5, Machianeyamacho, Toyonaka, Osaka, Japan
`eri-tana@let.osaka-u.ac.jp`, `l.g.fuad0809@gmail.com`
[2] Leibniz-Centre General Linguistics (ZAS), Berlin, Germany
`solt@leibniz-zas.de`

Abstract. This paper investigates the semantics and pragmatics of the Japanese equative marker *hodo*, which has the interesting property that it patterns as a negative polarity item on some but not all of its uses. We argue that the distributional patterns characterizing *hodo* derive from its weak existential semantics, which result in a trivial meaning in certain configurations. We further propose a pragmatic account of the presuppositional effects found with *hodo*, and discuss potential extensions to other data in Japanese and beyond. Overall, our findings add to other recent work demonstrating that the presence or absence of maximality represents an important dimension of cross-linguistic variation in the semantics of equative constructions.

Keywords: Equatives · Polarity effects · *hodo* · Existential semantics

1 Introduction

Cross-linguistic variation in the semantics of equative constructions has been the subject of considerable recent interest (see e.g. [2, 14, 15, 18]). Points of discussion have included the form of equative constructions in different languages, the use of the same equative marker to form scalar and non-scalar equatives, and the (im)possibility of negation in the standard clause.

We contribute to this body of research with an investigation of the Japanese equative marker *hodo*. What is interesting about *hodo* is that it exhibits a broader distribution than better-studied equative markers in languages such as English. In some of these uses, but not others, it is polarity sensitive, a pattern that has not to our knowledge been previously observed.

This work has been supported by "On Development of Logical Language and Mathematical Concepts", Osaka University International Joint Research Program (A), (Principal Investigator: Yoichi Miyamoto). Additional support was provided by the German Science Foundation (DFG) via grant SO1157-1/2 to the third author. We thank Luka Crnič for very helpful discussion.

© Springer Nature Switzerland AG 2020
M. Sakamoto et al. (Eds.): JSAI-isAI 2019, LNAI 12331, pp. 341–353, 2020.
https://doi.org/10.1007/978-3-030-58790-1_22

We propose an analysis of *hodo* according to which it does not express a relation between two maximal degrees, but instead has weak existential semantics. Polarity-based restrictions then arise as a result of triviality of meaning in certain configurations. We demonstrate that the analysis can be refined to account for prepositional effects in *hodo* sentences, and also extend the investigation to related data in Japanese and beyond.

2   Data

2.1   Polarity Sensitivity of *hodo*

The examples in (1a)–(1b) illustrate a use of *hodo* that corresponds to English '*as ... as*', where (1a) features a phrasal standard and (1b) a clausal standard. Here *hodo* appears to be a negative polarity item, being grammatical in the negative sentences but not their positive counterparts. In the positive sentences, *hodo* must be replaced with another equative marker, *kurai*, per (2a)–(2b).

(1)   a.   *Taro-wa   Jiro-hodo   se-ga   *takai/takaku-nai.*
           Taro-TOP   Jiro-hodo   height-NOM   tall/tall-NEG

           'Taro *is/is not as tall as Jiro.'

      b.   *Taro-wa   Jiro-ga   nonda-hodo biiru-o   *nonda/noma-nakat-ta.*
           Taro-TOP   Jiro-NOM   drank-hodo beer-ACC   drank/drink-NEG-past

           'Taro *drank/didn't drink as much beer as Jiro did.'

(2)   a.   *Taro-wa   Jiro-kurai se-ga   takai.*
           Taro-TOP   Jiro-kurai height-NOM   tall

           'Taro is as tall as Jiro.'

      b.   *Taro-wa   Jiro-ga   nonda-kurai (takusan) biiru-o   nonda.*
           Taro-TOP   Jiro-NOM   drank-kurai (much)   beer-ACC   drank

           'Taro drank as much beer as Jiro did.'

In this, *hodo* differs from equative markers such as English *as*, which is not polarity sensitive (e.g. *Taro is / isn't as tall as Jiro*).

Hodo, however, is not a negative polarity item in a standard sense. The clausal complement of *hodo* may include negation, in which case the matrix predicate has to be affirmative, as shown in (3). The sentence yields a comparative interpretation.

(3)   *Taro-wa   [Jiro-ga   noma-nakat-ta-hodo]*   *(takusan)   biiru-o*
      Taro-TOP   [Jiro-NOM   drink-NEG-Past-hodo]   (much)   beer-ACC
      *nonda/*noma-nakat-ta.*
      drank/drink-NEG-Past

      (Lit.) 'Taro drank as much beer as Jiro didn't drink.'
      'Taro drank more beer than Jiro did.'

Another case that differs from *hodo* in (1a)–(1b) is a context where a phrasal *hodo* is embedded in a relative clause and the whole sentence yields a superlative interpretation. *Hodo* in this context requires negation in the matrix predicate.

(4) *Taro-wa* [*Jiro-hodo* *se-ga*   *takai hito*]-*o*   *mita-koto-ga*
     Taro-TOP [Jiro-hodo height-NOM tall   person]-ACC saw-fact-NOM
     *aru/nai.
     be/NEG

'Taro has *seen/never seen a person as tall as Jiro.'

The example in (5), however, illustrates a distinct use of *hodo*, which corresponds more closely to English *'so... that'*. On this use, it is not polarity sensitive, being acceptable in positive as well as negative sentences.

(5) *Taro-wa*   *basukettobooru senshu-ni nar-eru-hodo*   *se-ga*
     Taro-TOP   basketball   player-to   become-can-hodo height-NOM
     takai/takaku-nai.
     tall/tall-NEG

'Taro is/is not so tall that he could become a basketball player.'

Thus *hodo* is quite unlike 'ordinary' polarity items, but instead displays an interesting and variable pattern of polarity sensitivity.

2.2 Additional Effects

Sentences with *hodo* exhibit additional presuppositional effects (cf. [3,5,10] on similar patterns with equative *kurai* and comparative *izyoo(-ni)*). Specifically, *'as'-hodo* sentences introduce standard-oriented presuppositions on both the standard of comparison and the subject. In an example such as (1a), the standard –here, Jiro – must count as a clear case of 'tall'; this explains why a *hodo* comparison to 209 cm tall Giant Baba is felicitous, whereas comparison to 145 cm tall Ikeno Medaka is odd:

(6) *Taro-wa*   *Giant Baba/#Ikeno Medaka-hodo se-ga*   *takaku-nai.*
     Taro-TOP Giant Baba/Ikeno   Medaka-hodo height-NOM tall-NEG

'Taro is not as tall as Giant Baba/#Ikeno Medaka.'

Likewise, the subject – here Taro – must also count as 'tall': (1a) conveys that Taro is tall but not as tall as Jiro, and would be infelicitous if Taro's being tall were not already part of the common ground.

In the case of *'so'-hodo*, there is similarly a presupposition on the standard of comparison; thus (5) would be odd if 'basketball player' were replaced with 'jockey'. But there is no presupposition on the subject; (5) could be felicitously uttered in a context where nothing was known about Taro's height.

Hayashishita [3,5] takes the similar effect on *kurai* and comparative marker *izyoo-(ni)* as lexically encoded comparison of deviation. These markers are claimed to encode differences between a contextually given standard and the degrees to which the subject/the standard reaches. The effect becomes conspicuous in a highly unlikely context where Taro's height and his 3 year old son's height are compared. In (7a), only *izyoo-ni* has a reasonable reading because the comparison is made between how far Taro's height is away from the average height of adults and how far his son is away from the average height of 3-year-olds. The use of *yori* here strikes us as odd, because of our common knowledge that a father should be taller than his 3-year-old son. If we apply this context to *hodo*, the result is that it resists it, as in (7b).

(7)   a.   *Taro-wa   san-sai-no   musuko-izyoo-ni/#yori se-ga   hikui.*
           Taro-TOP 3-year.old-GEN son-izyoo-ni/yori   height-NOM short

           (Lit.) 'Taro is shorter than his 3 year old son.'

      b.   *#Taro-wa san-sai-no   musuko-hodo se-ga   takaku-nai.*
           Taro-TOP 3-year.old-GEN son-hodo   height-NOM tall-NEG

           '#Taro isn't as tall as his 3 year old son.'

This suggests that *hodo* is not a *izyoo-ni* cousin with respect to a comparison of deviation analysis.

3   Explaining Variable Polarity Sensitivity

Standard degree-based semantic analyses treat equative markers as degree quantifiers that introduce a maximality operator, as in the following analysis of a simple English case (see e.g. [1] and references therein):

(8)   Taro is as tall as Jiro.
      $\max\{d : \text{Taro is } d\text{-tall}\} \geq \max\{d : \text{Jiro is } d\text{-tall}\}$

However, on the basis of differences in the behavior of equative constructions in English and Slovenian, Crnič & Fox [2] argue that maximality is not an inherent component of the semantics of the equative. Rather, they propose, equative semantics derive from the presence of separate existential and maximality operators, the latter of which is optional in some languages (in particular Slovenian), but is inserted when needed to avoid a trivial meaning.

The crucial data are the following: Both English *as . . . as* and Slovenian *tako . . . kot* can be used with a positive clausal standard, per (9). Both are analyzed as involving a maximality operator over the set of degrees introduced by the standard clause.

(9)   a.   John drove as fast [as Mary did].

    b.   *Janez se je   peljal tako hitro [kot se   je   Marija].*
        Janez self aux drive dem fast than self aux Mary

    'John drove as fast as Mary did.'

By contrast, the English example is bad with negation in the standard clause. Surprisingly, though, its Slovenian counterpart remains acceptable. The proposed explanation is that in English, maximality is obligatory; but in (10a), maximization fails (there is no maximum degree d such that Mary didn't drive d fast). In Slovenian, however, maximality may be optionally omitted, allowing (10b) to surface.

(10)   a.   *John drove as fast [as Mary didn't].

    b.   *Janez se je   peljal tako hitro [kot se   Marija ni].*
        Janez self aux drive dem fast than self Mary   neg.aux

    'John drove as fast as Mary didn't.'

As further support, the authors observe that the presence of a multiplicative modifier (as in *twice as fast*) requires maximality in the standard clause; when such a modifier is present in Slovenian, a negated standard clause is likewise ungrammatical.

We propose that Japanese *hodo* instantiates a third possibility: whereas maximality is mandatory in English and optional in Slovenian, our claim is that *hodo* never introduces maximality, but instead necessarily has weak existential semantics. Polarity-based distributional restrictions then result from triviality.

Formally, we assume that gradable predicates such as *se-ga takai* 'tall' relate individuals to degrees (as in [6]), and are monotonic, meaning that if Taro 180 cm tall, he is 170 cm tall, 160 cm tall, etc.:

(11) $[\![se\text{-}ga\ takai]\!] = \lambda d\lambda x.\mu_{HEIGHT}(x) \geq d$

We then propose the following lexical entry for *hodo*, on which it takes as arguments a set of degrees D, a gradable predicate P, and an individual x, and introduces a variable over degrees d^* which is constrained to be an element of D, and which is subsequently existentially bound, per (12):

(12) $[\![hodo]\!] = \lambda D_{\langle dt\rangle}\lambda P_{\langle d,et\rangle}\lambda x.P(d^*)(x)$, where $d^* \in D$

We apply this first to **'as'-hodo**, i.e. the use of *hodo* on which it may be paraphrased by English equative *as … as*. In (13) we give the constituency of the ungrammatical positive version of (1a).

(13)   Taro-wa [[Jiro-hodo] se-ga takai]
    Intended: 'Taro is as tall as Jiro.'

Here the first argument of *hodo* is provided by the proper name *Jiro*. On the surface this is not of the right semantic type, being of type e, whereas *hodo* requires an argument of type $\langle dt \rangle$. We propose that the type mismatch might be resolved in one of two ways. As one option, we might follow the approach of Hayashishita [4] for *yori* in taking the standard to be contextually determined on the basis of the complement of *hodo*, as shown in (14a). Alternately, we might take the standard in (13) to be covertly clausal (see again [1] and references therein for discussion), including an elided copy of the gradable predicate and null operator movement, as in (14b). For concreteness we assume the latter approach, though nothing crucial depends on this.

(14)   a. $f(\llbracket jiro \rrbracket) = \lambda d.\mu_{HEIGHT}(jiro) \geq d$

       b. $\llbracket Op_i \ jiro \ t_i \ \sout{se\text{-}ga \ takai} \rrbracket = \lambda d_i.\mu_{HEIGHT}(jiro) \geq d_i$

The following then presents the full derivation for (13). After existential closure over the variable d^*, the meaning we derive is that there is **some** degree of height that Jiro has that Taro also has. But with the monotonic semantics for *se-ga takai* 'tall' in (11), this meaning is entirely trivial: as illustrated in (16), there will always be some degree of height that the two individuals share. We take this to be the source of ungrammaticality.

(15)   a. $\llbracket jiro\text{-}hodo \ se\text{-}ga \ takai \rrbracket = \lambda x.\mu_{HEIGHT}(x) \geq d^*$,
            where $\mu_{HEIGHT}(jiro) \geq d^*$

       b. $\llbracket taro\text{-}wa \ jiro\text{-}hodo \ se\text{-}ga \ takai \rrbracket = \mu_{HEIGHT}(taro) \geq d^*$
            After existential closure:
            $\exists d^* : \mu_{HEIGHT}(jiro) \geq d^*[\mu_{HEIGHT}(taro) \geq d^*]$

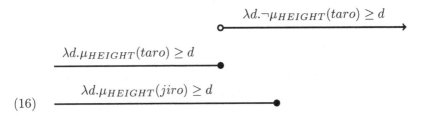

(16)

In (17) and (18) we present the corresponding constituent structure and semantic interpretation for the negative version of (1a).

(17)   Taro-wa [[Jiro-hodo] se-ga takaku-nai]
       'Taro isn't as tall as Jiro.'

(18) $\llbracket taro\text{-}wa \ jiro\text{-}hodo \ se\text{-}ga \ takaku\text{-}nai \rrbracket$
       $= \exists d^* : \mu_{HEIGHT}(jiro) \geq d^*[\neg\mu_{HEIGHT}(taro) \geq d^*]$

Referring back to the illustration in (16), the effect of negation in the matrix clause is to invert the set of degrees it introduces. The sentence thus expresses a relation between an upper-bounded set of degrees (the set of Jiro's heights) and a lower-bounded one (the set of heights that Taro doesn't have). In this configuration, an *'as'-hodo* sentence is not trivial: (18) says that there is some degree of height that Jiro has that Taro **doesn't** have, i.e. that Taro is shorter than Jiro.

Observe that in (18), existential closure takes scope over the negation operator introduced in the matrix clause. We assume that the opposite scope relationship is also in principle possible, but is blocked on account of triviality, being the negation of the trivially true (15b).

The analysis developed here also extends to clausal examples such as (1b), with a similar choice regarding how to derive a first argument of the right semantic type for *hodo*. It can also capture more complex examples such as (4), where *hodo* occurs in a relative clause: *hodo* composes in situ as shown in (20) and the composition proceeds as usual, with existential closure coming in at the end to bind the degree variable d^*. This yields the interpretation in (21), which states that there is some degree of height that Jiro has such that Taro has not seen a person of that height.

(19)   Taro-wa [Jiro-hodo se-ga takai hito]-o mita-koto-ga nai.
       'Taro has never seen a person as tall as Jiro.'

(20)   a. $[\![Jiro\text{-}hodo\ se\text{-}ga\ takai]\!] = \lambda x.\mu_{HEIGHT}(x) \geq d^*$,
            where $\mu_{HEIGHT}(jiro) \geq d^*$

       b. $[\![Jiro\text{-}hodo\ se\text{-}ga\ takai\ hito\text{-}o]\!] = \lambda x.person(x) \wedge \mu_{HEIGHT}(x) \geq d^*$,
            where $\mu_{HEIGHT}(jiro) \geq d^*$

(21) $[\![(19)]\!] = \exists d^* : \mu_{HEIGHT}(jiro) \geq d^*[\neg \exists x[person(x) \wedge \mu_{HEIGHT}(x) \geq d^* \wedge saw(taro, x)]]$

A possible objection to this analysis of *'as'-hodo* comes from the construction in which an external negation licenses *hodo*:[1]

(22)   [*Taro-ga*   *Jiro-hodo se-ga*   *takai to-iu-koto*   ]*-wa nai.*
       [Taro-NOM Jiro-hodo height-NOM tall   COMP-say-fact]-TOP NEG

       'It is not the case that Taro is as tall as Jiro.'

In (22), if the negation takes scope over the clause, the predicted interpretation would be trivial:

(23) $\neg \exists d^*$: $\mu_{\text{HEIGHT}}(\text{jiro}) \geq d^*$ $[\mu_{\text{HEIGHT}}(\text{taro}) \geq d^*]$

We claim that (22) does not give us a blow, because we assume that the existential semantics comes from existential closure and (22) is analyzed on a par with (4): *hodo* is composed in situ and negation comes next and existential

---

[1] We thank J.R Hayashishita for pointing this out.

closure is applied at the end to take scope over negation, which results in a non-trivial interpretation. The licensing of *hodo* thus exhibits a peculiar behavior, because a usual NPI, such as *nidoto* has to obey the clause-mate condition, as shown in (24).

(24) *[Taro-ga nidoto kuru to-iu-koto]-wa   nai.
      [Taro-NOM again   come   COMP-say-fact]-TOP   NEG
      'It is not the case that Taro comes again.'

Finally, we derive a prediction. Negation in the matrix clause had the effect of reversing the set of degrees it introduces, creating a configuration on which the resulting meaning is non-trivial. We then predict a parallel effect when negation is present in a clausal standard, such that it (rather than the matrix clause) introduces a lower-bounded set of degrees. This prediction is borne out, as illustrated by the previously discussed (3), which demonstrates that in the case of a negated clausal standard for *hodo*, it is the positive sentence that is grammatical, while the negated one is ill-formed.

We turn now to **'so'-hodo**, that is, the use of *hodo* on which it would be paraphrased with English *so ... that*. Here, we draw on Meier's [13] analysis of *so ... that*, according to which the clausal complement of *'so'-hodo* is covertly modalized, with the set of degrees derived as the standard of comparison being those degrees that are sufficient for the referenced state of affairs to obtain. In (5), whose structure is given in (25), the modalized proposition is as in (26a), and the corresponding set of degrees is the set of heights that would be sufficient for one to be a basketball player, per (26b). Importantly, this set is lower bounded, as illustrated in (27); e.g., if the minimum height to play basketball is 2 m, the relevant set of degrees is $\{d : d \geq 2m\}$.

(25)   Taro-wa [[basukettobooru senshu-ni nar-eru-hodo] se-ga takai]
        'Taro is tall enough to become a basketball player.'

(26)   a.   PRO is d tall in w → PRO $can_{w,h}$ become a basketball player in w

        b. $\lambda d.sufficient\text{-}to\text{-}play\text{-}basketball(d)$

$\lambda d.\mu_{HEIGHT}(taro) \geq d$

$\lambda d.sufficient\text{-}to\text{-}play\text{-}basketball(d)$

(27)

On this basis we derive the following as the interpretation for (25):

(28) $\exists d^* : sufficient\text{-}to\text{-}play\text{-}basketball(d^*)[\mu_{HEIGHT}(taro) \geq d^*]$

Crucially, (28) is not trivial but rather expresses the contingent proposition that Taro has some degree of height that would be sufficient for him to be a basketball player. In contrast to the case with *'as'-hodo* in a positive context, the sentence is therefore felicitous.

     A *'so'-hodo* sentence can be felicitously negated, as in (29). Here in contrast to the case of negated *'as'-hodo* we take existential quantification to scope under negation, as in (30a). Just as before we assume that the opposite scope (30b) is also in principle possible, but here would result in a trivial meaning (trivially true, since assuming that Taro has finite height there will necessarily be some degree of height that he doesn't have that would be sufficient to be a basketball player).

(29)   Taro-wa [[basukettobooru senshu-ni nar-eru-hodo] se-ga takaku-nai]
       'Taro isn't tall enough to become a basketball player.'

(30)   a. $\neg \exists d^* : sufficient\text{-}to\text{-}play\text{-}basketball(d^*)[\mu_{HEIGHT}(taro) \geq d^*]$ ✔

       b. $\exists d^* : sufficient\text{-}to\text{-}play\text{-}basketball(d^*)[\neg \mu_{HEIGHT}(taro) \geq d^*]$ ✘

To summarize this section, the variable polarity sensitivity of *hodo* on its *'as'* versus *'so'* uses can be related to difference between a standard that is a upper-bounded set of degrees and one that is an lower-bounded set.

4   Explaining Presuppositional Effects

As discussed in Sect. 2.2, *hodo* sentences exhibit additional presuppositional effects, which are similar but not identical to those observed for other Japanese comparative markers such as *izyoo-(ni)*. To briefly recap the relevant pattern, negated *'as'-hodo* introduces norm-oriented presuppositions on both the subject and the standard of comparison. By contrast, *'so'-hodo* has a presupposition on the standard but not on the subject.

     One possibility to account for these patterns would be to posit a lexical presupposition as a part of the semantics of *hodo* itself, along the lines proposed by Kubota [10] for *izyoo(-ni)* and *kurai* constructions. However, the lexical approach predicts that this presuppositional effect is not cancelled out in any context. We argue that this prediction is not borne out.

     Hodo may be appended by contrastive topic marker *wa* or concessive marker *mo* 'even'. As argued by Sawada [16], these markers may reverse the effects that comparative markers may have. In (31a), the standard is understood to be 'tall', while in (31b), the complement of *hodo* should be short.

(31) a. *Taro-wa   Giant Baba/#Ikeno Medaka-hodo-wa   se-ga*
          Taro-TOP   Giant Baba/Ikeno   Medaka-hodo-CT   height-NOM
          takaku-nai.
          tall-NEG

      b. *Taro-wa   #Giant Baba/Ikeno Medaka-hodo-mo   se-ga*
          Taro-TOP   Giant   Baba/Ikeno Medaka-hodo-even height-NOM
          takaku-nai.
          tall-NEG

If the lexical approach were on the right track, (31b) would be judged unnatural, because the effect of concessive *mo* and the alleged presupposition of *hodo* contradict. We thus will not take the lexical presupposition approach.

We also do not see an obvious way that Hayashishita's analysis of *izyoo-(ni)* in terms of comparison of deviation could be extended to *hodo*, given the differences in behavior between the two documented in Sect. 2.2.

We propose instead that a more parsimonious account of the presuppositions of *hodo* can be achieved by deriving them pragmatically. In this, we follow an approached developed by Simons [17] and Leffels et al. [12], according to which presupposition-like interpretive patterns are analyzed as manner implicatures relative to simpler alternatives. By way of example, Leffels and colleagues derive the implication (or presupposition) of *John was not very late* that John was late as an implicature that the simpler *not late* does not obtain.

With regards to *hodo* specifically, we take these patterns to arise as the consequence of competition with the structurally simpler form obtained by deleting the *hodo* constituent (cf. Katzir [7] on structurally defined alternatives). Here we observe a parallel to the account proposed for interpretive effects in 'compared to' constructions proposed by Sawada [16], which similarly relies on principles of economy.[2]

Following current practice, we analyze the unmodified form of gradable adjectives as involving a null 'positive' morpheme *pos*, which introduces a contextually determined threshold θ_c, as in (32); this yields (33) as the semantics of the simpler alternatives to the *'as'-hodo* sentences in (13)/(17).

(32) $[\![pos]\!] = \lambda P_{\langle d,et \rangle} \lambda x. P(\theta_c)(x)$

(33) a. *Taro-wa   se-ga   takai / takaku-nai.*
          Taro-TOP height-NOM tall / tall-NEG

          'Taro is / isn't tall'

      b. $\mu_{HEIGHT}(taro) \geq \theta_c$ / $\neg \mu_{HEIGHT}(taro) \geq \theta_c$

Consider the grammatical negative example in (18). If Jiro did not have some degree of height that is greater than the contextually determined standard θ_c,

---

[2] We thank a LENLS reviewer for bringing this parallel to our attention.

there would be no reason to describe an individual as *Jiro-hodo se-ga takaku-nai* 'not Jiro-hodo tall', since in that case it would be possible to use the simpler *se-ga takaku-nai* 'not tall'. Similarly, if Taro's height were not at least θ_c, he could likewise be described simply as *se-ga takaku-nai* 'not tall', without the need to invoke Jiro's height. Thus *'as'-hodo* sentences require a context of utterance in which it is established that both the complement of *hodo* and the subject have a measure that exceeds the contextual standard introduced by *pos*.

A similar explanation can be applied to the standard of comparison in *'so'-hodo* sentences: (25) is felicitous because 'basketball player' introduces a higher standard than simply 'pos tall'; if this were not the case, the simpler positive form could have been used instead. But since the *hodo* sentence in this case produces a more informative assertion about the subject (Taro) than its simpler alternative, it is not blocked by the latter; there are therefore no presupposition-like effects with respect to the subject.

We further note that our account might be refined by construing the degrees over which *hodo* quantifies not simply as degrees, but more specifically as possible thresholds θ_c for the positive form of *se-ga takai* 'tall'. On this view, (18) states that there is some possible threshold for tall according to which Jiro counts as tall but Taro does not; (25), that there is a threshold of tallness at or above which one can play basketball and Taro has at least that height. This would be to say that *hodo* sentences are a variety of positive construction. Such a view would be consistent with the observation that *hodo* cannot be used to express so-called crisp judgments (see [8]): (18) would be infelicitous if Jiro were only a few millimeters taller than Taro, but instead requires there to be a significant difference in height between the two. We also note a connection to Klein's [9] theory of comparatives, according to which *Taro is taller than Jiro* is analyzed essentially as expressing 'there is some way of construing *tall* such that Taro is tall and Jiro is not tall'. The difference in the present case is that to say that 'there is some way of construing *tall* such that both Taro and Jiro are tall' is trivially true, resulting in ill-formedness.

5   Extensions

In the preceding two sections, we have shown that the equative marker *hodo* can receive a unified analysis that covers both its *'as'* and *'so'* uses. We see potential to extend this account also to other uses of *hodo*, and potentially to other lexical items in Japanese and beyond.

To start, observe that *hodo* has a use on which it composes with a numerical expression to produce an approximative interpretation, per (34). The present analysis of *hodo* might be extended to such data by taking the numerical expression (here, *50-nin*) to supply a set of degrees that saturates the first argument position of *hodo*. This might be achieved by taking the interpretation of the numerical expression to be coerced to that of its pragmatic halo (see [11]). The resulting interpretation is that in (35).

(34) *50-nin hodo-no   hito-ga   paatii-ni kita.*
      50-CL   hodo-GEN people-NOM party-to came
      'About 50 people came to the party.'

(35) $\exists d^* \in HALO(50)\exists x[people(x) \wedge came\text{-}to\text{-}party(x) \wedge |x| = d^*]$

Although the compositional implementation remains to be worked out in detail, and may require a slightly different lexical entry for *hodo*, the core elements of the analyses of its *as* and *so* uses are retained.

Looking more broadly, it is interesting to consider whether aspects of the present analysis of *hodo* might be extended to the equative marker *kurai*, which also has presupposition effects, but which is a positive polarity item rather than a negative polarity item. A potentially promising direction to pursue in explaining the difference between the two items is that *kurai* obligatorily includes maximality as a part of its semantics. We must however leave a fuller exploration of this possible connection to future work.

Finally, we observe that the sorts of patterns under discussion here are not restricted to Japanese: German *dermaßen* 'to such an extent' exhibits similar behavior. Specifically, *dermaßen... dass* 'to such an extent that' is like *'so'-hodo* in being acceptable in both positive and negative sentences, whereas *dermaßen... wie* 'to such an extent as' is like *'as'-hodo* in requiring the presence of negation. Thus the present work draws attention to a previously unrecognized and perhaps more general pattern in equative semantics.

6   Conclusions

We have shown that the distributional and interpretive effects characterizing *hodo* can be explained on the basis of a weak existential semantics, which yields a trivial interpretation in certain configurations, coupled with pragmatic competition with the simpler positive form. Previous work by Crnič & Fox has shown that the obligatory versus optional presence of a maximality operator is a dimension along which the semantics of equative constructions may vary cross-linguistically. We have argued that Japanese *hodo* instantiates a third possibility (which may be present in other languages as well): *hodo* never introduces maximality, the consequence being a more restricted and seemingly idiosyncratic distribution relative to better-studied equative markers. Our findings thus contribute to a fuller picture of variation in the semantics of degree constructions across languages.

References

1. Beck, S.: Comparative constructions. In: Maienborn, C., von Heusinger, C., Portner, P. (eds.) Semantics: An International Handbook of Natural Language Meaning, vol. 2, pp. 1341–1389. Mouton de Gruyter, Berlin (2011)

2. Crnič, L., Fox, D.: Equatives and maximality. In: Altshuler, D., Rett, J. (eds.) The Semantics of Plurals, Focus, Degrees, and Times, pp. 163–184. Springer, Cham (2019). https://doi.org/10.1007/978-3-030-04438-1_9

3. Hayashishita, J.R.: *Izyoo(ni)*-and *gurai*-comparatives: comparisons of deviation in Japanese. Gengo Kenkyu **132**, 77–109 (2007)

4. Hayashishita, J.R.: *Yori*-comparatives: a reply to Beck et al. (2004). J. East Asian Linguist. **18**(2), 65–100 (2009). https://doi.org/10.1007/s10831-009-9040-5

5. Hayashishita, J.-R.: Reconfirming *izyoo(ni)*- and *gurai*-comparatives as comparisons of deviation. J. East Asian Linguist. **26**(2), 163–187 (2017). https://doi.org/10.1007/s10831-016-9152-7

6. Heim, I.: Degree operators and scope. In: Jackson, B., Matthews, T. (eds.) Proceedings of the 10th Semantics and Linguistic Theory Conference (SALT10), pp. 60–84. CLC Publications, Ithaca (2000). https://doi.org/10.3765/salt.v10i0.3102

7. Katzir, R.: Structurally-defined alternatives. Linguist. Philos. **30**(6), 669–690 (2007). https://doi.org/10.1007/s10988-010-9074-1

8. Kennedy, C.: Vagueness and grammar: the semantics of relative and absolute gradable adjectives. Linguist. Philos. **30**(1), 1–45 (2007). https://doi.org/10.1007/s10988-006-9008-0

9. Klein, E.: A semantics for positive and comparative adjectives. Linguist. Philos. **4**(1), 1–45 (1980). https://doi.org/10.1007/BF00351812

10. Kubota, Y.: The presuppositional nature of *izyoo(-ni)* and *gurai* comparatives: a note on Hayashishita (2007). Gengo Kenkyu **141**, 33–46 (2012)

11. Lasersohn, P.: Pragmatic halos. Language **75**(3), 522–551 (1999). https://doi.org/10.2307/417059

12. Leffel, T., Cremers, A., Gotzner, N., Romoli, J.: Vagueness in implicature: the case of modified adjectives. J. Semant. **36**(2), 317–348 (2019). https://doi.org/10.1093/jos/ffy020

13. Meier, C.: The meaning of *too, enough and so... that.* Nat. Lang. Semant. **11**(1), 69–107 (2003). https://doi.org/10.1023/A:1023002608785

14. Penka, D.: Degree equatives - the same as comparatives? In: Workshop on Equative Constructions. University of Cologne (2016)

15. Rett, J.: Separate but equal: a typology of equative constructions. In: Hallman, P. (ed.) Degree and Quantification. Brill, Leiden (in press)

16. Sawada, O.: Pragmatic aspects of implicit comparison: an economy-based approach. J. Pragmat. **41**(6), 1079–1103 (2009). https://doi.org/10.1016/j.pragma.2008.12.004

17. Simons, M.: On the conversational basis of some presuppositions. In: Capone, A., Lo Piparo, F., Carapezza, M. (eds.) Perspectives on Linguistic Pragmatics. PPPP, vol. 2, pp. 329–348. Springer, Cham (2013). https://doi.org/10.1007/978-3-319-01014-4_13

18. Umbach, C., Özge, U.: Scalar and non-scalar comparison across categories: the case of Turkish equatives. In: TbiLLC 2019 (2019)

An OT-Driven Dynamic Pragmatics: High-Applicatives, Subject-Honorific Markers and Imperatives in Japanese

Akitaka Yamada[(✉)]

Graduate School of Language and Culture, Osaka University,
1-8 Machikaneyama, Toyonaka, Osaka 560-0043, Japan
ay314@georgetown.edu

Abstract. The relation between a sentence type and an illocutionary force is 'one-to-many' but not 'one-to-any.' The goal of this paper is to provide a formal theory capable of describing this association. The primary data for this study comes from Japanese imperatives. In this language, the illocutionary force of an imperative sentence is determined by the interaction between high-applicatives and subject-honorific markers. Inheriting important insights from Portner et al. (2019), this paper develops the idea that all of these constructions are involved in the process of determining AUTHORITY among the discourse participants. Integrating the Optimality Theory into Dynamic Pragmatics, I propose that there are pragmatic constraints which are relevant in determining (i) who is in AUTHORITY and (ii) what illocutionary force is appropriate for a given sentence, before we update the structured discourse context.

Keywords: 'Point-of-view' applicatives · Subject-honorific markers · Imperatives · Optimality Theory · Dynamic Pragmatics

1 Introduction

This paper examines the Japanese imperative system and its interaction with high-applicatives and subject-honorific markers. Incorporating some important insights from the phonology of Optimality Theory (OT) (Prince and Smolesky 2004 [1993]; McCarthy and Prince 1993; Kager 1999), I propose that the speech act of an utterance is determined as a consequence of interactions between pragmatic constraints. To be more precise, this is a study of relation between the sentence type and the illocutionary force. In this study, the term SENTENCE TYPE is used to refer to a particular grammatical form of a sentence. For example, consider the sentences in (1). The sentence types of these sentences are a declarative, an interrogative and an imperative.

(1) **Sentence types and sentential forces**

a.	Bond gives every fish to Loren.	Declarative	*stating*
b.	Does Bond give every fish to Loren?	Interrogative	*asking*

© Springer Nature Switzerland AG 2020
M. Sakamoto et al. (Eds.): JSAI-isAI 2019, LNAI 12331, pp. 354–369, 2020.
https://doi.org/10.1007/978-3-030-58790-1_23

   c.   Give every fish to Loren, Bond!   Imperative   *directing*

In order to capture both similarities and differences, it is a common practice to "distinguish two aspects of the meaning of a sentence; its content—what [(1)a-c] seem (more or less) to have in common—and *sentential force*—what the grammar assigns to the sentence to indicate how that content is conventionally presented (Chierchia and McConnel-Ginet 1990: 164)." For instance, declarative sentences, such as the example in (1)a, are conventionally associated with the sentential force of *stating*, which stands in stark contrast to both *asking* (the sentential force of an interrogative) and *directing* (the sentential force of an imperative).[1]

At the most rudimentary level, these terminologies are helpful in clarifying the differences. However, the causal relation between a sentence type and its communicative effect is not so simple. Consider the following imperatives in (2).

(2)   **Sentence types and illocutionary forces**

    a.   Soldiers, <u>march</u>!   Imperative   [COMMAND]
    b.   <u>Have</u> some beer!   Imperative   [OFFER]
    c.   <u>Help</u> me!   Imperative   [ENTREATY]

Clearly, all three share the same sentence type. First, the verb takes the bare infinitive form. Second, the subject of the main clause is not present. Therefore, we can assert that they are all imperatives. Yet, their (prototypical) communicative effects are different. For instance, (2)a is typically used as a COMMAND; (2)b is usually considered to be an OFFER; and (2)c would be most likely be used as an ENTREATY. I use the term ILLOCUTIONARY FORCE to refer to such detailed communicative effects and, in what follows, small caps are used to refer to illocutionary forces.

Traditionally, a sentential force is considered as a function associated with a particular sentence type. So, this is something that all the imperative sentences have in common (if anything). In contrast, illocutionary forces are more closely related to social actions. Hence, the relation between a sentence type and an illocutionary force is 'one-to-many,' as demonstrated in (2). These theoretical concepts were each proposed in different historical backgrounds. The sentential force originates from Frege's attempt at content-force dichotomy (Frege 1918), a concept which proves useful when we assume that there is a core communicative meaning/function pertaining to all the declaratives; the notion of illocutionary force was originally proposed by researchers working on speech act theories (Austin 1962; Searle 1969; Searle and Vanderveken 1985); see also Portner (2018b) and Murray and Starr (in prep.) for the detailed review of the literature.

As previously stated, the purpose of this paper is to propose a formal device with which to analyze the relation between a sentence type (or a grammatical

---

[1] **Sentential force for an imperative:** For the purposes of explanation, the term *directing* refers to the sentential force of the imperative. This term could be improved, and one might propose or coin a better term. None of the information that follows depends upon the particular label give to this sentential force.

pattern) and an illocutionary force, *not* the relation between a sentence type and a sentential force. Particularly, this paper tries to elucidate the two seemingly opposing properties of illocutionary forces. First, the relation is 'one-to-many,' as mentioned previously. We do not want our theory to be too specialized to explain the diversity of possible illocutionary forces. Second, the relation is not 'one-to-any.' For example, whereas the imperative sentence type can be linked to many different illocutionary forces, it cannot be used as a question. So how do we capture the flexibility and limitations of the relation between the sentence type and the illocutionary force?

To consider this dilemma, this paper investigates Japanese imperatives and their interaction with subject-honorifics and high-applicatives. As shall be explained in the next section, the relation between a Japanese imperative and an illocutionary force is much more complicated than the example shown in (2); the illocutionary force assignment is sensitive not only to the sentence type but also to other grammatical profiles of a given sentence (Sect. 2). To account for this complexity, this paper integrates an OT-based perspective into dynamic pragmatics. The key idea is that after semantics are completed, discourse-oriented meanings are translated as 'violable' constraints, determining the type of combination between a sentence and an illocutionary force (Sect. 3). The article concludes with a summation of implications for future studies (Sect. 4).

2   Data

This section provides readers with the relevant Japanese data—(i) imperative suffixes, (ii) applicative markers, and (iii) subject-honorific constructions (Svahn 2016; Yamada 2019).

2.1   Imperative Suffix

Form. Japanese is an SOV, agglutinative language. A verb is followed by functional suffixes in an order which is, for the most part, in agreement with Baker's (1985) Mirror Principle. For example, observe the sentence in (3)a. The verb *nom-* 'to drink' is followed by a past tense marker *-ta*.[2]

(3)   **Consonant-base verb**

    a.   Watasi-wa biiru-o   non-da.   Declarative
          I-TOP   beer-ACC drink-PST
          'I drank beer.'

    b.   Biiru-o   nom{-e/*-ro}.   Imperative
          beer-ACC drink-IMP
          'Drink beer!'

---

[2] **Assimilation:** Due to an assimilation, *-ta* becomes *-da*. In addition, the last consonant *m* in *nom-* becomes *n* to match the articulation point of the following consonant.

The corresponding imperative is given in (3)b. In an imperative, a tense marker is suppressed as it is in English; a verb is followed by an imperative suffix -*e* 'IMP.'

This imperative suffix has a phonologically-conditioned allomorph. If a verb ends with a vowel, -*ro* 'IMP' is used in place of -*e* 'IMP.' For example, the verb *tabe*- 'to eat' is a vowel-base verb and thus the imperative form is *tabe-ro*, not *tabe-e.

(4)　　**Vowel-base verb**

    a.　Watasi-wa gohan-o tabe-ta.　　　　　　　　　Declarative
       I-TOP　　　rice-ACC eat-PST
       'I ate beer.'
    b.　Gohan-o tabe{*-e/-ro}.　　　　　　　　　　　Imperative
       beer-ACC eat-IMP
       'Eat rice!'

In general, unlike in English, a bare form of a verb cannot be used as an indicator of a directing force (though we will see some exceptions below shortly). For example, (5) is illicit.

(5)　　*Gohan-o tabe!
       beer-ACC eat
       'Eat rice! (intended)'

Illocutionary Force. As we saw, some imperatives are 'stronger' than others. Despite the fact that they share the same sentence type, the sentences in (2) differ on whether the addressee is obliged to act, showing a variation in illocutionary force (Portner 2018a).

One peculiarity of Japanese imperatives is that an imperative suffix does *not* result in a comparable variation in illocutionary force. Observe the Japanese corresponding sentences in (6).

(6)　a.　Koosinsi-**ro**!
       march-IMP　　　　　　　　　　　　　　[COMMAND]
       'March!'
   b.　Biiru-o　 nom-**e**!
       beer-ACC drink-IMP　　　　　　　　　[COMMAND/*OFFER]
       'Drink beer!'
   c.　Watasi-o tasuke-**ro**!
       me-ACC　 help-IMP　　　　　　　　　[COMMAND/*ENTREATY]
       'Help me!'

They are all interpreted as a COMMAND. These sentences are typically used by a person of high social status, taking the addressee's obedience for granted. Therefore, we cannot use these sentences when making an OFFER or an ENTREATY.

2.2 Applicatives

But what procedure do we employ if we want to make an ENTREATY or an OFFER? In such cases, a 'point-of-view' applicative morpheme must be present in the sentence.

Form. A 'point-of-view' applicative is an applicative construction that has a point-of-view restriction on its argument.[3] Here, let us see two such examples. First, observe the sentences in (7).

(7)   **Low applicative (non-honorific form)**

    a.   Sensei-ga   {watasi/*siranai hito}-ni ringo-o   **kure**-ta.
          teacher-NOM me/*stranger-DAT   apple-ACC give-PST

          'The teacher gave me an apple (*an apple to a stranger).'

    b.   Watasi-ni ringo-o   **kure**{*-e/*-ro/∅}.
          me-DAT   apple-ACC give(*-IMP)

          'The teacher gave me an apple.'

The verb *kure-* 'to give (me)' in (7)a is a low applicative denoting a giving-receiving relation between the event participants. In addition, this verb has a point-of-restriction that the referent of the indirect object (the recipient) must be the speaker or his associate(s). Therefore, *watasi* 'I' is a felicitous indirect object while *siranai hito* 'stranger' is ruled out because it is difficult to conceive of a stranger as the speaker's associate.

    The corresponding imperative sentence is given in (7)b. Importantly, neither *-e* nor *-ro* is a permissible sentence. Even though *kure-* 'to give' is a vowel-base verb, it cannot be accompanied by *-ro*. *Kure-* must be used in the bare form.

    Second, this verb also has a high-applicative use. Consider the sentences in (8) and (9). The baseline sentence is (8), which contains no applicative marker.

(8)   Sensei-ga hasit-ta.
      teacher-NOM run-PST
      'The teacher ran.'

If one wishes to express an applied argument, (9)a is used instead. In this sentence, the main verb *hasir-* 'to run' is followed by the converb suffix *-te* and the applicative element *kure-*. As a result, a beneficiary is introduced. As in the case of low applicative usage, there is a 'point-of-view' restriction: the newly introduced individual must be either the speaker himself or his associate(s).

(9)   **High applicative (non-honorific form)**

    a.   Sensei-ga   watasi-notameni hasit-te **kure**-ta.   Declarative
          teacher-NOM me-for   run-CV APPLн-PST

---

[3] **Non-'point-of-view' applicatives:** There are other applicatives that do not have this type point-of-view restriction. For example, the verb *watas-* 'give' is a ditransitive predicate which can take *a stranger* as its indirect object. This verb takes *-e* when used in an imperative (*i.e.,* *watas-e* 'give-IMP').

'The teacher ran for me.'
b.   Watasi-notameni hasit-te **kure**{*-e/*-ro/∅}.   Imperative
     me-for   run-CV APPLн(*-IMP)
     'Please run for me!'

As shown in (9)b, an imperative suffix is disallowed in this construction. The applicative morpheme must take the bare form to encode the *directing* sentential force.

Illocutionary Force. The bare form of the 'point-of-view' applicative is dedicated to the weak imperative in Japanese (Kikuchi 1997; Yamada 2019). Unlike in (6), the sentences in (10) are compatible with different illocutionary acts, akin to the variation in (2) (except for COMMAND).

(10)   a.   Koosinsi-te **kure!**
            march-CV APPLн   [WEAK ORDER/GIVING A CUE/ENTREATY/...]
            'March (for me)!'
       b.   Non-de **kure!**
            drink-CV APPLн   [WISH/ENTREATY/OFFER/...]
            'Enjoy (for me)!'
       c.   Tasuke-te **kure!**
            help-CV   APPLн   [ENTREATY/WISH/WEAK ORDER/ ...]
            'Help me (for me)!'

2.3   Subject-Honorifics

In Japanese, subject-honorific constructions exhibit an interaction with an imperative suffix.

Form. Japanese subject-honorific markers are divided into two clusters; (i) those that can never be used in an imperative and (ii) those that can be used in an imperative. First, some subject-honorific expressions are completely illicit in an imperative sentence. For example, the suffix *-are* is a subject-honorific suffix with which the speaker shows his respect for the referent of the subject noun phrase; in (11)a, the subject-honorific suffix *-are* is used to encode the speaker's respect for *the teacher*. Since this suffix ends with a vowel, it seems appropriate that *-ro* would be used when making the imperative. However, as shown in (11)b, neither *-e*, *-ro* nor ∅ is permissible.

(11)   a.   Sensei-ga   koosins-**are**-ta.   Declarative
            teahcer-NOM march-HONs-PST
            '(i) The teacher marched; (ii) the speaker respects the referent of the subject.'
       b.   *Koosins-**are**-{*-e/*-ro/*∅}!   Imperative
            march-HONs-IMP
            '(i) March!; (ii) the speaker respects the referent of the subject (intended).'

Likewise, there is a periphrastic subject-honorific construction *go/o-* (nominalized verb)-*ni nar*. (12)a is a declarative example. As shown in (12)b, with or without an imperative suffix, this subject-honorific construction cannot be associated with the *directing* sentential force.

(12) a. Sensei-ga   **go**-koosin-**ni**   **nat**-ta.   Declarative
          teahcer-NOM HON-march-DAT become-PST

          '(i) The teacher marched; (ii) the speaker respects the *teacher*.'

      b. *Go-koosin-**ni**   nar-{*-e/*-ro/*∅}!   Imperative
          HON-march-DAT become-IMP

          '(i) March!; (ii) the speaker respects the *teacher* (intended).'

Second, another subject-honorific morpheme (*nasar-*) can be used in an imperative. Consider the three sentences in (13). (13)a is a declarative example. As shown in (13)b, an imperative suffix cannot be attached to this suffix, just as (11)b and (12)b are unacceptable.[4] But this construction has a remedy. If *nasar-* is used without an imperative suffix or a tense marker (i.e., in the bare form), the sentence can be associated with the *directing* sentential force. This is illustrated in (13)c. Presumably due to a phonological constraint, namely, that CVC syllable structure must be avoided, the consonant *r* in *nasar-* changes to *i*.[5]

(13) a. Sensei-ga   koosin-**nasar**-u.   Declarative
          teahcer-NOM march-HONs-PRS

          '(i) The teacher march; (ii) the speaker respects the referent of the subject.'

      b. Koosin-**nasar**{*-e/*-ro}!   Imperative
          march-HONs-IMP   (with a suffix)

      c. Koosin-**nasai**!   Imperative
          march-HONs   (in the bare form)

          '(i) March!; (ii) the speaker thinks that the addressee is subordinate to the speaker.'

Illocutionary Force. An important restriction of this *nasai*-imperative is that it cannot be used when the referent of the subject is someone the speaker respects, despite the fact that *nasar-* itself is a subject-honorific morpheme. Rather, the addressee is supposed to be subordinate to the speaker and the speaker assumes that the addressee should take the requested action. For example, the sentence in (14) cannot be used when a speaker is talking to a teacher he respects. In previous studies, honorific meanings have been characterized by a non-at-issue, expressive meaning, which does not interact with other semantic

---

[4] **Historical change:** In the past, an imperative suffix could be attached to *nasar-* (i.e., *nasar-e*). Native speakers of contemporary Japanese can recognize the intended meaning, but this usage sounds archaic and is no longer widely used.

[5] **A change in syllable-ending consonants:** A comparable phonological change is observed in *nak-* 'NEG' to *nai*.

operators (Potts and Kawahara 2004; Potts 2007; McCready 2014, 2019; Portner et al. 2019; Yamada 2019). But the fact that the subject-honorific meaning is 'switched off' with a *directing* sentential force seems to suggest that it does interact with other meanings, challenging the common assumption.

The only illocutionary force compatible with this construction is COMMAND, not REQUEST, or OFFER. For instance, although *help me* is typically used as an ENTREATY in English, the sentence in (14) can never be used in this manner. It *must* be a COMMAND from a speaker who (arrogantly) assumes that the addressee should obediently take action to help him (e.g., the utterance of an arrogant princess).

(14)   Watasi-o tasuke-**nasai**!   Imperative
        I-ACC   help-HONs   [COMMAND/*OFFER/*ENTREATY]
        '(i) Help me!; (ii) the speaker thinks that the addressee is subordinate to the speaker.'

Yet (14) is not as blunt as (6)c. The speaker of (14) is more respectful to their addressee compared to the speaker of (6)c. In this sense, the original honorific meaning is still active (though attenuated to a substantial degree).

2.4   Subject-Honorific Applicatives

If a speaker wants to make a weak imperative with a subject-honorific expression, he must also use the 'point-of-view' applicative element.

Form. The high-applicative suffix *kure-* 'APPLh' has the suppletive subject-honorific form *kudasar-* 'APPLh.HONs.' A declarative example is given in (15)a. Similarly to *kure-*, it cannot be used with an imperative suffix, as shown in (15)b.[6] As in (15)c, it must be used in the bare form.

(15)   a.   Sensei-ga   koosinsi-te **kudasar**-u.   Declarative
             teacher-NOM march-CV APPLh.HONs-IMP

             '(i) The teacher marches for me; (ii) the speaker respects the *teacher*.'

        b.   Koosinsi-te **kudasar**{*-e/*-ro}!   Imperative
             march-CV   APPLh.HONs-IMP   (with a suffix)

        c.   Koosinsi-te **kudasai**!   Imperative
             march-CV   APPLh.HONs   (in the bare form)

             '(i) Please march!; (ii) the speaker respects the referent of the subject.'

Illocutionary Force. Subject-honorific applicative forms are associated with an illocutionary act other than a COMMAND in which the speaker respects the

---

[6] **Historical change:** In the past, *-e* can be added to the verb; *kudasar-e*. In fact, native speakers in contemporary Japanese can still understand the intended meaning of *kudasar-e* but they judge this sequence as an archaic and/or an obsolete expression.

addressee. For example, the following sentence can be used as an OFFER and as an ENTREATY.

(16)   Kyuusoku-o tot-te   **kudasai!**   Imperative
        rest-ACC   take-CV APPLh.HONs   [*COMMAND/OFFER/ENTREATY]

'(i) Please take a rest!; (ii) the speaker respects the referent of the subject.'

2.5   Interim Summary

The relation between a sentence type and an illocutionary force in Japanese is much more complicated than in English. The data can be summarized thusly:

- First, there are two distinct grammatical strategies to mark an imperative sentence (a sentence type); (i) to have an imperative suffix, which is associated with a COMMAND, and (ii) the bare form, which cannot be used with a simple verb.
- Second, the imperative suffix -*e*/-*ro* is associated with an illocutionary force of COMMAND.
- Third, in order for a sentence to be used as a weak imperative, (i) the imperative suffix must not be used and (ii) a 'point-of-view' applicative marker must be present.
- Fourth, subject-honorific meaning disappears or is attenuated when the sentential force is *directing*, irrespective of the presence/absence of the imperative suffix.

3   Proposal

The data presented in Sect. 2 would be difficult, if not impossible, to explain under the assumption that all the variations are due to semantics. In terms of descriptive adequacy, the denotation in (17) might be correct (n.b., a black circle separates meanings in different dimensions, aka., multidimensional semantics; Potts and Kawahara 2004; Potts 2005, 2007; McCready 2014, 2019; Yamada 2019). But this kind of conditional denotation brings a conceptually unmotivated complexity into semantics.

(17) $[\![\text{HONs}]\!] = \begin{cases} \lambda p. \ p \bullet \text{the addressee is subordinate to the addressee} \\ \qquad\qquad\qquad\qquad\qquad\qquad\quad \text{(if it is in an imperative)} \\ \lambda p. \ p \bullet \text{the speaker respects the addressee (otherwise)} \end{cases}$

In order to reconcile the dilemma, this study assumes that the interaction takes place not in the semantic derivation but in the pragmatics.

3.1   Backgrounds

Dynamic Pragmatics. The framework in which pragmatic rules play a pivotal role in context update is called DYNAMIC PRAGMATICS (Stalnaker 1978; Gazdar

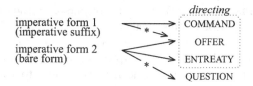

Fig. 1. Sentence type and illocutionary force

1981; Lewis 1979; Roberts 1996; Portner 2004). Deferring to Portner (2018a), who presents the most articulated characterization of Dynamic Pragmatics, I assume that (i) "sentences have standard static semantic values"; (ii) "the communicative effect of utterances in discourse is modeled as the effect they have on the discourse context"; and (iii) "the effect of a particular sentence is determined by pragmatic principles on the basis of syntactic or semantic features" (Portner 2018a).

To be more precise, I assume the relation between the imperative sentence type and its illocutionary force as shown in Fig. 1. First, Japanese employs two distinct forms for the imperative sentence type (i.e., (i) with an imperative suffix and (ii) the bare form[7]). Second, the mapping of the sentence type to illocutionary forces is specified via pragmatic principles. Finally, based on the given illocutionary force, the context is updated in an appropriate way. In this framework, the context is seen as a tuple of objects representing the relevant information in the discourse. For example, it can be structured as in (18), where cg, qs, tdl and h refer to the context set, the question set, the to-do list and the hierarchy relation. When COMMAND is selected as the illocutionary force of the given sentence, we update tdl and h, in such a way that (i) the content of the sentence is added to the to-do list of the addressee and (ii) the speaker exerts power over the addressee.

(18) $c = <cg, qs, tdl, h>$

Authority. The idea that the structured discourse context contains such a power hierarchy is extensively discussed in Portner et al. (2019). Examining the Korean addressee-honorification system, the idea that honorific expressions are involved with a power hierarchy is developed; there is a hierarchy among individuals and the job of honorific markers is to update this hierarchy structure.[8] For example, if

---

[7] **Morphology:** I assume that the choice of these strategies is a matter of morphology.

[8] **Pragmatic contribution of honorific markers:** In Yamada (2019), I mention the possibility that the pragmatic effect of content-oriented honorifics may be different that of utterance-oriented honorifics. Content-oriented honorifics (subject-honorifics and object-honorifics) seem more related to the power hierarchy at least in Japanese, whereas utterance-honorifics are less clearly related to the hierarchy although the social hierarchy relation is one important factor (Shibatani 1998; McCready 2014, 2019). I leave the issue to future studies as to whether all honorifics are involved in such a hierarchy. For studies that examine the Japanese honorification system

the speaker uses an honorific marker to refer to person x, the context is updated to reflect that x is superior to the speaker.

The details of their analysis are rather technical, so for the sake of brevity, I will opt to use a simplified model which captures the same intuition, by proposing the notion of AUTHORITY. First, authority here refers to the individual who dominates the conversation and is, thus, higher in the power hierarchy than the other discourse participants.

Second, each illocutionary force has a specification of authority. For example, in COMMAND, it is the speaker who has a power over the addressee; hence, the speaker is in authority. But in ENTREATY (e.g., *please help me!*), the addressee is in authority and the speaker conceives of himself as being subordinate to the addressee. In a similar vein, Japanese high-applicatives (*-tekure* and *-tekudasar*) are also involved with establishing authority; the referent of the applied argument is in authority, thanks to whom the speaker receives a benefit.

Third, h in (18) is an ordered pair taking two possible states, as in (19). The referent of the first element is seen as the person in authority and the referent of the second individual is the person subordinate to the referent of the first element. For example, $<sp, addr>$ means that the speaker is superior to the addressee in the power hierarchy.[9]

(19) $h \in \{<sp, addr>, <addr, sp>\}$

In addition to cs, qs, and tdl, this h is updated every time the utterance occurs.[10]

3.2   An OT-Driven Dynamic Pragmatics

An important property of this h is its consistency; it cannot take both $<sp, addr>$ and $<addr, sp>$ simultaneously. We must select one of the states.

(20)   **Consistency**: after the context update, the new h must be either $<sp, addr>$ or $<addr, sp>$, but it cannot take both simultaneously.

Imagine a situation where a sentence contains two expressions relevant to the update of h but they propose different power hierarchies. For instance, a sentence contains expression A, which suggests that the speaker is in authority, and expression B, which proposes that the addressee is in authority. If we maximally respect the meanings of these expressions, we must update h in such a way that the new state h' is both $<sp, addr>$ and $<addr, sp>$. But this results in a contradiction. Thus, such an update is ruled out by the principle in (20).

If such a problematic situation occurs, a pragmatic negotiation should take place, before the context update, so that we can decide to whom the authority

---

which do not excessively rely on the idea of social hierarchy, see Yamada (2019) and Oshima (forthcoming).

[9] **More individuals:** If we attempt to specify the relation of individuals beyond the speaker and the addressee, we need an elaborated model; see Portner et al. (2019).

[10] **Maintaining the hierarchy:** In some cases, the update to h is vacuous (e.g., h in the previous context is $<sp, addr>$ and h' is also $<sp, addr>$).

is attributed. I propose that this decision is made as a consequence of interaction among 'violable' constraints *à la* OT-phonology (Prince and Smolesky 2004 [1993]; McCarthy and Prince 1993; Kager 1999).

The summation of the analysis is as follows. First, a sentence can be potentially associated with any illocutionary force (aka., Richness of the Base in the OT-phonology). At the outset, we prepare combinations between the sentence, for example, *march!* and a variety of illocutionary forces which we refer to by using an ordered pair ⟨*SentM, IllocF*⟩. They are potential candidates for the relation. Second, these pairs are assessed by several pragmatic constraints which exclude some illicit combinations (or, we can put a weight to each constraint; cf., Harmonic Grammar, Boersma and Pater 2016). As a result of this assessment, only a few prototypical, felicitous illocutionary forces are selected as the best combinations. More specifically, I assume that the assessment is based on the following pragmatic constraints:

(21)   **Pragmatic constraints**

a.   Imperative sentence type (both -*e/ro* and ∅)
↔ The speaker is in AUTHORITY binding the addressee to take the action expressed by the content of the sentence.

b.   Semantics of APPLн
↔ The referent of the applied argument (= the addressee if used in an imperative) is in AUTHORITY who gives the speaker a benefit.

c.   Semantics of HONs
↔ The addressee is the AUTHORITY who speaker respects.

3.3   Examples of Illocutionary Force Assignment

Example 1. Let us consider the sentence in (6)a, which contains an imperative suffix. First, we make pairs of the sentence form and the illocutionary force. For example, the sentence can be paired with COMMAND, ⟨(6)a, COMMAND⟩, or with OFFER, ⟨(6)a, OFFER⟩. Consider the tableau in (22). Each row represents one such pair. Second, the columns express the constraints and their ranking. The most important constraint in this language is (21)b (APPLн). But the sentence in (6)a does not contain a 'point-of-view' applicative, so this constraint is not relevant for the current case. IMP is the next highest constraint (= (21)a), which requires that the speaker is in authority. Consequently, weak imperatives—⟨(6)a, ENTREATY⟩ and ⟨(6)a, OFFER⟩—are ruled out.

(22)

koosinsi-ro 'march-IMP'	APPLн	IMP	HONs
⟨(6)a, COMMAND⟩			
⟨(6)a, OFFER⟩		*!	
⟨(6)a, ENTREATY⟩		*!	

Example 2. Consider the sentence in (10)a. This sentence has a 'point-of-view' applicative morpheme and it cannot be used as a COMMAND. The same tableau makes the expected prediction. Observe the results in (23). First, we prepare all

the pairs between this given sentence and an illocutionary force. Second, each pair is assessed by the constraints. As the first row shows, $\langle(10)a, \text{COMMAND}\rangle$ is ruled out, because COMMAND requires that the speaker is in authority, which has a conflict with the constraint in (21)b (APPL$_H$); the 'point-of-view' applicative makes it so that the speaker is a benefit-recipient, who is therefore subordinate to the benefit-giver (the addressee). Other combinations are deemd appropriate as long as the authority is on the addressee's side. This is the answer to the problem of *one-to-many* property.

(23)

koosinsi-te kure 'march-CV APPL$_H$'	APPL$_H$	IMP	HONs
$\langle(10)a, \text{COMMAND}\rangle$	*!		
$\langle(10)a, \text{OFFER}\rangle$		*	
$\langle(10)a, \text{ENTREATY}\rangle$		*	

Example 3. Let us observe an example with a subject-honorific marker. Consider the sentence in (13)c and the tableau in (24). First, the pairs of the sentence and illocutionary forces are generated. Second, APPL$_H$ does not play a role, because the sentence does not contain an applicative suffix. Third, the bare form of the verb indicates that it is an imperative. The imperative sentence type requires the authority to be on the speaker's side. Therefore, neither ENTREATY, WISH nor any other illocutionary force in which the authority is on the addressee's side is a valid choice.

(24)

koosin-nasai 'march-HONs'	APPL$_H$	IMP	HONs
$\langle(13)c, \text{COMMAND}\rangle$			*
$\langle(13)c, \text{OFFER}\rangle$		*!	
$\langle(13)c, \text{ENTREATY}\rangle$		*!	

Example 4. When a high-applicative is present, the speaker is lower in the power hierarchy and the addressee is in authority, allowing for COMMAND, but not other illocutionary acts.

(25)

koosinsi-te kudasai 'march-CV HONs.APPL$_H$'	APPL$_H$	IMP	HONs
$\langle(15)c, \text{COMMAND}\rangle$	*!		*
$\langle(15)c, \text{OFFER}\rangle$		*	
$\langle(15)c, \text{ENTREATY}\rangle$		*	

4   Conclusion and Implications

In order to explain the 'one-to-many' and the '*one-to-any' property of illocutionary force assignment, this study has presented an OT-driven dynamic pragmatics. By assuming a set of 'violable' pragmatic constraints, the variation and the convergence in illocutionary force are easily explained: note that the 'one-to-many' property and the cancellation of subject-honorific meaning in (13) is hard to explain if the context update is automatically triggered by the subject-honorific morpheme. If the proposed analysis is on the right track, the relation between the semantics and the pragmatic update is considered as in (26):

(26)   form/meaning → AUTHORITY/force assignment → context update

First, the form of the sentence and the semantics are recognized. For example, the imperative suffix and the bare form tell us that the sentence is an imperative. Second, before updating the context, there is an interaction between constraints which reflect the form and the meaning of the given sentence. In our case, we check (i) the sentence type, (ii) presence/absence of a 'point-of-view' applicative, and (iii) presence/absence of a subject-honorific marker. The constraints are ranked, and based on the interaction between these constraints, we determine two things: (i) which discourse participant is in AUTHORITY and (ii) an appropriate illocutionary force for that sentence. Finally, based on this decision, the context is appropriately updated. Lack or attenuation of honorific meaning in (13) is possible because of the intermediate negotiation stage before the context update. This kind of interaction among pragmatic constraints is seen as a development of the spirit of dynamic pragmatics, and the objective of this paper is to formalize this pragmatic interaction within the framework of Optimality Theory.

In future studies, it would be valuable to ask whether the ranking among constraints is language-dependent, or universal, or whether it is better conceived of as a weight assignment (as in Harmonic Grammar; Boersma and Pater 2016). In addition, the relation between the imperative and the addressee-honorification system deserves further studies (Yamada 2019). Even though the subject-honorific marker can be present in an imperative (= (13)), the addressee-honorific marker is illicit in an imperative, as shown by the contrast in (27).

(27)   Addressee-honorific markers in imperatives   Contemporary Japanese
    a.   Ie-de   odor-e!
        house-at dance-IMP

        'Dance at home!' (a strong imperative)
    b.   *Ie-de   odori-**mas**-e!
        house-at dance-HONA-IMP

        'Dance at home!' (a weak imperative reading is intended).

However, in Edo period Japanese, -*mas* is permissible even in an imperative sentence, as illustrated in (28) (Yamada 2019: 176–177).

(28)   Tito o-mati-nasare-**mas-e.**   Edo period Japanese
    little HON-wait-HONs-HONA-IMP

    '(i) Wait a minute;
    (ii) the speaker respects the referent of the subject (< -*nasar*);
    (iii) the speaker respects the addressee (< -*mas*).' (Shinhanashi Warai Mayu, author is unidentified, 1712; Miyachi 1977: 250)

In addition to this diachronic change, typological variations are worth our attention. Imperatives in Punjabi can be made with an allocutive marker (Kaur 2019a, 2019b; Kaur and Yamada 2019). In Burmese, an addressee-honorific marker is preferred in an imperative: when people are conversing with friends,

-pà/bà 'HONₐ' is not used in a declarative clause but an addressee-honorific marker is commonly used (despite interpersonal closeness) in imperatives (p.c., with Atsuhiko Kato on 07/04/2018; n.b., the sentence in (29)a is not ungrammatical).

(29)   Burmese imperatives   (Kato 2018: 574)

    a. Ɂèiɴ-hmà kâ.   b. Ɂèiɴ-hmà kâ-**bà**.
       house-at dance   house-at dance-HONₐ
       'Dance at home!'   'Dance at home!'

Wheatley states that Burmese imperatives "can be softened by the addition of polite particle the 'polite' Pv, /-pa/, or 'tags', such as /-no/ or /-là/ 'won't you' (Wheatley 1982: 292)." This observation suggests that Burmese addressee-honorific markers play a similar role as Japanese 'point-of-view' applicatives. Examination of the way languages vary in strong/weak imperative distinction should shed new light on the relation between the sentence type and the illocutionary force and the relevant mechanism that intervenes between the syntax/semantics and the context update mechanism, providing a new direction in the study of dynamic pragmatics.

References

Austin, J.L.: How to Do Things with Words. Oxford University Press, Oxford (1962)

Baker, M.C.: The mirror principle and morphosyntactic explanation. Linguist. Inq. **16**(3), 373–415 (1985)

Boersma, P., Pater, J.: Convergence properties of a gradual learning algorithm for Harmonic Grammar. In: McCarthy, J., Pater, J. (eds.) Harmonic grammar and harmonic serialism, pp. 389–434. Equinox Press, London (2016)

Chierchia, G., McConnel-Ginet, S.: Meaning and Grammar. MIT Press, Cambridge (1990)

Frege, G.: Der Gedanke. Beiträge zur Philosophie des deutschen Idealismus I, pp. 58–77. Page references to English translation (1918 [1956])

Gazdar, G.: Speech act assignment. In: Joshi, A.K., Sag, I.A., Webber, B. (eds.) Eelements of Discourse Understanding, pp. 64–83. Cambridge University Press, New York (1981)

Kager, R.: Optimality Theory. Cambridge University Press, Cambridge (1999)

Kato, A.: Burmese. In: Tsunoda, T. (ed.) Levels in Clause Linkage: A Crosslinguistic Survey. Mouton de Gruyter, Berline (2018)

Kaur, G.: Allocutivity as the locus of imperative syntax. In: The Proceedings of the North-Eastern Linguistic Society, vol. 49, no. 2, pp. 165–174 (2019a)

Kaur, G.: Not all imperatives have a Jussive head: emphasizing the role of allocutivity in syntax. Presented at Person and Perspective: A Workshop Honoring the Work of María Luisa Zubizarreta, 3–4 May Los Angeles, University of Southern California, 3–4 May 2019b

Kaur, G., Yamada, A.: Embedded allocutivity and its reference. Presented at Person and Perspective: A Workshop Honoring the Work of María Luisa Zubizarreta, 3–4 May, Los Angeles, University of Southern California, 3–4 May 2019

Kikuchi, Y.: Keigo [Honorifics]. Kodansha, Tokyo (1997)

Lewis, D.K.: Scorekeeping in a language game. J. Philos. Logic **8**(1), 339–359 (1979)

McCarthy, J.J.: Prince, A: Prosodic Morphology: Constraint Interaction and Satisfaction. Rutgers University Center for Cognitive Science, New Brunswick (1993)

McCready, E.: A semantics for honorifics with reference to Thai. In: Pacific Asian Conference on Language, Information, and Computation (PACLIC), vol. 28, pp. 503–512 (2014)

Miyachi, K.: '-masuru' kara '-masu' e no zen'isoo: sharebon shishoo no koosatsu [Transition fom '-masuru' to '-mas': a reflection on sharebon texts]. Teikyoo Daigaku Bungakubu Kiyoo Kokugo Kokubungaku [J. Dept. Jpn. Lit. Teikyo Univ.] **9**, 1–50 (1977)

McCready, E.: The Semantics and Pragmatics of Honorification: Register and Social Meaning. Oxford University Press, Oxford (2019)

Murray, S.E., Starr, W.B.: The structure of communicative acts, Manuscript (in prep). http://williamstarr.net/research/the_structure_of_communicative_acts.pdf

Oshima, D. Y.: The logical principles of honorification and dishonorification in Japanese. In: Kojima, K., Sakamoto, M., Mineshima, K., Satoh, K. (eds.) New Frontiers in Artificial Intelligence: JSAI-isAI 2018 Workshops, JURISIN, AI-Biz, SKL, LENLS, IDAA, Yokohama, Japan, 12–14 November 2018, Revised Selected Papers. Springer, Heidelberg (forthcoming)

Portner, P.: The semantics of imperatives within a theory of clause types. Semant. Linguist. Theory (SALT) **14**, 235–252 (2004)

Portner, P.: Commitment to priorities. In: Fogal, D., Harris, D.W., Moss, M. (eds.) New Work on Speech Acts, pp. 296–316. Oxford University Press, Oxford (2018a)

Portner, P.: Mood. Oxford University Press, Oxford (2018b)

Portner, P., Pak, M., Zanuttini, R.: The speaker-addressee relation at the syntax-semantics interface. Language **95**(1), 1–36 (2019)

Potts, C.: The Logic of Conventional Implicatures. Oxford University Press, Oxford (2005)

Potts, C.: The expressive dimension. Thoret. Linguist. **33**(2), 165–197 (2007)

Potts, C., Kawahara, D.: Japanese honorifics as emotive definite descriptions. Semant. Linguist. Theory (SALT) **14**, 253–270 (2004)

Prince, A., Smolesky, P.: Optimality theory: constraint interaction in generative grammar. [Revision of 1993 technical report, Rutgers University Center for Cognitive Science] Blackwell, Malden, MA and Oxford, UK (2004)

Roberts, C.: Information structure in discourse: towards an integrated formal theory of pragmatics. In: Yoon, J. H., Kathol, A. (eds.) OSU Working Papers in Linguistics 49, Ohio State University Press, Columnbus, Ohio (1996)

Searle, J.R.: Speech Acts. Cambrdige University Press, Cambridge (1969)

Searle, J.R., Vanderveken, D.: Foundations of Illocutionary Logic. Cambridge University Press, Cambridge (1985)

Shibatani, M.: Honorifics. In: Jacob, M. (ed.) Concise Encyclopedia of Pragmatics, pp. 341–350. Elsevier, Amsterdam (1998)

Zhan, Z.: Assertion. Selenium WebDriver Recipes in C#, pp. 57–62. Apress, Berkeley (2015). https://doi.org/10.1007/978-1-4842-1742-9_10

Svahn, A.: The Japanese imperative. Ph.D. thesis, Lund University, Lund (2016)

Wheatley, J. K.: Burmese: a grammatical sketch. Ph. D. thesis, University of California, Berkeley, California (1982)

Yamada, A.: The syntax, semantics and pragmatics of Japanese addressee-honorific markers. Ph.D. thesis, Georgetown University, Washington D.C. (2019)

Comparatives and Negative Island Effect in Japanese

Mayumi Yoshimoto[1] and Eri Tanaka[2(✉)]

[1] Otemon Gakuin University, 2-1-15, Nishiai, Ibaraki, Osaka, Japan
m-yoshimoto@haruka.otemon.ac.jp
[2] Osaka University, Machikaneyamacho 1-5, Toyonaka, Osaka, Japan
eri-tana@let.osaka-u.ac.jp

Abstract. This paper contributes to the understanding of Japanese *yori*-comparatives, focusing on the alleged lack of negative island effect in this language. The lack of the effect has been taken to be one piece of evidence for the negative setting of the Degree Abstraction Parameter [1]. We argue that this parameter setting does not explain the whole picture of the negative island effect in Japanese comparatives and advocate a more traditional analysis that utilizes the maximality operator.

Keywords: Comparatives · Negative island effect · Japanese · Negation

1 Introduction

The literature on comparative constructions in natural language semantics has observed that they are not cross-linguistically uniform in their forms and semantic/syntactic properties. Included in the variations are, for example, scopal properties of comparatives, availability of subcomparatives, and negative island effects (NIE, hereafter). These variations have sometimes been attributed to a parameter setting, with a positive/negative setting of a parameter entailing these properties. One of such parameters is the one proposed by [1], the Degree Abstraction Parameter (DAP), which is to capture the lack of subcomparatives, scopal interaction of a comparative marker with another scope bearing element and NIE in Japanese. This paper focuses on NIE, presenting a new set of data to argue that Japanese does exhibit a NIE in *yori*-comparatives but it doesn't in other degree constructions such as *kurai*-equatives. We claim that the DAP is not responsible for NIE but another possible parameter which will be dubbed as Maximality Optionality Parameter (MOP) will explain the data.

This work has been supported by JSPS KAKENHI Grant Number 17K02810. Our gratitude goes to Kenta Mizutani for a helpful discussion.

© Springer Nature Switzerland AG 2020
M. Sakamoto et al. (Eds.): JSAI-isAI 2019, LNAI 12331, pp. 370–382, 2020.
https://doi.org/10.1007/978-3-030-58790-1_24

2   Negative Island Effects in Japanese

2.1   Background

It has been well known that downward entailing elements such as negation and negative quantifiers are not allowed in comparative and equative clauses, a phenomenon known as the negative island effect (NIE). This effect has been attributed to the undefinedness of the maximality of the degrees that the comparative/equative clauses denote, if we take the semantics of these morphemes incorporating the maximality operator, as in (1a)–(1b) (e.g., [3, 10, 12]). In (2a), the maximum in the comparative clause cannot be defined, because the set denotes infinitely many degrees. The maximality analysis is extended to equatives in an obvious way.

(1) a. *John bought a more expensive book than nobody did.

    b. *John is as tall as nobody is.

(2) a. $[\![\text{-er}]\!] = \lambda D1.\lambda D2.\ \max(D2) > \max(D1)$,
        where $\max(P) = \iota x \in P.\ \forall y \in P.\ x \geq y$.

    b. $[\![(1a)]\!] = \max(\lambda d.$ John bought a d-expensive book$) > \max(\lambda d.$ nobody bought a d-expensive book$)$

[1] claims that Japanese *yori*-comparatives cannot be analyzed on a par with (2b), taking the lack of NIE as one of the pieces of evidence. They propose a parameter called Degree Abstraction Parameter (DAP), according to which a language may differ whether a degree variable is syntactically abstracted or not. Japanese is, as they propose, a language whose DAP is set negatively. If a language lacks degree abstraction, there will be no sets of degrees that the maximality operator works on, which should lead to the lack of NIE.

(3) Degree Abstraction Parameter (DAP)
    A language does/does not have binding of degree variable in syntax.
    Beck et al. (2004)

This paper, however, argues that DAP is not the source of the alleged lack of NIE, considering cases where negation takes different scopes.

2.2   Negative Island Effects in *Yori*-comparatives

[1] claims that the complement clause of *yori* in *yori*-comparatives in Japanese may either be a nominalization or a relative clause, and semantically, it does not denote a degree but an individual.

(4)   *Taro-wa*   [*dare-mo*   *kawa-nakatta-*(no)]-yori*   *takai*
        Taro-TOP   [wh-mo   buy-neg.Past-(NOMINAL)]-than   expensive
        hon-o   *katta.*
        book-ACC   bought

(*) "Taro bought a more expensive book than nobody bought."
(OK) "Taro bought a more expensive book than the one nobody bought."
(example from [1])

In (4), the presence of nominalizer *no* is crucial in grammaticality. In the complement clause, a relativization (internally or externally) of an individual argument
is operated in either case, but with *no*, the set can be bound by ι operator.
Without it, it is bound by the maximality operator, which yields a NIE (on
individuals) effect.

(5)   a.   *dare-mo kawa-nakatta-no*
           LF: [[OP1 [dare-mo t1 kawa-nakatta] no]
           Semantics: THEc [λx. nobody bought x]
           "the one that nobody bought"

      b.   *dare-mo kawa-nakatta-∅*
           Semantics: max(λx. nobody bought x)
           the maximal individual that nobody bought

This argument, however, does not seem to be a fair argument, because if
what matters is *no*, then the data in (4) does not have any relevance to the
negative island effect in Japanese, as [5] notes.
We thus take on a different frame to test the availability of NIE in Japanese.
Consider the following:

(6)   a.   *Taro-wa*   [*Jiro-ga*   *se-ga*   *takaku-nai yori*] *se-ga*
           Taro-TOP   [Jiro-NOM   height-NOM   tall-Neg   yori]   height-NOM
           ??takai/takaku-nai.
           tall/tall-Neg

           "Taro has more "non-tallness" than Jiro does."

      b.   *Taro-wa*   [*Jiro-ga*   *hutottei-nai yori*] *??hutotte-iru/hutottei-nai*
           Taro-TOP   [Jiro-NOM   fat-Neg   yori]   fat/fat-NEG

           "Taro has more "non-fatness" than Jiro does."

(7)   a.   **Taro-wa*   [***dare-mo*** *se-ga*   *takaku-**nai** yori*] *se-ga*
           Taro-TOP   [who-mo   height-NOM   tall-Neg   than]   height-NOM
           takai/takaku-nai.
           tall/tall-Neg

           (Intended) "Taro has more "non-tallness" than no one does."

b.   *Taro-wa   [Jiro-ga   hutottei-**ta-koto-ga** **nai**   yori]   hutotteiru/hutottei-nai
     Taro-TOP [Jiro-NOM fat-Past-fact-NOM Neg than] fat/fat-Neg

(Intended) "Taro has more "non-fatness" than Jiro never has had."

All of these examples contain negation but no individual gap in the complement clause. In (6), the affirmative in the matrix is reported to be worse than its negative counterpart by our informants (including the authors themselves). As pointed out by a reviewer, even the "good" sentences in (6) may sound somewhat awkward, but its grammaticality is sharply contrasted with that of (7). All the informants (six Japanese native speakers) found that (6) with negation in the matrix is much better than (7), which are judged to be totally bizarre.

If we follow [1], the grammatical contrast between (6) and (7) should be reduced to the availability of (internally-headed) relativization or nominalization. This rationale, however, cannot be supported by the fact. Both of the complement clauses of yori in (6) and (7) show the *same* grammaticality with respect to relativization and nominalization:

(8)   Taro-wa   [{Jiro-ga/dono   gakusei-mo} se-ga   takaku-nai]-no-ni
      Taro-TOP [{Jiro-NOM/dono student-mo} height-NOM tall-neg]-no-DAT
      {??atta/odoroita}
      {met/was-surprised}

(Unavailable) "Taro met {Jiro, who is not tall/no student who is tall}."
"Taro was surprised by the fact that {Jiro is not tall/no student is tall}."

Note that *no* does not rescue the ungrammatical one:

(9)   *Taro-wa   [dare-mo se-ga   takaku-nai-no   yori] se-ga
      Taro-TOP [who-mo height-NOM tall-neg-NOMINAL than] height-NOM
      takai/takaku-nai.
      tall/tall-Neg

In spite of the ungrammaticality of (7), minimally different sentences with equative marker kurai (=(10a)) are fully acceptable as in (10b)–(10c). If the DAP is working, the affirmative versions of (10b)—(10c) are not mysterious, but we do not know why (7) should be ungrammatical. Notice also that (10b)–(10c) do not allow negated matrix predicates.

(10) a.   Taro-wa   Jiro-kurai {se-ga   takai/(takusan) tabe-ta}.
           Taro-TOP Jiro-as   {height-NOM tall/(alot)   eat-Past}

      "Taro is as tall as Jiro./Taro ate as much as Jiro did."

      b.   Taro-wa   **[dare-mo** hutottei-**nai** kurai] hutotteiru/*hutottei-nai
           Taro-TOP [who-mo fat-Neg   as]   fat/fat-Neg

      "Taro is fatter than anyone else is."

    c.   *Taro-wa*   *[Jiro-ga*   *(imamade)* *hutottei-**ta-koto-ga** **nai** **kurai]***
        Taro-TOP [Jiro-NOM (ever)   fat-Past-fact-NOM Neg as]
        *hutotteiru/*hutottei-nai*
        fat/fat-Neg

    "Taro is fatter than Jiro has ever been."

In sum: the grammatical contrasts in (6)–(7) and (10b/10c)–(7) do not follow from the negative setting of the DAP, because in one case the DAP is seemingly working, while in the other, it is not.

3 Analysis

The analysis we will pursue is a traditional one; the complement clause of *yori* may have a degree abstraction which is the target of the maximality operator.

3.1 Scope of Negation

Let us first look at the contrast between (6) and (7). As indicated in the translations, the interpretations of (6) is very similar to the one of so-called comparison of deviation observed in *The Brothers Karamazov is more long than The Dream of a Ridiculous Man is short.* (an example from [8], see also [4]). Here, what is compared is how far the heights of Taro or Jiro are away from what is considered to be the contextually determined standard degree.

    Furthermore, the negations in these examples scope differently: The one in (6) takes an *internal* scope, in the same way as *little* [7,13], while the one in (7) takes scope over the clause to license indeterminate (=*dare* "who") based NPI *dare-mo* or temporal existential marker *V-ta-koto-ga*, as in (11a):

(11) a. *Taro-wa*   *America-ni itta-koto-ga*   {*aru/nai*}
          Taro-TOP America-to went-fact-NOM {be/be.Neg}

          "Taro has been to the US./Taro has never been to the US."

      b. $\exists t.\ t \leq t0 \wedge$ Taro visits the US at t
          $\neg\exists t.\ t \leq t0 \wedge$ Taro visits the US at t $t0 =$ the speech time

Given the relational analysis of gradable adjectives (i.e. $\langle d, \langle e, t \rangle \rangle$), the internal negation is defined in (12a), following [13]. Here, the function of negation is to take the complement set of degrees that a non-negated gradable adjective denotes. When applied to a gradable adjective like *tall*, the internal negation yields the same meaning as its antonym (12b).

(12) a. $[\![\neg_{internal}]\!] = \lambda P_{\langle d,et\rangle}.\ \lambda d.\ \lambda x.\ \neg P(x)(d)$

  b. $[\![\neg\ tall]\!] = \lambda d.\ \lambda x.\ \neg height(x) \geq d = \lambda d.\ \lambda x.\ height(x) < d$
     $= short$

That *nai* in the *yori*-clause in (6) is indeed an internal negation is evidenced by the contrast given in (13), where Ikeno Medaka, who is a 149 149 cm-tall adult man, is acceptable as the subject, while a man with average height is not:[1]

(13) *Taro-wa* *[{Ikeno Medaka/#ano heikin shinchoo-no dansei}-ga*
   Taro-TOP [{Ikeno Medata/that average height-GEN man}-NOM
   se-ga   *takaku-nai yori] se-ga*   *takaku-nai.*
   height-NOM tall-neg   yori] height-NOM tall-neg

   "Taro is as short as {Ikeno Medaka/#that man in average height.} "

3.2 Max-Analysis of *yori*

We propose that *yori* has the equivalent meaning to *er*, (2a), crucially incorporating the maximality operator.

The hallmark of the construction we are discussing is that it yields a comparison of deviation-like interpretation. This means that the comparative clause as well as the main clause refer to a "standard" of gradable property: in (6a), for example, the comparison refers to a contextually relevant standard of height. Following the standard convention, we assume that a contextual standard is introduced by a phonetically null *pos*-operator, along the lines of [7] and [13]. In these papers, a contextually given standard is understood as an interval which is neutral about whether the individual related to it counts positive about the gradable property or not (=N). (14a) is Heim's version of semantics of *pos*. If we apply this to a gradable adjective with an internal negation, we will get (14c), where the complement set of degrees of John's height subsumes the neutral area, which successfully yields the interpretation where John is short.

(14) a. $[\![pos]\!]^c = \lambda P_{\langle d,t\rangle}.\ N_c \subseteq P$

  b. $[\![pos]\!]^c(\lambda d.\ John\ is\ d\text{-}tall) = N_c \subseteq \lambda d.\ height(John) \geq d$

  c. $[\![pos]\!]^c(\lambda d.\ John\ is\ not\ d\text{-}tall) = N_c \subseteq \lambda d.\ height(John) < d$

---

[1] One might wonder why the "¬tall" (=*short*) interpretation never arises in a matrix sentence (e.g., *Taro-wa se-ga takaku-nai.* "Taro is not tall."). We suspect that this is due to a competition with a sentence with its antonym as its main predicate: the internal negation of *tall* refers to the same set of degrees as *short* does, but the former is more complex than the latter, which would violate a conversational maxim.

I depart from the semantics given in (14a) in that there is another interval, I_N, defined based on N, which may denote either an interval that starts from the bottom of the scale (=0) to the maximal degree of N or one that starts from the minimum of N to infinity. Our *pos* is now defined as in (15):

(15) a. $[\![\text{pos}]\!] = \lambda d.\ \lambda D_{\langle d,t \rangle}.\ I_N \subset D \wedge D(d) \wedge \neg (I_N)(d).$

 b. I_N denotes either of
   (a) $\{ d \mid 0 \leq d \leq \max(N) \}$ or
   (b) $\{ d \mid \min(N) \leq d \}.$

The *pos* in (15) ensures that I_N should be a subset of the set of degrees to which an individual is related. This move is added to give us the difference between the maximum/minimum degree of N and the maximum degree that an individual reaches to yield a comparison of deviation interpretation.

I assume that *pos* has been moved from a position internal to AP, and another degree operator is moved to a higher position, as in (16b). With these set-ups, for a sentence like (16a), the *pos* operator gets us the set of degrees that fall within Taro's height but not within I_N (see Fig. 1(a)). We assume that the set is existentially closed at the end in this case. I will refer to "$\lambda d.$ height (Taro) $\geq d$" and "$\lambda d.$ height (Taro) $< d$" as "HEIGHT$_{Taro}$" and "¬HEIGHT$_{Taro}$", respectively, when possible, to enhance the readability.

(16) a. *Taro-wa   se-ga   takai.*
     Taro-TOP height-NOM tall

    "Taro is tall."

 b. LF: [Op1 [[t1 pos] [Op2 [Taro [[t2 tall]]]]]]

 c. $[\![(16a)]\!]$
    $= \lambda d.\ I_N \subset (\lambda d'.\ \text{height (Taro)} \geq d') \wedge \text{height(Taro)} \geq d \wedge \neg I_N(d)$
    $= \exists d.\ I_N \subset \text{HEIGHT}_{Taro} \wedge \text{HEIGHT}_{Taro}(d) \wedge \neg I_N(d)$
    Existential Closure

For comparatives, *yori*-clauses are taken to be a degree quantifier. When negation takes an internal scope within a *yori*-clause, the sentence will have the following structure:

(17) LF: [[[Op1 [t1 pos] 2 [Jiro-ga t2 [**neg** [se-ga takai]]]] yori] [3 [4 [t4 pos] Taro-wa t3 **neg** [se-ga takai]]]]

The compositional steps are given below. The LF in (17) produces what we want: the max of difference of Taro's height and I_N is greater than that of Jiro's (see Fig. 1(c)). Here, the maximal degree of such "differences" will be defined, as desired.

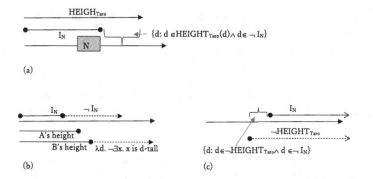

Fig. 1. Positives and comparatives

(18) a. $[\![$ the complement of *yori* $]\!]$
$= \lambda d. \, [\![\, pos \,]\!](d)(\lambda d'. \, \neg [\![\, tall \,]\!](Jiro))$
$= \lambda d. \, I_N \subset \neg HEIGHT_{Jiro} \wedge \neg HEIGT_{Jiro}(d) \wedge \neg I_N(d)$

b. $[\![\, matrix \,]\!] = \lambda d. \, I_N \subset \neg HEIGHT_{Taro} \wedge \neg HEIGHT_{Taro}(d) \wedge \neg I_N(d)$

c. $[\![\, (17) \,]\!]$
$= \mathbf{max}(\, \lambda d. \, I_N \subset \neg HEIGHT_{Taro} \wedge \neg HEIGHT_{Taro}(d) \wedge \neg I_N(d))$
$> \mathbf{max}(\lambda d. \, I_N \subset \neg HEIGHT_{Jiro} \wedge \neg HEIGT_{Jiro}(d) \wedge \neg I_N(d))$
max is defined.

(19a), where negation takes scope over *pos*, on the other hand, does not yield a coherent interpretation, because there will be infinitely many degrees that nobody reaches and are not in I_N (see Fig. 1(b)). The maximality operator fails here.

(19) a. LF: [[Op1 [**neg** [t1 pos] 2 [dare-mo [t2 se-ga takai]]]] yori] ...

b. $[\![$ the complement $]\!] = \lambda d. \, \neg \, [I_N \subset (\lambda d'. \, \exists x. \, height(x) \geq d') \wedge \exists x. \, x$ is d-tall $\wedge \, \neg I_N(d)]$

c. $[\![\, (19a) \,]\!]$
$= .... > \mathbf{max}(\lambda d. \, \neg \, [I_N \subset (\lambda d'. \, \exists x. \, height(x) \geq d') \wedge \exists x. \, x$ is d-tall $\wedge \, \neg I_N(d)])$ **max** is not defined.

(7b) is analyzed in the same way: the complement clause of *yori* denotes a set of degrees such that Jiro's weight has never reached it and it is not in I_N.

We claim that the contrast between the positive and negative versions of (6) is due to the non-uniformity of the predicates in the matrix and the *yori*-complement clause. The positive version of (6) yields the comparison between the difference from the contextual standard for *tall* and Taro's height and the one from the contextual standard for *not tall* =*short* and Jiro's height. This is not impossible, but it seems to require more effort to compare these than the difference from the same contextual standard.

[4] argues that Japanese has a comparative marker, *izyoo-ni*, which is lexically dedicated to the comparison of deviation. With this comparative marker, (20) seems to sound better than its *yori* counterpart. Our conjecture is that *izyoo-ni* is a genuine comparison of deviation marker, while *yori* requires that the two comparisons refer to the same contextual standard: Taro, as an adult, is usually understood to be taller than his 3-year-old son.

(20) *Taro-wa   san-sai-no   musuko-ga se-ga   hikui-izyooni/??yori*
      Taro-TOP 3-year.old-NOM son-NOM   height-NOM izyooni/yori
      se-ga   hikui.
      height-NOM short

  "Taro is shorter than his 3 year old son."

In summary: We claim that the crucial difference between (6) and (7) rests on the scope of negation. For (6), internal negation is a possible option, which makes it possible to have a comparison of deviation interpretation, while for (7), it is not a choice, due to a presence of an item that has to be taken scope over by negation. Note at this point that we are not claiming that the "wide" scope negation is impossible for (6); it just does not yield a possible interpretation due to the undefined maximality.

3.3 Equatives

Let us turn to equatives. The insensitivity of equatives to the NIE is not unknown in the literature. [2], for example, shows that Slovenian equative marker *kot* allows a DE environment in its complement, unlike its English counterpart, as in (21b).

(21) a. *John drove as fast as Mary didn't.

      b. *Janez se je   peljal tako hitro [kot   se   Marija ni].*
          John self aux drive dem fast [than self Mary   neg.aux]

[2] argues that equatives may be composed of existential quantification over degrees, but this yields a trivial proposition, as in (22a). The maximality operator (in the standard) is operative to avoid this:

(22) a. $\exists$d. John drove d-fast $\wedge$ Mary drove d-fast.   trivial

      b. $\exists$d. John drove d-fast $\wedge$ d = $\mathbf{max}$(λd. Mary drove d-fast)
          non-trivial, equative interpretation

This means that the maximality operator is not a mandatory component of the meaning of an equative marker. Rather, it is a parametric option: in a language like Slovenian, it is optional, while English-type languages require it. With this hypothesis, [2] explains the contrast in (21a)–(21b) in terms of the availability of the maximality operator. We call this hypothesis the Maximality Optionality Parameter (MOP).

(23)   The Maximality Optionaltiy Parameter (MOP)
        A language does/does not have an optional maximality operator.

In English-type languages, where MOP is negatively set, the standard clause is always quantified by the maximality operator, and thus the negation (or DE context) leads to undefined maximum. In Slovenian-type languages, on the other hand, the lack of the maximality operator results in a coherent interpretation, which is equivalent to a comparative interpretation (see [11]).

(24)   a. English-type languages ([−MOP]): max is obligatory
            $\exists d.\ speed(john) \geq d \land d = \mathbf{max}(\lambda d. \neg\ speed(bill) \geq d) \Leftarrow undefined$

        b. Slovenian-type languages ([+MOP]): max is optional
            $\exists d.\ speed(john) \geq d \land \neg\ speed(bill) \geq d$
            $\approx$ Bill's speed > John's speed

A reasonable conjecture, given the observation in examples (10a)–(10c) in Sect. 2, is that Japanese is a Slovenian-type language with respect to the MOP. With (10a), *kurai* has an equivalent interpretation with its English counterpart (see (22b)). With (10b)–(10c), on the other hand, it has just the existential semantics.

Applying the existential semantics to *kurai*-equatives, we will get the following result. The result is a coherent meaning where Taro's fatness reaches a degree that no one reaches (we omit an irrelevant part for the sake of readability), namely, a meaning where Taro is the fattest of all (see Fig. 2).

(25) $\exists d. \neg \exists x.\ FAT_{Taro}(d) \land fat(x) \geq d \land \neg(I_N)(d).$
        $\approx$ Taro is the fattest of all.

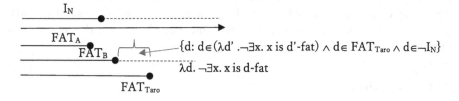

Fig. 2. Equatives

This reasoning explains why the negation in the matrix is not allowed. We attribute the ungrammaticality to its triviality. If the matrix predicate is negated, the whole sentence would mean that there is a degree among the set of "fat" degrees that nobody's weight reaches, including Taro's, has reached. This is too weak and trivially true, so it does not give us any clue to Taro's weight.

(26) $\exists d. \neg \exists x. \neg \text{FAT}_{Taro}(d) \wedge \text{fat}(x) \geq d \wedge \neg(I_N)(d).$

The reasoning here also implies that the MOP does not only serve as a parameter that differentiates degree constructions across languages but also as one that differentiates lexical semantics of standard markers: *yori* in Japanese obligatorily incorporates a max-operator, but *kurai* does not.

We finally would like to mention one additional aspect of *kurai*, the one argued by [4,6] (see also [9]). As we mentioned above, those works claim that *kurai* is an equative marker that lexically encodes a comparison of deviation, just like *izyoo-(ni)*. This effect is clearly observable in a case like (10a): the sentence denotes the equivalence between the gaps from the contextual standard for height for Taro and Jiro. Thus in (27a), the norm-relatedness cannot be cancelled. When this comes to the negated complement-*kurai*, the judgment does not seem to be as clear as the one in (27a):

(27) a. *Taro-wa*   *Jiro-kurai* *se-ga*   *takai* *ga,*   *#dochira-mo*
          Taro-TOP   Jiro-kurai   height-NOM   tall   but   which-mo
          se-ga   *hikui.*
          height-NOM   short

      "Taro is as tall as Jiro, but both of them are short."

      b. *Taro-wa* *[Jiro-ga*   *(imamade)* *hutottei-ta-koto-ga*   *nai kurai]*
          Taro-TOP [Jiro-NOM   (ever)   fat-PAST-fact-NOM   neg kurai]
          hutotteiru *ga,*   *(?)soredemo* *dochira-mo* *yaseteiru.*
          fat   but, still   which-mo   skinny.

      (Lit.) "Taro is as fat as Jiro has never been, but both of them are skinny."

We suspect that this could be due to the different roles that I_N plays in the semantics. With (10a), the difference in the gaps from the I_N crucially determines the truth conditions of this sentence. In (10b), on the other hand, someone's weight may or may not exceed I_N (see Fig. 2 again) in order to satisfy the truth condition in (22). In other words, the deviation from the standard is not crucial in this case.

4   Conclusion

We argue that the alleged evidence for the DAP in Japanese, NIE, may not serve as the evidence for that parameter. The internal and external negation cases exhibit a clear contrast, which is explained in terms of the maximality operator in the semantics of *yori*, thus indicating that the irrelevance of the DAP to Japanese comparatives. Our conclusion is consonant with [4,5], in that they also argue for the maximality operator in the semantics of comparatives in Japanese.

We would like to mention other pieces of evidence that [1] presents for the negative setting of DAP in Japanese.[2] One of them is lack of subcomparatives, (28a). We can see, however, that the grammaticality is greatly improved when we use the adjectives that bothpoint to vertical dimension, as in (28b):

(28) a. *Kono doa-wa   [kono teeburu-ga   nagai-yori] takai.*
          this   door-TOP [that table-NOM long-than] high.

          "This door is higher than that table is long."

     b. *Kono suisoo-wa   [ano doa-ga   takai-yori] hukai. Dakara,*
          This fish.tank-TOP [that door-NOM high-than] deep. So,
          kono suisoo-o   ano heya-ni ireru koto-wa   dekinai.
          this fish.tank-ACC that room-to put.in fact-NOM cannot

          "This fish tank is deeper than that door is high. So you cannot carry it into that room."

What we suspect is that the alleged ungrammaticality of (28a) comes from the comparing two different dimensions.

The present paper thus contributes to the body of debate about the status of Japanese with respect to the DAP and possible cross-linguistic degree-related parameters in general.

References

1. Beck, S., Oda, T., Sugisaki, K.: Parameteric variation in the semantics of comparison: Japanese vs English. J. East Asian Linguist. **13**, 289–344 (2004)
2. Crnič, L., Fox, D.: Equatives and maximality. In: Altshuler, D., Rett, J. (eds.) The Semantics of Plurals, Focus, Degrees, and Times, pp. 163–184. Springer, Cham (2019). https://doi.org/10.1007/978-3-030-04438-1_9
3. Gajewski, J.: More on quantifiers in comparative clauses. In: Proceedings of SALT, vol. 18, pp. 340–357 (2008)
4. Hayashishita, J.R.: *Izyoo(ni)*- and *Gurai*-comparatives: comparisons of deviation in Japanese. Gengo Kenkyu, pp. 77–110 (2007)
5. Hayashishita, J.R.: *Yori*-comparatives: a reply to Beck et al. (2004). J. East Asian Linguist. **18**, 65–100 (2009)
6. Hayashishita, J.R.: Reconfirming *Izyoo(ni)*- and *Gurai*-comparatives as comparisons of deviation. J. East Asian Linguist. **26**, 163–187 (2017)
7. Heim, I.: Little. In: Proceedings of SALT, vol. 16, pp. 35–58 (2006)
8. Kennedy, C.: Projecting the Adjective: The Syntax and Semantics of Gradability and Comparison. Garland, New York (1999)
9. Kubota, Y.: The presuppositional nature of *Izyoo(-ni)* and *Gurai* comparatives: A note on Hayashishita (2007). Gengo Kenkyu, pp. 33–46 (2012)
10. Rullmann, H.: Maximality in the semantics of Wh-constructions. Ph.D. thesis, University of Massachusetts, Amherst (1995)

---

[2] We thank a reviewer for LENLS 16 for bringing this point to us.

11. Schwarzschild, R.: The semantics of comparatives and other degree constructions. Lang. Linguist. Compass **2**, 308–331 (2008)
12. von Stechow, A.: Comparing semantic theories of comparison. J. Semant. **3**(1), 1–77 (1984)
13. von Stechow, A.: The temporal degree adjectives *Früh(er)/Spät(er)* 'early(er)/late(r)' and the semantics of positive (2007)

KANSEIAI 2019

Kansei and Artificial Intelligence 2019

Koichi Yamagata ⓘ

The University of Electro-Communication, 1-5-1 Chofugaoka,
Tokyo 182-8285, Japan
koichi.yamagata@uec.ac.jp

1 The Workshop

On November 11, 2019, a workshop of Kansei and Artificial Intelligence (KANSEI-AI) took place at Keio University. It was one of workshops of the JSAI International Symposia on AI (JSAI-isAI 2019), sponsored by The Japan Society for Artificial Intelligence (JSAI).

The porpose of this workshop was to share the progress of research and to share methodology by researchers studying the five senses. Various perceptions through the five senses are used in our decision making and executions. Our level of understanding and methodology differ in each of the five senses. Researches in visual-texture perception are said to be the most developed among all. However, the neural mechanism of visual-texture perception remains unclear for the most part. Thus, there is no established way to reproduce the mechanism with artificial intelligence. The scope of this workshop was research of science and engineering related to value judgements made through the five senses, such as image processing, tactile engineering, acoustics, machine learning, sensitivity engineering, and natural language processing.

This year's workshop was the first time to be held, with three speakers giving talks on texture and natural language processing. The first lecture was "Partial Image Texture Translation" by Dr. Gibran Benitez-Garcia (The University of Electro-Communications). The second one is "A New Way of Making Advertising Copies: Image as Input" by Dr. Nozaki (The University of Electro-Communications). The third one is "Product search system using onomatopoeia for texture" by Dr. Yamagata (The University of Electro-Communications). All of these studies were challenging and unique. From them, two researches were selected by the committee for papers of this volume.

2 Papers

There are two papers in the KANSEI-AI part of the present volume.

The first paper is "Partial Image Texture Translation" by Gibran Benitez-Garcia et al. This study is about style transfer method to change the texture of an object in a given image to a different texture. Existing original neural style transfer algorithm changes the style of an entire image including the style of background. They propose a partial texture style transfer method by combining neural style transfer with semantic segmentation. Their algorithm segments target objects using a weakly supervised segmentation method, and transfer the material of the style image to only segmented areas.

The second paper is "A New Way of Making Advertising Copies: Image as Input" by Nozaki et al. This study is about a model for generating advertising copies. Most of the previously reported advertising copy generators take specified keywords which a user wants to embed in a copy. Their method can take input of colored images and makes effective use of the sensibility derived from the images.

3 Acknowledgements

Let me acknowledge those who helped with the workshop. The program committee and organisers were Yuji Nozaki and myself. The organisers would like to thank JSAI for giving us the opportunity to hold the workshop.

Partial Image Texture Translation Using Weakly-Supervised Semantic Segmentation

Gibran Benitez-Garcia(✉), Wataru Shimoda, Shin Matsuo, and Keiji Yanai

Department of Informatics, The University of Electro-Communications,
Tokyo 1-5-1 Chofugaoka, Chofu-shi, Tokyo 182-8585, Japan
{gibran,shimoda-k,matsuo-s,yanai}@mm.inf.uec.ac.jp

Abstract. The field of Neural Style Transfer (NST) has led to interesting applications that enables to transform the reality as human beings perceive. Particularly, NST for material translation aims to change the material (texture) of an object to a different material from a desired image. In order to generate more realistic results, in this paper, we propose a partial texture style transfer method by combining NST with semantic segmentation. The original NST algorithm changes the style of an entire image including the style of background even though the texture is contained only in object regions. Therefore, we segment target objects using a weakly supervised segmentation method, and transfer the material of the style image to only material-based segmented areas. As a result, we achieved partial style transfer for only specific object regions, which enables us to change materials of objects in a given image as we like. Furthermore, we analyze the material translation capability of state-of-the-art image-to-image (I2I) translation algorithms, including the conventional NST method of Gatys, WCT, StarGAN, MUNIT, and DRIT++. The analysis of our experimental results suggests that the conventional NST produces more realistic results than other I2I translation methods. Moreover, there are certain materials that are easier to synthesize than others.

Keywords: Neural style transfer · Weakly-supervised semantic segmentation

1 Introduction

In 2015, Gatys et al. proposed to use Convolutional Neural Networks (CNNs) for applying painting styles on natural images [2,3]. They demonstrated that it is possible to exploit CNN feature activations to recombine the content of a given photo and the style of artworks. This method is known as Neural Style Transfer (NST), which is the process to render a content image in different styles using CNNs [6]. In other words, it enables us to modify the style of an image keeping its content recognizable. It replaces the information which are degraded

© Springer Nature Switzerland AG 2020
M. Sakamoto et al. (Eds.): JSAI-isAI 2019, LNAI 12331, pp. 387–401, 2020.
https://doi.org/10.1007/978-3-030-58790-1_25

while the signal of the content image goes forward through the CNN layers with style information extracted from the style image, and reconstructs a new image which has the same content as a given content images and the same style as a given style image, as shown in Fig. 1. NST introduced "style matrix" which was presented by Gram matrix of the feature maps, that is, correlation matrix between feature maps in CNN.

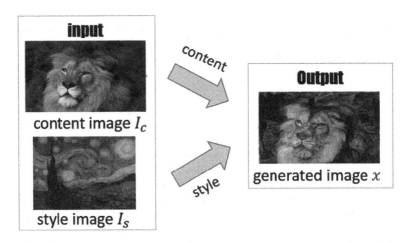

Fig. 1. An example result of the neural style transfer.

In this work, we apply this neural style transfer algorithm to changing the material of objects in an image. The method proposed by Gatys et al. [2,3] changes the style of an entire image including the style of background even though we want to change only object regions. Therefore, we need information of target object position, in order to transfer texture styles to only object regions in a given image. We segment the regions of the target materials using a weakly supervised segmentation method and transfer the style of the given materials to only the target regions [14]. Thus, we achieve partial style transfer for only specific material regions, which enables us to change materials of objects in a given image as we like. In addition, we analyze the material translation capability of state-of-the-art (SOTA) I2I translation algorithms, including the WCT [11], StarGAN [1], MUNIT [5], and DRIT++ [10]. As a material image dataset, we use Flickr Material Database (FMD) [12] which is widely used for material image analysis. We evaluate our experimental results quantitatively and qualitatively. Quantitatively, we use different metrics including: Inception Score (IS), Frechet Inception Distance (FID), and classification accuracy. Qualitatively, we show examples of synthesized images that can be evaluated by visual inspection. The analysis of our results suggests that the conventional NST produces more realistic results than other I2I translation methods. Moreover, certain materials such as glass and fabric are easier to synthesize than water and foliage.

2   Related Work

Image-to-image (I2I) translation can be divided into two types of methods, neural style transfer (NST), and generative adversarial neural networks (GANs). The seminal work of Gatys et al. [3] is part of the image-based optimization NST methods [6], since the style transfer is built upon an iterative image optimization in the pixel space. To enable faster stylization, model-based optimization methods train Conv-Deconv-Networks using content and style loss functions to approximate the results in a single forward pass [7]. Some approaches even aim to train one single model to transfer arbitrary styles [4,11]. Huang and Belongie [4] propose the adaptive instance normalisation (AdaIN) to achieve real-time performance. AdaIN transfers channel-wise statics between content and style, which are modulated with affine (trainable) parameters. Concurrently, Li et al. [11] propose a pair of whitening and coloring transformations (WCT) to achieve the first style learning-free method.

On the other hand, GAN-based methods achieve outstanding results for I2I translation. For example, CycleGAN [21] proposes the cycle consistency loss to achieve an unpaired I2I translation. StarGAN [1] extends this work to reach multi-domain I2I translation by learning I2I mappings from multiple domains with a single model. Moreover, Huang et al. [5] combine AdaIN with the adversarial and the perceptual loss functions to achieve multimodal unsupervised I2I translation (MUNIT). Concurrently, Lee et al. [9] proposes a method to disentangle the content and style information for producing diverse outputs without paired training images, which was extended in DRIT++ [10] to achieve multimodal with a single model. All of these methods can be applied to material translation, and Table 1 shows its main characteristics. Regardless of its clear disadvantages, the conventional NST is considered as a gold standard due to its visual quality [6]. Therefore, we build our proposal upon this method. Furthermore, we test with different SOTA methods to prove this statement.

Table 1. Comparision of image to image translation methods.

	NST	WCT	Cycle GAN	StarGAN	MUNIT	DRIT++
Single image optimization	✓	✓	–	–	–	–
Adversarial loss	–	–	✓	✓	✓	✓
Cycle consistency loss	–	–	✓	✓	–	✓
One single model	–	✓	–	✓	–	✓
Multi-domain generation	–	–	–	✓	–	✓
Multi-modal generation	–	–	–	–	✓	✓
AdaIN layers	–	–	–	–	✓	–
Disentangled representation	✓	✓	–	–	✓	✓

3   Proposed Method

3.1   Overview

Figure 2 shows the workflow of our proposed framework. We combine neural style transfer with weakly semantic segmentation to achieve partial image texture translation. The whole process of our proposal is described as follows.

1. Choose the content and style images to perform partial image texture translation.
2. Change the style of the material images by Gatys et al.'s neural style transfer method [2].
3. Estimate the regions corresponding to the given material by a semantic segmentation method.
4. Synthesize the image in which the material is changed by integrating the material regions of the transferred images and the background regions of the original images into the final output images.
5. Evaluate the synthesized image by automatically recognizing its new material.

3.2   Neural Style Transfer

First, we transform the style of an image using the conventional NST method proposed by Gatys et al. [2,3]. We represent an input image to be transformed as x_c, a given style image the style of which is transferred as x_s, and an output image which is a synthesized image with the content of x_c and the style of x_s as x_g. In the algorithm, we repeatedly modify x_g so that the content features of x_g extracted from CNN becomes close to the content features of x_c and the style features of x_g becomes close to the style features of x_s. After several tens of iteration, we obtain a synthesized image. This process is illustrated in Fig. 3.

Following [2], we use VGG19 [18] pre-trained with the imagenet dataset as a base CNN for feature extraction. We extract content features from conv4_2, and style features from five layers (conv1_1, conv2_1, conv3_1, conv4_1, and conv5_1).

We use activations (a 3D tensor) $F(x, l)$ of layer l as content representation of layer l. The loss function regarding content features which is the difference between $F(x_c, l)$ and $F(x_g, l)$ is represented by the following equation:

$$L_c(x_c, x_g) = \frac{1}{2} \sum_{i,j} (F_{i,j}(x_c, l) - F_{i,j}(x_g, l))^2 \tag{1}$$

On the other hand, according to [2], we use Gram matrix $G(x, l)$ of activations of layer l as a style representation. It is the original finding by Gatys et al. that Gram matrix of CNN activations represents a style of an image efficiently. The loss function regarding content features which is the difference between $G(x_s, l)$ and $G(x_g, l)$ is represented by the following equation:

$$G(x, l) = F(x, l)F^T(x, l) \tag{2}$$

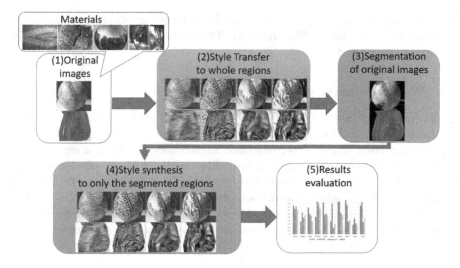

Fig. 2. Processing flow.

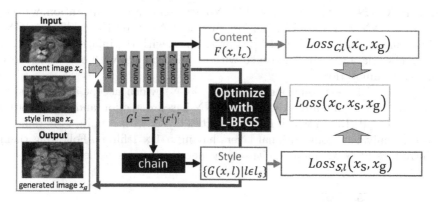

Fig. 3. The algorithm of neural style transfer.

$$Loss_{s,l}(x_s, x_g, l) = \frac{1}{4N_l^2} \sum_{i,j} (G_{i,j}(x_s, l) - G_{i,j}(x_g, l))^2 \tag{3}$$

$$Loss_s(x_s, x_g) = \sum_l w_l Loss_{s,l} \tag{4}$$

The loss function is represented by the following equation:

$$Loss(x_c, x_s, x_g) = w_c Loss_c + w_s Loss_s \tag{5}$$

where w_c and w_s are weighting constants. We estimate x_g so as to minimize this loss function with the L-BFGS method. The estimated x_g was the image with the content of x_c and the style of x_s.

3.3   Weakly-Supervised Semantic Segmentation

In this paper, we use a CNN-based weakly-supervised semantic segmentation proposed by Shimoda et al. [16] as a semantic segmentation method. With a weakly-supervised semantic segmentation method, we can train a segmentation model from training images having only class labels, without pixel-level annotation. In this method, they improved class-specific saliency maps proposed by Simonyan et al. [18] which was a back-propagation-based object region estimation method, and proposed a method to obtain "Distinct Class-specific Saliency Maps (DCSM)". DCSM can be used as unary potentials of dense CRF [8]. Figure 4 shows the procedure of the DCSM-based weakly-supervised semantic segmentation.

Training CNN. For preparation of CNN-based semantic segmentation, we need to train a CNN with a multi-label loss function. As an off-the-shelf basic CNN architecture, we use the VGG-16 [18] pre-trained with the imagenet dataset. In this framework, a CNN is fine-tuned with training images with only image-level multi-label annotation.

Recently, fully convolutional networks (FCN) which accept arbitrary-sized inputs are used commonly in works on CNN-based detection and segmentation such as [15] and [13], in which fully connected layers with n units were replaced with the equivalent convolutional layers having n 1×1 filters. Following them, we introduce FCN to enable multi-scale generation of class saliency maps.

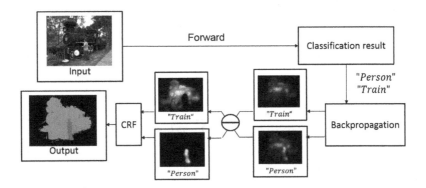

Fig. 4. The procedure of CNN-based weakly-supervised semantic segmentation.

Saliency Maps. Recently, a convolutional neural network (CNN) trained with only image-level annotation has been known to have the ability to localize trained objects in an image. Simonyan et al. [17] proposed class saliency maps based on the gradient of the class score with respect to the input image, which showed weakly-supervised object localization could be done by back-propagation-based visualization. However, their class saliency maps are vague and not distinct. When different multiple kinds of target objects are included in the image, the maps tend to respond to all the object regions. To tackle the weaknesses of their method, Shimoda et al. [16] propose a new method to generate CNN-derivatives-based saliency maps. The proposed method can generate more distinct class saliency maps which discriminate the regions of a target class from the regions of the other classes. The generated maps are so distinct that they can be used as unary potentials of CRF directly.

To make class saliency maps clearer, they propose three improvements [16]: (1) using CNN derivatives with respect to feature maps of the intermediate convolutional layers with up-sampling instead of an input image; (2) subtracting saliency maps of the other classes from saliency maps of the target class to differentiate target objects from other objects; (3) aggregating multiple-scale class saliency maps to compensate lower resolution of the feature maps.

Dense CRF. Conditional Random Field (CRF) is a probabilistic graphical model which considers both node priors and consistency between nodes. By using CRF, we can obtain smoother regions from roughly estimated region potentials. Because object class-specific saliency maps (OCSM) represent only probability of the target classes on each pixel and have no explicit information on object region boundaries, we apply CRF to obtain more distinct object boundaries. In the framework, we use Dense CRF [8] where every pixel is regarded as a node, and every node is connected to every other node. The energy function is defined as follows:

$$E(\mathbf{c}) = \sum_i \theta_i(c_i) + \sum_{i,j} \theta_{i,j}(c_i, c_j) \qquad (6)$$

where c_i represents a class assignment on pixel i. The first unary term of the above equation is calculated from class saliency maps $\hat{M}_i^c$. We defined it as $\theta_i(c_i) = -\log(\hat{M}_{x,y}^c)$.

In our work, we introduce background label extension in addition to the method by Shimoda et al. [16]. Using class saliency maps of the target classes, we estimate the background potential as follows:

$$M^{bg} = 1 - \max_{c \in \text{target}} M_{x,y}^c \qquad (7)$$

Note that the classes the likelihood estimated by the multi-class CNN of which exceed the pre-defined thresholds are selected as target classes.

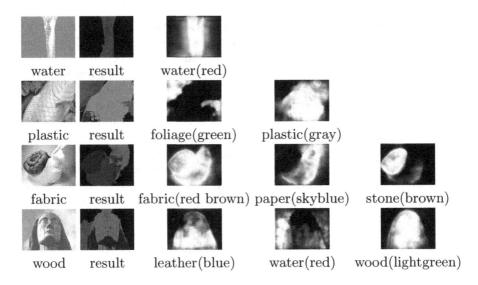

water   result   water(red)

plastic   result   foliage(green)   plastic(gray)

fabric   result   fabric(red brown) paper(skyblue)   stone(brown)

wood   result   leather(blue)   water(red)   wood(lightgreen)

Fig. 5. Examples of segmentation results and class-specific saliency maps of material images.

4 Experimental Results

In this paper, we use the Flickr Material Database (FMD) [12] which consists of ten kinds of material classes (fabric, foliage, glass, leather, metal, paper, plastic, stone, water, and wood), where each class contains 100 real-world images. The samples were selected manually from Flickr, and were manually annotated at pixel-level. Figure 5 shows the obtained saliency maps of some FMD material images by the weakly supervised segmentation method (DCSM [16]). In the experiments, we randomly selected 20 images from each class as style images (200 images in total), and we used two images per class as content images (20 in total), Fig. 6 shows all the content images.

We compare the results of our approach (using the conventional NST [3]) with a real-time learning-free NST method (WCT), and three SOTA GAN-based approaches: StarGAN [1], MUNIT [5], and DRIT++ [10]. In order to train the data-hungry GAN-based approaches, we use the extended version of the FMD dataset (EFMD [20]), which contains the same ten material classes, but includes 1,000 images per class (10,000 in total). We have trained the three models with 900/100 images as training/testing samples, using the default parameters provided in their open-source codes. Note that, to get optimum results, we train one MUNIT model per combination of different materials (45 models for ten classes). For WCT, we use the pre-trained model provided by the authors [11] with no further modifications.

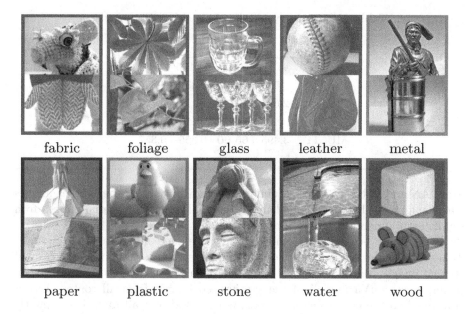

| fabric | foliage | glass | leather | metal |

| paper | plastic | stone | water | wood |

Fig. 6. Content images used in the experiments.

We quantitatively evaluated all methods using GAN and classification metrics. Specifically, we use Inception Score (IS), Frechet Inception Distance (FID), classification accuracy (Acc), and average classification score (Score). All metrics were calculated with an InceptionV3 [19] model pre-trained with imagenet, and fine-tuned on the ten classes using EFMD dataset [20]. Following the framework of Fig. 2, we apply partial image texture translation of each content image (20 samples) to the ten material classes (200 style images). So that, the quantitative results of each evaluated method are calculated using 4,000 synthesized images in total.

Table 2 shows the average statistics of all metrics from all evaluated methods. From this table, we can see that the conventional NST approach presents higher performance than other methods in all metrics except for the FID which MUNIT achieves the highest score. These results suggest that the conventional NST is better suited for partial image texture translation even though it has clear disadvantages such as the slow processing time due to its image-based optimization. Note that the GAN-based methods that use only one model to translate all material classes present significantly lower results than other methods.

The statistical results of Table 2 are confirmed in Fig. 7, which shows 10 results out of 4,000 synthesized images from all evaluated methods. This figure illustrates the synthesized results of ten materials from a content image of a stone object (shown in Fig. 6). It is clear that the NST-based approaches (NST and WCT) achieve more realistic results, especially for the fabric, glass and metal materials. On the other hand, MUNIT can successfully transfer the material style, however, the content information is lost to some extent. Contrastively,

Table 2. Quantitative results of all evaluated methods.

Method	IS ↑	FID ↓	Acc ↑	Score ↑
NST	**4.161**	66.54	**0.425**	**0.407**
WCT	3.518	65.61	0.355	0.350
StarGAN	2.673	103.80	0.110	0.107
DRIT++	2.662	106.70	0.110	0.106
MUNIT	3.495	**65.60**	0.355	0.357

StarGAN and DRIT++ present almost no modifications to the content images, which might be due to the challenge of generalizing ten material classes from significantly different objects in a single model.

We evaluate per-material translation performance of all evaluated methods. Table 3 shows the average classification score of each translated material from all content images (original material). So that, each class result is the average score (using InceptionV3 model) of the synthesized images from all content images translated to the corresponding class. As expected, not all materials show the same level of realism after the translation process, being glass the material that can be most easily translated on average among all methods. For the conventional NST approach, fabric and glass are the materials easier to synthesize, while water and foliage are certainly more challenging, as shown in Fig. 8. From this figure, we can see that generated objects of water and foliage are totally unrealistic, since the shape of the original objects contradicts the nature of the target material. However, this might be overcome if more suitable style images are chosen for the translation process. For example, a bouquet depicting a round shape might be better suited to synthesize a content image of a leather ball.

Finally, we also analyze the capability of each material-based object to be translated to the ten target materials. Table 4 shows the average classification score of each class of content images (original material) to all possible classes. So that, each class result is the average score of the synthesized images from the two content images of the corresponding class translated to all material classes. We can see that some objects are more natural to be translated from all evaluated methods, such as plastic, wood, and leather. In the specific case of the conventional NST approach, fabric, wood, and stone are the most accessible materials. This might be due to the shapes of the objects from these materials can be found in objects from different classes.

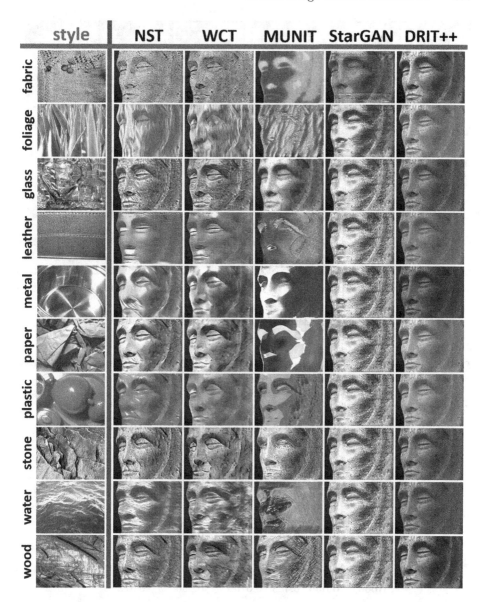

Fig. 7. Qualitative results (material-changed images) of all evaluated methods.

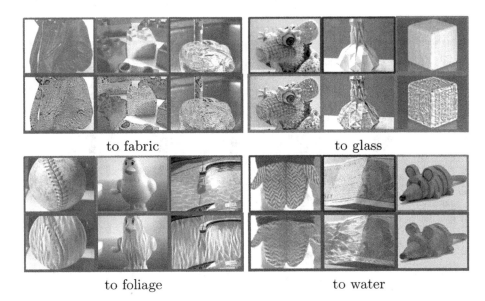

to fabric   to glass

to foliage   to water

Fig. 8. Translation results to different materials.

Table 3. Average classification score results (using InceptionV3 model) calculated from synthesized images of all content images to each material class.

Class	NST	WCT	StarGAN	DRIT++	MUNIT
Fabric	**0.631**	0.243	0.137	0.103	0.251
Foliage	0.193	0.337	0.102	0.100	**0.396**
Glass	**0.622**	0.610	0.142	0.108	0.412
Leather	0.194	0.395	0.092	0.094	**0.495**
Metal	0.304	0.317	0.241	0.117	**0.377**
Paper	**0.454**	0.239	0.037	0.111	0.361
Plastic	**0.586**	0.445	0.138	0.098	0.522
Stone	**0.485**	0.270	0.095	0.069	0.111
Water	0.045	0.206	0.014	0.169	**0.279**
Wood	**0.554**	0.438	0.070	0.096	0.372
Avg.	**0.407**	0.350	0.107	0.106	0.357

Table 4. Average classification score results (using InceptionV3 model) calculated from synthesized images of the two content images of each material class to all material classes.

Class	NST	WCT	StarGAN	DRIT++	MUNIT
Fabric	**0.552**	0.317	0.097	0.103	0.352
Foliage	0.113	0.101	0.100	0.100	**0.160**
Glass	0.254	0.234	0.094	0.108	**0.256**
Leather	0.398	0.420	0.114	0.094	**0.533**
Metal	0.458	**0.462**	0.105	0.117	0.327
Paper	**0.395**	0.304	0.111	0.111	0.246
Plastic	0.455	0.474	0.109	0.098	**0.492**
Stone	**0.510**	0.409	0.109	0.069	0.381
Water	0.395	0.359	0.115	0.169	**0.398**
Wood	**0.537**	0.421	0.114	0.096	0.431
Avg.	**0.407**	0.350	0.107	0.106	0.357

5   Conclusions

In this paper, we examined if neural style transfer technique could change the material of objects. To do that, we proposed a combination of neural style transfer and semantic material image segmentation. In the experiments, we analyzed 4,000 synthesized results from 2 content and 20 style images for each material class. As a result, in many cases, changing materials of objects were successfully done, and we observed the tendency that some materials were easy to synthesize. Especially, we found that for the conventional NST, fabric, and glass were accessible materials to transfer, while water and foliage were certainly harder materials. In addition, it turned out that also some materials are more suitable to be translated to the ten target materials. This is the case of plastic, wood, and leather.

For future work, considering the finding of this work, we will propose a method to select better style images or better part of style images automatically. In this work, we carried out style transfer and segmentation independently, and synthesize partial transferred images using both results. These two independent CNN-based processing sometimes made unnatural boundaries in the transferred images. Therefore, we plan to make an end-to-end network which realizes partial style transfer including both processing of segmentation and style transfer.

Acknowledgment. This work was supported by JSPS KAKENHI Grant Number 15H05915, 17H01745, 17H06100 and 19H04929.

References

1. Choi, Y., Choi, M., Kim, M., Ha, J.W., Kim, S., Choo, J.: StarGAN: unified generative adversarial networks for multi-domain image-to-image translation. In: Proceedings of the IEEE Conference on Computer Vision and Pattern Recognition, pp. 8789–8797. IEEE (2018)
2. Gatys, L.A., Ecker, A.S., Bethge, M.: A neural algorithm of artistic style. arXiv:1508.06576 (2015)
3. Gatys, L.A., Ecker, A.S., Bethge, M.: Image style transfer using convolutional neural networks. In: Proceedings of IEEE Computer Vision and Pattern Recognition (2016)
4. Huang, X., Belongie, S.: Arbitrary style transfer in real-time with adaptive instance normalization. In: Proceedings of the IEEE International Conference on Computer Vision, pp. 1501–1510. IEEE (2017)
5. Huang, X., Liu, M.Y., Belongie, S., Kautz, J.: Multimodal unsupervised image-to-image translation. In: Proceedings of the European Conference on Computer Vision, pp. 172–189 (2018)
6. Jing, Y., Yang, Y., Feng, Z., Ye, J., Yu, Y., Song, M.: Neural style transfer: a review. IEEE Trans. Vis. Comput. Graph. (2019)
7. Johnson, J., Alahi, A., Fei-Fei, L.: Perceptual losses for real-time style transfer and super-resolution. In: Leibe, B., Matas, J., Sebe, N., Welling, M. (eds.) ECCV 2016. LNCS, vol. 9906, pp. 694–711. Springer, Cham (2016). https://doi.org/10.1007/978-3-319-46475-6_43
8. Krahenbuhl, P., Koltun, V.: Efficient inference in fully connected CRFs with Gaussian edge potentials. In: Advances in Neural Information Processing Systems (2011)
9. Lee, H.Y., Tseng, H.Y., Huang, J.B., Singh, M., Yang, M.H.: Diverse image-to-image translation via disentangled representations. In: Proceedings of the European Conference on Computer Vision, pp. 35–51 (2018)
10. Lee, H.Y., et al.: Drit++: diverse image-to-image translation via disentangled representations. Int. J. Comput. Vis., 1–16 (2020)
11. Li, Y., Fang, C., Yang, J., Wang, Z., Lu, X., Yang, M.H.: Universal style transfer via feature transforms. In: Proceedings of the Advances in Neural Information Processing Systems, pp. 386–396 (2017)
12. Liu, C., Sharan, L., Adelson, E., Rosenholtz, R.: Exploring features in a Bayesian framework for material recognition. In: Proceedings of IEEE Computer Vision and Pattern Recognition (2010)
13. Long, J., Shelhamer, E., Darrell, T.: Fully convolutional networks for semantic segmentation. In: Proceedings of IEEE Computer Vision and Pattern Recognition (2015)
14. Matsuo, S., Shimoda, W., Yanai, K.: Partial style transfer using weakly supervised semantic segmentation. In: Proceedings of the IEEE International Conference on Multimedia & Expo Workshops, pp. 267–272. IEEE (2017)
15. Oquab, M., Bottou, L., Laptev, I., Sivic, J.: Is object localization for free? -weakly-supervised learning with convolutional neural networks. In: Proceedings of IEEE Computer Vision and Pattern Recognition (2015)
16. Shimoda, W., Yanai, K.: Distinct class-specific saliency maps for weakly supervised semantic segmentation. In: Leibe, B., Matas, J., Sebe, N., Welling, M. (eds.) ECCV 2016. LNCS, vol. 9908, pp. 218–234. Springer, Cham (2016). https://doi.org/10.1007/978-3-319-46493-0_14

17. Simonyan, K., Vedaldi, A., Zisserman, A.: Deep inside convolutional networks: visualising image classification models and saliency maps. In: International Conference on Learning Representations (2014)
18. Simonyan, K., Vedaldi, A., Zisserman, A.: Very deep convolutional networks for large-scale image recognition. In: International Conference on Learning Representations (2015)
19. Szegedy, C., Vanhoucke, V., Ioffe, S., Shlens, J., Wojna, Z.: Rethinking the inception architecture for computer vision. In: Proceedings of the IEEE Conference on Computer Vision and Pattern Recognition, pp. 2818–2826. IEEE (2016)
20. Zhang, Y., Ozay, M., Liu, X., Okatani, T.: Integrating deep features for material recognition. In: Proceedings of the 23rd International Conference on Pattern Recognition, pp. 3697–3702. IEEE (2016)
21. Zhu, J.Y., Park, T., Isola, P., Efros, A.A.: Unpaired image-to-image translation using cycle-consistent adversarial networks. In: Proceedings of the IEEE International Conference on Computer Vision, pp. 2223–2232. IEEE (2017)

A New Way of Making Advertising Copies: Image as Input

Yuji Nozaki⬤, Masato Konno, Koichi Yamagata⬤,
and Maki Sakamoto(✉)⬤

The University of Electro-Communication, 1-5-1 Chofugaoka,
Tokyo 182-8285, Japan
{na003169,maki.sakamoto}@uec.ac.jp

Abstract. Our impression can be effectively delivered by a color. In this paper we present a novel model for generating advertising copies using machine learning techniques. Unlike most of the previously reported advertising copy generators take specified keyword(s) which a user wants to embed in a copy, our proposed model takes one colored image as its input. We use the previously reported database that provides the potential color impression of a word for the purpose of selecting several words assumed to give a similar perceptual impression of the input image. We also use a deep neural network based binary classifier to extract appropriate words for advertising copies from an increased vocabulary. To output advertising copies of relatively natural expression out of the ones generated, we use a word embedding model of a shallow neural network called Skip-gram. The qualities of the advertising copies were evaluated by online survey and were compared with other copies generated by various models. As the result of the evaluation, our proposed model outperformed the other models.

Keywords: Text generation · Advertising copy · Color impressions · Neural networks

1 Introduction

In this paper we present a novel model for generating advertising copy using machine learning techniques. An advertising copy is a catchy short message used in the advertisement designed to develop an interest of target customers and to prompt them to purchase the product or the service.

As colors and emotions are closely linked [1–3], to choose adequate combination and proportion of color for advertising image is an important factor to give target customers an intended impression. As it is also reported that some words, such as "warm" or "cool", may have the effect of evoking colors to those who listen [4–6], the affinity of the color combination and the words is important in situations where color and copy are presented together.

While there has been substantial amount of work that focuses on generating sentences using machine learning techniques [7], as far as we know, none of the previously proposed copy generator system has been successfully developed on color combination

© Springer Nature Switzerland AG 2020
M. Sakamoto et al. (Eds.): JSAI-isAI 2019, LNAI 12331, pp. 402–411, 2020.
https://doi.org/10.1007/978-3-030-58790-1_26

input. Unlike most of the previously reported generating models take a specific key-word which a user wants to embed in the copy, our proposed model takes one colored image as its input. Though image captioning [8] and related techniques are regarded as ones of the most successful applications in image-based sentence generation, in this research, we only focus on the proportion of color in the given image as previous researches show that the color is a one of the most important factor for perceptual impression of humans [9, 10].

Note that our research is designed to generate Japanese copies. Thus, the databases and the corpuses that will appear later in this paper are also in Japanese, so we intro-duce them of translated into English.

The rest of this paper is structured as follows. Section 2 introduces the overview of our system and its principle. Section 3 describes the conditions and the details of the evaluation test. Section 4 shows the result of the test and Sect. 5 concludes the paper.

2 Advertising Copy Generation

2.1 Overview

This section presents the operating principle of our model. Figure 1 is the overview that summarizes the steps to generate advertising copies. Our model uses following pro-cedure to embed a potential color impression in advertising copy to be generated.

A. **Color vector for the input image.** As discussed earlier, in this research, we only focus on colors in the given image. The combination and the proportion of the colors used in the input image is converted to a color vector c. To define the color vector, we used 130 colors which links to a specific affective impression. The 130 colors were divided into 44 groups based on their tone and hue for simplicity, and then one (or two) representative color was selected from each group resulting in forming of 45 representative colors. Figure 2 shows the 45 colors used for the elements of color vector $c = (c_1 c_2 . . . c_{45})$. Each color corresponds to each element in the color vector. These colors are selected based on the psychological experi-ment carried out in the previous study [11]. To convert the input image into its color vector, we map all the pixels in the image to one of the 45 colors by calculating the distance. Let $c_{(i,j),n}$ be the distance between n-th color element in the 45 colors and the RGB value of pixel at (i,j):

$$c_{(i,j),n} = \sqrt{\left(R_n - R_{(i,j)}\right)^2 + \left(G_n - G_{(i,j)}\right)^2 + \left(B_n - B_{(i,j)}\right)^2} \tag{1}$$

where R, G, B (0–255) are values of Red, Green, Blue of the pixel. The n-th color that gives the smallest distance for the pixel was chosen for the pixel. Then, the vector was normalized to satisfy:

$$\sum_{i=1}^{45} c_i = 1 \tag{2}$$

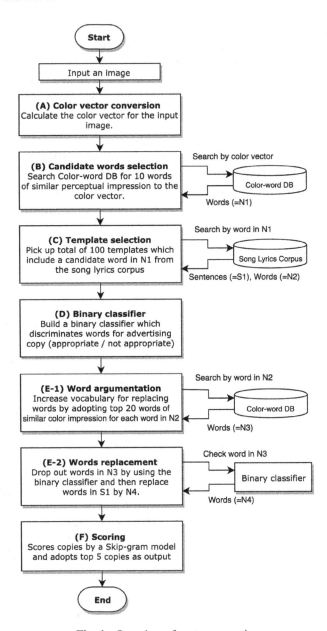

Fig. 1. Overview of system operation

B. **Candidate words selection.** The goal of this step is to choose 10 candidate words of similar potential color impression with the input image. For this purpose, we used the database (Color-word DB) previously reported by Konno et al. [12]. In the database, 710 words, that we call "Primitive word (PW)" which are assumed to

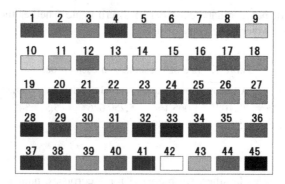

Fig. 2. 45 Color elements for color vectors

evoke some impression of color to those who listen, are related to their color vector of 45-dimension.

With the color vector of the input image, we calculate cosine similarity between all 710 PWs so as to find 10 words that gives the largest similarity. Let c_{image} be the color vector of the input image, and y_i be the color vector of the i-th PW,

$$similarity = \frac{c_{image} \cdot y_i}{\|c_{image}\| \|y_i\|} \tag{3}$$

C. **Template selection.** Though there has been reported several text generation models which use Markov chain (MC), or Long short-term memory (LSTM), these famous techniques are not very effective for advertising copy generation since structures and words used for copies are often different from those in basic conversations nor business documents. As we take notice that song lyrics shares some important features with advertising copies; for example, the degree of importance of sound of words, in this study, we decided to use song lyrics as "templates" for copies to be made. For this purpose, we used the song lyrics corpus previously reported by Suzuki et al. which contains the lyrics of 109,259 songs released from 1968 to 2017.

We search for 100 sentences include a PW chosen in step B were extracted from the corpus for the templates (10 sentences for each of PW). In the later steps, we will replace nouns in the templates so as to them to have similar color impression and to sound more closer as advertising copy.

D. **Binary classifier.** To make the model more expressive, we will later increase the vocabulary approximately 20 times in the step E. One natural strategy to increase a vocabulary is to consult a dictionary for synonyms, however, just using a dictionary is not to desirably work since very limited amount of words can be appropriately used as advertising copies (Table 1 will show how less words are used in actual advertising copies). Thus, in this step, we build and train a deep neural network based binary classifier to discriminate whether the given word is appropriate for advertising copy or not.

Table 1. Size of vocabulary in each corpus

Corpus	Ad copy	News paper	Journal article	Yahoo question
Vocabulary	70,109	1,065,168	5,250,626	5,517,342
Sentence	5,289	5,289	5,289	5,289

To train the binary classifier, we prepared for 4 corpuses, namely, an advertising copy corpus [13], newspaper corpus, journal article corpus, Yahoo question corpus. The advertising corpus was used to learn a positive example, and the others are used to learn a negative example. In the training process, as inputs for the neural network, a sentence is converted into bag-of-words representation and only nouns are retained as elements. We cropped the size of corpuses to 5,289 sentences for training. In a big corpus, the most frequent words occur millions of times and these words are usually not to be used as they provide less information value then the other words in natural language processing modeling. However, the purpose of training the classifier is to learn words which can be used for advertising copies. Thus, we use all the nouns appear more than one time in each corpus during training process. The numbers of vocabularies are summarized in Table 1.

As shown in Table 1. The vocabulary used in the corpus of advertising copy is significantly less than the other three corpuses. The trained DNN binary classifier provides 1 (which means the input word is appropriate for advertising copy) or 0 (is not).

E. **Word argumentation, template replacement.** In this step, we first increase the vocabulary to be used for replacing words in the templates by using the binary classifier and the Color-word DB.

First, for all the nouns contained in the 100 sentences chosen at step C, 20 words with similar color vector were picked up from the Color-word DB. The binary classifier is then used to shake words of inappropriate for advertising copy off from vocabulary. In our experiment, we averagely obtained 10 or less candidate words for replacing each noun in the sentence.

Finally, nouns in the sentence are replaced by a candidate word which randomly selected for each noun. By this processing, the color impression of the entire words included in the template can be brought to the color impression of the target image.

F. **Scoring the naturality by Skip-gram model.** In step F, we built a word embedding model using a shallow neural network called Skip-gram to evaluate sentences generated at the step E. This Skip-gram model is known as an efficient language modeling method for learning high-quality distributed vector representations that capture a precise syntactic and semantic word relationship [14]. We refer to Mikolov's method to build and train the Skip-gram model [15].

In our experiments, the Skip-gram model, which the size of the input layer 100, the size of the training window 5, negative sampling rate 10, was trained on the song lyrics corpus. We discarded from the vocabulary all words that occurred less than 50 times in the training corpus. Since the similarity of words obtained by Skip-gram model is originally a co-occurrence probability between words, we used the similarity as a score to measure the naturalness of sentences. The score of the sentence is calculated by the similarities between all possible pairs of words used in the sentence at the same time. Let w_i be the distributed representation of the i-th word in the sentence, N be the number of words in the sentence,

$$score = \frac{\sum_{i<j} similarity(w_i, w_j)_{ij}}{N(N-1)} \tag{4}$$

where

$$similarity(w_i, w_j) = \frac{w_i \cdot w_j}{\|w_i\| \|w_j\|} \tag{5}$$

We calculated the score for all the 100 sentences and takes 10 sentences as output in descending order of the score.

3   Evaluation of Copies

This section describes the evaluation design for comparing the quality of the copies obtained by various models. For the evaluation, we collected 20 advertising images with copies actually used in four categories; beverage and food, travel, beauty, and fashion.

3.1   Comparison with Other Models

We prepared copies made by 5 different ways; (A) original copies of product, (B) the proposed model described in Sect. 2, (C) the proposed model without step F, (D) the proposed model without step A, (E) Recurrent Neural Network (RNN) based model.

The model D in above directly uses a color vector of one keyword instead of an input image. For comparison, we prepared deep learning based method as model E. RNN is known as very powerful sequence model for text generation and has been used in a wide variety of application. We refer to Pytorch's reference method to build and train the RNN model [16]. The RNN model is trained on the corpus of advertising copy earlier introduce in Sect. 2. The trained RNN model generates a sequence of words until an end character is generated or the total length reaches 25 characters from an arbitrary word. We choose one specific keyword that we thought most likely meet to each of advertising image for input of D and E.

3.2   Test Design

The quality of the advertisement copy, including the degree of match with the image of the advertisement copy, is evaluated by 30 research participants (23 men, 7 women, average age 22.6) by online survey. A total of 20 images with 5 different copies were presented to the research participants. Participants were told to answer 2 general question and 4 evaluation questions for each individual copy on a scale of 1 to 7 (7 is the most positive reaction). Table 2 shows the evaluation questions.

Table 2. Questionnaires

	Type	Question	Answer
1	General	Have you seen this advertising image before?	Yes/No
2	General	Which copy do you think encourages you to buy the product/service?	(A)~(E)
3	Individual	Is the copy appropriate for this category?	1–7
4	Individual	Is the copy appropriate for advertising?	1–7
5	Individual	How do you evaluate the grammar of the copy?	1–7
6	Individual	Does copy match to the image?	1–7

4   Result

This section reports the result of the evaluation. As we used existing advertising images for this experiment, we discarded the answers for question 2–6 if a research participant answers "Yes" for the first question so as to obtain unbiased answers. This way, we obtained 13,200 valid answers. Figure 3 shows the number of times each model was selected in the Q1. While the model A (original copies) was turned out to be the most appropriate copy for the service and product, our model follows it and selected more times than the rest of models.

Table 3 summarizes the statistics obtained from the aggregated answers. The results show that while original copies achieve a respectable performance on each individual question, our proposed model also achieve much higher scores than the rest of the models (See Fig. 4).

To gain further insight into what step in our model contributes to this result, we looked into three models namely, B, C, and D; and then compared the models. Model B showed the highest average scores of three models. This suggests that both step F and step A works positively to heighten the quality of copies to be generated. While both C and D got total of 10 votes in online survey in the Q1, average scores on individual question (Q3–6) of C was much smaller than D. This suggests that step F has much impact on output of model than that of step A.

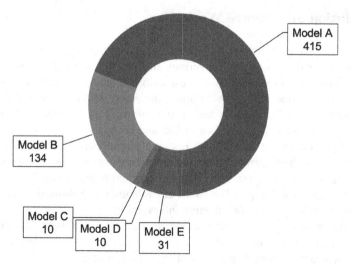

Fig. 3. Percentage of copies selected

Table 3. Survey statistics of 5 models on individual questions

Model	Q3	Q4	Q5	Q6
A	5.29 ± 0.07	5.75 ± 0.06	6.03 ± 0.06	5.37 ± 0.07
B	4.90 ± 0.07	5.17 ± 0.06	5.55 ± 0.06	4.22 ± 0.08
C	2.82 ± 0.07	3.15 ± 0.08	3.31 ± 0.08	2.51 ± 0.06
D	4.23 ± 0.08	3.92 ± 0.08	3.81 ± 0.09	3.20 ± 0.07
E	3.18 ± 0.07	2.74 ± 0.07	2.05 ± 0.06	2.75 ± 0.07

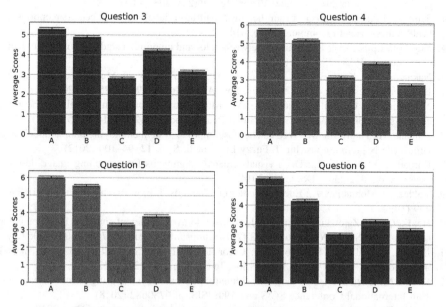

Fig. 4. Average scores and errors of models on question 3–6

5   Conclusion and Future Work

In this paper we studied a method for generating advertising copies from an image and the quality of copies generated by various model. We showed the way to build advertising copy generation model and to use colors as an input for the model. We also showed the way to choose words of similar impression with color and of appropriate for advertising copies by using a deep neural network based binary classifier. We successfully trained models on various of DB and corpuses.

As the results of the evaluation by research participants, we observed that it is possible to generate high quality attractive advertising copies using proposed method, compare to the other method including popular recurrent neural networks and keyword-based text generation technique. The result of evaluation also showed that using color information of an image is to be effective in several case.

However, as a drawback, our method focuses on expressing the impression delivered by color so it cannot reflect the effect or utility of the product in the copy. Neither, information of objects nor their spatial relation in a given image is not considered. Future research should consider the way to overcome these disadvantages so as to develop the quality higher.

References

1. Meyers-Levy, J., Peracchio, L.A.: Understanding the effects of color: how the correspondence between available and required resources affects attitudes. J. Consum. Res. **22**(2), 121–138 (1995)
2. Fuller, S., Carrasco, M.: Exogenous attention and color perception: performance and appearance of saturation and hue. Vision Res. **46**(23), 4032–4047 (2006)
3. Schuldt, J.P.: Does green mean healthy? Nutrition label color affects perceptions of healthfulness. Health Commun. **28**(8), 814–821 (2013)
4. Kaya, N., Epps, H.H.: Relationship between color and emotion: a study of college students. Coll. Stud. J. **38**(3), 396–405 (2004)
5. Nakamura, T., Kawanishi, K., Sakamoto, M.: A Possibility of Music Recommendation Based on Lyrics and Color. Trans. Jpn. Soc. Article Intell. **J94**(2), 85–94 (2011)
6. Nakamura, T., Utsumi, A., Sakamoto, M.: Music retrieval based on the relation between color association and lyrics. Trans. Virtual Reality Soc. Jpn. **27**(3), 163–175 (2012)
7. Yamane, H., Hagiwara, M.: Web catchphrase improve system employing onomatopoeia and large-scale N-gram corpus. Int. J. Fuzzy Log. Intell. Syst. **12**, 94–100 (2012)
8. Karpathy, A., Fei-Fei, L.: Deep visual-semantic alignments for generating image descriptions. arXiv:1412.2306, December 2014
9. Valdez, P., Mehrabian, A.: Effects of color on emotions. J. Exp. Psychol. Gen. **123**(4), 394–409 (1994)
10. He, L., Qi, H., Zaretzki, R.: Image color transfer to evoke different emotions based on color combinations. SIViP **9**(8), 1965–1973 (2014). https://doi.org/10.1007/s11760-014-0691-y
11. Ilba, S., Doizaki, R., Sakamoto, M.: Color and font recommendations based on mental images of text. Trans. Virtual Reality Soc. Jpn. **18**(3), 217–226 (2013)
12. Konno, M., Suzuki, K., Sakamoto, M.: Sentence generation system using affective image. In: 10th International Conference SCIS and 19th ISIS, p. 6780682 (2018)
13. make1, The catchcopy corpus. https://catchcopy.make1.jp/. Accessed 24 Sept 2019

14. Mikolov, T., Sutskever, I., Chen, K., Corrado, G., Dean, J.: Distributed representations of words and phrases and their compositionality. arXiv:1310.4546, October 2013
15. Mikolov, T., Chen, K., Corrado, G., Dean, J.: Efficient estimation of word representations in vector space. arXiv:1301.3781, January 2013
16. NLP from scratch: classifying names with a character-level RNN—PyTorch tutorials 1.2.0 documentation.   https://pytorch.org/tutorials/intermediate/char_rnn_classification_tutorial. html. Accessed 24 Sept 2019

Author Index

Printed in the United States
By Bookmasters

Printed in the United States
By Bookmasters